W9-AYQ-656

THE PRENTICE HALL SERIES IN MARKETING
Philip Kotler, Series Editor

Fourth Edition

STRATEGIC MARKETING
FOR
NONPROFIT ORGANIZATIONS

Philip Kotler

Northwestern University

Alan R. Andreasen

University of Connecticut

Prentice Hall, Englewood Cliffs, New Jersey 07632

Library of Congress Cataloging-in-Publication Data

Kotler, Philip.
    Strategic marketing for nonprofit organizations / Philip Kotler,
Alan R. Andreasen. -- 4th ed.
        p.   cm.
    Includes index.
    ISBN 0-13-851932-3 :
    1. Corporations, Nonprofit--Marketing.   I. Andreasen, Alan R.,
            . II. Title.
HF5415.K6312   1991
658.8--dc20   90-46176
                                                                      CIP

This book is dedicated to
MAURICE and BETTY KOTLER,
who provided my first introduction
to a nonprofit organization.

Philip Kotler

This book is dedicated to
JEAN MANNING,
whose love, encouragement, and insight
make all my work—as well as my life—
productive and joyful.

Alan R. Andreasen

Editorial/production supervision and interior design: **Maureen Wilson**
Cover design: **Ben Santora**
Manufacturing buyer: **Trudy Pisciotti**
Prepress buyer: **Robert Anderson**

 © 1991, 1987, 1982, 1975 by Prentice-Hall, Inc.
A Division of Simon & Schuster
Englewood Cliffs, New Jersey 07632

Printed in the United States of America
10 9 8 7 6 5 4 3

ISBN 0-13-851932-3

Prentice-Hall International (UK) Limited, *London*
Prentice-Hall of Australia Pty. Limited, *Sydney*
Prentice-Hall Canada Inc., *Toronto*
Prentice-Hall Hispanoamericana, S.A., *Mexico*
Prentice-Hall of India Private Limited, *New Delhi*
Prentice-Hall of Japan, Inc., *Tokyo*
Simon & Schuster Asia Pte. Ltd., *Singapore*
Editora Prentice-Hall do Brasil, Ltda., *Rio de Janeiro*

Contents

SECTION V   CONTROLLING MARKETING STRATEGIES

Preface

The fourth edition of *Strategic Marketing for Nonprofit Organizations* represents a major step forward in the evolution of this relatively young field. The first two editions of this book were pioneering works that sought to legitimize nonprofit marketing as a distinct discipline and codify some of its early principles and findings. They also fought negative stereotypes on the part of nonprofit managers who perceived marketing as unprofessional, if not outright malevolent.

The third edition was a major revision and repositioning of the material that reflected the maturing status of the discipline. No longer was it necessary to explain and apologize for marketing and to outline its major premises. As stated in the preface to the third edition, "the question is not whether one will use marketing but whether one will use it better than one's competitor or than one has in the past. . . . This means knowing the most sophisticated and advanced tools and concepts the field has to offer and being able to use them on a day-to-day basis."

The content and positioning of this fourth edition signifies two major milestones in the evolution of this young discipline. In its content, the book now makes much more use of inputs from practitioners in the field. The three earlier editions were largely designed to instruct, to share marketing wisdom drawn primarily from the private sector with those already doing nonprofit marketing and those students planning to enter the field some day on a full-time or avocational basis. Communication was largely one way: from the academy and the private sector to the nonprofit world.

This is no longer the case. The field now has produced a number of organizations and a large cadre of highly sophisticated practitioners who have much to share with the academy, other nonprofit managers, and even the executives in the private sector. This edition is therefore replete with checklists, hints, narratives of experiences, and sample materials drawn from nonprofit sources. Throughout the volume, well-known marketers from organizations such as the Girl Scouts, the Academy for Educational Development, Porter/ Novelli, and the United Way of America offer insights from their own experiences about the major and minor marketing problems this book addresses. The book is significantly richer for this input. At the same time, the two-way nature of the present volume is reflective of the arrival of the field at a plateau of sophistication approaching that of the private sector.

There has also been significant repositioning of material in this edition to reflect changes in the nature of the kinds of challenges facing the nonprofit sector in the 1990s. First, as identified in Chapter 1, the major need of the nonprofit sector now is not so much for techniques to implement marketing, but for assistance in strategic planning. Many nonprofits face significant declines in traditional sources of revenue, dramatic changes in their customer mix, and bold new competition. They need help rethinking where they are going and what broad strategies they should be using to get there. Thus, in this edition, the chapter on strategy has been expanded, rewritten, and moved earlier in the book to give it the centrality it now merits. This basic chapter has been supplemented by two chapters on key components of what we call the *core marketing strategy*. The first of these builds upon an earlier chapter on consumer behavior and treats extensively the problems involved in segmenting markets. The second is an entirely new chapter on positioning, a critical problem for nonprofits facing fickle markets and vigorous competition in the 1990s.

The material has also been expanded and repositioned to give increased emphasis to service and social marketing. Many nonprofit organizations are exclusively service enterprises and this aspect of their operations deserves greater attention (as it has been receiving in the private sector). More important, we argue in this edition that, in a sense, all marketing is service marketing in that what customers are seeking are not objects but something, someplace, or someone who will serve them benefits. Products are just one source of benefits. So are places and marketing people. And, on some occasions, target customers are the source of their own benefits, as when they begin a diet or exercise program.

The book also has a new chapter devoted exclusively to social marketing. Social marketing is undoubtedly the fastest-growing sector of nonprofit marketing. It is also one of the major sources of the two-way input from within the nonprofit sector that is lavished throughout this volume. It, too, deserves expanded treatment.

Despite these important changes, the book retains the customer focus emphasized in the third edition. We strongly believe that one of the things that sets marketing dramatically apart from other behavior-change disciplines is its placement of the customer at the center of all strategy development. No amount of strategic planning or development of core marketing approaches will succeed if they are not begun with the proper *marketing mind-set*. This customer-centered mind-set continues to be a central theme of virtually every chapter of the book.

ACKNOWLEDGMENTS

The first edition of this book was the result of a happy association with extremely creative and valued colleagues and students in the marketing department of the J. L. Kellogg Graduate School of Management at Northwestern University. The second edition benefited from dialogues with members of the marketing department: Bobby J. Calder, Richard M. Clewett, Jehoshua Eliashberg, Lakshmanan Krishnamurthi, Stephen A. LaTour, Sidney J. Levy, Trudy Kehret, Api Ruzdic, Louis W. Stern, Brian Sternthal, Alice M. Tybout, and Andris A. Zoltners. Excellent manuscript reviews of the second edition were provided by Professor Paul Bloom (University of Maryland); Professor Roberta N. Clarke (Boston University); and Professor Karen F. A. Fox (University of Santa Clara).

The third and fourth editions have reflected the input of many academics and nonprofit practitioners. Particularly valuable have been the insights of Jean Manning of Seyfarth, Shaw, Fairweather & Geraldson; William Smith of the Academy for Educational Development; Tom Walker of United Way of America; Dan Lissance of Population Services International; William Schellstede of Family Health International; Christopher Lovelock; and Bill Novelli of Porter/Novelli.

1

The Growth and Development of the Nonprofit Sector

As the National Geographic Society's coffers bulged with the fruits of its supremely successful efforts under the golden touch of Melville Bell Grosvenor in the early 1960s, the Society [in the 1980s] underwent a fundamental change. No longer a lean eleemosynary institution begging the world for a chance to fulfill its stated task—"the increase and diffusion of geographic knowledge"—the Society began to be a big and lucrative business.

From Gardiner Greene Hubbard's dream of bringing knowledge to the upper classes of provincial Washington, to Alexander Graham Bell's ideal of popularizing geography among the upper middle classes, to Gilbert Hovey Grosvenor's appeal to the vast and growing middle class, . . . under Melville Bell Grosvenor the Society became an institution of the masses, and a quite successful and wealthy one. But it was also, as a result of that success, far less a charitable educational institution than it was a giant commercial publisher and mail-order house.

On top of possessing a good product in an obviously desirable part of the publishing market, the National Geographic Society also had a handful of trump cards up its sleeves. For the Society wasn't run according to the rules followed by most of its fellow successful corporations and all of its competition [among] the commercial book and magazine publishers, atlas and globe makers, record producers, and the like—because the National Geographic Society was deemed a "nonprofit" organization under the rules of the Internal Revenue Service.

[Under IRS rules, the Society received important tax subsidies and] also took full advantage of another perquisite offered by the Congress: discounted postal rates. These discounts are offered to nonprofits on the assumption that their funds are limited and they thus need help with the costs of billing their members or distributing their appeals for funds. To the National Geographic Society, this assistance took a little different turn.

No doubt at least partially because of this discount privilege, the Society sends out an almost endless stream of full-color, high-quality mailings pitching its various goods and membership plans, the envelopes for each of which are clearly marked "Non-Profit Org." By 1984, according to Society officials, the postage subsidy was saving the organization $10 million a year.

As a result, the Society has become the fifteenth-largest mail-order house in America, according to Maxwell Sroge, a consultant who specializes in that industry. "[I think] they have really an unfair advantage" over the competition due to their tax-exempt status and their reduced-postage charges. Sroge estimated that the Society mails "several hundred million pieces" of promotional material every year.

Society founder Gardiner Greene Hubbard's goal was to create an organization of inquisitive, high-minded men both to help chart the globe and to inform other intelligent, curious people about their discoveries—in short, to promote "increase and diffusion of geographic knowledge." His successor, Alexander Graham Bell, wanted to fund this research, exploration, and publication chain by selling memberships to the masses, but still keeping the Society focused as an educational organization. Gilbert H. Grosvenor's goal was to funnel 15 percent of gross revenues into exploration and research.

[But by the 1980s, the Society was a great commercial success.] From the $60 million in gross income in 1968, the Society's gross revenue had reached $130 million in 1976. By 1984, the National Geographic Society was grossing $326,826,071 a year, had a net worth of at least $198 million, and recorded "profits" of more than $17 million, even under the peculiar rules that apply to it. In that same year, its interest and dividend income alone amounted to more than $18.7 million.

[But this success was not without controversy.] Astonishingly, in 1983 the National Geographic Society awarded research and exploration grants totaling only $3.18 million, less than 1 percent of its gross revenue. And even that figure is misleading, since many of those "grants" led to articles for the *National Geographic*, and would perhaps have been more accurately classified as publishing expenses. The next year, the Society reported that its research grants jumped to $4.3 million. But most of that increase involved projects destined for publication in a new research journal of very limited circulation that the Society was preparing.

Source: Adapted from Howard S. Abramson, "Geographic Travels Tax-Free; Nonprofit Status Gives Magazine Competitive Edge," *The Washington Post*, March 8, 1987, p. H1. Reproduced with permission.

The third edition of this book proudly noted that, by 1987, an idea that was once considered highly novel, the application to nonprofit organizations of marketing concepts drawn from the private sector, had reached its maturity stage. But this was maturity in the limited sense that the idea had been accepted by nonprofit funders and managers as "grown up" enough to be *considered* a necessary, even central, approach to solving many of their critical strategic problems.

The 1990s mark a dramatic leap forward for this newly matured discipline as it deepens its impact on areas in which it is already strongly entrenched and moves outward to conquer a wide range of new territory. This accelerated growth is partly driven by external factors. But it is also driven by the self-confidence of a newly grown-up discipline that is

1 *aware* of its applicability to a wide range of strategic and tactical situations, some defined as "marketing," many defined as something else but "marketing" at their heart (e.g., motivating employees or securing media coverage).
2 *proud* of the extent to which it has made major conceptual and strategic contributions back to the private sector context where it originated.
3 *confident* in its power to have a major impact on nonprofit performance.
4 *challenged* by social and economic circumstances that make it inevitable that nonprofit marketing will experience sharply rising interest and application in the decade ahead.

Indeed, management guru Peter Drucker argued in an article in the *Harvard Business Review* in the summer of 1989 that nonprofit organizations are becoming America's management leaders, especially in the areas of strategy and the effective use of boards of directors. Drucker claims "they are practicing what most American businesses only preach." Drucker continues:

> Twenty years ago, management was a dirty word for those involved in nonprofit organizations. It meant business, and nonprofits prided themselves on being free of the taint of commercialism and above such sordid considerations as the bottom line. Now most of them have learned that nonprofits need management even more than business does, precisely because they lack the discipline of the bottom line. The nonprofits are, of course, still dedicated to "doing good." But they also realize that good intentions are no substitute for organization and leadership, for accountability, performance, and results. Those require management and that, in turn, begins with the organization's mission.[1]

HISTORY OF AN IDEA

The idea of applying marketing to nonprofit organizations had its "birth" in a series of articles by Kotler and Levy,[2] Kotler and Zaltman,[3] and Shapiro[4] between 1969 and 1973. These articles argued that

> marketing is a pervasive societal activity that goes considerably beyond the selling of toothpaste, soap, and steel. Political contests remind us that candidates are marketed as well as soap; student recruitment in colleges reminds us that higher education is marketed; and fundraising reminds us that "causes" are marketed. . . . [Yet no] attempt is made to examine whether the principles of "good" marketing in traditional product areas are transferable to the marketing of services, persons, and ideas.[5]

The growth period of this idea's life cycle saw a dramatically steep rise in its acceptance. Driven partly by cost and competitive pressures and partly by the exciting promise marketing had to offer, practitioners in health care, education, and the arts rushed to embrace the new discipline and explore its possibilities. They were followed very shortly by the librarians, recreation specialists, politicians, and leaders of social service organizations and major charities. As this demand grew, so did the supply of scholars excited at the prospect of expanding the horizons of the discipline and testing the robustness of its concepts and tools. These scholars included both those inside academic marketing, such as the present authors and such people as Christopher Lovelock,[6] Charles Weinberg,[7] Michael Rothschild,[8] Paul Bloom,[9] Gerald Zaltman,[10] and numerous others, but also those outside the traditional field, such as Robin MacStravic in health care[11] and John Crompton in leisure and recreation.[12]

In the later 1980s, the nonprofit marketing idea reached the maturity phase of its life cycle. The evidence was everywhere. Several general textbooks had become available,[13] as well as trade and textbooks in specific subcategories such as the marketing of health care,[14] education,[15] and social issues.[16] Specialized readers, conference proceedings, collections,[17] and casebooks[18] abounded. Particularly robust was the growth in *social marketing* which saw texts by Manoff appear in 1985[19] and by Kotler and Roberto in 1989,[20] and a readings book by Fine in 1990.[21]

The 1980s also saw a number of nonacademic publications appearing that summarized experiences from practicing nonprofit marketers. Prominent among these was a series of reports on contraceptive social marketing from the Population Information Program at Johns Hopkins University,[22] a set of practical guides from SOMARC,[23] a marketing planning workbook from United Way of America,[24] handbooks for conducting focus group research[25] and carrying out communications programs for child survival[26] from the Academy for Educational Development, and a planner's guide on health communications from the Office of Cancer Communications in the U.S. Department of Health and Human Services.[27] These were supplemented by speeches and articles from a wide array of thoughtful practitioners, such as William Novelli, Mary Debus, and William Smith, writing and lecturing about their experiences in applying marketing in the nonprofit sector.[28]

In addition to a growing array of articles on nonprofits in traditional and not-so-traditional journals, several new journals have appeared, including the *Journal of Health Care Marketing*, the *Health Marketing Quarterly*, the *Praeger Series in Public and Nonprofit Sector Marketing*, the *Journal of Public Policy and Marketing*, *Healthmarketing*, *Hospital Public Relations*, the *Journal of Hospital Marketing*, the *Journal of Professional Services Marketing*, the *Journal of Marketing for Higher Education*, the *Journal of Marketing for Mental Health*, and the *Journal of Marketing/ Management for Professionals*. Journals in such diverse fields as library science, art history, leisure studies, occupational therapy, and hospital management have joined the marketing bandwagon. To take just one example, in a 1982 review of library journals, Norman found 87 articles, books, and monographs on some aspect of marketing.[29] Among the titles he found were "Marketing and Marketing Research: What the Library Manager Should Learn," *Journal of Library Administration* (Spring 1980); "The 'Marketization' of Libraries," *Library Journal* (1981); "Publicity and Promotion for Information Services in University Libraries," *Aslib Proceedings* (1974); and "Libraries: A Marketable Resource," *Canadian Library Journal* (1977).

In addition to this published output, by the late 1980s courses in nonprofit marketing were routinely demanded by MBA students at major universities as well as by swelling ranks of students from such diverse departments as health administration, public administration, arts administration, library science, law, social work, and leisure studies.

Major practitioner associations in nonprofit fields like the arts, health, and education included interest groups specifically concerned with marketing. Virtually all such associations find that they must routinely schedule marketing presentations at their annual professional meetings, and from time to time they organize special miniconferences on various aspects of marketing theory and practice.

In the field, marketing specialists in nonprofit organizations were no longer a rarity. They no longer had to hide behind deceptive job titles like director of development, education coordinator, or patient liaison officer, nor was it necessary that they carry more conventional titles like public relations manager or advertising manager when their real job was marketing. By 1987, there were over 2,000 high-level marketing executives working in U.S. hospitals. A wide range of consulting organizations sprang up in major centers, especially around Washington, D.C., to offer their services as marketing specialists in the nonprofit sector. To meet this new competition, the major traditional consulting firms found that they had to have special divisions or individuals dedicated to advising nonprofit marketing professionals.

After 15 years of rapid growth, it became no longer necessary to market marketing to nonprofit managers or to convince marketing students and scholars that it is both feasible and legitimate to study this new and exciting application. Today's textbooks, in contrast to earlier volumes, do not have to demonstrate in detail the diverse and sometimes unrecognized uses of marketing in a wide range of nonprofit, public sector, and individual contexts. It is no longer necessary to say in effect to readers, "I'll bet you didn't know that this was marketing or that you were doing marketing all along!"

The decade of the 1990s finds the idea of nonprofit marketing well accepted in most quarters, but now rapidly being broadened and deepened. As noted, this is partly the result of the self-confident proselytizing by nonprofit scholars, consultants, and marketers who argue that nonprofit marketing is highly effective and can have wide applicability. But it is also the result of four critical developments in the social and economic environment in which the nonprofit idea is nurtured. These developments have the effect of *accelerating* the spread of the "nonprofit idea."

Changes in the Political Environment in Several Countries Encouraging Increased Privatization of Public Services.   Countries in both the developed and developing world are becoming increasingly concerned about the efficiency and effectiveness of social programs and public services. As countries find themselves with both rising expectations on the part of their citizens and a growing number of alternative uses for public revenues (e.g., to reduce trade deficits), their governments have given increasing attention to "privatization" as an innovative means of lowering costs and improving the effectiveness of public programs.[30]

Privatization is the transfer to a private sector firm of some specific social program or service through one or more involvement mechanism. These include

1 short-term contracts or subcontracts for the delivery of specific services such as refuse collection or security in public buildings.
2 long-term monopoly franchises for the provision of basic services such as gas and electric power.
3 management contracts to run public services such as hospitals or food services in government buildings.
4 joint ventures between the government and private firms.
5 total divestiture of public programs.

In the United States, between 1981 and 1988, more than 45,700 federal jobs were contracted out to private sector firms at a savings to the U.S. taxpayer of $2.8 billion.[31] Even more contracting out has taken place at the state and local level where private sector firms have been given the tasks of running hospitals, managing prisons, and collecting garbage. The expectation is that privatization of public services will make them more efficient and more effective. As Arthur Young & Company put it,

> advocates tend to view contracting out as a way for their already money-strapped communities to cut the budget, hold the line on taxes yet continue to deliver essential services. The general belief is that the private sector has the flexibility, innovation, efficiency in management, and a controlling mechanism—

the profit motive—that enables it to provide goods and services more profitably than the public sector.[32]

While there is not universal agreement as to whether privatization is always desirable, particularly in sensitive areas like housing, health care, and prison management,[33] it is clear that privatization will continue to grow dramatically and this, in turn, will put greater pressure on public agencies who now have to learn to market their services in what was once a monopoly market and for-profit organizations who have to learn to market "public" services in an environment where major outcomes are not profits but social welfare.

Changes in the Social Climate Encouraging Increased Voluntarism.   At his presidential inauguration in 1989, George Bush pledged to make the United States a "kinder, gentler" nation, one in which people help other people and not rely solely on the government to meet social needs. He seeks a "thousand points of light" by which citizens volunteer for work in private nonprofit organizations and assume social burdens in a spirit of neighborliness that was commonplace in the earliest days in America. Many social observers have argued that the current drug scourge will not be eliminated unless citizens "take back the streets" or that AIDS will not be controlled unless individuals practice "safe sex" to protect themselves and others with whom they have contact.

One major effort in this direction is the "Give 5" program spearheaded by The Independent Sector in Washington. In the late 1980s, The Independent Sector established a prestigious panel of nonprofit and foundation leaders and members of other national organizations concerned about charitable funding to develop "Daring Goals for a Caring Society."

> After thorough study of the patterns and practice of American giving and volunteering and after long deliberations on the needs and aspirations of Americans, the task force put forth a challenge: that Americans double their charitable giving and increase volunteering 50 percent by 1991.
> These goals are based on solid evidence that Americans are developing the habit of "fiving"—a kind of contemporary version of tithing. Fivers give 5 percent or more of their income to charity and volunteer five or more hours a week to the causes of their choice. An estimated 20 million people are 5 percent givers and 23 million are fiver volunteers.[34]

This task force further recognized that achieving this lofty ambition involves achieving two broad goals:

- *Goal 1.* To establish a climate for giving and volunteering so that society as a whole and individuals in particular are conditioned to the importance of private philanthropy and volunteer service.
- *Goal 2.* To develop a far greater ability of voluntary organizations to raise money and involve volunteers.

What is significant about these basic goals is that they are both *marketing* goals. Society must be changed to take on a broader and deeper role in provision of social welfare services while at the same time, volunteer organizations must become first-rate generators of private financial and personnel support.

Changes in the Orientation of International Social Agencies According Social Marketing a Central Role.   After many years of only scattered interest in the application of marketing to major social problems, the 1990s are seeing dramatic growth of what has come to be called "social marketing" to a wide range of international social problems. The leader in this movement has been the U.S. Agency for International Development which is pouring millions of dollars per year into marketing programs affecting family planning, child survival, and AIDS in developing countries. Symbolic of this trend is the fact that USAID's recent RFP (Request for Proposal) to extend its multimillion-dollar child survival project once called "Communication for Child Survival" is now called "Communication *and Marketing* for Child Survival" (emphasis added).

Social marketing has proved effective in the public sector. It has saved U.S. taxpayers over $20 billion in losses due to forest fires through the Smokey the Bear campaign; helped many communities and international agencies recruit blood donors to meet growing hospital and research needs;[35] helped reduce infant mortality from diarrheal dehydration in Egypt and Honduras;[36] contributed to major antismoking programs;[37] and made family-planning products and services more accessible than ever in Mexico, the Dominican Republic, Thailand, Ghana, and Bangladesh.[38]

International social marketing is an idea whose time has clearly come.

Changes in Traditional Sources of Support for Nonprofits.   As noted in the next section, historically nonprofits in the United States and in many other countries have relied for their basic existence on three kinds of support, government subsidies or grants, corporate giving, and private giving. More recently, they have added sales of services and ancillary marketing (e.g., catalogues and retail outlets to supplement the traditional sources). In many nonprofit areas *all five* of these sources are either declining or are at risk. Barring a major shift in the political and social climate, several of them may be expected to play a diminished role in the next decade.

A case in point is the predicament of performing arts organizations. Performing arts organizations are today in serious financial jeopardy. Since 1986, major organizations such as the Dallas Ballet; the Denver, Oakland, and Oklahoma symphonies; the Boston Shakespeare Company; and the Alaska Repertory Theater have gone permanently or temporarily out of business.[39] The future for the remaining institutions does not look promising. Major environmental trends are working against the arts:

1   In the face of increasingly tight budgets, federal and state support for the arts has declined. Between 1981 and 1988, the federal budget for the National Endowment for the Arts declined 24 percent in real dollars. State governments have decreased funding for many arts councils and, in some cases, have threatened them with outright elimination.[40]

2 Corporate donations to the arts have leveled off or, in some specific cases, declined.[41] While it is hoped that this is a short-term aberration resulting from the stock market crash of 1987, many corporations are shifting priorities back to "bottom-line" investments.

3 There have been significant changes under the Federal Tax Reform Act of 1986 that reduce incentives for individuals to donate cash or other gifts to the arts, including museums.[42]

In addition to these changes in traditional support, the arts have also felt pressure on two other sources that have become increasingly important since the late 1980s:

1 Attendance at the performing arts has declined. A poll by Louis Harris and Associates showed that from 1984 to 1987 attendance declined 25 percent at plays, 9 percent at popular and classical music concerts (although *major* orchestras reported a 13 percent increase from the 1980–81 to 1985–86 seasons)[43] and 38 percent at opera and musical theater events.[44] Harris attributes this decline primarily to the significant shrinkage that has taken place in individual households' available leisure time as well as to higher ticket prices and, in many cases, a lack of availability of events and facilities.

2 Pending federal legislation threatens to tax a growing source of revenue for many performing arts organizations, for example, ancillary sales through gift shops, restaurants, and catalogues.

Of the five factors noted, the ones over which performing arts organizations have the most potential leverage are donations (corporate and private) and attendance. If the arts are to increase their survivability in the next decade, they must find new ways of expanding their audiences and their sources of financial investment. This inevitably means that marketing must play a more and more vital role as these organizations reach out for ways of making dramatic changes in their fortunes.

This means that, as the "Daring Goals" task force underscored, nonprofit marketers must significantly improve their skills. This book is designed to meet that challenge. It provides a motivated audience of students and practitioners with the concepts, techniques, and illustrations needed to make them first-rate nonprofit marketing managers. The book, therefore, is decidedly not introductory in the sense of acquainting the naive reader with marketing and its possibilities and motivating him or her to begin to use marketing in the day-to-day management of a nonprofit organization. Instead, the book assumes that the reader is already motivated and knows a little about marketing and what it might do but wants to know how actually to carry out marketing programs more extensively and more effectively.

As will be demonstrated repeatedly in the chapters to follow, it is our view that a first-rate marketing manager is one who has acquired (1) an ingrained appreciation of the *philosophy* of marketing, (2) a comprehensive and practical *process* for solving marketing problems, and (3) an *awareness and understanding* of the latest tools and techniques that can be used to make effective marketing decisions in specific areas. The book is organized around these objectives.

It is also a book *specifically* designed for the nonprofit sector. The "non-profit" distinction is not just an academic exercise. If there were not factors that were unique to the nonprofit context, there would be no point to a book like this; any of the many excellent general marketing texts would be perfectly satisfactory. But nonprofit marketing is not the same as for-profit marketing. The student and practitioner must appreciate the differences because they have major effects on what one can and cannot do as a marketing manager. We begin by considering the evolution of this new sector and the present significantly increased role for marketing.

Before proceeding, one definitional issue must be clarified. Some authors and several reporting agencies distinguish between two broad kinds of non-profits. On the one hand, there are publicly owned governmental agencies like the U.S. Postal Service, the Office of Cancer Communications of the National Cancer Institute, and the British Railway System; on the other hand, there are nongovernmental or "third-sector" nonprofits. Forms of ownership among the latter are very diverse; they range from corporations to cooperatives to individual enterprises. In our view, although nongovernmental and governmental nonprofits may differ in organizational form, they do not differ significantly in the unique marketing problems they face. Their differences from for-profit marketers are much more profound and are, indeed, the basis for this volume.

EVOLUTION OF NONPROFIT ORGANIZATIONS

Nelson Rosenbaum has proposed that since the American Revolution, the role of nonprofit organizations in society has evolved through four stages. The earliest stage conforms to what he terms a *voluntary/civic model*.[45] In Pilgrim times through the beginning of the present century, services that were not available from the government and were beyond the means of individual citizens were often provided by neighbors for each other. Thus, in those times—and in some rural areas and some fundamentalist religious communities today—citizens would band together to operate the volunteer fire department or to help a needy family build a barn. Such a model was (and in some cases, still is) appropriate to a world with homogeneous interests, personal philosophies based on sharing, and a generally low level of economic welfare.

As the country prospered, the industrial revolution concentrated great wealth in the hands of a few families. Whether out of a sense of social responsibility or plain guilt, extremely rich families like the Morgans, Rockefellers, and Carnegies developed a pattern of what Rosenbaum calls *philanthropic patronage.* This patronage significantly benefited major U.S. educational and cultural institutions during the early part of this century.

Following the onset of the depression and the rapid growth of government-supported social institutions and programs, America turned in the 1940s and 1950s to a nonprofit model based on *rights and entitlements.* Many groups argued that they were entitled to at least partial support out of public taxation funds for their work, their institutions, or both, in part because they served the general social interest.

The final stage is the one in which we presently find ourselves—the *competitive/market* stage. In the earlier three stages, nonprofits relied for support on (1) individual willingness to share, (2) the generosity of the wealthy, or (3) the largess of federal, state, and municipal governments. Although there is now growing interest in voluntarism, nonprofits are faced with two realities. First, they cannot rely on traditional sources of support. Second, as they increasingly turn to the marketplace for this support, they find other nonprofits there scratching for the same subsistence. The consequence is that in the 1990s, the greatest challenges facing nonprofit marketers are *competitive.* Marketers must not only, learn to find and attract new markets, they must learn how to accommodate their efforts to a flood of competitors.

This means that marketing *strategy* must be the dominant concern of marketing managers in the 1990s. They must learn how to choose target markets carefully, position their offerings effectively vis-à-vis competitors, and coordinate the many elements of their marketing programs to squeeze the most impact from the fewest resources.

IMPORTANCE OF THE NONPROFIT SECTOR[46]

The nonprofit sector is surprisingly large. A recent study by The Independent Sector found that in 1987 there were 1,368,000 private nonprofit organizations and government entities in the United States. These were distributed as follows:

Tax-exempt organizations reported to IRS	561,000	(41.0%)
Other nonprofits, tax-exempt	378,000	(27.6%)
Churches	346,000	(25.3%)
Government entities	83,000	(6.1%)

In the ten years from 1977 to 1987, the number of nonprofit and government entities grew 13.7 percent. However, this growth is much slower than the 38.8 percent increase for the business sector. The latter figure is not surprising in a decade mostly under Ronald Reagan when the promotion of private enterprise was a core objective of government policy.

The distribution of nonprofits tracked by the IRS for the years 1977, 1982, 1984, and 1987 is reported in Table 1-1.

The number of entities is deceiving since many nonprofits and government agencies can be very large. If one includes assigned values for unpaid volunteers

Table 1-1

NUMBER OF ACTIVE ENTITIES ON MASTER FILE
OF TAX-EXEMPT ORGANIZATIONS, 1977, 1982, 1984, AND 1987
(FISCAL YEAR ENDING SEPTEMBER 30)

Tax code number	Type of tax-exempt organization	1977	1982	1984	1987
501(c)(1)	Corporations organized under an act of Congress	1,072	24	24	24
501(c)(2)	Title-holding companies	5,223	5,522	5,679	5,977
501(c)(3)	Religious, charitable, etc.*	276,455	322,826	352,884	422,103
501(c)(4)	Social welfare	129,496	131,578	130,344	138,485
501(c)(5)	Labor, agriculture organizations	87,656	86,322	76,753	75,238
501(c)(6)	Business leagues	44,100	51,065	53,303	59,981
501(c)(7)	Social and recreational clubs	50,031	54,036	55,666	60,146
501(c)(8)	Fraternal beneficiary societies	141,138	116,549	92,431	98,979
501(c)(9)	Voluntary employees' beneficiary societies	6,486	8,703	10,145	10,927
501(c)(10)	Domestic fraternal beneficiary societies	12,410	18,570	16,116	17,813
501(c)(11)	Teachers' retirement funds	13	13	11	11
501(c)(12)	Benevolent life insurance associations	4,801	5,071	5,200	5,572
501(c)(13)	Cemetery companies	5,264	6,290	6,845	7,942
501(c)(14)	Credit unions	5,074	6,074	6,053	6,652
501(c)(15)	Mutual insurance companies	1,450	1,073	998	50
501(c)(16)	Corporations to finance crop operation	31	22	19	18
501(c)(17)	Supplemental unemployment benefit trusts	800	734	747	728
501(c)(18)	Employee-funded pension trusts	4	3	3	5
501(c)(19)	War veterans' organizations	14,305	23,851	22,100	24,749
501(c)(20)	Legal services organizations	–	90	140	210
501(c)(21)	Black lung trusts	–	9	14	21
501(d)	Religious and apostolic organizations	63	68	81	88
501(e)	Cooperative hospital service organizations	–	106	90	80
501(f)	Cooperative service organizations of operating educational organizations	–	–	–	1
521	Farmers' cooperatives	3,794	2,791	2,673	2,405
	Total	789,666	841,440	838,319	939,105

SOURCE: *Dimensions of the Independent Sector: A Statistical Profile*, 3rd ed. (Washington, D.C.: The Independent Sector, 1989). Reproduced with permission.

*All section 501(c)(3) organizations are not included because certain organizations, such as churches, integrated auxiliaries, subordinate units and conventions or associations of churches, need not apply for recognition of exemption unless they desire a ruling.

– = No cases.

and family workers, the importance of the nonprofit sector becomes much more significant. In 1987, the national income created by the three major sectors (in billions of dollars) is as follows:

Private, nonprofit	$ 247.1	(6.5%)
Government	$ 570.7	(15.0%)
Business	$2,983.0	(78.5%)

Thus, business, which makes up 93.7 percent of all entities, only contributes 78.5 percent of national income when values are assigned to voluntary work. And the latter figure has declined somewhat from 79.6 percent in 1977.

In terms of employment, there are almost 8 million full-time and part-time workers in the private nonprofit sector earning $130 billion in wages and salaries and almost 21 million in government service earning $420 billion. To these paid workers can be added 6 million volunteers in private nonprofits and almost 2.5 million in the public sector. Employment by nonprofits and government involved 28.7 percent of all those undertaking paid or unpaid work in 1987, a share that is up slightly since 1977.

Private nonprofits had operating expenditures of $290 billion in 1987, an increase of 35 percent *in constant dollars* since 1977 and 131 percent since 1960. Private nonprofits spent $896 for every person in the United States in 1987. This, too, is a significant 21 percent increase since 1977 and a 71 percent increase since 1960. The expenditures per capita rises to $1,208 if one includes an imputed value for the wages of unpaid volunteers.

Probably the most dramatic indicator of the growing importance of the so-called "third sector" is the fact that current operating expenditures of private nonprofits comprise 6.4 percent of the U.S. gross national product, a significant increase from only 5 percent as recently as 1970. This contribution to GNP has grown steadily since 1960 at which time the private nonprofit sector was only 3.6 percent of GNP.

Although the independent sector is huge, its problems are substantial. According to Smith and Rosenbaum, the independent sector reported that it obtained only 50 percent of its revenues from internally generated income (that is, from marketed products and services).[47] This varies greatly by subsector, from 7 percent for religious organizations to 79 percent for education and research institutions. The unmet resource needs for these organizations are made up by private philanthropy (25 percent) and government support (25 percent).

Analysis within the subsectors further delineates the potential for marketing in specific narrower fields. A 1983 survey of nonprofit income sources carried out by the Rockefeller Foundation reported the average percentages of earned income for one group, arts organizations. Their results are given in Table 1-2.

Outside the arts field, the Rockefeller study found that colleges and universities generated only 52 percent of their own income, private and secondary

Table 1-2

PERCENT OF INCOME THAT WAS EARNED
BY SELECTED NONPROFIT CATEGORIES, 1983

Organizations	% Income That Was Earned
121 Theaters	71
32 Major symphonies	56
32 Regional symphonies	55
91 Regional ballet companies	54
109 Opera companies	48
64 Media arts centers	46
4,409 Museums	42

SOURCE: James C. Crimmins and Mary Kiel, *Enterprise in the Nonprofit Sector* (New York: The Rockefeller Brothers Fund, 1983), p. 141.

schools 70 percent, zoos and aquariums 47 percent, and family service and child welfare organizations barely 14 percent.

DEFINING NONPROFIT MARKETING

The examples noted earlier of innovative marketing programs clearly indicate that marketing has a wide range of applications in nonprofit contexts. But it is also apparent that some of these applications are not very different from strategies and tactics one finds in profit-making organizations. Indeed, many governmental and nongovernmental nonprofits routinely carry on programs that are intended to be profit making. They consciously sell products and services to bring in needed revenue. For some, such as theaters and symphonies selling individual tickets and subscriptions or hospitals "selling" surgery and convalescent care, generating this revenue is their primary business. For others, selling products and services is a secondary business designed to supplement a more basic social mission. This is the case of the Girl Scouts selling cookies, the Sierra Club selling calendars, the American Red Cross selling first-aid kits, and most museums selling a wide diversity of gift items, reproductions, and food and drinks. These are not trivial businesses.

- Girl Scout Cookies constitute 10 percent of all cookies sold in the United States.
- Merchandise sales and royalties at New York's Metropolitan Museum of Art in 1986–87 generated sales of $53 million and earnings of $9.2 million or 14 percent of all of the Met's operating income.[48]
- The Washington State University bookstore is one of the biggest department stores in Eastern Washington State.

On the other hand, there are also *profit-making* organizations that carry out activities very much like those provided by nonprofit social service agencies.

Allstate Insurance has mounted a substantial attitude-change project designed to secure public, governmental, and auto manufacturer support for air bags for automobiles. Reynolds Metals urges consumers to recycle cans, and the local gas company tells us about ways to *save* energy (not buy it!). The liquor industry promotes sensible drinking. Exxon sponsors programming on public television, and the 7-Eleven minimarket food chain and others are active in the annual muscular dystrophy charity drive. Many supermarkets and mail order firms help in the search for missing children.

Public and Private Nonprofits

Confusion in the definition of "nonprofit" stems, in part, from the fact that now a number of quasi-governmental agencies like the postal service and Amtrak have emerged that appear to be neither traditional nonprofits nor profit-making organizations. As Lovelock points out, for example, the British Post Office became an independent corporation in 1961 and the U.S. Postal Service became an independent agency of the executive branch in 1971. These quasi-governmental organizations are often very large. For example, the British Railways Board holding company in 1980 operated a passenger rail service, a freight rail service, a shipping firm, eleven harbors, a hovercraft company, a food service company (for trains and stations), a locomotive and rolling stock construction company, an international consulting firm, and a North American passenger sales business.[49] As noted earlier, this trend to shift activities to the private sector through privatization is likely to accelerate.

Finally, it must be noted that not all the organizational alternatives available in the United States are possible in other countries of the world. In Thailand, for example, there is no legal entity like the U.S. nonprofit organization. As a consequence, Population Development Associates, a highly entrepreneurial rural developer and marketer of contraceptives, has been forced to set up a taxable enterprise but informally agree that any "profits" will be kept in the organization and not distributed to the nominal "stockholders."

CLASSIFICATION OF NONPROFIT ORGANIZATIONS

Since a welter of confusing organizational forms are doing "nonprofit marketing," it is essential that some definitions be established. A great many alternative definitions have been offered in recent years to distinguish "profits" from "nonprofits" and to separate various kinds of nonprofits from each other. Many authors suggest, as we have here, that the distinction between profits and nonprofits is not the only useful dichotomy, since even in the nonprofit sector there are public corporations like the postal service and state-run telephone and rail companies that are virtually indistinguishable from private corporations in their drive for sales and profits. Smith and Rosenbaum[50] suggest that *sources of funding* are a good basis for a typology, classifying organizations into those that are funded by (1) profit, (2) government revenues (taxes, grants, bonds, etc.), and (3) voluntary donations. Rados[51] suggests that within each area, a key distinction ought to be the organizational form of the venture (sole enterprise, association, corporation, partnership, or foundation). Fine,[52] on the other hand, emphasizes separating nonprofits and profits by the type of offering the organization is involved with (tangible products, services, or behavior changes).

Two authors propose a two-dimensional classification. Lovelock and Weinberg propose (after Smith and Rosenbaum) segregating public organizations in terms of their sources of financial support as well as by the extent of political control to which the organization is subject. They suggest that Amtrak and the U.S. Postal Service are examples of organizations under "tight political control," whereas British Railway and the U.K. post office are "largely independent of political control."[53]

A different kind of control is emphasized in Henry Hansmann's widely quoted partitioning of nonprofits according to two sets of characteristics. The first is whether the organization is *donative* or *commercial*, that is, whether it secures its revenues primarily from donations or from charges to users. The second is whether the organization is *mutual* or *entrepreneurial*.[54] Mutual organizations are primarily controlled by users, whereas entrepreneurial organizations are controlled by professional managers. For example, in the United States, the donative-mutual category would include many religions, local political organizations, and lobbying groups. The commercial-mutual category would include such groups as professional associations and nonprofit health or golf clubs. The donative-entrepreneurial category includes groups such as arts organizations, the Red Cross, and the Salvation Army. The commercial-entrepreneurial category would cover groups like nonprofit hospitals and contraceptive marketing programs.

A problem with many of these classification schemes is that they overlook the fact that nonprofit organizations often have different divisions that do different things, putting them simultaneously in different sectors of any typology. Thus, in Hansmann's classification scheme, the Los Angeles County Museum is donative-entrepreneurial with regard to amassing its collections yet commercial-entrepreneurial in its museum gift shop. Some hospitals are commercial-mutual in their outpatient services but donative-mutual in their candy striper patient services.

Legal Definition
and the Problem of Unrelated Income

One very important classification dimension is the legal one. One may always ask whether the organization is, in fact, a legally defined nonprofit. Section 501 of the Internal Revenue Code grants tax-exempt status to 24 different categories of organizations. Forty-five percent are covered under Section 501(c)(3), which includes charitable, religious, scientific, and educational institutions. Section 501(c)(4) of the Tax Code includes social welfare groups; section 501(c)(6), business leagues; and section 501(c)(7), social clubs (see Table 1-1).

It is essential that nonprofit managers obtain formal designation as a nonprofit for their organizations since a great many benefits are available to such enterprises. For example, U.S. nonprofits receive the following special treatments or exemptions:

- Exemption from federal, state, and local income taxes.
- Exemption from local property taxes in most cases.
- Exemption from unemployment insurance payments in some areas.
- Lower bulk postage rates.
- Exemption from the Robinson-Patman Act.
- Possible lower charges or none at all for federal services.
- Exemption from tort liability under common law.
- Hospitals and some other organizations can issue tax-exempt bonds.
- Charitable, educational, scientific, and certain other organizations can receive donations, gifts, and bequests that permit tax deductions for the giver.
- Access to donated space and air time from media.

Two rationales are typically offered for the special status of nonprofits. The most common is the "public goods" rationale, which argues that nonprofits provide services such as health care, education, and basic research that would not be provided were it not for the tax subsidy offered by the government. The second rationale, called the "quality assurance" rationale, argues that nonprofits provide services in areas in which consumers are ordinarily ill equipped to judge quality, such as health care and education. Having these services performed by tax-exempt nonprofits supposedly assures the public of quality and protection in situations where for-profit firms might charge excessive prices for inferior services.

In the past, government was relatively generous in granting special benefits to nonprofits. Ironically, however, the recent successes of marketing in the nonprofit sector have caused a major shift in federal thinking about nonprofits. As we shall note throughout this volume, many nonprofits have become extremely entrepreneurial, taking advantage of opportunities for direct revenue generation to supplement donative sources of funding. The Urban Institute estimates that about 10 percent of nonprofits now have some commercial enterprise.

Many nonprofits have dramatically pushed the frontiers of merchandising and greatly angered competing businesspeople and raised questions among the general public:

- The Metropolitan Museum of Art by 1989 had established boutiques selling its merchandise and gift items in shopping malls in New Jersey and Stamford, Connecticut, and within R.H. Macy's Manhattan store. It also licenses its name to manufacturers of "museum collections" of sheets and fabrics.[55] In 1987–88, the Met sold over $25.9 million worth of merchandise from its mail-order operations, up 19 percent over a year earlier. The Met earns overall *17 percent* on revenue, more than *three times* the average pretax profits for department store chains.[56]

- The Smithsonian Institution has nine retail outlets in Washington, D.C., and sends mail order catalogues to 5 million people a year. It recently began to make and sell its own videocassettes.[57]
- A large number of university bookstores sell not only textbooks and supplies to students but also blue jeans, computers at discount prices, and photo finishing services.[58] It has been estimated that nearby computer dealers may lose as much as $1 billion in sales to university bookstores each year.[59]

Ventures like these have led many in Washington to raise an alarm. These critics argue that the nonprofit sector, which was once dominated by donative organizations, is not only increasing its share of the GNP, but, more significantly, is becoming dominated by "commercial nonprofits."[60] This new breed, it is argued, secures substantial portions of their income from sales to those who can afford to pay, not to the poor and indigent whom the nonprofits were often granted their special status to serve. A major concern is that in these industries, nonprofits represent unfair competition for for-profit firms, especially small businesses. Analysts have suggested that nonprofits have become major factors in industries like audiovisual supplies, analytical testing, and research services where existing for-profit firms cannot easily exit from these industries due to their large investments. Thus, the nonprofits have caused an oversupply of firms, a decline in prices, and lower returns on investment. In other industries, it is claimed that nonprofits can underprice competitors (for example, in selling computers or in securing government contracts) because of their significant tax and other cost advantages.

The reason nonprofits have "gotten away" with these "business" activities is that the IRS simply looks at the overall purpose of the organization, not at individual ventures, to define nonprofit status. In 1950, however, the Congress determined that nonprofits must pay taxes on proceeds of "unrelated" business activities. Thus, even when an organization has been designated a nonprofit, the government still pays very close attention to its individual activities. The government's position is that any revenue-generating activity that is *unrelated* to the organization's basic mission must be taxed as would a for-profit enterprise. Thus, a manager must clearly understand whether any present or proposed ventures for which marketing plans are to be developed will be officially classified by the IRS as unrelated business activities. In some cases, it may be desirable to spin off an operation into a for-profit subsidiary. Boston University has spun off its bookstore operations which now include a clothing section and a restaurant. The New England Medical Center is putting some of its nonprofit revenues into a subsidiary that will develop computer software.[61]

Above all, managers should be extremely careful that the amount of unrelated, taxable activity does not grow to comprise too large a percentage of overall revenue. Hopkins has suggested that if this percentage rises above 35 percent, the organization should be concerned that it may lose its overall tax-exempt status.[62] The IRS will permit virtually any kind of unrelated business but will be very attentive to the *total* quantity of such ventures.

National Taxonomy of Tax-Exempt Entities

The problem of classifying nonprofits is important not only to tax collectors, but it is also important to those who wish to track the performance of the nonprofit sector. One solution to this dilemma recently proposed is the creation of a general taxonomy that would serve as the framework for all future statistical studies of the nonprofit sector. Such a framework has been developed by the National Center for Charitable Statistics (NCCS). Their "National Taxonomy of Exempt Entities" attempts to classify all nonbusiness and nongovernmental organizations in the United States with an emphasis on the philanthropic sector.[63]

The taxonomy is highly disaggregated in that it allows one to categorize individual programs within nonprofit organizations with three levels of specificity. First, each program can be classified into 1 of 24 broad service-area or organization categories. (These are listed in Exhibit 1-1.) Next, the program can be more narrowly defined to fit specific program categories. These can be one of nine categories common to all broad groupings (such as research) or a program category *specific* to the individual category. The latter includes over 350 designations developed by the National Center for Charitable Statistics (NCCS). Finally, the program can be defined in terms of the primary beneficiary group it is designed to serve.

The NCCS hopes that the taxonomy will be used by future scholars in their attempts to measure the contribution of the nonprofit sector to the general society as well as by individual organizations, such as foundations, to keep track of their own activities (e.g., fund allocations) over time.

MANAGERIALLY RELEVANT CLASSIFICATION

While the NCCS taxonomy may be useful for outside observers evaluating the nonprofit sector, it is of limited usefulness to *managers* of nonprofit enterprises. Managers need to know: "To what extent does the *type* of nonprofit I have to manage affect what I can do strategically?" Experience has shown that there are two key dimensions that affect what a manager can do in a nonprofit: (1) the nature of the relationship between the nonprofit and its regulatory and support environment and (2) the nature of the basic exchanges the organization is trying to create.

EXHIBIT 1-1

The National Taxonomy of Exempt Entities

The National Taxonomy of Exempt Entities (NTEE) assigns a four-digit code to each category of nonbusiness, nongovernmental organization in the United States. It is intended to classify organizations and not the programs they conduct. Each organization can be assigned a four-digit code. The first digit specifies the organization's major purpose. The next two digits specify the organization's major *program* focus. Finally, the last digit specifies the primary beneficiary of the entity's programs. The 24 major categories are the following:

1 Arts, Culture, Humanities
2 Education/Instruction and Related
3 Environmental Quality, Protection, and Beautification
4 Animal Related
5 Health: General and Rehabilitation
6 Health: Mental Health, Crisis Intervention
7 Health: Mental Retardation, Developmentally Disabled
8 Consumer Protection, Legal Aid
9 Crime and Delinquency Prevention, Public Protection
10 Employment, Jobs
11 Food, Nutrition, Agriculture
12 Housing, Shelter
13 Public Safety, Emergency Preparedness, and Relief
14 Recreation, Leisure, Sports, Athletics
15 Youth Development
16 Human Service: Other including Multipurpose
17 International, Foreign
18 Civil Rights, Social Action, Advocacy
19 Community Improvement, Community Capacity Building
20 Grant Making, Foundations
21 Research, Planning, Science, Technology, Technical Assistance
22 Voluntarism, Philanthropy, and Charity
23 Religion Related, Spiritual Development
24 Mutual Membership Benefit

SOURCE: National Center for Charitable Statistics, *National Taxonomy of Exempt Entities* (Washington, D.C.: The Independent Sector, March 14, 1987).

Nature of the Organization's Environment

Five key questions help define the organization's environment:

- Does the organization rely on donations in whole or in part?
- Is the organization's performance likely to be subject to public scrutiny?

- Is marketing seen as undesirable from the standpoint of some or all members of the organization or its major sponsors or reviewers?
- Does the organization rely extensively on volunteers?
- Is performance largely judged by nonmarketing measures?

We shall consider each of these questions before turning to distinctions associated with the specific *activities* a nonprofit might perform.

Is the Organization Donative?   If the proposed activity or the organization as a whole is funded through private philanthropy or government grants, how one *can* market and *ought to* market is influenced in two major ways. First, outside funding agencies may establish restrictions on what can be done. In such cases, the least bothersome problem but nonetheless an important source of irritation is procedural restrictions that formally specify the steps to be taken, the forms to be filled out, the individuals with whom one must "touch base," or all three. To cite a typical example, many government contracts put a substantial hurdle before nonprofit marketers who wish to carry out research by requiring that questionnaires be approved by the Office of Management and Budget before being taken into the field.

More troublesome are outright restrictions on certain activities. Donors may require that a funded program target specific audiences, even though this may be an inefficient and ineffective use of the nonprofit's resources in the short run. They may proscribe certain media, prevent the hiring of particular specialist staff members, or require that some products be used where better choices are available elsewhere.

One problem of government sponsorship is that nonprofit marketers may not be allowed to choose the segments to which they will market. In some situations they may not be permitted to segment at all, as when the postal service must charge the same price for a first-class letter between any sender and receiver no matter what the costs of the service or the ability or willingness of either party to pay for the service.

In some cases, nonprofit marketers are required by sponsors to tackle segments that are very difficult to reach and influence in comparison with other segments on which limited resources might be more efficiently spent. Contraceptive marketing programs in many developing countries, for example, must be directed at consumers with low literacy and limited awareness of the birth control issue in villages where conventional distribution facilities are nonexistent or primitive. Agencies that would prefer in the short run to build marketing skills and develop a stable revenue base by marketing to more sophisticated – but still needy – urban target audiences are often effectively barred (or at least discouraged) from doing so by sponsoring agencies.

The second consequence of an organization's donative status is that the marketing task is doubled. Not only do marketers have to plan programs aimed at final consumers, they must also consciously plan strategies to ensure continued – and preferably increased – outside support. This problem of having to market to multiple publics is not strictly unique to nonprofits. For-profit corporations must market to stockholders, investment specialists, regulatory agencies, town councils, and even labor unions. But in the private sector, these are typically relatively minor problems. Indeed, the interests of many of these secondary publics (for example, investors and town councils) are well served simply if the corporation's main customer marketing task is successful. More sales revenue means more profits, more jobs, more taxes. But it must be remembered that nonprofits get *50 percent* of their revenues from donations and grants. Support publics are therefore not at all minor concerns. Thus, nonprofits must arrange marketing strategies for *resource attraction* as well as *resource allocation.*

The problems of multipublic marketing will be taken up later in the book. At this point, it must be emphasized that marketing to multiple publics should, in fact, be a *marketing* activity. Too often, contacts with government agencies or major donors are left to the chief executive officer or chairman of the board with no input from the marketing staff.

Is There Public Scrutiny?   Nonprofits may find their marketing options severely restricted if they are subjected to constant public scrutiny. The kinds of problems that can occur are well illustrated by a 1980 situation involving the government of Canada. During the last years of the Trudeau administration, the Canadian government actively sought public support for its newly proposed constitution. To achieve this goal, the government decided to undertake a major advertising campaign at a cost of about $6 million. The campaign raised all sorts of questions about whether the government was doing "too much" marketing. Routine ads for agricultural products and job openings were quite acceptable, but government marketing of highly visible and controversial campaigns like that for the Constitution raised a number of public protests. Whereas it was estimated that federal government advertising in the United States cost about $146 million in 1979, in Canada, with one-twentieth the population, total expenditures were higher at $160 million. This amounted to about $6.66 for each Canadian citizen, compared with 65 cents per person in the United States. The U.S. federal government was the country's twenty-eighth largest advertiser, while in Canada it was the largest, up from seventeenth in 1969. The Canadian government's advertising expenditures, which now are three times those of the second largest advertiser, General Foods, have received extensive public criticism from both industry leaders and individual citizens. J.L. Foley, chairman of the Institute of Canadian Advertising, said that the growth in government advertising constitutes a threat to free speech, a waste of taxpayers' money and "a further emasculation of Parliament and parliamentary democracy." A reader of Toronto's *Globe and Mail* put it more simply. "Good government needs no advertising. It speaks for itself."[64]

The fact that a nonprofit organization is publicly accountable has other restrictive features. One consequence is that nonprofits feel they should ignore certain competitors or not compete with them. Bloom and Novelli distinguish between friendly and unfriendly competitors as follows:

> Social marketers must also be concerned about the impact of a type of competition that commercial marketers rarely face—the friendly competition provided by other social organizations fighting for the same cause. Thus, in developing a marketing plan for the smoking cessation program of the National Cancer Institute, it becomes necessary to consider the potential actions of the National Heart, Lung and Blood Institute, the U.S. Office of Smoking and Health, the American Cancer Society, the American Lung Association, the American Heart Association, and a host of others. Friendly competitors can help the social marketer in many ways, but they can also create fragmented efforts, funding problems, and other difficulties.[65]

Is Marketing Seen as Undesirable?   Over the years, marketing has had difficulty in gaining acceptance in a number of nonprofit organizations. One hindrance was the view that marketing really wasn't necessary. It was argued, for example, that good health does not need to be sold, that hospitals don't need to be marketed, that lawful behavior is simply a social requirement, and that one shouldn't have to advertise to drivers to get them not to speed.

Fortunately, the view that marketing is undesirable because it is unnecessary has faded away, in part because nonprofit managers and their supporters have learned the potential of marketing and in part because they have been starkly confronted with the *need* for it.

More vexing and more lasting is the sometimes not-so-subconscious opinion that at base marketing is *evil*. This opinion manifests itself in three views:

MARKETING IS SEEN AS WASTING THE PUBLIC'S MONEY.   As we have seen in the Canadian government case, a frequent criticism of marketing activities is that they are too expensive. In 1971, for example, the U.S. Army spent $10.7 million on advertising in a 13-week period in an effort to increase army enlistments, and this upset many people. Similarly, the U.S. Postal Service increased its cost of operations by establishing a marketing department within the postal service and giving it a large budget.[66] Many people carefully watch the marketing expenses of charitable organizations to make sure that they do not get out of line with the amount of money being raised.

Organizations, of course, should not add costs that do not produce an adequate return. Nonprofit organizations owe their publics an explanation of the benefits they are seeking to achieve through their marketing expenditures. They should not overspend and they should not underspend. At this stage, nonprofit organizations are more prone to underspend than to overspend on marketing. If the U.S. Army needs a certain number of recruits, $10 million spent on national television is probably the most efficient way to proceed. The issue should not be the absolute cost but the relative attraction cost per 1,000 new recruits. If the U.S. Postal Service needs to develop new and viable mail services for its users, its expenditure on marketing research, planning, testing, and promotion is proper if this expenditure is expected to yield a reasonable return.

MARKETING ACTIVITIES ARE SEEN AS INTRUSIVE.   A second objection to marketing is that it often intrudes into people's personal lives. Marketing researchers go into homes and ask people about their likes and dislikes, their beliefs, their attitudes, their incomes, and other personal matters. A health clinic, for example, sent out researchers to study the fears of married men about vasectomies (male sterilization) in order to formulate a more effective information campaign on behalf of vasectomies. There is a widespread concern that if various government agencies started doing a lot of marketing research, the information might eventually be used against individual citizens or in mass propaganda. Citizens also dislike the fact that their tax money is being spent to do the research.

Ironically, marketing research is primarily carried on to learn the needs and wants of people and their attitudes toward the organization's current products so that the organization can deliver greater satisfaction to its target publics. At the same time, organizations must show a sensitivity to the public's feelings for privacy.[67]

MAKETING IS SEEN AS MANIPULATIVE.   A third criticism is that organizations will use marketing to manipulate the target market. Many smokers resent the antismoking ads put out by the American Cancer Society as trying to manipulate them through fear appeals. Some congressmen were upset with the report that the Interior Department planned to spend more money on a high-powered campaign to tout itself and "its photogenic boss."[68] Image ads by police departments are seen by some citizens as manipulative.

Administrators should be sensitive to the possible charge of manipulation when they implement a marketing program. In the majority of cases, the nonprofit organization is seeking some public good for which there is widespread consensus, and it is using proper means. In other cases, the charge of manipulation may be justified and such efforts, unless they are checked, will bring a "black eye" to the organization and to marketing.

Critics have argued that ads for state lotteries are often uninformative or misleading, especially with respect to the odds of winning.[69] These critiques may be generalized to all of marketing. A headline in *U.S. News and World Report* in 1985 asked, "Is 'Showbiz' Ruining America's Big Museums?" Joseph Veach Noble, former director of the Museum of the City of New York, states the criticism: "This mercantile trend of our cultural institutions has been forced upon us, but it certainly isn't healthy. Aesthetic judgment must now take a back seat to whatever sells." Blockbuster shows produce excessive wear on facilities, divert money and personnel from work on the permanent collection, and alienate some regular museumgoers.[70]

Does the Organization Rely Heavily on Volunteers?   A significant proportion of nonprofit organizations rely upon unpaid volunteers for clerical assistance, fundraising, stuffing envelopes, conducting tours, and even attracting other volunteers. Weisbrod has estimated that as of the mid-1970s, volunteers provided over 20 percent of nonprofits' labor resources.[71] This amounted to 6 billion hours of effort, the equivalent of 3 million full-time workers (4 percent of the U.S. labor force). This can create two types of problems for the nonprofit manager. First, the need for a steady influx of volunteers means that a third "public" is added to those to whom the manager must market. Programs must be designed to attract and retain paid personnel, while a watchful eye must be kept on possible ramifications of proposed programs on existing volunteers. Directors of blood donation programs who rely heavily on volunteers, for example, often find that plans for extending collection hours or expanding into new, marginal, and sometimes unsavory neighborhoods meet with strong resistance from the volunteer segment of their staff. Blood program managers have succeeded in these needed outreach efforts when they have first marketed the program and its benefits to the volunteers.

The second problem with volunteers involves day-to-day management. A universal complaint of managers who have to work with volunteers is that they are unreliable. One manager has what he calls a "rule of thirds" for volunteers. According to his experience, one-third of all volunteers will be highly motivated, eager to help out, and highly responsive to superiors' directions. At the other extreme is the third who seem to want little more than to tell their friends that they volunteered. They seldom appear at all for work. Their promises of assistance are rarely kept, and when they do appear, they resist directions to do anything they don't *really* feel like doing. The third in the middle is the group that can make or break the organization. The ability to effectively motivate and direct this group is the true test of a nonprofit manager's interpersonal skills. Although, as we shall outline in Chapter 10, many of the principal techniques of personnel management in the private sector can and ought to be applied in nonprofit organizations, the simple fact that a manager doesn't have the "carrot" of a salary or the "stick" of potential firing to use to motivate and direct the people needed to make the marketing program successful is often a crucial hindrance in carrying out an effective and fast-moving marketing program.

Is Performance Judged Primarily by Nonmarketing Standards?   Those who judge marketing performance in nonprofit organizations have often been trained in other disciplines and have only a crude appreciation of the realities of day-to-day management. This can seriously affect the kinds of marketing goals that are set for the nonprofit marketer.

Expectations for success, for example, can often be highly exaggerated. Those who evaluate nonprofit programs often want "everyone" to wear seat belts or to stop smoking or to give to their charity. As Peter Drucker notes, "To obtain its budget, [the nonprofit] needs the approval, or at least the acquiescence, of practically everybody who remotely could be considered a 'constituent.' Where a market share of 22 percent might be perfectly satisfactory to a business, a 'rejection' by 78 percent of its 'constituents' . . . would be fatal to a budget-based institution."[72]

A second problem with nonprofit marketing objectives is that accomplishments may be very difficult to detect because of their intangibility. How does one *know*, for example, that museum visits or symphony attendance have become more "educational" or that they "improve the quality of life in the community?" Yet these are often set as the marketing goals of nonprofit institutions. They are perfectly legitimate goals; they just present serious measurement problems. Unfortunately, the combination of that measurement difficulty and the glare of public accountability that faces many nonprofits leads managers too often to seek to achieve what is *measurable* rather than what is important. There is a serious danger, for example, that the nonprofit organization will become a budget maximizer. As Peter Drucker has noted

> being paid out of a budget allocation changes what is meant by "performance" or "results." *"Results" in the budget-based institution means a larger budget. "Performance" is the ability to maintain or increase one's budget.* . . . . Not to spend the budget to the hilt will only convince the budget-maker that the budget for the next fiscal period can safely be cut.[73] (Italics in original.)

As we shall see, this is one of many distortions in planning and performance that the peculiar status of the nonprofit marketing task can give rise to.

Nature of the Exchanges the Organization Is Attempting to Influence

In addition to the differences just described in organizational milieu, nonprofit marketers' options are often affected considerably by the things they are attempting to market. The major *organizational* mission of a church or a synagogue involves the promulgation of religious values, whereas the major organizational mission of museums involves cultural education. But some of the specific *activities* of these two institutions could be virtually identical from a marketing standpoint—both, for example, could be involved in promoting lotteries or reselling goods such as Christmas cards or posters. On the other hand, the *way* identical marketing activities are carried out may be affected by the type of organization. A church, for example, might feel it had to be relatively dignified in promoting its lottery or its Christmas cards, a museum might feel it should have a relatively "classy" promotion, a neighborhood youth group might feel that its image required a more casual, folksy style.

As we will discuss further in Chapter 4, the market transaction that the nonprofit organization is trying to influence is most usefully conceived from a managerial standpoint as an *exchange*. Target audience members are asked to exchange something they value for something beneficial provided by the nonprofit organizations. As seen from the target consumer's perspective, he or she is being "asked" to incur costs or to make some sacrifices (that is, to give up something valuable) in return for some promised benefits. In the main, the kinds of costs consumers are usually asked to "pay" by nonprofit marketers are one of four types:

1 *Economic costs*—for example, to give up money or goods to a charity, or simply to buy a product or service.
2 *Sacrifices of old ideas, values, or views of the world*—for example, to give up believing that the world is flat, that women are inferior, that one is not getting senile, that one is not hooked on drugs, or that abortion is evil (or not evil).
3 *Sacrifices of old patterns of behavior*—for example, to start to wear seat belts or to let someone else meet some of your physical or psychological needs.
4 *Sacrifices of time and energy*—for example, to perform a voluntary service or give blood to a hospital or the Red Cross.

In return for these kinds of sacrifices, consumers in nonprofit enterprises receive benefits of three basic kinds: economic (both goods and services), social, and psychological. The combination of these kinds of sacrifices and benefits yield the matrix outlined in Table 1-3. Here we see that it is only the first 2 cells in the top left corner of the matrix that we typically identify as the domain of the profit sector—although, as we've noted, some nonprofits such as hospitals and schools promote these transactions as their primary objective. It is the other 14 cells that are truly in the nonprofit domain, since *by definition* they cannot generate a profit. What does it mean to be responsible for transactions in these 14 cells?

Table 1-3

**COST/BENEFIT MATRIX
FOR THE PROFIT/NONPROFIT SECTORS**

	Benefits			
Costs	*A Product*	*A Service*	*Social*	*Psychological*
Give up economic assets	Buy a poster	Pay for surgery or an education	Donate to alma mater	Donate to charity
Give up old ideas, values, opinions	Receive free Goodwill clothing	Support neighborhood vigilantes	Support Republicans	Oppose abortion
Give up old behaviors, undertake or learn new behaviors	Practice birth control and receive a radio	Undertake drug detoxification treatment	Go to geriatric group once a week	Wear seat belts
Give up time or energy	Participate in a study and receive a coffeemaker	Attend a free concert	Volunteer for Junior League	Give blood

THE UNIQUENESS OF NONPROFIT MARKETING

In a landmark article, Michael Rothschild implicitly raised the question: What difference does it make *from a marketing management standpoint* to be involved in activities surrounding exchanges other than those where the consumer makes economic sacrifices for economic benefits? Rothschild asks, Why is it so hard to sell brotherhood like soap?[74] Among the answers that he and other authors have developed are the following:

1 There is usually very little good secondary data available to the nonprofit marketer about consumer characteristics, behaviors, media preferences, perceptions, attitudes, and the like compared to what is available in commercial markets. Although studies are sometimes available in the general social science literature, they seldom address key marketing issues.

2 Because the sacrifices consumers are asked to make often involve very central ego needs as well as attitudes and behaviors with respect to controversial or taboo topics, it is often very difficult to secure reliable research data from consumers to serve as the basis for marketing decisions. As Bloom and Novelli point out, "While people are generally willing to be interviewed about these topics, they are more likely to give inaccurate, self-serving, or socially desirable answers to such questions than to questions about cake mixes, soft drinks, or cereals."[75]

3 Very often consumers are being asked to make sacrifices where they are often largely indifferent about the issue. (For example, who really worried about water conservation or the effects of speeding on a country's energy consumption before we were told about it?) This means, as noted above, that marketers will have a serious development marketing problem, which can be extremely costly.

4 Consumers are often asked to make 180-degree shifts in attitudes or behaviors. In the private sector, a marketer simply tries to get consumers to value a product or service *more* than they used to (or at least more than they value competitors' offerings). Seldom does the marketer have a mandate to convert those who are *against* the product to favor it. Yet nonprofit marketers are asked to do this all the time. They must try to entice "macho men" into wearing seat belts, timid souls into giving blood or taking medication around which swirl rumors about devastating effects on sexual potency, or aging citizens to finally admit they are infirm or otherwise need assistance.

5 In the private sector it is often possible to modify an offering to meet consumer needs and wants better, but this is often difficult in the nonprofit sector. There is only one way to obtain blood, for example. Pills must be taken if one is to control high blood pressure. So many notes must be played by an organized set of musicians in order to perform Beethoven's Fifth Symphony. On the other hand, as will be noted in later chapters, the fact that some basic physical or behavioral aspects of the transaction cannot be changed does not mean that other elements of the marketing mix cannot. One can give blood in a great many different, often very attractive physical environments and social settings, for example. Most emphatically, even though the basic offering cannot be changed to meet consumers' needs and wants, other elements of the marketing mix (such as how the offering is described and promoted) can be very responsive to consumer needs and wants.

6 Because the issues with which nonprofits deal involve very complex behaviors

and attitudes, especially in areas like health care or conservation, large amounts of information must be communicated to consumers. For example, to get consumers in developing countries to use oral rehydration therapy (ORT) correctly and regularly to keep their fragile offspring from dying from the loss of fluids and electrolytes during prolonged and severe bouts of diarrhea, they must learn (a) that dehydration *per se* is life-threatening for the child, (b) that ORT will solve the problem, (c) that the benefits of use exceed the costs, (d) that they must use it properly or else it will not be effective or, indeed, may cause more problems than it cures, and (e) that there are specific places where the salts can be obtained and that it will cost X units of the local currency.

7   Very often the benefits resulting from the sacrifice are not evident. If ORT is used properly and in time—that is, *before* the child becomes dehydrated—the mother will *not see* any benefits due to the action she took. A similar problem is faced by those trying to market high blood pressure control programs. High blood pressure is a health problem with no symptoms, and treatment with appropriate therapy does not result in immediately visible effects for its victims. As Rothschild points out, "In order to establish or maintain a behavior, there must be a positive reinforcer. . . . In many nonbusiness cases, neither positive nor negative reinforcements are perceivable."[76]

8   Another distinction in nonprofit marketing is that for some sacrifices, the benefits accrue to others and the individual making the sacrifice benefits little or not at all. A case in point is the 55-mile-per-hour speed limit. Drivers were asked to change their behavior in return for energy savings that would benefit the government, that would possibly keep prices for everyone down to some degree, and that would improve the bargaining position and perhaps the profits of U.S. oil companies. It is understandable that many drivers were not very responsive to marketing programs designed to get them to obey the new law.

9   Because many of the changes to be marketed involve intangible social and psychological benefits, it is often difficult to portray the offering in media presentations. Just how does one describe a symphony concert or the benefits of changed attitudes toward women or energy conservation? If a physical object is involved, its portrayal (for example, showing an orchestra or an army tank) simply does not capture the real benefits one is trying to communicate. Indeed, the product may simply carry the wrong connotations (for example, an orchestra in white tie and tails may connote an intimidating formal occasion; a tank may connote skill training that may not seem useful outside of an army setting).

SUMMARY

Marketing is no longer considered a radical approach to solving the problems of public and nonprofit organizations. It is well into its maturity as an effective management tool. Economic and social changes and a proven rate of success have led to rapidly broadened and deepened applications. In the 1990s, increased privatization of public programs, renewed interest in voluntarism, growing appreciation of the potential role of marketing in international social programs, and decreased support from traditional sources have converged to expand dramatically the importance of nonprofit marketing.

This fourth edition focuses on approaches and techniques that can significantly improve the practice of marketing management in the nonprofit sector on the part of existing and future managers. It emphasizes the development of (1) a proper *philosophy* of marketing, (2) a *systematic approach* to solving marketing problems, and (3) an awareness and ability to use the very latest *concepts and techniques* from the private sector.

The starting point for a consideration of strategic marketing in nonprofit organizations is a clear perception and understanding of the unique environment in which they operate. Nonprofit organizations can be defined legally, but it is more crucial to understand the organization's environment and the specific marketing activities that constitute its mission. The major factors affecting the organization's environment are (1) whether it is a donative or commercial organization, (2) whether its performance is subject to public scrutiny, (3) whether marketing is perceived to be undesirable, (4) whether the organization is largely volunteer, and (5) whether marketing is judged by nonmarketing standards.

The missions of nonprofit organizations differ depending on the type of demand they seek to influence and the type of activity they are engaged in. The organization's type of activity can be defined in terms of the key concept of exchange. On the one hand, target customers are asked to "pay" economic costs; sacrifice old ideas, values, and views of the world; sacrifice old patterns of behavior; or sacrifice time and energy. In return, they can expect products, services, social or psychological benefits, or some combination of these. Although nonprofits seek to influence exchanges of money for goods and services just like for-profit organizations, what makes them unique is their concentration on exchanges involving nonmonetary costs on the one hand and social and psychological benefits on the other. Influencing such exchanges requires different perspectives and modified techniques. Peculiarities of the present state of the nonprofit world make it hard to "sell brotherhood" like soap.

QUESTIONS

1. Governments in developing countries often are concerned that the application of marketing approaches to social programs in their countries would represent merely one more case of American cultural imperialism. How would you counter this argument?

2. Privatization brings for-profit managers into environments where they will be judged by standards other than bottom-line profits. How will these new standards affect the kinds of marketing that should and should *not* be undertaken?

3. It has been argued that promoting increased voluntarism is impossible in affluent and materialistic capitalist societies. How would you rate the likely success of The Independent Sector's "Give 5" campaign? Why?

4. The manager of a local photofinishing chain has challenged the president of

a university to close the photofinishing operation in the university's bookstore. The for-profit manager argues that the university has unfair advantages in competition. What are these advantages? How would you answer the manager's challenge?

5. Give five additional examples of nonprofit marketing projects that would fit within each of the 16 cells in Table 1-3.

NOTES

1. Peter F. Drucker, "What Business Can Learn from Nonprofits," *Harvard Business Review*, July–August 1989, pp. 88–93.

2. Philip Kotler and Sidney J. Levy, "Broadening the Concept of Marketing," *Journal of Marketing*, January 1969, pp. 10–15.

3. Philip Kotler and Gerald Zaltman, "Social Marketing: An Approach to Planned Social Change," *Journal of Marketing*, July 1971, pp. 3–12.

4. Benson Shapiro, "Marketing for Nonprofit Organizations," *Harvard Business Review*, September–October 1973, pp. 223–232.

5. Kotler and Levy, "Broadening the Concept of Marketing."

6. See, for example, Christopher H. Lovelock, "A Market Segmentation Approach to Transit Planning, Modeling and Management," in *Proceedings of the Sixteenth Annual Meeting of the Transportation Research Forum*, 1975, pp. 247–258.

7. See, for example, Charles Weinberg, "Marketing Mix Decision Rules for Nonprofit Organizations," in Jagdish Sheth, ed., *Research in Marketing*, Vol. 3 (Greenwich, Conn.: JAI Press, 1980), pp. 191–234.

8. See, for example, Michael L. Rothschild, *An Incomplete Bibliography of Works Relating to Marketing for Public Sector and Nonprofit Organizations*, 3rd ed. (Madison: Bureau of Business Research and Services, University of Wisconsin, 1981).

9. See, for example, Paul N. Bloom, "Evaluating Social Marketing Programs: Problems and Prospects," *1980 Educators Conference Proceedings* (Chicago: American Marketing Association).

10. Kotler and Zaltman, "Social Marketing."

11. Robin E. MacStravic, *Marketing Health Care* (Germantown, Md.: Aspen Systems Corporation, 1977).

12. See, for example, John L. Compton, "Public Services—To Charge or Not to Charge," *Business*, March–April 1980, pp. 31–38.

13. In addition to the first three editions of the present volume, there are now the following: Christopher H. Lovelock and Charles B. Weinberg, *Marketing for Public and Nonprofit Managers*, 2nd ed. (Redwood City, Calif.: The Scientific Press, 1989); David Rados, *Marketing for Non-Profit Organizations* (Boston: Auburn House Publishing Company, 1981); Armand Lauffer, *Strategic Marketing for Not-for-Profit Organizations* (New York: The Free Press, 1984); Larry L. Coffman, *Public Sector Marketing* (New York: John Wiley, 1986).

14. Philip Kotler and Roberta N. Clarke, *Marketing for Health Care Organizations* (Englewood Cliffs, N.J.: Prentice-Hall, 1986).

15. Philip Kotler and Karen F.A. Fox, *Strategic Marketing for Educational Organizations* (Englewood Cliffs, N.J.: Prentice-Hall, 1985).

16. Seymour H. Fine, *The Marketing of Ideas and Social Issues* (New York: Praeger, 1981).

17. For example, Ralph M. Gaedeke, ed., *Marketing in Private and Public and Nonprofit Organizations: Perspectives and Illustrations* (Santa Monica, Calif.: Goodyear, 1977); Michael P. Mokwa, William D. Dawson, and E. Arthur Priere, eds., *Marketing the Arts* (New York: Praeger, 1980); Michael P. Mokwa and Steven E. Permut, *Government Marketing* (New York: Praeger, 1981); Philip D. Cooper, *Health Care Marketing: Issues and Trends* (Germantown, Md.: Aspen Systems Corporation, 1979); Russell W. Belk, ed., *Advances in Nonprofit Marketing* (Greenwich, Conn.: JAI Press, 1985, 1990); Lee W. Frederiksen, Laura J. Solomon, and Kathleen A. Brehony, eds., *Marketing Health Behavior* (New York: Plenum, 1984).

18. Christopher H. Lovelock and Charles B. Weinberg, *Public & Nonprofit Marketing: Readings & Cases*, 2nd ed. (South San Francisco, Calif.: The Scientific Press, 1990); Philip Kotler, O.C. Ferrell, and Charles Lamb, eds., *Strategic Marketing for Nonprofit Organizations: Cases and Readings* (Englewood Cliffs, N.J.: Prentice-Hall, 1987).

19. Richard K. Manoff, *Social Marketing* (New York: Praeger, 1985).

20. Philip Kotler and Eduardo L. Roberto, *Social Marketing: Strategies for Changing Public Behavior* (New York: The Free Press, 1989).

21. Seymour H. Fine, ed., *Social Marketing* (Needham Heights, Mass.: Allyn & Bacon, 1990).

22. For example, Populations Reports, *Contraceptive Social Marketing: Lessons from Experience* (Series J, no. 30, July–August 1985); *Operations Research: Lessons for Policy and Programs* (Series J, no. 31, May–June 1986); and *AIDS Education—A Beginning* (Series L, no. 8, September 1989).

23. For example, Practical Guide #1, *Model Protocol for Tracking Promotional Campaigns*, Practical Guide #4, *Conducting an Effective Retail Audit*, and *A Program Manager's Guide to Media Planning*.

24. *The Marketing Planning Workbook* (Alexandria, Va.: United Way of America, 1989).

25. Mary Debus, *Handbook for Excellence in Focus Group Research* (Washington, D.C.: Academy for Educational Development, n.d.).

26. Mark R. Rasmuson, Renata E. Seidel, William A. Smith, and Elizabeth Mills Booth, *Communication for Child Survival* (Washington, D.C.: Academy for Educational Development, June 1988).

27. *Making Health Communications Work: A Planner's Guide* (Washington, D.C.: Office of Cancer Communications, U.S. Department of Health and Human Services, April 1989).

28. For example, William D. Novelli, "Can We Really Market Public Health? Evidence of Efficacy," paper presented to the Third National Conference on Chronic Disease Prevention and Control, Denver, Colorado, October 19–21, 1988; Mary Debus, "Lessons Learned from the Dualima Condom Test Market," SOMARC Occasional Paper, September 1987; and William Smith, "A Consumer Strategy for Health, Nutrition and Population," Academy for Educational Development, 1989.

29. O. Gene Norman, "Marketing Libraries and Information Services: An Annotated Guide to the Literature," *Reference Services Review*, Spring 1982, pp. 69–80.

30. John D. Donahue, *The Privatization Decision* (New York: Basic Books, 1989).

31. Margaret E. Kriz, "Slow Spin-off," *National Journal*, Vol. 20, no. 19 (1988) pp. 1184ff.

32. Arthur Young & Company, *Privatization* (New York: Arthur Young, 1987).

33. Robert Kuttner, "A Public Service Doesn't Always Require a Public Payroll," *Business Week*, April 18, 1988.

34. *Daring Goals for a Caring Society* (Washington, D.C.: The Independent Sector, 1988).

35. Patrick E. Murphy, "Recruiting Blood Donors: A Marketing and Consumer Behavior Perspective," in Belk, *Advances in Nonprofit Marketing* (1985), pp. 207–246.

36. B. Frost, *Social Marketing Oral Rehydration Therapy/Solution: A Workshop* (Washington, D.C.: Technologies for Primary Health Care Project, 1984).

37. Farquhar, J.W., N. Maccoby, J. Alexander, H. Breitrose, B. Brown, W. Haskell, A. McAlister, A. Meyer, J. Nash, and M. Stern, "Community Education for Cardiovascular Health," *The Lancet*, Vol. 1 (1977), pp. 1192–1195.

38. K. Higgins, "Marketing Enables Population Control Group to Boost Results," *Marketing News*, October 14, 1983, p. 2.

39. William H. Honan, "Arts Dollars: Pinched as Never Before," *The New York Times*, May 28, 1989, Section 2, p. 1.

40. Ibid.

41. Ibid.

42. Grace Glueck, "Gifts to Museums Fall Sharply After Change in the Tax Code," *The New York Times*, May 7, 1989, pp. 1, 17.

43. Andrew L. Yarrow, "Poll Finds Arts Attendance Has Declined," *The New York Times*, March 16, 1988, Section C, p. 19.

44. Charles Champlin, "Good News and Bad News for the Arts," *Los Angeles Times*, June 16, 1988, Part 6, p. 1.

45. Nelson Rosenbaum, "The Competitive Market Model: Emerging Strategy for Nonprofits," *The Nonprofit Executive*, July 1984, pp. 4–5. See also Paul J. DiMaggio, "The Nonprofit Instrument and the Influence of the Marketplace on Policies in the Arts," in W. McNeil Lowry, ed., *The Arts and Public Policy in the United States* (Englewood Cliffs, N.J.: Prentice-Hall, 1984), pp. 57–99.

46. Much of the material in this section is drawn from Virginia Ann Hodgkinson and Murray S. Weitzman, *Dimensions of the Independent Sector: A Statistical Profile*, 3rd ed. (Washington, D.C.: The Independent Sector, 1989).

47. Bruce L.R. Smith and Nelson Rosenbaum, "The Fiscal Capacity of the Voluntary Sector," paper prepared for delivery at the Brookings Institution National Issues Seminar on "The Response of the Private Sector to Government Retrenchment," Washington, D.C., December 1981.

48. Barnaby J. Feder, "Metropolitan Museum Shows a Retailing Bent," *The New York Times*, May 27, 1988, p. D1.

49. Christopher H. Lovelock, "An International Perspective on Public Sector Marketing," in Mokwa and Permut, *Government Marketing*, pp. 114–143.

50. Smith and Rosenbaum, "Fiscal Capacity."

51. Rados, *Marketing*.

52. Fine, *Marketing of Ideas*.

53. Lovelock and Weinberg, *Marketing for Public and Nonprofit Managers*.

54. Henry Hansmann, "The Role of Nonprofit Enterprises," *The Yale Law Journal*, April 1980, pp. 835–901.

55. Teri Agins, "Growth of Museum Shops Stirs Debate on Tax Status," *The Wall Street Journal*, February 27, 1989, p. B1.

56. Feder, "Metropolitan Museum."

57. Agins, "Growth of Museum Shops."

58. Erik Calonius, "There's Big Money in the 'Nonprofits,' " *Newsweek*, January 5, 1987, p. 38.

59. "Battling 'Nonprofits' for Profit," *Chicago Tribune*, April 16, 1989, p. 14.

60. *Unfair Competition by Nonprofit Organizations with Small Business: An Issue for the 1980s* (Washington, D.C.: Office of Advocacy, U.S. Small Business Administration, November 1983).

61. Calonius, "There's Big Money."

62. Bruce R. Hopkins, "The Tax Implications of Profit-Making Ventures," *The Grantsmanship Center News*, March–April 1982, pp. 38–41. See also Bruce R. Hopkins, *The Law of Tax-Exempt Organizations*, 3rd ed. (New York: John Wiley, 1979).

63. National Center for Charitable Statistics, *National Taxonomy of Exempt Entities* (Washington, D.C.: The Independent Sector, March 14, 1987).

64. Andrew H. Malcolm, "Ottawa Runs Into Protests Over Its Huge Advertising Costs," *The New York Times*, November 1, 1980, p. 10.

65. Paul Bloom and William D. Novelli, "Problems and Challenges in Social Marketing," *Journal of Marketing*, Spring 1981, p. 80.

66. See the case "U.S. Postal Service," in Christopher H. Lovelock and Charles B. Weinberg, *Cases in Public and Nonprofit Marketing* (New York: John Wiley, 1984), pp. 153–162.

67. The American Marketing Association has published a code of ethics for marketing research. A good discussion of ethical perspectives and problems in marketing research is found in C. Merle Crawford, "Attitudes of Marketing Executives Toward Ethics in Marketing Research," *Journal of Marketing*, April 1970, pp. 46–52.

68. Jack Anderson, " 'Blow Your Horn Louder,' Interior Department Told," *Chicago Daily News*, September 28, 1971, p. 13.

69. Charles T. Clotfelter and Philip J. Cook, "The Unseemly 'Hard Sell' of Lotteries," *The New York Times*, August 20, 1987.

70. "Is 'Showbiz' Ruining America's Big Museums?" *U.S. News and World Report*, February 25, 1985, pp. 64–65.

71. Weisbrod, *Statement*.

72. Peter Drucker, "Managing the Public Service Institution," *The Public Interest*, Vol. 33 (Fall 1973), pp. 43–60.

73. Ibid., p. 50.

74. Michael L. Rothschild, "Marketing Communications in Nonbusiness Situations or Why It's So Hard to Sell Brotherhood Like Soap," *Journal of Marketing*, Spring 1979, pp. 11–20.

75. Bloom and Novelli, "Problems and Challenges."

76. Rothschild, "Marketing Communications."

2

Developing a
Marketing Mind-set

A problem for many staff members of charitable organizations is that they believe in what they are doing! They think they have a cause that deserves widespread support—after all, *they* have devoted their lives to it. But very often this fervor leads them to see the fundraising challenge as one of convincing others to share their vision.

Just such a problem has faced United Way of America. As an agency collecting over $3 billion a year through its various programs and chapters, United Way rightly believes that it is a critical catalyst for helping Americans express their need for caring. However, over the years, it has not been uniformly successful in appealing to all segments of the American population. It has had particular difficulty in attracting a "fair share" of donations from young urban professionals who too often have proved resistant to traditional workplace solicitations and United Way promotions.

Research in the mid-1980s by Alan R. Andreasen suggested an alternative strategy for the United Way that has considerable promise for attracting this difficult group. However, the strategy required two important changes in United Way thinking.

First, United Way had to put itself in the minds of its target audiences and understand what it is that *they* want out of their charitable giving. Andreasen suggested that what young urban professionals want is to allocate their charitable expenditures sensibly—just as they allocate their investments and their family budgets. He then proposed that United Way put itself in the position of being the yuppies' "charity investment counselors." United Way's experience in studying the charitable market both in general and in specific communities represents a unique resource that no charity competitor possesses. And it is an asset that this overcommitted market would especially value.

The second change required in United Way thinking is that it become more liberal in its encouragement of "donor designation." Yuppies, it turns out, are independent-minded and resistant to United Way's traditional one-package strategy. However, the United Way possesses a second major differential advantage over most competitors in that it can offer a very elaborate *portfolio* of charities to its Yuppy markets. It needs to see that this market wants not only portfolios but *choices* of portfolios. Just as they seek investments of different risk levels or different country or industry concentrations, so too do they want the opportunity to invest in different charity portfolios. Some may want a portfolio of charities focused on children or the elderly. Others may want to help just major charities like the American Red Cross, or put their money behind "start-ups."

Tom Walker, United Way's Vice President for Marketing, comments on how United Way has adapted to this new perspective.

> Responding to donors, offering meaningful giving choices, adding value to the giving experience, providing regular performance evaluation reports, working together with donors and other community groups to solve problems—stated succinctly, tailoring the options available to donors—will provide the differentiating power for positively positioning the United Way System in the 1990s and beyond.
>
> A substantial number of United Ways have been moving in the direction of *choice* offerings since the early to mid-1980s. Despite United Way's excellent track record in assessing community need and providing funds to charities on the basis of criticality of need, most of the choice programs were focused on the ability to designate one's contribution to a particular agency or agencies, with very little guidance or consumer oriented direction provided by United Way.
>
> This new product offering of the 80s did not fit smoothly into the fabric of United Way, the nation's largest voluntary problem-solving charity. A new approach to this *choice* product was needed. In selected communities across America, the United Way portfolio concept is beginning to emerge. A variety of thoughtful giving investments or funds are being defined and offered to donor customers.

It is the central tenet of this book that one can be a successful marketer only if one has adopted the proper *marketing mind-set.* This means having a clear appreciation for what marketing comprises and what it can do for the organization. More important, it means developing a philosophy of marketing that puts the customer at the center of everything one does. We would argue that much of what is unattractive about marketing practice today is the result of a lack of appreciation of the proper way to go about *doing* marketing.

Marketing is not intimidation or coercion. It is not "hard selling" and deceptive advertising. It is a sound, effective technology for creating exchanges and influencing behavior that, when properly applied, *must be* socially beneficent. In the wrong hands (i.e., in the hands of those without the proper mind-set), what is called "marketing" can be manipulative and intrusive, and an embarrassment to those of us who use marketing as it ought to be used.

A major objective of this book is to develop this proper marketing mind-set in the reader to the extent that it will become second nature in their day-to-day future marketing practice.

THE BOUNDARIES OF MARKETING

One of the reasons for the rapidly growing interest in marketing is that it applies to such a wide range of situations in individuals' professional and personal lives. We would argue that *all* the following represent instances of *marketing:*

- McDonald's says, "You deserve the best today."
- Safeway supermarkets claims it has "lower prices overall."
- You (or your son or daughter) asks someone for a date to go to the movies.
- A subordinate asks for a raise in pay.
- You ask a coworker to join you as a volunteer in the upcoming United Way fund drive.
- Mikhail Gorbachev offers a unilateral arms reduction at the United Nations.
- Your local public TV station holds a pledge drive.
- You try to convince your teenage daughter to stop smoking.
- You request that a supplier give you an additional 3 percent discount if you commit to a larger order.
- You send a press release to a local TV station urging coverage of an upcoming workshop on the homeless.

What is common to all these situations is that someone (a marketer) is attempting to influence the behavior of someone else (a target market). Marketing is not just something that an organization such as Procter & Gamble or Pepsi-Cola does. It is something nonprofits do and something we do daily in our individual personal lives. And, given that all these situations involve marketing, they can all benefit from the application of the very best marketing management techniques.

We define marketing management as follows:

> **Marketing management** is the analysis, planning, implementation, and control of programs designed to create, build, and maintain beneficial exchange relationships with target audiences for the purposes of achieving the marketer's objectives.

The key feature of this definition is *that it focuses on exchanges.* Marketers are in the profession of creating, building, and maintaining *exchanges.* For example, I give you 79 cents and you give me a bar of sweet-smelling soap, or I walk two hours to get to the doctor's office, wait there three more hours, and worry that my house and children are being neglected, and the doctor gives my baby an immunization which protects her from measles. Because exchanges only take place when a target audience member *takes an action*, the ultimate objective of marketing is to influence behavior.

This definition permits us to distinguish marketing from several things it is *not.* Marketing's objectives are not *ultimately* either to educate or to change values or attitudes. It may seek to do so as *a means* of influencing behavior. However, if someone has as a final goal of imparting information or knowledge, that person is in the education profession not marketing. Further, if someone has as a final goal of changing attitudes or values, that person may be described as a propagandist, a lobbyist, or perhaps an artist, but not a marketer. While marketing may use the tools of the educator or the propagandist, its critical distinguishing feature is that its ultimate goal is to influence behavior (either changing it or keeping it the same in the face of other pressures).

Unfortunately, however, many of those who *could* use marketing principles do not do so because they do not see the relevance of marketing to their tasks. But we would argue that, in nonprofit organizations, public relations specialists, fund-raisers, volunteer recruiters, and employee supervisors are all at one time or another marketers. And, as such, they can all benefit from understanding the philosophy and approach to marketing outlined in this book.

On the other hand, there are many in nonprofit organizations (as well as in the private sector) who *think* they are marketers but who go about it the wrong way because they do not really understand what proper marketing is all about. Consider the following examples:[1]

- The director of an urban art museum describes her marketing strategy as "an educational task. I assemble the best works available and then display them grouped by period and style," she says, "so that the museum-goer can readily see the similarities and differences between, say, a Braque and a Picasso or between a Brancusi and an Arp. Our catalogues and lecture programs are carefully coordinated with this approach to complete our marketing mix."
- The public relations manager of a social service agency claims, "We are very marketing oriented. We research our target markets extensively and hire top-flight

creative people with strong marketing backgrounds to prepare brochures. They tell our story with a sense of style and graphic innovation that has won us several awards."

- A marketing vice-president for a charitable foundation ascribes his success to careful, marketing-oriented planning: "Once a year we plan the entire year's series of messages, events, and door-to-door solicitation. We emphasize the fine human-itarian work we do, showing and telling potential donors about the real people who have benefited from donations to us. Hardly a week goes by without some human-interest story appearing in the local press about our work. The donors just love it!"

Each of these executives thinks he or she understands what marketing is all about. *They do not.* But they are not alone. Permut sampled 88 arts administrators in the late 1970s and concluded that for this population, "marketing was seen as primarily sales promotion, heavily tied to advertising and selling activities (particularly for special programs or unusual events)."[2] In a more recent study, Fine surveyed 89 private nonprofits and 59 government agencies engaged in what he has called "idea and social issues marketing" (that is, marketing in which no tangible product or service is involved). The study concluded the following: "If stated objectives are indicative of organizational policy, it appears that public and nonprofit institutions share a pattern of disdain for their clients . . . less than 20% of public and nonprofit institutions and only 33% of the [business] firms consider their principal goal to be satisfying customers."[3] Further, the study found that nonprofit and public sector organizations were less familiar with key marketing concepts and concluded that "institutions sponsoring ideas and social issues certainly do engage in marketing practices, but for the most part, in an ad hoc manner."

Consistent with this view of nonprofit managers as having a narrow or distorted view of marketing is a study of museum directors that showed that, as compared to marketing practitioners, museum directors were

- Less likely to have secured "information from [their] customers regarding what they would like [the museum] to offer."
- More likely to see their product as desirable for everyone rather than as targeted at specific segments.
- Less interested in changing prices to increase revenues.
- Less willing to change their distribution strategy.
- Less willing in the future to "change the nature of the products and services [they] offer [their] customers."[4]

Despite this confusion about marketing, it is not uncommon for these managers to sprinkle their planning documents and casual conversations with terms like "benefit segmentation," "product positioning," "message strategies," "marketing mix," and so forth. But if one were to pay careful attention to the subtle nuances of these managers' attitudes toward their customers and toward what they are offering them, it would become strikingly clear that their approach to marketing resembles what one would have found 30 years ago in the private sector. This approach is very different from that permeating today's modern marketing management.

THE EVOLUTION OF MARKETING PHILOSOPHY

To understand modern marketing management, it is useful to trace the evolution of different business orientations toward marketing in the private sector over the last hundred years. Four orientations can be distinguished.

The Product Orientation

When marketing first emerged as a distinct managerial function around the turn of the century, it found itself in an era that venerated industrial innovation in the design of new products. It was a period that saw the development of the radio, the automobile, and the electric light. In this first period, marketing also was decidedly *product oriented.* The belief was that to be an effective marketer, you had simply to "build a better mousetrap," and, in effect, customers would beat a pathway to your door.

Even today, many organizations are in love with their product. They believe strongly in its value even if their publics are having second thoughts. They strongly resist modifying it even if this would increase its appeal to others. Thus, colleges continue to require their students to study a foreign language even though few ever learn the language and most students report the whole experience as a waste of time and money. Museums feature certain works of art year after year even though they attract the attention or interest of virtually no one. And many churches present the same dull Sunday morning sermons year after year as a matter of tradition, ignoring the changing interests of churchgoers and the steadily declining attendance. We define a product orientation as follows:

> **A product orientation** toward marketing holds that success will come to those organizations that bring to market goods and services they are convinced will be good for the public.

The Production Orientation

As the great opportunities for technological and service innovation peaked in the first decade or so of this century, entrepreneurs such as Henry Ford turned their attention to simplifying and making more efficient the production process itself. This was also the case with marketing. New forms of distribution sprang up—first the department store, then the chain store, and later the supermarket. At that point, developing low-cost mass consumption systems became the keystone of many organizations' marketing success. The key was to sell more and more and thereby sell it cheaper and cheaper.

Today one still finds that many organizations focus their attention on running a smooth production process, even if human needs must be bent to meet the requirements of that process. The personnel in many U.S. employment offices, for example, act as though they are processing objects instead of people. Job seekers come in, sit for long stretches, are asked routine questions, and are offered jobs if any are available. One does not have the impression that the personnel in the employment office exist to serve the job-seeking clientele, but rather that the job seekers exist to meet the needs of the "system." As another example, consider the bus driver who speeds past dozens of waiting commuters so that he can make his timetable. We define a production orientation as follows:

> **A production orientation** toward marketing holds that success will come to those organizations that have the lowest costs and most efficient production and distribution systems.

Sales Orientation

The depression of the 1930s dealt a fatal blow to those profit-centered marketers who defined successful marketing in product or production terms. Building ingenious products, producing them cheaply, and distributing them as widely as possible was a reasonable way to be a successful marketer as long as there were customers out there to buy them. But with the depression, demand shrank dramatically and both factories and distribution systems found themselves with large volumes of excess capacity. In response to this turn of events, marketers reconceived their objectives in competitive terms. The problem was no longer to grind out masses of low-cost, inventive products and distribute them broadly. Now the challenge seemed to be to convince consumers that (1) they should give up their hard-earned money for things other than the bare necessities; and (2) when they did, they should choose the marketer's offering over anyone else's. The key was to persuade consumers that the marketer's offering was *better* than buying nothing or buying competitors' products or services. This new orientation led to significant increases in the role of advertising and personal selling in the marketing mix. "Salesmanship" became the byword of successful marketing. In the 1930s, salesmen and the denizens of Madison Avenue achieved a central role in American folklore. Willy Loman and the "Man in the Grey Flannel Suit" became important symbols of the new business culture.

The selling orientation also continues to be pervasive today. Some organizations believe they can substantially increase the size of their market by increasing their selling effort. Rather than change their products to make them more attractive, these organizations increase the budget for advertising, personal selling, sales promotion, and other demand-stimulating activities. Thus the college president reacts to a decline in enrollment by increasing the budget of the admissions office to permit hiring more recruiters, sending out more direct mail, and improving the looks of the college's brochures. These sales-oriented steps will undoubtedly work to produce more customers in the short run. But their use in no way implies that the college has moved into a marketing orientation that would generate higher sales in the long run. A sales orientation is defined as follows:

> **A sales orientation** toward marketing holds that success will come to those organizations that best persuade customers to accept their offerings rather than competitors' or rather than no offering at all.

The Customer Orientation

The orientations that characterized the three earliest stages in marketing's historical development had one thing in common. They all began marketing planning with the organization and *what it wanted to offer.* In the first two stages, it was expected that grateful customers would come to the organization that had the best or the cheapest offerings. In the "selling" era, the task was somewhat different. The organization was forced to go out and convince customers that they had a really good—perhaps superior—offering. As the economy rebounded after the depression, however, consumers became wealthier and more sophisticated. Consumers became pickier, more responsive to custom-tailored options, less willing to settle for just anything the market tried to persuade them to buy.

At that point, a number of leading marketers came to a very important realization. They realized that they had the marketing equation turned backwards. They had been trying to *change consumers to fit what the organization had to offer.* But truly the customer was sovereign. Whatever he or she chose to buy determined the organization's success. Consumers ultimately decided when transactions were to be made—not the marketer. And if this was so, then *marketing planning must begin with the consumer, not with the organization. Outside-inside marketing must replace inside-outside marketing.*

This simple idea is the essence of the modern approach to marketing. It is, in fact, the philosophy that will guide this volume. We shall see that, for the organization, a marketing mindset of "customer-centeredness" requires that the organization systematically study customer's needs, wants, perceptions, preferences, and satisfaction—using surveys, focus groups, and other means. The organization must act on this information to improve its offerings constantly to meet its customers' needs better. The employees must be well selected and trained to feel that they are working for the customer (rather than the boss). A customer orientation will express itself in the friendliness with which the organization's telephone operators answer the phone and the helpfulness of various employees in solving customer problems. The employees in a marketing-oriented organization will work as a team to meet the needs of the specific target markets that are to be served.

A customer orientation toward marketing holds that success will come to that organization that best determines the perceptions, needs, and wants of target markets and satisfies them through the design, communication, pricing, and delivery of appropriate and competitively viable offerings.

This philosophic orientation has a great many implications for the way a nonprofit marketing program ought to be run. As we shall see, adopting a customer orientation does not, as many nonprofit managers fear, mean that the organization must cater to every consumer whim and fancy. It doesn't mean that a symphony conductor or theater manager must give up his or her artistic integrity. Nor does it mean that health care institutions must abandon their professional standards or that college professors must become classroom song-and-dance performers. Those who argue that these consequences will befall the organization if the devil (marketing) is let in the door simply misunderstand what a customer orientation truly means. To restate: It means that marketing planning must *start* with customer perceptions, needs, and wants. It means that, even if an organization can't or ought not change certain aspects of the offering, the highest volume of exchange will always be generated if the way the organization's offering is described, "priced," "packaged," and delivered is fully responsive to what is referred to in the current jargon as "where the customer is coming from."

Consider two small examples. For years, the Buffalo Philharmonic, like many other symphonies, had a serious problem in trying to broaden its audience. It was willing to change its program somewhat, but ultimately it felt that Mozart is Mozart and somehow customers must be made to change *their* attitudes and behavior. Then, in the early 1970s, a modest university research project revealed that many consumers who indicated that they thought they *might* like to attend a concert did not do so because they expected the occasion to be very formal. As these potential target consumers put it, "We can't go because we don't have the proper clothes. We would feel really uncomfortable around all those fancy-dressed people." The orchestra itself was seen as distant, formal, and forbidding. Once the Philharmonic realized that this was where these potential customers were "coming from," they took great pains to humanize the orchestra and the concert-going experience. Orchestra section members began playing shirt-sleeve chamber music programs at neighborhood art fairs and other local outdoor events. Contact was made with local primary and secondary schools. The orchestra itself even performed at halftime at a Buffalo Bills football game!

A new conductor, Michael Tilson Thomas, began appearing on local television and giving brief informal talks to audiences at specific concerts. Concertgoing never again had the sense of formality that was clearly keeping many potential patrons away. Attendance figures clearly reflected this new customer-centered orientation.

Another example is national in scope. For years, organizations committed to reducing the incidence of smoking in the United States believed that the major reason individuals did not quit was that they did not realize the consequences of continued smoking, or if they did, they were not frightened enough of these consequences to take action. As a result the marketing programs focused almost exclusively on communicating the very real dangers of smoking to target smokers. In a sense, they were trying to *sell* the stop-smoking idea to what they thought was an ignorant and reluctant audience.

It was only after an extensive review of a large number of consumer studies that organizations like the National Cancer Institute realized that the "product" they were trying to sell—that smoking is bad for you—had already been sold. Seven out of eight smokers reported that they either wanted to quit smoking or had tried to quit several times in the past. Further analysis revealed that these consumers perceived two extremely significant barriers to quitting. First, they felt they did not really know of a technique for quitting that would be effective for them. Second, even in cases where they were vaguely aware of a method that might work, they were reluctant to try to quit because they expected to fail. They had either heard of many who had failed, or had failed themselves many times in the past. For these very reasons, they tended to "turn off" most antismoking commercials, since they saw these commercials as, in effect, asking them to fail again!

Once the cancer organizations finally understood this consumer perspective, the marketing efforts of NCI and its sister nonprofits changed dramatically. Warnings of the dangers of smoking were, of course, continued to deter new, young potential smokers. At the same time, a major new marketing thrust was developed along two fronts. First, efforts were made to develop and get into the field a wide range of quitting techniques. Second, NCI and the American Cancer Society worked to persuade physicians and other health care workers to help smokers implement the newly available techniques and, just as important, to cope with smokers' often desperate fears of failing. The effects on cigarette consumption of this new customer-centered campaign have been considerable.

CUSTOMER-CENTERED ORGANIZATIONS

The Buffalo Philharmonic and NCI examples are dramatic examples of the way individual marketing programs can be developed to respond to consumers' needs, wants, and perceptions, and not just to the organization's own needs. But why, one must ask, did these organizations not develop these solutions sooner? The answer—and it is a crucial one—is that the organizations had not (and many still have not) developed a true customer-centered philosophy that had seeped into the consciousness of every member of the organization who had any managerial responsibility or contact of any kind with potential target customers. We define a customer-centered organization as follows:

> **A customer-centered organization** is one that makes every effort to sense, serve, and satisfy the needs and wants of its clients and publics within the constraints of its budget.

One result of a customer-centered orientation is that the people who come in contact with such organizations report high personal satisfaction. They make such comments as, "This is the best church I ever belonged to"; "My college was terrific—the professors really taught well and cared about the students"; "I think this hospital is fine—the nurses are cheerful, the food good, and the room clean." These consumers become the best advertisement for these institutions. Their goodwill and favorable word of mouth reach other ears and make it easy for the organization to attract and serve more people. The organizations are effective because they are customer-centered.

Most organizations are not highly customer-centered. They fall into one of three groups. The first group would like to be more customer-centered but lacks the needed resources or power over employees. The organization's budget may be insufficient to hire, train, and motivate good employees and to monitor their performance. Or management may lack the power to require employees to give good service, as when the employees are under civil service or are volunteers and cannot be disciplined or fired for being insensitive to customers. One inner-city high school principal complained that his problem was not poor students but poor teachers, many of whom were "burned out" in the classroom and uncooperative but who could not be removed.

A second group of organizations is not customer-centered simply because it prefers to concentrate on things other than customer satisfaction. Thus, many museums are more interested in collecting antiquarian material than in making the material relevant or interesting to museum-goers. The U.S. Employment Service may be more interested in the number of people they process per hour than in how much help each one really receives. When these organizations are mandated to exist or are without competition, they usually behave bureaucratically toward their clients.

Finally, there are always a few organizations that intentionally act unresponsively to the publics they are supposed to serve. A local newspaper exposed that one food stamp office chose to be inaccessible in order to minimize the public's use of its service: "There is no sign on the building indicating that the food stamp office is inside . . . there also was no sign anywhere in the building directing applicants to the basement, no sign on the door leading to the stairs, and no sign on the door to the office itself. The only indication that a food stamp office is located in the building is a small, handwritten sign on the door at the top of the stairs. Adding to the inconvenience, the food stamp office was closed from March 10 to April 8."[5]

A number of studies have demonstrated the extent to which nonprofits lack a customer orientation. Reilly and McCullough, for example, conducted extensive interviews with executives in 46 nonprofit organizations and performed a detailed analysis of the formal written objectives of 39 of these organizations. They concluded the following:

> Content analysis of these statements of purpose indicated a clear sales orientation for the most part. About 65% of the respondents mentioned sales volume or the number of exchanges occurring during a period as their criterion for success.

Only 20% reported the evaluation of consumer feedback as a criterion for defining successful operation.

When asked to define marketing, similar results were obtained. Sales was mentioned by 33% of the respondents while 35% described marketing in terms of advertising or promotion. Ten percent could not define marketing at all and the remainder (22%) define marketing in consumer terms. These results along with the statements of organizational purpose indicate that only a small minority of the firms are actually involved in marketing as represented by defining the organization's purpose in terms of the various constituencies of consumers served. Most were concerned with maximizing output or the stimulation of sales to existing consumers, neither of which is consistent with a marketing orientation.[6]

DETECTING AN ORGANIZATION-CENTERED ORIENTATION[7]

Conversations with nonprofit managers such as those quoted earlier make it abundantly clear that they *wish* to be customer centered and, in virtually all cases, truly believe they already are. In most cases, they are not. Fortunately, a number of "clues" exist that tend to give away an organization's *organization-centered* marketing philosophy. These clues, simply stated, are

1   The organization's offering is seen as inherently desirable.
2   Lack of organizational success is attributed to customer ignorance, absence of motivation, or both.
3   A minor role is afforded customer research.
4   Marketing is defined primarily as promotion.
5   Marketing specialists are chosen for their product knowledge or their communication skills.
6   One "best" marketing strategy is typically employed in approaching the market.
7   Generic competition tends to be ignored.

Each of these clues will be discussed more extensively in the sections to follow, since in some ways it is easier to see what marketing *should* be by seeing what it *should not* be.

Clue #1: The Offer Is Seen as Inherently Desirable

The very nature of the offerings promoted in the nonprofit sector often leads their sponsors to have an extremely high opinion of the value of their offerings. They simply see their product or service as inherently desirable. They find it hard to believe that anyone would turn them down!

Committed theater managers find it hard to believe that right-thinking people wouldn't wish to attend a well-acted play; charitable organizations cannot accept a consumer's unwillingness to give; and those who head up nonprofit social issues groups often can't see why people won't vote for, say, cleaner air or the ERA. One organization that overcame the notion that its offerings were inherently desirable is the National Canter Institute. Most women, NCI discovered, agreed that practicing breast self-examination was a good way to ensure early detection of breast cancer, and many knew how to do it. Yet the majority were not practicing breast self-examination, or did so only rarely at best. What was the problem? It turned out that among women who practiced self-examination, the discovery that there was no problem led to a sense of relief the first few times, but eventually the women became bored and stopped the procedure. At the same time, the prospect of finding a problem was so frightening to most other women that they never even tried self-examination. It was only when NCI understood the barriers perceived by the target audience to an obviously beneficial practice that it began to develop more user-oriented marketing programs. NCI's new stance, which is based on assuring women that lumps are often nonmalignant and that progress is being made in the fight against breast cancer, has resulted in significant increases in breast self-examination practices among American women.

Clue #2: Customer Ignorance and Lack of Motivation Are Seen as the Barriers to Success

It is, of course, not surprising to find that if a manager believes that wearing seat belts or giving to the United Way is something everyone should do, then if someone does *not* respond to a specific marketing effort, there are really only two explanations. Either potential customers do not *truly* understand the offering (that is, do not share the organization's inherent belief in it), or they are simply not motivated enough to take action. Some managers in nonprofits are willing to accept the "blame" for this deplorable state. They admit that they simply haven't yet found the right way to communicate the benefits of the offering or they just haven't found the right incentives to get target consumers to overcome their "natural" inertia.

These managers have a relatively benign view of consumers. There is, however, a very large number of nonprofit managers who feel—often unconsciously—much hostility toward consumers. Their basic perception is that customers are really *enemies*. The managers feel that it is these recalcitrant customers who are standing in the way of the organization's becoming more successful. Such views manifest themselves in the organization's treatment of consumers at the box office, on the telephone, in the field, or in any other personal encounter. They are evident in the disapproving look of the family planning specialist confronted by an impoverished family unwilling to practice birth control. They are apparent in the resentful faces of fund-raisers turned down by those who are "uninterested" or "too busy" and in the sarcastic voices of box office people trying to explain ticket availability to confused telephone customers.

It is not hard for the consuming public to sense in these encounters the organization's true colors and to perhaps respond in kind. And if they do, of course, they only convince the managers that they were right about consumers in the first place!

A key strategic assumption of managers in organizations with this attitude seems to be that the task of marketing is to get the customer to change to fit the organization rather than the other way around. They do not realize that (1) in a great many nonprofit marketing situations, customers are very hard to change, while the organization is not; (2) the organization is under the manager's control and the consumer is not; (3) changing the organization to accommodate customers, if fully carried out, ensures that consumer trends will be carefully monitored and followed.

Clue #3: A Minor Role Is Given to Consumer Research

That customer ignorance or lack of motivation is not always the key problem in causing an organization's lack of success was obvious in the National Cancer Institute smoking example discussed earlier. But many organization-centered marketing managers are unlikely to discover this through consumer research. Given their anticonsumerist view of the cause of their lack of success, their opinion about what research is needed is very straightforward. Since part of the problem is that too many consumers are too ignorant about the organization's offering, they believe one kind of study that is needed is research into the nature and extent of consumer ignorance and into the characteristics of who is ignorant. Further, since motivation is a major problem, research may also be needed to try to map the attitudes of those who are knowledgeable to show why they are so negative and unmotivated. Such research, it is hoped, will yield clues as to how to motivate them to take action.

The low level of consumer research by nonprofit organizations is relatively well documented. Permut, for example, found that of the 88 arts organizations responding to his questionnaire, only 1 in 4 said they had done any kind of audience research in the past 12 months.[8] And, given that the respondents in the study were the more responsible and better managed of Permut's sample of 383 organizations, the overall rate of research in the arts must be quite low. Permut found that no research was carried on by 58 organizations, while the most spent for an extensive audience study was $5,800. The latter was estimated to represent only 5.8 percent of the sponsoring organization's available funds.[9]

Despite this low level of research activity, the potential can be dramatic. As most profit-sector marketers will attest, research can challenge some managers' most fundamental assumptions about their customers. The example of the antismoking groups' assumptions about consumer ignorance of the dangers of smoking is probably the best case in point.

Clue #4: Marketing Is Defined as Promotion

If one sees the marketing challenge as one of eliminating ignorance and increasing motivation, then it is inevitable that the tool one will focus on is better communications. Managers will see the need for

- a better copywriter and better copywriting
- a better brochure
- a new image
- better salespeople with better sales presentations
- more posters in more places
- ads placed in prime time rather than in public service announcement (PSA) "media ghettoes"
- more and better press releases
- better relations with newspapers and TV news departments
- a new advertising agency!

Other elements of the marketing mix like pricing, product redesign, and better distribution are seen as "not really the problem." Again, to resort to Permut's study,

- Promotion was clearly viewed as the preeminent marketing variable, with 72 [arts] administrators (82 percent) rating it "most important."
- Distribution was a concept of apparent irrelevance to respondents.
- Only a handful of administrators mentioned that they viewed the product of their organization in terms of "social/aesthetic experience," "enhanced leisure time pursuits," "cultural development," or other, more broadly defined conceptualizations. This is indeed unfortunate, one might argue, since product intangibles abound in the performing arts.[10]

A good example of the consequences of viewing marketing problems as stemming from consumer ignorance and lack of motivation is found in efforts to secure blood donations. Many blood-collection agency heads believe that the best way to encourage donations is to tell consumers about the good things that donor's blood can do or to stress that giving blood is a civic duty. They believe that people hold back from giving because they don't appreciate the "gift's" virtues or because they are afraid. Thus, agency heads reason, the marketing task is to tell consumers as dramatically and convincingly as possible about the benefits to society of giving blood and to assure them that the costs are trivial, that, indeed, giving is not really such a "big deal."

While these messages work for some people, important segments respond to very different approaches that are not based on impersonal media. Many donation programs, for example, have become more successful by simply changing the distribution strategy and going to major customer groups rather than insisting that they come to the agency, or having the hours of service convenient for potential donors, not just for the medical staff. For example, many men, especially blue-collar workers, can be motivated by challenges to their masculinity. Contrary to the view of the typical donor, the macho man who can brag to his coworkers that he is a 20-gallon donor is really responding to benefits he sees for himself. He may care relatively little about "society." Even more perversely, it may be that the higher the costs of giving, the greater the pain and suffering in the process of giving, the greater the rewards. Thus, campaigns in factories that publicize individuals' giving records (bar charts or 10- and 20-gallon lapel pins) and that (contrary to the usual program) don't downplay the possible psychological and physical costs of giving can be highly effective. In such situations, informal group pressure, rather than persuasion, is the key marketing tool.

On the other hand, social, fraternal, and church group members can be motivated to give blood by the let's-all-participate aspects of a blood-mobile visit. They will respond to messages about camaraderie, about "feeling left out if you don't join in," or about letting the group down if you don't go. Messages of this sort have little to say about the occasion for the get together or its value to society, recognizing that for these potential donors the key distinction is also selfish: the desire to be wanted and loved by other members of a group. Here again, rather than brochures and advertisements, it is within-group word of mouth stimulated by key opinion leaders that does the job.

Clue #5: The Best Marketers Are Seen as Those Knowledgeable About the Offering or About Communications

In most for-profit organizations, marketing managers are typically selected for their skills at *marketing;* the best managers are those who know their consumer markets and competitors well. They make active use of consumer research and they know how to develop and implement systematic marketing plans. They possess insights and skills that in theory could be used to manage *any* functional area within marketing (for example, advertising, the sales force, or public relations) or to market any kind of product or service. Their assumption is that it is always possible to learn the essential mechanics of a particular marketing function or the details of a particular product or service in a few weeks, while it takes years to become a marketing expert. Marketing talent is, in a sense, a generic skill that can be used whenever and wherever it can be most effective.

By contrast, in the nonprofit sector, the situation has often been quite different. In the first stage of the marketing revolution in nonprofits, marketing specialists were typically drawn from within the organization. Those with similar responsibilities, for example the director of advertising or the public relations specialist, were simply encouraged to become "more marketing oriented" (that is, to become instant marketers). In the second stage, this approach persisted with the slight modification that some organizations drafted their marketing people from outside the organization but from similar enterprises. They took this approach because they seemed to believe rather strongly that only if one really knows the product or service (e.g., the Boy Scouts or the United Way) can one be a truly successful nonprofit marketer.

Thus, as recently as early 1983 a study of marketing executives in 800 nongovernmental hospitals showed that despite the fact that hospital marketing is one of the most advanced areas in the nonprofit world, "The data showed that hospitals have tended to make marketers out of planners and others without a marketing background. Three out of every four hospital marketing directors responding had a non-marketing background. . . . Of those who worked elsewhere before taking the hospital marketing post, 28% came from another hospital while another 29% had other healthcare or government-agency background."[11]

This personnel strategy is, of course, perfectly consistent with a product orientation toward marketing. It is also explainable by four other factors. First, since marketing is an unfamiliar subject to many nonprofit heads, they don't know how to evaluate marketing skills (while they *can* evaluate product knowhow).

Second, these managers often believe that nonprofit marketing is so different from profit-sector marketing that there can be little transferability of skills.

Third, many top nonprofit administrators accumulate most of their management experience using product-oriented marketing and so are more comfortable working with people who have that orientation. Many business managers of arts organizations, for example, were once active performers or were formally trained in music, theater design, or museum curatorship. Many hospital administrators have either medical or public health backgrounds, and college presidents usually have Ph.D.s in academic disciplines. Seldom are these administrators selected purely for their management skills.

Finally, the world of nonprofits is a fairly clubby one where key people know others in the same field around the country. Thus, a certain amount of favoritism prevails. A prospective staff member with the proper connections and the right vocabulary stands a much better chance of making it than a total outsider. The profit-sector marketing professional, who probably doesn't know what "needs assessment" or "audience development" means, is at a distinct disadvantage in the nonprofit job market. This means that the customer-oriented marketer who is not part of the "club" and who is brought in to turn an organization around will be seen (whether consciously or not) as a threat.

In the recent third stage of development, a few nonprofits now no longer insist on hiring *product* specialists for their marketing positions. They do tend, however, to choose from the ranks of those with *communications* skills. These potential hires are typically chosen from advertising agencies or advertising departments of other companies (sponsors, for example). They might come directly from the media (for example, magazine or newspaper writers) or they may be public relations specialists. What these potential "marketers" have in common is that they are good communicators. Of course, the emphasis on communications skills reflects a view of marketing only slightly different from that found in the product-oriented organization. The problem is still seen as reducing ignorance and providing motivation. But in this group of firms with marketers trained in communications, the emphasis is placed on *persuasion* rather than information. This emphasis on persuasion, it will be obvious by now, is perfectly consonant with a "selling" orientation toward marketing.

Clue #6: One Really Good Strategy Is Seen as All You Need

Since the nonprofit administrator is not often in as close touch with the market as a customer-oriented marketer would be, he or she may view the market as monolithic or at least as having only a few crudely defined market segments. Subtle distinctions are ignored or played down. As a consequence, most nonprofits tend to see the need for only one or two marketing strategies aimed at the most obvious market segments (e.g., young people, families, and the elderly). This climate of managerial certainty precludes experimentation either with alternative strategies or with variations across a number of subtle market subsegments. In this view, the problem is to inform and motivate, and the challenge is about the same for every target consumer.

Also encouraging this approach is the fact that nonprofit managers often come from nonbusiness backgrounds and may fear taking risks. Personal job survival and slow aggrandizement of the budget and staff are often their paramount objectives. And since such administrators are typically responsible only to a volunteer board—which meets irregularly and sometimes prefers to know little about day-to-day operations—they do their best to keep a low profile and avoid causing waves. Simple, consistent strategies that imply well-thought-out analysis are the best choice for career safety. Too much change, too much variation, too much experimentation may seem to imply that one really isn't too sure about what to do. Such a low-profile, risk-averting strategy is, of course, tactically sound if one's organization happens to make up their losses with fundraising or government allocations. In such cases, aggressive marketing strategies are not really necessary.

Clue #7: There Is Assumed to Be No Generic Competition

In the private sector, organizations compete at many different levels, from interbrand competition all the way back to competition at the generic or basic desire levels. In the nonprofit sector, while many organizations do, in fact, compete—the Heart Fund with the American Cancer Society, the Metropolitan Museum of Art with the Whitney or the Museum of Modern Art—many institutions don't have clear competitors because their services or so-called products are intangible or stress unique behavior changes. The competitors faced by those marketing, say, blood donations or forest-fire prevention are not immediately apparent. So it's not surprising that marketers ignore competition at more basic levels. But at the product level, blood banks, for example, undoubtedly compete with other charities (who seek dollars, not blood) for donors. Even institutions with easily identifiable organizational competitors often face product competition from unlikely quarters. Thus, art museums compete with aquariums for family outings, with books and educational TV for art lovers, and with movies and restaurants as places to socialize.

Nonprofit organizations rarely plan strategies to compete at the product level because they lack a customer perspective. And this failure is even more serious at the nonproduct level. Before people will write their congressperson in support of very strict environmental standards, for instance, they must give up their long-held ideas and divert their energies to the new cause. Inertia can be a powerful force, but enthusiastic nonprofit marketers can bring about the necessary rethinking. Inertia, too, is competition.

CHARACTERISTICS OF CUSTOMER-CENTERED MARKETING MANAGEMENT

The preceding sections have held up a mirror to the product-centered and selling-centered nonprofit organization. We have learned what a true marketing organization is *not*. What, then, are the characteristics that one observes in a nonprofit organization that has fully adopted a modern marketing orientation? It will have the following characteristics:

- It will be customer-centered.
- It will rely heavily on research.
- It will have a bias toward segmentation.
- It will define competition broadly.
- It will have strategies using all elements of the "marketing mix," not just communication.

Customer-Centeredness

In a sophisticated marketing organization, all marketing analysis and planning begins and ends with the *customer*. A customer-centered organization always asks

- To whom are we planning to market?
- Where are they and what are they like?
- What are their current perceptions, needs, and wants?
- Will these perceptions, needs, and wants be different in the future when our strategy is to be implemented?
- How satisfied are our customers with our offering?

Reliance on Research

Since the consumer is central, management realizes that it must have a profound understanding of consumer perceptions, needs, and wants and must constantly track changes in them so that the organization can respond to subtle shifts as quickly as they occur. Better still, to assure that it is not merely reactive but *proactive* in its strategic planning, an alert market-oriented management will have in place a forecasting capability that can *anticipate* changes in customer needs, wants, and perceptions.

This is not to say that a consistent reliance on research need be expensive. As we shall outline in Chapter 7, there are a great many techniques by which high-quality and clearly useful research can be carried out by imaginative managements at relatively modest cost. The critical requirement for achieving these benefits, however, is the proper mind-set. The truly customer-centered manager must continually "think research." The manager should assume that what he or she "believes" is not necessarily what is true. Intuition, casual observation, or "just common sense" do not constitute the ideal bedrock on which to build solid marketing strategies and sound tactical decisions.

Take the case of the Midwestern hospital marketer who believed he had a "foreign doctor" problem. The marketer knew that his hospital had more foreign doctors than major competitors in nearby cities. In part, this situation resulted from the fact that there was a major veteran's hospital nearby and many foreign doctors came there to do their residencies or to carry out a public service obligation. After such service, the doctors, many of whom had begun to develop modest practices in the area, quite naturally decided to stay on in the city permanently.

The marketing manager "knew" that their presence in his hospital constituted a serious problem. After all, he knew the hospital was statistically different in its physician profile. And, besides, he saw these doctors regularly in the building. He had heard patients and staff both complain about having difficulty understanding their "foreign doctors." Finally, the one major malpractice issue the hospital had recently faced had involved a foreign doctor. Thus, the manager *knew* he had a problem.

To cope with this "problem," hospital management began to develop strategies both to change the mix of doctors in the community (and therefore the hospital) and to change patient and staff perceptions about the "foreign doctor problem." Fortunately, at about this time the hospital decided to carry out a field study with about 500 past and potential patients. Among the other valuable insights gained from this study was the information that the marketing manager's presumption about consumer perceptions of his foreign doctors was entirely wrong! Consumers were indeed aware that there were many foreign doctors at the hospital, and a few acknowledged that communicating with these doctors was sometimes difficult. But on the whole, they did not see this as a serious problem. In fact, many in the patient sample felt that the foreign doctors were more conscientious and more caring for their patients than were some of their golf-playing, blasé U.S. counterparts! Several respondents said that they thought that cultural and language differences simply made the foreign doctors more conscientious about clearly understanding exactly what the patient really meant and what he or she needed. For many patients, then, the foreign doctors were not a problem but a boon to the hospital.

The lesson, of course, is that for a few thousand dollars (much of which was spent for information serving a wide range of other planning needs), the organization saved itself the cost of an extensive communication project that could well have boomeranged.

A Predeliction for Segmentation

Just as the customer-centered manager routinely thinks of the consumer and of the possible need for research before planning programs, so, too, should he or she habitually "think segmentation." That is, in designing any particular marketing program, the nonprofit manager should routinely assume, until shown otherwise, that the market ought best be thought of as a combination of a great many smaller subsegments that may deserve separate marketing programs.

Of course, many nonprofit marketing managers do think of segmentation from time to time, but in our experience, only in the most general terms. Managers of symphony organizations, for example, are well aware that their prospects are better in high- than in low-income households, among women than among men, among the well educated rather than the less educated, and among the young or old rather than the middle-aged. And this understanding does affect where they concentrate their budgets. But all too often these budgets are spent on a single "best" program, usually aimed at upscale households. (This of course stems from the familiar ignorance-and-motivation definition of the marketing "problem.")

Yet even within this market, many possibilities for more subtle segmentation exist and are all too often passed by. In a study for the National Endowment for the Arts, for example, one of the authors and a colleague revealed that, despite wide industry "intuition" to the contrary, the best predictors of likely symphony attendance were not at all the traditional demographic characteristics like income and education but life-style factors, attitudes toward actual attendance, past experience, and childhood training.[12] Considering only the life-style measure, the study clearly showed that there were not just one but *two* major life-style groups interested in symphony attendance. One group was the "traditional" Cultural Life-style Group. This group made cultural events the center of their leisure pursuits. They tended to patronize the theater, opera, and museums as well as the symphony. They were very much interested in the program content and artists at specific performances and tended to be swayed less by atmospherics and prices. They attended largely for the cultural experience it provided. This group is undoubtedly the one that many theater and symphony marketers have in mind when they design their "one best" strategy.

The research, however, identified a very different life-style group that also included excellent prospects for the symphony. This Socially Active Group were very outgoing in their life-styles. They went out a lot, not only to the symphony but to all sorts of nonclassical events. They liked to give parties and dinners and attend those of their friends. For this group, symphony attendance was largely a social experience. It was an opportunity to meet and talk with their friends. It was an occasion to plan a dinner beforehand and, perhaps, dessert or cocktails afterwards. *Going out* was the thing. What was actually on the program was of less interest than who among their friends were going, what restaurants might be worth trying before the concert, and so forth.

Clearly, the appropriate strategies to reach these two groups are very different. More importantly, a strategy designed to appeal to the one group might very well turn off the other. Suppose, for example, that a symphony manager designed a typical "one best," nonsegmented strategy stressing program elements. Print ads, public relations releases, and interviews by guest artists and the symphony staff would emphasize the works to be performed— perhaps highlighting a first performance locally of a particular composition, the debut of a precocious youngster, the innovativeness or difficulty of a particular program entry, or the conductor's mastery of the "oeuvre" of the composer featured at the concert. All this would be very appealing to those in the Cultural Life-style Group. At the same time, it might have just the opposite effect on the Socially Active Group. The latter might see the event as formal and stuffy, a program for the aficionados and definitely not one that they would understand and enjoy. Certainly it would not seem to them to be something that their friends would attend. The group, then, would be very much turned off by this "best" strategy.

On the other hand, a marketing strategy could be chosen that emphasized the informality of the audience and the event, described the possibilities of making "an evening" of the occasion, talked about the ease of parking, and implied that "just about everyone" would be there. The Socially Active potential attendees might well be very attracted by such a prospect. At the same time, the Cultural Group may find this set of appeals vaguely distasteful. The marketing program might signal to them that the concert program would not be very challenging or, perhaps, even particularly well performed. And, even worse, the campaign might suggest to the cultural sophisticates that all those untutored, unsophisticated social types would be in attendance, ill dressed and applauding in all the wrong places.

The lesson is obvious. Markets can usually be segmented much further and in much more sophisticated ways than the naive marketer usually imagines. But only if the marketer has a customer- and segmentation-oriented philosophy clearly in mind is he or she likely to look for these potentials. As this extended example shows, ignoring segmentation possibilities can mean not only missing chances for attracting new customers whom one is not now reaching, but driving away important audiences to whom one may have considerable appeal.

A Richer Conceptualization of Competition

An organization-centered marketer naturally defines the competition as "other organizations like us." Yet if one begins with customers, the definition of competition can become very different. Competition, in its most basic sense, really becomes whatever the *customer* thinks it is. Thus, if certain customer segments think of treating a particular medical problem *themselves*, then *that* is a hospital or clinic's competition. If a potential donor thinks that money given to the United Way is money that could have gone for a "needed" weekend ski vacation, then that vacation is the competition. If going to the symphony competes with working in the garden or having friends over for pizza in front of the TV, then those activities are the competition.

Using the Full Marketing Mix

In contrast to those who conceive of marketing largely in terms of communications strategies designed to change customers to fit the organization's offering, sophisticated marketers view the marketing function as more diverse and the marketing objective as, above all, meeting customer needs and wants. A diverse marketing program pays attention not only to communication but also to the nature of the *offering*, its cost to target audience members, and the channels through which it is made available. The true marketer's philosophy considers that it is the organization that must be willing to adapt its offering to the customer, and not vice versa. This necessarily means not just a willingness to talk about the offering in different terms but to actually change it (within the constraints set by artistic and professional standards and the organization's capabilities). The marketer must be willing to change the product, service, or idea *itself* that it wishes the customer to get. For instance, skilled political infighters in any legislature, national or local, are well schooled in the need to adjust proposed bills or regulations to fit the needs and wants of specific senators or members of Congress with whom they are trying to make an exchange. It is not usually effective to take the stance that one knows one's position is *right*. Often one must compromise. Compromising may be seen simply as adaptive marketing.

The marketers must also be willing to change the cost of the offering or the place of performance. The marketing director of the Mass Transit District in Champaign-Urbana has found that by offering free or minimal-cost bus service on the very coldest, snowiest days, he can induce auto owners who are averse to using buses (but who are perhaps *more* averse to driving and parking their own cars in terrible weather) to try using the bus. The director also cleverly puts extra emphasis on on-time performance at every stop on these nasty days, with the reasonable expectation that customers would believe that punctual performance under such terrible circumstances surely would predict excellent service on normal days. The director also varies the price of his offering through the use of a "generic bus" painted in "plain-wrap," white and black lettering. This bus is randomly assigned to the various city routes as a reward to those who regularly ride the route and as a spur-of-the-moment incentive to those who rarely take the bus. The fares on the generic bus are a bare-bones 25 cents, and "losses" on the routes are subsidized by a local supermarket chain that itself features plain-wrap products. Clearly, this nonprofit marketer has learned well that effective marketing is a lot more than just good advertising. It is the right offerings in the right place at the right time and at the right price.

Putting It All Together

Finally, a good modern marketer is someone who can put all of these elements together in an effective whole. Exhibit 2-1 shows how Maxene Johnston of the Weingart Center in Los Angeles has developed a fully customer-oriented approach to the challenges faced in her market.

EXHIBIT 2-1

Maxene Johnston on Developing a Customer Orientation at a Center for the Homeless

The Weingart Center is a facility that has been serving the homeless and poor in Los Angeles since 1984. In that year, the business community responded to the homelessness issue by creating the Weingart Center Association (WCA). The Association was formed to manage the renovated 12-story skid row hotel, now known as the Weingart Center. It has been my privilege to serve as president of the WCA since 1984, after concluding a rewarding period as part of the management team which gave the world the wonderful Los Angeles Olympic Games. In the years since 1984, the Weingart Center has become the largest multipurpose complex of health and human services for the homeless and poor in California. Of course, given California's hulking size, that makes us the largest provider of such services nationwide, too. However, it did not begin that way. In 1984, millions of dollars had been spent to rehabilitate and renovate this down-at-the-heel skid row hotel for the purpose of converting it into an alcohol rehabilitation and low-income housing facility. But by the time it opened its doors, the Center was deep in financial trouble, even threatened with imminent foreclosure for outstanding and mounting debt.

WCA—The Association—was actually formed to confront and, hopefully, surmount this looming crisis. We began—and I cannot stress this point too greatly—by developing a *business plan*. We set out to learn what people—both customers and investors—desired, and we gave it to them. It should not have been a surprise, though it continues to be just that for many, to learn that the majority of people using our center—our customers—want *exits* off the streets, a way out of the special despair that accompanies homelessness. For some it meant getting jobs, for some it meant finding an apartment, for some it meant getting needed medication, and for some it merely meant getting their government benefits.

Unfortunately, we all have myths about the homeless. We have pictures in our minds' eye about aging, disheveled ladies huddled in doorways against the cold of night, or perched on a bench somewhere for an afternoon's warmth, with a grocery cart of hefty-bagged personal belongings near at hand. Is that the center's customer, we asked? And I think many of us believed that that, together with the hapless denizens of skid row in general, was the correct answer.

But in fact it wasn't. And it isn't. In fact, that homeless majority is *mythical.*

The homeless form a diverse market. Families, increasingly, are joining individuals in this market. And then, too, there is the grand myth that the homeless are something like a rag-tag army of sun seekers on holiday who, as winter approaches, head for Southern California or other Sunbelt locales. The fact is, most homeless are our neighbors; they truly are *our* homeless.

So in implementing our strategy to be customer driven and entrepreneurial in approach, our first step was to face the fact that the homeless customers we were to serve were different one from another. Thus we segmented our market accordingly.

- Derailed—the "have-nots"
- Disabled—the "can-nots"
- Dysfunctional—the "will-nots"

As a second step in implementing the game plan, we made satisfying investor orientation a priority.

- Public investors wanted beds and buildings.
- Private investors wanted organizations and options.
- Brokers wanted better public policy and equity for the poor.

For our third step, we planned and built a multiservice organization with a shared vision.

And, finally, we provided customer-driven services:

- One-stop shopping
- Service brokers for nine independent service agencies operating under our roof

Service Results

The Center today serves more than 2,000 people each day. It is organized to deliver quality services with a one-stop shopping approach. Nine public and private service agencies, ranging from the county departments of mental health and health services, American Red Cross, and the state Departments of Housing and Corrections, to the federal Veterans Administration operate under one roof. The business community serves as the entrepreneur and broker among these entities, ensuring that the center, which operates from a mixture of public and private revenues, is responsive to those it was established to serve.

> Self-sufficiency, not temporary shelter, is our goal. One of the center's pro-
> grams, aimed at returning people who have never before been homeless back to
> the community with jobs, housing and self-respect, has a 62 percent success
> rate. *In 46 months, out of approximately 8,000 clients, almost 5,000 have succeeded in*
> *meeting their goals.*

SOURCE: Adapted from Maxene Johnston, "Tackling Social Ills with Business Skills,"
speech presented to the Foundation for American Communications, December 8, 1989.

INTRODUCING A CUSTOMER-CENTERED PHILOSOPHY

If marketing is to take its rightful place in nonprofit organizations, management
must not only understand and accept its function, but also take care to introduce
it effectively.[13] Recognizing several considerations can increase the chance that
marketing will be able to make a maximum contribution to the organization.
When seeking to introduce marketing formally to an organization, remember
that

1　Marketing should not be positioned as a substitute for organizational manage-
　 ment (a point we have already made).
2　Other pressures on the organization should be recognized (for example, the
　 need to maintain artistic or professional integrity, to secure major government
　 subsidies, etc.).
3　Limited understanding of marketing by present organization members should
　 be accommodated.
4　The translation of for-profit marketing to the specific nonprofit context should
　 not be done mechanically.
5　It should be granted that the organization is already doing many things that are
　 "marketing." Marketing will be accepted more rapidly if one adopts the existing
　 language, at least initially, rather than trying to change the organization's
　 accustomed language to fit current marketing jargon.
6　Many nonprofit managers have come to their positions from nonbusiness
　 backgrounds and may be defensive about their naivete (although not neces-
　 sarily hostile to marketing).
7　There should be a careful selection of early marketing projects. Lovelock and
　 Weinberg suggests that five criteria should be met by such programs:
　 • They should be evaluated by explicit performance measures.
　 • They should be completed within a short to medium time period.
　 • They should use a limited portion of available resources.
　 • They should be neither peripheral nor central to the organization.
　 • Their results should be obvious to key decision makers within the
　 　organization.[14]
8　In the final analysis, getting marketing accepted in an ongoing organization is
　 much more a *political* activity than a simple attempt to market marketing
　 through persuasion. Allies must be sought—most particularly the chief execu-
　 tive officer. "Enemies" whose view of the organization and of their own turf is

threatened by the new approach should be assumed to exist, whether visible or not, and dealt with directly.

9 Setbacks will occur and compromises will have to be made.

The issue of achieving organizational change is a subject beyond the scope of this book. Interested readers may wish to read the works of Argyris and Schon,[15] Quinn,[16] or Weick.[17] How the marketing function should eventually be structured in order to be effective in an ongoing, nonprofit organization will be discussed further in Chapter 11.

HOW FAR TO GO IN ADOPTING
A CUSTOMER ORIENTATION

We have argued in this chapter that marketing can be successful only if it tailors the organization's offering to customer needs and wants. But many professionals in nonprofit organizations fear that such an approach, taken to the extreme, would mean that anything goes to "please the masses." They fear that the basic mission of their hospital, museum, child care program, or university will be compromised. As Lewin notes,

> Many doctors are worried that a hospital's success may come to depend more on the quality of its marketing efforts than on the quality of the health care. "The whole thing turns my stomach," said one doctor at a New York hospital with an active marketing department. "I cringe every time I see one of our ads. The administrators here tell me it's important, but I think hospitals ought to be striving for clinical excellence, not publicity.[18]

First, we too share these concerns. Ultimately, we view marketing's role as one of supporting the organization in achieving its goals. It does this best by devising strategies that start with the customer and not with the organization. But note that marketing is designated as a *means* to achieve the *organization's* goal. It is a tool—really a process and set of tools wrapped in a philosophy—for helping the organization do what *it* wants to do. Using marketing and being customer oriented should *never* be thought of as goals; they are ways to achieve goals.

Marketing is a subarea of management. It is not necessarily at the top of the organization. Clearly and importantly, top management has a responsibility to decide what role it will allocate to marketing. *Management* must decide which goals marketing can help achieve and how. It is management's prerogative to say that certain decisions will be made with little or no attention to marketing concerns. Thus, the management of a theater company may decide that it will choose the season's program on the basis of the interests of its directors who, in turn, will consider both past programming and the availability of acting and production talent in choosing specific plays and performers. Marketing may *then* be assigned the task of maximizing audience revenues for that given program. It is important to realize, however, that this does not mean that marketing should fall back upon a selling philosophy. It means that marketing planning must simply start with customers in deciding how to describe, package, price, and distribute a given program. Marketers must merely recognize that the specific program cannot be changed.

At the other extreme, a theater manager may decide to be very customer driven. He or she may very carefully survey the potential audience, consider past revenues and audience reactions, and consider what artist and plays are available to maximize future attendance. This organization would then establish an offering that limits attention to achieving artistic objectives but that maximizes sales. Note that the two approaches were equally customer oriented. They simply differ in the management goals they were designed to achieve.

There are, of course, many variations on these two options. The theater management could always choose a middle ground between the two extremes by opting for one of the following approaches to program offering:

1 Mixing artist-driven and customer-driven performances over the season. (As early as 1929, conductor Serge Koussevitzky designed the Boston Symphony Orchestra season himself, except for the last concert, which he let the audience determine).[19]

2 Alternating seasons of artist-driven and audience-driven programming.

3 Deciding to be audience driven initially until revenues are great enough to permit the luxury of more artistic offerings later.

4 Letting the content of the season be artist driven, with talent, costuming, or place of performance audience driven.

Theater managers, therefore, have a great deal of flexibility in choosing how audience driven the programming will be for a particular planning period, although how they market the offering in the final analysis should always be purely customer centered. Other institutions by their very nature may have more or less latitude in the extent to which offerings are customer driven. At one extreme are organizations that seemingly ought to give marketing a very central role because achieving "sales" is virtually their only objective. This would apply to a great many charitable organizations, alumni associations, and other groups that have as their major objective getting customers to give funds, time, and other resources to the marketer. At the other extreme are organizations that cannot change many elements of their basic offering at all because these elements very much define who they are. Included in this group would be most religious organizations and research institutions.

To repeat, then, the question of "how far marketing should go" is really a variable always under the control of management. Since marketing is merely a means to other ends, those who wish to protect those other ends need not fear marketing. At the same time, it is very important to stress that management should not allow the fears of artists and professionals to compromise marketing's legitimate place. As we shall indicate throughout this volume, marketing can make major contributions to nonprofit success in areas where it is appropriate. It must be controlled by management but not hamstrung by those who are suspicious of it if it is to be truly effective.

SUMMARY

The starting point for an effective marketing strategy is the proper marketing mind-set. Historically, marketing has passed through four stages: a product orientation stage, a production orientation stage, a selling orientation stage, and finally, today's customer orientation stage. The first three stages are characterized by management putting the organization's own needs and desires at the center of the strategic process. It is only when management realizes that it is the customer who truly determines the long-run success of any strategy that the nonprofit firm can join the ranks of the sophisticated customer-centered marketing strategists typically found in the private sector.

Several clues can be used to identify a nonprofit that is still mired in an organization-centered perspective. They see their offering as inherently desirable. They see the ignorance or lack of motivation of their customers as the major barrier to the organization's success. Research plays a minor role in strategy formulation. Marketing tends to be defined as synonymous with promotion. Marketing specialists tend to be chosen for their product knowledge or for their familiarity with communications techniques. A "one best" strategy is typically used in approaching the market, and generic competition is typically ignored in the process.

By contrast, customer-centered strategists begin with the customer and the customer's needs and wants. They rely heavily on research findings about their customers. They routinely assume—unless shown otherwise—that markets ought to be segmented. Since they adopt the customer's perspective, they inevitably define competition as coming from widely diverse sources, not just from similar products or services. Finally, they use all elements of the marketing mix (design of the offering, cost reduction, distribution, and promotion) not just communication.

Indoctrinating a nonprofit organization from top to bottom with the proper marketing philosophy is not an easy task. The experience of those who have successfully achieved this objective suggests such strategies as recognizing the limited understanding of others about what marketing really is, allowing for other pressures on the organization that may temporarily mandate noncustomer-oriented approaches, picking visible, short-term projects for the first marketing applications, and recognizing that the introduction of a new philosophy is as much a political exercise as a matter of logic and persuasion. Allies must be sought and enemies deflected. Above all, it is essential to secure a top-management commitment to the new way of thinking. Without it, a true marketing orientation will not be achieved and customer-centered thrusts in one area will inevitably run afoul of organization-mindedness elsewhere.

QUESTIONS

1. It has been argued that, when customers are engaging in socially or personally destructive behaviors like smoking or taking illegal drugs, marketers *must* engage in manipulative tactics. Do you agree? Why or why not?

2. The text outlines five characteristics of customer-centered marketing management. How would you rank these in importance and why?

3. Managers have claimed that programs in Africa designed to address the growing AIDS problem cannot be truly customer-centered because it is difficult to conduct *any kind* of consumer research in cultures not accustomed to it and even more difficult when one is studying such a delicate subject. Given the seriousness of the problem, these managers wish to go ahead with a combination of what works in other countries and their own best judgment. How would you advise them? Is customer-centeredness basically irrelevant to them?

4. There are seven clues that signal a selling orientation in an organization. If you were to conduct a face-to-face interview with a nonprofit marketer, what ten specific questions would you ask the marketer so that you could determine his or her basic orientation? What answers to each question would lead you to conclude whether he or she is selling oriented or customer oriented?

5. How can you justify anything more complicated than simple segmentation for a small nonprofit program with a limited budget such as a local homeless shelter or a small church or synagogue?

NOTES

1. Alan R. Andreasen, "Nonprofits: Check Your Attention to Customers," *Harvard Business Review*, May-June 1982, pp. 105–110.

2. Steven E. Permut, "A Survey of Marketing Perspectives of Performing Arts Administrators," in Michael P. Mokwa, William M. Dawson, and E. Arthur Priere, eds., *Marketing the Arts* (New York: Praeger, 1980). pp. 47–58.

3. Seymour H. Fine, "Concept Sector Within the Economy," in Philip Kotler, O.C. Ferrell, and Charles Lamb, eds., *Cases and Readings for Marketing for Nonprofit Organizations* (Englewood Cliffs, N.J.: Prentice-Hall, 1983), p. 349.

4. Chris T. Allen and Charles D. Schewe, "An Empirical Assessment of the Relative Marketing Orientations of Museum Directors and Marketing Practitioners." Working Paper 81-14, School of Business Administration, University of Massachusetts, Amherst.

5. Bill Grady, "This Food Stamp Office Is Hiding," *Chicago Tribune*, May 22, 1980.

6. Mike Reilly and Jim McCullough, "A Survey of Marketing Activity in Nonprofit Organizations," in F. Kelly Shuptrine and Peter Reingen, eds., *Nonprofit Marketing: Conceptual and Empirical Research* (Tempe: Bureau of Business and Economic Research, College of Business Administration, Arizona State University, 1982), pp. 40–43.

7. Much of the material in this section was first presented in Andreasen, "Nonprofits."

8. Permut, "A Survey."

9. Ibid., pp. 52, 53.

10. Ibid., p. 51.

11. John A. Witt and Nelson L. McRoberts, "Lack of Expertise, Funding Shackles Marketing Moves," *Modern Healthcare,* April 1983.

12. Alan R. Andreasen and Russell W. Belk, "Predictors of Attendance at the Performing Arts," *Journal of Consumer Research,* September 1980, pp. 112–120.

13. See Philip Kotler, "Strategies for Introducing Marketing into Nonprofit Organizations," *Journal of Marketing,* Vol. 43 (January 1979), pp. 37–44; William R. George and Fran Compton, "How to Initiate a Marketing Perspective in a Health Care Organization," *Journal of Health Care Marketing,* Vol. 5, no. 1, (Winter 1985), pp. 29–37.

14. Christopher H. Lovelock and Charles B. Weinberg, *Marketing for Public and Nonprofit Managers* (New York: John Wiley, 1984), p. 561.

15. Chris Argyris and Donald A. Schoen, *Organizational Learning: A Theory of Action Perspective* (Reading, Mass.: Addison-Wesley, 1978).

16. James Brian Quinn, *Strategies for Change: Logical Incrementation* (Homewood, Ill.: Richard D. Irwin, 1980).

17. Karl E. Weick, *The Social Psychology of Organizing* (Reading, Mass.: Addison-Wesley, 1969).

18. Tamar Lewin, "Hospitals Pitch Harder for Patients," *The New York Times,* May 10, 1987, Section 3, pp. 1, 28.

19. Apparently Koussevitzky was copying an innovation begun sometime earlier by the Philadelphia Orchestra.

3

The Strategic Marketing Planning Process

Three men, one black, one white, and one Hispanic, are pictured above the line "We Want to Collar a Few Good Men." A young man strolls down a darkened hospital corridor puzzling over his career while a narrator says, "The work is hard but the rewards are infinite." At first glance they seem like just another series of recruitment ads for the armed forces. But they are promoting the priesthood for the Archdiocese of Detroit.

Television evangelists like Jerry Falwell and Oral Roberts recognized decades ago the power of television and radio to spread their message. Mainstream religious groups dabbled with advertising in the past, but were inhibited by the fear of offending members of their congregations. Now, however, they are increasingly turning to the kind of slick advertising and marketing campaigns used by consumer goods companies. Sharp marketing is considered a survival strategy.

Such mainline groups as the Mormon, Episcopal, Lutheran, and Unitarian churches are proclaiming the rewards of religion in television, radio, newspaper, magazine, and billboard advertisements. Even the bishops of the Catholic Church are considering a nationwide advertising program to encourage Catholics to return to their roots.

Churches may not be businesses, but they have many of the same concerns. They have to pay employees, attract "customers," build and maintain physical facilities and get a message through to the public—most of which boils down to one thing. As a piece of direct mail advertising for the Rhode Island Council of Churches puts it: "Whoever said money was the root of all evil never had to run a church."

The Archdiocese of Detroit was perhaps the first Catholic group to undertake a multi-media effort to raise public awareness of the need for priests. It began its six-month $300,000 ad campaign last spring. The fifth-largest archdiocese in the United States, with some 350 parishes, Detroit was desperate. Its 65-year-old seminary was foundering as the number of seminarian students dropped to 26 from a high of 850 in 1965. Half its parochial schools, the traditional means of recruitment, were out of business.

Over the next several months, the ads drew 450 phone calls requesting information on the requirements to enter the priesthood, five times as many as the archdiocese usually got.

"We're in an age of materialism and results, and we're talking about spiritual development that takes a lifetime," said the Rev. John West, vocations director of the archdiocese. "We need more leaders."

Source: Adapted from Aimee L. Stern, "Putting Faith in Madison Avenue," *The New York Times.* December 27, 1987, p. F4. Copyright © 1987 by The New York Times Company. Reprinted by permission.

Once management believes that it has understood and internalized the customer-oriented marketing mind-set, the next critical step in becoming an effective marketer is to develop *a systematic process* for actually doing marketing. Chapter 1 pointed out that the single most important challenge facing nonprofit managers today is developing an effective *competitive strategy*. This means determining what the target audience ought to be, how the organization should position itself vis-à-vis competitors, and what the detailed elements of its "marketing mix" ought to be to reach the target market with the chosen positioning strategy.

This competitive strategy is something that must guide the organization for a number of years. Thus, it must be farsighted and based not on today's competitive situation but on a careful study of the competitive situation the organization will face in the future. And since it will be the "spine" upon which the year-to-year details of specific marketing actions will be hung, it should be well articulated, thorough, and valid for relatively long stretches of time, typically three to five years.

This book is organized around this strategic marketing planning process. In the chapters to follow in this section of the volume, we offer both concepts and processes for carrying out several of the major subsections of the strategy formulation process. In the present chapter, we describe how a manager analyzes the internal and external marketing environment and sets the marketing mission, objectives, and goals. Chapter 4 then focuses in greater depth on the most critical element of the external environment, customers. Chapters 5 and 6 then turn to the two key problems in the determination of an organization's core marketing strategy, segmentation, and developing a clear and effective competitive position. Finally, Chapters 7 and 8 describe approaches to developing and using marketing research and forecasting information for both strategic planning and day-to-day decision making.

Section III of the book then discusses the problems of developing and organizing various kinds of resources to carry out the strategic plan and Section IV how to design elements of the marketing mix that are necessary to implementing the plan. Section V concludes the volume by presenting several systems for evaluation and control.

THE STRATEGIC MARKETING PLANNING PROCESS

The approach we shall advocate for carrying out strategic planning in marketing is what we shall call the *strategic marketing planning process (SMPP)*. Just as "customer centeredness" is the advocated way of *thinking* about marketing, SMPP is the advocated way of *doing* marketing. It is an approach that can apply equally well to the question of what to do over the next ten years and, in highly simplified form, what to do tomorrow.

The SMPP is a set of steps one must take to decide what to do in any given marketing situation. It is based on the assumption that marketing is a function that must operate within two environments. First, it operates within an organization. Therefore, what marketers do in the future must necessarily fit with what the organization as a whole wishes to do. As we shall see, this does *not* mean that the marketer must take the organization's goals and plans as given and slavishly adapt to them. On the contrary, assuming that the organization is run *openly* and the marketing function is properly located at the very highest level of the organization hierarchy, there should be continual interaction between marketing planning and organization planning. Marketers must tell organizational planners what can and cannot be accomplished in the way of developing or changing consumer markets. At the same time, organizational planners must tell marketers where and how and what they must do to meet the organization's overall needs and plans.

Second, marketers cannot plan willy-nilly to do anything they want (say, meet an observed customer need) without taking very serious account of the organization's *abilities* to take advantage of the opportunity the external world presents. It is essential, then, that any planning process systematically consider organization strengths and weaknesses before it makes suggestions for new ventures, particularly those that take the organization far afield from its present activities.

The strategic marketing planning process is outlined in Figure 3-1. It includes the following steps:

1   Analyze the organizationwide mission, objectives, goals, and culture to which the marketing strategy must contribute.

2 Assess organization strengths and weaknesses to respond to threats and challenges presented by the external environment.

3 Analyze the *future* environment the marketer is likely to face with respect to:

    a Publics to be served

FIGURE 3-1

Strategic Marketing Planning Process

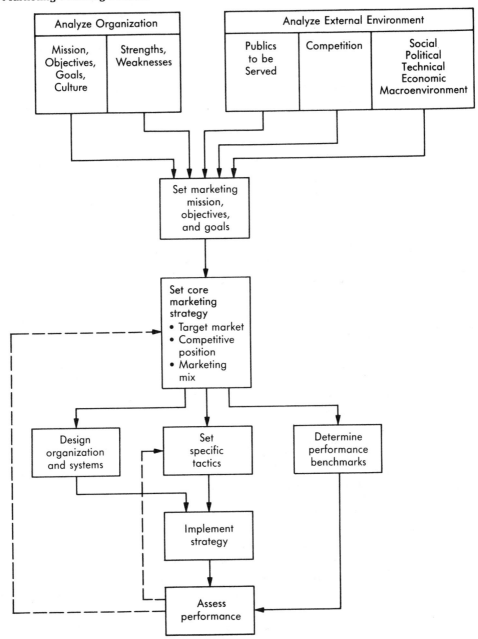

    b Competition
    c Social, political, technological, and economic environment.
4 Determine the marketing mission, objectives, and specific goals for the relevant planning period.
5 Formulate the core marketing strategy to achieve the specified goals.
6 Put in place the necessary organizational structure and systems within the marketing function to ensure proper implementation of the designed strategy.
7 Establish detailed programs and tactics to carry out the core strategy for the planning period, including a timetable of activities and assignment of specific responsibilities.
8 Establish benchmarks to measure interim and final achievements of the program.
9 Implement the planned program.
10 Measure performance and adjust the core strategy, tactical details, or both as needed.

The present chapter discusses the first four of these steps in general terms. Thus, we discuss internal assessment of organizational mission, objectives, goals, culture, and strengths and weaknesses and external assessment of key publics, competitors, and the macroenvironment to which the organization must be responsive. Finally, we describe how management translates these assessments into a marketing mission and a set of goals and objectives.

STEP 1: DETERMINING ORGANIZATION-LEVEL MISSIONS, OBJECTIVES, AND GOALS

A marketing program is not developed in a vacuum. It must adjust to both internal and external realities. The principal internal reality is where the organization as a whole wishes to go. If the organization is mature and well managed, it should have already completed an organizationwide strategic planning process like that outlined in Figure 3-1. That is, before marketing planning should begin, the organization's top-level managers (including the marketing manager) and its advisory boards should ideally have

1 Determined the organization-level *long-term* culture, mission, objectives, and goals.
2 Assessed the organization's likely future external environment (of which the *marketing* environment is a subset).
3 Assessed the organization's present and potential strengths and weaknesses (of which marketing strengths and weaknesses are a subset).

In this sense, strategic marketing planning can be seen as a *nested activity*, as suggested in Figure 3-2. That is, marketing strategic planning can—and should—be nested within organization-level strategic planning. Further, if the organization is large enough, the same kind of strategic planning ought to be

FIGURE 3-2

Nested Strategic Planning

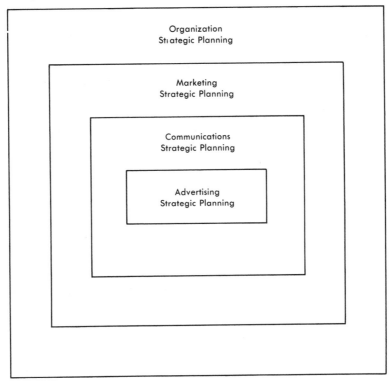

carried out by subunits *within* the marketing function. In general, the further down the planning hierarchy, the more detailed the planning and the shorter the planning horizons.

Plan formulation involves the organization in determining an appropriate mission, objectives, and goals for the current or expected environment. The three terms are distinguished as follows:

- *Mission:* the basic purpose of an organization, that is, what it is trying to accomplish.
- *Objective:* a major variable that the organization will emphasize, such as market share, profitability, reputation.
- *Goal:* an objective of the organization that is made specific with respect to magnitude, time, and responsibility.

We examine these concepts in more detail here. We shall also discuss the effect of *corporate culture* on marketing strategy.

Mission

Every organization starts with a mission. In fact, an organization can be defined as a *human collectivity that is structured to perform a specific mission through the use of largely rational means.* Years ago, Peter Drucker pointed out that organizations need to answer the following questions: *What is our business? Who is the customer? What is value to the customer? What will our business be? What should our business be?* Although the first question "What is our business?" sounds simple, it is really the most profound question an organization can ask. A church should not define its business by listing the particular services it offers. Consistent with a customer-centered philosophy, it should identify the underlying need that it is trying to serve. The church might decide that it is in the "feeling good" business, that is, helping people feel better about themselves and the world. Or it might decide that it is in the "hope" business, that is, helping people feel that they will eventually experience joy and fulfillment, either in this life or in the next. Ultimately, a church has to decide what its mission is so as not to lose sight and confuse it with a lot of intermediate goals and services that it might provide.

Clarifying the organization's mission is a soul-searching and time-consuming process. Different members will have different views of what the organization is about and should be about. One organization held numerous meetings over a two-year period before membership consensus developed on the real mission of the organization.

A helpful approach to defining mission is to establish the organization's scope along three dimensions. The first is *consumer groups*, namely, *who* is to be served and satisfied. The second is *consumer needs*, namely, *what* is to be satisfied. The third is *technologies*, namely, *how* are consumer needs to be satisfied. For example, consider a church that serves mainly senior citizens who only want a simple worship service every Sunday. By contrast, the mission of Northminster Presbyterian Church is to serve almost all age groups; to meet needs for worship, study, sociability, and charity; and provide services through the chapel, meeting rooms, classes, and outings.

Still other churches will have a different mission scope. A campus church will serve primarily students of a particular religious faith and meet a wide variety of needs (for belief, sociability, counseling, and so on) within the four walls of a religious house. On the other hand, Robert Schuller's church, Garden Grove Community Church (Garden Grove, Calif.) meets a wide variety of needs of 7,000 members and serves them through such modern technologies as radio, television, and cassettes, in addition to its $16 million "Crystal Cathedral."

An organization should strive for a mission that is *feasible, motivating,* and *distinctive.* In terms of being feasible, the organization should avoid a "mission impossible." The United Way of America has set its mission to double its level of volunteers and financial support in the 1990s and may discover this to be infeasible. United Way staff and volunteers must believe in the feasibility of this goal if they are to lend their support. An institution should always reach high, but not so high as to produce incredulity in its publics.

The mission should also be motivating. Those working for the organization should feel they are worthwhile members of a worthwhile organization. A church whose mission includes "helping the poor" is likely to inspire more support than one whose mission is "meeting the social, cultural, and athletic needs of its current members." The mission should be something that enriches people's lives.

A mission works better when it is distinctive. If all churches resembled each other, there would be little basis for pride in one's particular church. People take pride in belonging to an institution that "does it differently" or "does it better." By cultivating a distinctive mission and personality, an organization stands out more and attracts a more loyal group of members.

Here are some mission statements for major nonprofits:

- "To increase the organized capacity of people to care for one another" — *United Way of America*
- "To provide the knowledge, resources and perspectives needed by journalists and their sources to effectively communicate through the news information about important public issues." — *Foundation for American Communications*
- "To advance the family planning service delivery goals of the Office of Population (USAID) through the design, implementation and enhancement of contraceptive social marketing (CSM) programs around the world." — *SOMARC, The Futures Group*
- "To urge and assist the personal and professional development of our members and to advance the science and ethical practice of the marketing discipline" — *American Marketing Association.*

Objectives

The mission of an institution suggests more about where that institution is coming from than where it is going to. It describes what the institution is about rather than the specific objectives and goals it will pursue in the coming period. Each institution has to develop major objectives and goals for the strategy horizon separate from but consistent with its mission statement as well as objectives and goals for each annual planning period.

For every type of institution, there is always a potential set of relevant objectives, and the institution's task is to make choices among them. For example, the objectives of interest to a college are: increased national reputation, improved classroom teaching, higher enrollment, higher-quality students, increased efficiency, larger endowment, improved student social life, improved physical plant, lower operating deficit, and so on. A college cannot successfully pursue all these objectives simultaneously because of a limited budget and because some of them are incompatible, such as increased cost efficiency and improved classroom teaching. In any given year, therefore, institutions will choose to emphasize certain objectives and either ignore others or treat them as constraints. For example, if Beloit College's enrollment continues to fall, Beloit will make increased enrollment a paramount objective subject to not letting student quality fall below a certain level. Thus, an institution's major objectives can vary from year to year depending on the administration's perception of the major problems that the institution must address at that time.

Goals

The chosen objectives must be restated in an operational and measurable form called *goals*. The objective "increased enrollment" must be turned into a goal, such as "a 15 percent enrollment increase in next year's fall class." A goal statement permits the institution to think about the planning, programming, and control aspects of pursuing that objective. A number of questions may arise: Is a 15 percent enrollment increase feasible? What strategy would be used? What resources would it take? What activities would have to be carried out? Who would be responsible and accountable? How will we track achievement? All of these critical questions must be answered when deciding whether to adopt a proposed goal.

Typically, the institution will be evaluating a large set of potential goals at the same time and examining their consistency. The institution may discover that it cannot simultaneously achieve "a 15 percent enrollment increase," "a 10 percent increase in student quality," and a "12 percent tuition increase" at the same time. In this case, the executive committee may make adjustments in the target levels or target dates or drop certain goals altogether to arrive at a meaningful and achievable set of goals. Once the set of goals is agreed upon in the goal formulation stage, the organization is ready to move on to the detailed work of strategy formulation.[1]

The issue of determining organizational goals can be broken into two distinct steps: (1) determining what the current goals are, and (2) determining what the goals should be. Sometimes the task of determining present goals is straightforward because they are written down, widely disseminated, and most importantly, understood by everyone as meaning the same thing. But frequently the image of the current goals differs from person to person and group to group in the organization. The president of a college may see the primary goal as upgrading the quality of the student body, the vice-president for admissions may see the primary goal as increasing the size of the student body, and the vice-president for finance may see the primary goal as increasing the number of nonscholarship students in relation to scholarship students. The faculty as a whole may pursue the goal of a reduced teaching load to permit more time for research, whereas the administration may adopt the goal of an increased teaching load to reduce the cost of education. These differences reflect the fact that the organization is really a coalition of several groups, each giving and seeking different things from the organization. On the other hand, in some organizations differences in goals may signal a basic confusion that really ought to be corrected before planning proceeds much further.

Another disconcerting problem occurs when the marketing manager discovers that what the organization *says* its goals are and what they *actually* are constitute two very different things. In the late 1960s a major consumer goods marketer decided to make increased employment and upgrading of minority staff a central corporate objective. After three years of operation, however, the program was found to be languishing well behind its stated objectives. The reasons for the diminished activity were clear. Many local managers had conscientiously tried to meet what they believed were management's clearly expressed social goals. The steps they took, however, were internally costly. As a consequence, their year-end operating profits suffered. And, when they were called by top management to account for this reduced profitability, they quite naturally pointed to the many steps they had taken to seek out, train, and promote minority workers as management had directed them. Management's response was, in effect, "That's admirable. We are pleased that you are taking these important social initiatives. But we do notice that your bottom line has suffered . . . " Very soon these managers learned that the organization's *real* goals were not what management said they were: the real goals were what management *rewarded*.

There are two implications of this kind of experience. First, marketing managers must be aware that many organizations will, in practice, turn out to be schizophrenic in their goal setting, speaking and acting in different ways. Sometimes this is intentional. It is not so important to the marketing manager to know the true explanation, only that he or she be able to read the proper signals and either respond to what management *really* wants or, if the marketing manager believes management is misguided in what it is doing, try to bring the firm's real goals more in line with stated goals.

CORPORATE CULTURE
AND CULTURE CONFLICT[2]

A number of students of management have pointed out that the "corporate culture" of an organization may be the single most important determinant of what the organization can achieve and what will be expected of those (such as the marketing manager) who are challenged to achieve it.

Peters and Waterman, in their book *In Search of Excellence*, stress the central contribution of *corporate culture* to the success of their "best-run" organizations:

> Without exception, the dominance and coherence of culture proved to be an essential quality of the excellent companies. Moreover, the stronger the culture and the more it was directed toward the marketplace, the less need was there for policy manuals, organization charts, or detailed procedures and rules. In these companies, people way down the line know what they are supposed to do in most situations because the handful of guiding values is crystal clear.[3]

The success of organizations like J.C. Penney, Pepsi-Cola, AT&T, Chrysler, and Domino's Pizza reflects the impact of a clear, customer-centered, pervasive corporate culture. Analyses of these cultures make it clear that if a culture is too rigid or is not kept attuned to the dynamics of its marketplace, it will fail as did those of Twentieth Century Fox and People's Express. The lack of a clear, dominant culture can be equally undesirable. Both problems are demonstrated by the recent history of Apple Computer. In its infancy Apple had a clear, dominant culture reflecting the personalities of its two founders and emphasizing technological daring and loose work style. However, rigid adherence to this culture to the neglect of changes in the competitive and customer environment soon put Apple's sales growth and net profits at peril. A marketing "whiz" from Pepsi-Cola then was brought in, and Apple went through a long and well-publicized period during which the old technology-centered and the new market-driven cultures were at war. Only with the second founder's resignation (the other had resigned previously) was the crippling cultural conflict resolved, and the organization turned around to once again effectively challenge IBM's market dominance.

Culture Conflict

Many organizations in the nonprofit area appear to suffer from a significant, perhaps inherent, *culture conflict*. At minimum, this conflict severely inhibits nonprofit marketers' abilities to be effective in the marketplace and, at worst, threatens to tear their organizations apart through internal dissension.

The nature of the conflict is not unlike that experienced by Apple in its "middle period," as a battle between "original vision" and the realities of modern marketing is occurring. A significant number of health care programs and institutions were begun by individuals or ad hoc groups committed to doing something positive about an aspect of a population's health. Examples include hospitals such as the Mayo Clinic, the current "just say no" antidrug campaign, and the contraceptive social marketing programs in countries like Bangladesh and Thailand.

The early life of most of these organizations is typically dominated by what is called a *social service culture*. Those adopting this perspective see their mission as one of maximizing some aspect of the public's health status by "improving health" rather than by "being efficient." The organization is willing to overlook waste and misdirection in the short run as long as the effort is a case of "doing good." Senior managers, and most if not all of the staff, are trained in some basic health care discipline such as medicine, social work, or public health. They see themselves as professionals with strict codes of ethics and feel that they should serve everyone possible within the limits of time and economic resources. Camaraderie pervades the organization, in part because it is small, its members share the same training and goals, and there is a religious zeal to "have a real impact." In many respects, the organization and participation in it are ends in themselves to those involved.

A social service culture is ideal for such organizations in their beginning years. Often they lack resources, and employees must endure low salaries, inadequate equipment, limited staff assistance, and so on. Without the vision of significant social service payoffs, such deprivations might be "killing." The vision builds a close sense of camaraderie in the organization and helps members defend themselves from early critics and doomsayers.

The social service culture can survive for years for two reasons. First, the organization is undertaking something the public truly needs at a time of great pent-up demand and little competition. Many wasteful and misdirected approaches are tolerated because most work. Even if they do not, the culture tends to accept any "good-hearted" efforts as long as they are intended to have a social impact. Second, the organization is largely free to do "its own thing" because of a lack of outside supervision. Support is usually from a few individuals or small grants, often with few strings attached. The lack of competition reinforces a sense of freedom to pursue what organizational members personally believe is the right course of action.

These early conditions will inevitably change. If the organization initially meets a real need, over time it will attract more resources and with them more "watchdogs." As staff expands, the people who enter the once tight-knit work force will have less sense of mission than the founders and less inclination to overlook inefficiencies and misdirection of effort. The initial surge of demand will have been met and "sales" will tend to plateau. Competition then enters and, in some cases, will be nasty. As a result, the organization will feel threatened internally and/or externally.

The response of many nonprofit organizations to this threat in recent years has been to seek help from marketing and management specialists. Sometimes this outreach is enthusiastic (and often wildly so); other times it is very grudging ("I guess we must pay some attention to marketing if we are to be able to continue our good work"). In the early stages, marketing and management are seen as technologies that can be appended to the original organization to help in its mission. Unrecognized is the fact that marketing and management cannot be effective if *dominated* by the old culture.

Good marketers and business managers come from a *corporate culture.* This culture is significantly different from the social service culture and, to the extent the nonprofit organization is serious about becoming marketing oriented, a severe clash of cultures is inevitable. In the corporate culture, competitors are not viewed as benign and cooperative. Staff are expected to produce results and are not coddled as long as "their heart is in the right place." Strategic thinking replaces uncoordinated programs, resources are husbanded carefully, and ineffective programs that may be the personal fiefdoms of staff members are routinely called into question. Short-term tactics become equal in importance to long-term programs, and the organization is seen as a means to *achieving* ends, not an end in itself.

When nonprofit organizations bring these two cultures together, signs of culture conflict soon appear in subtle and not-so-subtle forms. The marketer is "shocked" by the extent of mismanagement in the organization and suspicious of pet projects lacking clear purposes. Questions are raised about costs and about the "fit" of tactics to general strategies. Concurrently, the founding professionals are equally "shocked" by the marketer's seeming lack of commitment to the organization's "real purposes." The professionals are suspicious of the corporate culture and scrutinize the marketer's every action for signs of the unethical, expedient, and manipulative behavior they are sure this alien culture promotes. The marketer, in turn, sees the professionals as having "their heads in the sand," not recognizing the realities of today's marketplace. The marketer will, indeed, accept the long-run mission of the organization, but will not understand why the specialists fail to realize that unless the organization becomes more effective and uses its resources better in the short run, there will be no long run!

Solutions

The most serious consequence of culture conflict is that the organization becomes schizophrenic. People are not sure what direction it is taking. Ill feelings and distrust develop among coworkers who have allegiances to different values. The organization vacillates between "giving in" to the marketers for a while and then "coming back to the (social service) basics."

Signals to the outside environment are mixed. Some organization members emphasize the social service mission of the organization and the many sacrifices being made by all participants. Members of the marketing culture may be describing the careful planning and efficient use of resources that mark the organization's new operating style. Some outsiders may feel there is cause to worry that the nonprofit organization has lost its original sense of mission.

In the private sector, cultural conflict is usually transitional. As with Apple Computer, stockholders eventually rebel and force some resolution or the company simply fails and goes out of business or is absorbed by others. In contrast, in the nonprofit field a number of market characteristics can prolong this period of conflict—perhaps interminably. For example, the bottom line is often not clear, no tough-minded board of directors or outside funders intervene, and/or no clear competitors move into the market vacuum.

Part of the problem is that top managers in nonprofit organizations are likely to be part of the conflict. They do not recognize it or see its implications for the organization and those allied with it. The first step in correcting any problem is to recognize its symptoms and face them squarely. The next step is to resolve the problem, which is not an easy task. Several suggestions can be offered.

1 Key members of the organization must learn to recognize the symptoms and then *admit* that, indeed, cultural conflict is present within the organization and that its effects are personally and professionally debilitating.
2 Specific time should be set aside for beginning to resolve the conflict, with the understanding that full resolution will probably (a) take a long time to be effectuated and (b) lead to some resignations.

3 Initial discussions should be guided by the assumption that unless one culture dominates, and those adhering to its rival accommodate themselves to that dominance, the organization is doomed at worst to failure or at best to continuing friction and a generally unpleasant working environment.

4 Because all parties are too close (both perceptually and emotionally) to the crisis, resolution can be achieved only under the guidance of an outside catalyst sensitive to the issues and skillful enough to help the participants face and resolve them.

5 Resolution is most likely if all key organizational members can be brought to articulate for themselves and others (a) what they feel the basic mission of the organization should be, (b) what they feel are the best means of achieving that mission, (c) what they feel are *inappropriate* means for the organization to use (on the grounds of either ethics or efficiency), and, most important, (d) what they *personally* wish to achieve through their participation in the organization.

6 Once these perceptions, wishes, and hopes are "on the table," there should be a mutual exploration, with minimal guidance, of how both the participants and the organization can maximize their goals. In the process, the exploration will inevitably lead to heightened empathy for others' dreams and aspirations and an open consideration of who will have to compromise or resign if the organization is to survive and grow. The participants also will recognize that, unless the latter goal is achieved, individual dreams are unlikely to be fulfilled.

7 The eventual outcome of this process will be not only a resolution of the cultural conflict, but also, through the consideration of the values of participants, a bonding of the remaining coworkers in a more empathetic and productive personal and organizational relationship.

In the end, this middle period of a nonprofit's growth with its inevitable culture conflict can be a time of vital reassessment of organizational means and ends. As in the Apple Computer case, this period can clear the air both internally and externally. It can mean the reassertion of organizational dynamism and growth. The danger in the nonprofit field is that because of the character of its participants and lack of the usual outside checks and balances, the conflict will go unresolved and the steps necessary to move forward into the third phase will not be taken. The organizational and personal costs of this sorry state can be extremely high.

STEP 2: ANALYZING ORGANIZATIONAL STRENGTHS AND WEAKNESSES

A second aspect of the internal analysis is a cold-blooded review of the organization's strengths and weaknesses. In many cases this analysis will be carried out *after* the assessment of opportunities in the organization's market environment. Clearly, an organization cannot think about tackling a great opportunity if it does not have—and is unlikely to develop—the needed capabilities.

Weaknesses come in two forms. First, there are weaknesses that are environmental or organizational constraints on what the organization is *allowed* to do. For example, the School of Business Administration at California State

University, Long Beach, may see a major opportunity to do significant management research on Pacific Rim organizations seeking to enter U.S. markets. However, a major program of high-quality research would require staffing by doctoral students who carry out much of the work, generate papers, and perhaps help train visiting businesspeople. Unfortunately, the California State legislature does not permit CSULB's School of Business Administration to offer a Ph.D. in business.

Many other nonprofits suffer similar restrictions. As noted in Chapter 1, the U.S. Internal Revenue Service sets implicit bounds on how much nonprofits can generate revenue from unrelated activities. Similarly, donors may set limits on what may be done with their money. Physicians may effectively limit what a hospital may do in the area of preventive care or holistic health. And, governments in developing countries may tell private voluntary organizations (PVOs) that they cannot duplicate activities carried out in the public sector and that they cannot engage in tactics that are offensive to the culture (e.g., advertising contraceptives).

A second form of weakness is more correctable. These are aspects of the organization's structure, strategy, and tactics that just are not very good. Not surprisingly, many managers are blind to these deficiencies. For this reason, it is important that management from time to time have an outside *audit* of the total organization, including the marketing function. A thorough audit typically covers both the external and internal environments. Thus, it can serve as a major vehicle for carrying out both steps 2 and 3 of the strategic marketing planning process. We consider it here because it can be used both to identify management areas that need to be improved and to identify organizational capabilities that constitute the *requirements for success* in the markets in which it operates or wishes to operate.

The Marketing Audit

The marketing audit is defined as follows[4]

> **A marketing audit** is a *comprehensive, systematic, independent,* and *periodic* examination of an organization's marketing environment, objectives, strategies, and activities with a view of determining problem areas and opportunities and recommending a plan of action to improve the organization's strategic marketing performance.

The four characteristics of a marketing audit are expanded upon in the following paragraphs

1   *Comprehensive.* The marketing audit covers all the major marketing issues facing an organization, and not only one or a few marketing trouble spots. The latter would be called a functional audit if it covered only the sales force, or pricing, or some other marketing activity.

2   *Systematic.* The marketing audit involves an orderly sequence of diagnostic steps covering the organization's marketing environment, internal marketing system, and specific marketing activities. The diagnosis is followed by a correc-

tive action plan involving both short-run and long-run proposals to improve the organization's overall marketing effectiveness.

3 *Independent.* The marketing audit is normally conducted by an inside or outside party who has sufficient independence from the marketing department to attain top management's confidence and the needed objectivity.

4 *Periodic.* The marketing audit should normally be carried out periodically instead of only when there is a crisis. It promises benefits for the organization that is seemingly successful, as well as the one that is in deep trouble.

A marketing audit is carried out by an auditor who gathers information that is critical to evaluating the organization's marketing performance. The auditor collects secondary data and also interviews managers, customers, dealers, salespeople, and others who might throw light on the organization's marketing performance. The auditor cannot rely on an internal management opinion, and must seek the opinions and evaluations of outsiders regarding the organization. Often the findings are a surprise, and sometimes a shock, to management.

Table 3-1 is a guide to the kinds of questions that the marketing auditor will raise. Not all the questions are important in every situation. The instrument will be modified depending on whether the organization is a museum, college, social service agency, government agency, and so on.[5] However, the sequence of topics should be maintained.

Table 3-1

MARKETING AUDIT GUIDE

Part I. Marketing Environment Audit
Macroenvironment
A. Demographic
1. What major demographic developments and trends pose opportunities or threats for this organization?
2. What actions has the organization taken in response to these developments?
B. Economic
1. What major developments and trends in income, prices, savings, and credit have an impact on the organization?
2. What actions has the organization taken in response to these developments and trends?
C. Ecological
1. What is the outlook for the cost and availability of natural resources and energy needed by the organization?
2. What concerns have been expressed about the organization's role in conservation and what steps has the organization taken?
D. Technological
1. What major changes are occurring in relevant product, service, and process technology? What is the organization's position in these technologies?
2. What major generic substitutes might replace this product or service?
E. Political
1. What new legislation could affect this organization? What federal, state, and local agency actions should be watched?
2. What actions has the organization taken in response to these developments?

F. Cultural
  1. What changes are occurring in consumer life-styles and values that might affect this organization?
  2. What actions has the organization taken in response to these developments?

Task Environment

A. Markets
  1. What is happening to market size, growth, and geographical distribution?
  2. What are the major market segments? What are their expected rates of growth? Which are high-opportunity and low-opportunity segments?
B. Customers
  1. How do current customers and prospects rate the organization and its competitors, particularly with respect to reputation, product quality, service, sales force, and price?
  2. How do different classes of customers make their buying decisions?
  3. What are the evolving needs and satisfactions being sought by consumers in this market?
C. Competitors
  1. Who are the major competitors? What are the objectives and strategy of each major competitor? What are their strengths and weaknesses? What are the sizes and trends in market shares?
  2. What trends can be foreseen in future competition and substitutes for this product?
D. Distribution and Dealers
  1. What are the main distribution channels bringing products to customers?
  2. What are the efficiency levels and growth potentials of the different distribution channels?
E. Suppliers
  1. What is the outlook for the availability of different key resources used in production?
  2. What trends are occurring among suppliers in their pattern of selling?
F. Facilitators and Marketing Firms
  1. What is the outlook for the cost and availability of transportation services?
  2. What is the outlook for the cost and availability of warehousing facilities?
  3. What is the outlook for the cost and availability of financial resources?
  4. How effectively is the advertising agency performing?
G. Publics
  1. What publics (financial, media, government, citizen, local, general, and internal) represent particular opportunities or problems for the organization?
  2. What steps has the organization taken to deal effectively with its key publics?

Part II. Marketing Objectives and Strategy Audit

A. Organization's Objectives
  1. Is the mission of the organization clearly stated in market-oriented terms? Is the mission feasible in terms of the organization's opportunities and resources?
  2. Are the organization's various objectives clearly stated so that they lead logically to the marketing objectives?
  3. Are the marketing objectives appropriate, given the organization's competitive position, resources, and opportunities?
B. Marketing Strategy
  1. What is the core marketing strategy for achieving the objectives? Is it a sound marketing strategy?

2. Are enough resources (or too many resources) budgeted to accomplish the marketing objectives?
3. Are the marketing resources allocated optimally to prime market segments, territories, and products of the organization?
4. Are the marketing resources allocated optimally to the major elements of the marketing mix, that is, offer quality, service, sales force, advertising, promotion, and distribution?

Part III. Marketing Organization Audit

A. Formal Structure
   1. Is there a high-level marketing officer with adequate authority and responsibility over those organizational activities that affect the customer's satisfaction?
   2. Are the marketing responsibilities optimally structured along functional, product, end user, and territorial lines?
B. Functional Efficiency
   1. Are there good communication and working relations between marketing and sales?
   2. Is the product management system working effectively? Are the product managers able to plan profits or only sales volume?
   3. Are there any groups in marketing that need more training, motivation, supervision, or evaluation?
C. Interface Efficiency
   1. Are there any problems between marketing and operations that need attention?
   2. What about marketing and R&D?
   3. What about marketing and financial management?
   4. What about marketing and purchasing?

Part IV. Marketing Systems Audit

A. Marketing Information System
   1. Is the marketing intelligence system producing accurate, sufficient, and timely information about developments in the marketplace?
   2. Is marketing research being adequately used by managers?
B. Marketing Planning System
   1. Is the marketing planning system well conceived and effective?
   2. Is sales forecasting and market potential measurement soundly carried out?
   3. Are sales quotas set on a proper basis?
C. Marketing Control System
   1. Are the control procedures (monthly, quarterly, etc.) adequate to ensure that the annual plan objectives are being achieved?
   2. Is provision made to analyze periodically the profitability of different products, markets, territories, and channels of distribution?
   3. Is provision made to periodically examine and validate various marketing costs?
D. New Product Development System
   1. Is the organization well organized to gather, generate, and screen new product ideas?
   2. Does the organization do adequate concept research and business analysis before investing heavily in a new idea?
   3. Does the organization carry out adequate product and market testing before launching a new product?

Part V. Marketing Productivity Audit

A. Profitability Analysis
   1. What is the profitability of the organization's different products, customer markets, territories, and channels of distribution?
   2. Should the organization enter, expand, contract, or withdraw from any market segments, and what would be the short- and long-run profit consequences?
B. Cost-Effectiveness Analysis
   1. Do any marketing activities seem to have excessive costs? Are these costs valid? Can cost-reducing steps be taken?

Part VI. Marketing Function Audits

A. Products
   1. What are the product line objectives? Are these objectives sound? Is the current product line meeting these objectives?
   2. Are there particular products that should be phased out?
   3. Are there new products that are worth adding?
   4. Are any products able to benefit from quality, feature, or style improvements?
B. Price
   1. What are the pricing objectives, policies, strategies, and procedures? To what extent are prices set on sound cost, demand, and competitive criteria?
   2. Do the customers see the organization's prices as being in line or out of line with the perceived value of its offer?
   3. Does the organization use promotional pricing effectively?
C. Distribution
   1. What are the distribution objectives and strategies?
   2. Is there adequate market coverage and service?
   3. Should the organization consider changing its degree of reliance on distributors, sales reps, and direct selling?
D. Advertising, Sales Promotion, and Public Relations
   1. What are the organization's advertising objectives? Are they sound?
   2. Is the right amount being spent on advertising? How is the budget determined?
   3. Are the ad themes and copy effective? What do customers and the public think about the advertising?
   4. Are the advertising media well chosen?
   5. Is sales promotion used effectively?
   6. Is there a well-conceived public relations program?
E. Sales Force
   1. What are the organization's sales force objectives?
   2. Is the sales force large enough to accomplish the organization's objectives?
   3. Is the sales force organized along the proper principle(s) of specialization (territory, market, product)?
   4. Does the sales force show high morale, ability, and effort? Are they sufficiently trained and incentivized?
   5. Are the procedures adequate for setting quotas and evaluating performances?
   6. How is the organization's sales force perceived in relation to competitors' sales forces?

Criteria of Audit Success.   The marks of a good marketing audit are the following:[6]

- *Comprehensiveness.* Have all the key dimensions of the organization's marketing program been investigated?
- *Objectivity.* To what extent have the evaluations been
    Quantified?
    Based on valid internal or external secondary data?
    (If subjective) replicated or cross-checked with other observers?
    (If original research) based on a valid, reliable research methodology?
- *Timeliness.* Was the examination based on up-to-date inputs and information?
- *Usefulness.* Was the report delivered in time to meet management decision-making needs? Were the recommendations relevant, affordable, and otherwise feasible?
- *Clear Communication.* Was the final report
    Simply, clearly written?
    Prefaced by an executive summary?
    Illustrated with forceful, necessary graphics?
    Concise and understandable?
    Supplemented by necessary documentation and appendices?

Marketing Audit Procedure.   A marketing audit is sometimes requested by a funding agency or a governing body. More often the management of the organization itself will request a marketing audit. The actual task of carrying out an audit for the first time can be divided into ten stages[7] (see Figure 3-3). Several stages can be modified or eliminated in subsequent audits. Although these stages are typically carried out in sequence, it is often necessary to return to earlier stages as later stages suggest new avenues of investigation. (On-site interviews, for example, may reveal new secondary sources to be reviewed which, in turn, may suggest additional questions for later interviews.) Some key issues to be addressed in several of these steps are listed next.

BACKGROUNDING AND INITIAL MANAGEMENT CONTACT. The auditor should begin by reviewing any previous studies of the organization that are available, including past marketing audits. Discussions should be held with those who requested the audit to ascertain their expectations for the audit's outcomes. At this stage, tentative final deadlines should be specified.

The auditor should next meet with the management of the organization audited in order to

1 Assure management that the audit is designed to assist management in developing a better marketing organization and better marketing strategies. Management must know and accept that the audit is *not* at all like an accounting audit, which looks for errors, deceptions, or other evidence of mismanagement. Instead, the marketing audit is a *forward-looking* document indicating to management what can and should be the focus of their strategic efforts in the coming months and years.

FIGURE 3-3

Steps in a Marketing Audit

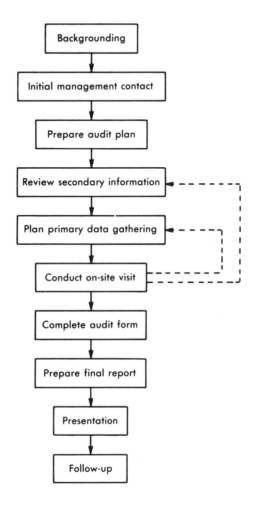

2 Introduce the auditor (or the auditing team) to management and explain to management that the audit will be based on hardheaded practical considerations that take full recognition of local conditions. A marketing audit is not an ivory-tower exercise that outlines ideal strategies or evaluates programs according to unrealistic standards. Rather, it is a down-to-earth set of guidelines to point the organization in directions consistent with the best marketing wisdom and experience.

3 Ascertain management's wishes and expectations for the audit's outcomes. It is important that the audit meet not only the needs of those individuals who initiate or pay for the audit, but also those of management.

4 Describe the audit procedure and review with management the specific audit instrument.

5 Present a formal request for archival information to learn from management what required information is available and when and how it can be obtained. A

checklist of the basic information to be requested should be prepared in advance.

6 Begin planning a site visit (or several visits) for first-hand observation and interviews with staff and knowledgeable outsiders.

7 Establish a procedure to keep management informed of insights secured during the audit, and test the feasibility of (and management's receptivity to) various courses of action that could be proposed. If the audit's recommendations are to be implemented, it is critical that they not come as surprises to management.

DATA GATHERING.   Background information to be obtained from the organization is not always available on the dates indicated by management. Some will turn out not to exist, some will be received late, and some will have to be secured from other sources. A bibliography of the material used in the audit, both internal and external to the organization, should be appended to the final report.

Secondary data must usually be supplemented by original research. This research might include

- Interviews with key staff.
- Review of documents not previously available.
- Observation of sales training meetings, sales calls, press briefings, and trade exhibits.
- Visits to outlets.
- Observation of advertisements, brochures, and point-of-purchase materials for the subject organization.
- Observation of competitors' products, packaging, advertisements, and point-of-purchase materials.

A specific audit form should be used to record the data from these investigations. This standardized document will facilitate comparisons from audit to audit and across units within a single audit.

FINAL REPORT AND PRESENTATION.   The audit form itself contains the raw material and detailed recommendations that will feed into the final report. The final report must contain three additional elements:

- An executive summary
- A presentation of recommendations
- An appendix

The appendix will contain exhibits, reports, questionnaires, tables, or sample materials to back up the audit report itself. Some of these may be original documents prepared by the auditor.

The first and second additional elements are more critical. The recommendations section should summarize and prioritize the audit's major recommendations, pointing out clearly how the results of the next audit should differ from the current one. The executive summary should briefly present the audit's major findings and recommendations.

The audit is valuable only if it is used. The auditor, therefore, has primary responsibility to make sure that the final report is clearly and thoroughly understood. This means not only that the report should be stated in the simplest, most direct, and most compelling language, but that it should also be discussed in person with all interested parties. Such discussion will ensure that major ambiguities are cleared up, that there is no misunderstanding of the auditor's major recommendations, and that management understands what is required of them to implement necessary changes. Finally, face-to-face presentation offers one additional opportunity to secure feedback about the report that may or may not necessitate revision.

FOLLOW-UP.   As already noted, the audit must be very explicit about what the organization must do to carry out the report's recommendations. In this regard, it is important that the date of the next audit be set, at least at the point of the final presentation, so that management can develop a timetable to achieve the goals implied by the audit. It may also be useful for management or the organization sponsoring the audit to identify interim benchmarks that would permit it, as well as the implementing organization, to make sure the goals of the audit will be achieved on schedule.[8]

STEP 2: ANALYZING EXTERNAL THREATS AND OPPORTUNITIES

A marketer operates in an external environment that is constantly changing. The internal environment tells the marketer what is *desired* and what is *permissible*. The external market tells the marketer what is *possible*. The external environment has three components:

1 The *public environment,* consisting of groups and organizations that take an interest in the activities of the focal organization. The public environment consists of local publics, activist publics, the general public, media publics, and regulatory agencies whose actions can affect the welfare of the focal organization.

2 The *competitive environment,* consisting of groups and organizations that compete for attention and loyalty from the audiences of the focal organization. The competitive environment includes desire competitors, generic competitors, form competitors, and enterprise competitors.

3 The *macroenvironment,* consisting of large-scale fundamental forces that shape opportunities and pose threats to the focal organization. The main macroenvironmental forces that have to be watched are the demographic, economic, technological, political, and social forces. These forces largely represent "uncontrollables" in the organization's situation to which it has to adapt.

We shall consider each of these environmental components in turn.

The Public Environment

When marketing managers turn to examining the external environment, they realize that it contains several publics, and the organization has to market to most or all of them. We define a public in the following way:

> **A public** is a distinct group of people, organizations, or both whose actual or potential needs must in some sense be served.

It is fairly easy to identify the key publics that surround a particular organization. Consider a university. Figure 3-4 shows 16 major publics with which a university deals and whose needs it must consider.

Not all publics are equally active or important to an organization. Publics come about because the organization's activities and policies can draw support or criticism from outside groups. Publics can be classified by their functional relation to the organization. Figure 3-5 presents such a classification. An organization is viewed as a resource-conversion machine in which certain *input publics* supply resources that are converted by *internal publics* into useful goods and services that are carried by *intermediary publics* to designated *consuming publics*. Here we will look at the various publics more closely.

Input Publics.   Input publics mainly supply original resources and constraints to the organization, and as such consist of donors, suppliers, and regulatory publics.

DONORS.   Donors are those publics who make gifts of money and other assets to the organization. Thus a university's donors consist of alumni, friends of the university, foundations, corporations, and government organizations. Each university runs a development office consisting of a staff of professional fund-raisers. This staff develops a philosophy of fund-raising and specific proposals that might excite possible donors. It tries to match its financial needs with the appropriate donor groups. It tries to build value in the eyes of its donors so that they can feel pride and other satisfactions from their association with the institution.

SUPPLIERS.   Suppliers are those organizations that sell needed goods and services to the focal organization. Nonprofit organizations often try to obtain price concessions or even free donations of goods and services but don't often succeed. In recent times, supply shortages and the rapidly rising cost of supplies have made skillful supply planning and purchasing more important than ever.

REGULATORY ORGANIZATIONS.   The third input public consists of regulatory organizations that impose rules of conduct. The regulatory publics of a university include federal, state, and local government agencies, trade unions, and various academic accreditation associations. The focal organization must keep in close contact with these regulatory organizations and be ready to argue against regulations that will harm their ability to create value for their clients.

FIGURE 3-4

The University and Its Publics

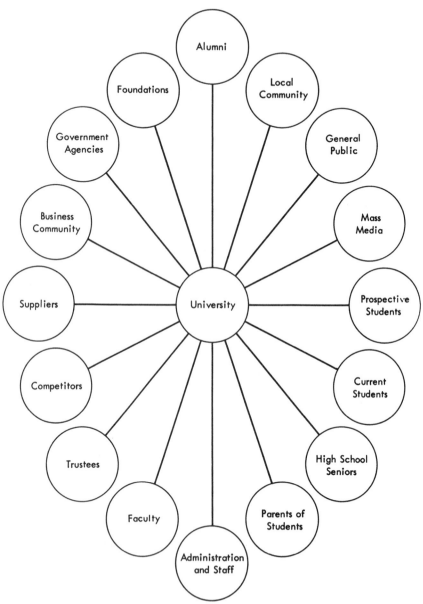

Internal Publics.   It has been argued that it is often as important to do effective internal marketing as external marketing. The internal publics of an organization define, refine, and carry out the organization's strategy. Thus, as we noted earlier, if marketing is to be effective, these internal publics must

FIGURE 3-5

The Main Publics of an Organization

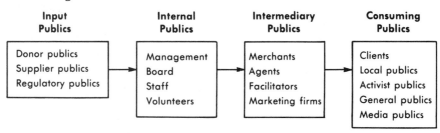

understand and internalize the marketing mind-set. They must also help carry out the marketing strategy. This applies to all four of the key internal publics of the organization: management, the board of directors, staff, and volunteers. (Public agencies often lack volunteers and may have a government agency or a legislative committee as their "board of directors.") We have already considered the requirement that marketing managers be responsive to those above them in the organization hierarchy, that is, top management and the board of directors. Marketing managers must also be responsive to those below them in the organization.

STAFF. The staff consists of the various employees who work on a paid basis. This would include middle management, secretaries, workmen, telephone operators, and so on. The staff would also include the skilled practitioners who deliver the organization's services to its consumers, such as the hospital's nurses, the college's professors, the police department's police officers, and the social agency's social workers.

Management faces the normal problems of building an effective staff: defining job positions and responsibilities, recruiting qualified people, training them, motivating them, compensating them, and evaluating them. Employee training is a critical task with significant marketing implications. Those employees who come in contact with consumers must be trained in a "customer service" orientation. A college whose professors are cold or indifferent to the students is much more likely to have falling enrollment than a college with student-oriented professors.

Motivating the staff takes careful planning. The staff wants several things from the organization: adequate salaries, fair treatment, respect and recognition, and the feeling of working for a worthwhile enterprise. Management must create these benefits if it expects to get in return solid work, high morale, and continuous support. As we shall discuss in Chapter 13, employees are a "market" to which management must creatively communicate and relate.

VOLUNTEERS. Many nonprofit organizations—churches, charities, hospitals—use volunteers as an important part of their operations. The volunteers perform work that usually requires less skill, and this helps to keep down the costs of running the organization. On the other hand, volunteers are less controllable and often less productive. They may not show up for meetings, resist doing certain tasks, and tend to be slow in getting their work done on time. Some organizations claim to be able to accomplish more by increasing the size of the paid staff and reducing the number of volunteers.

At the same time, a better answer might be for the organization to improve its skill in managing and motivating the volunteers. Volunteers are sensitive to small slights like not receiving recognition for a job well done or being pushed hard. They feel that they are giving their time free and want to be appreciated and respected.

The competent volunteer staff manager will be skilled in attracting good and reliable volunteers and in motivating and rewarding them. A marketing approach means understanding the volunteers' needs and meeting them in a way which draws their support and hard work. The volunteer staff manager is likely to sponsor social functions for volunteers, confer awards for many years of service, and arrange a number of other benefits that will recognize their contributions.[9]

Intermediary Publics.   The focal organization enlists other organizations, called marketing intermediaries, to assist in promoting and distributing its goods and services to the final consumers. A college, for example, may decide to offer off-campus educational services to consumers who cannot avail themselves of courses offered on campus. The college may work with four different marketing intermediaries to distribute and promote its educational services and products. They are described next.

Merchants.   Merchants are organizations such as wholesalers and retailers that buy, take title to, and resell merchandise. Suppose the college makes an arrangement with a local bookstore to carry and sell certain textbooks, where the bookstore cannot return the unsold books. The bookstore is performing a merchant role in the distribution system used by the college.

Agents.   Agent middlemen are organizations such as manufacturer's representatives, agents, and brokers that are hired by producers to find and/or sell to buyers without ever taking possession of the merchandise. Suppose the college signs a contract with a person who agrees to recruit new students for the college. This person is acting as an agent for the college. The college would have to negotiate the terms on which the agent would be remunerated for services.

Facilitators.   Facilitators are organizations such as transportation companies, real estate firms, and media firms that assist in the distribution of products, services, and messages, but do not take title to goods or negotiate purchases. Thus, the college will use the telephone company and the post office to send messages and materials to prospective students. These facilitators are paid a normal rate for their transportation, communications, and storage services.

Marketing Service Firms.   Marketing service firms are organizations such as advertising agencies, marketing research firms, and marketing consulting firms that assist in identifying and promoting the focal organization's products and services to the right markets. The college will hire the services of these marketing firms to investigate, develop, and promote new educational services. The focal organization has to select these firms wisely and negotiate terms that are mutually rewarding.

Consuming Publics.   Various groups have interests in the output of an organization, and in varying senses have needs the marketing manager must meet. These are: customers, local residents, activists, the general public, and the media. They are described here.

CUSTOMERS.   Customers represent the marketer's primary public, its *raison d'être*. For this reason, we shall consider them in much more detail in Chapter 4. Drucker insists that the only valid purpose of a business is to create a customer. He would hold that hospitals exist to serve patients, colleges to serve students, opera companies to serve opera lovers, and social agencies to serve the needy.

Various names are used interchangeably to describe customers, such as consumers, clients, buyers, and constituents. The appropriate term is elusive in some cases. Consider a state penitentiary. The prisoners are clearly the penitentiary's consumers. A psychiatrist in the prison will have certain prisoners as clients. The prisoners are not buyers in the sense of paying money for the service; instead, the citizens are the buyers, and they are buying protection from criminal elements through their taxes. The citizens are also the prison's constituents in that the prison exists to serve their interests. We might conclude that the citizens are the prison's primary customers.

What this illustrates is that a market can have a multiple set of customers, and one of its jobs is to distinguish these customer groups and their relative importance. Consider this issue in relation to a state college. Who is the state college's primary customer? Is it the students, because they consume the product? Is it the students' parents, who expect the college to transmit knowledge and ambition to their sons and daughters? Is it employers, who expect the college to produce people with marketable skills? Is it taxpayers, who expect the college to produce educated individuals? Or is it the college's alumni, who expect their alma mater to do notable things to give them pride?

Clearly, a college must take the interest of all of these "customer" groups into account in formulating its services and policies. At times, the college will aim to increase its service to one group more than to another. If the students complain about poor lectures and unavailable professors, then the administration will have to focus its energy on improving service to the students. This may require putting pressure on the professors to be more responsive to students. At other times, professors may complain that their teaching load is too heavy to get any research done, and the administration may seek additional money from alumni to finance lighter teaching loads. Most of the time the administration is busy balancing and reconciling the interests of diverse customer groups rather than favoring one group all the time at the expense of the other groups.

LOCAL RESIDENTS.   Every organization is physically located in one or more areas and comes in contact with local publics such as neighborhood residents and community organizations. These groups may take an active or passive interest in the activities of the organization. Thus, the residents surrounding a hospital usually get concerned about ambulance sirens, parking congestion, and other things that go with living near a hospital.

Organizations usually appoint a community relations officer whose job is to keep close to the community, attend meetings, answer questions, and make contributions to worthwhile causes. Responsive organizations do not wait for local issues to erupt. They make investments in their community to help it run well and to acquire a bank of goodwill. This, too, is a marketing activity.

ACTIVISTS.   Organizations are increasingly being petitioned by consumer groups, environmental groups, minority organizations, and other public interest groups for certain concessions or support. Hospitals, for example, have had to deal with demands by environmental groups to install more pollution control equipment and engage in better waste-handling methods.

Organizations would be foolish to attack or ignore demands of activist publics. Responsive organizations can do two things. First, they can train their management to include social criteria in their decision-making to strike a better balance between the needs of the clients, citizens, and the organization itself. Second, they can assign a staff person to stay in touch with these groups and to communicate more effectively the organization's goals, activities, and intentions.

GENERAL PUBLIC.   A marketer is also concerned with the attitude of the general public toward the organization's activities and policies. The general public does not act in an organized way toward the organization, as activist groups do. But the members of the general public carry around images of the organization that affect their patronage and legislative support. The marketer needs to monitor how the organization is seen by the public and to take concrete steps to improve its public image where it is weak.

THE MEDIA.   Media publics include media companies that carry news, features, and editorial opinion: specifically, newspapers, magazines, and radio and television stations. Marketers are acutely sensitive to the role played by the press in affecting their organizations' capacity to achieve their marketing objectives. Organizations normally would like more and better press coverage than they get. Getting more and better coverage calls for understanding what the press is really interested in. The effective press relations manager knows most of the editors in the major media and systematically cultivates a mutually beneficial relation with them. The manager offers interesting news items, informational material, and quick access to top management. In return, the media editors are likely to give the organization more and better coverage.

Marketing to all these publics is essentially the same. The organization needs to understand each public's needs and wants and how it perceives the marketing organization. In light of this information, the organization must show the target public that cooperating with it by running a press release, refraining from criticizing a particular program, or putting up a stop light opposite the organization's entrance (e.g., to protect handicapped clients or volunteers) will *meet the particular public's own needs.*

In Exhibit 3-1, Daniel Beckham of the Beckham Company describes how hospitals can involve a key public, physicians, in their planning process. In Chapter 20 on public relations, we will discuss further the specific application of these principles to relationships with the media, activists, and the general public. And, of course, we consider applications to *consumer* publics throughout the volume.

EXHIBIT 3-1

Daniel Beckham on Putting Physicians in the Marketing Planning Cycle

When hospital administrators speak of involving doctors in decision making, it's often with a groan. For years, the conventional wisdom has been that nothing is more certain to sabotage a planning process than having the doctors participate. The result was often a cat-and-mouse game with administration telling the doctors as little as possible and the doctors complaining bitterly about always being "the last to know."

But things have started to change. Competitive pressures and growing government intervention have caused both doctors and hospitals to recognize that they are very much in the same boat. In enlightened organizations, shared challenges give rise to shared responses. Many hospitals and doctors have found that a united front leads to more certain success for everyone involved.

At Lutheran General Hospital, a 700-bed teaching hospital outside of Chicago, executives verified in a 1985 market research study what many of them had already suspected. Their relationship with their doctors was deteriorating. And the most certain cause for the problem was poor communication. So they took the challenge in hand and made a simple, but bold (and frankly all too rare) move. They started opening up the channels of communication by systematically visiting doctors—in their practices. And they started to actively solicit physician input as they planned new services and marketing initiatives. The result has been impressive.

In a recent video program called *Physicians in the New Equation* produced by the American College of Healthcare Executives, physicians at Lutheran General talked positively about their "new partnership" with their hospital pointing to full beds in a tight market as evidence of what that partnership has meant. Vice President of Planning and Marketing at Lutheran General, John Kessler places a high priority on rubbing shoulders with his hospital's customers. "Active involvement of our medical staff in our planning and marketing efforts has been a cornerstone in our steadily growing market share." He adds that " . . . Lutheran takes seriously the notion of doctors as 'partners.' We've invested in their success and they have found that we're an ally they can depend on."

When planning with doctors, it makes sense to pick your teams with care and build a solid "fit" that recognizes unique differences in personalities and skills. Here are some suggestions based on my experience in working with doctors:

Build a "team" not a "committee."   As the old saying goes, "There are no statues built to committees." Although tradition or bureaucracy may dictate what you call a venture team, be sure that it is designed from the beginning to work as a harmonious group towards some attainable goal. Winning teams by definition can (and must) embody a variety of skills and perspectives. To be productive team members, physicians must share a commitment toward some common goal and motivation to work toward that goal.

Find a leader.   Teams must be led. Consultants should facilitate, they shouldn't lead. Physician planning teams are best led by physicians. Decide early on who will direct the team and what the parameters of the leadership role will be. There is a difference between leading the planning team and eventually leading the venture that emerges from the planning. A venture leader can evolve, but the planning team leader must be designated at the onset.

Tune the team for productivity.   No group mired in political stalemate or worse in outright internal conflict will achieve much. Complete team harmony may be just as dangerous. So a healthy level of group tension directed toward a definable set of objectives may be the ideal. To create that healthy mix recognize and manage the physician personality types you're likely to encounter:

- *Cynics*—Certainly this personality type has its counterparts outside of medicine. The cynic fails to see a "half-full glass" but always sees it as a "half-empty" one. It is the willingness to view every challenge as unsolvable and every solution as suspect that defines the cynic. Generally, it's best to keep the cynic off the planning team. (Internal medicine has a high percentage of cynics.)

- *Recluses*— There are "research" recluses and "clinical" recluses. They live only for their highly specialized work. Unless the planning venture involves their area of specialization, keep them off the team. (They probably won't show up for meetings anyway.)

- *Social Activist*—"Rebel with a cause." If there is a match between your team's purpose and this physician's social mission, he can make an excellent team member. He can bring an extremely high level of energy to the challenge. But beware if there's not a match between team purpose and the activist's mission. He'll either try to move the team to his agenda or he'll sabotage the effort in order to dislocate organizational focus. (High potential for activism: psychiatry, oncology, pediatrics.)

- *Overwhelmed*—Many physicians dedicate every ounce of energy to their practices (which often run them more than they run the practice). As much as these physicians may bring to the table, they can't be counted on to get to the table often enough to be of help. Save yourself the trouble of bringing them up to speed (and slowing down the team) by not including them to begin with. (Where you'll find the overwhelmed: OB/GYN, family practice, pediatrics.)

- *Entrepreneurs*—Ah, now here's a prize—the "physician entrepreneur." He can bring together that rare combination of medical expertise and business savvy. Doctors that demonstrate entrepreneurial skills often command the respect (admittedly sometimes begrudgingly) of their colleagues. Most physicians recognize that they are woefully inexperienced in the business arena (although they may not admit it). The physician entrepreneur brings a level of pragmatism and creditability that's invaluable to a planning team. (Good sources for entrepreneurs: cardiologists, radiologists, pathologists, pulmonologists.)

- *Lone rangers*—These doctors are not used to working as a team. They like to wander into the medical staff lounge or the board room "gun on hip" and tend to shoot quickly particularly at those who get in their way. Invite them to be on the team or invite them to certain meetings. They have little patience for consensus building but they won't play games either. Lone rangers tend to do their homework, give you their reaction quickly and honestly, then go back to work. They like to be center stage so be willing to tolerate some "grand standing." (Look for "lone rangers" among your surgeons, particularly the high-risk specialties like cardiovascular and neurosurgery.)

- *Opportunists*—These folks may look like entrepreneurs (and they may be) but they only have one agenda. They're in unabashed pursuit of self-interest. Their colleagues know what the opportunist's purpose is and they'll subvert them if they get a chance. Keep them off the team. (The classic opportunist M.D.: Fat sucking, tummy tucking cosmetic surgeons and cataract happy ophthalmologists.)

- *Politicians*—A surprisingly rare breed among physicians, the politician has often succeeded in coalescing some constituency within the medical community. He may have leveraged that constituency into representation in the formal organizational structure (medical executive committee or board of directors) or he may sit atop a more powerful (and perhaps more effective) informal power structure. Put him or one of his lieutenants on the team if the venture is big enough or controversial enough to need broad support. (Likely hot beds of political activity: internal medicine, OB/GYN, family practice.)

- *The patient advocate*—There are many doctors for whom the social contract with the patient is fundamental. These doctors make their decisions in light of their impact on the patient. "What's best for the patient" becomes the one governing principle. Put "patient advocates" on the team. (In my experience, hospital managers are much more likely to forget their responsibilities to be patient advocates than are doctors.) A "patient advocate" can serve as a reminder of why the team is there to begin with. (There are "patient advocates" in every specialty.)

The list above isn't intended to suggest that all internists are "cynics" or that all surgeons are "lone rangers." That's certainly not the case. It's important, however, to recognize that the success or failure of a planning team is often determined before it even meets by the composition of its members. The best combination for a productive physician planning team:

- Entrepreneurs, social activists, politicians, and patient advocates.
- Physician specialists of any ilk whose expertise is a central component of the venture (yes, you may have to tolerate an "opportunist' or drag a "recluse" to meetings).

- A circle of "technical advisors" who don't participate as team members but who may be invited occasionally or whose input may be solicited by a team member (this is a good way to involve an "overwhelmed" or a "lone ranger").
- A physician leader who can make them all work productively together.

Use numbers and research to make your case.   Ann Fyfe emphasizes that numbers appeal to the rational, analytic character of doctors. They are much less comfortable with qualitative and anecdotal input than are managers.

Present physicians with direct evidence.   Several hospitals have started using videotapes of interviews with referring physicians to make their point with specialists. Although a consultant's report that indicates a problem with communications and follow-up from specialists to referring physicians can be convincing, it's not nearly as compelling as hearing it from the referring doctor's mouth in full color video. (This technique works well with nurses too.)

Focus on a common foe.   A key to creating consensus is uncovering mutuality of interest among physicians. Divisions between doctors on the basis of personality, specialty and competition can run very deep, but identifying a common threat shared by all can often overcome those divisions. Research and other evidence that confirms a common danger can be a powerful tool in creating consensus.

Prioritize, discuss, prioritize again.   Physicians are surprisingly democratic. One way to build consensus and commitment is the old-fashioned way—by voting. In a planning session, for instance, a list of key issues can be generated. The issues then can be prioritized using a ballot system that allows physicians to "score" each issue. Scores are then averaged and fed back to the group. Those physicians who feel that the average score for an issue is too low or too high can state their case. Then the group prioritizes once again, this time with the benefit of everyone's advocacy and concerns in mind. The scores are averaged once more and then presented to the group as final ratings. The same approach can be used when evaluating any set of options. For instance, product/service characteristics can be assessed and prioritized in this manner.

Involve them in defining the situation.   Physicians are much more likely to agree with your assessment of a situation if they've had a hand in defining it. Doing work in advance of a critical meeting or planning session to insure advance input is a smart move. You create the environment for consensus by giving physicians ownership before decisions are made. (Savvy politicians line up their votes before the roll is called.) When a situation assessment is presented, physicians are gratified when they see their input incorporated. They feel (rightly) that their perspective has been given a fair hearing. There are other advantages to such advance work. It allows physicians to make controversial statements and provide unpopular perspectives outside the often inhibited environment of a group meeting. It allows the physician to elaborate in detail, which might otherwise interrupt the flow of a group meeting. It allows meeting leaders and those responsible for building consensus to identify stumbling blocks and controversy early so they can be addressed in advance of critical meetings (or at least surfaced with sensitivity).

Involve them in the solution.   It's amazing the extent to which critics can be transformed into advocates when they are given responsibility for creating a solution to a problem or given a role in building something. Involving physicians in the design of new services, the execution of strategies and in the development of policy and protocols is a sure-fire way to make supporters out of detractors. It's also a proven technique for engineering consensus.

SOURCE: Daniel Beckham, personal correspondence, January 3, 1990.

The Competitive Environment

As we noted in Chapter 1, the most significant characteristic of the nonprofit marketplace in the 1990s is the extent of competition. Unfortunately, many nonprofit organizations still deny the existence of such competition, feeling that this is only characteristic of private-sector markets. Thus, hospitals until recently did not like to think of other hospitals as competitors, museums tended to ignore other museums, and the Red Cross saw other blood banks as all seeking the same general public goal. They would rather think of their sister organizations as simply helping provide social services and not competing. Yet the reality of competition is driven home when one hospital starts attracting doctors and patients from another hospital, blood banks compete for donors, or YMCAs start losing members to local racquetball clubs and gymnasiums.

By contrast, there are also nonprofits who recognize the existence of potential competitors but seem to think that competing is "not nice." They feel that since all nonprofits, in some sense, are attempting to achieve the same (obviously desirable) social goals, any attention to competition would divert energies from what each competitor should *really* be doing. Sometimes nonprofit marketers are rudely awakened when a competitor doesn't "play fair."

Consider the case of Population Development Associates (PDA), the dominant nonprofit contraceptive marketer in Thailand. In 1984, PDA found their lowest-priced Mechai brand condom challenged by a new, similar priced brand whose package bore a very strong resemblance to PDA's own brand. This competitive brand—what in Western marketing circles would be considered a me-too brand—was brought to the market not by a private brander or by foreign competition but by a "sister" nonprofit organization, Thailand's affiliate of International Planned Parenthood Federation (IPPF). PDA's first reaction was one of shock. It complained to the IPPF affiliate that its tactics "weren't fair" and that they should concentrate on the larger issue of getting consumers to practice birth control and not try to beat each other out of sales in the marketplace. However, this reaction was fleeting, and PDA, a sophisticated nonprofit marketer, quickly developed a hard-nosed, strictly competitive reaction, drawn straight out of the private sector consumer goods marketing handbook. PDA simply came back with its own new, even-lower-priced competitive brand targeted specifically at gaining back market share lost to the IPPF products.

What PDA realized is that competition may help rather than hurt the nonprofit marketers' performance in two important ways. First, the existence of two competitors in the marketplace, clamoring for attention, spending two advertising budgets, commanding even more shelf space or media interest, can stimulate increases in *the size of the total market*. Thus, it is entirely possible that PDA might lose market share but discover that, because the entire market grows more than their share loss, PDA's total sales may be higher. And if the higher sales are great enough to cover the increased costs due to the new competition, PDA will clearly be better off after the copycat brand entry than before. More important, more total sales of contraceptives would mean that Thailand's population is also better off, which, of course is PDA's basic mission.

The second way in which competition can benefit the nonprofit is that it can sharpen the competitive skills of the embattled marketers. It is a serious danger in the nonprofit domain that marketers will become fat and happy by observing growing sales and pretending there is no competition. There is nothing like the effect of new competitive activity to give complaisant managers the needed slap to the side of the head. To compete, they have to rethink how their brand is positioned. They have to look to their customers more carefully to see if there are better ways to meet their needs and wants. They have to consider the possibility of changing prices, features, and advertising. This reevaluation and the continuing close attention to marketing details can only help the marketer's overall performance.

A marketer can face up to four major types of competitors in trying to serve a target market. They are

1 *Desire competitors*—other immediate desires that the consumer might want to satisfy.
2 *Generic competitors*—other basic ways in which the consumer can satisfy a particular desire.
3 *Service form competitors*—other service forms that can satisfy the consumer's particular desire.
4 *Enterprise competitors*—other enterprises offering the same service form that can satisfy the consumer's particular desire.

We will illustrate these four types of competitors as they were faced by a New York legitimate theater, the Neil Simon, offering the play *Orpheus Descending* with Vanessa Redgrave in the spring of 1989. Consider a young professional woman in New York deciding what to do on a particular evening. Suppose her options are evaluated as shown in Figure 3-6. She realizes that she has several desires she could satisfy—finishing a project at work, getting some exercise, meeting several household responsibilities, or being entertained. Once she determines that the *desire* she will satisfy is to be entertained, she has to consider various *generic* competitors, including TV at home, a movie, or a live performance. Choosing to be entertained by a live performance, she has to consider various *forms* of live entertainment—a symphony, a nightclub performance, a rock concert, or a legitimate play. Finally, after settling on a legitimate play, she has to choose the offerings of various *enterprises*—*Orpheus Descending* at the Neil Simon, *The Merchant of Venice* with Dustin Hoffman at the 46th Street Theater, or *Les Misérables* at the Broadway.

If the Neil Simon Theatre is experiencing poor sales, the causes may be poor marketing strategy at *any or all* of the four levels of competition. The Neil Simon may have chosen a poor offering and so loses out to other *enterprise competitors*. Or the play may be terrific, but too many consumers may be choosing other *form competitors* such as nightclubs or rock concerts. In the latter case, the marketing manager's challenge would be to focus on those who like live entertainment and convince them that legitimate theater is a better alternative. This could involve research into why the theater is losing out to other forms. It may be that competitors in other forms have discovered better ways to meet consumer needs that the theater might wish to copy (for example, reducing prices, selling popcorn or liquor). Or it might be that more people would choose the theater except for certain disincentives ("costs") that the marketer could correct. For instance, potential customers could fear for their safety in downtown parking lots (the marketer could build a new structure, put in stronger lights, or hire a bus service to bring fearful people up to the door from a distant, safe lot). Or they could feel their friends might not want to come. In that case, the marketers could offer two-for-one ticket bargains or a "bring-a-friend-free" promotion.

At the next level of competition, if the manager found that too many

FIGURE 3-6

Types of Competitors Facing a Legitimate Theater

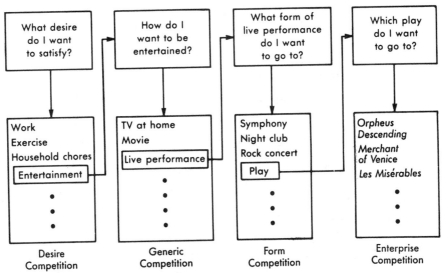

promising customers were not choosing live entertainment as the preferred generic form of entertainment, the theater manager might consider joint promotions with its generic comrades (symphony managers, rock concert promoters, nightclub owners) to get people out to "the live world of entertainment tonight." On the other hand, if the problem is at the *desire level* of competition, joint promotion by those in the entertainment industry (live performance promoters, movie house bookers, TV station managers) could compete with other desires by promoting the theme that "in this stressful, work-conscious world, you need more entertainment to relax, to replenish, to grow."

The most intensive competition is usually at the enterprise level. Nonprofit marketers must understand who their competitors are and what are their strengths and weaknesses. Information on competitors can be gained from sources such as those described in Table 3-2.

Table 3-2

SOURCES OF INTELLIGENCE ON COMPETITORS

From Competitors Themselves
- Annual reports
- Newsletters
- Planning documents
- Marketing brochures
- Advertisements
- Speeches and public statements
- Reports to regulatory agencies
- Want ads

From One's Own Organization
- Sales and service people
- Personnel department
- Economic or market researchers

Outside Observers
- Suppliers
- Trade associations
- Other competitors
- Newspaper articles
- Magazine articles
- Stock market analyses (Moodys, D & B)
- Court records
- Distribution channels
- Advertising agencies
- Financial institutions
- Former employees of competitor

Competitors' Customers
- Market research
  - Interviews
  - Focus groups
  - Surveys

Table 3-3

ST. MARY'S HOSPITAL SUMMARY OF COMPETITOR STRATEGIES

Hospital	Present Position		Plans	Apparent Strategy
	Strengths	*Weaknesses*		
A	• Strong local image • Good medical-surgical market share; relatively high utilization • Strong psychiatry services (range of services and utilization) • Developing women's program • High-visibility media promotion	• Heavy debt load	• Ambulatory care satellite • One-day surgery • Home health • Radiation therapy • Cardiac catheterization • Health Maintenance Organization	• Emphasis on primary/secondary care; outreach and on site
B	• Teaching affiliation • Increasing medical-surgical utilization • Stable psychiatric utilization • Some specialty programs— neonatal intensive care unit, radiation therapy, open-heart surgery	• Declining obstetrics and pediatrics utilization	• Oncology • Pain center • One-day surgery • Outreach satellites • Physician recruitment • Health Maintenance Organization	• Emphasis on market and program development
C	• Multihospital system • Teaching affiliation • Health Maintenance Organization affiliation (PRUCARE)	• Deteriorating utilization in all major services • Medical staff turnover • Underutilized open-heart surgery	• Wellness services • Elderly day care	• Emphasis on affiliations and development of non-inpatient services

Table 3-3
(Continued)

Hospital	Present Position		Plans	Apparent Strategy
	Strengths	Weaknesses		
D	• Increasing obstetrics utilization • Stable medical-surgical utilization	• Limited inpatient services—no pediatrics or psychiatry	• Physician office building • Computerized Tomography Scanner replacement	• Emphasis on primary care—attracting patients to site
E	• Increasing medical-surgical utilization • A few strong specialty services • Fourth-generation computerized tomography scanner • Alcoholism program	• Underutilized, declining obstetrics and pediatrics • Underutilized open-heart surgery	• $32 million expansion on site approved	• Emphasis on adult inpatient care on site

For an example of how a hospital (St. Mary's, a fictitious name) analyzed its enterprise competition, see Table 3-3. St. Mary's could base a strategy on challenging those hospitals that were not able to deliver comparable satisfaction to the same target customers. It could focus, for example, on Hospital G attempting to attract its better medical staff and promoting several major services to its potentially vulnerable patients and potential patients.

Macroenvironment

If strategic planning has its consequences in the future, it is crucial that nonprofit managers understand the broad forces creating the world in which they must operate. These broad forces can be divided into demographic, economic, technological, political-legal, and social-cultural categories. The nature of these forces varies, of course, by the country in which the nonprofit markets, and within a given country, their relative impact varies significantly by region and nonprofit sector. Demographic and political-legal trends are very important for strategic planning in social service agencies. Economic trends are important to charities, technological trends to hospitals and libraries, demographic and economic trends to the armed forces, and social-cultural trends to parks and recreation services and the performing arts.

The United Way of America is a nonprofit organization that believes strongly in conducting what it calls "environmental scanning" as a basis for its strategic planning. It maintains a volunteer group of futurists largely from the private sector called the Environmental Scan Committee, which publishes a document, *What Lies Ahead*, every two years. The major national planning assumptions it produced for the 1990s in a publication entitled *What Lies Ahead: Countdown to the 21st Century* are outlined in Exhibit 3-2. The Committee's chairman, Alfred F. Lynch, director of planning and research, J.C. Penney Company, Inc., notes

> This publication depicts the most likely scenario we expect to face in the years ahead. It is not intended—and should not be taken—as a guarantee of what the future will bring. Nine years of preparing reports such as this one have taught us that change is unpredictable. However, the difficulty of looking ahead with certainty should not stop our readers from . . . using [these] findings for informed decision making in their own organizations.[10]

EXHIBIT 3-2

Nine Leading Forces Reshaping American Society

The United States enters the final decade of the 20th century in the midst of a profound restructuring involving the economy, society, institutions, and even individual life-styles. United Way of America's Environmental Scan Committee expects this restructuring to move at an even faster pace during the 1990s, and has identified nine major ChangeDrivers, or lines along which it is proceeding.

Some of the ChangeDrivers are forces which will be quite disruptive; at the same time, many of the ChangeDrivers offer opportunities to strengthen America's social and economic fabric.

1. The Maturation of America

This trend starts with the maturing of the baby boom generation as these individuals move into their prime family-, household-, and asset-formation phase. It also includes trends pertaining to the "graying of America" – the growth of the age-65-and-over population, a more active, more affluent group than existed in previous generations. Accompanying the aging of the population is the related psychological phenomenon of a maturing and increasing sophistication of tastes. The U.S. is leaving an era obsessed with youth, and moving into one that will be more realistic, more responsible, and more tolerant of diversity.

2. Movement Toward a Mosaic Society

Rising levels of education, increased ethnic diversity, a growing population of elderly individuals, more single-person households, and other diversity-related trends are moving American society away from "mass society" toward a "mosaic society." Technology is enabling products to be customized for each of the parts of the mosaic, further reinforcing their distinctive identities. Alvin Toffler, author of *Future Shock*, refers to this phenomenon as "demassification." The mosaic, however, is not static; rather, it is similar to an ever-changing kaleidoscope.

3. Redefinition of Individual and Societal Roles

There will be a blurring of the boundaries which have traditionally defined the roles of the public sector versus the private sector, as well as those which have set the boundaries of individual versus institutional responsibilities.

a. Redefinition of Public Sector versus Private Sector

The impetus for redefinition of public-sector and private-sector roles is coming from both sides. The federal budget deficit will continue to constrain federal action on social problems, and both the federal and state governments are contracting with private-sector firms to perform many functions which have traditionally been carried out by government. At the same time, business is more directly involved in social issues (such as education, illiteracy, substance abuse, and AIDS), becoming a major player in an arena once dominated by government and the voluntary sector.

b. Redefinition of Individual versus Institutional

Individuals are taking on a greater share of responsibility in many areas, and are relying less on large institutions. The growing emphasis on wellness activities is an example of the shift of responsibility for personal health away from doctors and hospitals and more toward the individual. Individuals are also taking on more responsibility for their employment and careers, exemplified by the growth of entrepreneurial activity, self-employment, and multiple careers. Individuals are less willing to wait for large institutions to provide opportunities, and more willing to act on their own.

4. The Information-Based Economy

The spread of information and communications technology is creating an information-based economy, which is structured in a different way from the current industrial economy. These two economic types have a complex relationship and can be expected to remain distinct, but mutually influencing, throughout the 1990s.

5. Globalization

The movement of products, capital, technology, information—and ideas—around the world is continuing to increase. This is having several significant effects. (1) There is increasing foreign ownership of the U.S. industrial base, and a growing presence of U.S. firms in foreign countries. (2) The *relative* economic power of the United States is declining as other nations develop mature industrial economies. (3) U.S. consumers are experiencing more cultures through travel, imports, immigration, international organizations, and the media. An increasing globalization of tastes and ideas is occurring. (4) Americans are directing their volunteer time and their philanthropic dollars toward a range of global, as well as national, causes. (5) Meanwhile, foreign-owned firms are playing a growing role in American philanthropy.

6. Economic Restructuring

Global economic competition, deregulation, new information technologies, and diverse and changing consumer tastes are forcing an ongoing restructuring of American business. This is happening at many levels: (1) global economic activity is spread among more nations as newly industrializing countries (NICs) emerge as robust economies; (2) entire industries are being globalized and restructured as new entrants and new technologies change the rules of the game; (3) large corporations are cutting management layers and operating more like networks rather than hierarchies; (4) small firms are being created in unprecedented numbers; and (5) firms of all sizes are continuously reassessing their structure and offerings because market conditions are so volatile.

7. Increase in Concern for Personal and Environmental Health

Quality-of-life issues, particularly the health of the individual and the state of the environment, are beginning to emerge as key areas of public concern. During the 1990s, there is likely to be a sharper public perception of issues such

as the threat of global warming from the "greenhouse effect" and ozone deple-
tion, and of the link between personal behavior and disease risk. Quality-of-life
issues such as these tend to follow periods when economic growth has been
strong, and tend also to be vulnerable to economic downturns.

8. Family and Home Redefined

Many functions that once were handled predominately by families—such as
meal preparation and child care—are increasingly offered as services by commercial concerns such as restaurants and day-care centers. At the same time,
activities formerly available only outside the home—such as shopping and
viewing movies—have been brought into the home through videos and cable
television. Information technologies bring consumer services such as shopping
and banking into more homes and enable more Americans to work or run
businesses from their homes. Meanwhile, the family has become a diverse
institution, with many single-person households, single-parent families, and
two-income families. In a rapidly changing, often chaotic outside world, the
family will grow in importance as a stabilizing force. Yet, at the same time, the
evident stresses on family life may make the family less able to fulfill its support-
giving role without help from outside the family structure. Government assistance with child care is one example of such help.

9. Rebirth of Social Activism

After a decade of concentration on business and economic growth, the public-
agenda pendulum is swinging decisively in the direction of social concerns.
Environmental degradation, deterioration of public infrastructure (such as roads
and water-supply systems), pervasive homelessness, lack of affordable housing,
racial tensions, and extensive child poverty are some of the issues which are
gaining increased attention. Accompanying this shift is likely to be less tolerance
for business actions which the public perceives as harmful to society, such as
financial actions which harm the economy and pollution which threatens public
health.

SOURCE: United Way Environmental Scanning Committee, *What Lies Ahead: Countdown
to the 21st Century* (Alexandria, Va.: United Way of America, 1989). Reproduced with
permission.

STEP 4: SETTING MARKETING MISSION, OBJECTIVES, AND GOALS

Once the marketing manager has completed the first three steps of the strategic
marketing planning process, he or she must then integrate what has been
learned at these earlier stages into a long-term strategy for marketing. That is,
the opportunities and threats in the external environment (step 3) must be
compared to the organization's strengths and weaknesses (step 2) to determine

what long-term course of marketing action will best achieve what top management has communicated are its real mission and objectives (step 1).

Mission

One approach used by sophisticated marketing managers to incorporate both internal and external analyses into a long-range marketing mission is through the use of a grid that portrays existing or proposed offerings along two dimensions: (1) market attractiveness and (2) organizational strengths. The overall mission of the marketing function then is to achieve the previously determined organizationwide objectives through *balanced* development of a portfolio of offerings.[11]

This mission then gives guidance to annual plans that must decide

1 which products or services to pour additional resources into because their future looks bright (building opportunities)
2 which products or services to maintain essentially in their present posture as doing just fine (holding opportunities)
3 from which products or services to drain resources because they are not promising (harvesting opportunities)
4 which products or services to drop because their future doesn't look promising or because other product or service prospects look better (divesting opportunities)
5 which products or services to add to the portfolio over the planning period (new product opportunities)

In essence, the problem is like that of managing an investment portfolio where one must decide which stocks to buy or sell, how much to hold of each, whether to switch from stocks to bonds or real estate, whether to withdraw cash, and so on. The problem for the financial investor as well as for the marketing manager is constantly to evaluate the portfolio against changing market conditions and changing performances of individual units in the portfolio.

There are a number of approaches to the portfolio management problem. The most prominent are those commonly referred to as the Boston Consulting Group (BCG) and McKinsey/General Electric approaches. The approaches have a number of elements in common.

The first step in any portfolio analysis is to partition the organization's existing offerings into *strategic business units* (SBUs). These can be individual products and services or groups of similar products or services. Four criteria should be considered when deciding whether individual products and services belong together in a strategic marketing unit:

1 Do they market to essentially the same customers?
2 Are they marketed in essentially the same way? That is, do they use similar media for advertisements or common distributor channels?

3 Do they have essentially the same competitors?
4 Can they be planned for together?

Thus, in a family planning program, the sterilization marketing programs *could* be grouped with programs to market birth control pills and condoms for strategic planning purposes. Further analysis, however, would reveal that they more properly belong with other *medical services* offered by the family planning program. They have in common with the latter two important characteristics: (1) they are offered through the same distribution channel—medical clinics rather than drug stores, and (2) they face the same competitors—other clinics and other private physicians rather than other pharmaceutical manufacturers.

The next step is to assess the favorability of the market in which the SBU competes and the SBU's current performance.

McKinsey/GE's *strategic business planning grid* (see Figure 3-7) uses two basic dimensions, market attractiveness and organizational strength. The best programs to offer are those that serve attractive markets and for which the organization has high organizational strength.

Market attractiveness is a composite index made up of such factors as

- *Market size.* Large markets are more attractive than small markets.
- *Market growth rate.* High-growth markets are more attractive than low-growth markets.
- *Profit margin.* High-profit-margin programs are more attractive than low-profit-margin programs.

FIGURE 3-7

**General Electric Portfolio Approach
(Called the Strategic Business Planning Grid)**

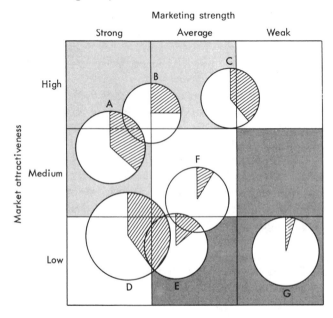

- *Competitive intensity.* Markets with many strong competitors are less attractive than markets with a few weak competitors.
- *Cyclicality.* Highly cyclical markets are less attractive than cyclically stable markets.
- *Seasonality.* Highly seasonal markets are less attractive than nonseasonal markets.
- *Scale economies.* Programs where unit costs fall with large volume production and marketing are more attractive than constant cost programs.
- *Learning curve.* Programs where unit costs fall as management accumulates experience in production and distribution are more attractive than programs where management has reached the limit of its learning.

Marketing strength is a composite index made up of such factors as

- *Program quality.* The higher the program quality relative to competitors, the greater its organizational strength.
- *Efficiency level.* The more efficient the organization is at producing the program relative to competitors, the greater its organizational strength.
- *Market knowledge.* The deeper the organization's knowledge of customers in that market and their needs and wants, the greater its organizational strength.
- *Marketing effectiveness.* The greater the organization's marketing effectiveness, the greater its organizational strength.

The factors making up each dimension are scaled and weighted so that each current SBU achieves a number indicating its market attractiveness and marketing strength and therefore can be plotted in the grid.

The grid is divided into three zones—green, yellow, and red. The green zone consists of the three cells at the upper left, indicating those SBUs that are located in attractive markets and for which there is marketing strength. The implication is that the organization should "invest and grow" these SBUs. The yellow zone consists of the diagonal cells stretching from the lower left to the upper right, indicating SBUs that are medium in overall attractiveness. Here the organization gives serious consideration to harvesting or divesting. Finally, the red zone in the three cells at the lower right represent definitely unattractive situations where divestment is in order.

For an example, consider program G shown in Figure 3-7. The graph indicates that program G is in an unattractive market and that the marketing group does not have strong strengths to bring to it. It is a fairly large volume program (indicated by the size of the circle) and the organization has only a small market share (indicated by the shaded wedge). The organization will want to consider phasing this program down or out.

Other portfolio approaches have been developed. As an example, consider a college administration trying to determine how much support to give to each academic department. One college developed the following criteria:

- *Centrality.* The degree to which an academic program is central to the mission of the college.
- *Quality.* The quality and reputation of the academic department relative to those in other colleges.
- *Market viability.* The degree to which the market for the academic program is sufficient in size and growth.

FIGURE 3-8

Academic Portfolio Model

Centrality

	High	Medium	Low
High	Psychology (MV–H) Decision: •Build size •Build quality		Home Economics (MV–H) Decision: •Build size •Build quality
Medium		Geography (MV–M) Decision: •Hold size •Hold quality	
Low	Philosophy (MV–L) Decision: •Reduce size •Build quality		Classical Languages (MV–L) Decision: •Reduce size or terminate

(Quality axis on left; levels High, Medium, Low)

The three criteria can be combined in the grid shown in Figure 3-8. Each criterion is divided into high, medium, and low. (Market viability is represented by MV and its level is represented by H, M, or L, for high, medium, or low, respectively.) According to Figure 3-8, the administration rates the psychology department high in centrality, quality, and market viability. Because the psychology department is one of the stars, the administration may want to increase its budget further. On the other hand, classical languages' rating falls in the lower right. The administration feels that classical languages are not central to its purpose, that the faculty is poor, and that the market viability is low insofar as few students enroll in the courses. The administration will give serious thought to reducing or dropping classical languages.[12]

The ultimate decision as to whether to change the portfolio may well depend on the marketing manager's or the organization's attitude toward risk. Some managers might on some occasion be quite averse to risk. A marketing manager hoping for a renewal grant from a funding agency, for example, would pursue a cautious, no-change strategy that would guarantee that the program would appear reasonably successful at the end of the period. The manager would prefer this to a riskier strategy that could look sensational but could also fail sensationally.

Opportunity Identification

Portfolio planning is very useful as a device for creating a mission as far as it goes. But it doesn't help the nonprofit manager with two of the most difficult problems the manager faces—determining (1) how to find and nurture new offers, and (2) how to *grow* new offers into stars.

Needed is a systematic approach to opportunity identification. A useful device for doing this is known as the product/market opportunity matrix (see Figure 3-9).[13] Originally a two-by-two matrix proposed by Ansoff, it is here expanded into a three-by-three matrix. Markets are listed at the left and offerings along the top.

Each cell in Figure 3-9 has a name. Potential opportunities—in this case, for a college—are listed in small letters. The administration should first consider cell 1, called *market penetration.* This cell raises the question of whether the college can maintain or expand its enrollment by deepening its penetration into its existing markets with its existing products. If further market penetration does not look likely, then it will have to look for ideas in another cell. Exhibit 3-3 shows how the Girl Scouts of the United States of America has attempted to increase its penetration in an underserved market.

Cell 2, *geographical expansion,* raises the question of whether the college should consider expanding into new geographical markets with its existing offerings. The college could open a branch in another part of the city, or in a new city, or start a new campus in another country. Southern Methodist of Dallas is

FIGURE 3-9

Product/Market Opportunity Matrix

Offerings

	Existing	Modified	New
Existing	1. Market Penetration	4. Offer Modification • short courses • evening program • weekend program • new delivery system	7. Offer Innovation • new courses • new departments • new schools
Geographical	2. Geographical Expansion • new areas of city • new cities • foreign	5. Modification for Dispersed Markets • programs offered on military bases or at U.S.-based firms abroad	8. Geographical Innovation
New	3. New Markets A. Individual • senior citizens • homemakers • ethnic minorities B. Institutional • business firms • social agencies	6. Modification for New Markets A. Individual • senior citizens • homemakers • ethnic minorities B. Institutional • business • government	9. Total Innovation • new courses • new departments • new schools

Markets

EXHIBIT 3-3

Frances Hesselbein, National Executive Director of the Girl Scouts of the United States of America on Reaching New Markets

Rapidly changing demographics, with racial/ethnic minorities growing into a majority of the population in some geographic areas, have presented an urgent marketing challenge to Girl Scouts of the U.S.A.

The nation's largest organization for girls, which relies on a proportionately large corps of adult volunteers, was founded in 1912 when traditions of the Anglo-American middle class were assumed to be the norm. It is repositioning itself for a pluralistic society, actively reaching out to girls and adults from all segments of the community.

As long ago as 1970, "a membership reflective of total population" was a stated national objective. The same idea, rephrased and elaborated, has been a corporate goal ever since the Girl Scouts' present system of strategic and tactical planning was introduced in 1977. *From 1978 to 1989, the proportion of minorities (as defined by the U.S. Census Bureau) to total Girl Scout membership more than doubled, from 6.6 percent to 13.7 percent* – thanks to the united efforts of Girl Scouts of the U.S.A. and its local councils.

The Girl Scouts recently established a National Center for Innovation, combining grass-roots market research with imaginative approaches to marketing problems. A national staff team was deployed to Southern California in July 1988; its assignment was to collaborate with nine Girl Scout councils in creating demonstration projects for recruitment of Hispanic, black, Asian, and American Indian girls and adults.

Five projects were developed in California over an 18-month period, then shared with 47 additional Girl Scout councils at an innovation conference on the East Coast in November 1989. Results up to that point were substantial enough to warrant a $2.3 million grant from the W. K. Kellogg Foundation for two-year operation of a Girl Scout/Kellogg National Innovation Center in Appalachia and another in Spanish-speaking areas of southern Texas.

SOURCE: Personal correspondence, December 19, 1989.

offering courses in its M.B.A. program in Houston. Similarly, Notre Dame now grants an M.B.A. in London, and Antioch operates campuses in several countries.

The administration then moves to cell 3, *new markets*, and considers possibly offering its existing programs to new individual and institutional markets. Colleges are increasingly recruiting nontraditional student groups such as senior citizens, homemakers, and ethnic minorities. Iowa State University, for instance, has instituted "Eldercollege," a program for retired and older adults, which meets once a week for two months. In addition, colleges are trying to interest business firms, social agencies, and other organizations in buying educational and training programs to be delivered in-house by the faculty.

Next the marketing manager can consider whether the organization should engage in *offer modification* to attract more of the existing market (cell 4). Standard courses can be shortened in the evening or on weekends. For example, Alverno College, a private women's school in Milwaukee, instituted a weekend college and drew large numbers of housewives and employed women. Some colleges are beginning to offer courses in the very late evening or very early morning, having discovered a number of working people for whom these hours would be more convenient.

Cell 5 is named *modification for dispersed markets.* The University of Maryland, for example, offers modified programs for members of the armed forces both domestically and abroad.

Modification for new markets (cell 6) may be a more realistic growth approach for colleges and universities. To penetrate the senior citizen market, for example, may require a modification of standard courses. Specifically, the time period might need to be shorter and less reading might be required, with more comfortable seats and probably books with larger print.

Offer innovation (cell 7) involves developing new courses, departments, or schools for existing markets. A business school, for example, might develop a new program in managing nonprofit organizations to offer to its students.

Geographical innovation (cell 8) involves finding new ways to serve new geographical areas. Illinois Bell, for instance, has developed an electronic blackboard that allows a professor to write on a blackboard in one location and have it transmitted over telephone lines to a distant city. With the advent of home computers, interactive television, and other new media technologies, it will be possible to offer courses to a national audience.

The final category, *total innovation,* refers to offering new offerings for new markets. The "university without walls" college where learning takes place away from a campus is an example.

The product/market opportunity matrix helps the administration imagine new opportunities in a systematic way. These opportunities are evaluated and the better ones pursued. The results of the product/market analysis and the previous portfolio analysis allow the organization to set its basic mission and carry out annual planning.

Objectives

There are a number of alternative marketing/financial objectives that might be pursued by nonprofit organizations. Some are more desirable from a social standpoint than others.

Surplus Maximization.   Some nonprofit organizations pursue the objective of maximizing their surplus. A performing arts group, for example, might want to accumulate as much cash surplus as possible in order to build a new theater. This does not mean that it will charge the highest possible ticket price, because this would reduce attendance. It would need to know how the quantity of tickets sold is affected by price, as well as how the donations are affected.[14]

Revenue Maximization.   An alternative objective is to maximize the total revenue even though high costs might be incurred. A public transportation company, for example, might feel that a high total revenue tells the market that the organization is important and doing a good job. Management might feel that increased revenue would lead to greater confidence in the organization.

Usage Maximization.   Many nonprofit organizations are primarily interested in maximizing the number of users of their services. Thus, art museums and zoological parks are eager to maximize the annual number of visitors, because this is taken as a sign that they are providing worthwhile educational and recreational services to the community. The city council will look at each institution's attendance growth to determine how much budget to grant it for next year.

Usage Targeting.   Organizations with fixed service capacities typically set their price and marketing expenditures to produce a capacity audience. For example, a symphony orchestra experiencing low attendance might lower its price in order to fill more of the seats in the auditorium. If the potential ticket-seekers exceed capacity, the orchestra would raise prices to improve its revenue while filling the auditorium.

Full Cost Recovery.   Many nonprofit organizations are primarily interested in breaking even each year. They would like to provide as much service as they can as long as their sales revenue plus donations and grants just cover their costs. Many universities want to be in the position of spending just short of the amount at which they would have to report a deficit. Many public agencies also have this objective, making sure to spend any remaining funds toward the end of the year to avoid showing a surplus that might lead to receiving a lower budget during the next year.

Partial Cost Recovery.   Other organizations operate with a chronic deficit each year. Examples in the past have included most performing arts organizations and many local public transportation companies. There is no reasonable price and marketing expenditure level that would bring these organizations close to breaking even. Instead, their aim is to keep the annual deficit from exceeding a certain amount. Public authorities or private foundations or individual donors are solicited to cover the annual deficit.

Budget Maximization.   Many nonprofits, particularly those in social services, act as if they are attempting to maximize the size of their staffs, the number of programs they offer, and their operating expenditures. They seem to seek program grants and donations without fully considering their ability to use the contributed funds effectively. They are also reluctant to trim programs or staff even in the face of evidence that these are nonproductive. Trimming operations would, of course, make the organization seem less "successful" in the staff's own eyes and—they believe—in the eyes of their peers.

Producer Satisfaction Maximization.   Many nonprofit organizations are as eager to satisfy the wants of their own staffs as those of the publics they serve. One often hears the criticism that hospitals place the needs of doctors ahead of those of patients and that colleges place the needs of faculty ahead of those of students. One can imagine the members of a symphony orchestra playing primarily music that pleases them, whether or not it attracts a large audience. This introduces a new variable not shown in the equation, maximization of producer satisfaction. According to Etgar and Ratchford: "the product is created mainly for the satisfaction of producers themselves. . . . The organization will modify its product away from the one which gives its own members the most satisfaction only insofar as is necessary to obtain enough revenue from these customer groups to survive financially."[15] McKnight goes further and argues that most nonprofit organizations and professionals are basically self-serving and oriented toward maximizing their own interests.[16]

Goals

Once the general marketing objectives have been set, the next step is to set specific goals to be achieved over the strategic planning horizon. These goals may be stated in terms of people served, revenues, costs, or some other factors over which marketing staff may be expected to have some influence. These goals should have the following characteristics. They should

1 Give direction to marketing staff.
2 Describe the basic pathway between the present and the planning horizon.
3 Provide benchmarks against which progress will be measured.
4 Provide triggers for implementation of contingency plans.
5 Motivate staff to achieve more than they have in the past.
6 Establish a basis for future performance rewards.
7 Communicate the organization's direction to "the outside world."
8 Identify needed marketing tracking information.

Philip Harvey and James Snyder point out that clear goal definition is relatively rare in nonprofit organizations for six reasons:

1 Many nonprofit managers fear accountability. They come to the job, in part, because they expect to have limited surveillance.
2 Many projects continue even when they no longer serve an organization's mission and no one wants to look hard at these projects' performance.
3 Nonprofits often undertake projects simply because there is money available for doing them.
4 Some nonprofit managers fear that management science will replace humanitarian concerns.
5 Nonprofit managers often equate busyness with doing something worthwhile.
6 Nonprofits seldom have financial report cards to tell them how they are doing.[17]

As the nonprofit world matures and managers are increasingly better trained in management techniques and in the value of careful strategic planning, these barriers to effective goal setting should wither away.

SUMMARY

Once management has developed the appropriate marketing mind-set, it must determine the basic direction the organization will take over the strategic planning horizon. The means by which this is carried out is called the strategic marketing planning process. The first step in this process is to identify the organization's overall mission, objectives, and specific goals and to understand the nature of its basic culture.

The next step is to analyze the strengths and weaknesses that the organization brings to the marketplace. A marketing audit is an effective tool for this purpose. Step 3 involves a careful analysis of the organization's external environment. First, management must identify and understand the key publics it must consider in its planning. Publics can be input publics (donors, suppliers, and regulatory organizations), internal publics (management, board, staff, and volunteers), intermediary publics (merchants, agents, facilitators, and marketing firms), and consuming publics (customers, local residents, the general public, and the media).

The second major environmental component is competition. Here, the organization must recognize that it has competitors on four levels: desire, generic, service form, and enterprise. It may be required to consider all four of them in its planning. The third component is the macroenvironment. The organization must understand major trends taking place in its social, political, technological, and economic environments. Many nonprofits conduct environmental scanning exercises with private-sector assistance for this purpose.

Step 4 of the strategic marketing planning process requires that planners take the information from the earlier steps and develop a specific mission and sets of goals and objectives for the marketing department. Strategic planning grids can be used to compare market opportunities with organization capabilities. If the organization decides it wishes its mission to focus on growth, it may do so by expanding into new products, into new markets, or some combination of both.

Decisions about the basic mission then lead naturally to the formulation of objectives for the planning period. These can include maximizing surpluses, revenues, usage, or budgets. Alternatively, the organization can set objectives in terms of usage targeting, full or partial cost recovery, or satisfaction of its own staff. These objectives must then be turned into detailed goals. These goals should give direction to the organization's staff and describe pathways to its future. They should offer benchmarks for measuring progress and provide triggers for contingency plans. Goals should be motivating for staff and provide a basis for assessing future performance. Finally, goals should communicate the organization's direction to the outside world and indicate needs for developing marketing tracking information systems.

QUESTIONS

1. A major professional theater company has decided that it can pursue both a differentiation and a cost leadership strategy simultaneously. It will offer the lowest-cost tickets of any of its competitors while differentiating itself as the only theater offering the latest in American and English plays. Michael Porter argues that most organizations cannot follow *two* basic core strategies simultaneously. Do you think the theater is acting against Porter's advice? If so, what do you believe are its chances of succeeding?

2. What are the major publics that the American Red Cross must consider in developing its marketing strategies? Describe three situations in which strategies directed at one public might alienate another.

3. Describe the corporate culture of your organization or university. How does that culture influence the type of marketing that (a) can be done and (b) should be done?

4. Offer suggestions for product and market expansion for a successful teen drug counseling program using the product/market matrix in Figure 3-9.

5. Suggest two specific numerical benchmarks that the New York Public Library might use to track its success in achieving seven of the eight marketing objectives listed in this chapter (omit "surplus maximization").

NOTES

1. For an advanced example of goal setting in a university environment, see David P. Hopkins, Jean-Claude Larreche and William F. Massy, "Constrained Optimization of a University Administrator's Preference Function," *Management Science,* December 1977, pp. 365–377.

2. The material in this section is drawn from Alan R. Andreasen and Jean M. Manning, "Culture Conflict in Health Care Marketing," *Journal of Health Care Marketing,* Vol. 7, no. 1 (March 1987), pp. 2–8.

3. Thomas J. Peters and Robert H. Waterman, Jr., *In Search of Excellence* (New York: Harper & Row, 1982).

4. For details, see Philip Kotler, William Gregor, and William Rodgers, "The Marketing Audit Comes of Age," *Sloan Management Review,* Winter 1977, pp. 25–43.

5. For a marketing audit guide for social service organizations, see Douglas B. Herron, "Developing a Marketing Audit for Social Service Organizations," in Charles B. Weinberg and Christopher H. Lovelock, eds., *Reading in Public and Nonprofit Marketing* (Palo Alto, Calif.: Scientific Press, 1978), pp. 269–271. For arts organizations, see Tom Horwitz, *Arts Administration* (Chicago: Review Press, 1978), pp. 81–85. For hospitals, see Eric N. Berkowitz and William A. Flexner, "The Marketing Audit: A Tool for Health Service Organizations," *HCM Review,* Fall 1978, pp. 55–56.

6. Alan A. Andreasen, *Problems in Practical Application of a Standardized Marketing Audit* (Washington, D.C.: The Futures Group, 1983).

7. Alan R. Andreasen, *A Marketing Audit Model for Contraceptive Social Marketing Programs* (Washington, D.C.: The Futures Group, 1983).

8. Ibid.

9. See David L. Sills, *The Volunteers—Means and Ends in a National Organization* (Glencoe, Ill.: Free Press, 1957). Also note that the National Center for Voluntary Action, 1785 Massachusetts Avenue, N.W., Washington, D.C., 20036, researches, runs seminars on, and disseminates up-to-date techniques on managing volunteers.

10. United Way Environmental Scanning Committee, *What Lies Ahead: Countdown to the 21st Century* (Alexandria, Va.: United Way of America, 1989).

11. As noted earlier, the portfolio approach is central to the new marketing strategies of the United Way of America.

12. For additional readings on portfolio analysis applied to universities, see Peter Doyle and James E. Lynch, "A Strategic Model for University Planning," *Journal of the Operations Research Society*, July 1979, pp. 603–609; and Gerald D. Newbould, "Product Portfolio Diagnosis for U.S. Universities," *Akron Business and Economic Review*, Spring 1980, pp. 39–45.

13. H. Igor Ansoff, "Strategies for Diversification," *Harvard Business Review*, September–October 1957, pp. 1123–1124.

14. See also Charles B. Weinberg, "Marketing Decision Rules for Nonprofit Organizations," in Jagdish N. Sheth, ed., *Research in Marketing*, Vol. 3 (Chicago: JAI Press, 1980), pp. 191–234.

15. Michael Etgar and Brian T. Ratchford, "Marketing Management and Marketing Concept: Their Conflict in Non-Profit Organizations," *1974 Proceedings* (Chicago: American Marketing Association, 1974).

16. John McKnight, "Professional Service Business," *Social Policy*, November–December 1977, pp. 110–116.

17. Philip D. Harvey and James D. Snyder, "Charities Need a Bottom Line Too," *Harvard Business Review*, Vol. 66, no. 1 (January–February 1987), p. 14.

4

Understanding
Consumer Behavior

The Boy Scouts of America have an image problem.

Boy Scouts have been part of American legend for over 80 years. They have had among their ranks such future leaders as Gerald Ford, Henry Fonda, and Neil Armstrong. For millions of young boys in the 1950s, 1960s, and 1970s, the chance to earn scouting badges or become an Eagle Scout was a chance to be "really somebody."

Unfortunately, times have changed. In the new, cool 1990s, members of the Boy Scouts all too often are seen as nerds. Focus group studies conducted in Kansas City, Minneapolis, and Los Angeles in 1989 found that the descriptor of scouts most frequently used by participants was "geek."

In part as a result of this image and in part as a result of changes in demographics and lifestyles, growth in enrollment in scouting has been relatively flat over the last decade. Trial rates for boy scouting remains disappointingly low compared to cub scouting. Although 55 percent of all boys enroll in Cub Scouts, only 21 percent enroll in Boy Scouts.

To make scouting more relevant to today's target consumer, the Boy Scouts of America proposes to change its image. They have hired an agency, Media Communications, Salt Lake City, to conduct a nationwide marketing campaign to promote scouting as one of life's really exciting adventures. TV and direct mail will be used to reach the target market of boys 10 to 12 years. Testing will be carried out in six markets in 1990 with a $15 to $20 million national campaign to follow.

At the same time, the Boy Scouts have begun to develop a range of specialized programs targeted at markets where they have recently not had particular success. For example, in western Los Angeles, the regional Boy Scout Council has developed an In-School Scouting program for hard-to-serve youth. In 1990, the program will be expanded to include Afterschool, Handicap, and Latchkey programs. The latter is particularly appropriate for the 1990s, offering "positive alternatives to youngsters who find themselves alone at home during their parents' working hours."

Source: Based on materials in Marcy Magiera, "Be Square? Scouts Stalk Cooler Image," *Advertising Age,* August 7, 1989, and In-School Scouting Program brochure of the Western Los Angeles County Council, Boy Scouts of America, 1989.

In our view, the bottom line of all marketing strategy and tactics is to influence behavior. Sometimes this necessitates changing ideas and thoughts first, but in the end, it is behavior change we are after. This is an absolutely crucial point. Some nonprofit marketers may think they are in the "business" of changing *ideas,* but it can legitimately be asked why they should bother if such changes do not lead to action. That is, why bother changing whites' attitudes towards blacks unless it leads to fair treatment socially and in the workplace? Is social marketing really successful if the attitudes of a specific white population (for example, teenaged boys in a given neighborhood) are made more positive while their behaviors continue to be prejudicial? If one argues that attitude change alone really does represent success because *eventually* behavior will change, one is simply reinforcing our fundamental position that the bottom line of nonprofit marketing really is—or ought to be—*behavior change.*

If the end product of a particular program is only a change in a mental state, this should more properly be called *educating* or *propagandizing.* It is not really marketing. A great many nonprofit organizations, of course, engage in a great deal of education or propagandization as well as marketing. Besides educational institutions, these include religious organizations and those seeking broad social reforms.

Our definition still leaves a very wide area for the application of marketing principles. Indeed, there are scholars like Bartels and Luck who believe that the arena for marketing is defined too broadly.[1] But all the following seem to us to be perfectly legitimate opportunities for the application of effective marketing:

- Sales of products and services
- Efforts to get individuals to undertake activities that will be good for their physical and mental health—from brushing their teeth or exercising regularly to undergoing surgery or entering psychoanalysis
- Efforts to get individuals to refrain from certain activities, such as smoking, excessive drinking, and taking harmful drugs
- Efforts of customers to influence *marketers*—for example, to get them to reduce prices, add free accessories, or give free installation

THE CENTRAL ROLE OF EXCHANGE

What do all of these contexts have in common? The parties involved all believe they can induce behavior change by offering the other party a *favorable exchange*. People—at least those who are mentally competent—behave in ways that they perceive will leave them better off than if they behaved in some other fashion. Since every action implies perceived costs (if only some anxiety about not taking an alternative action), it follows that people act in certain ways because they perceive *the ratio of the benefits to costs* to be better than for any alternative. Since the costs are in a basic sense the sacrifices the consumer must make to receive the benefits the action will bring, a diverse array of scholars have come to consider the *exchange* to be the most useful way to conceptualize the relationship between marketers and their target consumers. The marketer is offering what the consumer perceives to be benefits but the organization sees as costs, and receives in return what the organization sees as benefits but the consumer sees as costs or sacrifices. The simplest exchange can then be represented as follows:

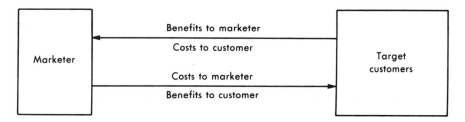

Formally speaking, the exchange perspective assumes that four conditions exist:

1 *There are at least two parties.* In the simplest exchange situation, there are two parties. If one party seeks an exchange more actively than the other, we call the first party a marketer and the second party a prospect. A marketer is someone who is seeking a behavior from someone else and who is willing to offer benefits in exchange. The marketer can be a seller or a buyer.

2 *Each can offer something that the other perceives to be a benefit or benefits.* If one of the parties has nothing that is valued by the other party, the exchange will not take place. Each party should consider what things might be perceived as benefits by the other party. Four categories of things tend to offer such benefits. The first is *physical goods*. A good is any tangible object—food, clothing, furniture, and so on—that is capable of satisfying a human want. The second is *services*. A service is any act that another person or institution might perform that is capable of satisfying a human want. The third category is *money*. Money is a generalized store of value that can be used to obtain goods or services. The final category is *time and effort* (including psychological effort). Many marketing exchanges involve marketers seeking to attract any of the previous resources from others. This could include getting others to give blood, serve as volunteers for a charity drive, or provide free advice to the organization's management.

3 *Each is capable of communication and delivery.* For exchange to take place, the two

parties must be capable of communicating with each other. They must be able to describe what is being offered and when, where, and how costs and benefits will be exchanged. Each party must state or imply certain warranties about the expected performance in the exchange. In addition to communicating, each party must be capable of finding means to deliver the values to the other.

4   *Each is free to accept or reject the offer.* An exchange assumes that both parties are engaging in voluntary behavior. There is no complete coercion. For this reason, every trade is normally assumed to leave both parties better off. Presumably each ended up with more value than he or she started with, since they both freely entered the exchange.

It is critical to recognize that in attempting to understand consumer behavior, one can distinguish between exchange as a *process* and exchange as an *outcome*. In the present context, exchange as an outcome will be considered a *transaction*. That is, the *process* of "exchanging" results in an outcome called a transaction. If either party is actively trying to create or influence the *nature* of an exchange, that is *marketing*. Merely accepting or rejecting the marketing of another is "exchanging," but by our definition, it is *not* marketing.[2]

Types of Exchanges

Exchanges can vary in whether they are *two party* or *multiple party* and whether they lead to transactions that are *continuing* or of *fixed duration*. Multiple-party exchanges occur in a number of contexts: the "additional" party can be (1) *allied with the customer*—for example, other family members, other members of the neighborhood, or other members of a buying group; (2) *allied with the marketer*—for example, an advertising agency or distribution channel member; (3) *independent* of either prime transactor but necessary to *facilitate* the transaction—for example, a credit card company; (4) *independent* of either party but *seeking to influence* the existence or content of an exchange—for example, a bystander urging a teenager not to take an offered cigarette or a national politician urging citizens to be sure to vote.

"Continuing transactions" are transactions where one or more parties must perform some continuing behavior as their part of the exchange agreement. "Fixed duration transactions" are, most commonly, specific product sales. However, renting a car or a motel room for several days or weeks is a transaction taking place over time but is of fixed duration. A great many of the transactions sought in the nonprofit sector, however, require the target consumer to change for a long time some behavior or set of behaviors. Examples include campaigns to induce children to brush their teeth regularly, teenagers to avoid drugs, adults to stop smoking, and couples to practice birth control. Implicit in continuing transactions—and therefore crucial to marketers—is the fact that marketing does not stop and *should not stop* with the parties' agreement to the transaction or when the exchange is first performed under the terms of the transaction. Marketers must continue to influence (i.e., reinforce) the desired behavior.

Marketers and the Exchange Process

To summarize, we have proposed the following:

1 Marketing is a set of activities designed to influence behavior.
2 Behavior by a target consumer is carried out at the end of an exchange process.
3 An exchange will result in a transaction whenever the target consumer perceives the benefits of the behavior the marketer seeks to exceed the costs or sacrifices the behavior entails *and* this ratio of benefits to costs is better than that achieved by "spending" the costs in any other conceivable way.
4 Behavior by the target consumer yields benefits to the marketer (which was the reason for marketing in the first place), while most of the benefits the consumer receives will involve costs for the marketer.
5 The outcome of an exchange may be of fixed duration or continuing.
6 There may be two or more parties, one or both of whom may be carrying on marketing.

Given the exchange framework, the challenge to the marketer in the case of a single consumer is relatively straightforward. To secure a transaction, the marketer must somehow induce the consumer to perceive the benefit/cost ratio to be more favorable than other alternative actions the consumer is considering −including doing nothing. Assuming that the consumer is not behaving as the marketer wishes, the task is either to increase the perceived benefits and/or reduce the perceived costs of this behavior (or in some cases, reduce the perceived benefits and increase the perceived costs of a competitive alternative). At the aggregate level, the marketer must choose a *set* of strategies to be directed at changing cost/benefit ratios of sets of consumers so that the marketer secures for itself the largest amount of the benefits it desires.

A Model of the Determinants of Exchange

Bagozzi has formulated a comprehensive model of the major determinants affecting exchange. The model is summarized in Figure 4-1. We will apply it to a hospital's problem of attracting a new physician to its staff.

First, we consider the two primary social actors involved in the exchange, namely, the chief of staff (source) and the prospective physician (receiver). The chief of staff and the prospective physician will engage in actions and communicate and exchange information to influence each other. The chief of staff's influence will be a function of several personal qualities, namely, attraction, similarity to the physician, expertise, prestige, trustworthiness, and status. The prospective physician's perception of these qualities will be influenced by his own self-confidence, self-esteem, sex, race, religion, social class, intelligence, and personality. The physician's ultimate decision will additionally be influenced by situational variables such as the availability of alternative sources of satisfaction (other hospitals and career opportunities), the opinion of other parties (wife, children, friends, and other colleagues), physical and psychologi-

FIGURE 4-1

A Model of the Determinants of Exchange

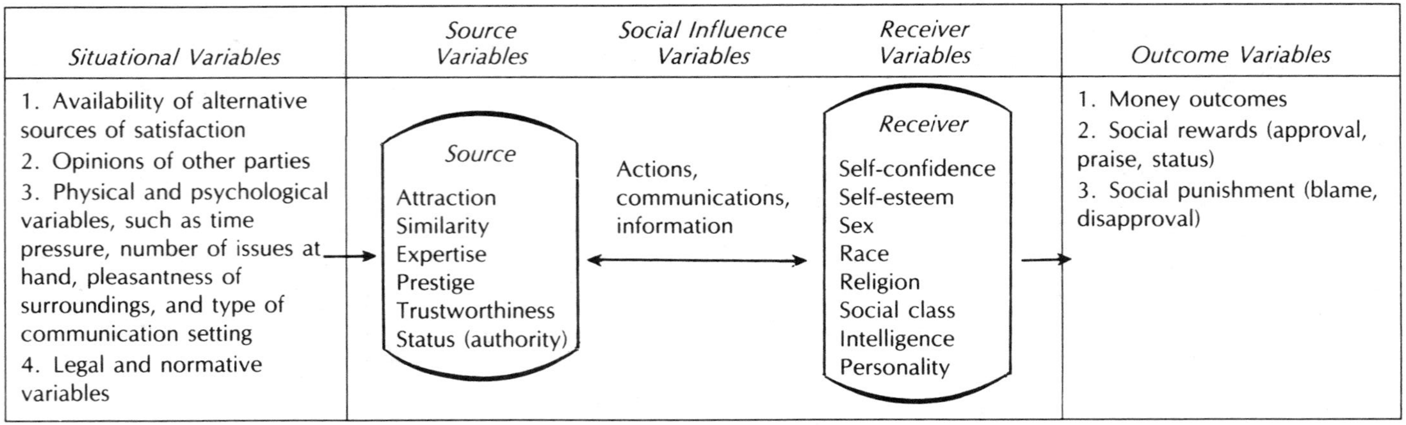

Situational Variables	Source Variables	Social Influence Variables	Receiver Variables	Outcome Variables
1. Availability of alternative sources of satisfaction 2. Opinions of other parties 3. Physical and psychological variables, such as time pressure, number of issues at hand, pleasantness of surroundings, and type of communication setting 4. Legal and normative variables	*Source* Attraction Similarity Expertise Prestige Trustworthiness Status (authority)	Actions, communications, information	*Receiver* Self-confidence Self-esteem Sex Race Religion Social class Intelligence Personality	1. Money outcomes 2. Social rewards (approval, praise, status) 3. Social punishment (blame, disapproval)

SOURCE: Diagram adapted by the authors from prose text in Richard P. Bagozzi, "Marketing as Exchange: A Theory of Transactions in the Marketplace," *American Behavioral Scientist*, March-April 1978, pp. 535–56.

cal variables (time pressure for making a decision, number of issues that have to be considered, pleasantness of the surroundings, type of communication setting), and legal or normative variables (his contract with his present hospital and any normative concerns that might be triggered by the thought of leaving his community).

The physician will also be influenced by his picture of the contrasting consequences associated with his staying versus leaving his present hospital. Three kinds of consequences are likely to be important. First, his money income will be influenced by the outcome. Second, he will experience different social rewards in the form of approval, praise, and status, Third, he might also experience some social punishment such as disapproval or blame.

LEVELS OF UNDERSTANDING CONSUMER BEHAVIOR

The marketing manager for a nonprofit organization must understand consumer behavior because the organization's success depends on it. There are four broad classes of management decisions for which an understanding of consumers is especially crucial. The decisions will determine

1 *How to aggregate consumers into similar groupings for purposes of marketing planning.* This is the issue of *segmentation,* which is taken up in the next chapter.
2 *How to market to each chosen segment, if at all.* These are the *marketing mix* decisions taken up in Section IV of this book. The marketer must decide what to offer in costs and benefits (offer and "pricing" decisions), how to communicate these (promotion decisions), and how to make them available (distribution decisions).
3 *How much to market to each segment.* These strategic allocation decisions involve questions about how many dollars in investment and operating budget to put into a particular market, how much personnel to use, and how much to use of one of the scarcest organizational resources—management's own time.
4 *When to apply the marketing efforts to the segment.* These timing decisions are also critical strategic choices. They involve allocations of resources over time as well as sequencing decisions for various tactics within a given strategy.

There are also four levels at which a manager may wish to understand consumer behavior so as to make these decisions better:

1 *Descriptive understanding.* At the simplest level, the manager may wish to profile the characteristics of the market at a given point in time. How many buyers of what age, sex, and occupational status are in market A, creating how many exchanges of type B, in month Y, costing X marketing dollars, and so on. At a more sophisticated level, the manager may wish to categorize consumers in terms of complex indexes such as their social class or family life cycle or their "psychographic profile."
2 *Understanding of associations.* At this level, the manager may desire to know what behaviors or characteristics in the profile are associated with what other behav-

iors or characteristics at a certain point in time. Thus, the manager may wish to know whether museum attendance is associated with occupation, theater attendance with gender, and attendance at both with age and family composition.

3 *Understanding of causation.* If a curvilinear association between family life cycle and arts attendance is found, a manager may wish to know whether getting older and having children *leads* to less performing arts attendance or whether the two sets of factors just happen to occur together for other reasons. This level of understanding moves beyond association to show determinancy. Such information is particularly valuable if the "cause" at issue is a marketing intervention the manager can control.

4 *Ability to explain causation.* Ideally, a manager would like to move beyond knowing that A causes B to know *why* this is so. That is, the manager may "know" that arts attendance has a curvilinear association with age and that the appearance of children *causes* a decline in attendance. But the manager may only have hypotheses as to why this is so. It is possible, for example, that the explanation is that the appearance of children puts a strain on budgets that precludes former luxuries like arts attendance (an economic explanation). Alternatively, it may be that younger family members put pressure on adult consumers to *not* attend the performing arts (a sociological explanation). Or, the appearance of children may change the consumer's personal priorities. He or she may decide to devote more time to being with the children or more time working to build a firm economic future for the family, which leaves no room for attending the performing arts (a psychological explanation). Quite obviously, what a performing-arts marketer should do to win back families with new children—or whether one should do anything at all—depends on which of these explanations is the most valid.

Developing a sophisticated understanding of various consumer markets is, of course, not easy. It comes with time and experience and the careful use of the formal and informal research approaches discussed in Chapter 7 to accumulate facts, understand relationships, and slowly form patterns from them. But personal observation and formal research are both likely to be much more effective if they are based on an awareness of what we already know about consumers. More important, it will be much more useful and effective if this observation, research, and past history are all based on a sound conceptualization or model of consumer behavior. The remainder of this chapter will offer such a conceptualization centered on the fundamental concept of exchange.

INDIVIDUAL DECISIONS

Unilateral Two-Party Marketing

We begin with a situation where a marketer is seeking to influence a consumer to undertake an exchange that is favorable to the marketer. For a *one-time exchange* to take place, a minimum of three steps must occur in the exchange process:

1 The consumer must *need or want* to make an exchange.
2 The consumer must *understand* that the marketer's offering will meet those needs or wants.
3 The consumer must *behave* as desired (that is, must complete the transaction).

While it is obviously a continuum, consumer behavior theorists make a distinction between *low-involvement* and *high-involvement* exchanges. They believe this difference affects the amount of cognition or problem solving a consumer will undertake during and after the exchange process. As defined by Engle and Blackwell, with respect to products and services,

> **Involvement** is the activation of extended problem-solving behavior when the act of purchase or consumption is seen by the decision-maker as having high personal importance or relevance.[3]

High personal involvement has been found to occur when one or more of the following conditions are operative

1 The behavior required of the consumer will reflect upon his or her self-image.
2 The economic and personal costs of behaving "incorrectly" are perceived as high.
3 The personal or social risks of a "wrong" decision are perceived as high.
4 Outside (nonmarketer) reference group pressures to act in a particular way are strong and the target consumer's motivation to comply is strong.

Thus, exchanges can vary in the extent to which they are personally involving. They can also vary in their *newness* to the decision maker. There are, of course, exchanges made for the first time and exchanges made after years and years of experience. Thus, we might expect very complex decision making to occur for exchanges that are highly involving and that are being made for the first time. As the consumer gains experience, however, decisions will be simplified to reflect this experience. At some point, given many repeats of the exchange process, the evaluation process may become relatively routine even though the subject of the exchanges is still highly involving. This distinction is indicated in Table 4-1.

There are also many exchanges, especially in the private sector, where consumers are not personally involved to any great degree. Whether or not they have had any relevant experience, they may make their decisions about what to do with little or no conscious evaluation of alternatives, certainly nothing elaborate. Such exchanges are sufficiently trivial to the individual that they may in fact *appear* to be behaving randomly. In such cases, attempts by marketers to try to develop some complex model of supposedly rational decision-making activity is not at all warranted. Engel and Blackwell warn that complex decision making may be much rarer than we think: "This [rational problem solving] occurs, however, with only a minority of product purchases. Most items, quite frankly, are not sufficiently important to justify this kind of activity."[4]

However, it is very likely that a great many of the exchanges nonprofit marketing managers are attempting to influence are high, rather than low involvement. The manager should be extremely careful, however, *not* to assume that the elaborate cognitive model outlined in the next section applies to all consumer decisions about behavior that many nonprofit marketers attempt to influence. It is possible that many other nonprofit exchanges, such as small donations, voting on trivial public issues, signing a simple petition, and so on, are really low-involvement actions. It is our experience that there is the real danger that a myopic company-oriented view of marketing will assume that the exchange is highly involving to consumers since it is to the marketer. The marketer then may seek to develop an elaborate level of understanding of an exchange that is basically relatively simple.

Having raised this important caution, we must repeat our position that a much larger number—perhaps the majority—of exchanges with which marketers in nonprofit organizations are involved are in fact considered high involvement and therefore highly cognitive. Decisions about changing health habits, voting for major candidates, choosing a school or a career, giving a significant donation of time or money, attending the arts, changing religious institutions, supporting tax referenda, obeying the laws, and so forth all may be characterized as

- Involving very elemental aspects of one's self-image
- Involving major personal or economic sacrifices
- Risking major personal or social costs if a wrong choice is made
- Involving considerable peer pressure for or against.

The Marketer's Task—An Overview

As outlined in Table 4-1, consumer decisions can exhibit various levels of complexity. They can be (1) extensive, (2) simplified, (3) routinized, and (4) unobservable. An understanding of these differences can be very instructive to a marketer. As in the private sector, a given market at any single point in time may contain consumers who differ significantly in the kinds of cognitive behavior they are undertaking. To illustrate the point, let us consider a hypothetical example of a political race for a seat on a city council between the incumbent, Dave Horne and his opponent, Irene Anderson. Exit interviews with a hypothetical family, the Evanses, might turn up the following differences in decision styles among the family members that represent the four levels of evaluation complexity. As will be seen, as one moves to simpler levels of complexity, decisions involve less cognition, less search behavior, simpler decision rules, and less personal involvement in the decision-making process.

Greg Evans, age 19, is an example of a highly complex decision maker

Table 4-1

A TAXONOMY OF CONSUMER
DECISION-MAKING APPROACHES

Experience	Degree of Personal Involvement	
	High	*Low*
None	Extensive decision making	Simplified decision making
Some	Simplified decision making	No observable decision making
Much	Routinized decision making	No observable decision making

undergoing extensive evaluation. This election was his first opportunity to exercise his citizen franchise. He was anxious to put to the test his high school civics lessons and to satisfy his commitment to himself that he would be a concerned citizen. Greg carefully read the campaign literature of both candidates and attended most of the debates sponsored by the local Junior League at Greg's high school. Greg talked about the candidates with his parents; his older sister; his girlfriend, Jean, a senior at State College; and a few politically astute friends. Greg paid careful attention to the endorsements of his favorite local newspaper columnist and the American Civil Liberties Union (to which he planned to belong someday). Greg changed his intentions at least once during the period leading up to the election and admitted he was not entirely certain of his choice until he entered the polling place to cast his ballot for Irene Anderson.

Bert, Greg's father, is an example of someone undergoing simplified evaluation. Bert had only recently become interested in politics. For years, as a foreman in the local dishwasher manufacturing plant, he didn't see how local politics affected him very much. But five years ago, when he moved into an executive position with the company, he realized how much local council actions could affect his firm. He voted for Horne last time but had not been comfortable with some of his votes on the council. Bert knew what he was looking for in a good council man and carefully studied the campaign positions of the two candidates before deciding that Horne's positions were still best for Bert and his company. His decision making could be characterized as simpler than that of his son due to his experience as a voter, but not as *routine* as was the case for his wife.

Jennifer Evans, Bert's wife, indicated that the exchange for her vote for the candidate's expected future services and positions on issues was a *routine decision* for her. She had lived in the area for over 18 years and had voted a number of times. In the last two elections she had voted for David Horne. She was satisfied with his performance in office and saw no reason to switch to an unknown at this time. She had intended to vote for Horne from the start and remained true to those intentions to the end of the campaign.

Theresa Evans, age 22, was largely an uninvolved decision maker in this election. She considered the race between Horne and Anderson just not worth her time and interest. She was off at college and was unsure whether she would ever return to her home community afterward. She felt that the winner would have little effect on her personal well-being. She might have thought more about this election race because the results would affect the rest of her family, but Theresa had become disenchanted with local politics in her hometown. She viewed both candidates as political hacks equally likely to be incompetent in office. Her views of politics were strongly influenced by her peers at college who debated "one-world" issues and tended, in their youthful enthusiasm, to see domestic politics as either irrelevant to what they felt were the broader issues or as downright divisive. Theresa and her friends felt that campaign rhetoric focused people's attention too much on nationalism and patriotic pride that, Theresa thought, got in the way of what she and her friends called "world empathy." For Theresa, casting her vote in the Anderson-Horne race (which she did) was a very trivial decision. One could not really detect any clear cognitive evaluation in her choice.

Thus, as the Evans family suggests, in any market it is important for the marketer to measure whether target segments are undergoing complex, simple, or routine evaluations or are simply uninvolved. As can be seen in the above example, the marketing manager's approach to each member of the Evans family would be very different simply because of the way they went about making decisions in this contest.

Several points about the makeup of markets according to decision style need to be made.

1   Because a particular target audience member adopts a particular style for a particular exchange does not mean that the marketer should assume that the audience member would use the same process for other decisions, even if they involve similar factors. Thus, Theresa Evans might turn out to be a highly complex decision maker with regard to a future Senate race because she feels that the candidates are actively debating important world issues. At the same time, Mr. and Mrs. Evans might be uninvolved in the same Senate election because the two of them are very local in their orientation and, in general, feel that who goes to Washington will have no effect on them. Thus, for a marketer to characterize an observed decision style with respect to one decision as a general approach applying to many situations would be incorrect. While it is entirely *possible* that a given consumer would treat a number of related decisions similarly (for example, treat all small charitable gifts or all conservation requests as simplified evaluations), a marketer should not automatically assume that this will occur.

2   Because a consumer adopts a decision style on one occasion doesn't necessarily mean that he or she will adopt it next time for the same decision. Three kinds of circumstances could make the next time different from this. First, the consumer could simply acquire more experience, and a highly complex decision could become simplified and then routinized. Next time around, Greg Evans could

just repeat his votes from this first time. Second, the consumer could change in his or her perceptions, needs, and wants. Theresa could move back home and, away from the influence of her college friends, see that local issues *can* have important effects on individual lives. This could lead her to decide to become a highly complex decision maker with respect to local political issues. Third, circumstances surrounding the next decision occasion could change. A charismatic new world-centered candidate could appear who would grab Theresa's attention even though she was still largely under the spell of her college values. Or, David Horne could die, be involved in a scandal or choose to run for a different office, leaving Jennifer with no chance to exercise her routine decision process (unless she chose to repeat what she may define as a "Republican" or "Democratic" choice). An individual's past decision behavior is not necessarily a good predictor of the future.

3   Although the consumers in a market at a given time will undoubtedly represent all four decision styles, the *majority* may be characterizable as one type or another. This may be the case when a crucial subject is at issue and everyone must choose for the first time (for example, choosing two new presidential candidates or voting for or against a new public nonsmoking ordinance or a sales tax referendum). Or it may just be that, although the decision is not new or unique, the behavior in question is one that is almost always routine (for example, perhaps contributing to the United Way or to a high school spring raffle) or always highly complex (for example, choosing a hospital or a church).

4   Although a certain type of exchange may most frequently involve a particular decision style for most consumers at one point in time, virtually everyone in the market may be predicted to change before the next time they decide. Again, this may be due to the passage of time and the maturing of a market over its life cycle. Thus, when consumers were first asked many years ago to consider relatively narrow antismoking ordinances, the decision for many was highly complex. Today, as society seems to have generally accepted such restrictions on individual freedom, voting on similar ordinances will be more simplified. Alternatively, markets may shift totally as major circumstances change. For years, patients have chosen physicians largely on the basis of word of mouth and have routinely stuck with their doctors despite sometimes less than satisfactory care. Growing sophistication by patients and the availability in some communities of published guides and evaluations of physicians have led many consumers to engage in much more complex doctor-shopping behavior. This doctor-shopping has added one more pressure to an already highly competitive marketplace.

Implications.   It is clear that the appropriateness and probable impact of various marketing strategies depends on the depth of cognition undertaken by the market segment to whom the marketing program is directed. To understand these implications, it is necessary to describe our current best understanding of the processes we believe are operative under each of the four decision styles.

We shall begin with highly complex decisions because they are, obviously, the most comprehensive and perhaps the most common in nonprofit marketing. We turn next to simplified and then routine cognitive decisions since, as we have indicated, they are by definition outgrowths of earlier, more complex processes. Finally, we shall shift our focus to decisions for which it is fruitless to attempt to understand consumers' cognitive activity. "Unobservable evaluations" will be assumed to occur for decisions that are very trivial for the individual. It is possible that such decisions really involve some kind of cognitive activity that is a *very highly* simplified version of the processes in the more elaborate cases. We shall assume, however, that the possibility of unearthing these cognitions is so remote or so costly that digging them out is simply not worth the marketer's troubles. Further, since the decisions are trivial, even if we could understand the cognitions behind a consumer decision today, the chances are good that they wouldn't apply tomorrow.

Highly Complex Decisions

For exchanges in which a consumer has relatively high involvement, a representation of the steps from need arousal to behavior (and repeat behavior) is outlined in Figure 4–2.

The core of this heavily cognitive model is the evaluation of alternatives. We shall consider this stage first. It involves three components: forming the choice set, determining evaluation criteria, and evaluating alternatives.

Forming the Choice Set.   Through the process of gathering information, the consumer arrives at an increasingly clear picture of the major available choices. He or she eliminates certain alternatives and moves toward making a choice among the few remaining alternatives.

This process of *choice narrowing* can be illustrated for Bob Jones as he faced the problem of what he should do after high school. Bob Jones considered a number of alternatives to college, including working, joining the army, traveling, and loafing. He decided that going to college made the most sense. Should

FIGURE 4-2

A Model of Complex Evaluations

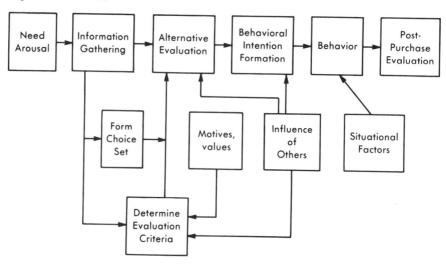

it be a community college, a state university, or a private college? Examining his needs and values, he decided to attend a private college.

We can now examine how Bob narrowed his choice to a specific set of colleges. Figure 4-3 shows a succession of sets involved in this consumer's decision process. The *total set* represents all private colleges that exist, whether or not the consumer knows about them; this list runs into the thousands. The total set can be divided into the consumer's *awareness set* (the colleges he has heard of) and the *unawareness set*. Of those he is aware of, he will only want to consider a limited number; these constitute his *consideration set*, and the others are relegated to an *infeasible set*. As he gathers additional information, a few colleges remain strong candidates, and they constitute his *choice set*, the others being relegated to a *nonchoice set*. (Some research has suggested that choice sets seldom exceed seven alternatives, plus or minus two.) Let us assume that the student sends applications to the four colleges in his choice set and is accepted by all four. In the final step, he carefully evaluates the colleges in the choice set (we shall examine this process shortly) and then makes a final choice, in this case Cornell University.

The implication of this choice-narrowing process is that a nonprofit marketer potentially competes with a large number of other choices for the consumer's interest. Therefore, before making plans to market to a particular segment, the nonprofit marketer must study consumers to learn (1) whether the

FIGURE 4-3

Successive Sets in Consumer Decision-Making

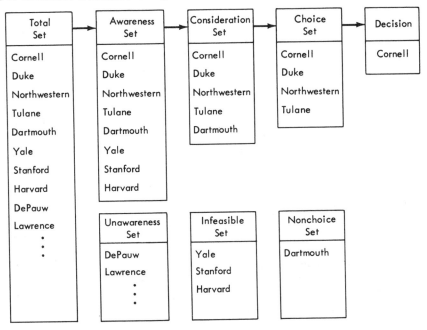

organization is in the segment's awareness, consideration, and choice sets and (2) if the organization *is* in the various sets, who the competitors are. If the organization is not in the choice set, for example, then the desired exchange will not be possible. The first marketing task, then, is to get the alternative into the choice set of the target buyers.

Another marketing task is to identify the major competitors. We saw how colleges compete not only with each other but also with alternatives to college, such as going to work or military service. If high school seniors start favoring some of these generic alternatives, then all colleges will suffer. As a result, colleges would have to constantly prove their value to high school students, either in terms of raising their ultimate incomes or their appreciation and enjoyment of life. In addition, each college must watch the trends in the intraform competition. If the high tuitions of private colleges drive more students into community colleges and state universities, private colleges will suffer. Finally, each college must undertake research to determine its closest "brand" competitors (i.e., other colleges) and monitor their strengths and weaknesses.

Forming Criteria.   To make an eventual judgment about which of the alternative behaviors he will select, Bob Jones must develop some basis for forming an overall evaluation of the alternatives in the final choice set. Presumably, developing these criteria is a step he could have taken before or—more likely— during the process of defining his choice set.

Clearly, if a college marketer wants to influence Jones, he ought to understand what is important to Jones. And finding what is important to Jones is really finding out two things: (1) what factors Bob Jones considers in judging the various alternatives and (2) the relative value he assigns to each factor. We shall refer to the former as *choice criteria* and the latter as *criteria weights*.

One of the key factors determining Bob Jones's criteria in choosing his college is his own needs. While individuals have many basic needs, the marketer must discover which ones apply in this specific case.

One of the most useful typologies of basic needs is Maslow's *hierarchy of needs* shown in Figure 4–4.[5] Maslow held that people act to satisfy the lower needs before satisfying their higher needs. A starving man, for example, first devotes his energy to finding food. If this basic need is satisfied, he can spend more time on his safety needs, such as eating the right foods and breathing good air. When he feels safe, he can take the time to deepen his social affiliations and friendships. Still later, he can develop pursuits that will meet his need for self-esteem and the esteem of others. Once this is satisfied, he is free to actualize his potential in other ways. As each lower-level need is satisfied, it ceases to be a motivator and a higher need starts defining the person's motivational orientation.

We can ask what basic needs are stimulated by the aroused interest in college. Some high school seniors become concerned about whether they can afford college and meet their basic needs for food and adequate housing. Others

FIGURE 4-4

Maslow's Hierarchy of Needs

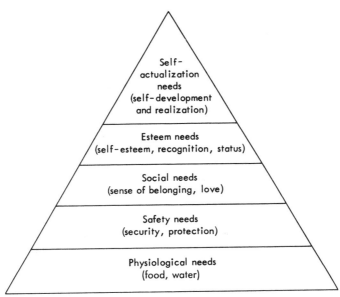

wonder about how safe they will be away from home. Still others are concerned with whether they can find people they like and who like them. And others are concerned with self-esteem or self-actualization. A college will not be able to give attention to all these needs. Thus, we find colleges that cater primarily to the need for belonging (small schools with small classes, a caring faculty, and a good social life), others to the students' need for esteem (many "name" colleges), and still others to the need for self-actualization (many "arty" schools).

Students often want to satisfy several needs, some of which are in conflict, by the same behavior. Thus, a student may have a high need for both achieving and belonging. This can create mental conflict, which can be resolved either by treating one need as more important or by fluctuating between the two needs at different times. Here is where the person's *values* come into play, namely, the principles the person employs to weight the various consequences that might follow a particular choice.

Measurement.   Maslow's hierarchy is only one way of looking at the criteria target consumers might apply in a particular decision context. Whatever model or checklist one uses, the nonprofit marketing manager must still discover what specific criteria and weightings apply in a specific complex (or simplified) exchange context. Criteria can be determined by any of four different methods: (1) direct questions, (2) indirect measurements, (3) perceptual mapping, or (4) conjoint analysis. These are outlined in Exhibit 4-1.

EXHIBIT 4-1

Methods for Determining Decision Criteria and Weightings

Direct Questioning

Most marketing researchers use direct questioning to assess consumer needs and wants. They may conduct an interview with a single individual or lead a focused group discussion. They may use open-end questions, such as "What courses would you like to see added to the college curriculum?" or "What recreational facilities would you like to see added on the campus?" Closed-end questions may also be included, such as "Rank the following activities in terms of your level of interest" or "Rate each of the following services on a scale from one to ten." Closed-end questions are simple to administer and code. They assure uniformity of responses across consumers (they are all responding to the same stimulus). But they have two major disadvantages in comparison to open-ended questions. First, they require that the nonprofit marketer know the "master list" of criteria in advance. The marketer, then, is really asking the consumer *which* of a set of criteria applies (and, perhaps, how heavily weighted each is or will be). Second, direct questions risk influencing how the consumer thinks about the behavior. By telling the interviewee in advance what the *marketer* thinks are the key dimensions, the questioner risks inducing the Heisenberg effect by which the thing being measured is changed by the process of measurement itself.

Indirect Methods

The direct questioning method assumes that consumers are aware of their own needs and wants and are willing to share the information with interviewers. But there are many issues on which they may not know or want to share their true feelings. College students, for example, may mention a desire for more study time when what they really want is less work. Or they may say they want younger teachers when they really believe that younger teachers will be less demanding, and less demanding teachers are what they really want.

Thus, the needs a person verbalizes may mask his or her real needs. Various projective techniques have been proposed to probe more deeply into the real needs of consumers. The four main projective techniques are

1   *Word association or sentence completion.* Here the person might be asked to name the word that first comes to mind when each of a set of words is mentioned. The interviewer might say "college" and the person might respond with "boring." By mentioning key words, the interviewer hopes to infer a pattern of needs and wants that people connect with a particular object or behavior.

2   *Projection.* Rather than being asked about himself or herself directly, the individual is asked about a vaguely defined "someone else." A

questioner, for example, might ask an individual what he or she thinks is the basic reason "most people" go to college. Another approach is to present a picture or drawing of someone and ask the subject what that person is thinking about when considering college. Alternatively, the person might be presented with a set of incomplete sentences and asked to finish them. One sentence might read: "College is for people who _____." The basic assumption of these techniques is that, in the absence of specific information about the other individuals, consumers will project onto them their own true feelings.

3 *Picture completion.* The person is shown a vague picture and asked to make up a story about what he or she sees (called the Thematic Apperception Test or TAT). Or he or she may be shown a cartoon involving two people talking to each other, with one of their remarks deleted. The person is asked to fill in the words, which are thought to reflect the respondent's own attitudes toward the subject.

4 *Role playing.* In this technique, one or more respondents are asked to act out a given role in a situation that is described in the briefest terms. One person, for example, may be asked to play the role of a successful business alumnus of a major university and the other the university president asking for a larger contribution. Through role playing, the respondents again project their needs and personalities into the amorphous situation, thereby providing useful clues on fundraising.

Perceptual Mapping

The direct and indirect approaches require that the respondents explicitly indicate both the nature and the relative weightings of alternative criteria. A newer approach, called perceptual mapping, permits the researcher or manager to *deduce* either the weightings or both criteria and weightings from consumer judgments about the available alternatives. Two techniques are typically employed in perceptual mapping: direct and indirect. In direct perceptual mapping, consumers are asked to rate the various alternatives on a set of dimensions supplied by the researcher. A mathematical technique called factor analysis is then applied to these responses to yield one or more statistically independent underlying dimensions that best represent the original responses. These factors can then be used to produce a "map" on which the alternatives can be placed.

Factor analysis assumes that the original responses contain a great deal of redundancy and are really just surface outcroppings of more basic underlying criteria (factors). Thus, for example, Bob Jones may constantly give similar ratings to different colleges on scales labeled "student centeredness," "classroom size," and "teacher approachability" because they all reflect an underlying "intimacy" factor that he believes is *really* the important difference between big state colleges and smaller private institutions.

The disadvantages of the direct approach were pointed out earlier: it assumes that the researcher knows all the relevant dimensions in advance, and the questioning process may well influence the consumer's judgments.

The indirect approach does not place these burdens on the research designer. The indirect approach simply asks respondents to rate the alternatives in terms of their similarity to each other, letting the individual apply to these "similarities judgments" whatever criteria he or she wants. Again, a computerized mathematical algorithm is used to reduce the similarities data to one or more underlying dimensions. While this technique does not bias the respondent by presenting dimensions in advance, it does require that the *researcher* label the dimensions after the fact. Such labeling is often as much an art as a science.

Conjoint Analysis

An even newer technique that can be used in this context is called conjoint analysis. Conjoint analysis was developed, in part, to remedy the problem of more naive direct rating approaches, namely that ratings of alternatives are developed with respect to one benefit or cost dimension at a time. The traditional approach ignores two important features of the real world. First, when target consumers are evaluating courses of action, they implicitly or explicitly realize that the actions will generate *bundles* of benefits and *bundles* of costs. Second, in judging these various bundles, people are often willing to make *trade-offs*. That is, Bob Jones, if asked directly, may say that he prefers small classes to large classes and tuition under $1,000 to tuition over $1,000. Suppose, however, that he were offered the two conjointly. How would he respond if given the choice of (1) classes averaging 12 students and a tuition of $2,500 versus (2) classes averaging 45 students and a tuition of $800? The answer is that it depends on how he makes trade-offs between the two criteria. This, in turn, depends on the weight he has in mind for the two dimensions. The mathematical algorithm underlying conjoint analysis is specifically designed to reveal these weights, which are known as "part-worths" in the conjoint lexicon.

Evaluating Alternatives.   The bottom line in understanding highly complex decisions is determining how consumers ultimately come to a conclusion about each alternative in the choice set. Although the range of approaches to this very difficult issue would fill several volumes, we prefer to adapt a model developed by a psychologist, Martin Fishbein, at the University of Illinois in the late 1960s and early 1970s.[6] The central features of this approach have received wide acceptance in the private sector and play a central role in basic consumer-behavior texts.

To understand Fishbein's approach, it is necessary to recall that our principal interest as a marketer is influencing behavior. Further, we proposed earlier that consumers choose whether or not to undertake a particular behavior on the basis of the benefits and costs they expect to result from taking that action. It logically follows that at any point in time, a consumer who has not yet decided whether to take a particular action or which of several actions to take will consider three things:

1. Each consumer will possess a set of perceptions (what we shall call *beliefs*) about the positive and negative consequences of undertaking each act in the choice set (that is, the benefits and costs). These can be stated as the perceived *probabilities* of the consequences that result from particular behaviors. Thus, in a research study, we might ask Bob Jones the following questions about what we will assume are his *only* relevant criteria.

   a. How likely is it that classes will be small if you choose to attend each of the following?

	Very unlikely							Very likely	
1. Cornell	.1	.2	.3	.4	.5	.6	.7	.8	.9
2. Duke	.1	.2	.3	.4	.5	.6	.7	.8	.9
3. Northwestern	.1	.2	.3	.4	.5	.6	.7	.8	.9
4. Tulane	.1	.2	.3	.4	.5	.6	.7	.8	.9

   b. How likely is it that you and your family will *not* make a major financial sacrifice if you choose to attend

	Very unlikely							Very likely	
1. Cornell	.1	.2	.3	.4	.5	.6	.7	.8	.9
2. Duke	.1	.2	.3	.4	.5	.6	.7	.8	.9
3. Northwestern	.1	.2	.3	.4	.5	.6	.7	.8	.9
4. Tulane	.1	.2	.3	.4	.5	.6	.7	.8	.9

   c. How likely is it that you will make many lifelong friends if you choose to attend

	Very unlikely							Very likely	
1. Cornell	.1	.2	.3	.4	.5	.6	.7	.8	.9
2. Duke	.1	.2	.3	.4	.5	.6	.7	.8	.9
3. Northwestern	.1	.2	.3	.4	.5	.6	.7	.8	.9
4. Tulane	.1	.2	.3	.4	.5	.6	.7	.8	.9

   d. How likely is it that you will have excellent teachers if you choose to attend

	Very unlikely							Very likely	
1. Cornell	.1	.2	.3	.4	.5	.6	.7	.8	.9
2. Duke	.1	.2	.3	.4	.5	.6	.7	.8	.9
3. Northwestern	.1	.2	.3	.4	.5	.6	.7	.8	.9
4. Tulane	.1	.2	.3	.4	.5	.6	.7	.8	.9

2. For each of the criteria used to evaluate the alternatives in the choice set, the consumer may be expected to have a sense of the value he or she places on the particular positive or negative consequence. These values we shall refer to as the *criteria weightings*. Thus, Bob Jones might be asked:

   a. Please allocate 100 points to the following consequences according to how important each is to your choice among colleges

	Points
Small college	_____
No large financial sacrifice	_____
Many lifelong friends	_____
Excellent teachers	_____
Total	100

3. Finally for each alternative in the choice set, the consumer's weighting of his or her beliefs on the various dimensions will result in a summary evaluation at that point in time which may be thought of as a "leaning" toward each of the courses of action. These "leanings" are termed *behavioral intentions*. Thus, one could ask Bob Jones the following kind of question

a. At the present time, considering all you know about the various alternatives, how likely is it that you will choose to attend the following colleges next fall?

	Very unlikely								Very likely
1. Cornell	.1	.2	.3	.4	.5	.6	.7	.8	.9
2. Duke	.1	.2	.3	.4	.5	.6	.7	.8	.9
3. Northwestern	.1	.2	.3	.4	.5	.6	.7	.8	.9
4. Tulane	.1	.2	.3	.4	.5	.6	.7	.8	.9

Modeling Attitudes.   If this view of highly complex alternative evaluation processes is the correct one, then careful research into our target population should reveal two things.

First, in the absence of significant new information (for example, Bob Jones learns of a rise in tuition at one of the alternative colleges) or some unexpected intervening event (for example, Bob Jones's mother is laid off by her employer), consumers' *behavioral intentions* ought to be very good predictors of their eventual behavior. As we suggested earlier, how good they are as predictors will in turn depend on how involved the given consumer is in the decision, how much experience he or she has had, and how much cognitive evaluation on this occasion he or she has completed at the time of the research.

Second, consumers' behavioral intentions should be predicted very well by their beliefs about the various consequences of taking the action *and* the relative importance of these consequences, assuming that these have been measured correctly. To make such a prediction, however, we still need to know how consumers combine (or process) the weightings and belief information.

To understand the possibilities, let us return to Bob Jones and assume that he has revealed his beliefs about the probabilities that his college alternatives will yield the consequences he considers important as indicated in Table 4–2. Table 4–2 also portrays Jones's allocation of an arbitrary 100 weighting points across the four basic criteria. How, then, might he "use" these beliefs and values to reach a decision about which school to attend?

We, of course, cannot know what most consumers really do. However, we can draw inferences from both decision theory and consumer research. Bob

Table 4-2

A HIGH SCHOOL STUDENT'S BELIEFS ABOUT FOUR COLLEGES

Alternative	Small Classes	No Large Financial Sacrifice	Many Lifelong Friends	Excellent Teachers
Cornell	.8	.3	.7	.7
Duke	.7	.2	.8	.7
Northwestern	.5	.5	.6	.9
Tulane	.3	.7	.6	.2
Weightings	40	20	30	10

Jones is most likely to proceed in one of two ways. On the one hand, he may begin by attempting to simplify the decision using one of the following rules[7]

1   *Elimination by Criteria.* Jones may eliminate any school that does not meet a minimum cutoff on *any* of the criteria (e.g., Duke is dropped because the probability of no financial sacrifice is too low).
2   *Elimination of Nondeterminative Criteria.* Jones could drop criteria where candidates vary little (e.g., "many lifelong friends").
3   *Evaluate One Attribute at a Time.* Jones could consider his most important attribute (small classes) and determine whether there is a clear winner (Cornell and Duke both score high). If not, he could proceed to his next most important attribute and see if there is a superior choice among those surviving at the first stage, and so on.

All three approaches may not yield a clear choice.

On the other hand (and if none of the preceding approaches is "successful"), Jones may attempt mentally to combine the information to yield a single overall "score" for each candidate and choose the one with the highest score. While there are a number of alternative formulas that consumer behavior theorists postulate are used, the most widely accepted is what is called *the expectancy-value model.*

LINEAR ADDITIVE EXPECTANCY-VALUE MODEL.   Here the consumer combines and then adds the beliefs and weighting data for each alternative. Each *expectation* about a consequence from choosing an alternative is weighted by the *value* of the consequence. All weighted consequences for a given alternative are then added to yield an overall "score" for that alternative. The weighted sum is then considered to be a mathematical representation of an *attitude* toward an act. Algebraically, this is

$$A_{act_j} = \sum_{i=1}^{n} b_{ij} a_i \tag{4-1}$$

where
A_{act_j} = attitude toward act j
b_{ij} = belief about the likelihood of experiencing consequence i from taking act j
a_i = value of consequence i
n = number of salient consequences

In the case of Bob Jones, we would have

A(Cornell)   = 40 (.8) + 20 (.3) + 30 (.7) + 10 (.7) = 66
A(Duke)   = 40 (.7) + 20 (.2) + 30 (.8) + 10 (.7) = 63
A(Northwestern) = 40 (.5) + 20 (.5) + 30 (.6) + 10 (.9) = 57
A(Tulane)   = 40 (.3) + 20 (.7) + 30 (.6) + 10 (.2) = 46

As a result of these (perhaps subconscious) computations, Bob Jones would be most likely to choose Cornell, followed by Duke, Northwestern, and Tulane, in that order.

Several comments need to be made about this model. First, it is the only model with which a choice is almost always determined. Thus, this processing approach typically comes into play in cases where one of the other models is not determinant. This is one reason that the linear additive model will be the major focus of our remaining discussions of highly complex consumer behavior. The second and more important reason is that the linear additive model has been shown empirically to be *an excellent predictor of behavioral intentions,*[8] and behavioral intentions are good predictors of behavior under certain conditions. All these conditions make the model potentially very useful for strategic marketing decisions.

There are, however, defects in the linear additive model. First, it does not take into account possible interactions among dimensions. Second, it is a *compensatory* model. That is, low scores with respect to one consequence can be compensated for by high scores with respect to another consequence. Thus, in Bob Jones's case, Cornell and Duke both compensate for their significantly poorer scores on financial sacrifice (that is, they cost more!) by having good scores on the other three dimensions. By contrast, Tulane is perceived to be very good on the financial dimension, but this cannot make up for poor scores in Jones's mind on the other three dimensions.

Key Features of the Expectancy-Value Model.   The first and perhaps most important feature of the expectancy-value model (in the foregoing version sometimes called "the Fishbein model") is that is captures the major inputs to the highly complex, highly cognitive decisions common in nonprofit marketing. These are Bob Jones's *perceptions* of the consequences of taking the action and his *internal weighting* of these consequences, which, in turn, are a function of his own personal needs and wants. This simply emphasizes the point that *to be effective marketers in situations where consumers make complex decisions, we must always start with a clear understanding of the target customers' perceptions, needs, and wants.* Further, because these perceptions, needs, and wants are interior to the consumer and not directly observable, some kind of formal research must be contemplated by anyone considering developing marketing strategies to influence these complex deliberations.

A second feature of the linear additive model is that it emphasizes *behavior.* The predicted consequences of behavior are a central determinant of action. Unfortunately, many marketers and researchers in both the profit and nonprofit sectors believe they ought to study individuals' perceptions of the *attributes of objects* involved in an exchange, rather than the behavioral consequences. In Bob Jones's case, these misguided researchers might try to study Jones's perceptions of Duke or Cornell itself, not his perception of going there. This approach can very often yield predictions that are far off the mark. If one were to ask Bob Jones to evaluate *colleges,* for example, he might indicate as important *attributes* such features as the reputation of the faculty for research and scholarship, the attractiveness of the campus, the innovativeness of curricula, and so forth. All of these may be very important to Bob Jones's evaluation of these college but have little or nothing to do with his evaluation of the opportunity to *attend* them. Questions about college attributes might never reveal that Jones was very concerned about whom he might meet there and turn into lifelong friends. It might not occur to him that this is what an interviewer meant when asking about the attributes of a college (an object) rather than going there (a behavior).

We are firmly of the opinion that in complex high-involvement decisions, it is behavioral intentions that determine behavior, and perceptions of consequences that determine behavioral intentions (along with other interpersonal factors to be noted shortly.) This approach will be central to our consideration of strategic planning throughout the rest of the book.

Influence of Others.   The evaluation stage leads consumers like Bob Jones to form A_{act_j}. Research has shown, however, that whether or not this is predictive of *behavioral intention* also depends on *the influence of others*. As David Reisman pointed out many years ago, many individuals go through life taking their cues about appropriate behavior largely from what are called by sociologists "significant others" or "referents." These referent individuals or groups could be people they know or people they've only seen or read about (for example, movie or rock stars). Further, they can be people they identify with (membership referents), envy and want to be like someday (aspiration referents), or people they *don't* wish to be like (negative referents). The latter would be exemplified by teenagers who refuse to go to the college where their parents went or to dress or to cut their hair as parents want them to. These referents can provide input into the criteria individuals use to form their personal attitude toward an act. They can also have *direct* influence on behavioral intentions by exerting pressure on the individual to act in certain ways.[9]

Some individuals may be directly influenced by several referents at once. Others may not be affected by referents at all. In the case of Bob Jones, to be able to obtain the best possible estimator of his behavioral intentions—and thus to have a true understanding of how his present perceptions affect his behavior—we must "add in" a factor for the possible influence of significant others. In a research context, this would involve three steps.

First, we must identify all of the definable sets of referents to whom Bob Jones might pay attention. These could include parents, high school counselors, brothers and sisters, and friends.

Second, we must ask Jones what he *perceives* each of the significant others as wanting him to do. Fishbein and his disciples refer to this as *normative behavior* and define it algebraically as NB_{kj} where k is an index referring to each set of significant others and j refers to the action in question.[10] Normative behavior is measured by asking Jones whether he believes each significant other wants him to take a particular action, that is, say, "Does not want it at all" or "Wants it very much." It must be emphasized once again that we must measure here what he *perceives* to be the position of others. Whether he has an accurate perception of reality does not matter. *"Reality" is what the consumer thinks it is,* a point we shall continue to emphasize.

Third, we must ask Jones how motivated he is, in general, to comply with the wishes of each referent group. This factor, defined as MC_k (motivation to conform), is in effect a *weighting factor* for each NB_{kj}. Thus, if one parent leans toward, say, Duke, and Bob listens to him or her most of the time, this influence on the ultimate choice could prove to be quite significant.[11]

With this consideration of the often important role of significant others on possible behaviors, we can now expand our model of the predictors of behavioral intention (*BI*) as follows:

$$BI_j = \left(\sum_{i=1}^{n} b_{ij}\, a_i \right) W_1 + \left(\sum_{k=1}^{m} NB_{kj} \cdot MC_k \right) W_2 \qquad (4\text{--}2)$$

It should be noted that this extended Fishbein model has one additional feature. There are two weighting coefficients, W_1 and W_2, which signify the relative importance of the individual and group influences on behavioral intention, respectively. In practice, these weighting coefficients are usually derived statistically—that is, they are the product of a statistical technique called multiple regression rather than of a question asked of consumers like Bob Jones. In this procedure, the components of the model set out in (1) above are used to predict behavioral intention (*BI*). If the best fit of the equation to Bob Jones's interview responses yields a value of W_1 greater than W_2, then we would conclude that Jones is what Reisman would call "inner directed," more driven by his own perceptions and needs. On the other hand, if we find that W_2 exceeds W_1, Jones could be characterized as relatively more "other directed," more driven by what he thinks and feels others expect of him.

Situational Factors.   Behavioral intention may not always directly lead to behavior in complex cases because of unexpected *situational* factors.[12] Bob Jones, for example, may postpone choosing any college until he acquires more money, his mother is reemployed, he gets a scholarship, or a friend agrees to enroll also. It is possible that all these situational factors may not clear up and cause Jones eventually to reconsider his intentions. Or, unexpectedly, he may not like the looks of the campus when he visits it. He may be turned off by some of the students or professors he meets. Marketers believe that unanticipated factors in the critical contact situation can have a great influence on the final decision.

Risk.   An individual may modify, postpone, or avoid a decision because of perceived risk. Marketers have devoted much effort to understanding exchange behavior as risk taking. Consumers cannot be certain about the performance and psychosocial consequences of their decisions. This produces anxiety. The amount of perceived risk varies with the amount of economic and social well-being at stake, the amount of consequence uncertainty, and the amount of consumer self-confidence. A consumer develops certain routines for reducing risk, such as avoiding decisions, gathering information from friends, and preferring national brand names and warranties. The nonprofit marketer must understand the factors that provoke a feeling of risk in the consumer and attempt to provide information and support that will help reduce this risk.[13]

Postdecision Assessment. Marketers must also be concerned with what happens after a decision. After going ahead with the behavior, the consumer will experience some level of satisfaction or dissatisfaction. Based on this, the consumer will engage in posttransaction actions that will have implications for the marketer. Here we want to look at the marketing implications of posttransaction satisfaction and subsequent actions.

What determines whether the consumer is satisfied with a choice? There are two major theories about this.

One theory, called *expectations-performance theory*, holds that a consumer's satisfaction is a function of the consumer's expectations and the perceived outcome.[14] If the outcome matches expectations, the consumer is satisfied; if it exceeds them, he or she is highly satisfied; if it falls short, he or she is dissatisfied.

Consumers form their expectations on the basis of messages and claims sent out by the seller and other communication sources. If the seller makes exaggerated claims, consumers who go ahead and take the recommendation will experience disconfirmed expectations, which lead to dissatisfaction. Thus, if Cornell fails to perform as Bob Jones was led to expect, Bob will revise downward his attitude toward Cornell and may drop out, transfer, or bad-mouth the college. On the other hand, if the college meets his expectations, he will tend to be a satisfied student.[15]

This theory suggests that the seller should be careful to only make claims that faithfully represent the likely outcomes so that consumers experience satisfaction. Some sellers might even want to understate performance levels so that consumers would experience higher-than-expected satisfaction with their choice of behavior.

The other theory of posttransaction satisfaction is called *cognitive dissonance theory*. It holds that almost every choice is likely to lead to some posttransaction discomfort; the issues are how much discomfort and what will the consumer do about it. As stated by Festinger: "When a person chooses between two or more alternatives, discomfort or dissonance will almost inevitably arise because of the person's knowledge that while the decision he has made has certain advantages, it also has some disadvantages. Dissonance arises after almost every decision, and further, the individual will invariably take steps to reduce this dissonance."[16]

Under this theory, we can expect Bob Jones to feel some posttransaction dissonance about his college choice. Problems with professors, other students, housing, or athletics are likely to stir doubts in his mind as to whether he made the right choice. He will undertake certain actions to reduce this dissonance.

The dissonant consumer seeks ways to reduce the dissonance because of a drive in the human organism "to establish internal harmony, consistency, or congruity among his opinions, knowledge, and values."[17] Dissonant consumers will resort to one of two courses of action. They may try to reduce the dissonance by *abandoning* the action, or they may try to reduce the dissonance by seeking information that might *confirm* its high value (or avoiding information that might disconfirm its high value). In the case of Bob Jones, he might withdraw from the college or, alternatively, he might seek information that would lead him to feel better about the college.

Organizations can take positive steps to reduce postpurchase dissonance and help buyers feel good about their choices. A college can send a warm congratulatory letter to recently admitted candidates. It can invite their suggestions and complaints after they have spent a few months on the campus. It can develop effective communications describing the college's philosophy and aspirations to reinforce the students' reasons for coming. Postpurchase communications to buyers have been shown to reduce the amount of consumer post-purchase dissatisfaction.[18]

Information Gathering.   In the process of making this decision, Bob Jones will seek and be offered information from a range of sources. Of key interest to the marketer are what these major information sources are and the relative influence each will have. Consumer information sources can be classified into four groups: (1) *personal nonmarketer controlled* (family, friends, acquaintances), (2) *personal marketer controlled* (sales representatives), (3) *nonpersonal nonmarketer controlled* (mass media, natural settings), and (4) *nonpersonal marketer controlled* (ads, catalogues). A consumer is normally exposed to all these sources. The marketer's task is to interview consumers and ask what sources of information they sought or received in the course of the decision process. On this basis, a picture can be drawn of the most frequent sources.

Different sources might appear at different stages of the process. For example, Bob Jones might report that his uncle initiated his interest in college by asking a year ago where Bob planned to go to college. His friends provided considerable information and influence about the types of colleges to consider. His parents acted both as influences and as buyers, since they were paying for his education. Bob Jones, however, made the final decision and was the user of the product.

Bob Jones not only received different information from each source, but he also placed different value on the information from each source. He consciously or unconsciously gave weight to the source's credibility in deciding how to use the information. An information source is more credible when the source is trustworthy, expert, and likable.[19] Thus, Bob would give more credence to the information provided by an older brother in college than to a college recruiter who is obviously biased.

Identifying the information sources and their respective influences calls for interviewing consumers and asking them how they happened to hear about the alternatives, what sources of information they turned to, what type of information came from each source, what credence they put in each source, and what influence each source of information had on the final decision. Marketers can use the findings to plan effective marketing communications and stimulate favorable word of mouth, issues we shall turn to in Chapter 18.

Two Examples. The extended model of complex decision making outlined above has been used by marketing researchers in nonprofit areas with considerable success. Ryan and Bonfield,[20] for example, used the model to predict loan application behavior of 93 faculty and staff members at a major southeastern university. The researchers measured beliefs about five outcomes, such as "the loan would be easy to obtain" or "I could get favorable terms," plus normative expectations for 4 referents: spouse, other family members, credit union employees, and friends and coworkers. Overall, Ryan and Bonfield were able to explain 23 percent of the variance in behavioral intentions using Fishbein's extended model. This is a highly respectable level of explanation in marketing. The contributions of the individual and group components (and their interaction) to the overall explanation of BI were as follows

	% *of Variance Explained*
Individual attitude	12
Normative influence	7
Joint effects	4
Total	23

The researchers also found that the two components plus behavioral intention explained 36 percent of the variance in actual loan application behavior.

A more complex test of the extended model using somewhat modified measures and a technique called causal modeling was conducted by Richard Bagozzi to predict blood donation behavior. Bagozzi[21] studied 157 male and female students, faculty, and staff at a medium-sized New England university one week prior to the first of two yearly campus blood drives. Ninety-five respondents who gave their names in the survey were then checked unobtrusively to see whether in fact they did or didn't give blood in the two drives as predicted.

Several interesting findings emerged from Bagozzi's study, including modifications of the basic model:

1 Citing earlier studies by Condie, Warner and Gillman,[22] and Pomazel and Jaccard,[23] and after his own pilot research, Bagozzi decided to include only *negative* consequences in his study (for example, "it would hurt my arm" or "my resistance to colds or infection would be lowered").

2 Attitudes were measured both by the linear additive expectancy-value approach advocated here and by semantic differential scales presumably tapping basic underlying feelings (affect) towards donating blood (for example, unpleasant/pleasant or safe/unsafe). The expectancy-value model performed consistently better.

3 "Social normative beliefs" were not found to be significant predictors of either BI or actual behavior. The measure of representative beliefs used, however, was

not as detailed as proposed here or as employed by Ryan and Bonfield. Bagozzi lumped together all significant referents as "people whose opinions you value the most."

4   Overall, the level of explanation of behavioral intention (depending on the definition of BI used) varied from 20 to 26 percent using the expectancy-value operationalization. This is very similar to the findings of Ryan and Bonfield and again is quite creditable.

5   On the other hand, Bagozzi had less success than Ryan and Bonfield in explaining behavior in the first blood drive. This is probably attributable to the much greater possibility that other situational factors will intervene between intentions and behavior for a blood drive than for a loan.

6   Finally, Bagozzi found that when measures of *past behavior* were used to predict behavioral intention, levels of explanation increased significantly (to 32 to 40 percent), although past behavior had no effect on the ability to predict actual behavior in the first drive. On the other hand, knowing that a person gave on the first drive permitted excellent prediction of behavior on the second blood drive (49 percent). This influence of past behavior is a point we shall return to.

Strategy Implications.   What then does a marketer *do* with research findings such as those hypothesized for Bob Jones? Suppose one is the marketing director for Tulane University—what can one do to improve the university's chances of attracting him (besides hope that the other three colleges turn Bob Jones down!)?

Tulane has five options with respect to Jones's personal attitudes (A_{act}):

1   *Change beliefs about alternatives.* Tulane could attempt to change Jones's beliefs about Tulane University (his b_{tj}'s) on key dimensions on which Tulane scores poorly. There are two alternatives here, depending on whether Bob Jones's perceptions are accurate or not.

    a   If Jones's perceptions *are* accurate and there are a great many otherwise highly attractive prospective students like him, Tulane might consider reducing its class sizes or improving the quality of its teachers (dimensions on which it scores poorly);

    b   If Jones's perceptions are *not* accurate and it is clear he and others have a misunderstanding of what Tulane is really like, then Tulane has a communication problem. By words, pictures, testimonials, informal research reports, and the like, Tulane must tell its story more effectively, being sure that it begins by responding to Bob Jones and his needs and perceptions rather than just telling him what *they* think he should know.

2   *Change beliefs about competitors.* Similarly, Tulane might attempt to change Bob Jones's beliefs about Tulane's competition (which the research has specifically identified as being in his choice set). This would be particularly appropriate if Tulane knew that Jones's perceptions were, in fact, wrong. That is, Tulane could offer comparative data (if such were available) showing that, for example, Tulane had below-average class sizes while major competitors had above-average class sizes.

3   *Change weightings.* A third strategy available to Tulane is to attempt to change the importance weightings assigned to the dimensions. One way to look at Tulane's problem is not that it is perceived badly but that the dimension on which it is rated highly, its lack of financial sacrifice, is not rated highly enough

by Bob Jones and his cohorts. Tulane would be the *most favored alternative* if it were to shift its target audience's weights for the four criteria as follows:

Consequence	Weight
Small classes	10
No large financial sacrifice	50
Many lifelong friends	30
Excellent teachers	10

  4 *Call attention to neglected favorable consequences.* Attendance at Tulane may have consequences that Bob Jones didn't realize. These might include better weather or the chance to visit nearby recreational or cultural centers. The college would attempt to have its target audience add these consequences to their salient criteria, especially if they are features that are not offered by competitors.
  5 *Add new favorable consequences.* Just as products add new ingredients or new packaging to revive flagging sales, so too could Tulane offer such new features as the chance to attend a new study-abroad program or participate in a local work-study option that would meet important basic needs of the target audience that they heretofore had not thought relevant to the college decision.

In addition to these actions, Tulane could seek to work through the reference groups found to be important to Bob Jones. Business alumni in Bob's hometown might be contacted to speak to Jones. Letters or phone calls could be directed to his parents. Possibly the applications of Jones and several of his friends could be treated as a "package."

Tulane will need to carefully evaluate these alternative strategies according to their feasibility and cost. The difficulty of implementing each strategy, such as repositioning the college or shifting the importance of weights, should not be minimized. But the marketer can take comfort that, at least for these kinds of first-time complex decisions, there are many points at which the decision can be influenced. As we shall see, however, the marketer's degrees of freedom decline as the consumer gains experience.

The reader should note that the beliefs and weightings data can also be used to segment markets, as can the measures discussed in the next section. We shall return to these considerations in Chapter 5.

Simplified Behavior

The complex process undergone by Bob Jones in evaluating his college is typical of many decisions nonprofits wish to influence because these decisions are highly involving. It was also complex because Jones was making the decision for the first time. If this were a decision that the consumer would be making a second, third, or fourth time, however, we would expect to observe some simplifications of the elaborate process outlined in Figure 4–2 as a result of experience. In such cases, we would still expect considerable information seeking and information processing to take place because the decision is an important one. Consumer behavior theory postulates, however, that three kinds of simplification will probably take place.

First, little information seeking and thinking will be devoted to defining the evaluative criteria. The first time around, say in evaluating charities, a consumer might be expected not only to try to learn about the charities to which she might give but also how she should go about evaluating her potential behavior. The consumer will take stock of what she really wants as benefits from charitable giving and what the costs might be. Friends and coworkers might be asked about how they choose charities. In these circumstances, the marketer has considerable opportunity to influence the criteria since they are still in their formative stage. (This would certainly be the case for the colleges communicating with Bob Jones.) With repeated behavior occasions (additional charity drives), however, it may be expected that after the first time the consumer will have fixed the criteria on which alternatives are assessed. Marketers thus will have very limited opportunity to intervene to change these criteria.

Second, the weights of the criteria may also be largely set, although they will be somewhat more changeable than the criteria themselves. That is, a consumer considering charitable donations from year to year may change the total amount dispensed depending on the *weightings* of a "financial sacrifice" dimension, which in turn might depend on personal economic fortunes or the relative desirability of other types of expenditures.

Third, the choice set may also be relatively well defined in second and third decisions. At least, a core subset of alternatives is likely to be constant from exchange to exchange with marginal alternatives coming and going at the periphery in response to new information or changing criteria or decision rules on the part of the individual consumer.

Thus, in complex cognitive exchanges, the experienced consumer will be primarily evaluating *given* choices on *given* criteria with relatively *constant* weightings. The marketer's first task in such circumstances, therefore, is to learn the contents of the choice set and the set of operative criteria as well as the consumer's beliefs about the consequences of accepting the marketer's alternative or those of competitors. Then, assuming that the marketer is a part of the choice set, the main option available is to devise marketing strategies to modify *beliefs* to secure greater market penetration. This may be the only area in which the marketer can maneuver. Relatively little can be done at this point to influence criteria or their weighting. In general, it may be expected that the less involving the decision, the faster the consumer will simplify the evaluation process with experience and the less flexibility the marketer will have to improve a flagging market share.

Routine Evaluation

After considerable experience on the consumer's part, one may observe the development of relatively habitual routine behavior. In such cases, relatively little cognitive evaluation will appear to be taking place. Future behavior will be better predicted by past behavior than by attitudes.

This brings us back to Bagozzi's study of prospective blood donors. Bagozzi found that if one only knew expectancy-value attitudes, one could explain from 10 to 22 percent of the variance in behavior at a blood drive one week away. If one knew how often the respondents had given in the past *and* what they did on the first blood drive, however, one could explain *40 percent of the variance* in behavior in the second drive. Since his study participants had given an average 13.08 times in the past five years, they were clearly experienced givers. For many, the behavior may well be described as having become highly simplified, if not routine. This would explain the greater role of behavioral over attitudinal predictors in Bagozzi's study. In such cases of routinized decisions, it is likely that the best approach to understanding the market is to study past behavior. Studying attitudes may not be particularly useful either because consumers cannot really recall what evaluation they went through many years ago or because their attitudes today have been simplified and aligned to support their behavior! Left with behavior only, the marketer can take several approaches.

1   Use past behavior frequencies to segregate the market and concentrate on the "heavy users" (see Chapter 5).
2   Seek to discover behavior modification strategies that "bypass" cognition—for example, use special incentives, free trials, and so on to change behavior (see Chapter 18).
3   Seek to discover persuasion strategies to "shock" habituated consumers into once again undertaking extensive cognitive activity.

Nonobservable Evaluations.   There are many situations in the private sector, and perhaps some in the nonprofit sector, where individual behavior involves virtually *no* active prior cognition. This does not mean that the behavior is not influenced to some extent by the brain and, therefore, that a marketer should always rule out possible influence strategies involving attitude change. But to the extent that they attempt to rely on this kind of approach, such strategies are likely to have very limited effect, in part because of the present crudeness of most of our attitude measurement technology. On the other hand, it is, of course, always true that marketers could attempt to influence trivial decisions as they do routinized, high-involvement decisions—that is through behavior modification or "shock tactics." But Krugman and other have postulated that a better way to view trivial exchanges is as instances of what is now called *low-involvement* or *incidental learning*.[24] Krugman points out that consumers in developed countries are inundated with hundreds of advertising messages daily. And when these messages are about exchanges about which the consumers are highly involved, they will become perceptually vigilant and process the information vigorously.

The question, then, is what happens to the remaining messages that aren't immediately relevant? Krugman suggests that, precisely because the exchange addressed in the message is one of trivial interest to the consumer, he or she will be neither perceptually vigilant nor perceptually defensive. The message, so the theory goes, bypasses the cognitive evaluation stage and goes directly into long-term memory to be stored in detail or as some vague overall impression. This trace then resides in memory until some cue at the time of purchase reactivates it (perhaps subconsciously). It *then* becomes a factor influencing the immediate choice. Since the more often a given message passes the consumer's sensory field, the more likely it is to become lodged in long-term memory, Krugman's postulation of low-involvement learning has led many marketers in "trivial" categories to emphasize memorable visual images (for example, cartoon characters, Morris the Cat, etc.), jingles or "haunting" melodies (for example, Coke or McDonalds) or out-right repetition (for example, the Mr. Whipple Charmin ads) to increase the probability that a subconscious memory trace will be built. Since most nonprofits cannot afford the budgets necessary to adopt these tactics, it may be expected that where they (reluctantly) conclude that a particular target segment considers the decision to be trivial, imaginative attempts must be developed to build trace recognitions through visual imagery, clever dialogue, or music that someday can be activated when an exchange is contemplated.

Emotion and Mood.   Under medium- to high-involvement situations, it is assumed that behavior follows what Ray has called the "think-feel-do" model of consumer behavior.[25] That is, consumers are assumed to take in information, form some emotional response and then act when the appropriate resources are available. However, Ray suggests there may be other sequences than think-feel-do.

One of those that has attracted considerable interest in private sector marketing recently is "feel-do-think." This model suggests that many consumers may be influenced to take actions not by their thoughts but by their feelings.[26] This may happen in low-involvement situations and potentially in high-involvement situations where the marketer is promoting such behaviors as drug rehabilitation or safe sex where very powerful feelings are relevant.

Attention to this alternative model has led to a growing interest in the private sector in manipulating emotions through television or magazine advertisements that communicate few "facts" but attempt to create feelings or moods and positive associations with an organization's offering. Thus, Pepsi commercials try to create an emotional response to "the Pepsi Generation" while Coke hopes we will feel "warm and fuzzy" when we hear its commercial refrain "I'd like to teach the world to sing in perfect harmony."

Many nonprofit marketers seek to influence behaviors where emotions could be used effectively as a key strategy component. Hospitals are a good example where dramatic portrayals of caring nurses and attractive maternity rooms may have a major impact on market share. Drug programs may have more effect by showing the warm, supportive camaraderie of a treatment group rather than emphasizing the facts about the harsh consequences of continuing drug abuse.

It may be expected that the use of such appeals will be given much more attention in the future.

GROUP DECISIONS

This chapter has so far given very extensive consideration to exchanges involving single individuals. But at the outset, we noted that many transactions can be multiparty. This means that the target consumer might not be a single person but a group. For nonprofits, important groups are *households* and *organizations*.

Multiparty decisions vary in the influence of different participants. First, there are occasions on which there will be true joint decisions in which each party shares more or less equally. Households in many cases are likely to function as joint decision makers when considering such exchanges as donations or legacies or when trying to decide on child-raising, family exercise, or dietary patterns.[27] Similarly, corporations may have committees jointly determining their charitable contributions. Foundations or government agencies may jointly determine budget allocations or decide on program acceptability. In these cases, the actions required in the exchange are actions that *all parties* must undertake.

The second general multiparty situation is the case where different roles involved in the exchange process are specifically allocated to different parties. There are five basic *roles* involved in any exchange:

1   *Initiator.* The initiator is the person who first suggests or thinks of the idea of becoming involved in a particular exchange.
2   *Influencer.* An influencer is a person who offers or is sought out for advice on the decision. This is not simply a *referent* but someone whose advice is heard.
3   *Decider.* The decider is the person who ultimately determines any or all parts of the decision to participate in the exchange: whether to take action, what action to take, how to take action, or when and where.
4   *Transactor.* The transactor is the person who completes the actual transaction.
5   *Exchanger.* The exchanger is the person(s) who then follows through on the transaction.

The decision by a household for a child to have his tonsils removed at a particular hospital, for example, is a situation where each role could be filled by a different person. The mother might be the *initiator*, noticing an increase in sore throat episodes. The family doctor may then come into play as a key *influencer* suggesting whether or not the problem is serious enough to merit action, making recommendations as to whether delay or urgent action is more appropriate and, finally, offering an opinion about surgeons and hospitals. If the household is strongly patriarchal, the father may be delegated the role of *decider* since "father ultimately pays the bills around here." The *transactor* could then be an older brother or sister who works near the chosen hospital who can sign the necessary admittance papers. And, of course, it is the child who is obviously the *exchanger*, the person whose tonsils are at issue. The implication of this example is, obviously, that if a hospital wishes to increase the amount of elective tonsillectomies performed at its institution, it would do well to know more about the role allocation strategies of target households in its market. The hospital may find that it will need different strategies to "win over" each of the different role types.

    1 *Initiators* need to be made aware of opportunities and needs for elective surgery they might not have thought about.
    2 *Influencers and deciders* need to have their perceptions, criteria, and choice sets subjected to a marketing program that ensures that the hospital will be the one chosen.
    3 *Transactors* need to find no impediments, clerical *or* psychological, to setting up the transaction.
    4 Finally, the *exchanger* needs to be contacted before, during, and especially after the exchange to ensure satisfaction, good word of mouth, and behavioral intentions that favor the hospital for future sickness episodes.

A third approach one can use when marketing to multiple-party exchangers like organizations is to consider the stages through which they go in taking an action. To see how this is, let us follow the approach the San Francisco Zoo might use to convince a large corporation to make a major grant toward building a new lion house.

Need Arousal Stage

The first step is for the marketer to identify corporate prospects and try to gain their attention and interest in the proposal. Thus, the San Francisco Zoo would approach corporations that have made generous civic gifts in the past. "Qualifying the prospect" can save the marketer a lot of time.

    The marketer's next step is to try to understand the basic needs and wants of target organizations. This is fairly straightforward in the case of corporations, whose main objectives are to make money, save money, and be good corporate citizens. The San Francisco Zoo cannot help corporations make or save money, but it can appeal to the corporation's wish to be a good corporate citizen. Most corporations welcome favorable publicity about their "good deeds"; in this way, they build a fund of goodwill that they can draw upon when adverse events take place. The Zoo can meet this need by offering to name the new lion house after the corporation or arrange for other publicity showing the corporation's generosity.

    The marketing organization needs to analyze the mission, goals, plans, and criteria of each prospect organization so that it can develop appropriate appeals. When the San Francisco Zoo seeks a corporate grant, it must respect the fact that money is tight and that the corporation expects the Zoo's needs to be convincingly presented. The Zoo will state its case in a way that meets the issues uppermost in the minds of the corporation.

Information Gathering Stage

The buying organization normally needs time to consider the proposition and gather information. The amount of information needed depends on the type of buying situation and on the buying organization's familiarity with the marketer. Robinson and others distinguished among three types of buying situations, called *buyclasses*, that are not unlike the categories outlined earlier for individual decision makers.[28] They are

1 *Straight rebuy.* Here the buying organization is buying something similar to what it bought before. Most corporations, for example, set new budgets every year, and in the absence of major new factors, they might approve a budget pretty much like last year's budget, which did or did not include the Zoo. This is analogous to "routinized response behavior" in the individual consumer buying situation. In a straight rebuy, the buyer does not need much information because she knows the proposition and the marketer from previous dealings with her.

2 *Modified rebuy.* The modified rebuy describes a situation in which the buyer is considering modifying something it has purchased in the past. The task calls for "decision making with experience" and hence requires more information than the case of a straight rebuy. Thus, a corporation might want specific information to evaluate whether the Zoo's lion house needs to be remodeled and what alternatives are available.

3 *New task.* The new task faces an organizational buyer when she is presented with a new offer of an unfamiliar kind from an unfamiliar seller. An example would be a Japanese corporation being asked to build a new lion house at the San Francisco Zoo to improve Japanese-American relations. The Japanese corporation faces a complex problem-solving situation and needs to gather considerable information prior to making any decision.

Another issue deals with the probable sources of information to which the organizational buyer will turn. One source is the marketer, and the marketer can be more effective by supplying relevant and credible information to the buying organization. The marketer should also anticipate other information sources that the organization buyer is likely to tap in developing its marketing plans and possibly work indirectly through them.

Decision Evaluation Stage

Each buying organization has certain well-established ways of evaluating different types of "purchases." Straight rebuy decisions may be in the hands of a single officer who makes the decision in a fairly routine way. Modified rebuys may be in the hands of a small middle-management committee with the members coming from different business functions. New tasks may be in the hands of a high-level management committee, again with members representing different kinds of expertise.

The marketer must attempt to identify the people in the buying organization who are likely to get involved in the buying process. Webster and Wind call the decision-making unit of a buying organization the *buying center,* which they define as "all those individuals and groups who participate in the purchasing decision-making process, who share some common goals and the risks arising from the decisions."[29] The buying center includes all members of the organization who play roles in the buying process.[30]

The marketer's task is to identify the members of the buying center and try to figure out (1) in what decisions they exercise influence, (2) what their relative degree of influence is, and (3) what evaluation criteria each decision participant uses. This knowledge can help the marketer know the key buying influencers who must be reached personally (through multilevel in-depth selling) or through nonpersonal communications.

Organization buyers are subject to many influences when they meet to make their buying decisions. Some of the process is highly rational in that the buyers rate proposals on such attributes as (1) marketer credibility, (2) marketer efficiency, (3) impact of the proposal on profits, costs, and other dimensions, (4) amount of goodwill created, and so on. To the extent that the process is a rational one, the marketer will want to make the strongest case in rational terms.

Marketers also recognize the role of personal motives in the organization buying process, such as buyers who respond to personal favors (self-aggrandizement), to attention (ego enhancement), or to personal risk containment (risk avoidance). A study of buyers in ten large organizations concluded, "Corporate decision-makers remain human after they enter the office. They respond to 'image'; they buy from companies to which they feel 'close'; they favor suppliers who show them respect and personal consideration, and who do extra things 'for them'; they 'over-react' to real or imagined slights, tending to reject companies which fail to respond or delay in submitting requested bids."[31]

This suggests that marketers should also take into account the human and social factors in the buying situations and address more emotional and interpersonal appeals.

Decision Execution Stage

After the buying organization has decided to favor the offer, it must put the finishing touches on it. The buyer and seller would have to negotiate the exact terms and timing of various steps. Thus, the corporation that agrees to make a gift to the San Francisco Zoo would need to decide on the exact amount, how to pay it, when to pay it, and what compliance conditions to establish. Any of these steps can involve further negotiation. The marketer should anticipate these issues of detail and be prepared to work them through smoothly.

Organization buyers have also been known to cancel or withdraw at the last minute, given new situational factors. The buyer may have heard something negative about the marketer or might have encountered a cash flow problem. The practical implication is that the marketer's work is not finished after receiving news of a favorable decision. The alert seller wants to keep in touch with the buyer to make sure that the agreement is enacted smoothly and that no snags develop.

Postdecision Assessment Stage

The buying organization usually undertakes a periodic performance audit to make sure that the marketer is performing according to expectations. It is in the marketer's interests to negotiate clear performance goals with the buying organization in the decision execution stage. Then the marketer knows what is expected, and it can periodically supply the buyer with relevant information on performance. The San Francisco Zoo, for example, can keep a large corporate donor informed of the way the money is spent and the results achieved with the grant. By demonstrating responsible performance, the zoo will be able to go back to the same corporate donor some years later and ask for another grant based on the satisfactory results it has produced.

SUMMARY

The ultimate objective of all marketing strategy and tactics is to influence target audience behavior. While the short-term focus may be communicating facts or changing attitudes and values, what distinguishes these activities from education or propaganda is that they are not ends but means to other goals. And since the ultimate goal is behavior change and the proper philosophy is customer centered, it is essential that all strategic planning start with understanding customer behavior.

The targets of nonprofit marketers' influence strategies can be as diverse as legislators, donors, journalists, or consumers. In all cases, the marketer's objective is to bring about exchanges wherein target audience members give up some costs in return for some expected positive consequences. Exchanges may involve two or multiple parties and be of fixed or continuing duration. The starting point for understanding customer behavior thus must be an understanding of the exchange relationship to be effected. Most importantly, that exchange must be seen from the target audience's perspective.

Exchanges in the nonprofit sector are usually high involvement and often concern target audience behaviors where audience members have little or no experience. In such highly complex decision situations, customers begin by gathering information to form a choice set of alternative behaviors and to determine the criteria that will eventually be used to choose among them. The criteria, in turn, will be affected by the customer's own needs and wants and by the influences of significant others.

The next step in the typical process is to evaluate the chosen alternative on the relevant criteria and to form attitudes and behavioral intentions toward each.

These behavioral intentions will again be influenced by others. In a similar way, the eventual course of behavior will be modified by situational factors such as the availability of funds or time. Finally, behavior will result in experience and subsequent evaluations that will influence both attitudes and behavioral intentions in the future.

Marketers have several options in seeking to influence complex exchanges that are not turning out as a marketer wishes. The marketer can attempt to change the target customer's perceptions of the probable outcomes of choosing the marketer's alternative and/or the alternatives of competitors. Weightings on the criteria can be changed—although this is more difficult—or the customer can be pointed toward new or neglected favorable consequences.

With experience, customers proceed to simplify and then routinize behavioral patterns. In such cases, criteria are relatively fixed and alternatives are narrowed considerably. At the routine stage, behavior may appear to occur with little conscious thought or even appear probabilistic. In cases of low-involvement decisions, relatively little cognition may be the norm even when the customer has little experience.

Not all decisions of interest to nonprofit marketers are individual. Where one is dealing with households or organizations, it is first necessary to understand the possible roles various members of the group can play. These roles include initiator, influencer, decider, transactor, and exchanger. But even for such groups, a given decision may be much like that which occurs for individuals in that it may be complex, simplified, or relatively routine.

QUESTIONS

1. Who are the "significant others" whom you, or others like you, would consider when deciding whether to join the armed forces? How could the military use this insight in developing marketing strategy?
2. Under what circumstances would the choice of performing arts events be a high-involvement decision and when would it be low involvement? How could a marketer learn which condition would apply for a particular event or for a particular consumer?
3. Changing the eating patterns of an overweight head of a household can be seen as a problem of influencing the household rather than the individual. Develop a model of the current and planned influence process and show how this model would influence marketing strategy.
4. Some consumers make evaluations not by absolute judgments but by comparing a potential choice to some standard. What might these standards be—other than simply another alternative? Devise an advertisement for a drug treatment clinic using each of the standards you propose.
5. How could the marketing director for a hospital use mood and emotion in an advertisement to achieve increased market share?

NOTES

1. Robert Bartels, "The Identity Crisis in Marketing," *Journal of Marketing*, October 1974, pp. 73–76; David J. Luck, "Broadening the Concept of Marketing—Too Far," *Journal of Marketing*, January 1969, pp. 53–54.

2. For additional discussion of the concept of exchange in marketing, see Richard P. Bagozzi, "Marketing as an Organized Behavioral System of Exchange," *Journal of Marketing*, October 1974, pp. 77–81; and "Marketing as Exchange," *American Behavioral Scientist*, March–April 1978, pp. 535–556.

3. James F. Engel and Roger D. Blackwell, *Consumer Behavior*, 4th ed. (Chicago: Dryden Press, 1982), p. 24.

4. Ibid.

5. Abraham H. Maslow, *Motivation and Personality* (New York: Harper & Row, 1954), pp. 80–106.

6. See Martin Fishbein and Icek Ajzen, *Belief, Attitude, Intention and Behavior* (Reading, Mass.: Addison-Wesley, 1975).

7. See Paul E. Green and Yoram Wind, *Multiattribute Decision in Marketing: A Measurement Approach* (Hinsdale, Ill.: Dryden Press, 1973), Chapter 2.

8. Fishbein and Ajzen, *Belief*.

9. Robert Burnkrant and Alain Cousineau, "Informational and Normative Social Influence in Buyer Behavior," *Journal of Consumer Research*, 1975, pp. 206–215.

10. Michael J. Ryan and Edwin H. Bonfield, "The Extended Fishbein Model and Consumer Behavior," *Journal of Consumer Research*, September 1975, pp. 118–136.

11. The reader will note that the relationship among the $NB_{kj}MC_k$ components is compensatory, as is the relationship among the a_i and b_{ij} factors.

12. Russell W. Belk, "Situational Variables and Consumer Behavior," *Journal of Consumer Research*, December 1975, pp. 157–164. See also Pradeep Kakkar and Richard J. Lutz, "Situational Influence on Consumer Behavior: A Review," in H.H. Kassarjian and Thomas Robertson, eds., *Perspectives in Consumer Behavior*, 3rd ed. (Glenview, Ill.: Scott, Foresman, 1981), pp. 204–214.

13. See Raymond A. Bauer, "Consumer Behavior as Risk Taking," in Donald F. Cox, ed., *Risk Taking and Information Handling in Consumer Behavior* (Boston: Division of Research, Harvard Business School, 1967); and James W. Taylor, "The Role of Risk in Consumer Behavior," *Journal of Marketing*, April 1974, pp. 54–60.

14. See John E. Swan and Linda Jones Combs, "Product Performance and Consumer Satisfaction: A New Concept," *Journal of Marketing Research*, April 1976, pp. 25–33.

15. See Ralph E. Anderson, "Consumer Dissatisfaction: The Effect of Disconfirmed Expectancy on Perceived Product Performance," *Journal of Marketing Research*, February 1973, pp. 38–44.

16. Leon Festinger and Dana Bramel, "The Reactions of Humans to Cognitive Dissonance," in Arthur J. Bachrach, ed., *Experimental Foundations of Clinical Psychology* (New York: Basic Books, 1962), pp. 251–262.

17. Leon Festinger, *A Theory of Cognitive Dissonance* (Stanford, Calif.: Stanford University Press, 1957), p. 260.

18. See James H. Donnelly, Jr., and John M. Ivancevich, "Post-Purchase Reinforcement and Back-Out Behavior," *Journal of Marketing Research*, August 1970, pp. 399–400.

19. Herbert C. Kelman and Carl I. Hovland, " 'Reinstatement' of the Communicator in Delayed Measurement of Opinion Change," *Journal of Abnormal and Social Psychology*, Vol. 48, 1953, pp. 327–335.

20. Michael J. Ryan and E.H. Bonfield, "Fishbein's Intentions Model: A Test of External and Pragmatic Validity," *Journal of Marketing*, Spring 1980, pp. 82–95.

21. Richard P. Bagozzi, "Attitudes, Intentions and Behavior: A Test of Some Key Hypotheses," *Journal of Personality and Social Psychology*, 1981, pp. 607–627.

22. S.J. Condie, W.K. Warner, and D.C. Gillman, "Getting Blood from Collective Turnips: Volunteer Donations in Mass Blood Drives," *Journal of Applied Psychology*, 1976, pp. 290–294.

23. R.J. Pomazel and J.J. Jaccard, "An Informal Approach to Altruistic Behavior," *Journal of Personality and Social Psychology*, 1976, pp. 317–326.

24. Herbert E. Krugman, "Low Involvement Theory in the Light of New Brain Research," in John C. Maloney and Bernard Silverman, eds., *Attitude Research Plays for High Stakes* (Chicago: American Marketing Association, 1979), pp. 16–22; and "The Impact of Television Advertising: Learning Without Involvement," *Public Opinion Quarterly*, Fall 1965, pp. 349–356. See also F. Stewart DeBruiker, "An Appraisal of Low-Involvement Consumer Information Processing," in Maloney and Silverman, *Attitude Research*, pp. 112–132.

25. Michael L. Ray, "Psychological Theories and Interpretations of Learning," in S. Ward and T.S. Robertson, eds., *Consumer Behavior: Theoretical Sources* (Englewood Cliffs, N.J.: Prentice-Hall, 1973), pp. 45–117.

26. See, for example, Meryl P. Gardner, "Mood States and Consumer Behavior: A Critical Review," *Journal of Consumer Research*, Vol. 12, no. 3, 1985, pp. 281–300; and Gerald Gorn, "The Effects of Music in Advertising on Choice Behavior: A Classical Conditioning Approach," *Journal of Marketing*, Winter, 1982, pp. 94–101.

27. For a review of the family decision-making literature, see Harry L. Davis, "Decision Making Within the Household," *Journal of Consumer Research*, March 1976, pp. 241–260.

28. Patrick J. Robinson, Charles W. Faris, and Yoram Wind, *Industrial Buying and Creative Marketing* (Boston: Allyn & Bacon, 1967).

29. Frederick E. Webster, Jr., and Yoram Wind, *Organizational Behavior* (Englewood Cliffs, N.J.: Prentice-Hall, 1972), p. 6.

30. Ibid, pp. 78–80.

31. See Murray Harding, "Who Really Makes the Purchasing Decision?" *Industrial Marketing*, September 1966, p. 76. This point of view is further developed in Ernest Dichter, "Industrial Buying Is Based on Same 'Only Human' Factors That Motivate Consumer Market's Housewife," *Industrial Marketing*, February 1973, pp. 14–16.

5

Developing a Core Marketing Strategy: Segmenting the Market

Although the Mexican Social Security Institute (IMSS) provides family planning services to approximately 3 million women a year, until recently, acceptors were not screened for risk on a systematic basis. By identifying a minimum set of demographic, biological and personal medical factors associated with elevated maternal and infant mortality, IMSS has developed a strategy which classifies each woman as normal or high-risk. To improve the quality of its services, IMSS wanted to test the feasibility of a strategy aimed at improving user education, strengthening the competence of IMSS service providers in the evaluation of reproductive risk, and providing an appropriate method for each woman seeking family planning services.

The intervention included components of in-service training, risk evaluation, user education and program management. The training included seminars on reproductive risk for IMSS physicians and paramedical staff in both family medicine clinics and hospitals. Subsequently, each woman who attended an IMSS clinic or hospital in the experimental area was evaluated for factors associated with reproductive risk. The educational strategy was designed in order to inform the IMSS health service users about the risk factors associated with maternal and infant mortality. It included radio spots, audiovisual presentations, brochures, discussions and posters. Particular emphasis was placed on the management aspects of a risk prevention program, including procedures for adequate screening, referral and follow-up of individual patients.

Two health areas with similar characteristics were chosen as experimental and control groups. Baseline and endline data were collected on more than 3000 women in the hospitals and clinics in both areas. The use of mini-surveys of users during supervisory visits ensured that the physicians and paramedical staff were performing the evaluation and educational activities correctly.

The results were as follows:

- In hospitals, more postpartum and post-abortion women accepted methods in the experimental area than in the control area. Among high-risk women, acceptance of either IUD or tubal ligation grew by 11 percentage points, compared to a 1 point increase in the control area. When considering all postpartum and post-abortion women, prevalence in the experimental area grew by 14 points, compared to 2 points in the control area.
- Among women using family medicine clinics in the experimental area, 39% of the users accepted their current method during the study period. However, in the control area only 23% accepted during the same period. The IUD and tubal ligation were the most frequently utilized methods among clinic users.
- Professional attitudes toward family planning were also improved during the study. Before the intervention, only about half of IMSS physicians routinely promoted family planning. Afterward, nearly 90% were routinely screening for reproductive risk. Many providers indicated that they were willing to promote family planning as a health intervention, but disapproved of it as a means of completing demographic goals.
- By classifying women as normal or high-risk, IMSS has developed a strategy to provide the most appropriate method for each woman, improve quality of care, and at the same time increase contraceptive prevalence. Focusing on women's reproductive health has been an effective way of increasing provider participation in family planning service delivery as well as improving user's awareness of personal risk.

The strategy has been well accepted by IMSS staff and users alike, and is being extended throughout the entire IMSS system in Mexico. Additionally, several other countries in the region have expressed interest in developing a reproductive risk program.

Source: Adapted from "IMSS Improves Quality of Care and Contraceptive Prevalence," *Alternatives,* March 1989, pp. 2, 8. Reproduced with permission.

The single most important stage in the strategic marketing planning process is determining the organization's *core marketing strategy*. A core marketing strategy comprises the basic thrust an organization wishes to take over an extended period of time to achieve the marketing objectives it has set for itself. This longer view then provides the framework within which detailed tactical elements are created and specific year-to-year plans formulated. It is the "skeleton" of the entire marketing program. The core marketing strategy has three elements:

- One or more *specific target markets*
- A clearly defined *competitive position*
- A carefully designed and coordinated *marketing mix* to meet the needs of the target markets while differentiating the marketer from major competitors.

In this chapter, we will outline the characteristics of an effective core marketing strategy and discuss its first component, segmentation. Chapter 6 will then consider positioning. Considerations to be kept in mind when developing the various elements of the marketing mix will be introduced in later chapters on offer development and management, pricing, distribution, and communications.

CHARACTERISTICS OF AN EFFECTIVE CORE MARKETING STRATEGY

An organization's core marketing strategy should flow naturally from the earlier stages of the strategic marketing planning process. There will already have been a careful assessment of organization mission and goals, trends in the market environment, characteristics of target customers, and the organization's present strengths and weaknesses. Marketing management will have begun to define marketing's own mission, objectives, and goals. The difficult part is translating all this insight and information into a basic strategy that will guide the marketing effort over three, five, or ten years. The core strategy is so important because it is the statement or set of statements that sets out just how the organization will tackle the market challenges.

IBM and Apple are both in the computer business. But the ways in which the two of them approach customers, advertise themselves, position and price their products and services, and work through distributors are very different. It is these elements of substance and style that make the organizations very different. CBS's approach to the news is different from CNN's. Sears tackles the retail market differently from Nordstrom's and both are different from Macy's. Yale is not MIT and Carnegie Hall is not Radio City Music Hall. There are many nondescript me-too organizations in every marketplace. What makes these successful organizations stand out is that each has a unique view of itself and its role in the marketplace.

This unique role in the marketplace is captured in the *core marketing strategy.*

An effective core marketing strategy will have the following characteristics:

1. It will be *customer centered*. It will have as its principal focus meeting the needs and wants of its target audiences. It will not be designed to sell a program or image that the marketer thinks needs to be sold.
2. It will be *visionary*. It will articulate a future for the organization that offers a clear sense of where the organization is going, what the "new" enterprise will look like, and what it will achieve when it meets with its expected success.
3. It will *differentiate* the organization from its key rivals. The marketer will stand out; it will offer target markets unique reasons to prefer its goods and services.

4   It will be *sustainable* for the long run and in the face of likely competitors' reactions. Strategies are not implemented in a vacuum. If they are successful, competitors will respond and the organization will anticipate this possibility and prepare for it.

5   It will be *easily communicated*. The central elements of the strategy will be simple and clear so that both target audiences and the marketers' own staff have an unambiguous understanding of just what the strategy is and why it should be supported.

6   It will be *motivating*. A successful strategy will have the enthusiastic commitment of those who will carry it out. This will not be the case if it is either little more than business as usual or so unrealistic as to be unimaginable by key participants.

7   It will be *flexible*. It should be sufficiently broad that it allows for diversity in the ways that individual staffers implement it and not so rigid and uncompromising that it is not adaptable to unforeseen contingencies.

Michael Porter, in his book, *Competitive Strategy*,[1] has proposed three basic core strategies an organization can adopt:

1   *Differentiation*. This approach means offering something that no or few other competitors can offer. Differentiation can be in terms of *real differences* in the products and/or services offered or in the distribution systems through which they are offered or *perceived differences* created primarily through promotion. Thus, a hospital might differentiate itself by:
   a   Offering live-in facilities for expecting fathers, gourmet meals, cable television, fax machines, and computers for long-term business patients, visitors, and so on (product/service differentiation).
   b   Offering "Doc-in-the-box" neighborhood emergency care or physical therapy in the home (place differentiation).
   c   Promoting the hospital as the most technologically advanced, the most experimental, or the most patient-friendly hospital (image differentiation).

2   *Cost Leadership*. This approach involves marketing the lowest-cost offerings in the marketplace. In an industry where overhead costs often run 50 to 80 percent of donations, the United Way can typically boast that it keeps its administrative costs below 15 percent.

3   *Focus*. This approach involves selecting a limited segment of the market—typically one not served by anyone else in the market—and concentrating on uniquely serving that market. Thus a program for the homeless might focus on a particular neighborhood such as homeless on the riverfront, a particular customer group such as American Indian homeless, or a particular kind of offering such as emergency mental care.

Notice that each of these approaches involves a unique combination of the three elements of the core marketing strategy: choice of market segments, positioning, and marketing mix. Porter argues that organizations should not attempt to carry out more than one core strategy at the same time. Further, the choice of core strategy should be based on the preceding steps of the SMPP (i.e., steps 1 through 4) and should recognize that each type of core strategy will require a different type of organization and often a different organizational culture and leadership style.

MARKET SEGMENTATION

The first element to be set out in the core marketing strategy is the organization's approach toward market segmentation. As we indicated in the preceding chapter, customers to be targeted in a particular kind of exchange relationship can vary in dozens—perhaps hundreds—of ways. A fundamental problem for marketing managers is how to deal with this complexity. Treating all customers the same may achieve economies of scale, but it ignores the diversity that is typically present in most markets, and it probably means that what is offered never meets anyone's needs very well. On the other hand, treating everyone individually is usually too expensive and impractical for most situations (except in fund-raising where individualized approaches to foundations, corporations, and major donors are certainly merited).

The solution is usually some strategy in between the two extremes. However, the appropriate solution will vary by organization and the market challenge it faces. It will also be a matter of preference. Two organizations faced with the same challenge may simply *choose* to proceed differently. Preferably, these differences will reflect differences in organization capabilities. It is, however, not uncommon to find choices mainly reflecting the tastes and preferences of particular managers and/or boards of directors.

Nonprofit organizations have gone through four stages in their thinking about how to segment markets:

- *Mass marketing.* Mass marketing is a style of marketing where the organization mass produces and mass distributes one market offer and attempts to attract every eligible person to its use. It is compatible with a selling orientation to marketing. Thus, the Philadelphia Transit Authority could conceivably offer only one form of transportation—buses—and try to attract all commuters to use that form. The argument for mass marketing is that it would result in the lowest costs and prices and therefore create the largest potential market. The mass marketer pays little or no attention to differences in consumer preferences.
- *Differentiated marketing.* Differentiation is a style of marketing compatible with a product orientation to marketing. With this approach, the organization prepares two or more market offers for the market as a whole. The market offers may exhibit different features, styles, quality, and so on. Thus, the Philadelphia Transit Authority could create a bus system and subway system and leave it to commuters to make the choice. The offers are designed, not so much for different groups, but to offer alternatives to everyone in the market.
- *Target marketing.* Target marketing is a style of marketing appropriate to a customer-oriented organization. In it the organization distinguishes between the different segments making up the market, chooses several of these segments to focus on, and develops market offers and marketing mixes tailored to meet the needs of each segment. The Philadelphia Transit Authority, for example, could develop a commuter train system designed to meet the needs of affluent commuters for a clean train and comfortable ride, albeit at a high price. At the same time, it could provide inexpensive, small "jitney" buses for those who want frequent, cheap, short rides, say in a downtown area.
- *Niche marketing.* Niche marketing is also customer oriented. This approach is

particularly appropriate for an organization with limited resources. Rather than spreading these resources across a wide array of segments, the organization chooses one or two segments on which it will totally concentrate. Its choice may be based on its own strengths, a perceived unmet market need, and/or a sense of competitor weakness. An example would be a commuter helicopter service that focuses only on meeting the transportation needs of a limited number of high status and/or time-pressured organizations and individuals in major congested urban markets.

Organizations can be found today practicing each style of marketing. As one might expect, however, there is a strong movement away from mass marketing and product-differentiated marketing toward target or niche marketing. At least three benefits of target marketing can be identified. First, organizations are in a better position to spot market opportunities. They can notice market segments whose needs are not being fully met by current offerings. Second, marketers can make finer adjustments of their offer to match the desire of the market. They can interview members of the target market and get a good picture of their specific needs and desires and track how these change over time. Third, sellers can make finer adjustments of their prices, distribution channels, and promotional mix. Instead of trying to draw in all potential buyers with a "shotgun" approach, sellers can create separate marketing programs aimed at specific target markets (called a "rifle" approach).

For the marketer wishing to adopt the more sophisticated *target marketing* approach, a process is needed to cope with the sheer enormity of the task. There are really *two* stages to this process. First is a conceptualization and research stage to identify and describe the groups the marketer *may* wish to target. This stage we shall refer to as *segmenting markets*. As can be seen in the left side of Figure 5-1, market segmentation requires (1) identifying the different bases for segmenting the market, (2) developing profiles of the resulting market segments, and (3) developing measures of each segment's attractiveness. The second stage is *target marketing*, the act of selecting one or more of the market segments and developing a positioning and marketing mix strategy for each. This chapter will describe the major concepts and tools for both stages.

FIGURE 5-1

Steps in Market Segmentation and Target Marketing

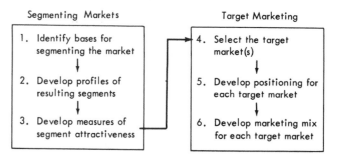

SEGMENTING MARKETS

There are three stages in the process of segmenting markets, identifying bases for segmentation, developing segment profiles, and assessing segment attractiveness. We begin by considering the criteria a manager may use in deciding whether to segment at all and, if so, whether the bases for the resulting segments are ideal.

Criteria for Segmentation

There are a great many ways in which a given market can be divided up for purposes of marketing strategy. In determining which way one ought to proceed, the manager should first consider *why* segmentation is to be carried out. Management may wish to consider segmenting a market[2] to help make the following strategic decisions:

1 *Quantity decisions: How much* of the organization's financial, human, and mental resources are to be devoted to each segment (if any)?
2 *Quality decisions: How* should each segment be approached in terms of specific offerings, communications, place of offering, prices, and the like?
3 *Timing decisions: When* should specific marketing efforts be directed at particular segments?

Given the seemingly infinite array of segmentation possibilities, management needs to decide which is best. In theory, the choice is relatively straightforward. A segmentation base is optimal if it yields segments possessing the following characteristics:

1 *Mutual exclusivity.* Each segment should be conceptually separable from all other segments. Breaking donors into present givers and past givers, for example, would be confusing for a respondent who could be both a past and present giver.
2 *Exhaustiveness.* Every potential target member should be included in some segment. Thus, if there is to be segmentation according to household status, one should have categories to cover relationships like unmarried couples and religious communes where the notion of "household head" really does not apply.
3 *Measurability.* This is the degree to which the size, purchasing power, and profile of the resulting segments can be readily measured. Certain segments are hard to measure, such as the segment of white upper-income teenage female drug addicts, since this segment is engaged in secretive behavior.
4 *Accessibility.* This is the degree to which the resulting segments can be effectively reached and served. Thus, it would be hard for a drug treatment center to develop efficient media to locate and communicate with white female drug addicts.
5 *Substantiality.* This is the degree to which the resulting segments are large enough to be worth pursuing. The drug treatment center is likely to decide that

white affluent female drug addicts are too few in number to be worth the development of a special marketing program.

6 *Differential responsiveness.* This is perhaps the most crucial criterion. A segmentation scheme may meet all of the above criteria but several or all segments may respond exactly alike to different amounts, types, and timing of strategy. In such cases, although it may be *conceptually* useful to develop separate segments in this way, *managerially* it is not useful.

The last point deserves a brief elaboration. Figures 5–2A and 5–2B show the allocation of a given advertising budget to two geographically separate markets we'll call East and West. Curves marked *aa* and *bb* depict the responsiveness of each market to different levels of advertising expenditure. The slope of curve *aa* as compared to *bb* indicates that the West market responds more dramatically than the East market for any given change in ad spending. (That is, the West market is more *advertising elastic* than the East market.)

The points A_{E_1} and A_{W_1} represent equal advertising expenditures in the two markets. This allocation strategy yields total response results of $(R_{E_1} + R_{W_1})$. But it can be seen that if, say, $1,000 is shifted from East to West to yield expenditure levels $(A_{E_2}$ and $A_{W_2})$, then total response $(R_{E_2} + R_{W_2})$ rises, even though *total* expenditures are unchanged. This is because the gain in shifting dollars to the West market $(R_{W_2} - R_{W_1})$ exceeds the loss in the East $(R_{E_2} - R_{E_1})$. One should continue shifting a given budget into the West market until such point as the incremental gain in the one market just equals the incremental loss in the other. In general, one should shift a given budget among differentially responsive markets until the point is reached where the *total* responses would be unchanged under any further fine-tuning one might do between markets. Technically, this is the point where the marginal responses[3] for the various segments are equal.

FIGURE 5-2

Hypothetical Responses of Two Markets to Advertising Expenditures

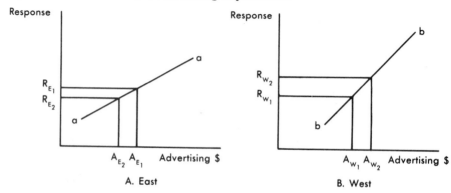

A. East

B. West

Alternative Segmentation Bases

As the preceding discussion indicated, it would be ideal if target consumers could be labeled as to how and how much they would respond to specific quantities, qualities, and timing of marketing strategy. Since consumers don't carry such labels, an ideal segmentation approach expressly requires specifications of the responsiveness of different potential segments. However, once specifications are determined either by assumption or through research, the requirement that the segments be differentially *reachable* still means that we must also know something about *where* they might be reached—for example, through what media, what outlets, what personal information sources, and so on—so that we might differentially apply our segmented strategies.

The ideal response-and-reachability-based approach is rarely achieved for two reasons. First, field research to determine responsiveness and information source behavior is costly and time consuming and not every organization has the funds and the patience to make the necessary investment. Second, the sheer *number* of segmentation decisions a manager must make precludes such care and attention except in rare, very important situations.

As a result, managers typically use *surrogates* for what they *ideally* would like to measure. Segmentation is often based on demographics, for example, because managers assume that such characteristics will be related to likely responses and reachability. Thus, one might choose to segment potential symphony customers on the basis of sex because it is believed (or past research has shown) that women respond more to communications focusing on the performance itself whereas men respond more to communications about the social aspects of attending the symphony *event*. At the same time, it may be found (or assumed) that ads placed in the sports section of a newspaper would reach a predominantly male audience and ads in the metropolitan news section would be an excellent way to reach females. Symphony marketers may initially conclude—with or without past research evidence—that the added costs of placing two such ads in a given paper may be justified by the better *total* responses achieved over a less costly, single ad that tried a middle approach or tried to combine the two approaches in one (possibly confusing) message.

But it should be reemphasized that in the demographic approach, responsiveness and reachability are typically estimated rather than known. As we shall note in Chapter 7, however, a strategy of flying blind needn't continue. A careful program of experimentation could directly test which segmentation approach (for example, separate or single ads) generated more mail orders or more box office sales. Once such a research base was begun, further research could experiment with other segmentation bases or use other strategies to attack the chosen segments. Over time, a careful, systematic, low-cost research program could accumulate considerable experience on the responsiveness and reachability of key market segments.

Variables that have been used to segment markets in particular cases vary according to whether they were *primarily* chosen to reflect expected differences in responsiveness or differences in reachability. Frank, Massy, and Wind have developed a useful two-by-two matrix that serves as a useful vehicle for categorizing segmentation approaches that may be used to achieve these ends.[4] These authors note that two important ways in which segmentation variables differ are in the extent to which they are (1) objective or inferred and (2) general or specific. See Figure 5–3. *Objective measures* are those that can be verified by an independent observer—for example, status indicators such as age, income, sex, and the like. *Inferred measures* are mental states peculiar to each respondent; included are such cognitive factors as perceptions, beliefs, benefits sought, and so forth. Inferred variables can only be measured through the candor and cooperation of a target consumer through answers to a questionnaire, a paper-and-pencil test, or similar assessment device.

General variables are those that might apply to any exchange, whereas *specific* variables are those that are unique to one type or class of exchanges, for example, the purchase of a particular brand or patronage of a particular hospital or museum. Thus, the extent to which an individual consumer possesses an "aggressive" or "risk-averse" personality would be a general inferred variable, whereas beliefs about the likelihood of getting friendly nursing service or the latest diagnostic procedures at Good Samaritan Hospital would be a specific inferred variable.

Objective General Measures.   In some respects, marketers would prefer to use objective rather than subjective measures as the basis for segmentation. There are several reasons for this. First, there is the *ease* of measuring target consumers. Most objective general measures such as sex and geographic location are instantly observable. Others, such as education level, occupation, household size, and family composition are relatively easily determined and verifiable. Unlike inferred measures, objective indicators do not always require consumer cooperation, nor is there a strong likelihood that an error in measure-

FIGURE 5-3

Bases for Market Segmentation

	General	Specific
Objective Measures	Age, income, sex Place of residence Status change Family life cycle Social class	Past behavior • Purchase quantity • Outlet/brand preference • Loyalty Decision role
Inferred Measures	Personality Psychographics/ life-styles (e.g., PRIZM) Values (e.g., VALS 2)	Beliefs, perceptions Benefits sought Personal influences Stage in decision

ment would be made either because the wrong wording was used for a question or because respondents did not know the answer or consciously or unconsciously distorted their responses. Second, target consumers can be fairly easily allocated to specific, nonarbitrary categories. Third, the measures can be adapted easily by different researchers to different contexts, permitting extensive comparison of segmentation findings across studies. This is typically not possible with inferred characteristics, where subtle changes in wording can yield major differences in results.

Finally, objective measures are often preferred because they are available in secondary sources. Thus, if one believes that households with young children are the best prospects for a charity drive, then publicly available census data can be used to discover cities or census tracts within cities that have above-average frequencies of households with that characteristic. Thus, socioeconomic characteristics are the principal criteria used by the National Center for Charitable Statistics to segment the target markets for exempt nonprofit agencies. Their taxonomy is reproduced in Exhibit 5–1.

Among the most commonly used objective general measures are the following:

GEOGRAPHICAL SEGMENTATION.   In geographical segmentation, the market is divided into different geographical entities, such as nations, states, regions, counties, cities, zip code areas, or neighborhoods, based on the notion that consumer needs or responses vary geographically. The organization either decides to operate in one or a few parts of the country as a specialist in meeting their needs or to operate broadly but pay attention to regional variations in needs and preferences. Geographic segmentation is often used as the basis for direct-mail campaigns. More recently, information on geographic location has been combined imaginatively with life-style information to yield descriptions of neighborhoods richer than traditional demographics. The new life-style approach is called *geoclustering*. It is typified by the PRIZM system.

PRIZM was developed by the Claritas Corporation. Claritas collects a vast amount of information on the 36,000 zip code areas in the United States, including standard demographics, product and service purchases, and media usage. Clustering procedures are used to group the zip code areas into 40 categories which are given colorful names such as "Shotguns and Pickups" and "Norma Rae-Ville" (see Exhibit 5–2). A nonprofit marketer can use the information in the PRIZM system to locate new markets or learn what would be appealing to existing markets. For a predetermined fee, the organization can acquire a list of all the zip codes in a selected area with life-styles that would suggest they are good targets for fund-raising or for products and services the organization offers. On the other hand, PRIZM can help define markets, telling the organization which zip code types are the best prospects for the organization's offering. PRIZM can

> tell you more than you probably ever wanted to know about [an] area's typical residents: what they like to eat; which cars they like to drive; whether they prefer scotch or sangria, tuna extender or yogurt, hunting or tennis . . . which

EXHIBIT 5-1

A Taxonomy of Beneficiaries of Nonprofit Organization Programs

I.   *General*
   1. All, general public, no specific beneficiary
II. *Age related*
   1. Infants, babies
   2. Children and youth
   3. Aging, elderly, senior citizens, and retired
III. *Sex*
   1. Boys 5 to 19
   2. Boys and men (i.e., males 5 and older)
   3. Girls 5 to 19
   4. Girls and women (i.e., females 5 and older)
   5. Men 19 and older
   6. Women 19 and older
IV. *Race*
   1. Asian, Pacific Islander
   2. Blacks
   3. Hispanics
   4. Native Americans, American Indians
   5. Other Minorities
   6. Minorities, general, unspecified
V.   *Other beneficiaries*
   1. Disabled, general, unspecified
   2. Disabled, physically
   3. Disabled, mentally, emotionally
   4. Immigrants, newcomers, refugees, stateless
   5. Member or affiliates (organizations)
   6. Member (individual)
   7. Military, veterans
   8. Offenders, ex-offenders
   9. Poor, economically disadvantaged

SOURCE: National Center for Charitable Statistics, *National Taxonomy of Exempt Entities* (Washington, D.C.: The Independent Sector, 1987).

magazines they read, which TV shows they watch, whether they are more likely to buy calculators or laxatives, whether they're single or are potential customers for a diaper service.[5]

In addition to PRIZM, there are other syndicated geoclustering approaches available nationally. These include ACORN ("A Classification of Residential Neighborhoods") from C.A.C.I. of Arlington, Virginia and ClusterPlus from Donnelly Marketing Information Services.

DEMOGRAPHIC SEGMENTATION.   In demographic segmentation, the market is divided into different groups on the basis of demographic variables such as age, sex, family size, family life cycle, income, occupation, education, religion, race, and nationality. Demographic variables have long been among the most popular bases for distinguishing consumer groups. One reason is that consumer wants, preferences, and usage rates are often highly associated with demographic variables. Another is that demographic variables are easier to measure than most other types of variables. Even when the target market is described in nondemographic terms (say, a personality type), the link back to demographic characteristics is necessary in order to know the size of the target market and how to reach it efficiently.

Here we will illustrate how certain demographic variables have been applied creatively to market segmentation.

Age. Consumer wants and capacities change with age. Thus churches have developed different programs for children, youths, singles, married adults, and senior citizens. The churches try to "customize" the religious and social experiences to the interests of these different groups. Some churches are even subsegmenting the senior citizens into those between 55 and 70 ("the young old") and 70 and up ("the old old"). The young old still feel vigorous and want challenge and variety in their lives, and the old old want to settle into a comfortable and routine existence.

Sex. Sex segmentation appears in many nonprofit sectors, such as male and female colleges, service and social clubs, prisons, and military services. Within a single sex, further segmentation can be applied. The continuing education department of a large university segments the female adult learners into "at homes" and "working outside the homes." The "at homes" are subdivided into homemakers and displaced homemakers. Homemakers are attracted to courses for self-enrichment and improved homemaking skills, while displaced homemakers are more interested in career preparation. The "working outside the home" segment breaks into two subsegments, clerical-technical businesswomen and management businesswomen. Each segment has a different set of motivations for attending college, and different educational programs are appropriate for each. Furthermore, each segment faces certain problems in attending college. By addressing the specific problems of each segment, the college is in a better position to attract more women to its campus.

Income. Income segmentation is another long-standing practice in the nonprofit sector. In the medical field, the standard health insurance policy pays for semiprivate rooms. Most hospitals, however, offer patients the option of a private room at an additional cost in order to cater to the preferences of higher income groups. Some hospitals have designed entire wings and even whole buildings to serve more affluent patients. Hospitals that establish outreach ambulatory centers vary the decor and service to match different income groups.

Race and Ethnicity. Two variables that are often used to segment nonprofit marketing programs are race and ethnicity. There are many reasons for this. One is that different issues impact different racial and ethnic groups. Hispanics and southeast Asians are particularly concerned with immigration issues while blacks are especially concerned with sickle-cell anemia. On the other hand, problems of drugs, poverty, education, and homelessness affect all groups.

Second, racial and ethnic groups differ in their media habits and organiza-

EXHIBIT 5-2

PRIZM™ Cluster Categories

1 *Blue-Blood Estates:* The richest of the rich; 1.1 percent.

2 *Money and Brains:* Swank townhouses, apartments and condos; 0.9 percent.

3 *Furs and Station Wagons:* New money in affluent suburbs; 3.2 percent.

4 *Urban Gold Coast:* Dense, white-collar enclaves; 0.5 percent.

5 *Pools and Patios:* Older, comfortable suburbs; 3.4 percent.

6 *Two More Rungs:* Dense suburbs with conservative buying patterns; 0.7 percent.

7 *Young Influentials:* A younger version of Money and Brains; 2.9 percent.

8 *Young Suburbia:* Child-raising families in outlying suburbs; 5.3 percent.

9 *God's Country:* Well-educated frontier types; 2.7 percent.

10 *Blue-Chip Blues:* The richest blue-collar neighborhoods; 6.0 percent.

11 *Bohemian Mix:* America's bohemia; 1.1 percent.

12 *Levittown, U.S.A.:* Suburban tract developments; 3.1 percent.

13 *Gray Power:* Middle-class retirement areas; 2.9 percent.

14 *Black Enterprise:* The black middle class; 0.8 percent.

15 *New Beginnings:* Archie Bunker's children; 4.3 percent.

16 *Blue-Collar Nursery:* Outlying towns and suburbs of small cities; 2.2 percent.

17 *New Homesteaders:* Less affluent version of God's Country; 4.2 percent.

18 *New Melting Pot:* New-immigrant neighborhoods; 0.9 percent.

19 *Towns and Gowns:* Midscale college towns; 1.9 percent.

20 *Rank and File:* Aging blue-collar suburbs; 1.4 percent.

21 *Middle America:* Midsize middleclass towns and outlying suburbs; 3.2 percent.

22 *Old Yankee Rows:* Blue-collar areas of older industrial cities; 1.6 percent.

23 *Coalburg and Corntown:* Small, peaceful towns like Lima, Ohio; 2.0 percent.

24 *Shotguns and Pickups:* Large families in crossroad villages; 1.9 percent.

25 *Golden Ponds:* Rustic villages near coasts, mountains, or lakes; 5.2 percent.

26 *AgriBusiness:* Ranching, farming, and lumbering areas; 2.1 percent.

27 *Emergent Minorities:* Minorities struggling up from poverty; 1.7 percent.

28 *Single City Blues:* Dense, urban, downscale singles areas; 3.3 percent.

29 *Mines and Mills:* Mining and mill towns where industry is king; 2.8 percent.

30 *Back-Country Folks:* Remote rural towns; 3.4 percent.

31 *Norma Rae-Ville:* Industrial suburbs; 2.3 percent.

32 *Small Downtowns:* Dense, old factory towns; 2.5 percent.

33 *Grain Belt:* Farm owners and less affluent tenant farmers; 1.3 percent.

34 *Heavy Industry:* Poorer version of Rank and File; 2.8 percent.

35 *Sharecroppers:* Southern-style tenant farms; 4.0 percent.

36 *Downtown Dixie Style:* Integrated, dense urban areas; 3.4 percent.
37 *Hispanic Mix:* The nation's Hispanic barrios; 1.9 percent.
38 *Tobacco Roads:* Unskilled rural laborers; 1.2 percent.
39 *Hard Scrabble:* The poorest rural areas; 1.5 percent.
40 *Public Assistance:* America's inner-city ghettos; 3.1 percent.

SOURCE: Claritas Corporation. Reprinted with permission. PRIZM and Claritas are registered trademarks of Claritas Corporation.

tional ties. In the United States, most major minority groups have their own newspapers, magazines, and, in some cases, radio and television programming. These permit very precise targeting of marketing messages.

Finally, the way one appeals to different races and ethnic groups is different. As shown in Figure 5-4, it is often essential to use different models and settings in ads for different audiences. Language and colloquialisms often should differ in communications to each segment as well as the basic appeals. Spokespeople will differ. For example, religious leaders can often be extremely effective in transmitting important social messages in Hispanic and black markets where preachers and priests are highly respected leaders.

Role in the Exchange Process. As shown in Figure 5-5, The Hospital of the Good Samaritan in Los Angeles has developed entirely separate brochures for its ambulatory care center for (1) potential patients, (2) physicians, and (3) businesses.

COMPLEX GENERAL OBJECTIVE MEASURES. As nonprofit marketers grow more sophisticated in their use of objective segmentation variables, two steps can be taken. First, marketers can be more precise in operationalizing the measures they use. Income, for example, is a frequently used variable in attempts to segment the charity market—for obvious reasons. Miller, however, has found that donation behavior in various zip codes in Oklahoma is often more closely associated with the source of income than the amount of income.[6] He found, for example, that the number of households in a zip code area receiving some form of interest income was a better predictor of total donations than was total adjusted gross income. Predictions of the *percentage* who would donate were better with measures of the percentage of households receiving dividends, or of the percentage receiving interest than with average household income. Clearly, routinely using total income in studies may miss insights that more careful measures might yield.

Complex measures can also be developed by combining objective measures in a single index. Two such combined measures, social class and family life cycle, have been used extensively in marketing.

Social class. Social classes are relatively homogeneous and enduring divisions in a society that is hierarchically ordered and whose members share similar values, interests, and behavior. Social scientists have distinguished six social classes: (1) upper uppers (less than 1 percent), (2) lower uppers (about 1

FIGURE 5-4

American Red Cross Advertisements for Different Racial Markets

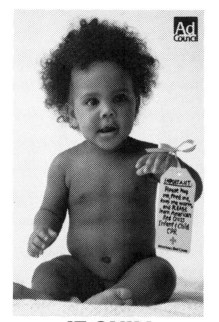

FIGURE 5-5

Brochures Designed for Consumer, Physician, and Business Markets

SOURCE: The Hospital of the Good Samaritan. Reproduced with permission.

percent), (3) upper middles (12 percent), (4) lower middles (32 percent), (5) upper lowers (38 percent), and (6) lower lowers (16 percent), using objective variables such as income, occupation, education, and type of residence. Social classes show distinct consumption preferences in the nonprofit area. A study of museumgoers attending the King Tut exhibit in New Orleans, for example, showed that attendance came heavily from the upper and middle classes, in spite of the mass marketing of this extraordinary exhibit.[7] Operas, plays, the ballet, symphonies, and lectures also attract the upper classes most heavily. Cultural institutions that wish to overcome their elitist image and attract lower-class audiences to appreciate their art form will have to develop separate marketing programs and strategies.

Family life cycle.   The family life cycle concept is based on the notion that over one's lifetime there are critical transition points when major changes in consumer behavior (and other behaviors) take place. These transition points are generally defined in terms of objective variables such as marital status, work force status, and the presence and age of children. Eight stages are typically specified as the modal family life cycle pattern:

1 Young single (under 40, not married, no children at home)
2 Newly married (young, married, no children)
3 Full nest I (young, married, youngest child less than 6)
4 Full nest II (young, married, youngest child 6 to 13)
5 Full nest III (older married, dependent children 14 or older)
6 Empty nest I (older married, no children at home, head working)
7 Empty nest II (older married, no children at home, head retired)
8 Solitary survivor (older single, working or retired)

In a recent analysis of performing arts attendance data, Andreasen found that family life cycle appeared to have an important effect on attendance at the six different types of performing arts. The proportions of households attending multiple events were as follows:

Young, single	17.9%
Young, married, no children	10.7%
Infants at home	8.7%
Children 6 or older	12.4%
Older, no children	15.4%
Elderly	8.8%

Obviously, the elderly represent a poor market. Among the remaining life-style categories, the relationship is clearly curvilinear: multiple attendance is high at each end of these life cycle categories but low in the middle. It would appear that the presence of children has a dampening effect on arts involvement. Undoubtedly, this is due to several factors including reductions in leisure time and discretionary income, changes in household priorities, and increased costs for "going out."[8]

It should be noted that while the family life cycle concept can prove a useful segmentation variable, it is not *exhaustive* in that it omits important groups of households. For example, older never-marrieds, and divorced or single parents with spouses absent are often not included.[9] For some nonprofit social service marketing programs, such households may be very important.

A third approach to using objective variables in combination is to use multivariate statistical procedures to develop customized *sets* of predictors that when considered together best segment target markets. These procedures consider *all* possible segmentation variables together and develop (1) a parsimonious subset that jointly does the best job of predicting the behavior in question, and (2) a measure of the relative contribution of each variable to the final predictions. Beik and Smith, for example, collected survey data on 2,261 households in Allegheny County, Pennsylvania, describing their charitable giving of all kinds. They also assembled objective data on the tracts in which the respondents resided.[10] By analyzing these results with a technique called multiple discriminant analysis, the researchers found they could best discriminate between households making donations of $50 or more to medical charities and all other households with the following equation:

$$Y_1 = .58328X_1 + .53414X_3 + .31493X_4 \tag{5-1}$$

where
  $Y_1 =$ donate \$50+ to medical charities (1 = yes, 0 = no)
  $X_1 =$ proportion of households with income $\geq$ \$15,000
  $X_3 =$ proportion of household heads $\geq$ 55 years of age
  $X_4 =$ proportion of household heads in managerial, professional, or entrepreneurial positions.[11]

Note three features of this analysis. First, to discriminate donation behavior, the researchers attempted to use objective variables other than age, income, and occupation such as the proportion of owned homes and the proportion of household heads who were college graduates. These variables, however, turned out in the multivariate analysis framework not to be useful for segmentation. Second, the coefficients in the final equation indicate that income contributed somewhat more as a predictor of medical donations than did age, while both were substantially more important than occupation. Finally, because the predictors are all available in government census data, if one assumed that the Oklahoma results applied elsewhere, one could—in theory—segment every area in the United States as to whether they are likely to be better or poorer prospects for solicitations by medical charities using the three variables and weightings reported in the above equation.

Objective Specific Measures.   For consumer decisions involving little or no cognitive activity, the best predictor of future responsiveness may well be past behavior in the exchange category or closely related exchanges. Among the objective specific variables relating to behavior often used in marketing are the following:

EXCHANGE SITUATION.   Buyers can be distinguished by the occasions when they purchase a product. Commuters using public transportation, for example, include those who are traveling to work, those who are shopping, those who are going to entertainment, and those who are visiting friends. Some public transit companies have launched campaigns to encourage the shopping segment to travel in off-peak hours and have even charged lower fares as an incentive.

USER STATUS.   Many markets can be segmented into nonusers, ex-users, potential users, first-time users, and regular users of a product or service. This segmentation variable is helpful to antidrug agencies in planning their education programs and campaigns. Much of their effort is directed at identifying potential users of hard drugs and discouraging them through information and persuasion campaigns. They also sponsor rehabilitation programs to help regular users who want to quit their habit. They utilize ex-users in various programs to add credibility to their effort.

In another example, Lovelock has found that one can separate target segments for mass transit in San Francisco as follows:

1   Never used (13.6 percent)
2   Nonuser, used in past (48.5 percent)
3   Occasional user (30.1 percent)
4   Regular user by choice (6.9 percent)

In his study, Lovelock found significant differences across these groups in perceptions of car, bus, and train travel and their knowledge of interurban bus service.[12] He concluded that "the findings presented from the San Francisco area represent a strong link between perceptions . . . and modal choice behavior." However, two features of this research need to be noted. First, the study uses specific rather than general objective measures (of behavior), so the implications about likely responsiveness are more obvious than they would be if general measures like automobile ownership, occupation, or place of residence were used and from which further inferences about transit patronage would have to be made.

Second, the study only showed *links* between the subjective measures and likely behavior. It did not discover the *direction* of the causation. Thus, it could be that favorable perceptions lead to public transit use, but it is also possible that public transit use leads to favorable perceptions. Thus, as Lovelock notes, only a longitudinal design could produce a causal explanation.

USAGE RATE.   Many markets can be segmented into light-, medium-, and heavy-user groups for the offer (called volume segmentation). Heavy users may constitute only a small percentage of the numerical size of the market but a major percentage of the unit volume consumed. Marketers make a great effort to determine the demographic characteristics and media habits of the heavy users and aim their marketing programs at them. An antismoking campaign, for example, might be aimed at the heaviest smokers, a safe driving campaign at those having the most accidents, and a family planning campaign at those likely to have the most children. Unfortunately, the heaviest users are often the most resistant to change. Fertile families are the most resistant to birth control messages, and unsafe drivers are the most resistant to safe driving messages. The agencies must consider whether to use their limited budget to go after a few heavy users who are highly resistant or many light users who are less resistant.

Semenik and Young segmented the audience attending opera into three attendance level segments—subscribers, frequent attenders, and infrequent attenders—and found significant differences.[13] Subscribers tended to be long-time patrons, attended as a married couple, and considered themselves to be opera fans. Frequent attenders had similar characteristics but were younger and lower in income and often attended with a friend rather than a spouse. Infrequent attenders did not consider themselves opera fans but attended because of a featured star or well-known opera. The identification of segment characteristics enables the development of separate market strategies designed to maximize attendance and loyalty.

LOYALTY STATUS.   Loyalty status describes the strength of a consumer's preference for a particular entity. The amount of loyalty can range from zero to absolute. We find consumers who are deeply loyal to a brand (Budweiser beer, Crest toothpaste, Cadillac automobiles), an organization (Harvard University, the Republican Party), a place (New England, Southern California), a person (Ralph Nader), and so on. Being loyal means preferring the particular object in spite of increased incentives to switch to something else.

Inferred General Measures.   Most of the measures in this category seek to identify consumers in terms of relatively enduring general intrapsychic predispositions that presumably would be operative over time and across exchange categories. The most widely used approaches are those that segment consumers by personality, by enduring needs, by values, and by life-style.

PERSONALITY.   It has long been believed that variations in consumer personality would be reflected in their marketplace behavior. However, in the main, general personality traits have not been useful in past studies, in part because they are very difficult to measure (that is, they are highly subjective and unreliable across studies) and therefore very hard to link to specific marketplace actions. On the other hand, studies have focused on relatively trivial behavior like beer preferences. It may be that in the future, personality measures may finally prove to be helpful in segmenting markets for the more highly involving exchanges that are of interest to nonprofit marketers.

VALUES.   A number of disciplines argue that individuals organize many of their choices in terms of the values they hold. Values consist of the beliefs individuals hold about what is right, fair, just, or desirable. Munson notes that they are used "in comparison processes when people establish standards, judge issues, debate options, plan activities, reach decisions, resolve differences, change patterns and exert influence." It affects how we present ourselves to others and how others are compared to us.

The best known scholar in this area, Milton Rokeach, distinguishes between *instrumental values* and *terminal values*.[14] Instrumental values guide our ongoing behavior to achieve certain end states. Terminal values guide our choices among those end states. Research has shown that values of both types are closely related to other segmentation variables such as age, family structure and life cycle, race and ethnicity, and geographic location. They are also closely related to attitudes and predispositions, product choices (e.g., automobiles), allocations of time between work and leisure, and use of various media.

Values are enduring but much less permanent than personality. Individuals slowly change in the values they use to guide their lives. For example, rural people moving to a competitive big city may come to value prudence over openness in their interpersonal relations. Values also change as societies change. Americans in the 1990s see value in many conservative programs (e.g., privatization of prisons) that would have been considered highly reactionary 20 years ago.

There are many approaches to studying values. One is to use Rokeach's value survey and then link it to specific attitudes, preferences, or behaviors of the target market. An alternative approach works backward from specific choices and preferences to discern fundamental values that drive these choices and preferences. The technique, called *laddering*, involves asking customers about preferences and then asking them to reveal reasons for those preferences (for example, to secure specific benefits or avoid certain costs). The interviewer then proceeds to seek the reasons for focusing on these benefits and costs and then seeks the reasons for those reasons and so on. One "moves up the ladder" finally to the basic values that characterize the particular customer and permit one to place him or her in a segment with other customers holding similar values.[15]

LIFE-STYLES.   Recent dissatisfaction with the overly general personality or dominant-need approaches to inferred segmentation has led to the very rapid growth of life-style research in the last twenty years. If segmentation by personality is based on the notion that "we do what we do because of the kind of person we are," then life-style segmentation is based on the notion that "we do

FIGURE 5-6

Activities and Interests of Leisure Life-style Groups

Passive Homebodies	*Active Sports Enthusiasts*
They agree with, or do, the following:	*They agree with, or do, the following:*
Television is my primary source of entertainment (interest).	Go bowling (activity).
I am a homebody (interest).	Go to a sports event (activity).
I watch TV in order to quietly relax (interest).	Play tennis (activity).
I would rather spend a quiet evening at home than go to a party (interest).	See a movie in a movie theater (activity).
My days seem to follow a definite routine (interest).	I like to attend sporting events (interest).
	I can't see myself going to an opera (interest).
They disagree with, or do not do, the following:	*They disagree with, or do not do, the following:*
See a movie in a movie theater (activity).	I would rather spend a quiet evening at home than go to a party (interest).
Go bowling (activity).	Many of my friends are interested in symphony concerts (interest).
Work on a sports event (activity).	Many of my friends are interested in the theater (interest).
Work on an arts or crafts project of my own (activity).	I usually know which symphony concerts are being performed around here (interest).
Go out to dinner at a restaurant (activity).	I am a homebody (interest).
Play tennis (activity).	I usually know which play is being performed around here (interest).

what we do because it fits into the kind of life we are living or want to live." A further distinction is that whereas personality is seen to be a very enduring, perhaps lifelong characteristic, life-style is seen as more transient, something that can change even from one year to the next.

There are several different approaches to identifying life-style groups in the population. Most, however, are based on measures of consumers' *activities, interests, and opinions* (AIOs). Life-style measures developed from these data can be general or more specific as in the case of one's leisure life-style. Life-style measures are also sometimes called *psychographics* to denote their combining psychological and demographic measurements.

Many life-style approaches are customized for specific research needs. For example, Andreasen and Belk used information on leisure time activities of respondents in four southern cities to group potential attenders at symphonies and theater in six broad categories. The six groups were labeled Passive Home-bodies, Active Sports Enthusiasts, Inner-Directed Self-sufficients, Active Home-bodies, Culture Patrons, and Social Actives. Responses of four of these groups are reported in Figure 5-6. As mentioned in Chapter 2, the researchers found

Culture Patron	*Socially Active*
They agree with, or do, the following:	*They agree with, or do, the following:*
Went to a play in the last 12 months (activity).	Go to a meeting of a social or service club (activity).
Went to a symphony orchestra concert in the last 12 months (activity).	Give or attend a party (activity).
Visited an art gallery or museum in the last 12 months (activity).	Go on a picnic (activity).
The arts are more important to me than to most other people (interest).	I usually know which plays are being performed around here (interest).
They disagree with, or do not do, the following:	*They disagree with, or do not do, the following:*
My major hobby is my family (interest).	I'd rather read a good book than a newspaper (interest).
Television is my primary source of entertainment (interest).	I would rather spend a quiet evening at home than go to a party (interest).
Watch television other than sports events (activity).	I can't see myself going to an opera (interest).
I watch television to relax quietly (activity).	I like to read nonfiction books (interest).
Watch a sports event on television (activity).	I have less leisure time compared to other people I know (interest).
If cultural organizations cannot pay their own way, they should go out of business (opinion).	

SOURCE: Alan R. Andreasen and Russell W. Belk, "Consumer Response to Arts Offerings: A Study of Theater and Symphony in Four Southern Cities," in Edward McCracken, ed., *Research in the Arts* (Baltimore, Md.: Walters Art Gallery, 1979), pp. 13–19.

that membership in the Culture Patron life-style group was a very good predictor of attendance at theater or symphony, presumably because the aesthetic benefits of symphony performances fit their life-styles. Further, membership in the Socially Active group predicted symphony attendance only, suggesting that it is the symphony performance *event* that meets the life-style needs of this group.

Life-style is a much better explanatory variable than any of the traditional socioeconomic characteristics, such as income and education, that are usually used to explain performing arts attendance. Andreasen and Belk suggest that these socioeconomic indicators may simply be masking what are really the more profound explanations—life-style compatibility.

Another customized psychographic approach has been developed for donors by the United Way of America using data developed by Burke Marketing Research. It is described in Figure 5-7.

FIGURE 5-7

Psychographic Segments in the Charity Market

The Burke psychographic segmentation grouped donors by their attitudes toward charity, their life-styles, and their values. Three key psychographic segments emerged from the analysis: the Social/Civic Minded, the Pressured Exchangers, and the Disconnected.

A. *The Social/Civic Minded*

Compared to people in the other two segments, the Social/Civic Minded are

- More active in community affairs
- More concerned about the quality of life for others in the community
- More likely to say they are frequently asked to give to charities
- Less suspicious of requests for charitable contributions
- More likely to feel that they give a reasonable proportion of their income to charities
- Much more likely to have a favorite charity they give to year after year.

In terms of demographics, the Social/Civic Minded segment is more affluent, has more formal education, and is more likely to be in professional or managerial positions than are people in the other segments.

B. *The Pressured Exchangers*

Compared to people in the other segments, the Pressured Exchangers are

- More likely to feel pressure when asked to give, either in the workplace or to a request received at home

- More likely to prefer giving to small charities
- More likely to prefer giving to a charity that will be personally helpful to them or someone they know; that is, they see giving as an exchange
- More likely to be uncertain about how to help others
- More likely to say that people have to help themselves.

Demographically, the Pressured Exchangers have somewhat lower incomes, less formal education, and lower occupational status than do the Social/Civic Minded. In this respect they resemble the third segment, the Disconnected.

C. *The Disconnected*

Compared to people in the other two segments, the Disconnected are

- Less active in community activities
- Less likely to attend church
- Less concerned about the quality of life for others in the community
- Place more importance on the charity making sure their money is well spent
- More likely to stress the importance of trusting a charitable organization before they donate.

Like the Pressured Exchangers, the Disconnected have somewhat lower incomes, less formal education, and lower occupational status than the Social/Civic Minded.

United Way Performance by Psychographic Segment

Performance can be measured in several ways. First, how effective is United Way in reaching the people in each segment with a request to donate? As one might expect, the Social/Civic Minded are most likely to be reached (49%), followed by the Pressured Exchangers (43%) and the Disconnected (39%).

Second, how successful is United Way with each group in terms of the percentage who give when asked? Here, perhaps because they do feel pressure, the Pressured Exchangers are most likely to give when contacted (61%), followed by the Social/Civic Minded (53%), who are about as likely to give as the Disconnected (51%).

Third, what is the size of gift United Way receives from the givers in each segment? Here, the $114 average donation of the Social/Civic Minded far exceeds the $77 donation of the Pressured Exchangers and the $69 donation of the Disconnected.

This means, for example, that although the Social/Civic Minded are 28% of the population, they account for 42% of United Way's donations. The Disconnected, 34% of the population, account for 22% of donations, and the Pressured Exchangers are 38% of the population and 36% of donations to United Way.

SOURCE: Adapted from *Market Research Review* (Arlington, Va.: United Way of America, undated). Reproduced with permission.

A widely accepted general psychographic approach is called VALS 2. The original VALS was developed by SRI International and introduced in 1978. At the time, it responded to a clearly felt need for some standardization in psychographic approaches. In contrast to many other contemporary approaches, VALS was not developed from multivariate statistical analyses but was theory driven. Using concepts developed by Abraham Maslow and David Reisman, Andrew Mitchell and his colleagues at SRI developed a set of nine categories reflecting individual values and life-styles (hence, the name VALS). Consumers were grouped on the basis of their resources and the extent to which their values emerged from observing others or were developed autonomously.

Although the original VALS was widely adopted, users felt that a few categories tended to dominate many analyses (e.g., the "belongers" and "achievers" groups) and that the VALS groupings did not predict buying behavior very well. Further, it was felt that VALS too greatly reflected the character of the U.S. population at the time. VALS 2 emerged in 1989 and was designed around unchanging psychological traits rather than shifting values and life-styles. Forty-three questions were developed that would allow SRI to categorize consumers into a matrix reflecting basic life-styles. These are described in Figure 5-8.[16]

FIGURE 5-8

VALS 2 Lifestyle Categories

VALS 2 is based on surveys of over 2,000 consumers. It divides consumers into eight segments along two dimensions: *resources* and *self-orientation*. Resources refers to much more than mere possessions or wealth. It includes all of the capacities on which consumers can draw, including education, income, health, self-confidence, and energy level. Self-orientation refers to the consumer's self-image and the attitudes and activities undertaken to reinforce this image. VALS 2 concludes that there are three basic types of self-orientation:

- *Principle-oriented consumers,* who are guided by their beliefs about right and wrong, justice, "the proper life," and so forth;
- *Status-oriented consumers,* who are guided by the actions, attitudes, and opinions of others; and
- *Action-oriented consumers,* who seek social and physical activity, variety, and risk taking.

VALS 2 divides those in each of these three self-orientation categories into those who have more abundant or more limited resources. The six groups that result are the following:

1 *Fulfilleds* (Principles-oriented with more abundant resources; 11 percent of the population). These are older consumers who are well-informed about the world around them. They value order, knowledge,

and responsibility and tend to be practical in their consumption deci-sions, looking first for value and durability.

2 *Believers* (Principles-oriented with more limited resources; 16 percent of the population). This older, traditional group is the largest VALS 2 segment. They have established routines involving their home, family, and social or religious organizations. They prefer American-made products and brand names.

3 *Achievers* (Status-oriented with more abundant resources; 13 percent of the population). These are successful career people who seek stability over risk taking. They work to achieve material goods and prestige. They are concerned about their "image" and buy products that will impress others.

4 *Strivers* (Status-oriented with limited resources; 13 percent of the pop-ulation). This group defines success in terms of money and sometimes they feel that life has been hard on them. They are easily bored and can be impulsive. They like to buy the impressive goods they see others having.

5 *Experiencers* (Action-oriented with more abundant resources; 12 per-cent of the population). This group is young, enthusiastic, and impul-sive. They experiment in order to help form their long-term lifestyles. They are enthusiastic shoppers for movies, videos, fast food, and clothing.

6 *Makers* (Action-oriented with limited resources; 13 percent of the pop-ulation). These self-sufficient individuals value family, practical work, and physical recreation. They buy practical items and not those which will impress others.

In addition to these six groups, there are two groups that are above and below the basic VALS 2 matrix.

7 *Strugglers* (14 percent of the population). This is the oldest, poorest segment. They must focus on getting by rather than defining some special self-orientation. They worry about their health and the needs of the present. They are cautious and so, although they do not spend much, they tend to be relatively loyal.

8 *Actualizers* (8 percent of the population). This small, elite group have enough resources to try any self-orientation they wish. They are leaders in business and government and have wide, frequently chang-ing interests. They tend to acquire goods and services reflecting a more refined style of life.

VALS 2 is now routinely included with other syndicated research services. Thus, one can learn what the distribution of VALS 2 groupings is for geo-demographic clusters developed by CACI (ACORN), Claritas (PRIZM), Don-nelley Marketing Information Services (ClusterPlus), and National Decision Systems. And one can learn media behavior of the VALS 2 groupings through the databases of Simmons Market Research Bureau and Mediamark Research, Inc.

Lifestyle information is valuable in many ways. One advantage is that it can give advertising creators rich portraits of their various target market seg-

FIGURE 5-9

Family of the Future Contraceptive Point-of-Sale Placard for the Cairo Market

SOURCE: Porter Novelli. Reprinted with permission.

ments. Figure 5-9 shows a point-of-sale placard aimed at relatively sophisticated Cairo women. The very same placard altered to fit the more traditional life-styles outside of Cairo is shown in Figure 5-10.

FIGURE 5-10

**Family of the Future Contraceptive Point-of-Sale Placard
for Non-Cairo Markets**

SOURCE: Porter Novelli. Reprinted with permission.

INFERRED SPECIFIC MEASURES.   Segmenting consumers subjectively for specific markets, of course, usually requires original field data. Rarely are such data available from secondary sources. In cases where the exchange at issue is highly involving, a very useful framework for such research is the Extended Fishbein Attitude Model described in detail in Chapter 4. It will be recalled that this model algebraically was as follows:

$$\text{Behavior} = BI_j = \left(\sum_{i=1}^{n} b_{ij}a_i\right) W_1 + \left(\sum_{k=1}^{m} NB_{kj} \cdot MC_k\right) W_2 \tag{5-2}$$

The model contains a wide array of specific subjective measures that can be used to segment markets. Referring to the algebraic notations, these measures and their segmentation possibilities include

1 j: the exchange alternatives in the evoked set (for example, segmenting those consumers that include your alternative separately from those that do not).
2 i: the criteria used to evaluate the alternatives (for example, segmenting those who *consider* consequences you offer from those who don't).
3 a_i: the pattern of weightings applied to the criteria (for example, segmenting those who give high weight to the set of consequences at which you excel from those who give them low weight).
4 b_{ij}: beliefs about consequences of taking particular action alternatives (for example, segmenting those who accurately see the consequences of choosing your alternative from those who have inaccurate perceptions or segmenting those who have more favorable beliefs about a competitive alternative than about yours from those for whom the reverse is true).
5 k: the significant others whose views about the behavior might influence behavioral intentions (for example, segmenting those who consider family only from those who consider peers only).
6 MC_k: the pattern of motivations to conform to the views of these significant others (for example, segmenting those who say they are heavily influenced by parents from those who are only "somewhat" influenced).
7 NB_{kj}: perceptions of the behavioral expectations of specific significant others (for example, segmenting those whose significant others are generally favorably disposed toward your alternative from those whose significant others are negative).
8 W_1/W_2: the relative weight of the person's own attitude versus the perceived views of significant others in affecting behavioral intentions (for example, segmenting those who are inner directed from those who are other directed).

BENEFIT SEGMENTATION.   Use of the a_i and b_{ij} measures means that buyers can be segmented according to the particular benefit(s) that they are seeking through the consumption of the offering. Benefits are reflected in the b_{ij} measures and their weights in the a_{ij} measures. Some consumers look for one dominant benefit from the offering and others seek a particular *benefit bundle.*[17] Many markets are made up of three core benefit segments: *quality buyers, service buyers,* and *economy buyers.* Quality buyers seek out the best reputed offering and are not concerned with the cost. A quality seeker in the college market would consider only the elite universities, and a quality seeker in the hospital market would consider only the best hospitals and surgeons. Service buyers look for the best value for the money and expect the service to match the price. A service seeker would choose a college that provides a good education and social life for the money, regardless of its reputation. Economy buyers are primarily interested in minimizing their cost and favor the least expensive market offer. An economy seeker would go to a community college to keep college costs to a minimum. Benefit segmentation, it should be added, works best when people's preferences for benefits are correlated with demographic and media characteristics, making it easier to reach them efficiently.

In a recent application, Bonaguro and Miaoulis developed eight benefit segments for a multiservice family planning agency. These segments are outlined in Table 5-1.

The eight segments were then combined into more manageable subsets. The Firefighters and Desperates were joined into a group that had in common a sense of urgency about health needs. They only seek information and take action in an emergency, at which point they are likely to be agitated, confused, and perhaps irrational. It was decided to ignore the Worriers and Infertile benefit segments because of the agency's limited budget and to group the four remaining original segments as Rationals. This combined group was likely to seek information on their own as a means of improving their families' health and future prospects. Print media, lectures, pamphlets, and posters all with longer messages were emphasized within the strategy destined for this group under the theme: "A brighter future–plan it now."

Note that in this example, the marketer segmented the market by benefits and then decided to concentrate on only those segments where it could have the best impact for its limited resources.

Table 5-1

BENEFIT SEGMENTS FOR A FAMILY PLANNING AGENCY

Benefits Sought	Segment Name
Immediate solution to a problem (pregnancy, breast lump, etc.), shoulder to lean on	1. Firefighters
Relief from feeling of desperation, financial stability, marital harmony	2. Desperates
Security about good health, relief from worry	3. Worriers
Conception, birth, children	4. Infertiles
Freedom of choice, control, financial stability, marital harmony	5. Married Rationals
Freedom of choice, financial stability	6. Married–No Children
Pregnancy prevention, financial stability, avoid social stigma	7. Married–With Children
Pregnancy prevention to avoid social stigma, retain independence, financial stability	8. Singles–Without Children

SOURCE: John A. Bonaguro and George Miaoulis, "Marketing: A Tool for Health Education Planning," *Health Education*, January–February 1983, p. 9.

SACRIFICE SEGMENTATION.   In Chapter 4, we noted that consumers are likely to undertake exchanges if the benefits outweigh the costs. And we further noted that in many cases, there is wide appreciation of the *benefits* of a particular action, while it is the *costs* that are the major inhibitors to action. In Chapter 4, we noted that Bagozzi, in his study of blood donors, found little difference among consumers in the perceived positive consequences that would follow from their behavior. Bagozzi found considerable variation in perceptions of *negative* consequences and learned that they were good predictors of behavioral intentions. These results give rise to the speculation that some markets could be usefully segmented in terms of the relative weight individuals attach to the various *barriers* to action rather than to the benefits. Thus, in the blood donation case, consumers could be subdivided into those who are highly sensitive to: physiological risks—infections, AIDS, physical pain; social risks—not being "brave" in the eyes of others; and psychological fears—fears of needles, blood, and "hospitals."

Bases for Segmenting Organizational Markets

Public and nonprofit organizations not only market to individual consumers but also have occasions to market to organizations. Museums need to identify appropriate foundations to solicit for financial support. Associations need to motivate their local chapters to improve their member services. Hospitals need to convince other hospitals to use their blood bank services and convince large nearby corporations to send their employees to the hospital's wellness and fitness clinics. In all these cases, the nonprofit is seeking to get other organizations to enter into exchanges for particular goods and services.

There are a number of bases that can be used to segment organizational markets. We discuss several that are particularly appropriate to fund-raising in Chapter 9. Bases that can be used for segmenting organizations are the following:

1 *Organization Size.* Larger organizations can afford more expensive purchases but typically have more complex purchasing processes. Medium and small organizations may have less to spend but can often be the focus for niching strategies. A museum might market sponsorship to major showings to large corporations while asking smaller, local firms to contribute advertising space or brochures for specific fundraisers.

2 *Interest Profile.* Organizations differ in their goals, their treatment of their staffs, and their time horizons. Organizations with a major commitment to the arts might be asked to agree to multiyear funding for a collection with their name on it. Organizations that pay close attention to the welfare of their employees could be asked to sponsor private museum tours for their staffs combined with a lecture and buffet.

3 *Buying Criteria.* Some organizations are concerned about cost-effectiveness, others about the potential for accruing prestige or specific payoffs to their organization's members. A museum may be required to provide detailed ac-

counting information for some potential sponsors and to establish clear means of publicizing the contributions of others.

4 *Buying Process.* Some organizations require a good deal of paperwork and a long time period before making a commitment. Others may act in a few days on the basis of a verbal promise and a handshake. Some use committees to make decisions; others may be dominated by a strong leader. The museum must have procedures to match a number of purchase styles.

5 *Degree of Local Autonomy.* Major national or international organizations differ in the degree to which they allow local representatives autonomy in making commitments to nonprofits. A museum may be able to deal with local decision makers for many organizations but have to contact corporate headquarters for others. The latter are more likely to require greater documentation and longer time periods to turn around requests.

Sometimes segmentation of particular offerings will involve both individual consumers and businesses. The Palm Springs Boys' Club faced such a problem in finding added revenue for their Pathfinder Ranch. Their experience is reported in Exhibit 5-3.

TARGET MARKETING

Market segmentation reveals the market segmentation opportunities facing the organization. The organization must next decide how to target these segments. There are three broad strategic choices.

1 *Undifferentiated marketing.* The organization can decide to go after the whole market with one offer and marketing mix, trying to attract as many consumers as possible (this is another name for mass marketing).

2 *Differentiated marketing.* The organization can decide to go after several market segments, developing an effective offer and marketing mix for each.

3 *Concentrated marketing.* The organization can decide to go after one market segment and develop the ideal offer and marketing mix.

Here we will describe the logic and merits of each of these strategies.

Undifferentiated Marketing

In undifferentiated marketing,[18] the organization chooses not to recognize the different market segments making up the market. It treats the market as an aggregate, focusing on what is common in the needs of consumers rather than on what is different. It tries to design an offer and a marketing program that appeal to the broadest number of buyers. It would be exemplified by a church that runs only one religious service for everyone, a politician who gives the same speech to everyone, and a family planning organization that tries to promote the same birth control method for everyone.

Undifferentiated marketing is typically defended on the grounds of cost

EXHIBIT 5-3

James Coston, Executive Director of the Boys' Club of Palm Springs, Inc., on Segmenting a Nonprofit Market

> The Pathfinder Ranch near Palm Springs, California, opened in 1965 as a summer camp for boys. By 1986, Pathfinder management still treated its marketplace as a monolithic entity, focusing almost exclusively on securing summer camp recruits through the local Boys' Clubs. However, because the facility was becoming more and more expensive to operate during the nonsummer months, the board of directors instructed its Executive Director to draft a plan either to close the Ranch from September through May or to increase substantially fee-generated revenues during that time period.
>
> A market analysis was conducted by the club's staff which identified the potential markets that might use the camp and the shortsightedness of the present strategy. In 1986, the Ranch was funded 50 percent by fees paid by summer campers and 40 percent by direct contributions. Three quarters of the year (i.e., the nonsummer months) only generated 10 percent of the revenue.
>
> Our solution was to segment our market into three revenue centers: (1) summer camp (which, although not self-sufficient, was viewed as a "sacred cow" because of its place in the origin and history of the camp), (2) church retreat groups (of the few groups using the facility prior to 1986, churches made up over 80 percent, and the number of churches within a two-hour radius of the camp was significant), and (3) outdoor education (since Proposition 13's impact on public funding had been fully felt, and because of increased interest in environmental issues, we believed it to be a viable potential market).
>
> The results have been staggering. Through November 30 of 1989, Ranch revenue is almost triple what it was in 1986. Share of revenue is now (1) summer camp, 19 percent; (2) contributions, 11 percent; (3) churches, 35 percent; (4) outdoor education, 35 percent. Contribution monies have increased as a total, but are no longer being used for operating. Over $400,000 in capital improvements have been made since 1987 due in part to the ability to focus that market toward physical improvements rather than operating expense.
>
> The most significant reason for increases in revenue has come from segmenting the viable markets and focusing on each of them as a revenue center rather than viewing the entire market singularly and not having significant penetration into any of them.

SOURCE: James Coston, personal correspondence, November 30, 1989.

economies. It is "the marketing counterpart to standardization and mass production in manufacturing."[19] Product costs, research costs, media costs, and training costs are all kept low through promoting only one offering. The lower cost, however, is accompanied by reduced consumer satisfaction through failure of the organization to meet individually varying needs. Competitors have an incentive to reach and serve the neglected segments, and become strongly entrenched in these segments.

Differentiated Marketing

Under differentiated marketing, an organization decides to operate in two or more segments of the market but designs separate offerings and/or marketing programs for each. For example, an art museum could attempt to develop a children's wing as a differentiated addition to its regular collection. Alternatively, it could take its basic offering and attempt to position it differently for different markets. The museum could show how its artworks meet the needs of those interested in the history of various cultures as well as those who have an interest in appreciating high artistic skill. Similarly, a hospital could take its basic set of services and emphasize (1) the "tender loving care" of its nurses to an elderly market, (2) the national reputations of its leading physicians to a young professional market, and (3) the cost efficiency of its entire operation to business personnel officers.

By offering product and market variations, the organization hopes to attain higher sales and a deeper position within each market segment. It hopes that a deep position in several segments will strengthen the customers' overall identification of the organization with the offer field. Furthermore, it hopes for greater loyalty and repeat purchasing, because the organization's offerings have been bent to the customer's desire rather than the other way around.

The net effect of differentiated marketing is to create more total sales for the organization than undifferentiated marketing. However, it also tends to create higher costs of doing business. The organization has to spend more in offer management, marketing research, communication materials, advertising, and sales training. Since differentiated marketing leads to higher sales and higher costs, nothing can be said in advance about the optimality of this strategy. Some organizations push differentiated marketing too far in that they run more segmented programs than are economically feasible; some should be pruned. The majority of public and nonprofit organizations, however, probably err in not pushing differentiated marketing far enough in the light of the varying needs of their consumers.

Concentrated Marketing

Concentrated marketing occurs when an organization decides to divide the market into meaningful segments and devote its major marketing effort to one or two segments. This is often referred to as "niche marketing." Instead of spreading itself thin in many parts of the market, it concentrates on serving a particular market segment well. Through concentrated marketing the organization usually achieves a strong following and standing in a particular market segment. It enjoys greater knowledge of the market segment's needs and behavior and it also achieves operating economies through specialization in production, distribution, and promotion. This type of marketing is done, for example, by a private museum that decides to concentrate only on African art; or an environmental group that concentrates only on the problem of noise pollution; or a private foundation that awards grants only to transportation researchers.

Concentrated marketing does involve higher than normal risk, in that the market may suddenly decline or disappear. The National Foundation for Infantile Paralysis almost folded when the Salk vaccine was developed. Fortunately, the National Foundation was able to turn its huge fundraising apparatus over to another medical cause.

Choosing Among Market Selection Strategies

The actual choice of a marketing strategy depends on specific factors facing the organization. If the organization has *limited resources,* it will probably choose concentrated marketing because it does not have enough resources to relate to the whole market and/or to tailor special services for each segment. If the market is fairly *homogeneous* in its needs and desires, the organization will probably choose undifferentiated marketing because little would be gained by differentiated offerings. If the organization aspires to be a leader in several segments of the market, it will choose differentiated marketing. If *competitors* have already established dominance in all but a few segments of the market, the organization might try to concentrate its marketing in one of the remaining segments. Many organizations start out with a strategy of undifferentiated or concentrated marketing and, if they are successful, evolve into a strategy of differentiated marketing. If the organization elects to use a concentrated or differentiated strategy, it has to evaluate the best segment(s) to serve. Each should be evaluated in terms of its relative attractiveness, the requirements for success within it, and the organization's strengths and weaknesses in competing effectively. The organization should focus on market segments that have intrinsic attractiveness and that it has a differential advantage in serving.

SUMMARY

Once an organization has analyzed its marketing environment and its internal strengths and weaknesses, it needs to develop a core marketing strategy. The core marketing strategy involves selecting key target segments, carefully positioning the organization, and then coordinating a set of marketing mix elements to implement the positioning to the target segments. The core marketing strategy must be customer-centered, visionary, differentiating, sustainable, easily communicated, motivating, and flexible.

Four approaches to market segmentation are mass marketing, differentiated marketing, target marketing, and niche marketing. Segmenting the market requires partitioning the market into subgroups that are mutually exclusive, exhaustive, measurable, accessible, substantial, and possessing differential responsiveness. Bases for segmentation are general or specific, objective or inferred. Many marketers think first of simple objective general measures such as age, income, geographic location, and marital status. Over the years, more complex general objective measures such as social class and family life cycle and inferred general measures such as values and life-styles have become more popular.

Specific bases for segmentation apply to the specific product or service. They include objective measures such as user status, usage rate, and loyalty. Inferred specific measures include beliefs, benefits, and perceived sacrifices. Organization markets can be segmented by organization size, interest profile, buying criteria, buying process, and degree of local autonomy.

Organizations can target their markets by undifferentiated, differentiated, or concentrated marketing. Choices among these options depend on organization resources, its strengths and weaknesses, the relative homogeneity of the segments, and competitive activity.

QUESTIONS

1. Outline four segmentation bases in each of the four quadrants of Figure 5-3 that could be the starting point for target marketing for a small college.
2. Under what circumstances would it be sound strategy for a family planning program in a developing country to carry out an undifferentiated segmentation strategy?
3. Suggest ten possible segments on which the symphony orchestra in your community (or one nearby) might focus. How should it choose which ones to focus on?
4. Under what circumstances would it be good strategy for the symphony orchestra discussed in Question 3 to adopt multiple strategies matched to various market segments? Under what conditions would this be extremely foolish?
5. Conduct a "laddering" exercise with a friend to learn the underlying basic values that led to his or her choice of a college or university. How could these values be used to develop a core marketing strategy for this institution?

NOTES

1. Michael E. Porter, *Competitive Strategy: Techniques for Analyzing Industries and Competitors* (New York: The Free Press, 1980).
2. A basic review of the segmentation literature is found in Ronald E. Frank, William F. Massy, and Yoram Wind, *Market Segmentation* (Englewood Cliffs, N.J.: Prentice-Hall, 1972). See also Yoram Wind, "Issues and Advances in Segmentation Research," *Journal of Marketing Research*, August 1978, pp. 317–337.
3. *Marginal response* is the change in response to a unit change in a control variable such as price or advertising expenditure.

4. Frank, Massy, and Wind, *Market Segmentation.*

5. Bob Minzesheimer, "You Are What You ZIP!" *Los Angeles*, November 1984, pp. 175–192.

6. Stephen J. Miller, "Source of Income as a Market Descriptor," *Journal of Marketing Research*, February 1978, pp.129–131.

7. See John E. Robbins and Stephanie S. Robbins, "Segmentation for 'Fine Arts' Marketing: Is King Tut Classless as well as Ageless?" in Neil Beckwith, Michael Houston, Robert Mittelstaedt, Kent B. Monroe, and Scott Ward, eds., *1979 Educator's Conference Proceedings* (Chicago: American Marketing Association, 1979), pp. 479–484.

8. Alan R. Andreasen, "Acquiring a Lifestyle: An Innovation Adoption Approach," working paper, Department of Marketing, California State University, Long Beach, 1988.

9. For a more complex approach, see Patrick E. Murphy and William Staples, "A Modernized Family Life Cycle," *Journal of Consumer Research*, June 1979, pp. 12–22.

10. Leland L. Beik and Scott M. Smith, "Practical Segmentation: A Fund Raising Example," Working Paper No. 68, College of Business Administration, Pennsylvania State University, February 1978.

11. Their analysis also included a second function using five variables to separate those who were not large medical givers into those who were large and small donors to all charities.

12. Christopher H. Lovelock, "A Market Segmentation Approach to Transit Planning, Modeling, and Management," *Proceedings, Sixteenth Annual Meeting Transportation Research Forum* (1975).

13. Richard J. Semenik and Clifford E. Young, "Market Segmentation in Arts Organizations," in Beckwith, Houston, Mittelstaedt, Monroe, and Ward, eds., *1979 Educators' Conference*, pp. 474–478.

14. Milton J. Rokeach, *The Nature of Human Values* (New York: The Free Press, 1973). See also Donald E. Vinson, J. Michael Munson, and Masao Nakanishi, "An Investigation of the Rokeach Value Survey for Consumer Research Applications," in W.D. Perrault, ed., *Advances in Consumer Research*, Vol. 4 (Atlanta, Ga.: Association for Consumer Research, 1977), pp. 247–252; and Robert E. Pitts, Jr., and Arch G. Woodside, eds., *Personal Values and Consumer Psychology* (Lexington, Mass.: Lexington Books, 1984).

15. Thomas J. Reynolds and Jonathan Gutman, "Laddering: Extending the Repertory Grid Methodology to Construct Attribute-Consequence-Value Hierarchies," in Pitts and Woodside, eds., *Personal Values and Consumer Psychology*, pp. 155–168.

16. Martha Frarnsworth Riche, "Psychographics for the 1990s," *American Demographics*, July 1989.

17. See Paul E. Green, Yoram Wind, and Arun K. Jain, "Benefit Bundle Analysis," *Journal of Advertising Research*, April 1972, pp. 31–36.

18. See Wendell R. Smith, "Product Differentiation and Market Segmentation," *Business Horizons*, Fall 1961, pp. 65–72.

19. Smith, "Product Differentiation."

6

Developing a Marketing Strategy: Positioning the Organization

Cities, like products and people, have images. Chicago is windy. Detroit is the home of snow and chicken wings. New York is frenetic and rude. Los Angeles is la-la land.

Images can attract tourists and they can repel them. Images can appeal to businesses or drive them elsewhere.

West Hollywood is a city with an image that it would like to change. Adjacent to Hollywood and Beverly Hills, West Hollywood is the home of much of Los Angeles's gay community and has been called the "Gay Camelot." Its city council is predominantly gay and it has some of the most liberal gay rights ordinances in the country.

And, while it is proud of its reputation, West Hollywood would also like the tourist and business worlds to know that it is a major center of creative expression in the Los Angeles area. To change its image, West Hollywood in 1987 established the West Hollywood Marketing Corp. and hired a marketing director, Rick Cole, to bring a new message to the rest of the world.

Since 1987, Cole's office has been the source of a continuing stream of brochures, street banners, catalogues, news releases, and speeches touting West Hollywood as an artistic and avant-garde community that can be compared to New York's Greenwich Village and Paris's Left Bank. Cole's strategy is to point out that West Hollywood derives more than 40 percent of its revenues from creative activities and should be a major destination for both adventurous tourists and "creativity" businesses that might wish to locate in an area "Where Creativity Gets Down to Business."

Source: Information contained in Alan Citron, "West Hollywood—Small Thinking Big," *Los Angeles Times,* July 10, 1989, Metro, Part 2, p. 1, and author's personal conversation with Rick Cole.

It is always possible for an organization to survive on the basis of a modest relative advantage. Small charities can always find some people who have a little cash to spare or a moderate interest in the charity's cause. A mediocre university can always count on students who appreciate the convenience of the campus location or the relatively low fees. An undistinguished hospital can always count on serving physicians who have nearby offices or who cannot obtain staff privileges at a major institution.

However, a lack of attention to positioning inevitably means that the organization's modest advantage can always be taken away by more aggressive competitors. Someone can offer slightly lower prices or move itself or a branch outlet closer to customers. To be truly successful in the long run, a nonprofit must establish a *differentiated market position* (1) that cannot easily be duplicated by competitors and (2) that causes potential target customers to bypass more accessible or lower cost marketers to patronize it. Positioning is a matter of both substance and perception. The organization must truly have a set of offerings and ways of presenting it that *can* differentiate it from the competition. However, it is important that customers *perceive* this different position.

MEASURING THE ORGANIZATION'S POSITION

The starting point for any positioning strategy is to understand how the organization is perceived at the present time in comparison to its major competitors. This involves measurement of what is often called "image." Image is a term that became popular in the 1950s and has been used to describe products (Ford Mustang, MacIntosh Computer), institutions (Harvard, McDonalds, the United Way, IBM), individuals (Donald Trump, George Bush), and places (San Francisco, Thailand, Brooklyn). Our definition of image is as follows:

> An **image** is the sum of beliefs, ideas, and impressions that a person has of an object.

This definition enables us to distinguish an image from similar-sounding concepts such as *beliefs, attitudes,* and *stereotypes.*

An image is more than a simple belief. The belief that the American Medical Association (AMA) is more interested in serving doctors than serving society would be only one element of a larger image that might be held about the AMA. An image is a whole set of beliefs about an object.

On the other hand, people's images of an object do not necessarily reveal their attitudes toward that object. Two persons may hold the same image of the AMA and yet have different attitudes toward it because of different weights they place on the beliefs.

How does an image differ from a stereotype? A stereotype suggests a widely held image that is highly distorted and simplistic and that carries a favorable or unfavorable attitude toward the object. An image, on the other hand, is a more personal perception of an object that can vary greatly from person to person.

Image Measurement. Many methods have been proposed for measuring images. We will describe a two-step approach: first, measuring how familiar and favorable the organization's image is and, second, measuring the organization's image along major relevant dimensions.

FAMILIARITY-FAVORABILITY MEASUREMENT. The first step is to establish, for each public being studied, how familiar they are with the organization and how favorable they feel toward it. To establish familiarity, respondents are asked to check one of the following:

Never heard of	Heard of	Know a little bit	Know a fair amount	Know very well

The results indicate the public's awareness of the organization. If most of the respondents place the organization in the first two or three categories, then the organization has an awareness problem.

Those respondents who have some familiarity with the organization are then asked to describe how favorable they feel toward it by checking one of the following:

Very unfavorable	Somewhat unfavorable	Indifferent	Somewhat favorable	Very favorable

If most of the respondents check the first two or three categories, then the organization has a serious positioning problem.

SEMANTIC DIFFERENTIAL. The organization must go further and research the content of its image. One of the most popular tools for this is the semantic differential.[1] It involves the following steps:

1   *Developing a set of relevant dimensions.* The researcher first asks people to identify the dimensions they would use in thinking about the object. People could be asked: "What things do you think of when you consider a hospital?" If someone suggests "quality of medical care," this would be turned into a bipolar adjective scale—say, "inferior medical care" at one end and "superior medical care" at the other. This could be rendered as a five- or seven-point scale. A set of additional relevant dimensions for a hospital is shown in Figure 6-1.

2   *Reducing the set of relevant dimensions.* The number of dimensions should be kept small to avoid respondent fatigue in having to rate n organizations on m scales. Osgood and his coworkers feel that there are essentially three types of scales:
    a   evaluation scales (good-bad qualities)
    b   potency scales (strong-weak qualities)
    c   activity scales (active-passive qualities)
    Using these scales as a guide, or performing a factor analysis, the researcher can remove redundant scales that fail to add much information.

3   *Administering the instrument to a sample of respondents.* The respondents are asked to rate one organization at a time. The bipolar adjectives should be arranged so as not to load all of the poor adjectives on one side.

4   *Averaging the results.* Figure 6-1 shows the results of averaging the respondents' pictures of hospitals A, B, and C. Each hospital's image is represented by a vertical "line of means" that summarizes how the average respondent sees that institution. Thus Hospital A is seen as a large, modern, friendly, and superior hospital. Hospital C, on the other hand, is seen as a small, dated, impersonal, and inferior hospital.

5   *Checking on the image variance.* Since each image profile is a line of means, it does not reveal how variable the image actually is. If there were 100 respondents, did they all see Hospital B, for example, exactly as shown, or was there little or considerable variation? In the first case, we would say that the image is highly *specific* and in the second case that the image is highly *diffused.* The organization will want to analyze whether a variable image is really the result of different subgroups rating the organization with each subgroup having a highly specific image.

DIRECT ATTITUDE MEASUREMENT.   An alternative to the semantic differential image model is the use of the expectancy-value *attitude* model described in Chapter 4. This approach involves developing an image measure that comprises

1   Beliefs about the positive and negative consequences of taking an action with respect to the attitude object (actions like entering a hospital, giving the hospital money, offering the hospital a tax break).

2   Weights attached subjectively to each of the consequences.

The advantage of the expectancy-value attitude measurement approach is that it focuses on *behavior,* which is usually what is critical to the nonprofit. The semantic differential more often focuses on an object or institution. The attitude measure also indicates weighting differences on the beliefs held by different critical publics. Since the latter reflect these publics' goals and values, such information can prove very valuable to the nonprofit manager when the time comes to try to *change* the organization's positioning.

FIGURE 6-1

Images of Three Hospitals (Semantic Differential)

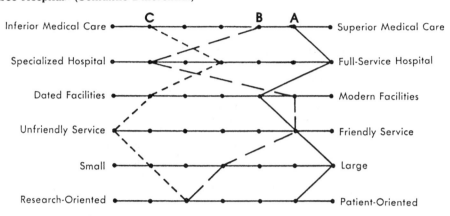

POSITIONING THE ORGANIZATION

Positioning Alternatives.   The specific positioning the organization adopts will depend very much on its analysis of its market segments, its competition, and its own strengths and weaknesses. Some organizations choose to leave their position relatively fuzzy in the hopes that disparate market segments will find something in the positioning that addresses their needs. While this may succeed on occasion (usually when there is no major competition), it is our view that, in an increasingly competitive nonprofit marketplace, it is the organization with the distinctly different competitive advantage that will survive and prosper.

We define positioning as follows:

> **Positioning** is the act of designing the organization's image and value offer so that the organization's customers understand and appreciate what the organization stands for in relation to its competitors.

It is possible to have different positions in different market segments. However, in the nonprofit sector, it is more typical for a single organization to attempt to develop a single image.

Optimally, the nonprofit should "own" the position it develops much as Hertz is seen as the world's largest car rental company, Disney as the premier children's entertainment company, and the American Red Cross as the United States' major blood collection agency.

As noted earlier, positioning involves (1) creating a real differentiation and (2) making it known to others. Ries and Trout, in their book, *Positioning: The Battle for Your Mind,*[2] argue that differentiation is largely a creative exercise carried out with an existing organization or product. They propose three strategies:

1 *Build upon your present strengths.* Avis capitalized creatively on what would appear to be a weak second place status with its "We Try Harder" positioning. In a similar manner, a hospital with only limited facilities could emphasize its concern with being very good in a concentrated number of very important areas of health care.

2 *Search for a niche.* If every hospital in an area understaffs its emergency room and uses interns and residents to treat most patients there, an innovative hospital could position itself as having an emergency room that treats everyone quickly and personally, and with the highest-quality medical staff.

3 *Reposition the competition.* Wendy's hamburger chain challenged the opposition by asking "Where's the beef?" A hospital without all the latest in medical technology could ask "Where are the people?" in an advertisement showing a high-tech hypothetical competitor treating a patient as merely a serial number!

In the majority of these cases, however, claimed differences must be backed with reality. A quick-serving emergency room must meet explicit turnaround objectives. A personalized hospital must stress and reward high-quality patient care.

The organization might strive for any of four long-term positions:[3]

- *Market leader.* If the organization has an excellent offering, is well regarded, has superior distribution, has broad resources for future battles, and competition is expected to be relatively weak, the organization can choose to maintain or enhance its leadership position. The U.S. Post Office has recently adopted this posture with considerable success.

- *Market challenger.* If the organization is not the market leader and the market leader is formidable and has clear long-term advantages, an organization has three options. The first of these is not to cede but to challenge the market leader or other firms in the industry. Contraceptive social marketers in several countries, while cooperating with larger government programs, have often acted as market challengers to prove that their way of marketing is superior in the long run.

- *Market follower.* Another option is to play follow the leader. There are many excellent reasons for adopting this strategy. First, it is a good choice if the market leader is tough or has substantial resources that would make a challenger strategy too costly. Second, imitating but not challenging a smart and innovative leader can lead to effective and efficient results. The market follower can save countless dollars and a great deal of managerial time and mental energy by not having to continually develop effective challenging strategies. Finally, a follower strategy often makes good sense as part of an overall portfolio strategy. A "follower" offering can often serve as a "cash cow," providing resources to other sectors of the enterprise. Thus, a me-too strategy is appropriate for book and gift shop operations in many museums and hospitals. These shops can watch what the Hallmark, Rizzolis, or Waldenbooks of the area are currently doing and follow their lead.

- *Market nicher.* This final strategy is one that is adopted by a number of nonprofits. The organization finds a set (or sets) of target customers whose needs are not well met by other marketers and devotes itself to that segment. Thus, a theater group in a large city might decide to specialize in producing only the plays of Shakespeare and therefore serve only the interests of theatergoers who love Shakespeare.

These four positioning options have further ramifications in terms of both choice requirements and tactical suboptions. Each will be discussed in turn.

Market Leader Strategies

In mature markets, there is usually a market leader who signals pricing changes, develops innovations, leads on legislative tactics, and so on. The leader may or may not be admired or respected. In the private sector, market leaders include General Motors, Kodak, and IBM. The nonprofit sector also has its leaders, including the Metropolitan Museum of Art in New York (art galleries), Harvard Business School (executive education programs), the United Way (charities), the Metropolitan Opera (opera companies), the Sierra Club (environmental protection agencies), Ralph Nader (consumer spokespeople), and the American Red Cross (blood donation agencies).

Unless the dominant firm enjoys a legal monopoly, it must maintain constant vigilance. Other firms will challenge its strengths or take advantage of its weaknesses. The dominant firm might look old-fashioned compared to newer and more aggressive rivals, as is the case for many old-line hospitals facing competition from high-tech, high-efficiency walk-in medical centers.

Dominant firms want to remain number one. This calls for action on three fronts. First, the firm must find ways to expand total demand. Second, the firm must protect its current market share through good defensive and offensive actions. Third, the firm can try to expand its market share further, even if market size remains constant.

Expanding the Total Market.   The dominant firm normally gains the most when the total market expands for one reason or another. If Americans are persuaded to allocate more to private charities, the United Way stands to gain the most. The United Way benefits if it convinces more people to give or persuades current givers to give more frequently, or to give larger amounts. In general, the leader should look for *new users, new uses,* and *more usage* of its products.

NEW USERS.   Every offering has the potential for attracting buyers who are unaware of the offer or who are resisting it because of its perceived cost or lack of certain features. An organization can search for new users among three groups. A university survey research center, for example, can try to convince academic departments that do not use research to do so *(market penetration strategy)*. It can convince private firms to start using the university's research capability *(new market strategy)*. Or it could sell its services in other cities or states *(geographical-expansion strategy)*. The University of Michigan's Survey Research Center has now developed a national and even an international clientele, to whom it sells special and continuing studies as well as reports, monographs, and books. Its survey of consumer buying intentions is eagerly awaited each quarter by business people, politicians, and the general media.

NEW USES.   Markets can be expanded by discovering and promoting new uses for a product or new ways of making exchanges. Thus, museums hold concerts, free admission days, or special tours or lectures as ways of promoting increased usage by their present attendees.

MORE USAGE.   The market leader can attempt to convince people to use more of the product or service per use occasion. Thus, universities and hospitals have devised a number of innovative estate planning arrangements to get wealthier individuals to transfer more of their wealth to the institution. Performing arts centers provide restaurants or bar facilities and operate gift shops as a means of getting higher expenditures from each visitor.

Protecting Market Share.   While trying to expand total market size, the dominant firm must continuously protect its current business against competitive attacks. The leader is like a large elephant constantly being stung by bees. What can the leader do to protect itself? The most constructive response is *continuous innovation,* in which the leader refuses to be content with the way things are and leads the industry in new product ideas, customer services, distribution improvement, and cost cutting. It keeps increasing real and perceived value to customers. The leader applies the military principle that the best defense is a good offense by exercising initiative, setting the pace, and exploiting competitors' weaknesses.

The leader, even when it does not launch offensives, must guard its fronts and not leave any flanks exposed. It must keep its costs down, and its prices must be consonant with the value the customers perceive in the offering. The leader must "plug holes" so that the challengers and nichers don't jump in. Thus, a major art museum may add a collection of contemporary art to forestall the formation of a new contemporary art museum.

Expanding Market Share.   Market leaders can also try to grow by increasing their market share, even if the total market has stabilized. A series of studies in the private sector has led some management experts to conclude that firms with higher market shares enjoy higher surpluses. Thus, the well-publicized *profit impact of management strategies (PIMS)* studies indicate that *profitability* (measured by pretax return on investment) rises linearly with *market share.*[4] The rationale offered for these findings is lowered costs. First, as an organization grows, it achieves scale economies not available to its smaller rivals. Thus, it can produce its products or services cheaper, buy its television or magazine advertising at less cost, and borrow its capital at lower rates. Second, as it grows, it learns how to produce and market in better ways. Thus, if one is producing five television ads or direct-mail pieces per quarter, one gets a lot better at it (especially if one continually experiments and conducts evaluation studies) than a rival who prepares only one ad or mailer per quarter.

Other studies have suggested that a V-shaped relationship between market share and profitability in many industries is "more correct."[5] Such industries have one or a few highly profitable leaders, several profitable small and more highly focused firms, and a large number of medium-sized firms with poorer profit performances. As an example, many medium-sized management consulting firms don't do as well as small specialized firms or the large leaders who share stronger reputations and resources. The message is that medium-sized organizations need to figure out how to break into the big league or else settle into specialized niches where they can do outstanding work.

Medium-sized organizations must not think, however, that gaining increased market share will automatically improve their performance. Much depends on their strategy for gaining increased market share, whether it is through offering higher quality, lower cost, or some other procedure. There are many high-market-share companies with low profitability and many low-market-share companies with high profitability. The cost of buying higher market share may far exceed its revenue value.

Market Challenger Strategies

The organizations that occupy second, third, and lower ranks in an industry can still be quite large in their own right, such as the Columbia Graduate School of Business and the New York City Opera Company. These runner-up firms can adopt one of two postures. They can attack the leader and other competitors in an aggressive bid for further market share (market challengers). Or they can simply watch the leader and mimic what seems to work for them (market followers).

A nonprofit organization that decides to be a market challenger must first define its strategic objective. Basically, the challenger can choose to attack one of three types of firms:

- It can attack the market leader. This is a high-risk but potentially high-payoff strategy and makes good sense if the leader is not a "true leader" and is not serving customer needs well. The "terrain" to examine closely is consumer need or dissatisfaction. If a substantial consumer group is unserved or poorly served by the leader, it offers a great strategic target. Alternatively, the challenger might attempt to outinnovate the leader across all segments.
- The challenger could attack organizations of its own size that are doing a poor job or that are underfinanced. Both consumer satisfaction and innovation potential should be examined for opportunities.
- The challenger could attack smaller organizations that are not doing the job and are underfinanced. Many major hospitals are growing not by taking away each other's customers so much as by gobbling up the "small fry" competitors.

Several strategic alternatives are available to the market challenger:

1 *Cost discount strategy.* Challengers can try to attract patrons with an offering comparable to the leader's at a lower cost (both economic and psychological). Thus, a college can charge a lower tuition but offer comparable quality. For a cost discount strategy to work, three assumptions must be fulfilled. First, the

challenger must convince buyers that its product and service are comparable to the leader's. Second, the buyers must be cost aware and cost sensitive. Third, the market leader must fail to respond to the competitor's cost discount.

2 *Cheaper goods strategy.* Another strategy is to offer the market a lower-quality product than the competitor's at a lower cost. This works when there are enough buyers who are primarily interested in the cost. Organizations that get established through this strategy, however, may be attacked by firms whose costs are even lower. In defense, they might try to upgrade their quality over time. Some mail-order nonprofit educational institutions appear to be following this strategy.

3 *Prestige goods strategy.* A market challenger can launch a higher-quality product and charge a higher price than the leader. Stanford, Wharton, and Northwestern all argue that they offer higher quality (for example, more analytical) executive programs than the leader, Harvard. Some prestige goods organizations later roll out lower-price products to take advantage of their prestige.

4 *Product proliferation strategy.* The challenger can attack the leader by launching a larger number of offerings. UCLA's Performing Arts Center offers its potential subscribers over a dozen different packages of events to compete with the nearby Ambassador Auditorium and the Los Angeles Music Center.

5 *Product innovation strategy.* The challenger may try to be more innovative than the leader. Thus, the New York City Opera offers less commonly performed quality operas, compared to the traditional fare of the Met. The public often gains the most from challenger strategies oriented toward offer innovation.

6 *Improved services strategy.* The challenger might find ways to offer new or better services to customers. A performing arts center that builds better parking facilities would be following this strategy.

7 *Distribution innovation strategy.* A challenger might discover or develop a new channel of distribution. Goodwill Industries in Los Angeles now places semi-trailers in shopping mall parking lots to make it easier for shoppers and nearby residents to donate used goods.

8 *Operating-cost reduction strategy.* The challenger might seek to achieve lower operating costs than its competitors through more efficient purchasing, lower labor costs, and more modern production equipment. The organization can use its lower cost to price more aggressively in order to gain more market share.

9 *Intensive advertising and promotion strategy.* Some challengers attack the leader by increasing their expenditures on advertising and promotion. Substantial promotional spending, however, is usually not a sensible strategy unless the challenger's product or advertising is distinctive or superior to the competitor's.

A challenger rarely improves its market share by relying on only one of the nine strategy elements. Its success depends on designing a strategy made up of several elements that will improve its position over time.

Market Follower Strategies

Many organizations do not attempt to wrest more share from the leader or others. They may be content to play a follower role.

A market follower needs to know how to hold current customers. The market follower must keep its costs low and its quality high. It must also enter new markets as they open up. Followership is not the same as being passive or a carbon copy of the leader. The follower has to define a growth path, but one that does not create competitive retaliation. Three broad followership strategies can be distinguished:

- *Following closely.* Here, the follower emulates the leader in as many market segments and marketing-mix elements as possible. Some followers act like parasites in that they put very little into stimulating the market, hoping to live off the market leader's investments.
- *Following at a distance.* Here, the follower maintains some differentiation but follows the leader in terms of major market innovations, general price levels, and distribution. This follower is quite acceptable to the market leader, who may see little interference with its market plans and may be pleased that the follower's market share helps the leader avoid charges of monopolization. The distant follower may achieve its growth through acquiring smaller organizations in the industry.
- *Following selectively.* This organization follows the leader quite closely in some ways and sometimes goes its own way. The organization may be quite innovative, yet avoid direct competition by following only some of the strategies of the leaders.

Market followers, although they have lower market shares, may be as profitable or even more profitable than the leader. A recent study reported that many companies with less than half the market share of the leader had a five-year average return on equity that surpassed the industry median.[6] The keys to their success were conscious market segmentation and concentration, effective research and development, profit emphasis rather than market share emphasis, and strong top management.

Market Nicher Strategies

Almost every industry includes organizations that specialize in parts of the market where they avoid clashes with the majors. These organizations occupy market niches that they serve effectively through specialization and that the majors are likely to overlook or ignore. These firms try to find one or more market niches that are safe and profitable. The niche should have the following characteristics:

- The niche is of sufficient size and purchasing power to be profitable, or at least self-paying.
- The niche has growth potential.
- The niche is of negligible interest to major competitors.
- The organization has the required skills and resources to meet the niche's success requirements.
- The organization can defend itself against an attacking major competitor through the customer goodwill it has built up.

The key idea in nichemanship is specialization. The firm has to specialize along market, customer, product, or marketing-mix lines. Here are several specialist roles open to a market nicher:

- *End-use specialist.* The organization specializes in serving one type of end-use customer. A welfare agency, for example, can specialize in serving only poor unmarried mothers.
- *Vertical-level specialist.* The organization specializes at some vertical level of the production-distribution cycle. A university research center, for example, could specialize in research design, field work, or data analysis.
- *Customer-size specialist.* The organization sells to small-, medium-, or large-size customers. Many nichers specialize in serving small customers who are neglected by the majors.
- *Specific-customer specialist.* The organization limits its selling to one or a few major customers. Some nonprofit consulting firms have the government as their only client.
- *Geographic specialist.* The organization sells only in a certain locality, region, or area of the world. Thus, the Chicago Trust limits itself to supporting good causes in the Chicago area.
- *Product or product line specialist.* The organization produces only one product line or product. Museums can specialize in one type of art, pianists in one type of music, and some small colleges in one type of curriculum (for example, liberal arts).
- *Product-feature specialist.* The organization specializes in producing a certain type of offering or offer feature. The University of Western Ontario specializes in the case method of teaching, while Carnegie Tech emphasizes quantitative analysis.
- *Job-shop specialist.* The organization produces customized products as ordered by the customer. Some colleges will design educational or training programs for particular firms.
- *Quality or price specialist.* The organization operates at the low or high end of the market. The University of Southern California specializes in the high-quality, high-price end of the executive education market in Los Angeles.
- *Service specialist.* The organization offers one or more services not available from other firms. An example would be a hospital that permits new fathers to sleep in the hospital room with the new mother and child.

Niching carries a major risk in that the market niche may shrink or be attacked. That is why *multiple niching* is preferable to *single niching*. By developing leadership in two or more niches, the organization increases its chances for survival. Even some large organizations prefer a multiple-niche strategy instead of serving the total market. Thus, Northwestern University has developed an excellent reputation in several professional education areas, including business, engineering, law, and medicine.

DESIGNING THE MARKETING MIX

One of the advantages of a carefully defined competitive position is that it makes transparently clear (1) the principal elements that must be in the marketing mix to carry out the positioning and (2) the need for careful coordination of that mix. If an organization adopts a "high-quality" positioning then its offerings should be of uniformly high quality, its prices should be above average, it should have high-quality facilities or outlets, and it should advertise in only the best media. If any one element of this mix is out of synchrony, the entire core strategy may be effectively sabotaged. A high-quality position can be undermined by "little things" such as low-quality stationery, handlettered signage, poorly dressed or ungrammatical customer contact personnel, sloppy accounting, and so forth.

We consider the issues involved in developing effective tactics within each element of the marketing mix in Chapters 12 through 21. A case study illustrating the design of an effective core marketing strategy is included in Exhibit 6-1.

EXHIBIT 6-1

Positioning the San Gabriel Valley: A Case Study

The San Gabriel Valley, a region of the Los Angeles metropolitan area, was concerned in 1989 that it had no "presence' in the highly competitive local market and had no unique appeal it could offer to prospective office and factory owners, residents, vacationers, or conventiongoers. It needed a marketing strategy that would not only increase its market presence but, more important, would meet its objectives of increasing *quality growth* while making the lives of its existing residents and workers more satisfying. After a careful internal study of the cities in the valley and external study of target markets and competitors, strategists concluded that there were three *basic target markets* for which the core marketing strategy would be aimed:

1 *External Sources of Commercial and Industrial Development.* These would include real estate developers, office location services, and *Fortune* 500 firms. Emphasis would be on *quality* firms that will bring upscale employment, attractive facilities, and a progressive and socially responsible attitude to the valley.

2 *Facilitating Agencies.* These would include banks and other financial agencies, advertising and public relations firms, local and national media, and other organizations who might be expected to assist in marketing the valley, either intentionally or unintentionally.

3 *Internal Supporters and Implementors.* These would include all individuals and agencies within the valley who can implement or support the strategic marketing plan:

   a Local government employees who will directly or indirectly deliver the products or services the program envisions.

   b Private sector support agencies that can take specific roles in the program. These would include Chambers of Commerce, local realtors, and financial institutions.

   c Existing businesses in the area who can "spread the word" as well as participate in specific tactical programs designed to carry out the strategic marketing plan.

   d Local citizens who also can spread the word and participate in the program.

In light of what was learned about (1) the site selection criteria used by external markets, (2) the image these markets held of the San Gabriel Valley and its two major competitors, and (3) the area's strengths and weaknesses, the following three elements were proposed to comprise the valley's *competitive positioning:*

1   The San Gabriel Valley should be positioned as comprising a rich *mosaic* of established, yet vibrant and progressive, neighborhoods representing many diverse cultures and physical environments at all levels of the economic spectrum.

2   The San Gabriel Valley should be positioned as a community just adjacent to the center of the Los Angeles metropolitan hub that has extremely convenient access by freeway to all of Southern California and by air and rail to all of the world.

3   The San Gabriel Valley should be positioned as a place where government and business is devoted to being totally "user-friendly" in its public and private services.

The core marketing strategy chosen for the San Gabriel Valley meets the criteria for an effective strategy as follows:

1   It *addresses the needs of external target markets* for good location choices. The San Gabriel Valley can argue that it has a diversity of neighborhoods to meet the needs of corporations who want an area where (a) they can find all types of labor and/or (b) all their staff can find areas to live *nearby* that fit their life-styles and pocketbooks.

2   It *addresses the needs of external target markets* for relative ease and efficiency in the *process* of building facilities, relocating, and/or running their enterprises. The San Gabriel Valley can argue that its governments are committed to being as responsive and user-friendly as possible. The field survey noted that three of the top 20 traits ranked by developers involved some aspect of government management (e.g., attitude toward growth, quality of local government management, and accessibility of local government officials). At the same time, they saw *no differences* in the quality of management among the three competing governments, although they perceived the one competitor, "the Inland Empire," to be more accessible and more in favor of high growth (which the majority of those interviewed preferred). It is critical to the proposed strategy that the San Gabriel Valley supplant the Inland Empire as *most accessible.*

3   It *addresses the needs of residents* offering them a basis for pride in the valley as a whole as well as in the individuality of their own communities.

4   It *addresses the needs of community leaders.* Leaders can be challenged to find ways to accentuate even more the special character of their neighborhoods. Businesspeople and government staffers can make their stores and services even more user-friendly.

5   The positioning clearly *differentiates* the valley from its two major competitors in a way that is, with some work, *sustainable* in that the other two competitive markets, Orange County and the Inland Em-

pire, will find it difficult to argue that they have similar accessibility and neighborhood diversity. The user friendliness is theoretically something that the other two areas *could* imitate. However, if the San Gabriel Valley (a) moves rapidly to become the *first* to adopt this positioning and (b) is *best* at making sure that reality matches the promise of user-friendliness, it should be able to make this positioning uniquely its own.

6   The positioning is *flexible* in that it allows each community, each government, and each set of private-sector enterprises within the valley to decide what it will do on its own to implement the "mosaic" and "user-friendly" concepts. It is also flexible in that it can be described in different ways for different submarket segments. "User-friendly" can be described one way to developers and another way to potential new residents or new retailers.

7   The positioning is *easily communicated* both internally and externally. The concepts are clear and can be elaborated in a number of ways in both pictures and words. The graphic possibilities for showing the diversity of neighborhoods would appear to be almost endless. Similarly, user-friendliness can be made concrete by simple, dramatic human case histories.

8   All three features, user-friendliness, geographic accessibility, and the mosaic of neighborhoods, provide *excellent story opportunities* for facilitator markets such as news media.

9   The "mosaic" concept makes the ethnic diversity of the valley a source of esteem rather than a "problem." Residents of the valley can celebrate, not fear, their cultural diversity.

SOURCE: Prepared by Consultants to Public Technology, Inc. Reproduced with permission of the City of West Covina.

REMAINING STEPS IN THE SMPP PROCESS

Developing Structure, Tactics, and Benchmarks

The next phase of the strategic marketing management process outlined in Figure 3-1 is to take three steps more or less simultaneously to set the stage for implementing the core marketing strategy defined in the preceding stage. These steps are the following:

1   Developing an *organizational structure* and a set of *management systems* within the marketing group to carry out the marketing strategy. In any particular strategic planning cycle, this may involve adjusting an existing structure or set of systems or may require the development of entirely new ones. We take up these issues in Chapter 11. It may also involve creating bases of support from others in terms of goods, services, and/or skills (discussed in Chapter 10) or implementing specific fund-raising activities (discussed in Chapter 9).

2   At the same time, detailed *tactics* must be specified for carrying out each aspect

of the core strategy. This will involve decisions about what offerings to make (Chapters 12, 13, 14, and 15); what channels to use and how to use them (Chapter 17); how to manage consumer costs (Chapter 16); and what communications tactics to use through advertising and sales promotion (Chapter 19); personal selling (Chapter 21); and public relations (Chapter 20).

3 *Benchmarks* must be developed reflecting the core strategy's goals and objectives so that, after implementation, marketing management can learn whether its strategy, structure, and tactics are achieving what is expected of them.

Implementing and Assessing Marketing Strategy.   If the strategic planning process has worked well, the task of implementation should be straightforward. However, it is extremely important that everyone who must carry it out—or at least not get in its way—understand what it is all about. Many organizations produce attractive booklets summarizing their strategic approach for both internal and external distribution. Some find that a graphic representation is very effective. Figure 6-2 shows how the United Way of America communicates to others its mission and how that mission is carried out by five core strategies and eight supportive programs.

Finally, it should be noted that the strategic marketing planning process is not complete until management consciously and systematically assesses how well it is performing. While we discuss these issues in more detail in Chapter 22, management must realize that this assessment step is crucial both to permit short-run and on-the-run fine tuning of core strategy, marketing organization structure, and marketing tactics and to feed into subsequent cycles of this critical strategic marketing planning process.

SUMMARY

Organization positioning involves setting the organization apart from competitors to secure a lasting, defensible place in the marketplace. Positioning involves both establishing a unique set of products and services and making sure the target market perceives them (and the organization) distinctly. This calls for image measurement. Two of the most common approaches to measurement are the semantic differential and direct attitude measurement.

Positioning involves establishing a competitive advantage for the organization that differentiates it from other marketers and then communicating that advantage clearly to target customers. Alternative positionings can build on present strengths, create a niche, or reposition competitors. The positioning strategy chosen then sets the parameters for the marketing mix and makes clear that it needs careful coordination.

In mature industries the organization must decide whether to pursue a market leader, market challenger, market follower, or market nicher strategy. Market leaders have to decide further whether they will emphasize expanding the total market, protecting market share, or expanding market share. Challengers must decide whom to challenge—the market leaders, other firms their

FIGURE 6-2

Figure Portraying the United Way of America Mission, Core
Strategies, and Support Programs

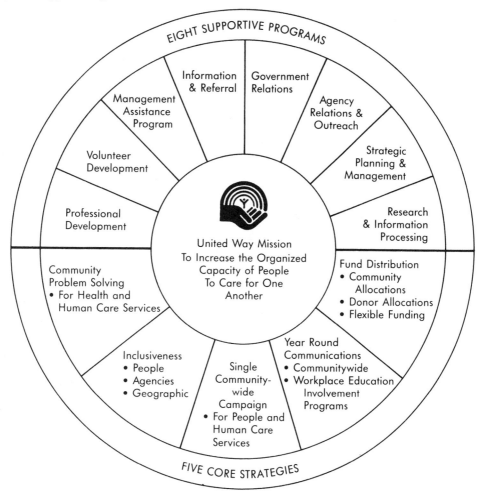

SOURCE: United Way of America. Reproduced with permission.

own size, or firms smaller than themselves. Market followers must decide
whether to follow closely, at a distance, or selectively. The market nicher must
decide on the basis of its niching strategy. For many, a multiple-niching strategy
is the most effective and safest.

The positioning strategy makes clear what the principal elements of the
organization's marketing mix must be to round out the core marketing strategy.

Once the core marketing strategy is set, the strategic marketing planning
process is completed by developing an organization structure and management

systems to carry out the marketing strategy. Next, specific tactics are established for each element of the marketing mix, and benchmarks set by which progress toward marketing goals is assessed. The final steps then involve implementation of the plan and careful assessment of its overall effects in preparation for the next round of strategic marketing planning.

QUESTIONS

1. Religion is a mature market. Characterize the marketing strategies of five religious organizations serving your community, including (if you wish) "televangelists."

2. Fitness programs at many YMCAs are in the decline stage of the offer life cycle. How should each of these Ys evaluate the effect of these programs on their market position and decide whether changes ought to be made?

3. A marketing department at a "second-tier" university in a major metropolitan area wishes to develop a niching strategy. What options are open to it? How would it choose which one to pursue?

4. The Museum of Science and Industry in a major metropolitan area wishes to measure its image using a semantic differential. It also wishes to measure the images of the local zoo, art museum, and children's museum. Suggest ten pairs of adjectives that it might use for this task. How will the Museum of Science and Industry use the results of this study to improve its market position?

5. Suppose the Museum of Science and Industry described in Question 4 learns that its image has much higher variance on six out of ten of its semantic differential scores than all of its competitors. Should it be concerned about this? How can the museum find out what it means?

NOTES

1. C. E. Osgood, G. J. Suci, and P. H. Tannenbaum, *The Measurement of Meaning* (Urbana: University of Illinois Press, 1957). Other image-measuring tools exist, such as *object sorting* (see W. A. Scott, "A Structure of Natural Cognitions," *Journal of Personality and Social Psychology*, Vol. 12, no. 4, 1969, pp. 261–278), *multidimensional scaling* [see Paul E. Green and Vithala R. Rao, *Applied Multidimensional Scaling* (New York: Holt, Rinehart and Winston, 1972)], and *item lists* [see John W. Riley, Jr., ed., *The Corporation and Its Public* (New York: John Wiley, 1963), pp. 51–62].

2. Al Reis and Jack Trout, *Positioning: The Battle for Your Mind* (New York: Warner Books, 1982).

3. This material is adapted from Philip Kotler, *Marketing Management: Analysis Planning and Control*, 5th ed. (Englewood Cliffs, N.J.: Prentice-Hall, 1984), Chapter 12. For another approach, see Michael E. Porter, *Competitive Strategy: Techniques for Analyzing Industries and Competitors* (New York: Free Press, 1980).

4. Robert D. Buzzell, Bradley T. Gale, and Ralph G. M. Sultan, "Market Share—a Key to Profitability," *Harvard Business Review*, January–February 1975, pp. 97–106.

5. John D. C. Roach, "From Strategic Planning to Strategic Performance: Closing the Achievement Gap," *Outlook*, Spring 1981, p. 22.

6. R. G. Hamermesh, M. J. Anderson, Jr., and J. E. Harris, "Strategies for Low Market Share Businesses," *Harvard Business Review*, May–June 1978, pp. 95–102.

7

Acquiring and Using
Marketing Information

BARRINGTON, IL. Back in the summer of 1975, an aspiring young
minister and a few of his friends went door to door throughout the
Northwest Chicago suburbs to find out why people didn't go to church.

"Boy, did we get an earful," recalled the boyish-looking Bill Hybels.
"Church is boring, church is predictable, church is irrelevant to my life."

And the No. 1 complaint: "The church is always bugging me for
money."

Based on his marketing study, Hybels decided to found Willow Creek
Community Church, a radically different kind of congregation designed to
attract alienated, "unchurched" people.

Willow Creek is one of a very few churches in the nation shaped by a
targeted "customer" survey. It is also a huge success. From a modest
gathering of 125 people who first met in a rented movie theater 14 years
ago, it has grown to its current position as the nation's No. 2 Protestant
congregation in terms of weekend attendance, second only to an
independent Baptist congregation in Indiana.

Hybels, 37, is rhapsodic about the church's future. "We're on the verge
of making kingdom history," he proclaims, "doing things a new way for a
whole new generation."

Hybels felt the call to the ministry at age 22 and walked out of the
family's lucrative produce business. Becoming a church youth leader, he
focused on events to draw in non-believers and quickly built up the group
from 25 to 1,000.

Next, Hybels asked three friends to help him canvass the Northwest Chicago suburbs to find out why adults didn't attend church.

The answers, in order of frequency: They always ask for money; I don't like the music; I can't relate to the message; the services are boring, predictable and irrelevant; the pastor makes me feel guilty and ignorant, so I leave feeling worse than when I came.

The follow-up question: What kind of church *would* attract you?

The survey respondents wanted non-threatening anonymity, elementary-level teaching, excellence, "high take-home value" and "time to decide."

"Non-churched Harry told us, 'Don't turn the screws tighter while I'm trying to find meaning in life and answers to perplexing ethical questions. Give me time,' " Hybels remembers.

Everything about Willow Creek Church—from the plain but massive sign on the highway to the "neutral corporate setting" of the campus—is designed to "impress . . . seekers with excellence but not ostentatiousness," says Hybels, who for five years was chaplain to the Chicago Bears football team.

Hybels tailored the church's program to the needs and gripes people registered in his door-to-door survey. As a result, the congregation:

- Doesn't have conventional "church worship" on weekends, yet fills its 4,550-seat auditorium on Saturday nights and twice on Sunday mornings.
- Has no altar, cross, vestments or other religious trappings, yet stresses "radical discipleship" to Jesus Christ.
- Has no choir, organ, hymnals or song books, yet produces professional-quality music, ranging from rock and jazz to country and classical.
- Doesn't use offering envelopes, ask for pledges or hold fund-raising dinners, yet through voluntary giving surpasses its budget and recently built a $10-million complex on 120 acres.

Willow Creek's colorful, precisely planned, multimedia services attract 1,000 new churchgoers each year. Between 400 and 700 adults are baptized annually. And about 2,500 members meet weekly in scores of small groups to study the Bible and pray.

Its weekend services are for beginners in the faith ("Christianity 101 and 201," says Hybels) and not intended to provide worship for believers; meatier fare for "born-again" Christians ("Christianity 301 and 401") is served on Wednesday evenings.

That service, called "New Community," plus 75 "subministries"—everything from staffing Willow Creek's extensive food pantry for the needy to producing Christian dramas for the elderly—make up the "core of the church," according to the Rev. Don Cousins, 32, Willow Creek's associate pastor for ministries.

"The weekend services are the front door, but the church inside has to be the real thing," he told a group of 580 attentive church leaders at one of Willow Creek's conferences for pastors, "or else people will go right out the back door."

Source: Excerpted from Russell Chandler, " 'Customer' Poll Shapes a Church," *Los Angeles Times*, December 11, 1989, pp. Al, A28–A30. Reproduced with permission.

We saw in the preceding chapters the critical role marketing research must play in understanding customer attitudes and behavior and planning marketing strategy. We define marketing research as follows:

Marketing research is the planned acquisition and analysis of data measuring some aspect or aspects of the marketing system for the purpose of improving an organization's marketing decisions.

Marketing research can be very diverse. It can involve conducting one-time field research studies. It can comprise the analysis of data provided by internal record systems or by secondary sources of information. It can involve experiments or panel studies. What distinguishes it from simple observation and systematic reflection is that it is (1) planned and (2) tied to specific decision-making situations.

MARKETING RESEARCH IN NONPROFIT ORGANIZATIONS[1]

Nonprofit organizations carry out much less marketing research than they can *or ought to*. This is a consequence of their limited budgets, their relative newness in the marketing field, and their limited research expertise. Increasing the amount of marketing research, therefore, calls for both education and motivation, showing nonprofit executives what marketing research can do and how to do it properly as well as encouraging them to do it more often.

Five myths keep nonprofit managers from engaging in more marketing research.

- The "big decision" myth
- The "survey myopia" myth
- The "big bucks" myth
- The "sophisticated researcher" myth
- The "most-research-is-not-read" myth

If nonprofit managers are to even consider doing more research, these five myths must be directly challenged.

The "Big Decision" Myth

Too often marketing research is considered necessary only for decisions involving large financial stakes, and in such cases it should always be carried out. But research should be viewed from a cost/benefit perspective. Its costs are usually of two types—the expenses for research itself and the amount of sales and competitive advantage lost by delaying a decision until the results are in. The benefits are measured in improvements in the decision under consideration. The value of the improvements, in turn, is a function of the stakes involved and how certain the manager is about the rightness of the contemplated decision.

The cost/benefit ratio may often come out against research even when the stakes are high. Take the case of the hospital manager who was thinking of adding an outpatient plastic surgery clinic and investing in a series of advertisements to promote this new service. He called in a research professional to design a study of consumer interest in plastic surgery that would show how likely acceptance of such a service would be. Although such a study could cost several thousand dollars, the researcher determined in extended discussions with the manager that unless the survey found virtually no interest in outpatient plastic surgery, the manager should go ahead with the decision to add the clinic.

The manager was highly uncertain about the market, but he was certain that his decision to add the clinic was best. The researcher convinced the manager that the research expenditure was unnecessary and that the money could more productively be used to ensure that the new clinic got the advertising send-off needed to have the best chances of succeeding.

On the other hand, research can often be justified even when the amount at stake is not very great. This is the case whenever the research can be done inexpensively, will not take very long to complete, and will help clarify which actions to take.

These conditions often accompany advertising copy decisions. While total expenditures are small, managers usually have two or three candidate ads, each of which seems to have potential worth. Showing the ads to a small but representative set of prospective target customers—very modest research—usually reveals one superior candidate, or at least, by pointing out serious defects in one or two candidate ads, allows the choice to be narrowed. This process has the fringe benefit that once in a while it produces extremely good suggestions for entirely different ads.

Research may also be justifiable when the stakes initially appear modest but later turn out to be high. In this regard, it is generally useful to think through the monetary consequences of making a poor decision. When one considers the possible side effects of a bad decision on such things as the organization's reputation, its ability to attract funding and staff, and its sales of related products, the costs may be very high indeed. Such is often the case when nonprofits venture beyond their national borders and assume that what works in their home countries will work overseas. The international community is replete with horror stories of marketing gaffes with long-term consequences that could have been avoided with a little research.

One may grant these arguments but then assert that there is no low-cost research to meet these challenges, that the research suggestions made previously involve the proverbial quick-and-dirty study that may well be worse than no research at all. The only good research, one might argue, is a survey carefully done. This contention leads to the second major misconception about the use of research.

The "Survey Myopia" Myth

Any reliable information that improves marketing decisions can be considered marketing research. If one takes this view, many alternatives to formal survey research come to mind. Consider a contraceptive social marketing manager thinking of introducing a new intrauterine device who has no idea whether the target market will accept the product or, once it is accepted, how quickly it can be expected to break even. If successful, the new product would produce profits of only a few thousand dollars in the first few years. The manager could conduct a survey to reduce this uncertainty. However, to make the research 95 percent certain of being within two percentage points of the break-even market share figure of 10 percent, the manager must use a sample of nine hundred people.

An experienced survey researcher would estimate that, assuming the questionnaire and sampling plan are already designed and ignoring analysis and report preparation costs, simply completing the interviews would cost in the U.S. between $4,000 and $8,000. (The amount would depend on the duration and type of interviews done.)[2]

Clearly, such research would eat up the manager's initial years' contribution profits. More important is the question of whether the research would yield valid data in any case. One should ask whether it is reasonable to expect respondents to be candid about or even to know their likely behavior with respect to this new IUD, especially if many do not want to disappoint the interviewer or the research sponsor by showing little enthusiasm for the product.

How else, then, might the survey research objectives be achieved at lower cost? The company could try test marketing in representative markets. This approach has the virtue of not only lowering costs but yielding useful data (that is, it shows what people will actually do, not what they say they will do). Testing in a number of markets also allows alternative marketing strategies to be systematically evaluated.

Another low-cost approach would be to commission focus group interviews of 8 to 12 members of the target audience at a time.[3] Although the results are not strictly projectable to the larger market because the groups are not randomly selected, these results can cut the cost of interviewing by a quarter or a half. Interviewers can sometimes develop richer data in the relaxed, chatty format of the focus group. Also, the groups can alert management to problems with the new product. When a company commissions several focus group sessions covering the range of people likely to be target market members for the new IUD, officials can spot serious problems mentioned by a modest number of participants and, if necessary, abort the product launch. Elaborate probability sampling designs are simply not necessary to satisfy this objective.

The "Big Bucks" Myth

We have already seen that there are often low-cost alternatives to the kinds of field surveys most nonprofit managers normally consider. To be knowledgeable users of marketing research, managers must know how and when to do traditional survey research and how and when to use a wide range of alternative low-cost research techniques. We shall consider these low-cost research techniques in later sections since nonprofits typically have seriously restricted budgets.

The "Sophisticated Researcher" Myth

Just as marketing research need not involve complex sampling and elaborate designs, a high level of sophistication in sampling techniques, statistics, and computer analysis is not essential. Of course, executives of nonprofits planning to undertake research programs should acquaint themselves with at least the rudimentary principles of probability sampling, questionnaire design, and graphic presentation of results.

Even when managers need high levels of sophistication—for example, if elaborate experiments or careful field study projects are being planned—they can get low-cost assistance on an ad hoc basis. Professors at local colleges are one resource. An alternative particularly appropriate to nonprofit organizations is the voluntary help of local professional researchers. Nonprofits contemplating extended research programs may want to ask marketing research professionals to sit on their boards of directors.

The "Most-Research-Is-Not-Read" Myth

Executives who would rather not bother with research or who subconsciously fear the results use this last rationale for their inaction. Poor research certainly is undertaken, but when it is, it is usually a testimonial to poor planning. In our experience, few pieces of *well-planned* research are rejected as unhelpful, although they may be ignored on other, often political, grounds.

How can one ensure that research will not be wasted effort? The responsibility rests with both the manager requesting the research and the researcher doing it. Research will be most valuable when

1   It is undertaken after the manager has made clear to the researcher what the decision alternatives are and what it is about those decisions that necessitates additional information.
2   The relationship between the results and the decision is clearly understood.
3   The results are communicated well.

MARKETING RESEARCH STRATEGY

Marketing research can be an extremely valuable management tool, especially in a customer-oriented organization. But, if marketing research is to be impactful, it must be *planned strategically*. That is, marketing research in a nonprofit organization should *not* comprise a series of studies undertaken as need arises but should be a system of information steadily flowing into management decisions. The sophisticated nonprofit manager should plan to invest in a *marketing information system*.

MARKETING INFORMATION SYSTEMS

As we have seen, nonprofit managers need timely, accurate, and adequate market information as a basis for making sound marketing decisions. We shall use the term *marketing information system* (*MIS*) to describe the organization's system for gathering, analyzing, storing, and disseminating relevant marketing information. More formally

> A **marketing information system** is a continuing and interacting structure of people, equipment, and procedures designed to gather, sort, analyze, evaluate, and distribute pertinent, timely, and accurate information for use by marketing decision makers to improve their marketing planning, execution, and control.[4]

The role and major subsystems of an MIS are illustrated in Figure 7-1. At the left is shown the marketing environment that marketing managers must monitor—specifically, target markets, marketing channels, competitors, publics, and macroenvironmental forces. Developments and trends in the marketing environment are picked up in the company through one of four subsystems making up the marketing information system—the internal reports system, the marketing intelligence system, the marketing research system, and the analytical marketing system. The information then flows to the appropriate marketing managers to help them in their marketing planning, execution, and control. The

FIGURE 7-1

The Marketing Information System

MARKETING ENVIRONMENT

Target markets
Marketing channels
Competitors
Publics
Macroenvironmental forces

Marketing information

MARKETING INFORMATION SYSTEM

Internal reports system

Marketing research system

Marketing intelligence system

Analytical marketing system

Marketing information

MARKETING MANAGERS

Planning information
Executing information
Control information

Marketing decisions and communications

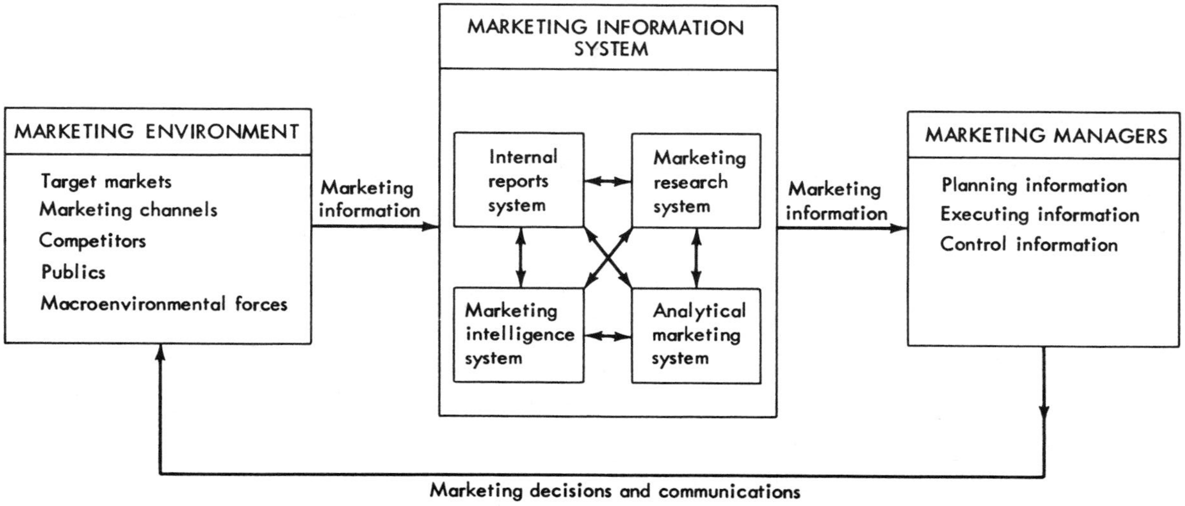

resulting decisions and communications then flow back to the marketing environment.

We will now expand on the four major subsystems of the organization's MIS.

Internal Records System

The oldest and most basic information system used by managers is the internal records system. Every organization accumulates information in the regular course of its operations.

A hospital will keep records on its patients, including their names, addresses, ages, illnesses, lengths of stay, supplies and room charges, attending physicians, complaints, and so on. From these patient records, the hospital can develop statistics on the number of daily admissions, average length of patient stay, average patient charge, frequency distribution of different illnesses, and so on. The hospital will also have records on their physicians, nurses, costs, billings, assets, and liabilities, all of which is indispensable information for making management decisions.

A museum will keep several record systems. Its contributor file will list the names, addresses, past contributions, and other data on its contributors. Its campaign progress file will show the amount raised to date from each major source, such as individuals, foundations, corporations, and government grants. Its cost file will show how much money has been spent on direct mail, newspaper advertising, brochures, salaries, consultant fees, and so on.

Every internal records system can be improved in its speed, comprehensiveness, and accuracy. Periodically, an organization should survey its managers for possible improvements in the internal records system. The goal is not to design the most elegant system, but one that is cost effective in meeting the managers' information needs. A cross-section of managers should be queried as to their information needs. Table 7-1 shows the major questions that can be put to them. Once their opinions are gathered, the information system designers can design an internal records system that reconciles (1) what managers think they need, (2) what managers really need, and (3) what is economically feasible.

Marketing Intelligence System

Whereas the internal reports system supplies executives with *results data*, the marketing intelligence system supplies executives with *happenings data*. Our definition is:

> The **marketing intelligence system** is the set of sources and procedures by which marketing executives obtain their everyday information about developments in the external marketing environment.

Managers carry on marketing intelligence mostly on their own by reading

Table 7-1

QUESTIONNAIRE FOR DETERMINING MARKETING
INFORMATION NEEDS OF MANAGERS

1. What types of decisions are you regularly called upon to make?
2. What types of information do you need to make these decisions?
3. What types of information do you regularly get?
4. What types of special studies do you periodically request?
5. What types of information would you like to get that you are not now getting?
6. What information would you want daily? weekly? monthly? yearly?
7. What magazines and reports would you like to see routed to you on a regular basis?
8. What specific topics would you like to be kept informed of?
9. What types of data analysis programs would you like to see made available?
10. What do you think would be the four most helpful improvements that could be made in the present marketing information system?

newspapers and trade publications and talking to various people inside and outside the organization. In this way, they are able to spot important developments. At the same time, their casual approach to gathering marketing intelligence can also result in missing or learning too late of some other important developments, such as a fund-raising opportunity with an important donor or a new law that might hurt the organization's nonprofit status.

An organization can take some concrete steps to improve the quality of the marketing intelligence available to its managers. First, the organization must "sell" its managers and staff on the importance of gathering marketing intelligence and passing it on to others in the organization. Their intelligence responsibilities can be facilitated by designing information forms that are easy to fill out and circulate. Managers should know the kind of information that would be useful to other managers.

Second, the organization should encourage outside parties with whom it deals—advertising agencies, professional associations, lawyers, and accountants—to pass on any useful bits of information. A museum's lawyer, for example, may hear about a wealthy donor who is revising his will, and this information can be useful to the development office of the museum.

Third, the organization could hire people to carry on specialized intelligence-gathering activities. Many organizations hire "mystery shoppers" to canvass their own organization and competitors' organizations. A mystery shopper might visit the admissions offices of several colleges and report back on the quality of their "customer handling." In one case, the "bogus student" reported receiving widely different receptions, some of which were absolute "turnoffs" and others of which were highly effective. Mystery shopping is also an important means for learning whether the organization's own staff is really practicing a customer orientation in its dealings with the public.

Fourth, the organization can establish an office that is specifically responsible for gathering and disseminating marketing intelligence. The staff would perform a number of services. It would scan major publications, abstract the relevant news, and disseminate the news to appropriate managers. It would install suggestion and complaint systems so that clients and others would have an opportunity to express their attitudes toward the organization. It would develop a master index so that all the past and current information could be easily retrieved. The staff would assist managers in evaluating the reliability of different pieces of information. These and other services would greatly enhance the quality of the information available to marketing managers.

Marketing Research System

From time to time, managers need to commission specific marketing research studies in order to have adequate information to make pending decisions. Administrators of nonprofit organizations are increasingly finding that they need marketing research, such as when a hospital wants to know whether people in its service area have a positive attitude toward the hospital, when a college wants to determine what kind of image it has among high school counselors, or when a political organization wants to find out what voters think of its candidates and other candidates. Many studies could prove worthwhile to an organization, but in the face of a limited budget, the organization must have know-how to choose marketing research projects carefully, design them efficiently, and implement the results effectively. We return to this problem below.

Analytical Marketing System

The marketing information system contains a fourth subsystem called the analytical marketing system. The analytical marketing system consists of a set of advanced techniques for analyzing marketing data and marketing problems. These systems are able to produce more findings and conclusions than can be gained by only commonsense manipulation of the data. Large organizations tend to make extensive use of analytical marketing systems. In smaller organizations, managers resist these approaches as too technical or expensive.

An analytical marketing system consists of two sets of tools known as the statistical bank and the model bank (see Figure 7-2). The *statistical bank* is a collection of advanced statistical procedures for learning more about the relationships within a set of data and their statistical reliability. They allow management to go beyond the frequency distributions, means, and standard deviations in the data.

Managers often want answers to such questions as:

- What are the most important variables affecting my performance, and how important is each one?
- If I raise my price 10 percent and increase my advertising expenditures by 20 percent, what will happen to sales?

FIGURE 7-2

Analytical Marketing System

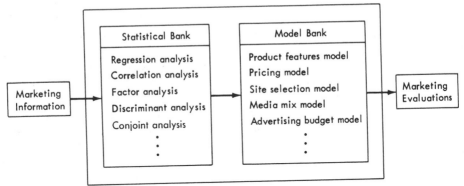

- What are the most discriminating predictors of which persons are likely to change their behavior in response to my marketing strategy?
- What are the best variables for segmenting my market, and how many segments should be created?

The statistical techniques are somewhat technical, and the reader is advised to consult other sources for understanding and using them.[5]

The *model bank* is a collection of models that will help marketers make better marketing decisions. Each model consists of a set of interrelated variables that represent some real system, process, or outcome. These models can help answer "what if?" and "which is best?" questions. In the last twenty years, marketing scientists have developed a great number of models to help marketing executives do a better job of pricing, designing sales territories and sales call plans, selecting sites for outlets, developing optimal advertising media mixes, developing optimal size advertising budgets, and forecasting new product sales.[6]

This concludes our review of the nature of a marketing information system and its main subsystems—internal reports, marketing intelligence, marketing research, and analytical marketing. Such a marketing research capability does not come about without careful planning. This requires that the nonprofit organization have (1) a marketing research mission, (2) a long-range strategy, (3) a budget, (4) an approach to carrying out individual projects, (5) an organization, and (6) a system of evaluation and control. We will comment in detail on (1) through (4) here and mention (5) and (6) briefly at the end of the chapter.

The Marketing Research Mission

A marketing information system has as its basic mission: helping marketing managers make better decisions. Thus, the first place to start when planning such a system is with managers' decisions. The research manager should think through the major kinds of decisions that managers will be making over the planning horizon for which marketing research might be useful. These include *routine decisions* to be made over and over, such as where to place advertising, which products or services to promote, what to do with prices and channels of distribution, and so forth. The planning period typically also includes *one-time decisions* such as whether to add a specific new product or service, reposition the enterprise, focus on a new target group, seek new funding sources, drop certain products, services, or customers, and so on. Some of these one-time decision needs can be anticipated and built into the mission statement, but some cannot. The manager must build excess capacity into the research system, the amount of which can be more precisely estimated with experience. For nonprofit organizations with very limited budgets, we would argue forcefully that *no* market research should be undertaken unless it leads directly into a decision.

However, where one has a generous budget, a nonprofit marketer might wish to establish capabilities to undertake one or both of two other kinds of research. One is *basic research*. Basic research has no immediate application to specific management decisions but is generally expected to lay the groundwork for better decisions somewhere down the road. Thus, the Association of College, University, and Community Arts Administrators has used part of its members' dues to explore the potential of life-style research—specifically, the VALS approach—to understand consumers' reactions to the performing arts.[7]

The other type of research a nonprofit might undertake alone or jointly is *methodological research*, that is, research designed to improve the organization's ability to do more effective research in the future. Organizations involved in contraceptive marketing programs in developing countries, for example, have invested in two kinds of methodological research in recent years. One research stream has focused on figuring out how to measure the impacts of contraceptive marketing programs on a country's marketing system. The organizations need to know whether contraceptive program sales come at the expense of existing private-sector firms or whether subsidized contraceptive marketing programs expand the entire market. In this connection, SOMARC, one of the key groups involved in international contraceptive social marketing has sponsored research in Bangladesh to develop a standardized *retail audit* methodology for tracking condom and oral contraceptive sales for all brands in the markets they serve.[8]

Another more difficult methodological problem in family planning programs is how to get valid information on consumer attitudes and behavior concerning family planning. In this highly sensitive subject area, respondents very often distort the truth, withhold information, and make claims of use (or nonuse) that simply do not reconcile with, say, known sales data. In some cultures, research has discovered significant differences even within given households with respect to relatively simple matters such as whether the family has ever actually used a particular method. Tackling this crucial methodological dilemma must be part of the marketing research mission of one or more of the key players in the social marketing arena over the next several years.

Research designed to be *applied* is likely to serve one of three purposes: description, explanation, or prediction.

Description.   Marketing research can be designed to tell a nonprofit manager what his or her marketing environment is like. It can, for example, tell a hospital manager how many patients were served in each hospital facility each hour of each day of each year and indicate the sex and home address of each patient, his or her attending doctor, any previous admissions to the hospital, and the diagnosis.

While internal records can often provide these data to hospital management, additional descriptive information could be acquired from a telephone survey to ascertain the patient's family status, occupation, education, media habits, satisfaction with various hospital services, and intentions as to word of mouth and future patronage. At the same time, the manager could acquire from published sources descriptive data on competitors' pricing and advertising expenditures as well as information on national trends in payment methods, wages of specific hospital departments, cost of equipment, and so on. All of these data have in common the fact that they are descriptions of one point in time or descriptions of trends or pattern changes over time. Descriptive data usually serve management decisions in three ways: (1) monitoring performance to indicate whether strategy changes are needed, (2) describing consumers for segmentation decisions, and (3) serving as the basis for more sophisticated analysis.

Explanation.   Usually a manager is not satisfied with merely seeing what the market environment looks like. He or she would typically like to know what makes it "tick." In principle, there are really three possible levels of explanatory sophistication that a manager could attempt to build into the nonprofit organization's marketing research system. Each succeeding level has higher costs and greater resource requirements than the one preceding it, but it also has higher potential payoff.

ASSOCIATION.   The simplest level of explanation is to discover what seems to be associated with what. Thus, the hospital manager might like to know which socioeconomic and demographic characteristics of patients characterize those who are repeat users of the hospital, or those who are satisfied or dissatisfied with past services, or those who are not favorably disposed toward competitors' offerings. Such data would be very useful in helping management decide which segment to address through what channels with which general strategy.

CAUSATION.   A nasty feature of associations data that is learned by every freshman statistics student is that association is not the same as causation. Thus, the hospital manager may find that OB/GYN patients are more satisfied with their hospital care than those who were admitted for treatment of, say, urological problems. The manager may be tempted to think that the OB/GYN service is doing a better job than Urology in terms of the technical quality and warmth of service offered. But suppose the manager had data like that displayed in Figure 7-3 showing patients' perception of the hospital before and after admission. The manager would quickly see that at admission, urology patients thought worse of the hospital than OB/GYN patients, but that the attitudes of OB/GYN patients *worsened* over the course of their treatment in the hospital, while the attitudes of urology patients improved. An "association" level of explanation would have given misleading indications about causation. For a manager to be sure of taking appropriate action, he or she must know what causes what. If the hospital manager subsequently took action to improve OB/GYN satisfaction scores, it would be critical to know whether these actions in fact led to the necessary changes. Only when the research strategy is specifically designed to trace antecedents and consequents, to measure effects under very controlled conditions, or to be subject to rather rigorous statistical procedures, does the strategy yield causative explanations.

REASONS WHY.   The ultimate level of explanation for marketing researchers is to know not only that A caused B, but *why* A caused B. Thus, the hospital manager looking at the data in Figure 7-3 may be willing to conclude that treatment by the urology service leaves patients satisfied, while treatment by the OB/GYN service does not. Before rushing to reward one service and castigate the other, the manager should have a better understanding of the nature of the causation, that is, of the "reasons why." To consider just one possibility, it may be that a significant number of patients in urology at the time of the study were there for treatment of kidney stones and were simply relieved to have them removed. Any set of nurses or doctors who treated them in *any* way, from very competently and warmly to very incompetently and coldly, would have found them happier after treatment than before. If treatment per se, not staff, is the reason for the pattern of causation in Figure 7-3, then clearly rewards are not due to the urology staff. Indeed, there could even be serious problems on the urology floor that the warm afterglow of treatment is hiding. Management must often dig beneath simple causation if research is to lead to the right decision and action.

Prediction.   Of course, descriptions or explanations of what exists or existed in the past are only useful to the manager if they tell about the future. As we noted in Chapter 3, marketing decisions play out in the future. Suppose the

FIGURE 7-3

Hypothetical Attitudes Toward Hospital Service Before and After Admission

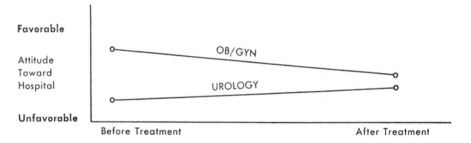

hospital manager in our hypothetical example finds that the reason for the posttreatment decline in OB/GYN patients' perceptions of the hospital is real and is due to the professional style of the staff, who emphasize doing the job right and efficiently rather than investing a lot of time in being solicitous and talkative with patients. But suppose it is also true that there are many patients who prefer this style—for example, those who have more education, those who are not having their first child, and those who are having birth complications. For the hospital manager to make a judgment about whether to try to change the style of the OB/GYN service to emphasize "warmth," it is essential to know what the future pool of potential patients will be and which strategic competitors will attack them. This clearly requires a different set of information than is available from a typical descriptive or explanatory study.

Research Strategy

Assuming that a nonprofit organization wishes to carry out a program of applied research, the next question is what specific kinds of research should be conducted this year and who should do it?

The range of specific studies open to a researcher is indicated in a 1983 American Marketing Association study of 599 private-sector companies in consumer and industrial goods, advertising, and financial services.[9] Table 7-2 shows the proportions carrying out each of 33 kinds of research.

The *kinds* of studies most heavily used in Table 7-2 are the ones that also should be used most heavily by mature nonprofits. These include

- Determination of market characteristics
- Short- and long-range forecasting
- Trend studies
- Competitive offerings studies
- Measurements of market potentials
- Market share analyses
- Sales analyses

The development of a specific research plan for a particular organization should not be difficult. An example of a master plan for a hospital marketing research strategy is outlined in Figure 7-4.

Budgeting

The next research planning problem is setting the overall research budget. While not all nonprofits have a marketing research department, specific funds for research purposes must be set aside annually. Four basic methods are used in both the nonprofit and for-profit sectors. Despite their popularity, they are decidedly inferior to the cost/benefit approach outlined in the next section.

Table 7-2

RESEARCH ACTIVITIES OF 599 RESPONDENT COMPANIES

	% Doing
Advertising Research	
A. Motivation research	47
B. Copy research	61
C. Media research	68
D. Studies of ad effectiveness	76
E. Studies of competitive advertising	67
Business Economics and Corporate Research	
A. Short-range forecasting (up to 1 year)	89
B. Long-range forecasting (over 1 year)	87
C. Studies of business trends	91
D. Pricing studies	83
E. Plant and warehouse location studies	68
F. Acquisition studies	73
G. Export and international studies	49
H. MIS (Management Information System)	80
I. Operations research	65
J. Internal company employees	76
Corporate Responsibility Research	
A. Consumers "right to know" studies	18
B. Ecological impact studies	23
C. Studies of legal constraints on advertising and promotion	46
D. Social values and policies studies	39
Product Research	
A. New product acceptance and potential	76
B. Competitive product studies	87
C. Testing of existing products	80
D. Packaging research: design or physical characteristics	65
Sales and Market Research	
A. Measurement of market potentials	97
B. Market share analysis	97
C. Determination of market characteristics	97
D. Sales analysis	92
E. Establishment of sales quotas, territories	78
F. Distribution channel studies	71
G. Test markets, store audits	59
H. Consumer panel operations	63
I. Sales compensation studies	60
J. Promotional studies of premiums, coupons, sampling, deals, etc.	58

SOURCE: Dik Warren Twedt, *1983 Survey of Marketing Research* (Chicago: American Marketing Association, 1984), p. 41. Reprinted with permission.

- *Historical increment.* The manager simply looks at the research budgets of the last several years and adjusts the figures upward or downward by some percentage based on the expected activity level of the organization in the current year.
- *Percent of revenues.* The manager applies a standard percentage to the amount of expected revenues. If private sector experience is any guide, this percentage could range anywhere from 0.1 percent to 0.8 percent of revenues.

FIGURE 7-4

Proposed Marketing Research Strategy for a Hospital

	Questions To Be Answered	Research Components						
		Hospital Records Analysis	Patient Survey[1]	Physicians' Survey[2]	Secondary Source Data Analysis	Market Area Survey[1] (Population)	Market Area Survey (Physicians)[2]	Market Area Survey (Hospitals)
Recent Patients	• Who are the Hospital's recent patients and how is the mix of patients changing?	X	X					
	• What Hospital services have patients experienced and what are their attitudes toward the Hospital?		X					
	• To what extent are patients aware of the Hospital's services which they have not experienced?		X					
	• What needs do patients have which might be served by the Hospital but currently are not being met?		X					
Affiliated Physicians	• Who are the Hospital's affiliated physicians?	X						
	• What experiences have these physicians had and what are their attitudes toward the Hospital?			X				
	• To what extent are these physicians aware of the Hospital's total services?			X				
	• What needs do these physicians have which might be served by the Hospital but currently are not being met?			X				
General Population/ Service Area	• Who lives in the Hospital's geographic market (services) area and how is the population mix changing?					X	X	
	• What experiences has this population had with health care organizations and what are their attitudes toward those organizations?						X	
	• To what extent is the population aware of the Hospital's services and what are their general attitudes toward the Hospital?						X	
	• What health care needs does the population have which might be served by the Hospital and might not be available through health care institutions serving the Hospital's geographic market area?						X	
Nonaffiliated Physicians	• Who are the nonaffiliated physicians serving the Hospital's geographic market area?					X		X
	• To what extent are these physicians aware of the Hospital's services and what are their general attitudes toward the Hospital?							X
	• What needs do these nonaffiliated physicians have which might be served by the Hospital and are not now available at other health care institutions in the area?							X
Competitors	• What organizations compete with the Hospital in providing health care services to residents in the Hospital's market area and how do they compete?		X			X	X	X

[1] Patient and market area general population survey may use a combined survey instrument.
[2] Physician and market area general population survey may use a combined survey instrument.

SOURCE: Dennis J. Cunningham and William C. Jackson, "Marketing Research in a Competitive Health Care Environment," *Health Care Focus*, Vol. 6, no. 3, June–July 1980, p. 3. Arthur Young & Co., Publisher. Reproduced with permission.

- *Competitive matching.* An estimate is made of either the dollar amount or percentage of revenues spent on market research by major competitors or similar organizations last year. The manager then sets the nonprofit's own budget to equal, stay proportionate with, or exceed these comparison organizations.
- *Affordable.* Budgets are first set for other "necessary" activities. Then the amount that is left over from projected revenue levels is divided between advertising and marketing research.

Collectively, there are a number of defects with these four approaches:

1   They imply that market research is a discretionary expenditure rather than an essential tool for effective management.
2   They ignore the fact that one should expect applied marketing research to produce better revenues. Rather than setting a research budget that would help increase revenues, these four approaches use revenues to determine marketing research budgets.
3   They are cyclical by definition. When revenues are up, more will be allocated to marketing research, and when revenues are down, less will be allocated. Yet a good case can be made for making marketing research budgets contracyclical. That is, in strong, buoyant markets where revenues are up, a wide range of decisions may prove successful. In such cases, marketing research can improve management decisions only marginally. By contrast, when the market is difficult, management will be much more uncertain about which way to go, and wrong decisions can be devastating. In such cases, marketing research will be more helpful. Obviously, when research can be more helpful, more should be spent on it.
4   Rule-of-thumb approaches to budgeting marketing research ignore enterprise life cycles. When many new activities are being proposed or just getting off the ground, much more research ought to be carried out, yet this is often a period when relatively little revenue is available to "pay" for such research.

The Cost/Benefit Approach.   The cost/benefit approach calls for the manager to follow the procedure suggested above for specifying research *needs* for the planning period and then costing out the research and comparing these costs to the expected benefits. Specifically, the steps are

1   List all possible projects that might be undertaken for the planning period. Develop this list by asking marketing managers to ascertain their upcoming information needs.
2   Estimate the costs for meeting each set of information needs, noting whether they can be met by secondary analysis of existing data, purchase of outside services, or whether they require original research.
3   Estimate the likely improvement in organizational performance as a result of each proposed study, that is, the study's "benefits." This involves considering several factors. First, the marketing research manager should ascertain the stakes involved in the various decision alternatives that the line manager is considering. An attempt should be made to estimate the economic *opportunity loss* of choosing the *wrong* course of action in each instance and the probability that such a loss might occur. This "expected" opportunity loss would then constitute the research's maximum possible benefit. This figure would constitute an upper limit on the amount that could be spent on aiding the manager's

decision making through research. This figure is often called the *cost of uncertainty*.[10]

4   Adjust the calculated benefit from the research by the probability that the research at the proposed budget level will, indeed, provide right answers as to which decision to make.

5   Compare costs to expected benefits and include *all* projects where the latter exceed the former. The total of these project costs will comprise the year's research budget.

Implementation

Once the marketing research strategy is worked out, the researcher is ready to design and carry out the specific studies. The research manager will be concerned about two criteria: *effectiveness* and *efficiency*. Effectiveness in the research context can be measured in terms of the study's *usefulness* for making management decisions. Efficiency is achieving usefulness at the lowest possible cost. We shall discuss low-cost research techniques later in the chapter. We consider here the more difficult problem of making research projects effective.

Being effective in research is the result of three major factors. First, the researcher needs a *research design process* that gives the greatest likelihood that the research will meet management's needs. Second, the researcher needs to know the *full array of methodologies* that might be used to solve the particular problem. Third, the researcher needs to know how to minimize the *research bias*.

In the following sections, we will first consider the problem of developing an effective *process* for researching. Next, we will outline several alternative research techniques, and finally, we will point out some major biases that the unwary researcher might expect in carrying out a specific research design.

THE RESEARCH PROCESS[11]

The standard approach to the research process is to start by defining the problem. The problem is then translated into a research methodology. This leads to the development of research instruments, a sampling plan, coding and interviewing instructions, and other details. The researcher takes to the field, examines the resulting data, and writes a report. The executive then steps in to translate the researcher's findings into action. The executive has, of course, already devoted some thought to the application of the results.

In the more typical case, however, managers leave the problem vague and general. They say, in effect, "Here are some things I don't know. When the results come in, I'll know more. And when I know more, then I can figure out what to do." This approach makes it highly likely that the findings will be off target.

We advocate instead a procedure that turns the traditional approach to research design on its head. The procedure stresses close collaboration between researcher and decision makers. It markedly raises the odds that the organization will come up with findings that are not only "interesting" but also actionable.

The "backward" approach advocated here rests on the premise that the best way to design usable research is to start where the process usually *ends* and then work backward. Each stage in the design is developed on the basis of what comes after it, not before. The steps in the procedure are outlined in Figure 7-5. They are

1 Determine what key decisions are to be made using the research results.
2 Determine what information will help management make the best decisions.
3 Prepare a prototype report and ask management if this will best help them make their decisions.
4 Determine the analysis that will be necessary to fill in the report.
5 Determine what questions will be asked to provide the data required by the analysis.
6 Ascertain whether the needed questions have been answered already.
7 Design the sample.
8 Implement the research design.
9 Analyze the data.
10 Write the report.
11 Assist management to implement the results.
12 Evaluate the research report and contribution.

While this process is costly in terms of the time commitments it requires of management, in the long run it can reduce significantly the cost of the overall research program by ensuring that unnecessary research is avoided and that all research actually carried out is directly on target.

As one might expect, the two first steps in the "backwards" process are the most important.

Steps 1 and 2

To most managers, the research "problem" is seen as a lack of important information about their marketing environment. The manager of a social services program might say, "The problem is that I don't know who I am serving and who I am not serving." Or "The problem is that I don't know whether my clients are more satisfied with my program than my major competitor's clients are satisfied with hers."

If the problem is defined this way, the "solution" is simply to reduce the manager's ignorance. Research is carried out that simply describes the patient population or that measures the level of satisfaction with alternative programs. These data may be very "interesting" and may give managers a great deal of satisfaction in revealing things they didn't know. But satisfaction can quickly

FIGURE 7-5

"Backward" Marketing Research

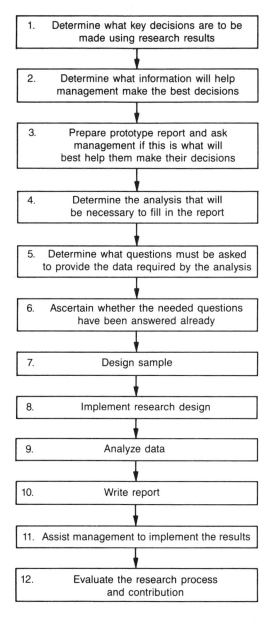

SOURCE: Alan R. Andreasen, *Cheap But Good Marketing Research* (Homewood, Ill.: Dow Jones-Irwin, 1988), p. 65.

turn to frustration and disappointment when the executive tries to use the results.

Take, for example, a life-style study done not long ago on over-the-counter drugs. Some respondents who claimed they were always getting colds and the flu frequently went to doctors, but the doctors were never of much help. They thought that the over-the-counter drugs were often very beneficial, but they weren't sure why. This information, together with other details, caused the researchers to label this group "the hypochondriacs."

What can be done with these results? As is usually the case with segmentation strategies, there are quantity and quality decisions to make. The company has to decide whether to pump more marketing resources into the hypochondriac group than its proportion of the population would justify. The marketing vice-president might first say yes because the hypochondriacs are heavy drug users.

But the picture is more complicated than that. Perhaps hypochondriacs are sophisticated buyers, set in their purchase patterns, and very loyal to favorite brands. If so, money aimed at them would have little impact on the market shares. Light users, on the other hand, may have fragile loyalties, and throwing money at them could entice them to switch brands. Of course, just the opposite might be true: the hypochondriacs, being heavy users, might prove to be very impressionable and responsive to compelling ads.

On the qualitative side, life-style research could be much more helpful. Since it generates a rich profile describing each group's jobs, families, values, and preferences, this research could tell the company what to say. But the frustrated manager is not likely to know *where* to say these things. There is no *Hypochondriac's Journal* in which to advertise, and there may be no viewing and reading patterns that apply to heavy users specifically—hypochondriacs or not.

A self-selection strategy could be tried in which the organization develops an ad speaking to hypochondriacs' fears and worries in the hope that they will see the message and say to themselves, "Ah, they're talking about me!" But nonhypochondriac heavy users who read the ad might say, "Well, if this product is really for those wimpy worrywarts, it certainly is not for sensible, rational me! I'll take my patronage elsewhere." In this case, the research will be very interesting (fine fodder for cocktail party banter) but not actionable.

But suppose that the company had first laid out all the action alternatives it might take after the study. If the marketing vice-president had made it clear that his problems were (1) whether to allocate marketing dollars differently and (2) whether to develop marketing campaigns aimed at particular, newly discovered segments, he would have launched the project in a more appropriate direction.

In the first case, discussions with the researcher would help the vice-president determine the criteria that would justify a different allocation. The manager needs research on the likely responses of different segments to advertising and promotional money. In the second case, the manager needs to know whether there are effective channels for reaching these segments. Only by first thinking through the decisions to be made with the research results will the project have a high likelihood of actionability.

Step 3

After step 1, management should ask, "What should the final report look like so that we'll know exactly what moves to make when the findings are in?" Now the collaboration between the researcher and the manager should intensify and prove both dynamic and exceedingly creative.

Scenarios are a good technique for developing ideas for the contents of the report. The initiative here lies with the researcher, who generates elements of a hypothetical report and then confronts management with tough questions, like "If I came up with this cross-tabulation with these numbers in it, what would you do?"

The first payoff from this exercise arises from improvements in the research itself. The exercise can move the project forward by sharpening the decision alternatives and backward by indicating the best design for the questionnaire or how the analysis of the findings should be carried out.

Suppose an arts manager is considering canceling a multiple-purchase discount offer because most of the people taking advantage of it may be loyal customers who are already heavy users, are upscale, and are largely price inelastic. The manager speculates that the discount mainly represents lost revenue. To decide whether to eliminate the discount, one must of course predict the responses of old and new customers to this step. The researcher hypothesizes tables showing various results.

Suppose the first iteration shows long-time customers to be price inelastic and new customers to be price elastic. This result suggests to the manager to offer no discount except to new customers. In considering this alternative, the manager will need to know whether potential new customers can be reached with the special offer in a way that will minimize or eliminate purchases at a discount by long-time customers.

This new formulation of the decision leads to a discussion of results set out in another set of dummy tables showing responsiveness to the proposed one-time discount by past patronage behavior. Other tables would then reveal what television shows various consumer segments watch and what they read or listen to, which will indicate whether they are differentially reachable. And so goes the process of recycling between the decision context and the research design.

The recycling will reveal what research is needed. Sometimes, the researcher will present contrasting tables of regression results only to discover that management would take the same course of action no matter what the results. This is actually a prima facie case for doing away with that part of the research design altogether.

Management participation in the design decision has other advantages. It serves to win managers' support of marketing research and deepens their understanding of research details. That understanding permits the researcher to simplify the report immeasurably. Working with contrasting, hypothetical tables can make the manager eager for the findings and unlikely to be startled by surprising results. Participation will also sensitize management to the study's limitations. Managers are often tempted to go far beyond research "truth" when implementing the results, especially if the reported truth supports the course of action they prefer to take anyway.

Step 4

The form of the report will clearly dictate the nature of the analysis. If management is leery of multivariate analysis, the researchers should design a series of step-by-step cross-tabulations. If management is comfortable with the higher reaches of statistics, the researcher can draw on more advanced analytic procedures. In general, the analysis phase should be straightforward. If the exercise of scenario writing has gone well, the analysis should amount to little more than filling in the blanks.

Step 5

The backward approach is very helpful in data gathering. In one study, management wanted to gauge young consumers' knowledge of and preferences for the organization's offering. Not until the researcher had prepared mock tables showing preference data by age and sex did the manager's wishes become clear. By "young," the manager meant children as young as 10. The manager also believed that preteens, being a very volatile group, undergo radical changes from year to year, especially as they approach puberty. Design plans to set a low age cutoff for the sample at 13 and to group respondents by age category—such as 13 to 16 and 17 to 20—went out the window. If the researcher had been following the usual design approach, the manager's expectations may not have surfaced until the study was well under way.

Backward design can also help determine the appropriateness of using strict probability techniques. If, for example, management wants to project certain findings to some universe, the research must employ precise probability methods. On the other hand, if the manager is chiefly interested in frequency counts (say, of words used by consumers to describe the organization's offerings or of complaints voiced about its staff), sampling restrictions need not be so tight. Researchers often build either too much or too little sampling quality for the uses the organization has in mind. Similarly, scenario writing will often also reveal that management wants more breakdowns of the results, requiring larger sample sizes or more precise stratification procedures than initially planned. Through simulating the application of the findings, the final research design is much more likely to meet management's needs with substantially lower field costs.

Steps 6–10

The first five steps encompass the major advantages of the backward technique. Steps 6 through 10 revert to a traditional forward approach that implements the research decisions and judgments made earlier. If all parties have collaborated well in the early stages, steps 6 through 10 should merely carry through what has already been decided.

Steps 11–12

The traditional research project concludes when the report is dropped on the manager's desk. This, however, is premature and shortsighted. The process began with the researcher and the manager thinking collaboratively about what the research would do to help management decision making. Now that the data are in hand, the researcher should continue to be involved because he or she (1) understands the database and its nuances and (2) has already thought hard about what the results should mean to the manager. Their continued teamwork through the application stage will ensure not only good decisions, but that the data are mined as thoroughly as possible and that they are not subject to inadvertent misinterpretations (for example, when the manager *wishes* to believe that a finding is present when it really isn't).

The last step in the process is equally necessary if the research project is not to be a unique event but is to fit into an organization's long-run research strategy. Sometime after the application steps have been inaugurated, the researcher and manager should review the entire research process and ask whether there were any ways in which it could have been carried out better. Only through such careful reflection will the entire research enterprise be perfected and the nonprofit get the most out of the limited resources it allocates to this critical function.

RESEARCH ALTERNATIVES

The second requirement for effective implementation is to choose the right research methodology. When the nonprofit researcher thinks of carrying out primary research, the technique that usually comes to mind first is the one-time field survey, usually a mail or telephone study using conventionally designed questionnaires. However, this technique can be very expensive. Later in the chapter we shall describe some techniques for reducing its costs. Here we wish to suggest some approaches that can either materially upgrade the value of the traditional one-time survey or can substitute for it.

In upgrading the traditional survey, the mature researcher should consider sophisticated attitude measures, conjoint analysis, and panel studies.

Sophisticated Attitude Measures

As noted in Chapter 4, consumers typically undertake complex decision processes in deciding whether to take a particular action in which nonprofit marketers are interested. Tapping into that process with the types of measures and models described in Chapter 4 can be very useful. Andreasen and Belk, for example, found that a complex expectancy-value attitude model best predicted likely future attendance at a symphony and theater in the South. The attitude measures proved not only good predictors but also offered a number of diagnostic insights for strategy.[12]

Using Conjoint Research Techniques

As also noted in Chapter 4, consumers make choices among alternatives. Traditional approaches that ask about choices one at a time ignore the reality that most choices involve trade-offs among desired benefits. That is, a patient facing a hospital stay may have to choose among

Hospital A: Low cost and close enough for the patient's spouse and children to visit frequently but with poor food and somewhat dated equipment.

Hospital B: Medium cost with better equipment in some medical services but equally poor food and a 20-minute drive time.

Hospital C: High cost, good food, and the very latest equipment but located in an urban center 1 hour distant.

Which hospital the patient will choose will depend on how he or she "trades off" the various qualities. Conjoint research techniques are specifically designed to capture this process. They permit analysts to estimate the importance to an individual or group of each quality or attribute and to project the likely success of new choices not in the original set.

Currim, Weinberg, and Wittinck used this technique for the Lively Arts Program (LAP) at Stanford University.[13] A mail survey of current LAP subscribers asked respondents to rank order three randomly chosen paired comparisons of attributes of a subscription series drawn from the following set of factors.

Attribute	Levels
Driving time	≤ 30 min; > 30 min.
Number of series events	5; 8
Seating priority	Yes; no
Single ticket price	$5; $8; $12
Subscription discount	30%; 15%; none
Performer renown	World; national; regional

Only three comparisons were needed since the researchers could reasonably assume a preference ordering for the levels of each attribute (that is, everyone would prefer less driving to more, seating priority over no priority, a ticket for $5 over one at $8, and so forth). By looking at the trade-offs consumers made among these factors, the researchers concluded that driving time was most important, followed by performer renown, price, seating priority, number of events, and percentage discount.

The power of the conjoint techniques is found in the interactions it can detect.

Panel Studies

Researchers who wish to monitor the performance of a target market over time can choose among four change measures. For example, they can study changes in consumer behavior

1   *Retrospectively,* by asking a single sample of consumers what they are doing now and what they did at some past point in time;

2   *Cross-sectionally,* by comparing behaviors of a single sample of consumers presumed to be earlier or later in a process (for example, comparing seat-belt usage of 21- to 30-year-olds with that of 31- to 40-year-olds, or those never exposed to a particular campaign with those exposed for two, four, and six months).

3   *Cross-sectionally over time,* by asking about behaviors of different samples at two points in time (for example, as in traditional polling).

4   *Longitudinally over time,* by taking behavioral measures of the same panel of consumers at different points over time.

The value of the last approach, panel studies, as compared to cross-sectional polls, is suggested in the following hypothetical but realistic example. Suppose a political candidate, Frank Allison, makes a major statement on a key issue, say, in favor of paying women and men equally for jobs of comparable worth. Further, suppose that polls before and after the speech using *different* samples showed that the proportion of female voters planning to vote for him rose from 40 to 50 percent. Understandably, the candidate would be pleased with such results. But this pleasure is based on a belief that if one studied the same consumers before and after the speech, the shifting of consumer preferences over time would look like the figures shown in Table 7-3a. The true result in a worst case scenario, however, could be like Table 7-3b.

In Table 7-3a, Allison's speech added nicely to his present core of supporters. In Table 7-3b, his speech alienated three-quarters of his core supporters and attracted a third of his opponents' supporters and *all* those previously undecided. Under the 7-3b scenario, Allison would realize he had to move fast to win

Table 7-3

HYPOTHETICAL PANEL STUDY RESULTS

| | *a* | | *b* | | |
| | *After Speech* | | *After Speech* | | |
Before Speech	*Prefer Allison*	*Prefer Opponent*	*Prefer Allison*	*Prefer Opponent*	*Total*
Prefer Allison	40%	0%	10%	30%	40%
Prefer opponent	10%	20%	10%	20%	30%
No preference	0%	30%	30%	0%	30%
Total	50%	50%	50%	50%	100%

back "his people" while at the same time trying to hold onto the possibly fickle "undecideds" who have just switched over to him. Learning this crucial information is *only* possible with panel data. Only panel data can show *who* changed. Such data may be absolutely crucial to an organization that wishes to move quickly and correctly in a volatile marketplace.[14]

Other Low-Cost Techniques

There are a number of other useful techniques for carrying out research at lower cost.

Qualitative Research.   There are many situations in which management may wish to carry out research that does not require projections to broader populations or the use of sophisticated statistical techniques. In such situations, *qualitative research* techniques are appropriate. Among the uses of qualitative research by nonprofits are the following:

1 Identifying a problem.
2 Preparing for a subsequent quantitative study:
   a Learning about the problem from subjects
   b Generating ideas and hypotheses
   c Learning appropriate language for questions
   d Pretesting questionnaires.
3 Helping interpret a prior quantitative study.
4 Pretesting alternative advertisements, product concepts, packaging, or brochures.
5 Generating ideas for new products or services.
6 Generating ideas for advertisements or product positioning.

Two approaches that are frequently used for qualitative research are *individual depth interviews* and *focus groups*. Individual depth interviews involve lengthy questioning of a small number of respondents (rather than brief questioning of large samples) one at a time often using disguised questions and minimal interviewer prompting. Focus groups involve bringing together groups of five to ten consumers, usually (but not always) a relatively homogeneous group, to discuss a specific set of issues under the guidance of a leader trained to stimulate and focus the discussion. Figure 7-6 indicates conditions under which each of these techniques might be used.

The objective of both in-depth interviewing and focus groups is to get beneath the surface of some issue. They are based on the presumption that individuals will reveal more either when they talk at length with a sympathetic and resourceful interviewer or when they are in a relaxed group setting and are stimulated by the camaraderie and comments of others (the "kaffee klatch" model). The "trick" in both circumstances is to bring out "hidden" or deeper aspects of a subject or issue. Mary Debus of Porter/Novelli has suggested several techniques that skilled interviewers and group moderators use to achieve this. These are listed in Figure 7-7.

FIGURE 7-6

Which to Use: Focus Groups or Individual Depth Interviews?

Issue to consider	Use focus groups when . . .	Use individual depth interviews when . . .
Group interaction	interaction of respondents may stimulate a richer response or new and valuable thoughts.	group interaction is likely to be limited or nonproductive.
Group/peer pressure	group/peer pressure will be valuable in challenging the thinking of respondents and illuminating conflicting opinions.	group/peer pressure would inhibit responses and cloud the meaning of results.
Sensitivy of subject matter	subject matter is not so sensitive that respondents will temper responses or withhold information.	subject matter is so sensitive that respondents would be unwilling to talk openly in a group.
Depth of individual responses	the topic is such that most respondents can say all that is relevant or all that they know in less than ten minutes.	the topic is such that a greater depth of response per individual is desirable, as with complex subject matter and very knowledgeable respondents.
Interviewer fatigue	it is desirable to have one interviewer conduct the research; several groups will not create interviewer fatigue or boredom.	it is desirable to have numerous interviewers on the project. One interviewer would become fatigued or bored conducting the interviews.
Stimulus materials	the volume of stimulus material is not extensive.	a large amount of stimulus material must be evaluated.
Continuity of information	a single subject area is being examined in depth and strings of behaviors are less relevant.	it is necessary to understand how attitudes and behaviors link together on an individual pattern basis.
Experimentation with interview guide	enough is known to establish a meaningful topic guide.	it may be necessary to develop the interview guide by altering it after each of the initial interviews.
Observation	it is possible and desirable for key decision makers to observe "firsthand" consumer information.	"firsthand" consumer information is not critical or observation is not logistically possible.
Logistics	an acceptable number of target respondents can be assembled in one location.	respondents are geographically dispersed or not easily assembled for other reasons.
Cost and timing	quick turnaround is critical, and funds are limited.	quick turnaround is not critical, and budget will permit higher cost.

SOURCE: Mary Debus, *Handbook for Excellence in Focus Group Research* (Washington, D.C.: Academy for Educational Development, n.d.), p. 10. Reproduced with permission.

FIGURE 7-7

Suggestions for Soliciting Responses in Focus Groups

---

1   *Build the relevant context information*—What are the experiences or issues that surround a product or a practice that influence how it/he/she is viewed?

2   *Top-of-mind associations*—What's the first thing that comes to mind when I say "family planning"?

3   *Constructing images*—Who are the people who buy Panther condoms? What do they look like? What are their lives about? (Or) Where are you when you buy condoms? Describe the place. What do you see? What do you feel? What do you do?

4   *Querying the meaning of the obvious*—What does "soft" mean to you? What does the phrase "it's homemade" mean to you?

5   *Establishing conceptual maps of a product category*—How would you group these different family planning methods? How do they go together for you? How are groups similar/different? What would you call these groups?

6   *Metaphors*—If this birth control pill were a flower, what kind would it be and who would pick it? If this group of products were a family, who would the different members be and how do they relate to each other?

7   *Image matching*—Here are pictures of ten different situations/ people. . . . Which go with this wine and which do not? Why?

8   *"Man from the moon" routine*—I'm from the moon; I've never heard of Fritos. Describe them to me. Why would I want to try one? Convince me.

9   *Conditions that give permission and create barriers*—Tell me about two or three situations in which you would decide to buy this chocolate and two to three situations in which you would decide to buy something else.

10   *Chain of questions*—Why do you buy "X"? Why is that important? Why does that make a difference to you? Would it ever not be important? (Ask until the respondent is ready to kill the interviewer!)

11   *Benefit chain*—This cake mix has more egg whites; what's the benefit of that? (Answer: "It's moister.") What is the benefit of a moister cake? (Answer: "It tastes homemade.") And why is homemade better? (Answer: "It's more effort.") And what's the benefit of that? (Answer: My family will appreciate it.") And? (Answer: "They will know I love them.") And? (Answer: "I'll feel better; they'll love me back.")

12   *Laddering (chains of association)*—What do you think of when you think of Maxwell House Coffee? (Answer: "Morning.") And when you think of morning, what comes to mind? (Answer: "A new day.") And when you think of a new day? (Answer: "I feel optimistic.")

13   *Pointing out contradictions*—Wait a minute, you just told me you would like it to be less greasy and now you're telling me it works because it's greasy and oily—how do you explain it?

14   *Sentence completions and extensions*—The ideal ORS product is one that . . . The best thing about this new product is . . . It makes me feel . . .

15   *Role playing*—Okay, now you're the Chairman of the Board, or the Mayor of this city. What would you do? (Or) I'm the Mayor, talk to me, tell me what you want.

16   *Best-of-all-possible-world scenarios*—Forget about reality for a minute. If

> you could design your own diaper that has everything you ever wanted in a diaper and more, what would it be like? Use your imagination. There are no limits. Don't worry about whether it's possible or not.
>
> **17** *Script writing*—If you were able to tell a story or write a movie about this company or city (or whatever), what would it be about? Who are the heroines and heroes? Does the movie have a message? Would you go see it? Who would?

SOURCE: Mary Debus, *Handbook for Excellence in Focus Group Research* (Washington, D.C.: Academy for Educational Development, n.d.), pp. 32–33. Reproduced with permission.

Experimentation.   A major problem with survey research is that it relies upon information volunteered by consumers. The quality of the measurements can well be compromised by interviewee or interviewer bias. Many private organizations have sought to develop more objective behavioral measures through experimentation. Experimental opportunities abound. Too many non-profit organizations ignore excellent opportunities to learn about their marketplace by applying differing marketing strategies to different subsamples of the population. For example,

- A fund-raiser could divide a mailing list into three groups and send out solicitations with varying degrees of "personalization."
- A manager of an adolescent drug program could place a television set in the waiting rooms of half their centers and video games in the other half and observe the effects on return rates of patients.
- A museum's cafeteria manager could systematically change prices on their assorted cheesecakes every day over a three-month period and estimate the price-volume relationship.
- Hospital rooms could be decorated in different colors or nurses' uniforms changed on different floors to assess their effects on patients' satisfaction with the quality of care.

These experimental manipulations often require little effort in the part of managers. Often they can be done as simple "wrinkles" in marketing projects that would be undertaken anyway. In contrast to surveys and many qualitative techniques, they usually can be carried out *unobtrusively*, that is, without the target audience knowing they are part of a study. Researchers, however, should avoid thinking that "just trying something" makes for good experimentation. Careful attention must be paid to random assignment of experimental treatments across subjects, use of control groups wherever possible, and monitoring the surrounding circumstances for possible confounding effects.[15]

Convenience Sampling.   A nonprofit organization with a very limited budget often can get useful data (although again not projectable) from respondents close at hand. Hospitals, for example, could study patients, visitors, and service delivery people coming into the hospital. These groups would obviously know more about the hospital and may be more biased than strangers. Still, the hospital might argue that these people are their target market and knowing more about them (and the differences among them) could be very useful.

Snowball Sampling. Participants in the above study could be asked to suggest the names of others "like them" who could be contacted. This would add a group that (1) did not have the familiarity biases of the first group, (2) would be likely to cooperate in the study (especially if the initial respondents allowed their names to be used as references), and (3) would closely *match* the first sample in all other socioeconomic characteristics but that which characterized the initial sample (for example, people already coming to the hospital). Snowball sampling is a particularly good technique for finding rare populations. A hospital trying to broaden its appeal to hemophiliacs, for example, might ask those hemophiliacs already attending the hospital to identify others. Conducting a full-scale random sample to find rare populations like paraplegics or handicapped bus riders or the deaf would be prohibitively expensive. Yet members of such rare groups may well be known to many others like themselves.

Piggybacking. Nonprofit organizations may be able to add questions onto studies undertaken by others. Several national research organizations regularly conduct omnibus surveys that combine questions from a number of sponsors. Nonprofits could add questions for close to the incremental cost of the question or questions. These or other private firms with a public service inclination may be willing to add such questions at no charge or at reduced rates.

Volunteer Field Workers. Nonprofits such as hospitals or charities may enlist volunteers to conduct telephone, mail, or "convenience" interviews, or to tabulate questionnaires.

Student Projects. Students in business schools and sometimes in psychology and sociology departments are frequently looking for outside, real-world term projects. They can be an excellent source of thought and legwork for nonprofit organizations. However, certain caveats should be observed. First, student interviewers are not the same as trained professional interviewers. The nonprofit manager must give them guidance or be sure that a professor is overseeing the research process. Second, plenty of lead time is necessary. Student projects must fit within semester or quarter academic systems. Third, the nonprofit manager should set time aside to consult with the students—they are doing this to learn. Finally, the nonprofit manager should be sensitive to the university's research norms. The students cannot be ordered to do the research in a particular way, the professor cannot be treated as a paid consultant or a field supervisor, and the professor may request that the results be made public (although possibly in disguised form).

Secondary Sources. Various published sources can provide comparative data or suggestions for question wording, sample design, and data analysis. Trade articles, marketing journals, and government reports can all prove very valuable, especially at the beginning stages of a project.

Board of Directors. Most nonprofit organizations select board members who will serve the nonprofit in some beneficial way. A typical board has lawyers, bankers, accountants, and individuals who have access to influential financial and political figures. There is every reason to add a marketing research professional (and advertising, public relations, and other marketing professionals) to the board. Such experts can provide useful advice, and possibly offer the services of their agency gratis or at reduced rates.

RESEARCH BIASES[16]

Research can only be effective if it avoids major sources of error. Detailing all of the things that can go wrong with field research is beyond the scope of this book. The nonprofit manager should be aware, however, of the major pitfalls. First, it should be made clear that there are two major kinds of error: sampling error and systematic bias.

Sampling error is the error brought about because only a sample was taken from the universe. This type of error can be reduced by simply increasing the sample size or by adopting sophisticated stratification techniques.

Systematic bias is more difficult to handle. It refers to all those "glitches" that cause the expected value of the sample to be different from the true value. The "expected value" is the value the research would yield if the design were repeated a very large number of times. As shown in Figure 7-8, in an unbiased sample, the expected value for the mean ($E(\bar{x}_1)$) is the same as the true value for the mean (μ). The standard error ($\sigma_{\bar{x}}$) would be a measure of the sampling error around this expected value. Its size would depend on (1) the true variability of the value being studied in the overall universe, which the researcher cannot influence, and (2) the sample size, which the researcher can influence. As shown in Figure 7-8, *bias* is the difference between the expected value from the particular research procedure and the true value (that is, $\mu - E(\bar{x}_2)$) when they are *not* the same.

FIGURE 7-8

Sampling Error and Systematic Bias in Field Research

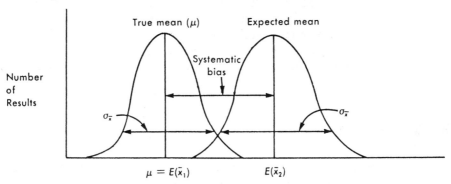

Systematic bias in a survey usually comes about in the following ways:

1   *Frame bias.* This is caused by drawing a probability sample from a poor representation of the universe. For example, estimating the proportion of households who moved in the last 12 months by sampling from the telephone directory would systematically underestimate the true value since recent movers are much less likely to be listed in a given directory.

2   *Selection bias.* This is caused when the procedure for drawing actual sample members *always* excludes or underrepresents certain types of universe (frame) members. This would occur if telephone interviewers only telephoned during the day, thus underrepresenting men and households where everyone works. It would also occur in field surveys where interviewers were allowed to pick and choose whom to interview. If interviewers were told to stand at a street corner or at a shopping mall and interview people "selected at random," they would probably ignore "unsavory characters" as well as people hurrying and people who had pestering children. "Nice" people or people with characteristics similar to the interviewer's would have a much better chance to be interviewed.

3   *Nonresponse.* This results when a particular group of those contacted declines to participate out of lack of interest, antagonism, or busyness.

4   *Interviewer bias.* In this situation, an untrained interviewer deliberately or inadvertently leads the respondent to deviate from the truth. This can occur, for example, when interviewers read or "clarify" a question in a way that suggests that a particular answer is preferred.

5   *Questionnaire bias.* Systematic error can arise due to poor or confusing wording, leading questions, identification of the research sponsor, or omission of important possible responses.

6   *Respondent bias.* In this instance, the respondent misremembers something, lies, or unwittingly distorts an answer. Often this source of bias results not from malice, but from a misplaced attempt to "help out," as when an interviewee tries to please the interviewer by "yea-saying" everything.

7   *Processing bias.* This would occur if the interviewer (or respondent in a written study) wrote down the wrong answers, the office entered the answers into the computer incorrectly, or—heaven forbid—the computer analysis was programmed incorrectly.

Catching all these glitches is not easy. It takes careful attention to the design process, to interviewer training, to checking on data processing, and so on. It should be said that research funds are often better spent on catching glitches than on increasing the sample size. As one can see in Figure 7-8, the band of sampling error around the expected mean could be reduced somewhat by increasing N, but the potential for reduction of systematic bias is *much greater*. Dollars spent reducing the latter will undoubtedly have much greater impact than just dragging in more (biased) sample members.

ORGANIZATION[17]

We noted earlier many ways in which the research function can be organized. Among the key questions to be decided are

1   Is the marketing research function to stand alone, or is it to fit within a broader marketing or management information system? The answer depends on management's perception of the research mission (whether it is largely to provide descriptive, explanatory, or predictive information) and also on the overall budget.

2   Which of the marketing research functions are to be farmed out to outside suppliers and which kept in-house? New nonprofit research departments will farm more functions out and with maturity gather them back in.

3   Where should the research function be placed in the organization? We believe it should be high in the organization, since we believe that effective marketing is informed marketing. It should not be placed in a position (for example, in accounting) where its value may be compromised and its use limited.

Evaluation and Control

The nonprofit's marketing research strategy should be routinely and formally evaluated. Questions should be raised about methodologies and personnel. Managers should be queried about the value of the information they received and asked for possible improvements. From time to time, an independent outside consultant should be brought in to ascertain the quality of the research given the available budget.

SUMMARY

Most nonprofit organizations carry out much less marketing research than they should. This is because they have accepted certain myths. They assume that marketing research should only be used for major decisions, that it involves big surveys and takes a long time, that it is always expensive, that it requires sophisticated researchers, and, when it is finished, that it is usually not read or used. But research using a diversity of techniques, many at low cost, can be extremely valuable to a wide range of decisions.

Research, like any other management activity, must be planned strategically with a mission, strategy, budgets, implementation plan, organization, and control. Eventually, the nonprofit organization should develop a marketing information system. A marketing information system has four major subsystems, an internal records system, a market intelligence system, a marketing research system, and an analytical marketing system.

Research can help managers by describing, explaining, or predicting market characteristics. Most nonprofit research is applied, although some could be basic or methodological research. The applied nature of the research provides a good framework for decisions about budgets and for designing specific research projects.

There are several approaches to budgeting research, including historical increment, percent of revenues, competitive matching, and affordable budgeting. A cost/benefit approach is preferable, however, because it explicitly takes account of the uses to which the study's results are to be put. The actual amount to spend would then depend on the likely quality that the expenditure could achieve.

An applied orientation also recommends a "backward" research design process. Here the research manager first looks to the decisions to be made using the research results and then works backward to design a study that would best inform such decisions. An important step would be determining what report format would provide the most managerially useful information. The report form would then suggest the type of analysis needed, which, in turn, would specify how the data are to be collected and processed.

Research can be quantitative or nonquantitative, high cost or low cost. Qualitative research, such as in-depth interviewing or focus groups, can be useful in identifying a problem, gathering background for later quantitative studies, interpreting past studies, pretesting advertisements, product concepts, packaging and brochures, and generating ideas for new products, services, and advertisements. Other techniques for keeping research costs low are experimentation, low-cost sampling designs, and use of secondary data and volunteer assistance.

Management of individual projects must involve careful attention in advance to potential biases and then to a careful evaluation of accomplishments or failures after the project has been completed. Such evaluation and control is especially essential as the organization develops a continuous program of strategic research over several years.

QUESTIONS

1. Develop an outline for carrying on a focus group discussion with groups of MBAs about three alternative study-abroad concepts. Describe techniques to be used for the situations where one or two individuals dominate the group.

2. A research director for a social service program aimed at Hispanic neighborhoods proposes a telephone study to determine community needs for new programs. She plans to interview 500 respondents picked by means of a reverse directory of area telephone listings. The budget will be $7,000. Under what circumstances would you advise her to reduce the sample size and spend the money saved on reducing other potential biases?

3. What are the major secondary sources a library director might use in constructing an estimate of potential lending volume for branch libraries in four alternative small towns? Construct a quantitative index the director could use to rank the candidate towns in order of potential.

4. What information could a museum director collect from a panel of area residents that would not be available from a one-time survey? Would this information justify the expenditure of an additional $2,000 a year? Explain.

5. A charity fund-raiser will send out four mailings to area residents over the next 12 months. He is willing to conduct one experiment with each mailing. Describe an experimental strategy where the set of experiments would build upon one another to improve management decision making.

NOTES

1. This section draws upon Alan R. Andreasen, "Cost-Conscious Marketing Research," *Harvard Business Review*, July–August 1983, pp. 74–77.
2. For further information on research costs, see Seymour Sudman, *Reducing the Costs of Surveys* (Chicago: Aldine, 1967).
3. See, for example, James B. Higgenbotham and Keith K. Cox, eds., *Focus Group Interviews: A Reader* (Chicago: American Marketing Association, 1979).
4. The definition is adapted from Samuel V. Smith, Richard L. Brien, and James E. Stafford, "Marketing Information Systems: An Introductory Overview," in their *Readings in Marketing Information Systems* (Boston: Houghton Mifflin, 1968), p. 7. See also Lee G. Cooper and Daniel Jacobs, "Marketing Information Systems for the Profession and Science of Arts Management," *The Journal of Arts Management and the Law*, Vol. 14, no. 1, Spring 1984, pp. 77–89.
5. See David A. Aaker, ed., *Multivariate Analysis in Marketing: Theory and Applications* (Belmont, Calif.: Wadsworth, 1971).
6. Various models are described in Gary L. Lilien and Philip Kotler, *Marketing Decision Making—A Model Building Approach*, 2d ed. (New York: Harper & Row, 1983).
7. *The Professional Performing Arts: Attendance, Preferences and Motives* (Madison, Wisc.: Association of College, University, and Community Arts Administrators, 1977).
8. Alan R. Andreasen, *Conducting an Effective Retail Audit*, Practical Guide #4 (Washington, D.C.: SOMARC/The Futures Group, 1988).
9. Dik Warren Twedt, *1983 Survey of Marketing Research* (Chicago: American Marketing Association, 1984).
10. This approach makes use of Bayesian analytic techniques. For an introduction to this approach, see Robert Schlaifer, *Probability and Statistics for Business Decisions* (New York: McGraw-Hill, 1979). For other cost/benefit treatments of this problem, see Frank M. Bass, "Marketing Research Expenditures: A Decision Model," *Journal of Business*, January 1963, pp. 77–90; and Ralph L. Day, "Optimizing Marketing Research Through Cost Benefit Analysis," *Business Horizons*, Fall 1966, pp. 45–54.
11. This section is drawn from Alan R. Andreasen, " 'Backward' Marketing Research," *Harvard Business Review*, May–June 1985, pp. 176–182.
12. Alan R. Andreasen and Russell W. Belk, "Predictors of Attendance at the Performing Arts," *Journal of Consumer Research*, September 1980, pp. 112–120.
13. Imran Currim, Charles B. Weinberg, and Dick R. Wittinck, "Design of Subscription Programs for a Performing Arts Series," *Journal of Consumer Research*, June 1981, pp. 67–75. For other examples, see Yoram Wind and Lawrence K. Spitz, "Analytical Approach to Marketing Decisions in Health-Care Organizations," *Operations Research*, September–October 1976, pp. 973–990, and Linda J. Golden, Mark I. Alpert, and John F. Betak, "A Programmatic Research Approach to Transit Marketing," *Traffic Quarterly*, Vol. 34, no. 4, October 1980, pp. 627–647.
14. For further discussion, see Seymour Sudman and Robert Ferber, *Consumer Panels* (Chicago: American Marketing Association, 1979).

15. A good introduction to alternative field experimental designs is found in Donald T. Campbell and Julian C. Stanley, *Experimental and Quasi-Experimental Designs for Research* (Chicago: Rand McNally, 1966). For a good example of a nonprofit experiment, see Richard A. Winett, Ingrid N. Lecklite, Donna E. Chinn, and Brian Stahl, "Reducing Energy Consumption: The Long-Term Effects of a Single TV Program," *Journal of Communications*, Summer 1984, pp. 37–51.

16. See Gilbert A. Churchill, Jr., *Marketing Research: Methodological Foundations*, 3rd ed. (Chicago: Dryden, 1983), pp. 412–420. See also Leslie Kish, *Survey Sampling* (New York: John Wiley, 1965), especially Chapter 13.

17. See, for example, Lee Adler and Charles S. Mayer, eds., *Readings in Managing the Marketing Research Function* (Chicago: American Marketing Association, 1980).

8

Estimating and Forecasting Markets

Demographic changes are playing havoc with the performing arts. The Baby Boom Generation has shown a remarkable reluctance to be interested in the theater, ballet, classical concerts, or opera. The 76 million Baby Boomers born between 1946 and 1965 are overworked and overcommitted. And when they think of leisure activities, their taste turns to avant-garde restaurants, comedy clubs, and movies.

Audiences for symphony orchestras around the country are aging rapidly. At least half of those subscribing to concerts in New York and Los Angeles are over 55. And a recent study for the Los Angeles Philharmonic found that 43.5 percent of its subscribers were over 65!

Baby Boomers are less likely than the generation before them to have been exposed to the classical arts during their childhood. Cuts in public and in-school programs make it likely that the next generations will be even less prepared to appreciate the "finer arts" when they grow up.

Even when Baby Boomers are bitten by the classical music bug, they more often turn to their stereos and CD players. The idea of dressing up and going downtown appeals to them a lot less than staying home with a good recording and some fine wine.

Many symphony orchestras have tried to lure the Baby Boomers to their halls with informal concerts and canapes at intermission. They have scheduled more photogenic and popular artists and conductors and used "pops" concerts as an entry-level inducement to future serious concert-goers. But the future looks bleak when they contemplate trying to attract an audience used to MTV and hyperelectronic rock concerts to a serious evening of Brahms and Beethoven, let alone Wagner and Philip Glass.

Source: See also Barbara Isenberg, "Marketing Music: Can You Say 'Baby Boomer'?" *Los Angeles Times*, November 19, 1989, pp. 6ff.

A great many marketing decisions require a full understanding of the current and probable future market for a good or a service. Whether a nonprofit should venture into a new market or whether it is getting a reasonable share of the existing market are questions that can be answered only after present and future market potential have been carefully determined. This in turn requires that the manager be able to answer the following questions:

1   Who is the market? (market definition)
2   How large is the current market? (current market size measurement)
3   What is the probable future size of the market? (market forecasting)

These questions will be examined in the following sections.

DEFINING THE MARKET

Every organization faces the task of defining who is in its market. It knows that not everyone is a potential customer of its market offer. Not everyone is in the market for a college education, or day care center services, or cancer treatment, or a job with the police department. Organizations must distinguish between their customers and noncustomers.

To define the market, the organization must carefully define its market offer. Take the case of a small private college. We can talk about the market for the college's bachelor's degree, or for its sociology program, or for its specific course on the sociology of religion. The market definition and size would vary in each case. Even the market for the course on the sociology of religion would be affected by the cost of the course and the place and time it is offered. The more specifically we can define the product, the more carefully we can determine the market's boundaries and size. We define a market as follows:

> **A market** is a set of actual or potential customers who might engage in a given exchange.

Two comments are in order. The term "customers" is shorthand for a number of other possible terms such as buyers, clients, adopters, users, and responders. Furthermore, customers can be individuals, families, groups, or organizations. Also the term "given exchange" is shorthand for all offers of tangible goods, services, or programs to which target customers can respond.

As noted in Chapter 4, those in the market for something have three characteristics: *interest, the ability to transact,* and *access.* To illustrate this, consider the following situation:

> The chairman of a French department at a small college is concerned with the declining number of students signing up for French. One faculty member has already been dismissed, and another will be dismissed if the market for studying

French continues to shrink. The French department chairman is thinking of offering an evening noncredit course on French culture to adults in the community. He is interested in estimating whether enough adults in the community would be in the "market" for this course.

The first thing to estimate is the number of adults in the community with a potential interest in a course on French culture. There are a number of ways to do this. The chairman could contact other colleges offering this course and find out their enrollment levels as a proportion of their area's adult population. A more direct approach would be to phone a random sample of adults in the more affluent and educated sectors of the community and ask about their level of interest in a French culture course. The following question could be asked: "If a noncredit French culture course is offered in the evening at our college, would you definitely take it, probably take it, or not be interested in taking it?" Suppose 4 out of 100 say they would definitely take the course, 6 say they might take it, and 90 say they would not take it. At the most, it appears that 10 percent have an interest in this course.[1] This percentage can be multiplied by the adult population in the community to estimate the potential market for this course. We define the potential market as follows:

> The **potential market** is the set of consumers who profess some level of interest in a defined market exchange.

Consumer interest is not enough to define a market. If a price is attached to the offer, potential consumers must have adequate income to afford the purchase. They must be able to buy besides being willing to buy. Furthermore, the higher the price, the lower the number of people who will stay in the market. The size of a market is a function not only of the interest level but also of the ability to transact.[2] In certain circumstances, this "ability" would include goods or time to donate, blood with adequate hemoglobin to give, and so on.

Market size is further cut down by personal *access* barriers that might prevent response to the offer. Interested consumers may not be able to take the French course at the place and time it is offered. Access factors make the market smaller. The market that remains is called the available market. We define the available market as follows:

> The **available market** is the set of consumers who have interest, ability to transact, and access to a particular market exchange.

In some market offers, the organization will establish some restrictions regarding with whom they will transact. Although a college sells football tickets to everyone in the community wishing to attend a game, it may not be willing to accept everyone who wants to take a course in French culture. The college may choose to accept only adults who (1) are 24-years-old or older and (2) have a high school diploma. These adults constitute the qualified available market:

> The **qualified available market** is the set of consumers who have interest, ability to transact, access, and qualifications for the particular market exchange.

Now the college has the choice of going after the whole qualified available market or concentrating its efforts on certain segments. In the latter case, we need the concept of the target market. We define the target market as follows:

> The **target market** is the part of the qualified available market that the organization attempts to attract and serve.

Suppose the college prefers to attract primarily middle- and upper-class adults to its evening classes and, as a result, promotes the French culture course primarily in certain sections of the city. In that case, the target market would be somewhat smaller than the qualified available market. The target market may be served by any number of marketers. Those who choose a particular marketer's offering are called the penetrated market. We define the penetrated market as follows:

> The **penetrated market** is the set of qualified available consumers who are actually participating in the marketer's exchanges.

The organization's market share is the ratio of the penetrated market to the portion of the target market served by all markets.

Figure 8-1 brings all the preceding concepts together. The bar on the left illustrates the ratio of the potential market—all interested persons—to the total population, here 10 percent. The figure on the right illustrates several break-downs of the potential market. The available market—those who have interest, ability to transact, and access—is 40 percent of the potential consumers. The qualified available market—those who would meet the college's admissions requirements—is 20 percent of the potential market, or 50 percent of the available market. The college is actively trying to attract half of these, or 10 percent of the potential market. Finally, the college is shown as actually enrolling 5 percent of the potential market in the course.

These definitions of a market are a useful tool for marketing planning. If the organization is not satisfied with the size of its penetrated market, it can consider a number of actions. First, it could try to attract a larger percentage of people from its target market. If it finds, however, that the nonenrolling part of the target market has chosen to study French culture at a competing college, this college might try to widen its target market by promoting the course in other parts of the city. Beyond this, the college could relax the qualifications for admission, thus expanding the qualified available market. The next step would be to consider expanding the available market by lowering tuition, improving the location and time of the course offering, and doing other things to reduce cost and access. Ultimately, the college could try to expend the potential market

FIGURE 8-1

Levels of Market Definition

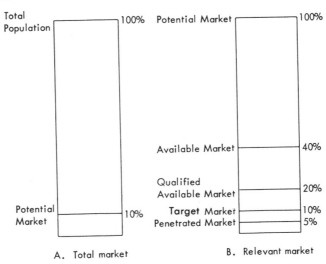

A. Total market   B. Relevant market

by launching a campaign to convert noninterested consumers into interested consumers.

MEASURING CURRENT MARKET DEMAND

We now are ready to examine practical methods of estimating current market demand for a market offer. There are four types of estimates that an organization will want to make: *total market demand, segment market demand, total industry demand,* and *organization market share.*

Estimating Total Market Demand

Total market demand is defined as follows:

> **Total market demand** is the total volume of exchanges with all marketers that would be made by a defined consumer group in a defined geographical area in a defined time period in a defined marketing environment under a set of defined marketing programs.

The most important thing to realize about total market demand is that it is not a fixed number but a function of the specified conditions. One of these conditions, for example, is the marketing programs (psychological and economic cost, product features, promotional expenditure level, etc.) of all marketers, and another is the state of the economy. The dependence of total market demand on these conditions is illustrated in the response curve in Figure 8-2. The horizontal axis shows different possible levels of marketing expenditure by industry organizations in a given time period. On the vertical axis is shown the resulting demand level. The curve represents the estimated level of market demand associated with different marketing expenditure levels by the industry organizations. We see that some base volume (called the *market minimum*) would take place without any demand-stimulating expenditures. Positive marketing expenditures would yield higher levels of demand, first at an increasing rate, then at a decreasing rate. Marketing expenditures higher than a certain level would not stimulate much further demand, thus suggesting an upper limit to market demand called the *market potential*.

The distance between the market minimum and the market potential shows the overall *marketing sensitivity of demand*. We can think of two extreme types of markets, the *expansible* and the *nonexpansible*. An expansible market, such as a market for a new sport such as paddle ball, is quite affected in its total size by the level of marketing expenditures. In terms of Figure 8-2A the distance between Q_0 and Q_1 is relatively large. A less expansible market, such as the market for opera, is not much affected by the level of marketing expenditures; the distance between Q_0 and Q_1 is relatively small. The organization operating in a low-expansible market can take the market's size (the level of *primary demand*) for granted and concentrate its marketing resources on getting a desired market share (the level of *selective demand*).

Only one of the many possible levels of marketing expenditure will actually be chosen by the various organizations in the market. The market demand corresponding to this expenditure level is called the *market forecast*. The market forecast shows the expected level of market demand for the expected level of organizational marketing expenditures in the given environment.

If a different environment is assumed, the market demand function would have to be freshly estimated. The market for theatergoing, for example, is higher during prosperity than recession because market demand is income-elastic. The dependence of market demand on the environment is illustrated in Figure 8-2B.

The main point is that the marketer should carefully define the situation for which market demand is being estimated. The marketer can use a method known as the *chain ratio method* to form the estimate. The chain ratio method involves multiplying a base number by a succession of percentages that lead to an estimation of the defined consumer demand. Here is an example:

> The U.S. Navy seeks to attract 112,000 new male recruits each year from American high schools. The question is whether this is a high or low target in relation to the market potential. The market potential has been estimated by the chain ratio method as follows:

Total number of male high school graduating students	10,000,000
Percentage who are militarily qualified (no physical, emotional, or mental handicaps)	× .50

Percentage of those qualified who are potentially interested in military service	× .15
Percentage of those qualified and interested in military service who consider the Navy the preferred service	× .30

This chain of numbers shows the market potential to be 225,000 recruits. Since this exceeds the target number of recruits sought, the U.S. Navy should not have much trouble meeting its target, if it does a reasonable job of market-

FIGURE 8-2

Market Demand

A. Market demand as function of marketing expenditure
(assumes particular marketing environment)

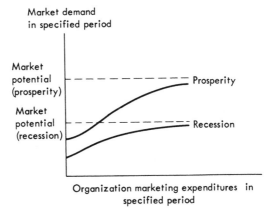

B. Market demand as function of marketing expenditure
(two different environments assumed)

ing. But many of the potential recruits are lost somehow. They are not contacted; their parents talk them out of military service; they hear negative things from friends; they form a bad impression at the recruiting office. The result is that the Navy barely manages to recruit the targeted number. Knowing the market potential therefore provides the Navy with a basis for knowing whether it is doing well or poorly in comparison to what it *could* do.

Estimating Total Industry Demand

Besides measuring potential demand, an organization will want to know the current number of exchanges taking place in its market. This requires identifying the other organizations serving the same market. This is not as simple as it sounds because of the many definitions of a market. Grant Hospital, for example, would have to identify other alcoholic treatment centers in the greater Chicago area where some of its potential consumers might have gone. Should this include Highland Park Hospital, which is a long distance away but might have some alcoholism patients? The organization must carefully define its real competition as the first step in developing an estimate of total sales and its share of sales.

Then the organization has to estimate the volume for each competitor. How can this information be obtained? In some situations, secondary databases may already exist, often as the result of mandated government reports. The next easiest way is to contact each competitor and offer to exchange information. In this way, each organization can measure its performance against every other organization and against the total volume for the industry. However, this solution is not always available. Trading competitive information is illegal in some industries. In other cases, particular competitors are not willing to divulge this information. In the latter case, the organization can still compare its performance to that of the cooperating organizations.

Another solution calls for a trade association to collect the data and publish the results of each organization, the industry total, or both. In this way, each organization can evaluate its performance against specific competitors or the industry as a whole. If such a trade association does not exist, nonprofit competitors may see the need for comparative data as the very reason to create a trade association.

If this solution is not available, the organization must estimate the volume of one or more competitors through indirect methods. Grant Hospital, for example, might infer the number of inpatient alcoholism treatments at a particular competitive hospital by knowing the number of beds, the size of the staff, or other clues. In the industrial world, a company may estimate the sales of another company by finding out how many shifts the factory is operating or how much raw material it is ordering from suppliers. In the retail sector, this if often accomplished by multiplying square footage of competitors' outlets by estimated sales per square foot (based, for example, on one's own sales per square foot).

Estimating Organization Market Share

The organization's own volume does not tell the whole story of how well it is doing. Suppose the organization's volume is increasing at 5 percent a year and its competitor's volume is increasing at 10 percent. This organization is actually losing its relative standing in the industry. Organizations will therefore want to compare their volume with that of competitors.

Organizations can estimate at least three market share figures. Ideally, the organization should know its (1) share of the total market, (2) share of the target market, and (3) share relative to the leading competitor or leading three competitors. Each of these measures yields useful information about the organization's market performance and potential.

FORECASTING FUTURE MARKET DEMAND

Having looked at ways to estimate current demand, we can now examine the problem of estimating future demand. Very few industries lend themselves to easy forecasting. The few cases generally involve a product or service whose absolute level or trend is fairly constant and whose competition is nonexistent or stable. In the vast majority of markets, total market demand and specific organization demand are not stable from year to year, and good forecasting becomes a key factor in effective performance. This is particularly true for nonprofits in which these problems are compounded by a lack of good historical data. In such cases, poor forecasting can lead to excess or insufficient personnel and supplies. The more unstable the demand, the more critical is forecast accuracy, and the more elaborate is forecasting procedure.

In approaching forecasting, one should list all the factors that might affect future demand and predict each factor's likely future level and effect on demand. Consistent with the SMPP (Chapter 3) the factors affecting demand might be classified into three categories: (1) *noncontrollable macroenvironmental factors* such as the state of the economy, new technologies, and legal developments; (2) *competitive factors* such as competitors' prices, new products, and promotional expenditures; and (3) *controllable organizational factors* such as the organization's prices, new products, and promotional expenditures.

In view of the many factors that might be involved, organizations have turned to various approximation methods to forecast future demand. Six major methods are discussed below. They arise out of three information bases for building a forecast. A forecast can be based on *what people say, what people do,* or *what people have done.* The first basis—what people say—involves systematic determination of the opinions of buyers or of those close to them, such as salespersons or outside experts. It encompasses three methods: (1) buyer intentions surveys, (2) intermediary estimates, and (3) expert judgments. Building a forecast on what people do involves another method: (4) market testing. The final basis—what people have done—involves using statistical tools to analyze records of past buying behavior, using either (5) time-series analysis or (6) statistical demand analysis. Each of these methods is described and illustrated below.

Buyer Intentions Surveys

Forecasting is particularly difficult when one is dealing with new offerings or markets that have dramatically changed. One way to form an estimate of future demand is to ask a sample of target buyers either individually or in focus groups to state their buying intentions for the forthcoming period. Suppose a college is trying to estimate the number of majors to expect next year in each of its disciplines. The objective is to schedule enough courses and faculty to service the level of demand for the various majors. A small number of sophomores can be asked to indicate their intended major next year. If 20 percent say that they intend to make economics their major, the college can multiply this against the size of the sophomore class and infer the number of actual students who plan to major in economics.

The reliability of buyer intentions forecasts depends on (1) buyers having clear intentions, (2) buyers being likely to carry out their intentions, (3) buyers being willing to describe their intentions to interviewers, and (4) little time elapsing between the forecast and the behavior. To the extent that these assumptions are weak, the results must be used with caution. Suppose a theater at midseason asked its subscribers about their intentions to renew their subscriptions for the following year. The problem is that the current subscribers may not have thought about renewal and they may want to finish the series before forming their intentions. Buyer intentions data in this case would be weak.

They would also be weak in the case of new products, services, or ideas with which consumers are unfamiliar. Thus, asking voters in 1991 about their intention to support a "flat" income tax may yield highly unreliable estimates. Consumers are also notoriously poor predictors whenever much time elapses before the predicted behavior itself. Certainly, Jimmy Carter would have dropped out of the presidential race of 1976 if he had believed that a poll indicating that less than 10 percent of the population intended to vote for him was a good predictor of the eventual outcome.

Buyer intentions could be assessed in a number of ways. A yes-or-no form of the question would be: "Do you intend to buy a season ticket next year?" This requires the respondent to make a definite choice. Some researchers prefer the following form of the question: "Will you (a) definitely buy, (b) probably buy, (c) probably not buy, or (d) definitely not buy a season ticket next year?" These researchers feel that the "definitely buys" would be fairly dependable as a minimum estimate and some fraction of the "probably buys" could be added to arrive at a forecast. More recently, some researchers have recommended using a *full purchase probability scale*:

Do you intend to buy a season theater ticket for next year?

.00	.10	.20	.30	.40	.50	.60	.70	.80	.90	1.00
No chance	Very slight possibility	Slight possibility	Some possibility	Fair possibility	Fairly good possibility	Good possibility	Probably	Very probably	Almost certain	Certain

The researcher uses various fractions of the positive responders to form an estimate. The researcher can improve the system over time by checking the forecasts against the actuals and seeing what weights would have improved the forecasts.

Finally, it may be noted that even when the *absolute* levels of demand derived from buyer intentions are unreliable, the relative levels are often reliable. Thus, if a nonprofit organization measures buyer intentions over several years, it may know that *each* estimate is fallible but that if the buyer intention index is up 20 percent between periods, demand may be expected to rise. Even where past indexes are unavailable, forecasts of *relative* demand for different kinds of market offerings can be derived by asking target audience members a series of "what if" questions (see Exhibit 8-1).

EXHIBIT 8-1

Expanding the Audience for Symphony and Theater

Traditional approaches to forecasting demand for the arts have relied on trend extrapolation or econometric models describing the relationship between selected socioeconomic characteristics and past attendance behavior. These approaches are of limited value for arts marketers interested in *changing* past relationships to broaden the base of arts attendance. To remedy this, Andreasen and Belk collected data forecasting the probable responses of theater and symphony audiences in four southern cities to a series of "what if" questions.

The approach adopted was designed, not to forecast absolute levels, but to provide indexes of the relative effectiveness of specific concrete strategies known to be available to most arts marketers. Thus, past attenders and nonattenders of theater and symphony were asked to indicate whether they would increase or decrease (if possible) their attendance *if* certain changes were made. Among the changes suggested were:

1 *Product changes*
    a   Changes in types of performance
    b   Changes in the quality of performances
    c   Increases in the amount of explanation about performances
2 *Place changes*
    a   Performances nearer to home
    b   More informal dress at performances

3 *Price changes*
  a   Increases or decreases in individual ticket prices
  b   Changes in series ticket discounts
  c   Offering half-price tickets the day of the performance
  d   Offering second tickets at half price
  e   Offering telephone credit purchases

These strategic changes were attempts to reflect plausible offerings and trade-offs. An indication of the kinds of responses in the case of symphony offerings is reported in Table 8-1. Figures are reported as numbers showing greater or lesser effects compared to an "average impact" score of 100. Results are reported for both past attenders and nonattenders and in total.

The final columns of Table 8-1 indicate clearly that the two most potent means of increasing symphony patronage among this set of alternatives is offering second tickets at half price or scheduling more famous conductors or performers. Least effective would be more choral music or more modern compositions. These options had the same effect on both past attenders and nonattenders. Thus, unfortunately, a powerful means of attracting past nonattenders, offering a second ticket at half price, is just as attractive to past attenders, implying that new revenues from such a strategem will be offset by losses from regular attenders who take advantage of the offer but who would have paid full price. Two cases showing major differences between attenders and nonattenders are having a more convenient site and making the occasion seem less formal. Nonattenders find these options significantly more appealing. However, the potential user of these results is confronted by the dilemma in Table 8-1 where regular attenders appear potentially turned off by such moves.

These results cannot be taken to indicate *absolute* levels of response to the various offerings. The results of asking consumers about future behavior in hypothetical situations must be interpreted cautiously. *If* one is willing to assume that biases are constant across offerings, however, then the data can be interpreted to indicate the *relative* effectiveness of each offering.

Intermediary Estimates

If reaching ultimate buyers is difficult or too expensive, another way of developing a forecast is to ask people who are close to the buyers what those buyers are likely to do. The college that is trying to anticipate enrollments to different majors, for example, might ask each department chairperson to estimate these enrollments. The chairpersons will examine past data and what they have recently heard and prepare a forecast. Some chairpersons will overestimate (the optimists) and some will underestimate (the pessimists). If individual chairpersons are fairly consistent overestimators or underestimators, their forecasts can be adjusted by the administration for their known bias before using the forecasts for planning purposes.

Table 8-1

INDEXES OF EFFECTIVENESS OF SYMPHONY OFFERINGS
AMONG PRIOR ATTENDERS AND NONATTENDERS

Offerings	Past Year Symphony Attenders		
	Attenders	Nonattenders	Average
Product Variations			
Type of performance:			
More classical music	102	107	105
More romantic music	107	90	97
More modern music	53	54	54
More concertos	56	57	57
More choral music	31	49	43
Quality of performance:			
More famous performers/conductors	150	166	161
More learning opportunities:			
Short talk	101	121	114
Context Variations			
Location/convenience:			
Nearer, less attractive, 20% discount	76	112	100
Formality of atmosphere:			
Dressing more informally	61	100	87
Price Variations			
Couples discount:			
Second ticket one-half off	199	180	186
Clearance discount:			
One-half off day of performance	106	121	116
Effort to secure tickets:			
Telephone/credit purchasing	77	81	80
Base ticket price decrease	112	124	120
Base ticket price increase	99	84	89
Series discount	96	112	107
Favorite program with ticket price increase	93	87	89
Average	100	102	100

SOURCE: Alan R. Andreasen and Russell W. Belk, *Audience Development: An Examination of Selected Analyses and Prediction Techniques Applied to Symphony and Theatre Attendance in Four Southern Cities* (Washington, D.C.: National Endowment for the Arts, 1981).

When business firms use this method, they ask for estimates from their sales force, distributors, and dealers, since all of these are presumably closer to the customers and can render an opinion about likely demand. Nonprofit organizations can also find similar "experts." Thus a national fund-raising organization can ask its regional chairpersons to make estimates, and they in turn can ask their individual fund raisers for estimates. Asking people who come in contact with the buyers for their estimates is called "grass-roots forecasting." In using the method, the grass-roots forecasters should be given a set of basic assumptions about the coming year, such as the state of the economy, the organization's tentative marketing plans, and so on. This is preferable to allowing each expert to make personal assumptions about major demand influences that will operate next year.

Grass-roots forecasting has a number of advantages. People will have more confidence in the derived sales quotas they get back and they will have more incentive to achieve them. Also, grass-roots forecasting results in estimates broken down by product, territory, customer, and estimator, which makes the setting of individual quotas easier.

Expert Forecasts

Buyer intentions or middlemen predictions may be helpful for near-term forecasting, especially for new offerings. When carrying out long-term forecasting, however, these groups may not have sufficient perspective, experience, or wisdom to be able to see the forest for the trees. Take, for example, the problem of the marketing manager of UCLA's executive education program in trying to estimate the long-run demand for MBA degree programs for senior executives. Several techniques may be used for such longer-range forecasts. The most casual approach is to subscribe to one or another expert social trend forecasting service such as those offered by SRI International or Public Policy Forecasting, and attempt to extrapolate their insights to the executive MBA problem.

SRI International in Menlo Park, California, has a Business Intelligence Program (BIP) that produces the publication *Scan*. This program involves 50 expert SRI consultants in California, Washington, Tokyo, and London looking routinely for signals of change. They then use electronic mail to share abstracts of their findings with other experts. Once a month, 15 experts assemble in Menlo Park to see if the "weak signals" from the field constitute a potential trend.

Public Policy Forecasting is the brainchild of Graham T.T. Molitar. Molitar assumes that shifts in public policy in European countries toward social, environmental, and health care issues are good predictors of what will happen later in the United States, usually 8 to 22 years later. He feels Sweden and Norway are particularly relevant and spends several weeks each year sniffing out trends for corporate (AT&T, Citibank, Coca-Cola, Standard Oil), university (Stanford, MIT, Harvard) and government (Federal Trade Commission, General Accounting Office, Federal Food and Drug Administration) clients.

These techniques, however, are not usually very specific to an organization or industry. Another possibility is what might be called "scenario analysis." This technique, championed by the Hudson Institute, takes past and present developments and offers several pathways into the future. Thus, in UCLA's case, they may propose these possibilities:

Scenario 1: General demand for executive MBA programs will rise through 1998 as managers promoted to senior ranks continue to have formal undergraduate training in areas other than business (for example, engineering) and need MBAs. At the same time, competition for this executive market will accelerate even faster, resulting in a decline in UCLA's market share toward the end of this period. After 1998, industry demand will drop sharply, competitors will be slow to leave the market, and UCLA's enrollment will drop sharply.

Scenario 2: Industry demand will increase through 1998 but competitors will not increase as fast as the industry, particularly competitors at UCLA's "quality level." After 1998, declining demand will encourage other high-quality competitors to leave the market rapidly, leaving UCLA with a growing market share in a declining market.

Scenario 3: Industry demand will increase to 1998 and then drop as far as senior executives are concerned. The fact that more senior executives enter the top ranks after 1998 with business training, however, will put even greater pressure on these remaining managers who lack MBAs and this will sustain the upward trend in the industry into the twenty-first century.

Managers and the scenario writers may then apply probability estimates to each scenario (and others that could emerge) to serve as their forecast. A major virtue of this technique is that it forces the nonprofit manager to think about contingency plans should the most likely scenario not take place.

A competing technique called the *Delphi method* permits interaction among diverse experts, who can be widely separated geographically.[3] The Delphi approach is based on a forecast-feedback-reforecast process as follows:

1 In the first round, experts are asked to (a) extrapolate past trends to some distant future point, and (b) write down the major environmental factors they considered in making their extrapolations.
2 The results of the expert forecasts are then pooled, the key environmental factors summarized, and the findings reported back to the original survey group.
3 The experts are then asked to revise their forecasts if they wish and to indicate any new considerations they have introduced.

This pattern may be repeated over additional cycles until a consensus is reached and the variance around the group's estimates is reduced considerably. The technique is costly but the Stanford Research Institute (SRI) found it extremely useful in attempting to estimate how the American populace will budget their time and expenditures for leisure activities 15 to 30 years in the future.

Market Tests

In the case where buyers do not plan their future behavior carefully or are very erratic in carrying out their intentions and where experts are not likely to be very good guessers, a more direct market test of probable behavior is desirable. A direct market test is especially desirable in forecasting the sales of a new product or the probable sales of an established product in a new channel of distribution or territory. Where a short-run forecast of likely buyer response is desired, a small-scale market test is usually a highly accurate and reliable method.

Time-Series Analysis

As an alternative to costly surveys or market tests, many organizations prepare their forecasts on the basis of a statistical analysis of past data. The underlying logic is that past time series reflect causal relations that can be uncovered through statistical analysis. The findings can be used to predict future demand.

A time series of past performance can be analyzed into four major components.

The first component, *trend (T)*, reflects the basic level and rate of change in the size of the market. It is found by fitting a straight or curved line through the time-series data. The past trend can be extrapolated to estimate next year's trend level.

A second component, *cycle (C)*, might also be observed in a time series. Many behaviors such as needs for poverty-related programs are affected by periodic swings in general economic activity. If the stage of the business cycle can be predicted for the next period, this would be used to adjust the trend value up or down.

A third component, *season (S)*, would capture any consistent pattern of movements within the year. The term "season" is used to describe any recurrent hourly, daily, weekly, monthly, or quarterly pattern. The seasonal component may be related to weather factors, holidays, and so on. The researcher would adjust the estimate for, say, a particular month by the known seasonal level for that month. Seasonal effects are especially important in predicting likely blood collections. Holiday periods are particularly difficult times.

The fourth component, *erratic events (E)*, includes strikes, blizzards, fads, riots, fires, war scares, price wars, and other disturbances. This erratic component has the effect of obscuring the more systematic components. It represents everything that remains unanalyzed in the time series and cannot be predicted in the future. It shows the average size of the error that is likely to characterize time-series forecasting. If it is very large, it may suggest that other forecasting methods, such as statistical demand analysis should be preferred.

Here is an example of how time-series forecasting works:

> A county historical museum had 12,000 visitors this year. It wants to predict next year's December attendance in order to schedule enough guards. The long-term trend shows a 5 percent attendance growth rate per year. This implies attendance next year of 12,600 (= 12,000 × 1.05). A business recession is expected next year, however, and this generally depresses attendance to 90 percent of the expected trend level. This means attendance next year will more likely be 11,340 (= 12,600 × .90). If attendance is the same each month, this would mean monthly attendance of 945 (= 11,340 ÷ 12). December is an above-average month, however, with a seasonal index standing at 1.30. Therefore, December attendance may be as high as 1,229 (= 945 × 1.3). No erratic events, such as public transportation strikes or new competitive exhibits, are expected (but they may occur). Experience has shown that such events could leave a forecast off plus or minus 3 percent. Therefore, the best estimate of next December's attendance is 1,229 with a possibility it could be as high as 1,276 or as low as 1,201.

Statistical Demand Analysis

Numerous real factors affect the demand for anything. *Statistical demand analysis* is a set of statistical procedures designed to discover the most important real factors affecting behaviors and their relative influence. The factors most commonly analyzed in the case of products and services are prices, income, population, and promotion.

Statistical demand analysis consists of expressing sales (Q) as a dependent variable and trying to explain sales variation as a result of variations in a number of independent demand variables $X_1, X_2 \ldots, X_n$; that is,

$$Q = f(X_1, X_2, \ldots, X_n) \tag{8-1}$$

This says that the level of sales, Q, is a function of the levels of independent factors $X_1, X_2 \ldots, X_n$. Using a technique called multiple-regression analysis, various equation forms can be statistically fitted to the data in the search for the best predicting factors and equations.[4]

Here is an example:

A central library wanted to forecast book circulation next year at each of its ten branch libraries. The following equation was fitted to past data:

$$Q = 5000 - 300X_1 + 1000X_2 \tag{8-2}$$

where
  X_1 = age of the branch library in years
  X_2 = average years of education in the branch's neighborhood

For example, the Lincoln branch library would be 10-years-old next year and was located in a neighborhood whose residents averaged 12 years of formal education. Using (8-2), we would predict that book circulation would be:

$$Q = 5000 - 300(10) + 1000(12) = 14,000 \tag{8-3}$$

If this equation predicts book circulation satisfactorily for the various branches, then the central library can assume that it has identified two key factors influencing book circulation. It may want to explore the exact influence of these factors, as well as other factors that might be added to improve the equation's forecasting accuracy.

Note, however, that this technique requires an independent estimate of the predictor variables. Thus, if the library wanted to forecast circulation ten years hence, somebody would have to first make a forecast of education levels. Sometimes good estimates are available from other sources. Sometimes the managers must make their own "guesstimates." If the issue is important enough, management may wish to develop a second, prior equation predicting a value that is then "plugged into" the forecasting equation.[5]

A structural model was used by Hanssens and Levien to study the effects of environmental and marketer-controlled factors on U.S. Navy recruitment.[6] Using measures for 30 variables collected at 43 Navy recruiting districts between January, 1976 and December, 1978, the researchers constructed and estimated a multiplicative (log-linear) model to explain the number of advertising leads secured and delayed-entry and direct-shipment recruitment contracts achieved. They concluded the following:

> Overall, changes in the environment have a more dramatic impact on re-cruiting performance than changes in marketing efforts . . . [I]ncreased marketing spending does not fully compensate for a much more difficult recruiting environment (e.g., a declining unemployment rate). At the district level, differences in youth attitudes toward the Navy, degree of urbanization, proportion of high school seniors and blacks in the target market are primarily responsible for the variability in recruiting performance across [Navy Recruiting Districts], in spite of the fact that poorly performing NRDs have received more recruiters, local advertising and recruiter aid support on a per capita basis.[7]

SUMMARY

In order to carry out their responsibilities for marketing planning, execution, and control, marketing managers need measures of current and future market size. We defined a market as the set of actual and potential consumers of a market offer. Being in the market means having interest, ability to transact, and access to the market offer. The marketer's task is to distinguish various levels of the market that is being investigated, such as the potential market, available market, qualified available market, target market, and penetrated market.

The next step is to estimate the size of current demand. Total current demand can be estimated through the chain ratio method, which involves multiplying a base number by a succession of appropriate percentages to arrive at the defined market. Estimating actual industry demand requires identifying the relevant competitors and using some method of estimating the sales of each. Finally, the organization should compare its sales to industry sales to find whether its market share is improving or declining.

For estimating future demand, the organization can use one or any combination of six forecasting methods: buyer intentions surveys, middleman estimates, expert estimates, market tests, time-series analysis, or statistical demand analysis. These methods vary in their appropriateness with the purpose of the forecast, the type of product, and the availability and reliability of data.

QUESTIONS

1. Develop a chain ratio formula for estimating the number of homeless likely to be needing services in the next five years in the major metropolitan areas in your state.

2. Compare buyer intention and expert surveys as alternative approaches to estimating the number of likely attendees at three different packages of opera performances in the next opera season.

3. A research manager for a large museum recommends that management conduct a series of experiments to estimate the demand for various *types* of products it might carry in its museum retail store. How would you recommend they carry out these studies?

4. The United Way of America relies on volunteers from the private and public sectors to collect donations for it. The leaders of these organizational volunteers are typically well-trained junior managers on the way up in their organizations. Each is relatively close organizationally to his or her target market. What are the advantages and disadvantages of using these volunteer leaders to develop estimates of market demand?

5. For which kinds of nonprofit organizations would time series forecasts be especially effective and why?

NOTES

1. Some analysts use all the "definites" and some arbitrary fraction of the "probablys" to estimate the demand level. Thus, they may say that the demand is made up of four "definites" and half of the six "probablys," namely, seven people, or 7 percent of the population.

2. It must be added that for many nonprofit organization markets, income is not a defining variable, because the consumer is not expected to pay for the service. Thus, in such cases as the Girl Scouts, U.S. Army, cigarette smokers, and so on, the target consumer's income is not a factor in the size of the market.

3. See Philip Kotler, "A Guide to Gathering Expert Estimates," *Business Horizons*, October 1970, pp. 79–87.

4. See William F. Massy, "Statistical Analysis of Relations Between Variables," in David A. Aaker, ed., *Multivariate Analysis in Marketing: Theory and Applications* (Belmont, Calif., Wadsworth, 1971), pp. 5–35.

5. For other statistical approaches, see Gary L. Lilien and Philip Kotler, *Marketing Decision Making: A Model Building Approach*, 2nd ed. (New York: Harper & Row, 1983).

6. Dominique M. Hanssens and Henry A. Levien, "An Econometric Study of Recruitment Marketing in the U.S. Navy," *Management Science*, Vol. 29, no. 10 (October 1983), pp. 1167–1184.

7. Ibid. Quotation reprinted by permission of *Management Science*. © The Institute of Management Sciences.

9

Fund-raising

Colleges and universities, facing many of the same competitive pressures as big corporations, are trying to raise huge amounts of money to prepare for the 1990's, a decade that many educators think will bring expensive and potentially disruptive changes to their institutions.

Prestigious private schools like the University of Pennsylvania are aiming for a billion dollars or more. The major state universities, long used to being supported largely by public money, are increasingly matching the major private institutions in their fund-raising ambitions. And less well-known colleges and universities, like Ball State University in Muncie, Ind., which says it needs $40 million in outside donations over the next five years, have joined the now-crowded field.

To be sure, the major private universities as a group remain the most proficient fund-raisers, according to a study in the recent issue of *Currents*, the magazine of the American Association of Fund Raising Counsel.

But John A. Dunn, Jr., vice president of planning at Tufts University in Medford, Mass., one of the study's authors, notes that now 6 of the 20 most successful fund-raisers are public institutions, among them the University of Minnesota, the University of Illinois and the University of Wisconsin at Madison.

Over all, Mr. Dunn says, public universities account for 20 of the top 50 institutions in total gifts.

And institutions which have previously done relatively little fund-raising have joined in the hunt. For example, the College of William and Mary in Williamsburg, Va., is trying to raise $65 million in its first major effort.

Giving to higher education fell last year for the first time since 1976 even as total gifts to philanthropy increased. Experts attributed the decline, to just under $8.2 billion from $8.5 billion the previous year, to the impact of the Tax Reform Act of 1986, which affected big donors by tightening some rules on deductions for charitable giving. Fundraisers expect the figure to rebound this coming year.

"We've raised our tuition by 6 percent, but that's our limit," says John E. Worthen, Ball State's president. "We're loath to go higher, because then we'd be pricing ourselves out of range of the students we think we can attract."

Finding Their Niche

Dr. Worthen said the campaign's other compelling cause was to secure a "niche" as a teaching university.

"We're a mid-sized university," he said. "Our people do research, but they do less of it, so we can't compete with an Indiana or an Illinois. But we can be excellent in teaching undergraduate and graduate students." Officials at major institutions talk about their niche as well, but their eyes are set on the very top of higher education's pecking order.

Sheldon Hackney, Pennsylvania's president, speaks of his university being part of "a new set of leadership institutions" among the major research universities—those which having planned properly, will emerge from the coming decade rich and strong.

Source: Adapted from Lee A. Daniels, "Raising Money Tops Agenda of Many Colleges for 1990's," *The New York Times*, December 17, 1989, pp. 1, 21. Reproduced with permission.

The major resource attraction problem of nonprofit organizations is attracting money to carry on their activities. For-profit organizations get their funds primarily through issuing equities and debentures. They cover the costs of these "borrowed" funds by charging prices for their goods and services that exceed their costs. Nonprofit organizations, in the absence of owners and profit-oriented price setting, must rely on other sources of funds to support their activities. Public organizations receive their funds primarily from the public treasury through the mechanism of taxation. Private nonprofit organizations rely mainly on gifts from generous donors. Fund-raising strategy is, therefore, an essential component of all nonprofit organizations.

The total amount of charitable money raised by all organizations in the U.S. in 1988 was $104.37 billion. Eighty-three percent of these contributions came from *individuals* ($86.70 billion), with the remainder coming from *bequests* ($6.79 billion), *foundations* ($6.13 billion), and *corporations* ($4.75 billion). Forty-six percent of the money was raised by religious organizations ($48.21 billion); the rest was raised by human service organizations ($10.49 billion); educational institutions ($9.78 billion); health-related groups ($9.52 billion); arts, culture, and the humanities ($6.82 billion); public and societal benefit organizations ($3.02 billion); and other groups ($16.53 billion).[1]

The art of fund-raising has passed through various stages of evolution. Its earliest form was *begging*, in which needy people and groups would implore more fortunate people for money and goods. Beggars perfected many techniques to gain the attention and sympathy of their target audience, such as simulating pain or blindness or showing their children with bloated stomachs. The next stage consisted of *collection*, in which churches, clubs, and other organizations would regularly collect contributions from a willing and defined group of supporters. In recent times, *campaigning* emerged in the form of fund-raising; organizations appoint a specific person or group to be responsible for soliciting money from every possible source in a systematic fund-raising campaign. Most recently, fund-raising has been reinterpreted as *development*, in which the organization systematically builds up different classes of loyal donors who give consistently and receive benefits in the process of giving. Today's organizations vary considerably in their concept of raising money, some seeing it as begging, others as collection, others as campaigning, and still others as development.

STAGES OF MARKETING ORIENTATION

Organizations that raise money typically pass through three stages of marketing orientation in their thinking about how to carry on fund-raising effectively.

- *Product orientation stage.* Here the prevailing attitude is "We have a good cause; people ought to support us." Many churches and colleges operate on this concept. Money is raised primarily by the top officers through an "old boy network." The organization relies on volunteers to help raise additional funds. A few loyal donors supply most of the funds.
- *Sales orientation stage.* Here the prevailing attitude is "There are a lot of people out there who might give money, and we must go out and find them and convince them to give." The institution appoints a development director who eventually hires a staff. This staff raises money from all possible sources, typically using a "hard sell" approach. The fund-raisers have little influence on the institution's policies or personality since their job is to raise money, not improve the organization. A majority of large nonprofit organizations are in this stage.
- *Strategic marketing stage.* Here the prevailing attitude is "We must analyze our position in the marketplace, concentrate on those donor sources whose interests are best matched to ours, and design our solicitation programs to supply needed satisfactions to each donor group." This approach involves carefully segmenting the donor markets; measuring the giving potential of each donor market; assigning executive responsibility for developing each market; and developing a plan and budget for each market based on its potential. More and more large nonprofit organizations have moved into this stage as fund-raisers become aware of the differences between a sales approach and a marketing approach.

A signal that an organization has shifted from a sales to a strategic marketing orientation in its fund-raising is when it treats its donors and potential donors not as targets but as potential partners. Sophisticated fund-raisers realize that they need not only individual gifts and grants but also lasting *relationships* with their target markets.

Public television station WTTW in Chicago has developed an innovative approach to relationship building. In 1990, it issued some 200,000 membership cards to individuals who gave $40 or more in the previous year. The card entitles members to discount admissions to most of the city's major museums, restaurants, and other businesses. Commenting on the program, Maggie Schmid, director of Chicago's Lincoln Park Zoological Society, notes that "like the Zoo, they are free. It doesn't cost anything to watch WTTW and there are many viewers who don't contribute. Trying to guilt trip them [into pledging] may or may not work. With this they have created a package of perceived value." Presumably, members will now feel a closer relationship with WTTW, particularly since all of their contributions go directly toward station programming.[2]

This chapter will analyze fund-raising from a marketing perspective. The first section will examine four major donor markets: individual givers, foundations, corporations, and government. Section two will examine how organizations organize their fund-raising effort internally. Section three will consider the important task of setting fund-raising objectives and strategies, while section four will take a look at the multiplicity of fund-raising tactics. The fifth section will consider how organizations can evaluate and improve their fund-raising effectiveness.

ANALYZING DONOR MARKETS

An organization can tap into a variety of sources for financial support. The four major donor markets are *individuals, foundations, corporations,* and *government.* Small nonprofit organizations frequently solicit funds primarily from one source — often wealthy individuals — to meet their financial needs. Larger organizations tend to solicit all sources and, in fact, make specific executives responsible for each market. Ultimately, they seek to allocate the fund-raising budget in proportion to the giving potential of each donor market. Here we will examine the institutional and behavioral characteristics of each donor market.

Individual Givers

Individuals are the major source of all charitable giving, accounting for some 83 percent of the total. Almost everyone in the nation contributes money to one or more organizations each year, the total amount varying with such factors as the giver's income, age, education, sex, ethnic background, and other characteristics. Thus relatively more money is contributed by high-income people, people in their middle years, and people of high education. At the same time, giving levels vary substantially within each group. Some wealthy individuals give little and some lower-income individuals give a lot. Among wealthy people, for example, physicians tend to give less than lawyers.

Charitable causes vary in their appeal to individuals. In a study sponsored by Save the Children Foundation, the public was asked: "Which of the five (categories of charity) would rate as the most worthwhile?" The ranking turned out to be (1) needy children, (2) disaster victims, (3) medical research, (4) aid to the handicapped, and (5) religious organizations.[3] That is, Americans would be most ready to give to a cause involving needy children, followed by disaster victims, and so on. Paradoxically, they give relatively small amounts to these causes in relation to the amounts they give to their churches.

Within each category of charity, the appeal levels also vary greatly. For example, within medical charities people give readily to the American Cancer Society ($257.6 million), American Heart Association ($163.3 million), March of Dimes ($110.5 million), Muscular Dystrophy Association ($102.9 million), and National Easter Seal Society ($88 million) (figures as of 1988).[4]

Some of the difference in the amount raised is due to the fact that these organizations have different life spans and different degrees of effectiveness at fund-raising. A larger part of the difference in giving levels is due to the opinions people hold about specific diseases, particularly about the disease's *severity, prevalence,* and *remediability.* Thus, heart disease and cancer are severe diseases—they kill—whereas arthritis and most birth defects are considered less serious since they do not kill. Cancer has a higher prevalence than muscular dystrophy and therefore attracts more support. Finally, people believe that cures or preventions are possible for heart disease and less so for birth defects and this leads to more giving. Figure 9-1 shows the hypothetical positions of four diseases on the three variables. If the March of Dimes wants to attract more funds for its cause—birth defects—it must try to increase the perceived severity, prevalence, and remediability of birth defects.

Why do individuals give to charity? Nonprofit organizations need a good understanding of the motives for giving to be effective at fund-raising. The

FIGURE 9-1

Public Perception of Different Medical Causes (Hypothetical)

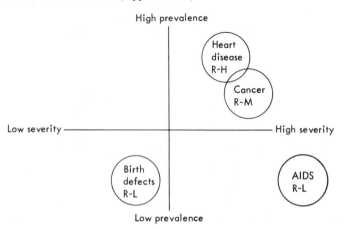

Note: The third variable, remediability (R), is shown for each disease with an indication of level: low (L), medium (M), and high (H).

Table 9-1

INDIVIDUAL GIVING MOTIVES

1   *Need for self-esteem.* These people attempt to build their self-esteem and self-image by playing "God," or feeling good from giving. The opposite of this would be shame or guilt.

2   *Need for recognition from others.* These people attempt to build their social status or enhance their prestige in the eyes of others. They have a strong need to belong.

3   *Fear of contracting the problem.* This need centers on people's fear that they or members of their families will contract a particular disease or fall into poverty or neglect in their old age. They hope in some sense to buy "protection."

4   *The habit giver.* These people give out of habit for no real reason other than a desire not to be embarrassed by not contributing to the cause. They are indifferent to contributions, but feel that they must give to someone because everyone else does. A benefit may be not having to agonize over choosing charities (for example, *not* giving to a needy cause).

5   *Nuisance giver.* These people only give to get rid of the caller. They feel that contributing to a cause is of no real significance, but would rather donate a few dollars than be troubled by others.

6   *Required to give.* These people are required to give at work; they feel they are under pressure from superiors to donate part of their checks to a fund. They therefore demand efficiency and credibility from the organization that they contribute to.

7   *Captive givers.* These people feel real sorrow for someone they know who has a particular problem. They are other centered in that they earnestly would like to aid the victim in some way. Givers in this category may contribute at the death of a friend rather than sending flowers, etc.

8   *People-to-people givers.* These people have a real feeling of the "commonness of man," a solidarity with other people. This group of people has internalized the idea of helping others because they want to.

9   *Concern for humanity.* This segment of givers is concerned about others for religious reasons and because they are "God's children." They feel a moral obligation to contribute to a charity. They have accepted the love-for-humanity idea because it is a requirement of their faith.

answer called "altruism" tends to mask the complex motives that underlie giving or helping behavior. The position of this book is that the individuals give in order to get something back. In other words, donations should not be viewed as a *transfer* but as a *transaction.* The question is, what does the donor *get?* Table 9-1 lists several motives underlying giving behavior. People give to get response or recognition, reduce fear, reduce social pressure, or feel "altruistic."

   Is there such a thing as giving without "getting"? Some people give and say that they expect nothing back. But, actually, they have "expectations." They expect the organization to use the money efficiently, they expect the fund-raiser to show gratitude, and so on. Even the anonymous giver who wants no acknowledgment may privately enjoy the self-esteem of being "big enough" to give money without requiring recognition.

   The various motives for giving provide clues to marketing strategy for fund-raisers. Harold Seymour has suggested that in many mass donor markets, one-third of the people are *responsible* (they donate without being solicited), one-third are *responsive* (they donate when they are asked), and one-third react to *compulsion* (they donate because of pressure).[5] Each market can be investigated further to discover the specific motive segments that exist. One group of givers to a university might respond to "pride," another to "let's catch up to the competition."

Too many organizations ask people to give to them as a needy organization rather than to support promising programs. The former approach is close to begging. The latter is more effective. People respond to what they sense as the relevance, importance, and urgency of a giving opportunity. Seymour suggests that the case for giving must be bigger than the institution. And it must be presented in a way that catches the eye, warms the heart, and stirs the mind.

Fund-raising must be segmented. One important basis for segmentation is the donor's "giving potential." Fund-raisers distinguish between small, medium, and large donors. Many fund-raisers prefer to concentrate all or most of their energy on large potential donors, feeling that attracting a few large gifts would produce more funds than attracting many small gifts. It is not uncommon to hear fund-raisers claim that 10 to 20 percent of the givers generate 50 to 80 percent of gifts. If a college fund-raiser spends 30 hours with a wealthy alumnus who ends up giving $1 million either directly or in a bequest, the fund-raiser's productivity is much greater than trying to raise $100 each from 10,000 alumni. Because large donations looked so attractive, many college fund-raisers in the past neglected building up the number of alumni donors and concentrated instead on increasing the size of the average gift received.

Other bases that fund-raisers use for segmentation are geographic area (e.g., urban, rural, zip code), connection with the organization (volunteer, audience member, relative of client), and past giving history (long-time giver, first gift, first repeat). These bases are used to determine how much effort to spend on each group, what medium to use (mass media, telephone, direct mail, personal contact), and what themes to emphasize.

Seeking the "large gift" from individual givers is still the most important part of fund-raising for many organizations. It involves careful personal selling, often over long periods of time, using many of the private-sector selling principles outlined in Chapter 21. One of the solicitation models used by many fund-raisers involves five steps: *identification, introduction, cultivation, solicitation,* and *appreciation.* They first identify wealthy individuals who could conceivably have a strong interest in the organization. They identify others who might supply information and arrange an introduction. They cultivate the person's interest without asking for any money. By asking too early, they may get less than is possible. Eventually, they do ask for money and, upon receiving it, they express their appreciation.

Large individual gift fund-raising is most effective when the organization has developed a "wish list" of exciting projects to show the prospective donor. Large hospitals classify their wished-for gifts in several financial sizes, ranging from the small pieces of medical equipment for under $10,000 to the building of an entire wing for over $3 million. One of the most powerful appeals is to allow donors to have their names (or names of loved ones) attached to physical facilities, research funds, distinguished chairs, and the like. Here, the exchange is very clear and dramatic. In addition, fund-raisers can offer these individuals all kinds of ways to make their gifts, including direct cash payments, gifts of stock and other property, and bequests in which they will assign part or all of their estate to the organization upon their death. Organizations have worked up a variety of gift plans that can be tailored to the needs of individual wealthy donors.

Foundations

Currently there are over 27,000 foundations in the United States, all set up to give money to worthwhile causes. They fall into the following groups:

1 *Family foundations*, set up by wealthy individuals to support a limited number of activities of interest to the founders. Family foundations typically do not have permanent offices or full-time staff members. Decisions tend to be made by family members, counsel, or both.

2 *General foundations*, set up to support a wide range of activities and usually run by a professional staff. General foundations range from extremely large organizations such as the John D. and Catherine T. MacArthur Foundation and the Ford and Rockefeller Foundations, which support a wide range of causes, to more specialized general foundations that give money to a particular cause, such as health (Johnson Foundation) or education (Carnegie Foundation).

3 *Corporate foundations*, set up by corporations and allowed to give away up to 5 percent of the corporation's adjusted gross income.

4 *Community foundations*, set up as a vehicle for pooling bequests from many private sources, including individuals, corporations, foundations, and non-profit organizations. There were 62 community foundations in 1987 with assets of over $4.7 billion making grants of $316 million, primarily for education, human services, arts and humanities, and health.[6]

With 27,000 foundations, it is important for the fund-raiser to know how to locate the few that would be the most likely to support a given project or cause. Fortunately, there are many resources available for researching foundations. The best single resource is known as the Foundation Center, a nonprofit organization with research centers in New York, Washington, and Chicago which collects and distributes information on foundations. In addition, many libraries around the country carry important materials describing foundations and how to approach them. The most important materials are

1 *The Foundation Grants Index*, which lists the grants that have been given in the past year by foundation, subject, state, and other groupings. The fund-raiser, for example, could look up visual arts and find out all the grants made to support the visual arts and identify the most active foundations in this area of giving.

2 *The Foundation Directory*, which lists 6,615 foundations that either have assets of over $1 million or award grants of more than $500,000 annually. The directory describes the general characteristics of each foundation, such as type of foundation, types of grants, annual giving level, officers and directors, location, particular fields of interest, contact person, and so on. The directory also contains an index of fields of interests, listing the foundations that have a stated interest in each field and whether or not they gave money to this field last year.

   3 *The Foundation News,* which is published six times a year by the Council on
   Foundations and describes new foundations, new funding programs, and
   changes in existing foundations.
   4 *Fund Raising Management,* which is a periodical publishing articles on fund-
   raising management.

The key concept in identifying foundations is that of *matching.* The nonprofit organization should search for foundations matched to its *interests* and
scale of operation. Too often a small nonprofit organization will send a proposal to
the Ford Foundation because it would like to get the support of this well-known
foundation. But the Ford Foundation accepts about one out of every 100 proposals and may be less disposed toward helping small nonprofit organizations
than more regional or specialized foundations would be.

After identifying a few foundations that might have strong interest in its
project, the organization should try to estimate more accurately their level of
interest before investing a lot of time in grant preparation. Most foundations are
willing to respond to a letter of inquiry, telephone call, or personal visit and
indicate how interested they would be in the project. The foundation officer may
be very encouraging or discouraging. If the former, the fund-seeking organization can then make an investment in preparing an elaborate proposal for this
foundation.

Writing successful grant proposals is becoming a fine art, with many
guides currently available to help the grant-seeker.[7] Each proposal should contain at least the following elements:

   1 *A cover letter* describing the history of the proposal, and who has been contacted, if anyone, in the foundation
   2 *The proposal,* describing the project, its uniqueness, and its importance
   3 *The budget* for the project
   4 *The personnel* working on the project with their résumés

The proposal itself should be compact, individualized, organized, and readable.
In writing the proposal, the organization should be guided by knowledge of the
"buying criteria" that the particular foundation uses to choose among the many
proposals that it receives. Like any other marketing communication, it must be
customer-centered. Many foundations describe their criteria in their annual
reports or other memos, or their criteria can be inferred by looking at the
characteristics of the recent proposals they have supported or talking to knowledgeable individuals. Among the most common guiding criteria used by foundations are

   1 The importance and quality of the project
   2 The neediness and worthwhileness of the organization
   3 The organization's ability to use the funds effectively and efficiently
   4 The importance of satisfying the persons who are doing the proposing
   5 The degree of benefit that the foundation will derive in supporting the proposal

If the proposing organization knows the relative importance of the respective criteria, it can do a better job of selecting the features of the proposal to emphasize. If the particular foundation is likely to be influenced by who presents the proposal, for example, the organization should send its highest-ranking officials to the foundation. On the other hand, if the foundation attaches the most importance to the quality of the proposal, the organization should put a lot of effort into fine-tuning the writing of the proposal.

Nonprofit organizations should not contact foundations only on the occasion of a specific proposal. Each organization should cultivate a handful of appropriate foundations in advance of specific proposals. This is called "building bridges" or "relationship marketing." One major university sees the Ford Foundation as a "key customer account." The development officer arranges for various people within the university to get to know people at corresponding levels within the foundation. One or more members of the university's board arrange to see corresponding board members of the foundation each year. The university president visits the foundation's president each year for a luncheon or dinner. One or more members of the university's development staff cultivate relations with foundation staff members at their levels. When the university has a proposal, it knows exactly who should present it to the foundation and whom to see in the foundation. Furthermore, the foundation is more favorably disposed toward the organization because of the long relationship and special understanding they enjoy. Finally, the organization is able to do a better job of tracking the proposal as it is being reviewed by the foundation.

Corporations

Business organizations represent another distinct source of funds for nonprofit organizations. Corporations have been especially supportive of such causes as higher education, the United Way, and health, civic, cultural, and social services. In 1988, American business contributed $4.75 billion of the $104.37 billion received in total charity. This amounts to less than 1 percent of business's pretax income. Since business organizations are allowed by law to give up to 5 percent of their pretax income to charity, considerable potential for more corporate giving exists.

Corporate giving differs from foundation giving in a number of important ways. First, corporations regard gift-giving as a minor activity, in contrast to foundations where it is the major activity. Corporations vary their giving level with the level of current and expected corporate income. They have to be sensitive to the feelings of their stockholders, to whom they have the first obligation both in terms of how much to give to charity and what particular charities to support. Corporations are more likely to avoid supporting controversial causes than are foundations. Corporations typically handle the many requests for support they receive by setting up a foundation so that corporate officers are not personally drawn into gift decision-making. Others will have a specific senior staff member such as a vice-president for community relations, who is given responsibility for corporate donations.

Second, corporations pay more attention than foundations to the personal benefit that any grant might return to them. If they can show that a particular grant will increase community goodwill (as a grant by a cigarette company to a cancer research foundation) or train more labor that they need (as a grant by an engineering company to an engineering school), these grants will be more acceptable to their board of directors and stockholders.

Third, corporations can make more types of gifts than foundations can. Thus, as will be discussed in the next chapter, nonprofit organizations can approach the business firm not only for *money*, but also for *securities, goods* (asking a furniture company for furniture or a computer firm for PCs or software), *services* (asking a printing company for free printing or printing at cost), and *space* (asking a company for the use of its auditorium for a program). In the extreme, the nonprofit organization should often be able to get office equipment, marketing research, advertising, and so on, free or at cost if it can identify the right corporate prospects to approach.

Effective corporate fund-raising requires that the nonprofit organization know how to identify good corporate prospects efficiently. Of the millions of business enterprises that might be approached, relatively few are appropriate to any specific nonprofit organization. Furthermore, the nonprofit organization ordinarily does not have the resources to cultivate more than a handful of corporate givers. The best prospects for corporate fund-raising have the following characteristics.

1 *Local corporations.* Corporations located in the same area as the nonprofit organization are excellent prospects. A hospital, for example, can base its appeal on the health care it offers to the corporation's employees, and a performing arts group can base its appeal on its cultural offerings. Both improve the local climate and thus help corporations attract and keep top-flight talent. Corporations find it hard to refuse to support worthwhile organizations in their area.

2 *Kindred activities.* Corporations located in a field kindred to the nonprofit organization's are excellent prospects. Hospitals can effectively solicit funds from pharmaceutical companies, and colleges can attract funds from companies that hire many of their graduates.

3 *Declared areas of support.* Nonprofit organizations should target corporations that have a declared interest in supporting that type of nonprofit organization.

4 *Large givers.* Large corporations and those with generous giving levels are excellent prospects. Yet fund-raisers must realize that these corporations receive numerous requests and favor those nonprofit organizations in the local area or a kindred field. Regional offices of major corporations are often not in a position to make a donation without the approval of the home office.

5 *Personal relationships or contacts.* Nonprofit organizations should review their personal contacts to obtain clues to which corporations they might solicit. A university's board of trustees consists of influential individuals who can open many doors for corporate solicitations. Corporations tend to respond to peer influence in their giving. It is a maxim of fund-raising that people do not give to institutions or causes: *people give to people.* This is especially true in corporate fund-raising.

6 *Specific capability*. The fund-raiser may identify a corporation as a prospect because it has a unique resource needed by the nonprofit organization. Thus, a charity hospital might solicit a paint manufacturer for a donation of paint to repaint the rooms in an old wing of the hospital.

The preceding criteria will help the nonprofit organization identify a number of corporations that are worth approaching for contributions. Corporations in the organization's geographical area or field are worth cultivating on a continuous basis ("relationship marketing") aside from specific grant requests. When the organization is seeking to fund a specific project, however, it needs to identify the best prospects and develop a marketing plan from scratch. We will illustrate the planning procedure for securing corporate contributions in connection with the following example:

> A well-known private university was seeking to raise $5 million to build a new engineering library. Its existing library was wholly inadequate and a handicap to attracting better students to the engineering school. The university was willing to name the new library after a major corporate donor who would supply at least 60 percent ($3 million) of the money being sought. This donor would be the "bell cow" that would attract additional corporate donors to supply the rest.

The first step called for the university to *identify one or more major corporations* to approach. The fund-raisers recognized that major prospects would have two characteristics: they would be wealthy corporations and they would have a high interest in this project. The fund-raisers developed the matrix shown in Figure 9-2 and proceeded to classify corporations by their giving potential and their interest potential. In classifying corporations, they realized that oil companies fell in the upper left cell. Oil companies have high profits ("giving potential") and a high interest in engineering schools ("interest potential"). They also want to give money to good causes to win public goodwill. The university decided that approaching an oil company would make good sense.

Which oil company? Here the university applied additional criteria. An oil company located in the same geographical area had already given a major donation to this university for another project; it was ruled out. The university

FIGURE 9-2

Classifying Propective Corporate Donors by Level of Interest and Giving Potential

		Giving Potential		
		High	Medium	Low
Interest Potential	High			
	Medium			
	Low			

considered whether it had any good contacts with other oil companies. The university identified one oil corporation in the East in which several of its graduates held important positions. In addition, a member of the university's board of trustees—a major bank president—knew the president of the oil company. It was decided on the basis of these and other factors to approach this oil company for support.

The next step called for preparing a *prospect solicitation plan*. As a start, the university fundraisers researched the oil company's sales, profits, major officers, recent giving record, and other characteristics. This information was useful in deciding whom to approach at the corporation, how much to ask for, what benefits to offer, and so on. A decision was made to approach the corporation's chairman, ask for $3 million for the new engineering library, and offer to name the library after the corporation.

The final step called for *plan implementation*. The bank president arranged an appointment to visit the oil corporation's chairman, who was an old friend. He was accompanied by the university's president and also the vice-president of development. When they arrived, they met the chairman and the oil company's foundation director. They made their presentation, and the chairman said the proposal would be given careful consideration. A subsequent meeting was held on the university's campus, and ultimately the oil corporation granted the money to the university.

The oil company responded positively to this solicitation because the proposal stood high on its major criteria. The oil company foundation rated each proposal on four criteria:

1 The proposal had to be worthwhile from a societal point of view. In this case, an engineering library would contribute toward better trained engineers in the United States.
2 The corporation had to feel that the soliciting institution was worthwhile and would handle the grant well. Here, the oil company had full confidence in the particular university.
3 The proposal should create some direct benefit, if possible, for the oil company. In this case, the oil company recognized a number of benefits: it would have an "in" with the best new graduates, it would memorialize its name on the campus, and it would get good publicity for supporting this private university.
4 The oil company foundation placed value on the personal relationships involved. The fact that an important bank president had taken the time to personally present the proposal to the oil company chairman was an important factor in having the proposal carefully considered.

In general, corporations pay attention to these criteria in considering whether to "buy" a particular proposal, and therefore the seller (fund-raiser) should weave them into its planning and presentation.

Government

Another major source of funds is government agencies at the federal, state, and local levels that are able to make grants to worthwhile causes. As an example, the federal government set up the National Endowment for the Arts (NEA) to make grants to support museums, ballet companies, art groups, and other arts organizations, large and small. Other government agencies make grants to support health care, university teaching and research, social services, and other worthwhile causes. Large nonprofit organizations appoint a staff member as director of government grants to concentrate on cultivating opportunities in this sector. The director monitors announcements of government grant opportunities that might have potential for his or her organization, as well as spends time in Washington and elsewhere getting to know officers at these various agencies.

Government agencies normally require the most detailed paperwork in preparing proposals. On the other hand, the agencies are very willing to review proposals, placing the main weight on the proposal's probable contribution to the public interest. Certain topics become "hot," such as cancer research, environmental health, and so on, and the granting agencies look for the best proposals they can find on these topics. They pay less attention to agency benefit or to personal relations with the requesting organizations.

ORGANIZING FOR FUND-RAISING

Nonprofit organizations must develop a strategic approach to fund-raising. They cannot simply rely on chance personal contacts or on money coming over the transom; this would make funding too erratic. Small organizations normally rely on one person who is chiefly responsible for fund-raising. This person may be the organization's head or a director of development. He or she will be responsible for identifying fund-raising opportunities and activating others—officers, employees, and volunteers —to assist when possible.

Large nonprofit organizations such as the American Red Cross and American Heart Association have entire departments of development consisting of dozens of staff members plus volunteers numbering in the thousands. In these large organizations, development staff members take responsibility for specific *donor markets, services, marketing tools,* or *geographical areas.* We shall illustrate this by showing how a large private college typically organizes its fund-raising.

A model organization for university fund-raising is shown in Figure 9-3. The board of directors has the ultimate responsibility for overseeing the financial health of the university and does this by making personal and company contributions, arranging donor contacts, and suggesting new fund-raising ideas. The college president is the chief fund-raiser when it comes to meeting important people and asking for money. The vice-president of development is the chief planner of the fund-raising strategy for the institution and also personally asks for money from potential donors. Day-to-day administration is often handled by a director of development to free the vice-president of development for strategic planning and outside travel. The remaining development staff carry out specialized activities. Some staff specialize in donor markets—thus, there are directors of alumni affairs, foundations, corporate giving, and so on. Other staff members manage marketing functions such as public relations, research, and volunteers.

Others handle various schools, where they get to know the faculty and fund-raising needs and opportunities. Finally, some staff members may manage regions of the country. Cornell, for example, at one time ran offices in eight cities to handle fund-raising, alumni relations, and public relations.

The staff's effectiveness is amplified by a large number of volunteers such as alumni, wealthy friends of the institution, deans, faculty, students, and so on. In the mid-1970s, Stanford, for example, ran a special program called the Inner Quad program for those who gave (or could have given) over $1,000 annually to Stanford. This program was run by 8 professional staff members working through 250 volunteers operating in 16 regions of the country.[8] In this case, the staff really functioned to activate the volunteers who were the main fund-raising arm of the university. Stanford University is particularly effective in segmenting its program efforts and adjusting both the types and levels of solicitation to each segment.

The university's effectiveness in fundraising is also influenced by the quality of its information system. The development office needs to maintain up-to-date and easily accessible files on donors and prospects (individuals, foundations, corporations, etc.) so that past and potential givers can be identified and

FIGURE 9-3

A Large University Fund-raising Organization

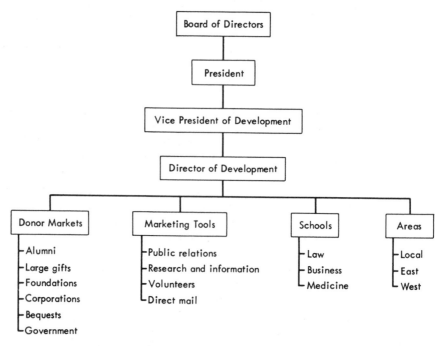

previous solicitations can be reviewed. To the extent that these files are computerized and data can be retrieved by year, school, giving level, and other key variables, the fund-raiser is in a much better position to allocate his or her time effectively.

Universities can help each other out in the organization of charity solicitations by coordinating the vast resources represented by their student bodies. In October of 1985, 75 university presidents under the leadership of the presidents of Brown, Georgetown, and Stanford Universities announced a program "to match students seeking volunteer work with agencies that need help."[9]

FUND-RAISING GOALS AND STRATEGY

Organizations must set annual and long-range goals for fund-raising. As an example, the March of Dimes set the following goals:

- To become the leading charitable organization in the area of birth defects
- To increase annual contributions received each year by an average of 10 percent
- To keep the expenses-to-contributions ratio below 20 percent
- To increase the median size of contributions by 10 percent
- To increase grants from the government by 15 percent

Presumably, these goals would have to be checked for consistency and prioritized in terms of importance.

Every organization tends to set an annual goal for contributions because this allows the organization to (1) know how much to budget for fund-raising, (2) motivate the staff and volunteers to high exertion, and (3) measure fund-raising effectiveness. Organizations use several different approaches to arrive at their fund-raising goal.

1 *Incremental approach.* Here, the organization takes last year's revenue, increases it to cover inflation, and then modifies it up or down depending on the expected economic climate. Thus, the American Heart Association may decide to raise about 15 percent more than it did in the preceding year.

2 *Need approach.* Here, the organization forecasts its financial needs and sets a goal based on its needs. Thus, a hospital's administration will estimate future building needs and costs, staff salaries, energy costs, and so on, subtract other funds sources, and set the portion that has to be covered by fund-raising as its target.

3 *Opportunity approach.* Here, the organization makes a fresh estimate of how much money it could raise from each donor group with different levels of fund-raising expenditure. It sets the goal of maximizing net surplus.

The opportunity approach is the soundest because it is customer centered. The vice-president of development would be responsible for analyzing the potential for each donor group. If this goal is accepted, the vice-president of development knows how much staff effort to allocate to each donor group.

After setting its fund-raising goal, the organization has to develop a core marketing strategy. As outlined in Chapter 3, it must decide on what target markets to solicit, what positioning stance to adopt and how to coordinate and implement a full marketing mix. The American Heart Association, for example, has to decide whether to position itself to respond to customer needs for "hope," "fear reduction," or some other major motive for giving. It has to decide how to allocate scarce staff time to different donor groups and geographical areas.

The role of the vice-president of development in influencing the organization's objectives and strategies varies greatly among organizations. Most organizations treat the development officer as a technician rather than a policymaker. The president, board, or both decide how much money is needed, select the broad fund-raising strategy, and then assign its implementation to the development officer. This unfortunately robs the organization of a valuable contribution that the development officer can make. Some organizations grant more scope to the development officer. This officer participates with the other officers in developing the organization's institutional positioning and personality. By helping the organization develop a better position in the market, the development officer can raise money more easily.

FUND-RAISING TACTICS

Fund-raising strategy sets the overall parameters for the fund-raising effort, which the development officer must fill with specific actions. The organization's job is to send messages to the potential donors through the most effective message channels and allow the donors to return money through the most efficient collection channels. This view of the channel options is shown in Figure 9-4.

The various channel opportunities give rise to a whole set of specific, well-known fund-raising tactics. Table 9-2 lists the major tactics that are effective in four market segments considered by most fund-raising organizations: the mass anonymous small gift market, the members and their friends market, the affluent citizens market, and the wealthy donors market. The tactics are adapted to both the nature and potential of each segment.

The *mass anonymous small gift market* consists of all citizens who might be induced to contribute a small sum (say, under $50) to a cause. The key idea is to use low-cost methods of fund-raising, since the contributions from this market are expected to be low. One of the oldest forms of mass fund-raising is the use of volunteers for street and sidewalk solicitation. The volunteers stand in high traffic areas holding out a can (Crippled Children), offering tags (Veterans' Day), ringing bells (Salvation Army), or distributing religious materials (Hare Krishna). Somewhat more costly is door-to-door solicitation because more time is involved and many people won't be home. Yet door-to-door canvassing is the preferred method of the American Heart Association (AHA), which has a massive army of volunteers organized by city, neighborhood, and block, who

FIGURE 9-4

Communication and Collection Channels for Fund-raising

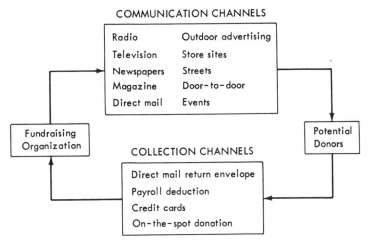

COMMUNICATION CHANNELS

Radio	Outdoor advertising
Television	Store sites
Newspapers	Streets
Magazine	Door-to-door
Direct mail	Events

Fundraising Organization

Potential Donors

COLLECTION CHANNELS

Direct mail return envelope
Payroll deduction
Credit cards
On-the-spot donation

ring doorbells once a year for the AHA. Block volunteers are typically home-makers who solicit their neighbors for money and make a substantial contribu-tion themselves. Some charities enlist retailers to keep donation cans in their establishments near the cash register where people might deposit their spare change.

In recent years, direct mail has become an extremely important marketing tool to reach the mass anonymous small gift market. There are three reasons for this. First, the cost of the personal solicitation has increased dramatically. Sec-ond, the growing availability of *highly* specialized mailing lists permits careful targeting of the market. And, third, the emergence of the personal computer has permitted charitable organizations to use and refine mailing lists at very low costs. Direct mail is relatively easy to get started. The first year's returns largely pay back the cost of the mailing lists and the system. This investment then pays off in subsequent years. With computers, charities can personalize correspon-dence and keep records in their data files of who responds to what. With special mailing lists, they can tailor appeals to segments with known interests and lifestyles. Each mailing allows the charity to build in more experience and fine-tune its approach. While small organizations can start up a direct-mail program for $300 to $400, one national charity invested $200,000 at the beginning and in 1981 was taking in $30 million annually from direct mail.[10] Mailings to acquire new donors vary in their results. The Zoological Society of San Diego found that by investing $80,000 in a high-quality, computer-personalized letter, modest premiums (free passes to the children's zoo and a zoo decal), and high-quality graphics, it generated $130,000 in membership revenues. Lists are carefully tested and analyzed and mailings are coordinated with television, radio, news-

Table 9-2

FUND-RAISING METHODS

Mass Anonymous Small Gift Market	
Charity cans in stores	Affinity cards
Direct mail	Raffles
Door-to-door solicitation	Rummage sales
Street and sidewalk solicitation	Sporting events
TV and radio marathons	Tours
Thrift shops	Walkathons, readathons, bikeathons,
Plate passing	danceathons, jogathons, swimathons
Cause-related marketing	Yearbooks
Members and Their Friends Market	
Affinity cards	Book sales
Anniversary celebrations	Dances
Art shows	Dinners, suppers, lunches, breakfasts
Auctions	Fairs
Benefits (theatre, movies, sports	Fashion shows
events)	Parties in unusual places
Bingo games	Phonathons (also called telethons)
Affluent Citizens Market	
Convocations	Parlor meetings
Dinners (invitational and/or	Telephone calls from high-status
testimonial)	individuals
Letters from high-status individuals	
Wealthy Donors Market	
Bequests	Testimonial dinner for wealthy
Celebrity grooming	individuals
Committee visit to person's home,	Wealthy person invited to another's
office	home or club
Memorials	

papers, and outdoor ads. The ads create an "awareness umbrella" that helped triple the Zoological Society's membership from 45,000 to 118,000 in just seven years.[11]

Telemarketing is another technique that is increasingly used for the mass anonymous small-gift market. Banks of telephones are assembled at campaign time and lists of potential donors are contacted by volunteers or hired solicitors one by one with carefully tailored solicitations. Appropriate lists can be obtained from secondary sources or simply developed directly using reverse telephone directories that list telephone numbers of households on streets or neighborhoods that are expected to have particularly high potential. Telemarketing has the advantage of bringing a personal touch to the solicitation process. However, overzealous organizations often lose this advantage through lack of adequate training and control. While telephone solicitors can be much more effective than direct mail in securing donations, they can also be much more damaging to an organization's reputation than mere pieces of paper if they are rude or pushy.

A final technique for attracting major contributions from the small gift market is cause-related marketing, described in the next chapter. In cause-related marketing, individuals can give to their favorite nonprofits *indirectly* by buying specific products and services.

The *members and their friends market* consists of the people who belong to the organization and their friends, who have a personal interest in supporting the organization. This market can be tapped for donations in a number of ways. Art museums, for example, favor raising money through selling memberships and running theater benefits, dinners, and tours. Churches, on the other hand, typically raise money by sponsoring bingo games, rummage sales, cake sales, plate passing, and raffles. Each of these fund-raising methods requires careful planning in order to maximize its potential revenue. Fashion shows, for example, have to be planned and promoted far in advance of the day of their occurrence; the same can be said of dances and fairs. Fund-raising consultants can be found who specialize in each method and know how to stage it for maximal effectiveness. These consultants can recommend the most effective and appropriate fund-raising methods to an organization. Furthermore, they continue to invent new approaches each year.[12] No sooner had walkathons become popular than other organizations created "readathons," bikeathons," and "jogathons." Each organization seeks to give a special or distinctive twist to its events. The Boys Clubs of Chicago, for example, once looked for an unusual place to hold a dinner for its members and decided on a black-tie dinner dance to be held in the Lion House of Lincoln Park Zoo, with the lions stalking around as the dinner guests dined and danced.

Members and their friends are also the major target of the so-called affinity card marketing programs. In these cases, individuals sign up with a particular credit card sponsor such as Citibank. They receive a special credit card, often with the nonprofit's logo on it, and for every dollar they spend using this card, the card's sponsor makes a small contribution (often one-half of 1 percent) to the nonprofit.

The *affluent citizens market* consists of persons whose income and interest in the organization or cause could lead them to give anywhere from $50 to several hundred dollars as a donation. the affluent citizens market is worth pursuing with more than direct mail. A highly effective technique is to issue invitations for special dinners or events. Political parties, for example, run $100- or $1,000-a-plate dinners to raise money for aspiring political candidates. Or the dinner might be free, with donations solicited after a round of enthusiastic speech making and drinking, both calculated to loosen the purse strings. Another popular method is letters and phone calls from supporters of the organization to their affluent friends asking for donations.

The *wealthy donors market* consists of persons whose wealth and potential interest is such that they might be induced to contribute anywhere from $1,000 to several million dollars to a cause or organization. These wealthy donors are usually well known in their community, and they are solicited by many organi-zations for financial support. Many of them set up foundations to handle these solicitations so that they do not have to be personally bothered. Yet some fund-raisers spend inordinate amounts of time cultivating these individuals in the hope of attracting a major grant to their institutions. One fund-raiser from a major private Eastern university has already spent seven years cultivating the friendship of a wealthy Chicago widow without yet receiving a major grant, yet he is not giving up. Some universities are skillful in putting on weekend retreats for wealthy donors in order to attract substantial money. One well-known private university invited 50 of its wealthiest alumni to an all-expense-paid weekend on the campus, flying them in on private planes from their homes in various parts of the country. These alumni were put up in the best hotels, treated to some fine lectures, led in a religious service by the university presi-dent, and treated to a football game won brilliantly by the school's team. Their spirits were so high that the typical alumnus attending that weekend gave a check to the university for over $100,000.

Many nonprofits such as churches and some charities carry on year-round fund-raising activities. Most, however, organize their efforts under the umbrella concept of a campaign. We define a campaign as follows:

> **A campaign** is an organized and time-sequenced set of activities and events for raising a given sum of money within a particular time period.

Fund-raisers distinguish between an *annual campaign* and a *capital campaign*. Colleges, hospitals, churches, and charitable organizations such as the United Way plan an annual campaign to raise a target amount of money each year to be used for various program operations. The campaign spells out the "case," goals, events, and so on. A well-known person may be invited to be the campaign chairperson to energize and symbolize that year's campaign.

Capital campaigns are not carried out annually but are a special set of activities designed to raise a large amount of money for one-time major under-takings or expansions. These campaigns require the most careful planning. Here are some of the major considerations:

1   An organization cannot run a capital campaign too often. After Stanford ended its five-year capital campaign, it would not launch another capital campaign for at least three to five years. This "spacing" is necessary if the capital campaigns are to retain their specialness in the minds of the donors.

2   The organization has to make decisions about the capital campaign's goal and duration. The goal should be achievable, for there is nothing more embarrass-ing than failing to reach the goal. And the campaign should not last too long because it will eventually lose its momentum.

3   The organization should try to add a matching gift feature to the campaign, where some wealthy donors or organizations promise to match, say $1 for $1,

the money raised from other sources. Early in the planning, the organization has to find and cultivate challenge grants.

4   The organization should prepare an attractive booklet showing the main items that the money will buy (called a *wish list*). Thus, MIT prepared a booklet showing what different amounts of money would buy, including buildings, endowed chairs, and so on.

5   A capital campaign should not be begun until much of its goal *has already been reached*. That is, larger donors must be solicited for major grants before announcing the campaign kickoff. This will give the campaign significant momentum right at the start, creating a *bandwagon effect* and erasing doubts that the project is not needed or that it will not soon achieve its goal.

An issue in designing a campaign is to decide whether potential donors should be "coached" in how much to give or whether this should be left to their judgment. In fact, there are three possibilities:

1   Don't specify any amount.
2   Suggest a specific dollar amount on the low side.
3   Suggest a specific dollar amount on the high side.

The first approach is the most common. People differ in what they can give, and it is felt that this is best left to their individual judgments.

Suggesting a specific amount on the low side is seen as accomplishing two things. It helps prospects know what is considered a minimum proper amount to give. And the "low-amount feature" allows people to get into the habit of giving (the "foot-in-the-door" theory).[13] While there is the problem that many people might have given more, research suggests that the technique can be quite effective. Brockner and others found that in a campaign for a relatively obscure charity, the National Reye's Syndrome Foundation, concluding the sales presentation with the phrase "even a dollar will help" resulted in *twenty times* as much money being raised as when this suggestion was not made.[14] Further, this was more effective than saying "even five dollars will help." The researchers found that the latter yielded more total dollars than the control condition (no request), but *less* than the "even a dollar" condition. This was due to increased frequency of donating under the "dollar" condition, rather than larger amounts being donated. Finally, the research found that the technique applies to both telephone and face-to-face solicitation. Citing earlier research, they also claim that the technique has been shown to work for at least three different charities, Reye's syndrome, the American Cancer Society, and the Heart Association.[15]

Suggesting a high amount to give works on the theory of the "door-in-the-face." It stretches people's idea of what they should give, and it is hoped that they will give this much or something close to it. Thus, the Give Five Program suggests that citizens give 5 percent of their income and/or 5 percent of their time each week to help others. Most people regard these amounts as too high, but end up giving more than they normally would (see also Exhibit 9-1).

EXHIBIT 9-1

How Not to Ask for Money in a Face-to-Face Situation

A successful young lawyer has a recent experience that graphically illustrates several subtle points about personal solicitation. He received a phone call from a person who said that he was from the lawyer's alma mater and would like to make an appointment to talk to the lawyer. At the appointed time the visitor appeared, a tall good-looking man with gray hair who looked like a college president. The visitor started to talk about the university's plan for the eighties and showed pictures of new buildings that the university needed. The lawyer now knew that the visitor was a development officer seeking a donation. After describing the university in glowing terms for fifteen minutes, the development officer came to the point: "In view of our needs and your affection for the university, I would like you to consider making a donation of $10,000 to your university." The lawyer at this point felt stunned by this request ("door-in-the-face"). He had never been asked for such a large contribution by any organization. He felt flattered that someone could think he could make such a large contribution; this meant that he had "arrived." On the other hand, he felt somewhat miffed to be asked without warning for such a large amount of money by a relative stranger. He told the development officer that he appreciated learning about his university's needs and would think it over, and hopefully would give, if not that amount, something substantial in any event. The officer looked a little disappointed, but thanked him for his time and left. At the time of this writing, the lawyer still had not made any donation to his university.

This episode illustrates several mistakes in the development officer's approach to the particular prospect. (Try to imagine these mistakes before reading on.) The development officer should have said over the phone who he was and his purpose for visiting. He should have sent an advance mailing describing the university's campaign, needs, and accomplishments. He should have considered bringing along an eminent lawyer who had also graduated from the same university. He should have done less talking and more listening, asking the lawyer how he felt about the university and what memories he had. The development officer should have asked for a more reasonable gift—say, $5,000. When the lawyer balked, the officer should have continued to try to "close the sale." He might have said that the lawyer could make a contribution of $5,000 over a five-year period in $1,000 annual amounts; this would ease the financial burden. Or he could have suggested a tangible benefit that would flow from this gift, such as a scholarship named after the lawyer to support a worthwhile student. Or he could have said that this would be a leadership gift, and the lawyer's name would be listed along with those of other leading contributors. Or he could have said that he would phone in two weeks to see how much the lawyer might be able to give. The development officer did not do any of these things, and his approach showed poor planning of this sales call.

EVALUATING FUND-RAISING EFFECTIVENESS

Each fund-raising organization must make a continuous effort to improve the effectiveness of its strategies through evaluating its most recent results, especially in the face of increasingly sophisticated competition and scarce funds. The organization can evaluate its results on the macro and micro levels.

Macroevaluation

Organizations use several methods to evaluate overall fund-raising effectiveness. They are described in the paragraphs that follow.

Percentage of Goal Reached.   For organizations that set an annual goal, the first thing to look at is how close they came to achieving the goal. Every organization wants to achieve at least its goal or better. This creates a temptation to set the goal low enough to be achieved. Often, the development officer favors a low goal so that he or she will look good. The organization's president, however, is tempted to set a high goal to induce the development office to work hard.

Composition of Gifts.   The organization should examine the composition of the money raised, looking at trends in the two major components:

Gifts = numbers of donors × average gift size

NUMBER OF DONORS.   Each organization hopes to increase the number of donors each year. The organization should pay attention to the number of donors in relation to the potential number of donors. Many organizations have a disappointing "reach" or "penetration." For example, if 29 percent of Stanford's alumni have given each year, the question is not why Stanford has 29 percent penetration but why 71 percent of its alumni do not give. The development officer should interview a sample of alumni nongivers and identify the importance of such reasons as: "Did not enjoy Stanford as a student," "Do not like the way Stanford is evolving," "Disagree with policies of the school in which I graduated," "Couldn't care less," "Was never asked," and so on. Each of these reasons suggests a possible plan of action.

AVERAGE GIFT SIZE.   A major objective of the fund-raising organization is to increase the size of the average gift in given donor segments. The development office should review the size distribution of gifts. It should estimate the potential number of gifts that might be obtained in each size class and compare it to the current number to determine the size classes of gifts that deserve targeted effort in the next period.

Comparison to Competitors.   For some organizations, comparisons with comparable organizations can be revealing about whether the institution is doing a competent job. A private Midwestern university, for example, compared its results to the results of five comparable universities and found it was trailing in the number of alumni givers and in the amount raised through government grants. This led to more effort being directed to these two donor directions. As another example, the Chicago Lung Association found that while it managed to raise more dollars each year, its rank among charitable causes had slipped from third place to eighth place. It was losing its "share of heart" in the giving community and needed to find ways to reverse this relative decline.

Expense/Contribution Ratio.   The fund-raising organization is ultimately interested in its net revenue, not gross revenue. At one time the American Kidney Fund spent $740,000 to raise $779,434 and created a scandal. It is more normal for the expense-to-contributions ratio to run between 10 and 20 percent, and the public generally accepts this. Many large donors, including corporations, look at this key ratio before they decide whether to support an organization. A low expense ratio can be a potent marketing feature since many donors believe that these ratios are very high—over 30 and 40 percent!

Microevaluation

The organization should also rate its individual staff members on their fund-raising effectiveness. This is not always done. One university vice-president of development said he had a general idea of the funds brought in by each staff member but not specific numbers. Many gifts were the result of several staff people working together: one identifying the prospect, another grooming him or her, and still another getting the check. Still, it would be worthwhile evaluating each individual to help train them better or dismiss them if they are not tapping the existing potential. As an example, one university rates the staff that solicits funds from foundations by using the following indicators (the numbers are illustrative):

Number of leads developed	30
Number of proposals written	20
Average value of proposal	$40,000
Number of proposals closed	10
Percentage of proposals closed	50%
Average value closed	$39,000
Average cost per proposal closed	$6,000
Cost per dollar raised	$.15

SUMMARY

One of the major problems of nonprofit organizations is fundraising. Organizations are gradually shifting from a product orientation to a sales orientation and then to a marketing orientation. A marketing orientation calls for carefully segmenting donor markets, measuring their giving potential, and assigning executive responsibility and resources to cultivate each market. Marketers assume that the act of giving is really an exchange process in which the giver also gets something that the organization can offer.

The first step in the fund-raising process is to study the characteristics of each of the four major donor markets: individuals, foundations, corporations, and government. Each donor market has its own giving motives and giving criteria.

The second step is to organize the fund-raising operation in a way that covers the different donor markets, organization services, marketing tools, and geographical areas.

The third step is to develop sound goals and strategies to guide the fund-raising effort. Goals are set on either an incremental basis, need basis, or opportunity basis. Strategies require selection of target markets, positioning and coordination of a full marketing mix.

The fourth step is to develop a mix of fund-raising tactics for the various donor groups. Different tactics are effective with the mass anonymous small-gift market, the members-and-their-friends market, the affluent citizens market, and the wealthy donors market.

The fifth step is to conduct regular evaluations of the fund-raising results. A macroevaluation consists of analyzing the percentage of the goal reached, the composition of the gifts, comparison to competitors, and the expense/contributions ratio. Microevaluation consists of evaluating the performance of each individual fund-raiser.

QUESTIONS

1. Develop a script for solicitors to use in a telemarketing campaign for a political candidate. Begin the script with questions to identify customer needs. Draft alternative follow-through messages for five different sets of identified needs.
2. How should the Los Angeles County Museum of Art segment its market when preparing a $40 million capital campaign to build a new structure to house a pre-Colombian art exhibit?
3. What macro and micro evaluation system would you establish to track the

capital campaign described in Question 2? Identify several interim results that would cause you to redirect the campaign.

4. Assume that the following figures represent the breakdown of the $12 million in charitable giving in a Midwestern city in 1989:

Religious organizations	42%
Hospitals and other health care	19%
Arts organizations	8%
Social services	16%
Other	15%

How would you go about forecasting the total level of giving and the breakdown for 1994?

5. Assume that you have been asked to do an image study of four arts organizations: a museum, a ballet company, a symphony orchestra, and a chamber music society. How would you do this so that the results would suggest fund-raising strategies for each organization for the coming year?

NOTES

1. *Giving USA: The Annual Report on Philanthropy for the Year 1988* (New York: AAFRC Trust for Philanthropy, 1989), pp. 8–9.
2. Rick Kogan, "Goodbye, 'Beg-a-thons': Public TV's New Ticket to Fundraising," *Chicago Tribune*, January 18, 1990, Section 5, pp. 1, 11.
3. "How Do We Choose the Charities We Support?" *Chicago Tribune*, July 30, 1972, Section 5, p. 9.
4. *Giving USA*, pp. 109–114.
5. Harold J. Seymour, *Designs for Fund-Raising* (New York: McGraw-Hill, 1966).
6. Eugene A. Scanlan, ed., *Community Foundations at 75: A Report on the Status of Community Foundations* (Washington, D.C.: Council on Foundations, 1989).
7. Here are some useful books and articles on grantsmanship. Virginia P. White, *Grants: How to Find Out About Them and What to Do Next* (New York and London: Plenum, 1975); Lois DeBakey and Selma DeBakey, "The Art of Persuasion: Logic and Language in Proposal Writing," *Grants Magazine*, Vol. 1, no. 1 (March 1978), pp. 43–60; F. Lee Jacquette and Barbara J. Jacquette, *What Makes a Good Proposal* (New York: Foundation Center, 1973); and Robert A. Mayer, *What Will a Foundation Look For When You Submit a Grant Proposal?* (New York: Foundation Center, 1972).
8. See "Stanford University: The Annual Fund," in Christopher Lovelock and Charles B. Weinberg, eds., *Cases in Public and Nonprofit Marketing* (Palo Alto, Calif.: Scientific Press, 1977), pp. 73–88.
9. Fox Butterfield, "Universities Take Lead in New Volunteer Efforts," *The New York Times*, October 17, 1985, p. 12.
10. Belinda Hulin-Salkin, "Strategies of Charities," *Advertising Age*, January 19, 1981, pp. 5–22ff.
11. Cliff Underwood, "Building Donor Relationships Strengthens Zoo's Membership," *Fundraising Management*, January 1984, pp. 37–43.

12. For several examples, see Suzanne Seixas, "Getting More From Givers," *Money*, September 1976, pp. 79–82.

13. In a study by Freedman and Fraser, the experimenters asked subjects to comply with a small initial request. Two weeks later, they were contacted and asked to comply with a large request. It was found that 76 percent of the experimental participants *agreed* to comply with the large request, compared to a 17 percent compliance rate by those subjects approached with *only* the large request. See J.L. Freedman and S. Fraser, "Compliance Without Pressure: The Foot-in-the Door Technique," *Journal of Personality and Social Psychology*, Vol. 4, 1966, pp. 195–202. See also Chapter 18.

14. Joel Brockner, Beth Guzzi, Julie Kane, Ellen Levine, and Kate Shaplen, "Organizational Fundraising: Further Evidence of the Effect of Legitimizing Small Donations," *Journal of Consumer Research*, June, 1984, pp. 611–613.

15. Peter H. Reingen, "On Inducing Compliance With Requests," *Journal of Consumer Research*, September 1978, pp. 96–102; Robert B. Cialdini and David A. Schroeder, "Increasing Compliance by Legitimizing Paltry Contributions: When Even a Penny Helps," *Journal of Personality and Social Psychology*, October 1976, pp. 599–604.

10

Acquiring Volunteer
and Corporate Support

A donation by Apple Computer to the Peace Corps will put personal computers in the African bush and other remote areas to work on such exotic tasks as tracking killer bees and monitoring well digging.

Apple Computer has given the government agency $216,000 worth of Macintosh personal computer systems for 35 of its overseas offices. Microsoft Corp., Bellevue, Wash., and Claris Corp., Mountainview, Calif., are contributing software.

"We are just thrilled," about the donation, says Susan Coates, management information specialist for the agency's international operations. "It has met a need that has been unmet for a long time."

Apple seems equally excited by the chance to help volunteers overseas, something it doesn't do very often.

"The Peace Corps offered a wonderful opportunity and a very thorough support plan," explains Apple's Beverly Long, adding that Apple makes few donations to groups working overseas because proper training and support is difficult when the volunteers work in the bush.

Ms. Long notes that her company was attracted to the plan because it is targeted at volunteers and because the Peace Corps promised thorough training for those using the new systems. In addition, shipping of the computers overseas with all its potential problems will be made easier by the Peace Corps.

Tracking Bees

Ms. Coates says the computers will be used by the "volunteers to support their work in the field in whatever area they are working on."

For example, beekeeping has become an important source of income in some developing countries. With the computer, the volunteers can help track bee populations, record the quality and quantity of the honey harvests and even monitor movements of the Africanized, or so-called "killer," bees.

They can be used in the same way to help projects dealing with agriculture, health, water quality and urban planning, she says.

In education, the desktop publishing capabilities of the computers could have a huge impact on the teaching of math, science, English, adult literacy, etc.

"In many of the places there is no funding for books or papers so that students arrive in class with no materials," Ms. Coates says, adding that often teachers must come early to write worksheets and other materials on the blackboard, if there is one, and then students spend class time copying it down.

"By automating the teacher's handouts, questions and quizzes, classroom instructors will have immediate teaching materials available for the students," she says. "This will provide more time for real learning."

Source: Adapted from "Apple Computer Helps Peace Corps Switch to High-Tech," *The Nonprofit Times*, August 1989, p. 3. Reproduced with permission.

For one who wishes to manage a nonprofit or public service marketing organization, it is essential to understand the special place society accords these organizations and the implications that special place has for managerial effectiveness. As is evident from both its actions and its attitudes, society considers nonprofit and public service organizations and those who work for them to be motivated not just by different goals but by *higher* goals. Elsewhere in this volume, we have suggested several of the disadvantages this status has for nonprofit organizations. We have noted that a major problem facing most nonprofit organizations is that they lack adequate time, work force, skills, and financial resources to achieve the mission they or society has established for them. To be successful, they have to augment these resources by securing the assistance of others. In addition to financing, this assistance comes in three forms, work force, skills, and volunteered or reduced-cost goods and services. Some of this assistance is provided routinely either as required by law (for example, tax concessions) or by common agreement (for example, the provision of free television air time for public service announcements). For the most part, however, securing assistance is itself a *marketing* task. Those who could assist must be brought to the point where they agree to exchange their goods and services (or their "normal" markup or profit) in return for certain benefits.

It is our position that while the special elevated status of nonprofit and public service organizations offers a highly positive platform for seeking help, the organization must also explicitly or implicitly have other benefits to offer as well. This is in part due to the fact that all nonprofits have real competition. Doctors who could help with an antismoking campaign or contribute to a charitable activity may agree that what you're doing is admirable and ought to be supported. But they may have many demands on their time by other organizations and, indeed, make their social contribution by providing free services to impoverished patients. To get their help, the nonprofit marketer must make them see that the benefits exceed the cost of the help and the benefit/cost ratio for this contribution is better than anyone else's.

In Chapter 7, we suggested the use of boards of directors as sources of volunteer help, and in Chapter 9, we outlined strategies for attracting funds from individuals, foundations, businesses, and the government. In this chapter, we will be concerned with attracting three other kinds of resources: volunteer staff, specialized skills, and specific goods and services. It should be pointed out, however, that we consider the special status of nonprofits that affords them these leveraging possibilities to be a *mixed* blessing. Put most simply, when goods and services are acquired at more or less full price on the open market, the acquirer has almost total discretion over how they are to be used. As the expression goes, he who pays the piper calls the tune. When the provider of the acquired goods or services offers a special dispensation, all too often they want a say in what the "tune" will be. The transaction has strings, and these strings may seriously impair the performance capability of the nonprofit. In the sections to follow, we shall alert the manager to these possibilities and suggest methods for coping with them.

RECRUITING AND MANAGING VOLUNTEERS

One common feature of many nonprofit organizations in their use of volunteers, both to keep down expenses and to provide a channel for high-minded people to contribute time to a cause they believe in. Among the organizations that make heavy use of volunteers are hospitals, political parties, trade associations, arts organizations, charitable institutions, churches, and social reform organizations. Also, smaller volunteer units are found in schools and social service organizations.

The core concept of voluntarism is that individuals participate in spontaneous, private, and freely chosen activities that promote or advance some aspect of the common good, as it is perceived by the persons participating in it. These activities are not coerced by any institution in society, and the behavior is not engaged in primarily for financial gain. A survey conducted by the Gallup Organization for The Independent Sector in March 1988 found the following:[1]

- 80 million Americans (45.3 percent of adults 18 years or older) volunteered an average of 4.7 hours per week in 1987.
- Total volunteered time amounted to 19.5 billion hours. Of this, about 14.9 billion (76.4 percent) was formal volunteering to specific nonprofit organizations.
- Formal volunteering to nonprofits amounted to the equivalent of 8.8 million employees with an estimated value of $150 billion.

A distribution of the jobs performed by volunteers in 1987 is reported in Table 10-1.

Trends in volunteering over time are difficult to establish. Nonprofit executives have been worried that volunteering would suffer as more women entered the labor force and workweeks became longer. Data from the Gallup study on respondents' *perceptions* of changes in their volunteer activity from 1984 to 1987 indicates that this fear may be groundless. Thirty-seven percent of the sample said they were volunteering more, and 25 percent were volunteering less. Increased volunteering was more often reported by women; men said they volunteered the same number of hours in 1987 as 1984. Perceived increases were also greatest among those ages 18 to 34 and in the $20,000 to $75,000 and over $100,000 household income brackets. The most often cited reasons for giving more time were more free time (35.8 percent) and an increase in concern or desire to help (23.4 percent).

While the pool of volunteers may not be shrinking, their motivations and the nature of their involvement has changed. Schindler-Rainman and Lippitt suggest several of the trends:[2]

1   While people are still volunteering because they feel it is a good thing to do, new motivations are emerging, such as
    a   The desire to change society.
    b   The desire to obtain experiences that can eventually be useful on a "regular" paid job.
    c   The desire to help a specific cause, such as improving the environment, electing a specific candidate, helping the elderly, removing discrimination, and so on.
    d   The desire to improve one's life through meeting others and attempting to make a difference.
    e   The desire to prepare for a volunteer career upon retirement.
    f   The desire to get inside important institutions (for example, government or a social movement) to see what it is doing and to make sure it is doing what it says it is doing.
2   A wider spectrum of people are volunteering. Rather than just the healthy, vigorous middle classes, we now find the "served" (for example, the elderly or the handicapped) and professionals also offering their services.

Table 10-1

DISTRIBUTION OF VOLUNTEER JOBS (BOTH FORMAL AND INFORMAL)*

Jobs	Percentage	Jobs	Percentage
Aide/assistant to paid employee	6.2	Blood bank or blood donation station	1.2
Aide to clergy	4.0	Assistant at nursing home	2.4
Assisting the elderly or handicapped	7.7	Visiting nurse	0.4
Baby-sitting (not part of an organization or group)	5.9	Fire or rescue squad volunteer	0.7
		Coach, director, recreational volunteer	3.3
Choir member or director	2.0	Librarian or aide	0.6
Church usher	1.5	Teacher or tutor (not as aide to paid employee)	3.5
Deacon or Deaconess	1.0	Youth group leader or aide	3.3
Parish visitor or missionary	0.9	Community coordinator	1.2
Sunday school or Bible teacher	3.3	Counselor (Big Brother/Big Sister, substance abuse prevention)	0.9
Driver	2.5	Social service counselor	0.6
Fund raising for local organization	5.3	Arts volunteer (theater, arts, and music)	1.6
Board member or trustee	2.3	Usher, guide, or tour leader	0.4
Office personnel, office work, or telephone answering	2.1	Civic or social group spokesperson	1.1
Organization officer (elected or appointed)	1.3	Meeting or convention planner	1.7
Committee member	4.9	Poll taker	0.4
Campaign worker or election day worker	1.6	Other	1.3
Cleaning or janitorial work	1.3	Don't know	32.7

Question: *In which of these areas have you done some volunteer work in the past month?*

*For the 39 percent of respondents who did volunteer work in the past month.

SOURCE: *Giving and Volunteering in the United States* (Washington, D.C.: The Independent Sector, 1988). Reproduced with permission.

3 Volunteers are more demanding. They want more "input" into what they are doing and are no longer willing to only be a drone in a larger enterprise.

4 Some groups are challenging the ultimate social desirability of volunteerism. While unions have traditionally worried that volunteerism was taking employment from those who could have been paid, the women's movement has recently challenged volunteerism as perpetuating the notion that what women do (that is, housework, volunteering) is not really valuable because it is unpaid.

These trends are putting pressure on nonprofit organizations to improve their abilities to recruit volunteers and to manage them once they are recruited. We shall consider these problems in turn.

Recruiting Volunteers

Recruiting volunteers is simply another marketing task and should proceed in a planned strategic way. The nonprofit organization should first be clear about its own organization mission, particularly as it relates to recruiting volunteers. Next, it should carefully research its environment—especially social trends, its target customers, and its competitors. It should understand its own strengths and weaknesses. Then, in light of all this input, it must carefully choose target segments on which it will closely focus, establish a differentiated market position vis-à-vis competition (which includes *not* volunteering and merely giving cash), and develop a coordinated marketing mix to implement the core strategy.

The most important element in all this is undoubtedly understanding the target market. This means understanding who volunteers are and why they volunteer. The characteristics of volunteers will tell the nonprofit whom to target and data on motivations will tell it how to "speak" to them. A starting point to understanding the target market is the characteristics of the organization's present volunteers. This is a task that each nonprofit can undertake for itself, learning the characteristics of their volunteers and, if possible, comparing them to the characteristics of (1) their city or region, (2) volunteers at competitive organizations, and (3) those who did volunteer to the organization once, but have since dropped out.

One point of comparison is the Gallup study for The Independent Sector mentioned earlier. This study reported an overall volunteering rate of 45.3 percent (both formal and informal volunteering). Volunteering rates associated with several key socioeconomic traits are shown in Table 10-2. These data suggest that, in general, the best prospects for volunteering are women, whites (or "other" races), individuals 35- to 44-years-old, those with incomes over $50,000, professionals or managers, those educated beyond high school, married people, those living in the Midwest, those in large households with two or more children under 18 years, members of a nonmainstream religion, and homeowners.

Surveys are also a useful way to learn about what motivates volunteers. The Gallup study produced a great deal of information on motivations of

Table 10-2

RATES OF VOLUNTEERING BY SELECTED DEMOGRAPHIC
CHARACTERISTICS

All respondents	45.3%	Elementary school	23.3%
Men	43.8	Some high school	25.0
Women	46.7	High school graduate	40.7
White and other	47.5	Trade, technical school	51.5
Black	27.7	Some college	57.7
Hispanic	26.8	College graduate	63.5
Age			
25–34	44.6	Married	49.9
35–44	53.9	Single	39.7
45–54	47.5	Divorced, separated	36.9
55–64	47.1	Widowed	31.9
65–74	40.0		
75+	28.6	East	41.3
		Midwest	56.5
Income		South	39.1
Under $10,000	23.4	West	46.1
$10,000–19,999	40.0		
$20,000–29,999	49.5	One-person household	32.9
$30,000–39,999	51.2	Two-person household	43.5
$40,000–49,999	43.5	Three-person household	45.7
$50,000–74,999	57.4	Four or more persons	50.4
$75,000–99,999	50.3		
100,000 and more	62.3	No child under 18	43.5
Occupation		One child under 18	40.8
Professional	63.3	Two children under 18	52.6
Manager	61.3	Three + under 18	50.7
Owner	47.7		
Skilled worker	46.0	Catholics	38.9
Semiskilled worker	30.2	Protestants	46.5
Clerical	37.0	Jews	45.8
Sales worker	41.4	Other religions	61.1
Service worker	34.7		
Retired	34.7	Own home	49.7
Housewife	40.4	Rent home	34.7

SOURCE: *Giving and Volunteering in the United States* (Washington, D.C.: The Independent Sector, 1988), pp. 13–20. Reproduced with permission.

volunteers and how they became connected to their nonprofit organization. The most frequently mentioned motivations for first volunteering were the following:

Wanted to do something useful	55.8%
Thought I would enjoy the work	33.5%
Family or friend would benefit	27.2%
Religious concerns	21.8%

These motivations vary by socioeconomic status as shown in Table 10-3. For example, women are somewhat more likely to mention that a friend or family member would benefit or that they had free time. Men are more likely to mention that they had previously benefited or had religious concerns. Single people responded to appeals that mentioned rewarding learning experiences and were much less likely to indicate religious motivations. Potential benefits to close friends and family members appear to be a powerful motivator for those ages 25 to 44. The principal reasons given for *not* volunteering were lack of time (50.8 percent) and health reasons (11.8 percent). The latter were much more likely to be mentioned by the elderly and those with low incomes (who often *are* the elderly).

Another approach to understanding motivations is to use focus groups. Focus groups undertaken by the United Way of America underlined the importance to volunteers of having a meaningful work experience.[3] There were two dimensions of meaningfulness. One was helping society. As one participant said,

> By working for the United Way I really felt like I was helping the needy.

Another said:

> It gave meaning to my own life.

The other dimension was the feeling that one is making an impact through one's own special skills. Consider the following comments:

> I felt like I was using my professional skills in this job: how to identify and define a problem, how to talk to people, how to organize people into productive, efficient action.

> To be honest, I didn't always keep in mind where the money was going but I loved the challenge of organizing an account that hadn't gone well before or making new contacts.[4]

A number of studies have shown that having motivation to volunteer is not enough to promote action; individuals have to make a concrete connection. Sometimes this is by being asked to volunteer by someone else; sometimes it is by participating in an organization either themselves or through the experiences of a family member or friend. Volunteers told Gallup that they learned of their present activity through the following means:[5]

Asked by someone	40.4%
Participated in organization	39.3%
Family or friend benefited	27.6%
Sought on their own	19.2%
Saw an advertisement	5.3%

Table 10-3

REASONS FOR FIRST VOLUNTEERING BY SELECTED SOCIOECONOMIC CHARACTERISTICS* (PERCENTAGE OF RESPONDENTS)

Demographic Characteristic	Thought I Would Enjoy the Work	Wanted to Do Something Useful	Wanted to Learn, Get Experience	Family Member or Friend Would Benefit	Previously Benefited From the Activity	Religious Concerns	Had a Lot of Free Time	Other	Don't Know
Total	33.5	55.8	9.4	27.2	9.9	21.8	8.6	3.0	4.5
Sex									
Male	33.9	56.2	10.4	24.2	11.3	24.1	6.8	0.6	3.7
Female	33.0	55.5	8.5	29.9	8.7	19.9	10.1	1.3	5.2
Race									
White	33.3	56.3	9.5	27.9	10.1	21.3	8.1	0.9	4.6
Black	34.7	52.3	5.7	19.2	5.0	26.2	12.2	1.7	3.1
Hispanic†	19.9	50.3	12.5	29.0	5.2	16.8	11.7	1.3	6.1
Age									
18–24	38.3	53.9	19.1	18.5	10.4	12.1	10.4	2.2	5.5
25–34	36.2	47.9	8.6	37.1	12.0	19.9	7.3	0.7	4.1
35–44	30.6	54.5	8.6	41.0	8.6	18.0	6.2	0.4	3.2
45–54	30.6	60.3	11.6	26.3	15.3	23.7	7.2	2.4	3.9
55–64	27.6	68.9	3.7	10.6	7.4	34.7	9.5	–	7.1
65+	39.7	56.2	6.1	11.4	4.9	26.9	14.3	0.7	4.7

Income									
Under $10,000	25.2	55.8	8.0	16.2	5.2	26.9	12.3	—	10.6
$10,000–$19,999	36.4	57.2	7.6	24.2	9.2	19.8	11.9	0.1	6.0
$20,000–$29,999	28.5	51.2	7.2	24.6	4.5	23.2	9.4	1.1	4.4
$30,000–$39,999	36.0	52.8	9.2	32.1	8.0	23.7	8.5	2.6	3.4
$40,000–$49,999	36.6	51.5	7.1	30.4	15.4	23.2	8.4	0.6	4.8
$50,000–$74,999	34.4	61.2	12.5	32.3	15.4	21.1	6.4	—	3.0
$75,000–$99,999	41.4	64.8	17.3	17.1	15.2	22.5	0.8	2.8	3.3
100,000 +	28.4	63.8	12.7	30.2	12.8	10.0	5.1	0.7	1.3
Marital Status									
Married	32.4	56.5	7.8	30.4	9.9	25.4	7.8	0.7	4.4
Single	39.7	54.5	17.4	15.5	11.4	12.6	9.2	2.7	6.0
Divorced, separated, or widowed	30.1	59.7	6.2	26.2	7.5	14.9	15.6	—	2.7

Question: *For what reasons did you first become involved in your volunteer activities?*

*Data from the 45 percent of respondents who volunteered in the past year as of March 1988. Respondents could give multiple responses.

†Hispanics may be of any race.

— Too few cases to be reliable.

SOURCE: *Giving and Volunteering in the United States* (Washington, D.C.: The Independent Sector, 1988), p. 29. Reproduced with permission.

The importance of being asked by someone suggests opportunities for increasing volunteer participation. Gallup found a number of groups that were much *less* likely to be asked to volunteer than others: blacks, 18- to 25-year-olds, those over 65, and those with incomes under $10,000.

Retaining Volunteers

As with any marketing task, it is usually much easier to market to present customers than to new customers. Thus, a nonprofit must pay particular attention to the problems of retaining present volunteers. One approach is to survey "dropouts" to ascertain what it is that made them quit. Another is to conduct periodic assessments of present volunteers' satisfactions and dissatisfactions. Among the sources of dissatisfaction that frequently surface in these studies are the following:

1 Unreal expectations when volunteering. This is sometimes the recruit's own fault in that he or she has unrealistic fantasies about how exciting it would be to join the Peace Corps, participate in a political campaign, or become part of the "United Way team," or about how much time would be involved. But just as often the culprit is the nonprofit organization, which, in its zeal to get recruits, paints an excessively optimistic picture of the volunteer's time commitment, type of work, and probable influence.
2 Lack of appreciative feedback from clients and coworkers.
3 Lack of appropriate training and supervision.
4 Feelings of second-class status vis-à-vis full-time staff.
5 Excessive demands on time.
6 Lack of a sense of personal accomplishment.

It is clear that training and supervision are a major source of dissatisfaction. Thus, a third approach to understanding what is needed to retain volunteers is to ask them what could be done to create an "ideal" situation for them in the nonprofit. Recently, volunteers to the United Way of America proposed the following set of ideal characteristics for their participation:

1 *Recognize professionalism.* The volunteers want to be treated as professionals, not with "kid gloves."
   • Involve experienced volunteers in the training.
   • Take each volunteer's expertise and experience into account when assigning responsibilities or providing training.
   • Cover more than a "model" campaign or contact with a company. Incorporate sequences of what *could* happen. Keep in mind that volunteers must deal with a wide range of companies, attitudes, and issues to resolve.
   • Provide more role-play activities.
   • Give more information about how to use United Way's printed communications materials and how to modify them for different situations.
   • Rework case books to include background on individual companies that is relevant to the new volunteer.

2 *Increase awareness of the impact of the United Way on the community.* Volunteers feel this information would help them motivate donors as well as themselves.
- Provide information about specific cases of "how people are helped."
- Educate volunteers about the needs and social conditions of the community.
- Inform volunteers on the progress of the campaign.

3 *Encourage internal, personal fulfillment.*
- Help the volunteers personalize their tasks.
- Encourage volunteers to get to know each other and foster a "team spirit" among all volunteers.
- Help volunteers understand the impact their volunteer work will have on other people. For example, take volunteers to visit a United Way–supported agency so the volunteers can actually see United Way dollars at work.
- Help volunteers identify with the cause. Let them know they play an important role in resolving local community problems and issues.[6]

Managing Volunteers

The use of volunteers is not an unmixed blessing for a nonprofit organization. The mix of volunteers and full-time staff can be a volatile one. There can be problems on both sides. On the side of the volunteer, many have the attitude that because they are donating their services to the nonprofit and are not paid by them (1) they don't really *work* for the organization and so shouldn't be *told* what to do, rather, they should be *asked* if they would be willing to do something; (2) they should have a great deal to say about the content and timetable for their assignments; and (3) they deserve continual appreciation for their generosity and commitment. Further, some individuals volunteer, not because they really want to work, but because they have been coerced into volunteering by an employer or peers or because they wish to add an item to their resume. One manager of a large volunteer force has developed what he calls his "rule of thirds." One-third of his volunteer force works avidly with very little direction and encouragement. One-third will work only with considerable motivation and are only effective with careful supervision. And one-third will not work at all under any circumstances and are best ignored (unless they are causing morale problems among those who do work).

On the organization side, there is considerable opportunity for friction to develop if the professional full-time staff looks on the volunteers as second-class workers. Among the opinions professionals have been known to offer are

1 Volunteers are dilettantes. They are not there for the long haul and so don't have to live with the consequences of their impulsive or lethargic performance.
2 Volunteers never really pay attention to their training and instruction because they are only part time and so commit tactical and ethical missteps that hurt the organization.
3 Volunteers often come from occupations in which they boss others and so cannot or will not take direction.
4 Volunteers are often well-to-do members of the leisure classes who (a) consider themselves better than the professional staff (the "Junior Leaguers") and (b) are unwilling to perform grubby tasks like licking envelopes or cleaning bedpans.

The potential for conflict between volunteers and professional full-time employees is therefore considerable. The situation can be exacerbated if management does not take firm control of the situation. Again, it is a matter of *attitude*. If management's attitude is dominated by feelings of gratitude that these individuals have so kindly volunteered, all is virtually lost. Management will be unwilling to ruffle the feathers of volunteers. This will only encourage the volunteers' tendencies toward undisciplined performance. At the same time, management will be likely to squelch grumblings of the paid staff for fear that they will upset these needed volunteers. This will only cause further unrest and surreptitious insubordination among the staff. The result will be that management loses control of *both* full-time and volunteer staff.

The solution that the more experienced programs have developed is simply to treat volunteers as much as possible as professional, full-time workers indistinguishable from paid staff. Among other things, this means using the following standards and managerial practices:

1 Assessing the volunteer's skills and, as nearly as possible, matching these skills to the tasks to be performed in the organization.
2 Setting out job responsibilities clearly and in detail in advance.
3 Setting specific performance goals and benchmarks.
4 Clearly informing the volunteers of these goals and of the fact that they are expected to achieve them.
5 Informing the volunteers that if they do not perform satisfactorily in their job, they will be let go or assigned elsewhere (the most difficult task).
6 Following through on the standards of accountability, knocking heads and dismissing volunteers until the word gets around that management is serious in its commitments (the most crucial task).

This straightforward, professional style of volunteer management may seem risky to the inexperienced manager. But both volunteer and professional staff respond very favorably to it. Most volunteers like to be taken seriously and challenged. They appreciate the opportunity to be well trained and well supervised. Those who do not are the one-third you do not want anyway. Full-time paid staff appreciate management's firmness and the fact that they, too, can treat the volunteer seriously, giving orders as necessary and reprimands as required. Performance standards for both groups improve enormously and the nonprofit's effectiveness, efficiency, and morale rise noticeably. Indeed, the organization's volunteer positions can be highly coveted.

Peter Drucker argues that "the steady transformation of the volunteer from well-meaning amateur to trained, professional unpaid staff member is the most significant development in the nonprofit sector."[7] Drucker says that, to attract the knowledgeable worker who will be the backbone of the volunteer movement in the future, nonprofits must treat volunteers as professionals, give them chances to put their competence and knowledge to work, and provide meaningful achievement recognition. Drucker says that the new professional volunteers require three things: a clear organizational mission, training, and personal accountability.

Drucker believes that this move toward professionalized volunteerism "may be the most important development in American society today." He concludes:

> We hear a great deal about the decay and dissolution of family and community and about the loss of values. And, of course, there is reason for concern. But the nonprofits are generating a powerful countercurrent. They are forging new bonds of community, a new commitment to active citizenship, to social responsibility, to values. And surely what the nonprofit contributes to the volunteer is as important as what the volunteer contributes to the nonprofit. Indeed, it may be fully as important as the service, whether religious, educational, or welfare related, that the nonprofit provides in the community.

ATTRACTING SKILLS, GOODS, AND SERVICES

A great many nonprofits are too small to be able to afford to hire specialized skills, goods, and services that could measurably improve their operations. And they are also too small or inexperienced to produce these themselves. Two areas in which assistance is often needed are advertising and marketing research. Some of the possible sources of help in these areas are described in the following sections.

Commercial Advertising Agencies

Probably the best-known source of leverage for nonprofits is professional advertising agencies willing to donate their skills and services in the public interest. Almost every major community has advertising agencies that are willing to make such contributions. There are a number of reasons why they contribute their services:

- They believe that the nonprofit organization will have important community executives among its other volunteers and so a volunteer campaign will be a major opportunity to make business contacts.
- Goodwill can be obtained by such public-spiritedness.
- Agency executives and staff can achieve personal psychic benefits from working on important social issues rather than just "selling soap."
- Opportunities in the campaign for individual creativity, agency creativity, or both may be considerably greater than when a paying client is "calling the tune." The agency may see a chance to make a major public impression with a highly innovative campaign.
- The campaign presents an opportunity to give experience to junior staff people where a major client is not at risk.

Like volunteers, contributed advertising services can be a mixed blessing. First, if the donated campaign is costly, the agency may skimp on production values. If it assigns junior people, the execution may not be of the highest quality. On the other hand, if the agency focuses too narrowly on the campaign as merely a chance to make a major creative impact, it may lose sight of the nonprofit organization's basic advertising goals. If nonprofit managers are alert to these potential dangers, however, they can typically be avoided with timely interventions. Again, as with volunteers, it is up to the nonprofit to treat the donated relationship *as if* it were a professional, fully-paid-for relationship rather than a "charity case" for which the nonprofit organization should be grateful (and thus noninterfering).

Probably the best-known example of donated advertising agency services is the operation of the Advertising Council. The Council was founded in 1942. In 1987–88, the Ad Council produced 37 national campaigns through the donated services of 34 different advertising agencies, including the most powerful in the country.[8] Over $1.2 billion in space and time was contributed in 1988 by over 22,000 media outlets, almost one-half from network television. Several of the campaigns promoted by Ad Council Agencies in 1987–88 are outlined in Figure 10-1. The history of one of the best known of these, Smokey the Bear, is described in Exhibit 10-1 along with a sample promotion seeking media cooperation in Figure 10-2.

FIGURE 10-1

Selected Advertising Council Campaigns 1987–88

Campaign	Theme	Agency
AIDS prevention	"Help stop AIDS. Use a Condom."	Scali, McCabe, Sloves, Inc.
Aid to higher education	"Give to the College of your choice."	Laurance, Charles, Free & Lawson, Inc.
Buckle your safety belt	"You can learn a lot from a dummy—buckle your safety belt."	Leo Burnett U.S.A.
Child abuse prevention	"Take time out. Don't take it out on your kid."	Lintas: Campbell-Ewald
Crime prevention	"Take a bite out of crime."	Saatchi & Saatchi
Drug abuse prevention	"Just say no."	DDB Needham Worldwide, Inc.
Forest fire prevention	"Smokey says: Only you can prevent forest fires."	Foote, Cone & Belding Communications
Peace Corps	"The toughest job you'll ever love."	Baker Spielvogel Bates Worldwide, Inc.
Take pride in America	"Bad guys abuse public lands. Good guys save them."	W. B. Doner and Company Advertising
United Negro College Fund	"A mind is a terrible thing to waste."	Young & Rubicam, Inc.

FIGURE 10-2

Promotion Seeking Media Cooperation

SOURCE: Foote, Cone & Belding. Reprinted with permission.

EXHIBIT 10-1

Smokey the Bear Program for the U.S. Forest Service, U.S. Department of Agriculture, and the Advertising Council

The Forest Service account has been a public service client of Foote, Cone & Belding's Los Angeles office since 1942. The Smokey the Bear Program is the longest-running public service campaign on record, and it has been handled by FCB since its inception. Further, an awareness study done by the U.S. Advertising Council in 1976 showed that Smokey the Bear is the second most widely recognized advertising symbol in America, second only to the Coca-Cola bottle.

The Ad Council's study also showed that 98 percent of the respondents not only recognize Smokey the Bear but also know that he stands for forest fire prevention. In addition, more than half the respondents can complete the Smokey the Bear slogan, "Only you . . ." can prevent forest fires.

The Smokey campaign, for which new material is created by FCB every year, includes public service advertising materials as well as posters and handouts for use by foresters and teachers to help teach children to be careful with fire in the forest.

History of Smokey the Bear

Smokey celebrated his fortieth birthday in 1984 and is the subject of a television documentary.

Smokey the Bear has a long history.

During the Second World War, a Japanese submarine shelled the Southern California coast, and forestry officials were afraid that future attacks might start widespread forest fires. The government was alerted to the danger to its national forests. Because of this, the Cooperative Forest Fire Prevention campaign was organized by the USDA Forest Service.

The campaign needed to take its message directly to the American people, so the newly formed Wartime Advertising Council was asked for their advice. The Council agreed to help, and Foote, Cone, & Belding of Los Angeles became the volunteer advertising agency.

At first, during 1942 and 1943, wartime slogans were used on forest fire prevention posters. Then Walt Disney's Bambi was used on a 1944 poster. After Bambi's success, the Forest Service and the Wartime Advertising Council decided to choose their own animal to represent forest fire prevention. The agreed-on animal: a bear. This bear was described as follows: "nose short (panda type), color black or brown; expression appealing, knowledgeable, quizzical; perhaps wearing campaign (or Boy Scout) hat that typifies the outdoors and the woods."

The first poster (1944–1945) showed the bear, named "Smokey," pouring water on a campfire.

When the war was over, the Wartime Advertising Council was renamed the Advertising Council. But they continued to sponsor public service campaigns, including Smokey the Bear's message. The famous message, "Only *you* can prevent forest fires," was created in 1947. It is still in use today.

By 1952, Smokey the Bear had become so well known that his image needed protection by law. So Congress passed the Smokey the Bear Act. The act did several things: (1) it prohibited the use of Smokey the Bear without permission of the Forest Service, (2) it permitted the Forest Service to license the use of Smokey the Bear and collect royalties, and (3) it allowed the Forest Service to keep the royalties and put them into a fund to be used only for forest fire prevention. The act also prohibited the wearing of a Smokey the Bear costume without permission.

The first Smokey the Bear stuffed toy was made in 1952 by Ideal Toys. With permission from the Forest Service, a card was inserted with each toy to be mailed to the Forest Service as an application to become a "Junior Forest Ranger." Children readily responded. By 1955 there were 500,000 Junior Forest Rangers.

Elementary school children were taken with the message of Smokey the Bear. State forestry people and Forest Service rangers visited classrooms, telling the students about forest fire prevention. Children were encouraged to write Smokey for their very own Junior Forest Ranger Kit. By 1965, Smokey was given his own zip code number. Requests for Junior Forest Ranger Kits from children are still being sent to Smokey today.

Has all this effort to prevent forest fires had a result? In 1942 over 10 million acres of wildlands were burned. In 1981, only 3 million acres were burned—representing a savings of over $20 billion for the American taxpayers.

SOURCE: Foote, Cone & Belding, Chicago.

Advertisements from several Ad Council campaigns being run in 1989 are reproduced in Figures 10-3 to 10-8. The effectiveness of one campaign, "Take a bite out of crime," is reported in Exhibit 10-2.

EXHIBIT 10-2

A Research Evaluation of "Taking a Bite Out of Crime"

The public service campaign, "taking a bite out of crime," was begun in October 1979, under the sponsorship of the U.S. Department of Justice and the Coalition Against Crime. The campaign features an animated dog, "McGruff,"who is dressed in a trenchcoat and describes a real example of someone personally combating a crime and asking the audience to follow this example. The PSA campaign focused heavily on television but also included radio, magazines, and newspapers. In the first phase, the campaign offered individuals suggestions on protecting houses and property. The second phase encouraged individuals to observe and report suspected criminal behavior. The third phase promoted the organization of neighborhood and local groups to support various community crime prevention activities.

In an attempt to assess the effects of this campaign over its first two years, the National Institute for Justice carried out an evaluation study through the University of Denver. This study relied upon data from two sources (1) a national probability sample of 1,200 households conducted in November 1981 and (2) reinterviews in November 1981, of 426 panel respondents in three cities who were previously interviewed three months before the beginning of the campaign (September, 1979).

Both the national survey and the panel data showed that a very broad range of the population was exposed to and influenced by the campaign. In particular, the studies found that those exposed to the campaign reported (1) they now knew much more about crime prevention, (2) they felt more positively about the likely effectiveness of private citizens taking actions against crime, and (3) they felt more personally competent in protecting themselves against crime. On the other hand, the campaign didn't make them feel more threatened by crime and, in fact, the panel felt less likely to be burglarized.

Effects on actual behavior were also apparent. The PSAs appeared to influence the panel to (1) leave outdoor lights on, (2) have neighbors watch the house, (3) use timer lights, (4) watch the neighborhood themselves, (5) report suspicious behavior to the police, and (6) join with others to prevent crime. All were advocated by the PSAs. Curiously, the study also found an increase in the proportion of the households "acquiring a dog for security purposes." Clearly McGruff had other influences besides the specific measures he advocated.

SOURCE: Adapted from Garret J. O'Keefe, " 'Taking a Bite Out of Crime': The Impact of a Public Information Campaign," *Communication Research*, Vol. 12, no. 2, April 1985, pp. 147–178.

FIGURE 10-3

To all the people who think the press goes too far sometimes, consider the alternative.

waters about 80 miles from the closest point of the Okinawa island chain and only about 200 miles

WASHINGTON (AP) — New details about the Navy's 1965 lo

comment.

d an associate, Joshua said their

To learn more about the role of a Free Press and how it protects your rights, call the First Amendment Center at 1-800-542-1600.

If the press didn't tell us, who would?

A public service message of The Ad Council and The Society of Professional Journalists.

FREE PRESS CAMPAIGN
NEWSPAPER AD NO. FP-89-1522—2 COL.

SOURCE: Free Press Campaign Newspaper Ad No. FP–89–1522–2 COL.

FIGURE 10-4

REACH
FOR THE POWER.
TEACH.

No other profession has this power. The power to wake up
young minds. The power to wake up the world. Teachers have
that power. Reach for it. Teach. For information call:

1-800-45-TEACH.

Recruiting New Teachers, Inc.

SOURCE: The Advertising Council. Reproduced with permission.

FIGURE 10-5

FOOD STAMPS CAMPAIGN
NEWSPAPER AD NO. FS-88-1396—2 COL.

SOURCE: The Advertising Council. Reproduced with permission.

FIGURE 10-6

AIDS CAMPAIGN
NEWSPAPER AD NO. AIDS-88-1380—2 COL.
(8⅜″ x 14″) AD NO. AIDS-88-1379

SOURCE: The Advertising Council. Reproduced with permission.

FIGURE 10-7

IF YOU'RE NOT RECYCLING YOU'RE THROWING IT ALL AWAY.

A little reminder from the Environmental Defense Fund that if you're not recycling, you're throwing away a lot more than just your trash.

You and your community can recycle. Write the Environmental Defense Fund at: EDF-Recycling, 257 Park Avenue South, New York, NY 10010, for a free brochure that will tell you virtually everything you need to know about recycling.

© 1988 EDF

ENVIRONMENTAL DEFENSE FUND CAMPAIGN
NEWSPAPER AD NO. EDF-88-1364—2 COL.
TABLOID SIZE (9⅜" x 14") AD NO. EDF-88-1363

SOURCE: The Advertising Council. Reproduced with permission.

FIGURE 10-8

CRIME PREVENTION CAMPAIGN
NEWSPAPER AD NO. CP-89-1466—3 COL.

SOURCE: The Advertising Council. Reproduced with permission.

Marketing Research Agencies

Marketing research agencies can also be helpful. Research organizations can provide advice on specific design strategies, research instruments, and analysis plans. They can carry out the research on a voluntary or at-cost basis. Finally, they can add research questions of interest to the nonprofit organization to questionnaires designed for other purposes.

Business Firms

Sometimes business firms will contribute staff time to meet other nonprofit requirements. Computer firms will assist with data processing. Major accounting firms will help keep the books, conduct audits, and prepare annual reports for nonprofits routinely as part of their "pro bono" professional responsibilities. Similarly, law firms and some management consultants will devote some of their staff time, albeit junior staff time, to pro bono work. They often provide this help collectively, as in the case of Business Volunteers for the Arts— Chicago. Under this umbrella organization, 64 executives from 36 corporations offered time and skills to metropolitan Chicago's nonprofit arts organizations in 1985.

Business organizations often will offer the use of their own premises for nonprofit activities. This can involve relatively simple contributions such as allowing charity gum machines to be placed in their retail stores or permitting the use of a conference center or meeting room for nonprofit board meetings or staff retreats. Major firms allow the United Way of America to conduct attitude and motivation studies on their employees using the companies' reproduction facilities, mail systems, and computers.

Charities have also benefited for years from the free goods and services provided for their fund-raisers and staff events by the soft drink, beer, and food industries. Firms will often announce charity campaigns in their employee publications, permit blood drives on their premises, and loan executives to give lectures or demonstrations at schools and civic meetings. Two of the most elaborate are the series of contributions from the private sector involved in the 1984 Summer Olympics and the annual Muscular Dystrophy drive.

Firms can also provide equipment and supplies. In a recent innovative contribution, Rubbermaid, through its Rubbermaid Foundation donated the first building ever constructed for a United Way chapter in Wooster, Ohio. It also acquired and renovated the Walnut Street School next door and converted it into a community arts center.[9]

Affinity Cards and Cause-Related Marketing.   Two of the most dramatic developments in recent years in the potential of leveraging corporate contributions to nonprofits have been *affinity credit cards* and *cause-related marketing*. In both these cases, for-profit marketers promote their regular products and services but give some percentage of their revenues to designated nonprofits. Thus, in the case of affinity credit cards (see Exhibit 10-3), members of a nonprofit organization sign up for a major credit card—often with no initial fee and a lower interest rate—and the credit card company rebates to the nonprofit a preset percentage of charges on the cards.

EXHIBIT 10-3

Marketers of Credit Cards Show New Affinity for Nonprofit Groups

In an unusual alliance, Bay Area nonprofit organizations are joining forces with banks to market credit cards, and they are taking a cut of the action for their efforts.

In 1987 KQED, Inc., San Francisco's public broadcaster, announced it was offering Visa cards issued by a Maryland bank to its nearly 250,000 members. By taking "royalties," one-half of 1 percent of the value of all transactions made on the cards, KQED estimates it could bring in $3.5 million to $5 million over a five-year period from the cards.

In 1986 San Francisco-based Sierra Club, the environmental organization, began a similar program with its members in conjunction with Chase Lincoln First Bank of Rochester, N.Y. The club said it is close to gathering $225,000 in revenue from the program this year.

But Bay Area nonprofits aren't alone.

A spokesman for San Mateo-based Visa International said the credit card company had approved more than 500 such programs throughout the United States.

Vietnam Veterans of America also has a Visa card program, in connection with Dollar Dry Dock Bank in New York. The largest, and one of the oldest groups, is the American Automobile Association's Visa program, which has issued 3 million credit cards.

"Affinity cards are a very, very fast growing area in the credit card industry," said David Brancoli, director of public relations for Visa. "And it's a program that brings benefits to everyone."

Affinity cards—the term comes from groups such as university alumni associations, airline frequent flyers and auto clubs, whose members are well-defined and share common goals or interests—have become increasingly popular for several reasons.

For banks, it represents a more "targeted" approach to marketing credit cards. Visa statistics showed the average response rate for a bank credit card solicitation by mail is 1 to 3 percent, Brancoli said. The response rate among affinity group members is 6 to 20 percent.

Although Visa does not have solid statistics, Brancoli also said preliminary indications are that affinity group members use their cards more frequently than other cardholders. They also tend to be more reliable about paying their bills.

For affinity groups, often nonprofit organizations scrambling for funds, the credit cards represent a much-needed new source of revenue.

In the first month of its credit-card program, the Sierra Club signed up 10,000 new card members for Visa, said Leonard Levitt, director of finance. After its first full year, the club has 24,000 cardholders. "We had budgeted receiving about $180,000 from the program," Levitt said, "but it looks like we'll probably do 25 percent better than that."

Although $225,000 is only about 1 percent of the Sierra Club's annual budget, "It's a nice piece of money coming in that we can readily use," he said.

And the income is likely to grow. Right now, about 6 percent of the Sierra Club's members have signed up for their Visa cards. Levitt expects that percentage to go to more than 10 percent.

The consumer benefits, too.

For many affinity groups, members pay slightly lower interest rates. KQED members will pay 17.8 percent—16.8 percent if they take advantage of a 1 percent year-end rebate, which can be donated to the broadcaster instead. Sierra Club members are charged 18 percent, lower than the 19.8 percent levied by most major banks.

In addition, KQED members do not have to pay the first year's annual credit card membership fee of $25. The fee is waived for four years for Sierra Club members.

SOURCE: Adapted from Kenneth Howe, "Marketers of Credit Cards Show New Affinity for Nonprofit Groups," *San Francisco Business Times*, August 7, 1987, Section 1, p. 4. Reproduced with permission.

Nonprofit affinity card projects have become highly competitive:

- Mastercard International program "Choose to Make a Difference" donates seven-tenths of a cent to a pool shared by six charities each time a MasterCard product is used during the Christmas season. Consumers also fill in ballots to indicate how the proceeds are to be used. In 1988, MasterCard donated $3.1 million to the six causes 12 percent more than it gave in 1987, the first year of its program.[10]
- Sears, Roebuck and Co. counters by offering to pay 10 cents to a charitable foundation for sick children each time its Discover Card is used to buy a toy.[11]
- In June of 1989, Marine Midland Bank of New York introduced an "ice cream affinity card" in cooperation with Breyers Ice Cream, a division of the Kraft General Foods group. These cards were offered during a Child's Miracle Network Telethon and a simultaneous advertising and newspaper insert campaign. Breyers paid $2.00 to children's hospital for every affinity card opened. Marine Midland then contributed one-half of 1 percent of the monthly balance on the accounts.[12]

In cause-related marketing, the objective is more short run. For-profit marketers decide to help out a specific event or charity drive and donate a percentage of sales from a particular product or service to the cause for a specified period of time. Cause-related marketing was "invented" by the American Express Company in 1984 to assist in the restoration of the Statue of Liberty. In this campaign, American Express agreed to donate a penny to the restoration cause for use of its card—and a dollar for most new cards issued in the United States. In one fiscal quarter, card usage increased 28 percent over the year earlier and the number of new cards issued rose 45 percent. American Express donated $2 million from this campaign to the Statue of Liberty.[13]

Other successful cause-related marketing efforts have been the following:

- General Foods distributed cents-off coupons for orange-flavored Tang as part of its "March Across America" campaign and gave Mothers Against Drunk Driving (MADD) 10 cents for every proof of purchase. MADD received $100,000 and sales of Tang were up by 13 percent.[14]
- Frito-Lay indirectly contributed $2 million in 1988 to the national antidrug marketing effort by printing the "Just Say No" slogan on 120 million bags of potato chips. A more modest contribution was the decision by Prince George County, Maryland car dealer, Bob Cairns, to put up a highway billboard saying: "Kids, it's not cool to use drugs. But it's cool to work hard and study hard for that new car."[15]
- Scott Paper Company has an entire product line, Helping Hand, positioned as meeting dual needs. The toilet paper, trash bags, and paper towels provide for household cleaning needs. But the product labels also say: "Every time you buy Helping Hand, you help children with special needs." For every purchase, Scott contributes 5 cents to a fund for six charities involved in childhood diseases. Over $1.6 million had been donated by mid-1988.[16]

The benefits to marketers are believed to be substantial. There are direct sales benefits. Scott believes that, although profits per unit are lower, sales of Helping Hand tap new market segments and do not eat into existing Scott brand shares. Other marketers believe that charitable ties provide indirect benefits to a company or brand's image. Still others are simply pleased to combine their entrepreneurial and social instincts.[17]

But cause-related marketing is not without its critics. Many believe that private-sector moneymakers are simply appropriating the image and credibility of worthwhile social causes for more crass commercial ends. For example, Procter & Gamble has been accused of trying to boost brand sales by obtaining the indirect blessing of Former First Lady Nancy Reagan by supporting her "Just Say No" campaign. Many executives appear to agree. One-third of CEOs contacted in a survey by the Council on Foundations felt that linking charity and marketing was *not* appropriate.[18]

Critics also fear that firms doing cause-related marketing will cut back on other contributions they make to the nonprofit sector. Finally, there is worry that individuals will assume that their indirect gifts to charity through their purchases will reduce or eliminate the need for their traditional charitable giving.

Ironically, American Express Travel Related Services, which pioneered this whole development, has recently shifted from broad-based national programs to sponsorships and promotions focusing on local community needs. In 1989, it was receiving over 1,100 proposals a year for potential sponsorship.[19]

Universities and Colleges

Universities and colleges can be important sources of advice and personnel. University faculty can provide advice on technical matters like research design and analysis. They can develop seminars for nonprofit staffers on marketing principles. They can also serve as consultants on specific nonprofit marketing problems.

Students can also be helpful. We have already noted their value as volunteers. Many marketing and management courses and even entire degree programs may require some kind of field study experience. Nonprofit organizations usually qualify for such projects as much as for-profit enterprises. Similarly, marketing research and advertising students are often looking for places to complete a term project or otherwise apply their newly developed skills. In some institutions, students' involvement with the nonprofit may be under close faculty supervision. In other cases it may not, and one should obviously be cautious in accepting advice and analysis from students who have limited experience and training. On the other hand, with the proper supervision, students may often provide workers to carry out research studies, experiments, forecasts, or other marketing projects that would otherwise not be completed for lack of personnel, skills, or both. Our experience has been that students find these experiences to be very rewarding both personally and professionally.

A good example of what is possible is shown by Stanford University. In 1988, Stanford's voluntary Public Management Program (PMP), which helps prepare students for leadership in public service, enrolled 17 percent of the school's MBAs. Many students work at internships in the public sector supported by the Stanford Management Intern Fund. This fund pools donations from the salaries of students working in private-sector internships to help subsidize those who choose lower-paying public service work. In 1988, 82 percent of first-year students pledged 1 percent of their salaries to support 12 classmates working in agencies such as San Francisco's AIDS office, a children's center in Massachusetts, and the Department of Education in New Jersey.[20]

In addition, 125 students participated in the student-run Business Development Association which assigns student volunteers to public service agencies, small businesses and start-ups. Similar programs are found at major business schools like those at Northwestern University, University of California Berkeley, Duke, and University of Virginia.[21]

Associations

As the nonprofit field has matured, organizations have sought to develop mechanisms for self-support. Perhaps the most ambitious of these is the Washington-based Independent Sector. Formed in March 1980, The Independent Sector now has over 700 members split between donors (foundations and corporations) and national voluntary organizations. It is a major source of statistics on the nonprofit "industry" and, recently, an active sponsor of the "Give Five" program to stimulate individuals to give 5 percent of their time and 5 percent of their income to voluntary organizations. Other Independent Sector programs include:

- *Public education* about the contributions and problems of the independent sector
- *Government relations efforts* at the national, state, and local levels to influence critical legislation and regulatory activity

- *Research* to build the knowledge base of the independent sector
- *Communication* among members about community problems and opportunities through periodicals, research reports, monographs, and conferences

A major concern of The Independent Sector is improving management skills in the nonprofit area.

SECURING OUTSIDE ASSISTANCE

Leveraged assistance for nonprofits is of two types, one-time and continuing. Securing one-time assistance for a particular charity drive or a research project involves three steps. First, the nonprofit must define its project and frankly recognize where it should not attempt some parts or all of an activity and should seek outside help. Second, the universe of possible sources of assistance from universities, firms, service agencies, individuals, and the like should be arrayed and ranked according to (1) degree of potential contribution, and (2) likelihood of offering help. In the latter regard, the nonprofit agency should put heavy weight on the possible benefits that each potential contributor will recognize—or can be made to recognize—as following from their cooperation and to minimize as many of the real and perceived costs it can. However, it must be recognized that, like a lot of other volunteer help, free goods and services may well come with strings, which should be carefully assessed. Experienced but opinionated professionals may insist on doing things their way or not at all. Inexperienced amateurs may want to do things their own way and may botch an otherwise potentially useful contribution.

The final step is, of course, to market directly to executives in the top-ranked potential contributor. This means also playing up the personal benefits they might derive and playing down any costs or inconveniences. Certainly, this is much easier if the match between project needs and the contributor's needs is high. When it is not, marketing creativity must be brought into play. The reputation of the nonprofit organization is certainly a major factor. Well-known community nonprofits have relatively more success in getting outside help. Indeed, they often have more offers of help than they need. More obscure agencies (for example, minor charities, neighborhood service agencies, and the like) have a much more difficult time. The nonprofit should *not* simply assume, however, that because the marketing is difficult it should not be attempted. Going it alone may have even greater costs.

One way of securing *continuing* help from for-profit organizations and individuals is to create a blue-ribbon marketing advisory board (in addition to the board of directors), bring key marketing professionals onto the nonprofit's board of directors, or both. Nonprofits are usually farsighted enough to see the need to put partners from major accounting firms and law firms in their communities onto their boards. Yet, as noted earlier, very useful continuing advice can be obtained by adding to the board a senior vice-president of marketing from a for-profit organization (preferably from a consumer goods or service company), the head of a local major advertising agency, or the director of one of the area's largest marketing research agencies. Not only will these executives provide useful ongoing advice, but they will often volunteer their organizations' facilities or services (or they can be *asked* to volunteer them) for specific one-time marketing needs.

SUMMARY

Nonprofits have limited resources. As a consequence, they must become experts at securing additional manpower, skills, and financial resources. This, too, is a marketing task. Others must be convinced that the benefits of helping exceed the costs.

Nonprofits are unique in needing volunteers to help them accomplish their basic goals. Strategies for recruiting and managing volunteers must take into account changes in the environment. Today's volunteers cover a wider spectrum of people. They are more demanding and have different motivations than they had in the past. More importantly, some groups are challenging the basic value of volunteer service.

Recruiting volunteers involves knowing the target audiences through segmentation, prospect, motivational, or image studies. The nonprofit should also know how to retain volunteers. Studies of former volunteers and the satisfaction and dissatisfaction of present volunteers can be helpful in this regard. Problems that may emerge may involve volunteers' expectations, training, supervision, and feedback.

Managing volunteers can also be a problem if the organization is not truly professional in its approach. Many volunteers work hard and effectively with little incentive or guidance. Some hardly work at all under any circumstances. Most, however, respond best to being treated as professionals. This means matching responsibilities to skills, setting clear, achievable goals, and then holding volunteers to achieving them.

Nonprofits must also secure important outside help in critical skill areas like advertising and marketing research. Commercial agencies may be quite willing to help out for both altruistic and self-interested reasons. The Advertising Council is a prime example of such help. Business firms can also help by loaning space, staff, or equipment and by providing specific advice. Recently, affinity cards and cause-related marketing have been major sources of leverage from private sector firms. Faculty and students at local colleges and universities are another major source of assistance. An effective vehicle for coordinating all of these efforts is through a Marketing Advisory Council.

QUESTIONS

1. Outline the costs and benefits that may be perceived by a local public utility in allowing the American Cancer Society to (a) conduct a recruiting drive on its premises and (b) include a solicitation and pledge card in the utility's monthly customer invoices. How could the American Cancer Society make the benefit/cost ratio for the utility better?

2. List three major charities with which you might volunteer and three you would not. What are the criteria you used in making your selections? How would a knowledge of these criteria help a given charity develop a recruiting strategy for the future?

3. Assume you have a volunteer who is the son of a major donor to your charitable organization. You have given this individual responsibility for planning a major fund-raising dinner but he is (a) well behind schedule, (b) uncommunicative about plans and progress, and (c) testy whenever you bring up problems. You have decided that something must be done. How would you solve this problem in the short run? What policies would you set to ensure that it does not happen recurrently?

4. Nonprofit agencies are springing up everywhere to deal with the problems of the homeless. Assume that there is no national association of such agencies and you have been asked to help create it. What mission would you set for this association? What activities would you have it undertake in year 1, year 2, and year 3? How would you determine a fee schedule?

5. Assume that you have been asked to do an image study for an art museum in your area among potential volunteer fund-raisers. Respondents in the study will be residents of neighborhoods in the top 10 percent of the income distribution in your area. Outline the dimensions that you would measure, the hypothetical competitors whose images you would also assess, and the personal or household characteristics you would include to give you the basis for a volunteer recruiting strategy for the 1990s.

NOTES

1. *Giving and Volunteering in the United States* (Washington, D.C.: The Independent Sector, 1988).
2. Eva Schindler-Rainman and Ronald Lippitt, *The Volunteer Community: Creative Use of Human Resources*, 2nd ed. (La Jolla, Calif.: University Associates, 1977), pp. 21–45.
3. *Volunteering and the United Way* (Alexandria, Va.: United Way of America, 1989), p. 19.
4. Ibid.

5. *Giving and Volunteering in the United States.*

6. *Volunteering and the United Way,* p. 21.

7. Peter F. Drucker, "What Business Can Learn from Nonprofits," *Harvard Business Review,* July–August 1989, p. 91.

8. Ad Council, *Moving America to Action: Report to the American People '87–'88* (New York: The Advertising Council, 1988).

9. "Rubbermaid Donates United Way Building," *HomeWorld Business,* January 15, 1990, p. 48B.

10. Yvette D. Kantrow, " 'Choose' Program Raises Volume: MasterCard Also Adds $3.1 Million to Charity Coffers," *American Banker,* February 10, 1989, p. 3.

11. Jeffrey Kutler, "Discover Joins Rivals with Charity Benefit Plan," *American Banker,* October 13, 1988, p. 2.

12. Donald Schoutz, "Visa Entry Is Hardly Plain Vanilla: Marine Midland's Breyers Card to Aid Children's Hospitals," *American Banker,* May 18, 1989, p. 6

13. Fritz Jellinghaus, "Business Forum: Doubts About 'Cause-Related' Marketing; Profits Have a Place in Philanthropy," *The New York Times,* March 29, 1989, Section 3, p. 2.

14. Ibid.

15. Jonathan M. Moses, "Advertisers Plug Products With Antidrug Message: Marketing Experts Say Theme Has Cachet, Crosses All Cultural, Economic Classes," *The Washington Post,* September 2, 1988, p. F3.

16. S.J. Diamond, "Firms Wrap Philanthropy in New Package," *Los Angeles Times,* July 22, 1988, Part 4, p. 1.

17. Ibid.

18. Zachary Sciller, "Doing Well by Doing Good," *Business Week,* December 5, 1988, p. 57.

19. Judith Graham, "Warner Canto; AmEx exec on prowl for special events," *Advertising Age,* p. 26.

20. "B-School Students Contribute to Their Communities' Bottom Lines," *AACSB Newsline,* Vol. 20, no. 1, October 1989, pp. 1, 2.

21. Ibid.

11

Organizing
for Implementation

Trees Atlanta Inc. is the kind of organization that might have been run in years past by a variation on the little-old-lady-in-tennis-shoes. But executive director Marcia Bansley, a former corporate lawyer, is a prototype of the new manager at organizations such as foundations, hospitals and universities.

"In the not-for-profit business, where the [money] pie is shrinking, you've got to have someone with a competitive background," says J. Nicholas Hurd of Russell Reynolds Associates Inc., a search firm.

While a university might once have considered a slate of candidates for president that included "eight academics and two retired academics," it will now look at recruits from business and government as well, says Stephen Garrison, Chairman of Ward Howell International Inc., a search firm. Managers of "the University of Wisconsin or Exxon are getting more similar," he adds. Both deal with "rates of inflation, labor unions, money management."

Conveniently, say consultants, there is a new supply to meet the demand: baby boomers who want more meaningful work and many middle managers who have lost their jobs in corporate restructurings.

Ms. Bansley of the Atlanta group, which plants and conserves trees, says she worked for years as a volunteer before realizing she enjoyed that more than her paid work. But her business experience got her this job, which involves motivating volunteers, raising funds, and dealing with her board. And in various battles around the city, she adds, "it helps to understand what a tort is."

Source: Julie Solomon, "For-Profit Chiefs for Nonprofit Concerns," *The Wall Street Journal*, June 12, 1989, p. B1. Reproduced with permission.

As we noted in Chapter 1, the concept of marketing has progressed through three stages of acceptance in the nonprofit sector: introduction, growth, and its present entry into the maturity phase. This has also been the typical pattern within individual nonprofit organizations.

The introductory phase within an organization is the period when marketing is first proposed as a philosophy and set of techniques for improving the organization's performance. This introduction typically comes about in one of two ways. One pattern is for marketing to be *pushed* into the organization by one or more key individuals who have been exposed to its potential in outside seminars or in formal academic training. This is a pattern that is common in the performing arts, and, in earlier days, in education. These potential change agents shuttle about the organization trying to convince others, most importantly the CEO, of the wisdom of their newfound views. They frequently encounter considerable intraorganization resistance, which is often reflected in disparagement of the marketing function and frequent allusions to its nastier manifestations. Unless the change agents are very highly placed in the organization or are extremely convincing in their promotion campaigns, the introduction period is likely to be quite prolonged under a "push" scenario.

The other common pattern for the introductory period is for marketing to be *pulled* into the organization by environmental forces. This condition occurred in health care in the 1980s as market conditions increased the pressures on nonprofit hospitals to improve performance. Marketing comes to be viewed as a potentially highly useful approach to such improvement. Pressures to introduce marketing are further heightened if one or more direct competitors begins to use marketing or is rumored to be beginning soon. Marketing is likely to be introduced much faster under a "pull" scenario than if it is "pushed" into a sometimes reluctant institution.

In the growth phase following marketing's introduction, attempts are made to expand marketing's role and formalize its position in the organization. Typically, marketing is first formalized as a staff function *coordinating* programs and providing advice to others. Only later, as marketing proves its value and/or environmental pressures become more intense, is it often changed into a specific line function with its own staff and responsibilities for programs and specific volume results.

Even when marketing becomes a formal department during the growth phase, its role may be inconsequential. The mature phase can therefore be identified by the transition of marketing from being just another division or function to being a top-level management concern. In this phase, marketing philosophy has permeated much of the organization's planning. Marketing has relatively few detractors and virtually no effort is needed to market marketing itself. Concern has shifted to the issue: how to market *well*.

We will now consider some organizational issues that marketing must face during each development phase.

THE INTRODUCTION STAGE

In the beginning, there will be much resistance to setting up a formal marketing function. Among the arguments against formally accepting marketing are the following:

- Some organizations think that formal marketing is inappropriate. Thus, the faculty of a college might be contemptuous of the notion that education has to be marketed.
- Some organizations think that marketing is everyone's job. They fear that appointing a marketing director will lead employees to think that marketing is something done by a marketing director rather than by everyone in the organization, and they will sit around expecting the marketing director to miraculously solve their problems.
- Some organizations feel that they are getting all the marketing they need from their directors of public relations, fund-raising, planning, and/or development. They identify marketing with these functions.
- Some organizations feel that they would be better off hiring marketing expertise as needed—from marketing consultants, advertising agencies, and marketing research firms—instead of hiring a full-time marketing director.
- Some organizations feel that a director of marketing would not contribute enough to pay for his or her salary. They believe that they can buy more important things with the same money.
- Some organizations are too small or too poor to afford a marketing director.

Some of these arguments undoubtedly reflect personal biases against what the individual believes marketing to be. The majority reflect an absence of a formal assessment of whether the organization really needs a marketing person, department, or program. At the outset, it should be realized that whether an organization should install a formal marketing function is not the issue of whether it should do marketing. All organizations do marketing whether or not they organize it in a formal way. Colleges, for example, search for prospects (students), develop products (courses), price them (tuition and fees), distribute them (announce time and place), and promote them (college catalogues). Also they engage in other activities such as lobbying, fund-raising, and public relations that are also, at base, marketing. When this dawns on a nonprofit organization, the response is much like that of Molière's character in *Le Bourgeois Gentilhomme* who utters, "Good heavens! For more than 40 years I have been speaking prose without knowing it."

Some organizations feel that they are not only doing marketing but that they already have formal staff positions responsible for marketing. Therefore, they don't need to add another staff position called "marketing." A college president may feel that the admissions director, the public relations director, the planning vice-president, and the development vice-president are the institution's professional marketers. This may or may not be correct, however. Many admissions directors are sales oriented rather than marketing oriented. They are good at "pounding the pavement" to reach prospective students but not skilled in marketing research and marketing strategy that would make this selling job easier. Most public relations directors are skilled in journalism and communication but are not trained in analyzing, researching, and planning for markets. Planning vice-presidents may concentrate on developing the physical plant and on financial problems without having much marketing knowledge or aptitude. Development vice-presidents are often sales oriented and fail to put their fundraising efforts on a modern marketing management basis. Though these officers should be professional marketers handling their respective markets, they typically are not.

The president may acknowledge this but feel that there are several ways to get marketing resources without going through the expense of establishing a formal marketing position. In fact, the nonprofit organization that cannot afford or chooses not to install formal marketing can get some marketing resources in the following ways:

1   Appoint a private-sector marketing executive to the board of directors, hoping to get help or advice from this marketing executive as needed. Also, invite voluntary help from other marketing executives in the community.
2   Invite help from the marketing faculty of a business school, such as using a marketing research class to research a problem facing the organization.
3   Hire a marketing consulting firm, marketing research firm, or advertising agency to do specific projects when needed.
4   Send key staff to marketing seminars and workshops to learn marketing.

Although these makeshift ways of acquiring marketing knowledge and services do not do the full job of creating a market-oriented organization, they normally produce good value in the short term. But certain cautions must be exercised. In drawing on the voluntary services of marketing executives in the community, it should be realized that they will be offering advice without the benefit of research data or much time to analyze the problem. Furthermore, they will be heavily influenced by their own industry background. A P&G soap marketing executive will put heavy emphasis on advertising spending because this is what works in the soap industry; an IBM marketing executive will put heavy emphasis on personal selling because this is what works in the computer industry. Every marketing executive has biases as to what works best and the nonprofit organization must maintain a critical attitude. If extensive use of such part-time advisors is contemplated, however, briefly introducing them to some of the differences between profit and nonprofit marketing as outlined in Chapter 1 would be helpful.

If the nonprofit organization decides to get marketing help by hiring marketing firms as needed, it must be able to discriminate between good, average, and poor firms. A poor advertising agency, for example, will try to solve a membership decline by creating an instant advertising campaign. An average ad agency will ask management questions to help clarify the nature of the membership decline and then create an advertising campaign. A good ad agency will ask about the organization's overall mission, goals, and plans and do some research with members and ex-members before developing an advertising campaign. Naturally, the nonprofit organization will get the most value from a market-oriented advertising agency.

At some point, the organization should appoint a marketing committee charged with three objectives:

1 Identifying marketing problems and opportunities facing the organization
2 Assessing the felt need of different department heads for professional marketing assistance
3 Recommending whether the organization should establish a formal marketing position

The marketing committee should include representatives from a cross section of the organization's departments that might have a stake in marketing. Thus, a university's marketing committee should include the vice-president of faculty, some deans and department chairpersons, the admissions director, the public relations director, the development vice-president, the planning vice-president, a board member, and possibly a student representative. The marketing committee might also include an outside marketing executive or paid marketing consultant to provide professional guidance. This committee should gather information from various groups (deans, chairpersons, students) as to how they see the environment (its opportunities and threats), the organization's strengths and weaknesses, the organization's strategy, the organization's marketing problems and possible solutions, and so on. Many surprising, if not shocking, things will be discovered in this process.

The committee should digest the information and prepare a report for the president. This report of marketing findings and recommendations is called a *marketing audit* (see Chapter 3). Although it is an inside audit done by a committee of nonprofessionals, it is likely to be highly useful. The organization always has the option of hiring a marketing consulting firm to do a full-scale marketing audit, which will cost more and be likely to yield even greater value because of the marketing auditor's independence, objectivity, and experience in doing marketing auditing in a large number of industries.

THE GROWTH PHASE

Eventually, the nonprofit organization will become committed to installing a formal marketing function. The organization may find the makeshift use of outside marketing resources to be too costly or unreliable, or it may find that its marketing needs are extensive enough to hire a full-time person. The organization should recognize that establishing a marketing function is undertaken at some risk if the rest of the organization is still resistant or the new appointee is not given sufficient authority to carry out his or her responsibilities. If the organization decides to move forward it must decide on (1) the level at which to hire, (2) the job description, and (3) the recruiting strategy.

The major issue concerning level is whether marketing will initially be a staff or a line function. The decision operationally is whether to hire a *director of marketing services* who would advise but not have direct responsibility over programs and people or *a vice-president of marketing* who would have line responsibility. The former person is hired at a middle-management level and basically acts as a resource person or internal marketing consultant to various other managers in the organization who need marketing services. In effect, marketing services director is a staff position, not a line position. This director can help define marketing problems, arrange for marketing research, and hire advertising agency services as needed. He or she may be located in the planning department under the vice-president of planning or in public relations or development, though these functions might overspecialize the use to which marketing is put. Some hospitals and colleges have preferred to position the person as an "assistant to the president" who reports directly to the president.

Alternatively, the organization might establish a vice-president of marketing. This is an upper-level management position that gives more scope, authority, and influence to marketing. A vice-president of marketing not only coordinates and supplies services to others in the organization but also participates in the setting of policy and direction for the institution. This person has a better chance to help create a marketing orientation throughout the organization. The position is much closer to being a true line position. The vice-president of marketing would be responsible for planning and managing relations with several publics of the institutions. In fact, if full delegation of line authority were given, this person would manage client relations, donor relations, public relations, and government relations. The person's title might be "vice-president of institutional relations" or "vice-president of external affairs" to avoid unnecessary semantic opposition to the term "marketing." A vice-president of marketing would cost the institution more but might ultimately contribute more to the institution.

Which position should it be initially? Some organizations prefer to make marketing a staff position on the assumption that the position costs less, its value can be tested, and, if the director proves effective and intraorganizational opposition is diffused, he or she can be promoted to a line position. Other organizations feel that a staff marketer can only accomplish minor things because he or she would not have the ear of the president, would not participate in strategy formulation, and would not have the necessary line authority. The authors favor establishing a vice-president of marketing with line responsibility initially because marketing's most important initial job is to transform the thinking of top management into a marketing mode.

Suppose, however, that the organization decides initially to hire a staff director of marketing services. A job description that outlines the functions, responsibilities, and major liaison relations associated with the job is needed. A sample job description for a university director of marketing services is shown in Table 11-1.

Before searching for a qualified person to fill the job the organization will want to define further the desirable years and type of marketing experience, salary range, and planned budget for the job. The organization may decide that

Table 11-1

JOB DESCRIPTION:
A UNIVERSITY DIRECTOR OF MARKETING SERVICES

Position title: Director of Marketing Services

Reports to: Vice-President, University Relations

Scope: Universitywide

Position concept: The Director of Marketing Services is responsible for providing marketing guidance and services to university officers, school deans, department chairpersons, and other agents of the university.

Functions: The Director of Marketing Services will:
1. contribute a marketing perspective to the deliberations of the top administration in its planning of the university's future.
2. prepare data that might be needed by an officer of the university on a particular market's size, segments, trends, and behavioral dynamics.
3. conduct studies of the needs, perceptions, preferences, and satisfactions of particular markets.
4. assist in the planning, promotion, and launching of new programs.
5. assist in the development of communication and promotion campaigns and materials.
6. analyze and advise on pricing questions.
7. appraise the workability of new academic proposals from a marketing point of view.
8. advise on new student recruitment.
9. advise on current student satisfaction.
10. advise on university fund-raising.

Responsibilities: The Director of Marketing Services will:
1. contact individual officers and small groups at the university to explain services and to solicit problems.
2. prioritize the various requests for services according to their long-run impact, cost-saving potential, time requirements, ease of accomplishment, cost, and urgency.
3. select projects of high priority and set accomplishment goals for the year.
4. prepare a budget request to support the anticipated work.
5. prepare an annual report on the main accomplishments of the office.

Major liaisons: The Director of Marketing Services will:
1. relate most closely with the President's Office, Admissions Office, Development Office, Planning Office, and Public Relations Department.
2. relate secondarily with the deans of various schools and chairpersons of various departments.

it wants a person with substantial marketing training and experience in industry rather than a person who has worked in its field—whether education, health, the arts—but who has only weak training in marketing. The organization normally finds it easier to educate a person about the field than to train a person from the field as a marketer.

The kinds of individuals recruited into nonprofit marketing in the mid-1980s reflect the characteristics of the growth period. This was demonstrated in the 1984 "National Hospital Marketer's Survey" by Allied Research Associates.[1] The study showed clearly that those who had been in a hospital marketing position for six or more years were more likely to have degrees no higher than a B.A. or B.S. and to come from a communications background. This lack of formal marketing training is a serious problem. The report stated that "the older hospital marketers who come from a nonmarketing background are frustrated because they don't know how to cope with the new demands of hospital marketing." By contrast, the growing maturity of the field was reflected in the fact that those who reported that they had come into hospital marketing in the previous year were more likely to have a master's degree, to be trained in marketing, and to be paid a higher salary. That marketing was not yet in the maturity phase in many hospitals, however, was indicated by the fact that almost half the marketers in these hospitals had formal titles involving public relations or community relations.

A broader based survey of 800 hospitals in 1983 by Witt Associates, Inc., confirmed these patterns. This study showed that in 1983 hospital marketers typically came from nonmarketing backgrounds and needed further training to be effective marketers. Three out of four came from nonmarketing backgrounds. In larger hospitals and chains, they tended more often to come into marketing from a planning role while in smaller hospitals they came from public or community relations. When hospitals hired from outside their own organizations they tended to hire those with experience in health care "who lack[ed] functional marketing skills or understanding."[2]

As might be expected, marketing was not a full-time responsibility for many participants in the 1983 study. Administrators or CEOs held marketing responsibilities in 29 percent of the hospitals studied. Marketing people in another 47 percent of the reporting hospitals had other responsibilities besides marketing. The researchers concluded that in 1983 "hospital marketing hadn't yet come of age in terms of acceptance, understanding and use. Rather many institutions seemed to favor the make-do or do-it-yourself approach. The many job titles that hospital marketing directors held underscore the tentativeness and fragmentation of health care marketing."

Developing Initial Marketing Projects

If marketing is to achieve a steep upward trajectory during the intraorganization growth phase, the new marketing director will want to demonstrate that marketing thinking can contribute to the organization. Many members of the organization will be critical of marketing, arguing that it is inappropriate or a waste of money, or that the money could be spent better elsewhere. Others will be puzzled about what marketing is or does. Only a few will see it as a strong opportunity for the organization.

In the face of this skepticism, the new director must carefully choose initial projects which, if successfully executed, demonstrate the value of marketing. The marketing director can devise these projects, but it would be better if he or she meets key groups and conducts a needs assessment to get ideas on important marketing needs. For example, a new marketing director at a hospital should meet with department heads, individually or in groups, describe the work that can be done (marketing analyses, new program assessment, communication planning, and so on), and ask about any projects they might be interested in seeing done. This approach will build goodwill and understanding with various people in the organization and lead to many project ideas, often more than can be handled by a single marketing director operating with a small budget. The director should not promise to do work on any project until he or she reviews the possible projects and chooses the best ones. The best early projects to undertake would have four characteristics:

1 A high impact on making money or saving money for the institution
2 A relatively small cost to carry out
3 A short period of time for completion
4 A high visibility potential if successful

Presumably, some projects will stand up better than others under these criteria. The main thing is to avoid major projects that will take a long time, cost a lot of money, and not yield definitive results. The organization will not have the patience to support costly, drawn-out marketing projects, at least not until the marketing function is well established and respected.

Expanding the Market Function

If the organization director does a good job that is recognized by others in the organization, more resources will be made available and more responsibility will be accorded.[3] The marketing executive may want to hire one or more assistants to specialize in marketing research, advertising, new services evaluation, and other marketing functions. It pays to hire a full-time expert in any specialized marketing function that the organization needs to cover on a continuous basis.

THE MATURE STAGE

As the organization matures, marketing people will become well accepted and marketing planning will be better integrated into the corporate planning cycle. The number of people in the marketing department can grow substantially. This can come about as organizational designers recognize that heretofore separate functions like fund-raising, public relations, and customer education need to be coordinated in one place. Such coordination would be consistent with the view proposed here that nonprofit organizations are already doing marketing in many parts of their enterprise—they are trying to influence behaviors of different target audiences whether they be potential donors, politicians, customers, the media, the general public, or employees. At the mature stage, then, the marketing department will be given (1) the responsibility for maximizing the number of exchanges between the organization and its various clienteles, and (2) line authority over most, if not all, of the tools within the organization needed to get the job done. This can lead to the establishment of a separate marketing department with its own budget and a substantial staff.

Organizational Design

As the marketing department grows in physical size, how to organize it internally becomes a critical question. This will affect not only how the department is run but what kinds of people can be employed. The options typically found in the private sector as design alternatives can be adapted to nonprofit marketing with limited rethinking. These alternatives are (1) functional organization, (2) product/service–centered organization, (3) customer-centered organization, and (4) mixed organization.

Functional Organization.   Most growing nonprofit marketing units first take on the appearance of a functional organizational structure as shown in Figure 11-1A.

As the marketing group absorbs once separate functions such as public relations, advertising, and marketing research, it is natural to keep them as separate functional units within marketing. Each function may initially be the responsibility of a single employee. As the marketing group grows, the functional units inevitably grow, and each function may well have its own manager. The kinds of functions a large mature organization such as the post office, YMCA, or Red Cross, could eventually *possibly* have (although few will have all of them) are outlined in Table 11-2.

The organization may choose to retain a functional structure for a long time. One obvious reason for this would be if the subunits never become larger than one or two persons. But even if they did, many in the private sector believe that keeping marketing people aligned with their functional specialty has many advantages:

1   *Economies of scale.* A single public relations or advertising group can produce mass communications programs at much less cost or can develop more "clout" with significant outside agencies than can individual advertising or public relations people scattered throughout a complex nonprofit organization.

FIGURE 11-1

Alternative Organizational Designs

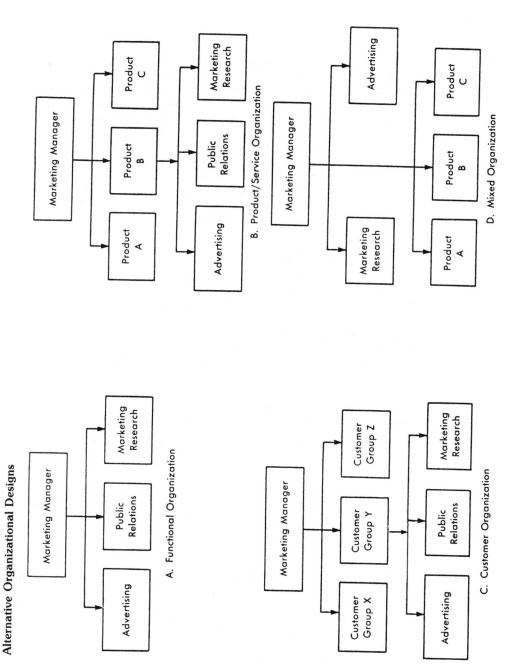

A. Functional Organization

B. Product/Service Organization

C. Customer Organization

D. Mixed Organization

Table 11–2

GENERIC MARKETING POSITIONS

> MARKETING MANAGER
> 1. Other names: vice-president of marketing, marketing director, chief marketing officer, marketing administrator, director of marketing services.
> 2. The marketing manager heads the organization's marketing activities. Tasks include providing a marketing point of view to the top administration; helping to formulate marketing strategy for the organization; planning, staffing, directing, and coordinating marketing activities; and proposing new products and services to meet emerging market needs.
>
> PRODUCT MANAGER
> 1. Other names: program manager, brand manager.
> 2. A product manager is responsible for managing a particular product or program of the organization. Tasks include proposing product objectives and goals, creating product strategies and plans, seeing that they are implemented, monitoring the results, and taking corrective actions.
>
> MARKETING RESEARCH MANAGER
> 1. Other names: marketing research director.
> 2. The marketing research manager has responsibility for developing and supervising research on the organization's market environment, competitors, and publics, and on the effectiveness of various marketing tools.
>
> COMMUNICATIONS MANAGER
> 1. Other names: advertising manager, advertising and sales promotion director.
> 2. The communications manager provides expertise in the area of mass and selective communication and promotion. Person is knowledgeable about the development of messages, media, and publicity.
>
> SALES MANAGER
> 1. Other names: vice-president of sales, service operations manager.
> 2. The sales manager has responsibility for recruiting, training, assigning, directing, motivating, compensating, and evaluating customer contact personnel and agents of the organization and coordinating their work with that of the other marketing functions.
>
> NEW-PRODUCTS MANAGER
> 1. Other names: new products director, program development manager.
> 2. The new products manager has responsibility for conceiving new products and services; screening and evaluating new product ideas; developing prototypes and testing them; and advising and helping to carry out the innovation's introduction in the marketplace.
>
> DISTRIBUTION MANAGER
> 1. Other names: channel manager, physical distribution manager, logistics manager.
> 2. The distribution manager has responsibility for planning and managing the distribution systems that make the organization's products and services available and accessible to the potential users.
>
> PRICING MANAGER
> 1. Other names: pricing executive.
> 2. The pricing manager is responsible for offering advice about or actually setting prices for the organization's services and programs.

CUSTOMER RELATIONS MANAGER
1. Other names: customer service manager.
2. The customer relations manager has responsibility for managing customer services and handling customer complaints.

GOVERNMENT RELATIONS MANAGER
1. Other names: legislative representative, lobbyist.
2. The government relations manager provides the organization with intelligence on relevant developments in government and manages the organization's program of representation and presentation to government.

PUBLIC RELATIONS MANAGER
1. Other names: public information officer.
2. The public relations manager has responsibility for communicating and improving the organization's image with various publics.

TERRITORY MANAGER
1. Other names: regional manager, district manager.
2. The territory manager has responsibility for managing the organization's products, services, and programs in a specific territory.

2 *Functional skill synergies.* Several advertising or public relations people working together in physical proximity will stimulate each other to produce much higher-quality work.

3 *Professional affinities.* A functional organization is consistent with the natural affiliations of those it hires. That is, other things being equal, advertising people will feel more comfortable with other advertising people, public relations people with other public relations people. Even if they are initially located apart, they will gravitate toward each other. Therefore, why not put them together in the first place?

In mature organizations, functional structures are desirable under two conditions. First, the product and customer mix should be relatively homogeneous. Second, the industry to be served should not be particularly dynamic. If the former is not the case, there is serious danger that functionally oriented specialists will ignore product or customer groups that don't interest them. In rapidly changing markets, focus on individual specialties and not on products or customers may lead functionally oriented departments to miss major changes in consumer behavior, competitive strategies, or both.

The functional approach also has other disadvantages.

1 Informal criteria of performance may become centered on what the *function* values and not on what is good for the nonprofit enterprise. Thus, advertising people working with each other may tend to feel rewarded for "impressive" advertisements. Public relations people may pride themselves on industry awards for their brochures or public education campaigns. Peer accolades will take the place of market performance.

2 Coordination is more cumbersome. If the organization has several products or services, the general marketing manager will have to spend a lot of time running between functional specialists to ensure that campaigns complement each other, that work is done on time and in proper sequence, and so on.

3 Bottom-line responsibility is diffused. If a product or service is unsuccessful or if a major customer group is stolen away by a competitor, functional specialists will blame "the other guy." If, for example, a new adult extension program in a hospital is a flop, the advertising people may blame the public relations people for not getting enough free TV time or news releases in local papers describing the program. For their part, the public relations people may blame the adult education staff for not being customer oriented enough in actually running the classes. No one person takes final responsibility for the disappointing performance.

Product/Service–Centered Organization.   Many of the leading private sector marketers have turned their functional departments into product/service–centered organizations as shown in Figure 11-1B. One person is put in charge of a specific product or service (or a set of relatively similar products and services) and charged with making them a success. Responsibility is inescapable. If the organization is large enough, each product/service manager would manage his or her own advertising, public relations, and marketing research specialists. In smaller organizations such as one often encounters in the nonprofit sector, it may be necessary to adopt a mixed form of organization like that in Figure 11-1D which attempts to capture at least the major features of the product/service design. In the mixed format, functional *staff* departments are established along with product/service departments. Each product/service manager then "buys" their services, coordinating their use and ensuring that the "purchased" service provider pays strict attention to market performance.

The product/service–centered organization has a number of advantages:

1 Responsibility is clear. If the product or service fails, there is only one person to blame. If it succeeds, one person probably deserves most of the credit (and the rewards that go with it).
2 This single responsibility forces close attention to market dynamics, shifts in customer tastes and preferences, and competitors' current and planned strategies and tactics. The product/service structure typically is much "faster on its feet" than the functional system.
3 General management skills are developed. Marketing proves to be a good training ground for future top managers. Since all product/service managers have their own little enterprises to manage, they should become very good at overall strategic planning, budgeting, coordination and personnel management, all skills that should quickly qualify them for higher-level management positions.
4 Small products or services are not neglected.
5 Intraorganizational competition is fostered. Hospital OB-GYN marketing programs could be set in competition with its programs for emergency or outpatient care or for adult education. This internal competitiveness in the private sector seems to keep marketers even more alert and aggressive than other structural designs.

Despite these important advantages, the product/service manager system can have serious limitations. Some are inherent. Broad general management skills are necessary in this kind of system, but often the product/service managers filling the ranks are young and not yet experienced enough to handle the complex managing job effectively. Further, a product/service emphasis can mean relatively weak skill development in functional areas. Thus, the product/service manager may not be particularly strong in advertising or marketing research or public relations and will need to defer too much operational responsibility to functional specialists. Finally, the product/service structure may encourage top management to assign product/service roles to persons with deep product/service knowledge rather than marketing skills and customer sensitivity. Thus, an older nurse with a large family may be seen as the best person to head up the OB-GYN marketing program. The adult fitness program may be assigned to the hospital "fitness freak," while the outpatient program is assigned to the young woman who dropped out of medical school for a management career.

Clearly, the major disadvantage of the product/service manager approach is that the manager is not given direct line authority over his or her functional specialists. Thus, product/service managers need great persuasive skill to get staff functional specialists to do what is needed *when* it is needed. With other product/service managers competing for the same staff specialists, there is a great chance that programs will be poorly coordinated. Further, where authority does not equal responsibility, product/service managers will feel considerable frustration at being held accountable for things they cannot totally control.

If there is the danger of this frustration occurring, three steps must be taken. First, top management must back up the product/service manager by according them an important role in the overall organization and by stressing to functional staff people that their job is to serve the product/service managers and not to decide what should or should not get done. Second, product managers should be chosen partly for their interpersonal and persuasive skills. Third, reward systems should explicitly make allowances for situational factors the product/service manager cannot control.

Customer-Centered Organization.   If, as we have argued, successful marketing organizations should be customer centered, then it might reasonably be asked why this shouldn't apply to their marketing systems as well (see Figure 11-1C). Take the case of the YMCA, for example. The Y has many "products"—physical fitness programs, arts and crafts programs, educational programs, and so on. A product management system would call for appointing a person to head each major program. Thus, a physical fitness director would study people's needs and interests in physical fitness and would develop plans for expanding the offerings and attracting more users, as well as for pricing the programs. This person would advise various local Y units on how to make their physical fitness programs stronger.

The Y also serves a variety of markets divided by sex (male, female) and age (teens, young adults, adults, senior citizens). In a marketing system organized by customer group, a person would be appointed to focus on each major market. Thus, the market manager for teens would study their needs and develop programs that satisfy their needs. This person would consult local Ys that are having trouble attracting teens and propose new programs that might be offered.

The potential for such a shift to a customer-centered orientation is captured in the experience of the Office of Cancer Communications at the National Cancer Institute, as shown in Exhibit 11-1.

EXHIBIT 11-1

A Proposal for a Customer-Centered Organization at the National Cancer Institute

The Office of Cancer Communications at the National Cancer Institute (OCC/NCI) is responsible for a number of communications programs dealing with detecting, treating, and helping families cope with various kinds of cancer. Among the programs they actively promoted in the early 1980s were those dealing with breast cancer, smoking, and industrial workplace cancers (for example, those contracted by some workers handling asbestos). These programs were initially organized by type of cancer (that is, by program). Over time, the first two programs evolved two separate and distinct marketing thrusts.

One thrust aimed at the general public. The other thrust was directed at potential cooperating organizations. Thus, the smoking program managers developed an effective liaison with physicians who became key educators about the consequences of smoking and communicators of how-to-quit information. Simultaneously, the breast cancer program recruited major corporations with large female work forces such as AT&T to help develop communications materials for their workers and to organize training sessions in breast self-examination.

A 1983 audit of these two programs recommended switching to a customer-centered program development system:

> It is recommended that reorganization along *customer* lines be explored. Under such a reorganization, staff would be specialists for specific target customer groups, rather than being "smoking" or "breast" specialists. Thus, someone would be responsible for *all* cancer communications programs directed at physicians and nurses, another for those directed at blue collar worksites or schools, still another for those directed at unions or the elderly or Hispanic or rural "customers." This market-centered organizational innovation is gaining increased use in the private sector.* It is used by Xerox, Mead, and Heinz. The latter, for example, has specialists for groceries, commercial restaurants, and institutions, with the latter further divided into schools, colleges, hospitals, and prisons.

For OCC, this organizational design would have several advantages:

1 It would reinforce efforts to make staff more customer-oriented. They would have clear motivation to understand better the needs, wants, and perceptions of their particular clients since staff, in effect, would be rewarded in terms of their success in creating behavior changes in these groups. (As it is now, each program deals with so many clients that it is just not possible to learn a great deal about any one.)

2   It will permit separation of those working with intermediaries from those working with "final consumers." The skills, insights, and approaches needed for the one are very different from those needed for the other. It is not unlike the split in sales forces and other marketing specialists between industrial or retail/wholesale buyers and final consumers in private sector companies.

3   Successful programs with specific target audiences can be followed up quite naturally with other programs. For example, if the breast cancer education program with AT&T or the smoking program with the Navy is successful and a good working relationship has developed, the customer specialist can be thinking ahead to introducing the next program (e.g., breast cancer education in the Navy, or antismoking at AT&T).

4   The synergism possible by applying research findings from one subject area to another can be enhanced.

5   OCC's image and capabilities can become sharper in target customer eyes since OCC will be personified by only one or two specific staff members. As it is now, a given customer group could conceivably be contacted by different OCC staff people not altogether clear on what each other is doing. Customers will prefer dealing with *one* OCC contact.

6   There would be incentive for OCC to promote the visibility and credibility of the staff person in the eyes of the target audience. Thus, staff might well be selected or assigned in terms of whether they will impress the target audience (e.g., having the "right" educational background, the "right" experience). They can be encouraged to participate in conferences attended by target audiences (especially intermediaries) and from time to time give papers or present workshops.

7   There would be incentive for the staffer to develop extensive contacts among target audience members. Thus, they would learn who the key media gatekeepers are and who opinion leaders/early adopters are in the target population. They could develop and then continually refine a computerized mailing list for all of the target audience or at least its key members.

8   Duplication of effort would be reduced. For example, if under the present system, a breast program was to be developed for the Navy, much already known about the Navy to the OCC smoking staff person would have to be acquired and contacts already made would have to be made by a second person.

9   Since there may be a certain diminished enthusiasm on the part of some staffers who have been involved a long time in one or the other programs, such a reorganization would revitalize them. In particular, the necessity of trying to apply what was learned in one program to other existing and new programs could prove particularly stretching.

10   Specific, important target customer groups (e.g., rural, minorities, the elderly) are less likely to be ignored.

11   Advisory committees could be formed from each target group as a

means of providing program inputs and of heightening OCC's profile. Such a grouping may be more "natural" than the present grouping by program.

12 Recruiting business financial support for publishing and/or promotional activities may well be easier since businesses more often identify with audiences than with programs. Thus, for example, a given business marketing to the Navy might be approached to help produce a booklet on smoking and, if that didn't spark an interest, a series of posters on breast cancer or colon-rectal cancer or on toxic chemicals could be proposed until something is found that is mutually rewarding.

*See Mack Hanan, "Reorganize Your Company Around Its Markets," *Harvard Business Review*, November–December 1979, pp. 63–74.

SOURCE: Alan R. Andreasen, *Second Marketing Audit of Smoking and Breast Cancer Program* (Washington, D.C.: Office of Cancer Communications, National Cancer Institute, 1981).

IMPLEMENTING A CUSTOMER ORIENTATION

Establishing the marketing structure appropriate to a particular organization does not necessarily make the organization market oriented. Indeed, it is crucial that the departments and key managers and staff elsewhere in the institution have the proper philosophy. Inculcating this philosophy may be the marketing manager's most important task. The marketing manager has a limited influence on how others in the organization think and behave toward customers and other publics. The marketing officer in a college, for example, cannot order professors to show a stronger interest in their students. A marketing vice-president in a hospital cannot require nurses to smile and act promptly to meet patient needs. The marketing manager, instead, must work patiently to build up a market-oriented organization. It is not possible for a nonmarket-oriented organization to be transformed into a fully responsive market-oriented organization overnight. Installing the marketing concept calls for major commitments and changes in the organization. As noted by Edward S. McKay, a long-time marketing consultant,

> It may require drastic and upsetting changes in organization. It usually demands new approaches to planning. It may set in motion a series of appraisals that will disclose surprising weaknesses in performance, distressing needs for modification of operating practices, and unexpected gaps, conflicts, or obsolescence in basic policies. Without doubt, it will call for reorientation of business philosophy and for the reversal of some long-established attitudes. These changes will not be easy to implement. Objectives, obstacles, resistance, and deep-rooted habits will have to be overcome. Frequently, even difficult and painful restaffing programs are necessary before any real progress can be made in implementing the concept.[4]

Any attempt to reorient an organization requires a plan. The plan must be based on sound principles for producing organizational change. Achieving a customer orientation calls for several measures, the sum of which will hopefully produce a market-oriented organization within three to five years. These measures are described below.

Top Management Support

An organization is not likely to develop a strong marketing orientation until its chief executive officer (CEO) believes in it, understands it, wants it, and wins the support of other high-level executives for building this mind-set. The CEO is the organization's highest "marketing executive," and has to create the climate for marketing by talking about it and agitating for it. The CEO of a university, for example, must remind the faculty, bursar, housing director, and others of the importance of serving the students. By setting the tone that the organization must be service minded and responsive, the CEO prepares the groundwork for introducing further changes later.

Effective Organization Design

The CEO cannot do the whole marketing job. Eventually, a marketing manager must be added to the organization, in either a staff or a line position.

As we saw earlier, a staff marketing director essentially operates as a *resource manager* who takes responsibility for building and coordinating marketing resources and activities. A marketing director operates as a high-level *strategy and policy manager*, capable of influencing other top managers to take a market-oriented view of the organization's customers and publics. The cost of failing to establish an adequate marketing function is described below:

> An illustration of the failure to position the marketing function properly within the organization is that of a large city hospital which made the mistake of assigning the organization's marketing to a mid-level supervisor already overloaded with administrative tasks. Not only was the supervisor unable to spend adequate time analyzing the hospital's major markets and competitive stance, but also the supervisor found that he was unable to obtain support for the few (quite reasonable) marketing actions he recommended. Because no one in top management had initiated the analysis from which the recommendation came and no top level manager was responsible for the marketing function, no one with the power to implement the recommended marketing actions would support them. The result was a frustrated supervisor who spent a good deal of his overallocated time on a nonproductive task and a hospital which missed out on two substantial market opportunities.[5]

In-Company Marketing Training

An early task of the new marketing executive should be to develop a series of workshops to introduce marketing to various groups in the organization. These groups are likely to have incorrect ideas about marketing and limited understanding of its potential benefits.

The first workshop should be presented to top corporate and divisional management. Their understanding and support is absolutely essential if marketing is to work in the organization. The workshop may take place at the organization's headquarters or at a retreat; it may consist of a highly professional presentation of concepts, cases, and marketing planning exercises. From there, further presentations can be made to the operations people, financial people, and others to enlist their understanding. These presentations should cover such topics as market opportunity identification, market segmentation, market targeting and positioning, marketing planning and control, pricing, selling, and marketing communication.

Better Employee Hiring Practices

Training can only go so far in inculcating the right attitudes in employees. If a college faculty has grown accustomed to concentrating on research instead of good teaching, it will be hard to change their attitudes. However, the college can gradually rectify the imbalance by hiring faculty who are more teaching and student oriented. The first principle in developing a caring faculty is to hire caring people. Some people are more naturally service minded than others, and this can be a criterion for hiring. Delta Airlines does much of its flight attendant recruiting from the deep South where there is a tradition of hospitality; it minimizes hiring in large northern cities because people from these cities tend to be less hospitable. Delta operates on the principle that it is easier to hire friendly people than to train unfriendly people to be friendly.

New employees should go through a training program that emphasizes the importance of creating customer satisfaction. They can be taught how to handle complaining and even abusive customers without getting riled up. Skills in listening and customer problem solving would be part of the training. This topic is developed further in Chapter 14.

Rewarding Market-Oriented Employees

One way for top management to convince everyone in the organization of the importance of customer-oriented attitudes is to reward those who demonstrate these attitudes. The organization can make a point of citing employees who have done an outstanding job of serving customers. Many colleges have "best teacher" awards based on student voting. Some hospitals carry a picture in their employees' magazine showing the "nurse of the month" and describing how this person handled a difficult situation. By calling attention to examples of commendable customer-oriented performance, it is hoped that other employees will be motivated to emulate this behavior.

Planning System Improvement

One of the most effective ways to build a demand for strong marketing is to improve the organization's planning system. Suppose the nonprofit organization has neither strong marketing nor strong planning. The organization might first design and install an organization planning system. To make this system work, strong marketing data and analysis are necessary. The planners will see that organization plans must begin with an analysis of the market. This will require strengthening the organization's marketing function. Top management will see that organization planning is largely an empty gesture without good marketing data and analysis.

SUMMARY

The role of marketing in a nonprofit organization typically evolves through three stages. In the introductory stage, there is resistance because organization members are opposed to marketing in principle or because they feel they are already doing it. If the organization wishes to proceed without a formal department, it can make use of outside resources. Should a formal marketing function be contemplated, a marketing committee should carefully consider what form it should take and how it should be introduced.

Marketing will clearly be a separate function during the growth phase. At this point, a major issue is whether marketing should be established as a line or a staff function. There may also be a question of what kind of background is appropriate for marketing positions. While it may be expedient to use someone with an advertising or journalism background initially, most organizations eventually turn to individuals with formal marketing training.

Initial projects for the marketing group should have a high economic impact yet be relatively inexpensive to implement. They should be completed in a short period of time and have high visibility if successful.

Once the mature phase is reached, marketing is well established. The organizational question at this stage is what form is best. The major alternatives are a functional orientation, a product/service orientation, a customer orientation, or some mixture. While the specific form chosen should depend on the experience, market conditions, and mission of the organization, the customer-centered form most explicitly incorporates the philosophy emphasized in this book. And even when the customer-centered form is not chosen, it is essential that the organization adopt such a perspective. This can be accomplished by careful hiring and training, explicit top management support, and a reward structure that reinforces customer-centered behavior.

QUESTIONS

1. Describe from the marketing director's point of view the composition of an ideal board of directors for the Brookhaven Center for child abuse. The center provides short-time housing, individual and family counseling, and, where necessary, foster home placement in a Midwestern city of 750,000 population.

2. The Homeview Hospital chain has five hospitals in medium-sized cities and employs functional marketing specialists for advertising, public relations, and customer services. It wishes to change to a "product" organization. How should it go about doing so?

3. The public relations director of a nonprofit charity is resisting an organizational restructuring that would put her under a newly created marketing manager position. How would you deal with this problem at both the logical and emotional levels?

4. An advertising agency vice-president, desiring to broaden his agency's public service portfolio, offers to serve as the marketing and advertising staff of a small but rapidly growing charitable organization. The organization has never had a marketing position before. What are the advantages and disadvantages of this relationship? What would you recommend?

5. Outline four initial marketing projects that a brand new marketing director for the Western Los Angeles Council of the Boy Scouts of America should undertake. Justify your choices.

NOTES

1. "A New Breed of Marketer Evolves as Hospitals Get Serious about Marketing," *Marketing News*, January 18, 1985, p. 8.

2. John A. Witt and Nelson L. McRoberts, "Lack of Expertise, Funding Shackle Marketing Moves," *Modern Health Care*, April 1983.

3. Sometimes, unfortunately, the reverse happens. At one college, the director of marketing helped improve recruitment effectiveness substantially. At this point, the president terminated the position, feeling that all the value had been obtained. Needless to say, other marketing problems emerged down the road, and the president realized that he had been hasty. Marketing is not a "fair weather" function, but one that has a continuous job to perform in an organization.

4. Edward S. McKay, *The Marketing Mystique* (New York: American Management Association, 1972), p. 22.

5. Roberta N. Clarke, "Marketing Health Care: Problems in Implementation," *HCM Review*, Winter 1978, p. 24.

12

Planning and Budgeting the Marketing Mix

During the last five years, hospital occupancy rates nationwide have dropped from more than 75 percent—where they had hovered for a decade—to the 1986 average of 63 percent. In good part, the falling rates were prompted by the Federal Government's shift to a Medicare reimbursement plan that makes it more profitable for hospitals to discharge patients quickly. But since hospitals with very low occupancy rates run the risk of being closed, they are competing ever more desperately for patients—and dreaming up increasingly elaborate marketing campaigns to woo them.

Despite . . . misgivings, hospitals—like other formerly low-profile institutions such as universities and law firms—have begun advertising with a vengeance, on television and radio, on buses, subways and billboards.

They are offering new amenities, too: candlelight dinners for new parents, and concierge services, gourmet menus and more stylish furniture for private patients.

Some hospitals are now creating clubs, like HealthExpress at Lee Memorial Hospital in Fort Myers, Fla., whose 10,000 members get a membership card, a discount on certain outpatient services—and a steady stream of mail from the hospital, which uses the club to build up, and refine, its mailing list.

Other hospitals have created trademarked brand-name "product lines." At hospitals owned by the Republic Health Corporation, these include

"You're Becoming" (cosmetic surgery), "Gift of Sight" (cataract surgery), and "Step Lively" (podiatric surgery).

Many hospitals now have neighborhood centers—known as "Doc in a Box"—for cash customers who want quick, cheap medical advice on cuts, colds and other problems not serious enough to warrant an emergency room visit. Many also have free physician referral services, to attract new patients to specialists affiliated with the hospital.

Source: Tamar Lewin, "Hospitals Pitch Harder for Patients," *The New York Times,* May 10, 1987, Section 3, pp. 1, 26. Copyright © 1987 by The New York Times Company. Reprinted by permission.

Once the core marketing strategy has been developed in light of the manager's analysis of target customers, probable future environmental changes, potential competition, and the organization's strengths and weaknesses, and once the appropriate organization structure and resources have been put in place, the next critical strategic planning task is choosing and developing cost-effective marketing programs. This chapter examines the planning and budgeting tools available to marketing managers in the nonprofit sector to make such determinations. Later chapters examine specific marketing mix elements—product, price, place, and promotion.

To be cost effective in its marketing programming an organization must face the following three issues:

1. How can the organization choose among competing marketing programs? (benefit/cost analysis)
2. How much should the organization spend on marketing? (optimal marketing expenditure level)
3. How can the organization determine the best mix of marketing tactics? (optimal marketing mix)

CHOOSING AMONG COMPETING PROGRAMS THROUGH BENEFIT/COST ANALYSIS

A common problem facing nonprofit organizations is choosing between alternative programs that all fall within the scope of the organization's objectives. Consider the following situations:

- The American Cancer Society is trying to decide between sponsoring a national cervical cancer detection program or a national breast cancer detection program.
- A public school system is trying to decide between establishing a gifted children program or a retarded children program.

- A police department is trying to decide between a campaign to educate people against pickpockets or adding a few more permanent policemen to the force.
- An art museum is trying to decide between establishing an arts library within the museum or adding a few more major paintings to its collection.
- A university is trying to decide between building some badly needed dormitories and building a badly needed student union.
- A public library is trying to decide between adding a bookmobile to bring books into neighborhoods or using the same funds to permit opening the library on Sundays.

These examples involve organizations facing a choice between two programs. They can choose one of the programs or allocate funds to both programs and operate them on a smaller scale than planned. In principle, the nonprofit organization can make a calculation similar to that of a profit organization. It should attempt to measure the benefits and the costs expected from each program. The benefits are all the contributions that the particular program will make to the organization's objectives. These benefits can include benefits to target customers and society as well as to the organization itself. The costs are all the deductions that the particular program will require from alternative organization objectives. A particular program is considered worthwhile when its benefits exceed its costs.

Theory of Benefit/Cost Analysis

Suppose a nonprofit organization is considering a choice between three programs, X, Y, and Z. All programs are estimated to cost about the same—say, 10 (in thousands of dollars). The programs, however, are estimated to yield different levels of benefits. The data on the three programs are shown in Table 12-1A.

All three programs show a positive net benefit $(B - C)$ as well as a benefit/cost ratio (B/C) greater than one. On both criteria, the best program is X, the next Y, and the last Z. If the organization has funds of only 10, it should invest in program X. If the organization has funds of 20, it should invest in programs X and Y. If the organization has funds of 30, it should invest in all three programs, because in all programs the benefits exceed the costs.

Now consider the data in Table 12-1B, where the three programs differ in costs as well as benefits. In this case, the net benefits and the benefit/cost ratios do not show the same rank order. Program X stands highest in net benefit but lowest in benefit/cost ratio. Which criterion should dominate? Generally, the benefit/cost ratio is the more rational criterion because it shows the productivity of the funds. If funds of 5 are available, they should be spent on Z because they will yield four times the benefit per dollar of cost. If funds of 15 are available, they should be spent on Y and Z to yield total benefits of 50, which is an average benefit/cost ration of $3^1/_3$ per dollar of cost. Notice that program X, although yielding net benefits of 30, only shows a benefit/cost ratio of 2. The only time program X would be preferred would be if the three programs were mutually

Table 12-1

EXAMPLES OF BENEFIT/COST COMPARISONS

Program	*B* Benefits	*C* Costs	*B–C* Net Benefit	*B/C* Benefit/Cost Ratio
		A. Equal Costs		
X	60	10	50	6
Y	30	10	20	3
Z	20	10	10	2
		B. Unequal Costs		
Program	*B* Benefits	*C* Costs	*B–C* Net Benefit	*B/C* Benefit/Cost Ratio
X	60	30	30	2
Y	30	10	20	3
Z	20	5	15	4

exclusive, funds of 30 were available, and the objective was to maximize the net benefit.

We will now ask how these benefits and costs can be quantified in the first place.

The organization is usually in a position to quantify the dollar costs of a program. If the program leads to some social costs, these are harder to estimate. A city government, for example, typically looks at the cost of building a cross-town expressway in financial terms. But an expressway destroys certain neighborhoods and increases local pollution and noise. These social costs should be included in the total evaluation of costs.

Evaluating benefits poses many tough problems. Identified benefits tend to fall into three groups. They are

1 Monetarily quantifiable benefits—benefits whose total value can be expressed in dollars

2 Nonmonetary quantifiable benefits—benefits whose total value can be expressed in some specific nonmonetary but numerical measure, such as "lives saved"

3 Nonquantifiable benefits—benefits whose total value cannot be expressed quantitatively, such as amount of happiness created, fear relieved, or beauty produced.

Suppose a certain program is estimated to have several benefits, all of which can be measured in dollars. This is the easiest case to handle.

A second possibility occurs when all the benefits can be measured in terms of a common nonmonetary value, such as "lives saved." In this case, we sum up the lives saved as a result of each benefit of the program. (If one assigned a dollar value to each of those lives, then the problem could be considered under the first category.)

A third possibility occurs when the various benefits do not all share a common value. Some analysts prefer to make a two-stage analysis, the first stage including only the quantifiable benefits and costs. If the benefit/cost ratio in quantifiable terms exceeds one, the program is considered good unless there is a conviction that the nonquantifiable costs substantially exceed the nonquantifiable benefits. If the quantifiable benefit/cost ratio is less than one, the program may nevertheless be good if the nonquantifiable benefits substantially exceed the nonquantifiable costs.

The value of trying to quantify the benefits in dollars or some other common denominator is readily apparent. It makes programming decision making more rational. This has led to a number of ingenious ways to try to determine the dollar value of a hard-to-quantify benefit. The first approach is to try to find an existing market price for this benefit. If a school dropout prevention program persuades a certain number of students to stay in school, the present value of their increased lifetime earnings can be used as a measure of the value of the program. If a fertilizer-education program increases farm output, the expected market value of the additional crops attributable to the educational program could be used as the monetary value of this benefit.

The second approach is used when there is no existing market price for the type of benefit being created by the program. Here people can be asked how much they would be willing to pay for that benefit. If a tennis court is being considered for a local park, local residents could be asked how much they would pay per hour to use it or how much additional taxes they would accept. If the National Aeronautics and Space Administration is contemplating a ten-year program to send astronauts to Mars, it might ask people how much they would be willing to pay personally over a ten-year period to achieve a successful mission.

Problems in Benefit/Cost Analysis

Some of the problems in putting benefit/cost analysis to practical use should now be apparent. Even if one manages to devise dollar values for the various benefits and costs, the technique makes certain assumptions that should be stated clearly.

First, the technique assumes that the program, if adopted, would not yield outputs sufficient to change the market prices that were used to estimate the benefits of the program. If school dropout prevention programs are introduced throughout the country, for example, they will increase the skill level of the population and probably result in a fall in the market price of skilled workers. Therefore, the life earnings calculation based on today's earnings of skilled workers overstates the market value of the benefit.

Second, the technique makes no allowance for redistributional benefits caused by the program. A vocational education program and a gifted children program, for example, may both improve lifetime incomes to the same extent.

But the vocational education program may improve the incomes of the poor and a gifted children program may improve the incomes of the well-off. Some analysts believe the technique should give weight to desirable redistribution effects.

Third, the technique assumes that economic value should be given the main weight in deciding between programs. Critics resent the notion that everything worthwhile can be measured in dollars or that the growth of the GNP is the major goal. They see the value of a school dropout prevention program not so much in increased dollars of earnings but in terms of increased self-esteem and improved social attitudes.

The technique also assumes that the rank ordering of projects is insensitive to the particular measure of benefit used. In a study of the net benefit of investing in different disease control programs, the ailment of arthritis did not seem important when the criterion "lives saved" was used because arthritis does not kill people. On the other hand, arthritis rates as a high-priority research problem when the criterion "dollars saved through avoiding medical treatment" is used.[1] Thus, various programs may rank differently depending on the benefit measure used.

These difficulties are not created by the technique but exist because the world is complex. The technique was never intended to replace judgment, but to systematize and quantify it where possible. Benefit/cost analysis suggests which important factors should be considered and what information is needed. It introduces relevant data into what otherwise would be a wholly subjective act of decision making. It rests on the premise that organized ignorance is preferable to disorganized ignorance in making decisions.

Finally, it has the advantage that it can be used to make programming decisions and also to evaluate programs once they are completed.

DECIDING ON THE OPTIMAL LEVEL OF MARKETING EXPENDITURES

Many nonprofit organizations that turn to formal marketing raise the question, "What is the proper amount to spend on marketing?" One college president specifically asked: "How many marketing dollars should we budget to increase our enrollment by 10 percent?" Unfortunately, the answer is not simple. We will describe the five major approaches available to organizations to establish their marketing budgets.

Affordable Method.   Many organizations set the marketing budget on the basis of what they think they can afford. Thus, a museum manager will assess all the competing claims for funds and arrive at an arbitrary residual amount that can be spent on audience development, retail sales, publicity, and fund-raising efforts. Setting budgets in this way is tantamount to saying that the relationship between marketing expenditures and sales is unknown and unknowable. As long as the organization can spare some funds for marketing, this will be done as a form of insurance. The basic weakness is that this approach leads to a changing level of marketing expenditure each year, making it difficult to attain consistent long-run results.

Percentage-of-Sales Method.   Many organizations prefer to set their marketing budget as a specified percentage of sales (either current or anticipated). Thus, a private college might decide to spend 5 percent of the average annual tuition per recruited student to cover admissions office salaries, advertising, and brochure preparation. If the college aims to recruit 2,000 freshman and 5 percent of the average tuition is $100, then the admissions office would receive a budget of $200,000.

The main advantage of the percentage-of-sales method is that it leads to a predictable budget each year, once the sales goal is set. It also keeps marketing costs within reasonable control. Nevertheless, the method has little else to recommend it. It does not provide a logical basis for the choice of a specific percentage, except what has been done in the past or what competitors are doing. Most important, it is countercyclical since if revenues are down, by this method marketing expenditures would decline also. Yet, this is often when one should be spending *more* on marketing.

Competitive-Based Method.   Some organizations set their marketing budgets specifically in relation to competitors' outlays. Thus, an opera company may decide on its marketing budget by investigating what its main competitor is spending on marketing. The opera may decide to spend more, less, or the same. Assuming that other arts organizations are roughly the same size, it would spend more if it wants to overtake or surpass the other arts organizations. It would spend less if it believes that it can use its funds more efficiently or influentially. It would spend the same if it believes that the competitor has figured out the proper amount to spend or if it believes that maintaining competitive parity would avoid an aggressive reaction by the competitor.

Knowing what the competition is spending on marketing is undoubtedly useful information. Basing one's spending on this information alone is not warranted, however. Marketing objectives, resources, and opportunities are likely to differ so much among organizations that the budget of one organization is hardly a guide for others to follow.

Objective-and-Task Method.   The objective-and-task method calls upon marketers to develop their budget by (1) defining their marketing objectives as specifically as possible, (2) determining the tasks that must be performed to achieve these objectives, and (3) estimating the costs of performing these tasks. The sum of these costs is the proposed marketing budget.

As an example, consider the private college that seeks to recruit 2,000 freshmen. The admissions office might estimate, on the basis of past experience, that the college would have to mail 20,000 letters to select high school seniors, which would result in approximately 8,000 inquiries, which would produce

4,000 applications, 3,000 admissions, and finally 2,000 acceptances. Each step requires a specific set of activities, the cost of each of which can be estimated. Table 12-2 shows a hypothetical estimate of costs involved in recruiting 2,000 freshmen. The admissions director builds the marketing budget by defining the objectives, identifying the required tasks, and costing them.

This method of setting the marketing budget is superior to the preceding methods. It requires that management think through its objectives and marketing activities. Its major limitation is its failure to consider alternative marketing objectives and marketing budgets in the search for the optimal course of action. We now turn to what is theoretically the soundest method for setting the marketing budget.

Response Optimization Method.   Response optimization requires that the manager estimate the relation between a market's response and alternative levels of the marketing budget. The estimate is captured in the response function, which is defined as follows:

> **A response function** forecasts the likely response of a market during a specified time period associated with different possible levels of a marketing element.

The best-known response function is the demand function, illustrated in Figure 12-1A. This function shows that the lower the price, the higher sales are in any given period. In the illustration, a price of $24 leads to sales of 8,000 units in that period, but a price of $16 would have led to sales of 14,000 units in that period. The illustrated demand curve is curvilinear, although other shapes are possible.

Suppose that the marketing variable is not price but total marketing dollars

Table 12-2

HYPOTHETICAL BUDGET FOR COLLEGE RECRUITING

20,000 leads	Purchase of names	$ 4,000
	Mailing cost	20,000
	Office processing	6,000
	Staff costs, including travel	50,000
	Advertising	33,000
8,000 inquiries	Staff cost	16,000
	Mailing cost	24,000
4,000 applications	Staff cost	40,000
	Mailing cost	2,000
2,000 acceptances	Staff cost	4,000
	Mailing cost	1,000
		$200,000

Note: Cost per recruited student = $200,000 / 2,000 = $100.

FIGURE 12-1

Sales Response Functions

A. Price function

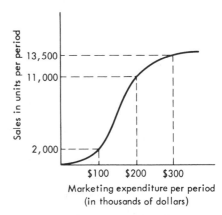

B. Marketing expenditure function

spent on sales force, advertising, and other marketing activities. In this case, the sales response function is likely to resemble Figure 12-1B. This function states that the more the organization spends in a given period on marketing effort, the higher the sales are likely to be. The particular function is S-shaped, although other shapes are possible. The S-shaped function says that low levels of marketing expenditure are not likely to produce many sales. The reason is that in most competitive markets a minimal level of marketing effort is necessary merely to attract notice. Higher levels of marketing expenditures per period produce much higher levels of response. Very high expenditures per period, however, may not add much more and would represent "marketing overkill." Thus, at the high end of the curve, responses would again flatten out.

The occurrence of eventually diminishing returns in response to increases in marketing expenditures is plausible for a number of reasons. First, there is an upper limit to the total potential demand for any particular offering. The easier prospects are attracted first; the more recalcitrant prospects remain. As the upper limit is approached, it becomes increasingly expensive to stimulate further responses. Second, as the organization steps up its marketing effort, competitors are likely to do the same, with the net result that each organization experiences increasing resistance. Third, if responses were to increase at an increasing rate throughout, natural monopolies would result. A single organization would tend to take over in each industry because of the greater level of its marketing effort. Yet this is contrary to what we observe in industry.

How can a marketing manager estimate the response function? Essentially, three methods are available. The first is the *statistical method,* in which the manager gathers data on past responses and levels of marketing mix variables and estimates the response functions using statistical estimation procedures.[2] Despite its apparent attractiveness, there are a number of problems with this method. First, a relatively large amount of data is required for the estimation to be reliable. Second, it requires enough variation in the marketing mix variables that a significant range of the response function is covered. Third, it requires that each historical data point represent a glimpse of the same response function and not the results of, say, two or three significantly different functions. The latter situation, however, may not be a serious problem if industry and competitive conditions have remained relatively stable over the analysis period.

The second method is the *experimental method,* which calls for deliberately varying the marketing expenditure levels in matched samples of geographical or other units and noting the resulting volume.[3] The third is the *judgmental method,* in which experts are asked to estimate the probable response.[4]

Once the response function is estimated, how is it used to set an optimal marketing budget? We would have to define the organization's objective. Suppose the organization wants to maximize its surplus. Graphically, we must introduce some further curves to find the point of optimal marketing expenditure. The analysis is shown in Figure 12-2. The key function that we start with is the response function. It resembles the S-shaped sales response function in the earlier Figure 12-1B except for two differences. First, response is expressed in terms of dollars of revenue instead of sales units, so that we can find the surplus-maximizing marketing expenditure. Second, the response function is shown as starting above zero sales on the argument that some revenue might be generated even in the absence marketing expenditures.

To find the optimal marketing expenditure, the marketing manager subtracts all nonmarketing costs from the *revenue response function* to derive the *gross surplus curve.* Next, marketing expenditures are drawn in such a way that a dollar on one axis is projected as a dollar on the other axis. This amounts of a 45° line when the axes are scaled in identical dollar intervals. The *marketing expenditures curve* is then subtracted from the *gross surplus curve* to derive the *net surplus curve.* The net surplus curve shows positive net surplus with marketing expenditures between M_L and M_U which could be defined as the rational range of marketing expenditure. The net surplus curve reaches a maximum at M. Therefore, the marketing expenditure that would maximize net surplus is $M.

DEVELOPING A COST-EFFECTIVE MARKETING MIX

The impact of a given marketing budget on demand depends not only on the size of the budget, but also on how the budget is allocated to the various marketing activities. An organization has many options concerning how to spend a given budget. A charity, for example, can spend the marketing budget on fund-raising staff, direct mail, media advertising, marketing research, publicity, and so on. The key task is to decide, for any given marketing objective, on the most cost-effective marketing mix.

FIGURE 12-2

Relationship Between Volume, Marketing Expenditures, and Surplus

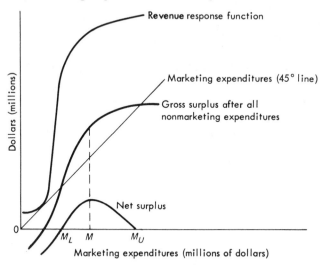

Before looking at how the marketing mix *should be* established, let us consider how it *is* established in practice. Most organizations develop rules of thumb to guide the budget's allocation to marketing activities. One college may find that sending out recruiters to select high schools produces the greatest number of applications and thus decide to commit over 50 percent of its budget to supporting a recruiting staff. Another college may find that direct mail works well in producing inquiries and make this the largest part of its budget. After a certain division of the funds gets established, management tends to adhere to it year after year. Management only gives thought to a drastic redeployment of its budget if major changes occur in the known effectiveness or cost of different marketing tools. The cost of travel, for example, has recently increased so much that college recruiters are reducing the number of high school campuses they visit and increasing the use of mail and telephone recruiting. In principle, each marketing element can substitute for another to some extent. A college can seek more students by lowering tuition, or increasing the number of recruiters, or using more direct mail. The organization must constantly try to assess the relative sales productivity of these different tools. This is another reason why marketing departments should be created—mainly to achieve administrative coordination over all the interrelated tools of marketing.

Theory of the Optimal Marketing Mix

We want to explore how the optimal marketing mix would be determined in principle. Assume that a college recruiting office uses advertising and a sales force as the two major elements of the marketing mix. Clearly, there are an infinite number of combinations of spending on these two items. Theory indicates that, for a given marketing budget, the money should be divided among the various marketing tools in a way that gives the same marginal profit on the marginal dollar spent on each tool. A geometrical version of the solution is shown in Figure 12-3. A constant-budget line is shown, indicating all the alternative marketing mixes that could be achieved with this budget. The curved lines are called *iso-sales curves*. An iso-sales curve shows the different mixes of advertising and sales force that would produce a given level of sales. Figure 12-3 shows iso-sales curves for three different sales levels: 75, 100, and 150 units. Given the budget line, it is not possible to attain sales of more than 100 units. The optimum marketing mix is shown at the point of tangency between the budget line and the last-touching iso-sales curve above it. Consequently, the marketing mix (A^*S^*), which calls for somewhat more advertising than sales force, is the sales-maximizing (and in this case profit-maximizing) marketing mix.[5]

Practical Method for Determining the Optimal Marketing Mix

The preceding theory can be turned into a practical method for evaluating different marketing mixes. Suppose a college admissions director, Ms. Ann Roche, has to make three decisions regarding the recruitment program: the application fee (P), the amount to spend on advertising (A), and the amount to spend on the sales force (S). Last year, the office charged $16 for an application fee and spent $10,000 on advertising and another $10,000 on sales force. The office now wants to consider possibly departing from this low price, low sales force strategy, which has drawn around 12,400 inquiries. Ann Roche is considering raising the application fee to $24, and possibly spending as much as $50,000 on either advertising or sales force or both. She develops a set of alternative

FIGURE 12-3

Optimal Marketing Mix for a Given Marketing Budget

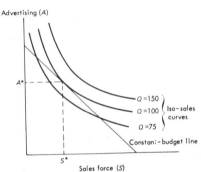

marketing mix strategies from among which to make a choice. Suppose Ms. Roche generates the eight strategies shown in the first three columns of Table 12-3 (the first listed strategy is the one used last year). These strategies were formed by assuming a high and low level for each of the three marketing variables.

Her next step is to estimate the likely number of inquiries (Q) that would be attained with each alternative mix. These estimates cannot come out of statistical analysis of past data because her office never charged an application fee of $24 or spent more than approximately $20,000 on marketing. She and her associates have to make educated guesses based on their "feel" for the market. The resulting estimates are shown in the next-to-last column of Table 12-3. The whole table represents Ann Roche's picture of the sales response function $Q = f(P, A, S)$, where the number of inquiries is a function of price, advertising, and sales force.

The optimal marketing mix strategy will depend on the organization's objective. If the college wants to maximize the number of inquiries, the best strategy is marketing mix number 4, consisting of a low application fee of $16 and a high expenditure of $50,000 each on advertising and sales force. But the college should be aware of the cost of this marketing mix strategy. Suppose the admissions office's fixed costs are $38,000 and unit variable costs are $10 for each inquiry handled. Using a surplus equation where surplus ($) is a function of price (P), variable cost (c), quantity sold (Q), donations, (D), grants (G), total fixed costs (F), and total marketing costs (M), we find:

$$\$ = (P - c) Q + D + G - F - M$$
$$\$ = (16 - 10) \, 22,600 + 0 + 0 - 38,000 - \$100,000 = -\$2,400$$

That is, the admissions office will contract a deficit of $2,400 by using this strategy. The surpluses (deficits) yielded by the other strategies are shown in the last column of Table 12-3.

Table 12-3

MARKETING MIXES AND ESTIMATED NUMBER OF INQUIRIES

Marketing Mix No.	Price (P)	Advertising (A)	Sales Force (S)	Inquiries (Q)	Surplus ($)
1.	$16	$10,000	$10,000	12,400	$16,400
2.	16	10,000	50,000	18,500	13,000
3.	16	50,000	10,000	15,100	-7,400
4.	16	50,000	50,000	22,600	-2,400
5.	24	10,000	10,000	5,500	19,000
6.	24	10,000	50,000	8,200	16,800
7.	24	50,000	10,000	6,700	-4,200
8.	24	50,000	50,000	10,000	2,000

Suppose the admissions office wanted to avoid a deficit and in fact wanted to maximize its surplus at the inquiry stage of the recruiting process to help pay for the costs of evaluating applications later. Then the optimal marketing mix strategy would be number 5, a fee of $24 and a low budget of $10,000 each spent on advertising and sales force. Unfortunately, although it will yield a high surplus of $19,000, this mix will produce only 5,500 inquiries, far fewer than the number needed to result in the target level of enrollment. The main point is that Ms. Roche should prepare these sales response estimates in order to determine the strategy that would produce the best balance among the competing objectives of inquiries and cost. Marketing mix strategy number 2 would produce substantially more inquiries than last year (18,500 instead of 12,400) at a slightly lower surplus ($13,000 instead of $16,400), and thus seems to be more attractive than last year's strategy.

Using Cost-Effectiveness Analysis for Marketing Mix Determination

Once a global marketing mix strategy is chosen, there are further marketing mix decisions of a more tactical nature to make. Suppose the admissions office decided to use global marketing mix number 4 because it is anxious to produce the largest possible number of inquiries, even though this will cause a deficit at this stage of the admissions process. In deciding to spend $50,000 on advertising, it must allocate this to competing advertising media, such as direct mail, newspaper ads, and radio ads. As an aid to determining the optimal media mix, the admissions office can use *cost-effectiveness analysis*. Cost-effectiveness analysis is the general name given to researching the effect of variations in cost on results. Figure 12-4 shows Ann Roche's estimates of how many inquiries would be produced by using different advertising media at different levels. She sees direct mail producing a linear growth in inquiries. Newspaper advertising is seen to produce a low level of response if used at a low level, increasing returns if used at a medium level, and diminishing returns if used at a high level. Radio is seen to produce a high number of inquiries if used at a low level and rapidly diminishing incremental returns thereafter.

Given the cost-effectiveness functions shown in Figure 12-4, which method is the most cost effective to produce inquiries? The answer depends on how many inquiries the college is seeking. If the college would be satisfied to attract fewer than n_1 inquiries, then radio is the most cost-effective medium. If the college is trying to attract between n_1 and n_2 inquiries, then direct mail is the most cost-effective medium. If the college is trying to attract between n_2 and n_3 inquiries, then newspaper advertising is the most cost-effective single method. If the college is trying to attract more than n_3 inquiries, then direct mail is once again the most cost-effective single medium.

If these media reach entirely different segments of the market, it would be better to use a combination of media to attract a given number of inquiries. Each

FIGURE 12-4

Cost-Effectiveness Functions

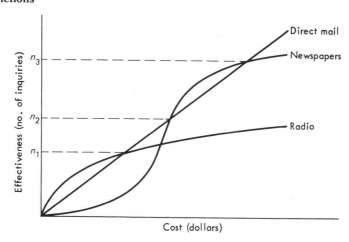

medium would be used to a level at which the marginal productivities of all media are equal.

Additional Factors Influencing the Choice of the Marketing Mix

We have examined the appropriate marketing mix in terms of response functions. We will now go behind those response functions to see what real factors influence the appropriate mix. The appropriate marketing mix is influenced by the following four factors: (1) the type of consumer—household versus organization, (2) the communications task to be accomplished, (3) the stage of the offer life cycle, and (4) the economic outlook.

The Type of Consumer—Household versus Organization.   Historically, there has been a considerable difference in the marketing mixes used by organizations selling services to households and those selling to other organizations. The mix differences are illustrated in Figure 12-5A. Advertising is believed to be the most important tool in marketing to households and personal selling the most important tool in marketing to organizations. Sales promotion is considered to have a smaller influence, but one that is equally important in both markets. And publicity is considered to be even less important, but again its influence is equal in both markets. These proportions, however, are not to be taken as authoritative, and many cases exist where marketers adopted different proportions with good success.

The Communications Task.   The optimal marketing mix also depends on the stage of buyer readiness at which the market is presumed to be. Figure 12-5B

FIGURE 12-5

Communications Mix as a Function of Type of Market and Buyer
Readiness Stage

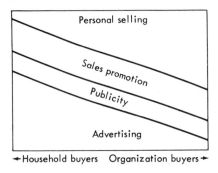

A. Normal marketing mix for
household buyers versus
organization buyers

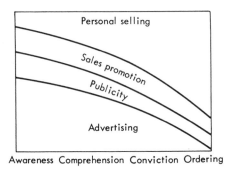

B. Marketing mix cost
effectiveness at different
buyer readiness stages

shows the general findings of a number of studies.[6] Advertising, sales promotion, and publicity are the most cost-effective tools at the initial stage in building buyer awareness; they are better than "cold calls" from sales representatives. Advertising is highly cost effective in producing comprehension at the next stage, with personal selling coming in second. Buyer conviction is influenced most by personal selling, followed by advertising. Finally, placing an order is predominantly a function of the sales call, with an assist from sales promotion.[7]

These findings have important practical implications. First, the organization could effect promotional economies by cutting back on the involvement of salespeople in the early stages of the selling job so that they can concentrate on the vital phase of closing the sale. Second, when advertising is relied on to do more of the job, it should take different forms, some addressed to building awareness and some to producing comprehension.

The Stage of the Offer Life Cycle.   The effectiveness of marketing expenditures varies at different stages of the offer life cycle, as will be discussed in greater detail in Chapter 15. The typical offer life cycle has four stages: introduction, growth, maturity and decline.

Advertising and promotion are important in the introduction stage because the market is not aware of the offer, and the cost per exposure is low. Sales promotion in particular stimulates interest in and trials of the new offer.

In the growth stage, word-of-mouth processes begin to work for the new offer and partially replace or supplement the organization's promotion efforts. If the organization wants to build its market share, it should continue to promote vigorously during the growth stage.

The maturity stage is marked by intensified promotional expenditures to meet competition and to advertise new uses and features. There is generally an increase in sales promotion effort relative to advertising effort.

In the decline stage, many organizations reduce their promotion expenditures to improve their profit margins and turn their offerings into "cash cows." Publicity is cut down, the sales force gives the offer only minimal attention, and advertising is cut down to a reminder level. Sales promotion is probably the most exercised promotion tool at this stage.

The Economic Outlook.   Organizations would do well to revise their marketing mixes with shifts in the economic outlook. During inflation, for example, buyers become highly price conscious. They look for value. The organization can do at least three things to respond: (1) it can increase its sales promotion relative to advertising, since people are looking for deals, (2) it can emphasize value and price in its communications, and (3) it can develop messages that help customers know how and where to buy intelligently.

SUMMARY

This chapter deals with three tasks in developing and choosing cost-effective marketing mixes.

The first task is to choose between alternative products or programs. Here cost/benefit analysis is helpful. The programs with the highest benefit/cost ratio are preferred. To calculate benefits and costs, monetary and quantitative measures are preferred, although ultimately nonquantifiable benefits should be taken into account.

The second task is to decide on the marketing expenditure level. Organizations decide on their expenditure level using one of five methods: affordable method, percentage-of-sales method, competitive-based method, objective-and-task method, and the response optimization method.

The third task is to develop an optimal marketing mix of product, price, place, and promotion. The optimal marketing mix can be set if the response function for each separate marketing mix element is known. The appropriate marketing mix varies with the type of buyer (households or organizations), the communication task, the stage of the offer life cycle, and the economic outlook.

QUESTIONS

1. Assume that the figures in Table 12-3 are changed as follows: price = $18 and $30, advertising cost = +10%, sales force cost = +20%. Assume inquiries are unchanged. Which mix would you recommend and why?

2. List the noneconomic costs and benefits for two competing programs: (a) a $100,000 three-year cocaine addiction treatment program in a low-income community expected to treat 50 persons a month and (b) a $80,000 two-year program for temporary housing and job training for the homeless in a waterfront area expected to help 100 persons per month. How should a foundation with only $10,000 to grant choose between the two?

3. List the tasks involved in a campaign to recruit 100 volunteers for a museum's fund-raising campaign. Estimate (or assume) the costs for each task. How do you decide whether the resulting total costs are worth it? What cost level would be too much and why?

4. In the past, a local chapter for a major national "disease" charity evaluated their marketing expenditures by comparing themselves to chapters of similar size elsewhere in the country. What are the advantages and disadvantages of this approach? What alternative should they consider, if any?

5. How could a national charitable organization set up a series of experiments to estimate response functions for different elements of its marketing mix? What could go wrong with these experiments and how would you minimize the potential danger?

NOTES

1. "Benefit/Cost Analyses for Health Care Systems," *Annals of the American Academy of Political and Social Science,* January 1972, pp. 90–99, especially p. 94.

2. As an example of this method, see David B. Montgomery and Alvin J. Silk, "Estimating Dynamic Effects of Market Communications Expenditures," *Management Science,* June 1972, pp. 485–501.

3. As an example, see Russell Ackoff and James R. Emshoff, "Advertising Research at Anheuser-Busch," *Sloan Management Review,* Winter 1975, pp. 1–15.

4. See Philip Kotler, "A Guide to Gathering Expert Estimates," *Business Horizons,* October 1970, pp. 79–87.

5. For additional theory, see Robert Dorfman and Peter O. Steiner, "Optimal Advertising and Optimal Quality," *American Economic Review,* December 1954, pp. 826–836; and Robert Ferber and P.J. Verdoorn, *Research Methods in Economics and Business* (New York: Macmillan, 1962), p. 535.

6. "What IBM Found About Ways to Influence Selling," *Business Week,* December 5, 1959, pp. 69–70; and Harold C. Cash and William J. Crissy, "Comparison of Advertising and Selling," in *The Psychology of Selling,* Vol. 12 (Flushing, N.Y.: Personnel Development Associates, 1965).

7. Swinyard and Ray have challenged the finding that advertising is more effective when it precedes the sales call. They found that female household residents who were contacted by a Red Cross volunteer followed by some mailings expressed a higher intention to donate blood than a similar group who first received the mailings and then received the sales call. See William R. Swinyard and Michael L. Ray, "Advertising-Selling Interactions: An Attribution Theory Experiment," *Journal of Marketing Research,* November 1977, pp. 509–516.

13

Managing Products and Services

Buffeted by competition and declining demand for their services, nonprofit hospitals are moving into new business lines, including some projects far removed from medicine, such as hotels, travel agencies and bill collection.

In 1987, the Roanoke Hospital Association, a nonprofit group that runs several hospitals in Virginia, purchased an advertising agency to go along with its other for-profit ventures, including two health clubs, an interior decorating firm, a pharmacy, and a helicopter ambulance service.

The Fairfax Hospital Association, a group of four Northern Virginia hospitals, invested nearly $3 million in venture capital from 1982 to 1987 in commercial projects. They include walk-in clinics, an in-vitro fertilization center, a weight-loss program, a home health equipment company, and a bill collection agency. These businesses produced $1.9 million in profits in 1986 on $22 million of revenue, according to Donald Harris, the association's senior vice-president.

In Baltimore, Johns Hopkins Hospital, several affiliated hospitals, and Johns Hopkins University created Dome Corp., a for-profit real estate development and management firm. Among the company's many projects is a $500 million biomedical research park on the grounds of the Francis Scott Key Medical Center in the eastern part of the city.

Increasingly, the nation's 3,500 private, nonprofit hospitals have started or are considering diversifying into commercial services. They are diversifying not only for new sources of income but also to attract doctors and patients.

"I think it's an unfortunate necessity of the times," said Dr. Arnold Relman, editor of the *New England Journal of Medicine.* "I think it is unfortunate the voluntary institutions should feel driven as a matter of survival to do these things. But I cannot fault them on ethical and social grounds."

Dr. John J. Lynch, a former president of the D.C. Medical Society, said: "If you are a nonprofit in another venture, and you are dumping profits back into the hospital, I can live with that. If that's what it takes to keep going, you've got to do it."

Source: Adapted from Michael Abramowitz, "Nonprofit Hospitals Venture into New Lines of Business: Moves Generating Funds and Criticism," *The Washington Post,* February 15, 1987, p. A1. Reproduced with permission.

The single most important element of the organization's marketing mix is *its offer.* Marketing's ultimate objective is to influence the behavior of target audiences by offering bundles of benefits and minimal costs in exchange for a desired behavior. Nonprofit organizations promote these exchanges largely to benefit the target audience and/or the society at large, and only secondarily to meet the organization's own needs for survival and growth. Nonprofits do not have stockholders with paramount claims.

Most organizations, for profit and nonprofit, cannot survive for very long if they do not offer something fundamentally attractive. Further, they cannot grow if they cannot distinguish their offer in significant ways from competition, even when the "competition" is inaction or the status quo. Even the most creative and dramatic advertising cannot "sell" a fundamentally weak offering. The latter is a marketing "truth" learned the hard way by such diverse "marketers" as Coca-Cola ("New Coke"), Jim Bakker ("the PTL Ministry"), and the U.S. Treasury ("the $2 bill").

In this chapter, we discuss the problems of designing and managing an organization's offer mix. We pay particular attention to the differences involved when the central benefit of the offer involves a product or a service provided by the marketer. Social marketing, discussed in the next chapter, more often involves offers in which the personal or social benefit is one that the target customer provides himself or herself (e.g., satisfaction at having overcome a drug addiction or having voted for a deserving candidate or statute). In Chapter 15, we consider the problems of developing and launching *new* offerings that can enhance the organization's societal contribution and its own growth.

DEFINING THE OFFER

In the private sector, it is conventional to divide offerings into two primary categories, products and services. We continue this distinction here. However, a unique feature of the nonprofit sector is that many of its organizations are involved in marketing activities that do not involve products or services, such as antilittering campaigns and many of the programs of the President's Council on Physical Fitness and Sports. Further, our definition of the boundaries of marketing outlined in Chapter 1 encompasses strategies to influence employees, political adversaries, and spouses or potential dates, again where marketing does not involve offering a particular product or service.

A broader definition of an offer is therefore needed. The key to our definition is rooted in our view of the nature of the influence process. As we outlined in Chapter 4, we believe that much of the behavior that nonprofit marketers wish to influence is undertaken because the target audience believes, consciously or unconsciously, that the consequences of the proposed action or actions will be positive on balance and will exceed the consequences of taking any other action (or maintaining a no-action status quo). We therefore define a marketing offer as follows:

> **A marketing offer** is a proposal by a marketer to make available to a target customer a set of positive or negative consequences if, and only if, the customer undertakes a desired action.

These consequences may flow from the acquisition of a physical product or a set of products from the marketer, as in the case of oral pills and condoms sold as part of a contraceptive social marketing program or food or gift items sold in a museum. They may also result from a contract for a service from a person (social worker, teacher), or a place (museum, zoo), or for rental products (library books or videos) or equipment (crutches or a physical therapy apparatus). Finally, they may result from the target customer's *own* actions, as when a donor simply feels happy to have given a few dollars to a Salvation Army captain standing on a snowy corner at Christmastime.

The tripartite distinction among products, services, and self-help is artificial in two important ways. First, what is significant about all three is that they are really alternative vehicles for the delivery of consequences. Indeed, we would argue that, at bottom, what customers are looking for is the set of consequences and only evaluate the delivery mechanism in terms of its ability to provide those consequences. In many cases, all three alternatives are available. Thus, a homeless person in a cold climate seeking to become warmer at night (the consequence) could (1) purchase a product, say a Hibachi, at a swap meet for a few cents and heat scraps of wood in it at night, (2) acquire a service such as a bed in a "rescue mission" (for which "payment" may be attendance at a daily religious service), or (3) provide for his or her own needs by sleeping in an area that provides more shelter (e.g., an abandoned building or storm duct) or more natural heat (e.g., over a grating or in an underground subway station).

The tripartite distinction is also arbitrary in that a great many offers are really *combinations* of products, services, and self-help. For example, an indigent elderly person on Medicare with a health problem may go to a clinic and see a doctor who gives advice (a service), purchase some antibiotics at the clinic's pharmacy (a product), and improve her eating and exercise patterns (self-help).

Even in the private sector, a product purchase is seldom pure. For example, a new car is a product, but it also comes with certain free service for the first few thousand miles and warranty provisions providing for free service later. Further, if the buyer is seeking as a major *consequence* of this "product" purchase that the car deliver its transportation benefits for a very long time, he or she must undertake certain personal actions such as nonabusive driving and regular maintenance.

A great many nonprofit organizations simultaneously engage in marketing in all three categories, as the following examples show:

- Population Development Associates in Thailand sells condoms, T-shirts, and aspirins; rents hotel rooms; provides day care services; and lobbies to get legislators to pass a law creating a new form of nonprofit (and nontaxed) private organization.
- The Krannert Center for the Performing Arts at the University of Illinois sells cream cakes and espresso; rents seats to concert attendees; and sponsors arts awareness programs for school children.
- The U.S. Postal Service sells commemorative stamps to collectors; "rents" its mail service to corporate and private subscribers; and from time to time tries to induce oversight committees to allow them to raise prices.
- The American Marketing Association sells publications; sends members on tours; offers them conferences; and tries to improve the public's perception of the field of marketing.

Different challenges face the marketing manager designing an offer strategy when the core benefit is delivered by a product, a service, or the target audience member himself or herself. In this chapter, we examine the challenges involving products and services. We begin with the problems of managing product offerings but give this topic somewhat less attention. There are two reasons for this. First, product marketing is typically not central to the mission of most nonprofits. Organizations in the major nonprofit categories of education, health care, politics, social service, religion, and the arts are all basically service or self-help enterprises. For most, product marketing either is supplementary to their primary mission (e.g., drugs for hospitals, uniforms for the Girl Scouts) or is part of fund-raising (e.g., Girl Scout cookies, KCRW T-Shirts, sweatshirts, and totebags).

Second, excessive focus on products as *things* whose attributes must be promoted ("highest-quality ingredients"; "tested by experts") encourages the unwary marketer to practice organization-centered marketing rather than the customer-centered approach we advocate here. It is tempting to any marketer to want to brag about the fine qualities of their products (service marketers are known to brag about their services as well) in their own terms ("we're great"). The point they miss is that, fundamentally, customers acquire products *for what these products can do for them*, that is for the consequences they deliver. Customers do not want highest-quality ingredients, they want something that will taste good or perform well, will impress their friends, or will not have to be replaced very often. They do not want a product tested by experts because it certifies how great the product is but because it is an indicator that the product will meet their own high performance standards, will incur low maintenance costs or will last a long time.

Products are only "consequence-delivery" objects as far as the consumer is concerned. Marketers must keep this at the center of their offer management strategies.

PRODUCT MARKETING

Marketers offer products as individual items, product lines and product mixes. For clarity, we will use the following definitions:

> A **product** is anything that can be offered in tangible form to a market to satisfy a need.

> A **product mix** is the set of all product lines and items that a particular organization makes available to consumers.

> A **product line** is a group of products within a product mix that are closely related, either because they function in a similar manner, are made available to the same consumers, or are marketed through the same types of outlets.

> A **product item** is a distinct unit within a product line that is distinguishable by size, appearance, price, or some other attribute.

Product Item Decisions

In developing a product to offer to a market, the product planner has to distinguish three levels of the concept of a product: the core, tangible, and augmented levels.

Core Product.   At the most fundamental level stands the core product, which answers the questions; What is the consumer really seeking? What need is the product really satisfying? UCLA markets textbooks, but students seek future earning power. The Sierra Club sells calendars, but purchasers are buying an organizing tool, aesthetic pleasure, and feelings of helping a "good cause." The marketer's job is to uncover the essential needs hiding under every product so that product benefits, not just product features, can be described. The core product stands at the center of the total product, as illustrated in Figure 13–1.

Tangible Product.   The core product is always made available to the buyer in some tangible form. That is, potential mothers seek family planning because it gives the core benefits of more free time and better economic circumstances. Birth control, however, comes in the form of tangible items like pills, intra-uterine devices, spermicidal tablets, and condoms. A tangible product can be described as having up to five characteristics. First, it has certain *features*; for example, the birth control pill has high or low hormone levels or does or does not contain iron. Second, it has certain *styling*; some birth control pills are brightly colored and monogrammed, others are drab and featureless. The tangible product also has a certain *quality level*; it is made well or badly. Fourth, it has a certain *packaging.* Birth control pills come in various kinds of blister packs and purse-sized compacts designed to make the product appealing and method of

FIGURE 13-1

Three Levels of Product

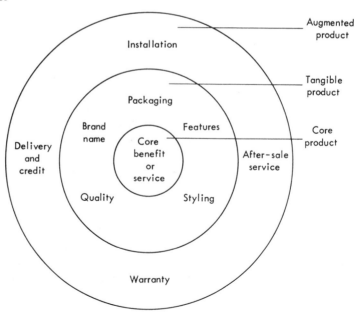

use straightforward. An attractive compact case for a birth control pill may increase its appeal; by contrast, an inconspicuous but high-quality package may be just right for a condom. Fifth, the tangible product can have a *brand name.* Thus, the birth control pills used in Egypt are known to their users as Noridette, Norminest, Triovular, Microgynon, and so on. We will examine these five controllable characteristics of a tangible product in more detail.

FEATURES.   Features represent individual components of the tangible product that could be added or subtracted without changing the product's style or quality. Consider a calendar marketer seeking to expand sales to international travelers. It might offer the following feature improvements:

1   Reference materials on the back of the calendar (U.S. and International time zones, foreign currency values)
2   Days and months in several languages
3   Dates of major foreign holidays

The use of features has many advantages. Features are a tool for achieving product differentiation vis-à-vis competitors. The organization can go after specific market segments by selecting features that would appeal to these segments. They have the advantage of being easy to add or drop, or they can be made optional at little expense. They are often newsworthy and can attract free media publicity.[1]

STYLING.   Styling means giving a product or service a distinctive look or "feel." Much of the competition in durable goods—such as automobiles, watches, and electronic products—is style competition. The style of a product can be established before or after the target market is identified. An American condom manufacturer can try to sell one style of condom without modification in, say, Egypt. Or the manufacturer could adopt a market-oriented view and design the style for the intended audience by introducing a package cameo figure that represents a more "Egyptian" countenance.

QUALITY.   Quality is the perceived level of performance in a product. Products that have a service component in particular are tremendously variable in quality, depending upon who is providing the service and how much control the organization exercises over its service providers. A basic issue is how sales response varies with the level of quality in a particular market.

PACKAGING.   Good packaging can add significant value to the core product. It can make the product easier to use as is the case with single-serving oral rehydration salt packages containing just the right quantity of chemicals for a suffering child's dehydrated system. It can keep the product safe or fresh for a long time as is the case for foil-wrapped lubricated condoms. It can add psychological value to a product as in the case of the attractive packages for contraceptive social marketing products differentiating them from products available at government clinics. Many women in developing countries will pay a little more for something that is tastefully packaged and not identified with "poor people's clinics." Examples of condom packages from two contraceptive social marketing programs in developing countries are shown in Figure 13–2.

BRANDING. Most products are branded, that is, given a name, term, sign, symbol, design, or some combination of these, which identifies them as the marketer's and differentiates them from competitors' offerings. Branding can also benefit the user, helping the user recognize a product, know its quality in advance, and so on. The seller might also gain. The Family of the Future (FOF) repackaged its basic condom in a new gold-and-white wrapper and branded the new offering as "Golden Tops." Although the tangible product was unchanged, the image of quality permitted FOF to reap a one-third higher price per unit with no loss in sales. (Indeed, the higher price itself probably added to the "quality" image.)

The brand name can also help define the product. We are offered Girl Scout Cookies and "Instant Lottery" tickets. The brand name or trademark can tie together a line of items and indicate a general standard of quality, as when all Family of the Future birth control products are marked with the organization's official symbol.

The creation of a brand name to symbolize the organization's product can contribute a number of values to the organization itself. An organization feels a proprietary interest in its brand name and normally works hard to ensure the quality and consistency of its offerings. It wants its brand name to create buyer confidence in its offerings and lead to consumer brand preference and repeat purchases.

Augmented Product. The marketer can offer to the target market additional services and benefits that go beyond the tangible product, thereby producing an augmented product. Thus, a physician offering a Family of the Future IUD can offer to insert it (utilizing training given him or her by FOF) and provide a booklet about IUDs that FOF has prepared. Organizations augment their tangible products to meet additional consumer wants, to differentiate their products from the competition, or both. Final outcomes depend as much or more on the augmented benefits as on the tangible product. As stated by Levitt, "The *new competition* is not between what companies produce in their factories, but between *what they add to their factory output in the form of packaging, services, advertising, customer advice, financing, delivery arrangements, warehousing, and other things that people value.*"[2]

Product Mix Decisions

An organization's product mix can be described in terms of its length, width, and depth. These concepts can be illustrated in a hypothetical example. Figure 13–3 shows a simplified product mix of a museum cafeteria. We see that the product mix, in terms of its length, consists of three product lines: main courses, desserts, and beverages. Each product line has a certain width. Thus, the dessert

FIGURE 13-2

Contraceptive Marketing Packages from Two Countries

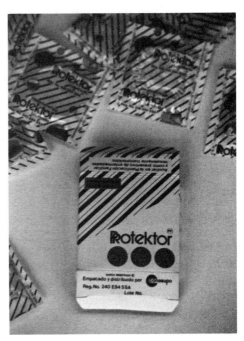

SOURCE: Porter/Novelli and SOMARC, The Futures
Group, Washington, D.C. Reproduced with permission.

FIGURE 13-3

Length, Width, and Depth of a Museum Cafeteria's Product Mix

	Main Courses	Desserts	Beverages
	Egg Dishes (4)	Ice Cream (18)	Soft Drinks (4)
	Mexican Dishes (3)	Pastries (10)	Coffee/Tea (2)
	Sandwiches (5)		Beer (3)
	Salads (6)		Wine (3)

(← —————————— Product Mix Length —————————— →)

(↑ Product Line Width ↓)

line includes ice creams and pastries. Finally, each product item has a certain depth: there are 18 ice cream flavors and 10 pastries.

Suppose the museum's cafeteria operated at a profit and the museum wanted to attract more sales. It could choose any of three alternatives. It could lengthen its product mix by adding a line of appetizers or breakfast combinations. Or it could widen one or more of its product lines, perhaps adding Italian or French entrees to its main course line, fruit or cheese offerings to the dessert line, or mineral water or fruit juices to its beverages. Finally, it could deepen any of its present ten product items, for example, by adding ten foreign beer brands, three imported wines, another sandwich variety, or six new ice cream flavors. The museum would have to assess which of these product mix choices would increase volume, patronage, or profit the most, depending on its objective.

On the other hand, the museum may want or need to prune the product mix in order to save money, free management time and energy, or focus its image better. Again it has three alternatives. It could make some product items "shallower." A more serious move would be to cut out an item altogether. Most radical, of course, would be to eliminate an entire line.

In reviewing the product mix, we should recognize that the products differ in their roles and contributions to the enterprise. Some are the enterprise's core products and others are its ancillary products. Furthermore, certain products play a major role in attracting patrons. They are called *product leaders* or *flagship products*. Often, an organization seeks to add a star product to its mix. The restaurant may offer a well-publicized torte from a famous Vienna restaurant for which customers save up their calories for weeks. An organization can showcase its flagship product as a symbol in its literature and promotion. The high cost of acquiring one crown jewel is often well repaid by the public relations value it produces.

Eliminating Old Products

A problem with many offer mixes is that they too often retain products that have "passed their prime." Most offer forms and brands eventually enter a stage where total volume declines. The decline may be slow, as in the case of barbershop quartet singing, or rapid, as in the case of politicians who fall out of public favor, or exhibit a scalloped pattern with occasional rebounds as in the case with "basic books" curricula in high schools and colleges. Volume may eventually plunge to zero and the offer may be withdrawn from the market. Or volume may petrify at a low level and continue for many years at that level. Many universities have witnessed a long-term decline in their schools of education and social work and have wrestled with decisions about what to do with these weakening offerings.

Volume declines for a number of reasons. Technical advances may give birth to new forms and brands, which become effective substitutes. Changes in fashion or tastes may lead to customer erosion. These developments intensify overcapacity and competition.

As volume declines, some organizations withdraw from the industry to invest their resources in more attractive markets. Those remaining in the industry tend to reduce their number of offerings. They withdraw from smaller market segments and weaker distribution channels. The promotion budget is reduced. Prices may also be reduced to halt the decline in demand.

Unless strong reasons for retention exist, carrying a weak offering is very costly to the organization. The cost of maintaining a weak offering is not just the amount of uncovered cost. No financial accounting can adequately convey all the hidden costs. The weak offering tends to consume a disproportionate amount of management's time; it often requires frequent tactical adjustments; it requires both advertising and sales force attention that might better be diverted to making the "healthy" offerings more successful; its very unfitness can cause customer misgivings and cast a shadow on the organization's image. The biggest cost imposed by carrying weak offerings may lie in the future. By not being eliminated at the proper time, these offerings delay the aggressive search for replacements; they create a lopsided offer mix, long on yesterday's breadwinners and short on tomorrow's breadwinners; they reduce current resource inflow; and they weaken the organization's foothold on the future.

The Drop Decision

When an offering has been singled out for elimination, the organization faces some further decisions. First, it has the option of selling or transferring the offering to someone else or dropping it completely. Second, it has the option of dropping the offering quickly or slowly. Third, it can keep the level of service to existing customers high or low.

Recently, various government units have adopted "sunset" proposals for the review and termination of government programs on a regular cycle. Each federal program would receive a review on a five- or six-year cycle. The reviewing government committee would determine whether the current program had met its objectives and whether it should be continued at the same budget level or with higher or lower funding, if any.

Well-managed marketing organizations do not wait until the last minute to jettison their weak products. They routinely seek to identify them through systematic analysis. Six steps are involved:[3]

1   An offer review committee is appointed with the responsibility for developing a system for periodically reviewing weak offerings in the organization's mix.
2   This committee meets and develops a set of objectives and procedures for reviewing weak offerings.
3   The controller's office fills out data for each offering showing trends in market size, market share, prices, and costs.
4   This information is run against a computer program that identifies the most dubious offerings. The criteria include the number of years of sales decline, market share trends, and cost trends.
5   Offerings put on the dubious list are then reported to the managers responsible for them. The managers fill out forms showing where they think sales and costs will go with no change in the current marketing program and with their recommended changes in the current program.
6   The review committee examines the offer rating form for each dubious offer and makes a recommendation to leave it alone, to modify its marketing strategy, or to drop it.

SERVICES MARKETING

A substantial majority of nonprofit organizations are basically in the service business. People enter into exchanges with them because the exchanges provide (1) *people* who educate, conduct art museum tours, or perform surgery; (2) *places* where customers can play golf, see exotic animals, or sunbathe; and/or (3) *the use of objects or equipment* so that customers can read a library book, view the distant stars through a high-powered telescope, or travel across a continent on a train. We define a service as follows:

> A **service** is any activity or benefit that one party can offer to another that is essentially intangible and does not result in the ownership of anything. Its production may or may not be tied to a physical product.

Services are of a great many types. Christopher Lovelock has pointed out that services have at least nine dimensions that affect how they should be marketed. These dimensions are outlined in Figure 13–4. Although there is high diversity in the nature of services, they tend to exhibit five important characteristics. A service is typically

- Intangible
- Inseparable from its producer
- Variable in its characteristics
- Perishable
- Dependent on the involvement of the customer in its production

FIGURE 13-4

Types of Services

Services can differ along the following dimensions:

1 Recipient:
   a   Done to people (like health care)
   b   Done to things (like plumbing repair)
2 Tangibility:
   a   Tangible (like a physical exam)
   b   Intangible (like psychotherapy)
3 Length of the service relationship:
   a   One-time (like a tire repair)
   b   Continuing (like telephone service)
4 Connection to customer:
   a   Subscriber (like telephone service)
   b   Nonsubscriber (like a police service)
5 Extent of possible customization:
   a   Low (like movies or public transportation)
   b   Medium (like education)
   c   High (like plumbing or health care services)
6 Stability of demand:
   a   High fluctuation (like hotel or police service)
   b   Low fluctuation (like insurance)
7 Adjustability of supply:
   a   High (like utilities)
   b   Low (like movie theaters)
8 Location of delivery:
   a   Customer comes to the service (like banking)
   b   Service comes to the customer (like plumbing)
   c   Service is provided at a distance (like TV programming)
9 Role of products versus people:
   a   Mostly products and equipment (like car leasing)
   b   Mostly people (like haircutting)
   c   A mix of products and people (like hospitals)

SOURCE: Christopher H. Lovelock, "Classifying Services to Gain Marketing Insights," *Journal of Marketing*, Vol. 47 (Summer 1983), pp. 9–20.

Intangibility.   Services are intangible; that is, they cannot be seen, tasted, felt, heard, or smelled before they are bought. Thus, a patient getting plastic surgery cannot see the result before the purchase; a patient walking into a psychiatrist's office cannot know the content or value of the service in advance since there is no tangible product involved. Under the circumstances, one makes a purchase on the basis of secondary cues and one's confidence in the service provider.

Inseparability.   A service is inseparable from the source that provides it. The very act of creating the service requires that the source, whether a person or a machine, be present. Thus, production and consumption occur simultaneously with services. This is in contrast to products, which continue to exist whether or not their source is present. Consider going to a Billy Crystal benefit performance. The emotional impact is inseparable from the performer. It is not the same service if an announcer tells the audience that Billy Crystal is indisposed and that they will play his record instead, or that John Smith will substitute. What this means is that the number of people who can experience a Billy Crystal benefit is limited by the amount of time Billy Crystal is willing to give to performances.

Variability.   Since a service is so closely linked to its source, it can be highly variable, depending on who is providing it and when it is being provided. A heart operation by Milton DeBakey is likely to be of higher quality than the same operation performed by a recently graduated M.D. And Doctor DeBakey's quality can vary depending on his energy and mental state at the time of the operation. Purchasers of services are aware of this high variability, and when there is a good deal at stake, will engage in extensive risk-reducing behavior such as talking to others and trying to learn who is the best provider.

Perishability.   Services cannot be stored. A car can be kept in inventory until it is sold, but the revenue on an unoccupied theater seat is lost forever. The reason many doctors charge patients for missed appointments is that the service value only existed at that point when the patient did not show up. The perishability of services is not a problem when demand is steady, because it is easy to staff the services in advance. When demand fluctuates heavily, however, service firms have difficult problems. Public transportation companies, for example, have to use much more equipment because of peak demand during rush hours than they would if public transportation needs were steady during the day.

Customer Involvement.   Many service exchanges involve the customer as an integral part in the production of the service itself. The customer therefore plays a crucial role in the ultimate nature and quality of the experience. At one extreme is client-centered psychological counseling, in which much of the value of the experience depends on the patient. Another example is the patient in the foreign hospital who cannot understand the staff, cannot figure out the telephone system, and cannot make his or her food preferences known and so considers foreign hospitals inferior and unpleasant, a judgment that can easily be projected onto the quality of care.

Each of these characteristics poses a special problem for the management of service offerings. Most fundamentally, they make the traditional distinctions between production and marketing and production and consumption extremely fuzzy. A plumber repairing your faucet, a clerk renting you a car or a motel room, and Itzhak Perlman playing a Brahms violin concerto are not just delivering some fixed commodity, they are creating the offering on the spot. They are both producers and marketers. At the same time, the way the customer advises the plumber about the nature of the plumbing problem, uses the rental car or motel room, or experiences the concerto will affect the quality of the outcome of the service encounter. They are both (partial) producers and consumers.

We focus on five major challenges in the design of service offerings.

MAKING THE INTANGIBLE TANGIBLE.   Services are difficult to evaluate because they do not involve products and are not made in advance. Consumers, therefore, look to other signs of potential quality. Diplomas can signify the quality of a physician or a mechanic. Plaques and awards are signs that a restaurant or museum is especially noteworthy. "Brand names" like the American Red Cross or the United Way can make a service more memorable and concrete.

Special attention must be paid to "atmospherics."[4] The way a service clerk is dressed, the quality of the brochures used to describe the offerings, and the character of the external architecture and interiors of the marketer's building can all affect the way the customer expects the service to be delivered. Car repair shops that keep their shop floors spotless will find that customers believe that their cars will get the same level of attention. A church or synagogue building that is modern in style will create a different set of expectations from one that is traditional and fitted with antiques and ornate decorations. A college building made of steel and glass will be suitable for an engineering school or an art department, while a granite structure with one or two fireplaces will be ideal for English or philosophy.

Service marketers can also make their offerings tangible by leaving behind concrete signs of their efforts. Some motels leave strips of paper around toilet seats or plastic wrap on drinking glasses as tangible signs of a high level of cleanliness. Restaurants offer a take-home sweet at the end of an evening to memorialize a pleasant experience. Many customer-oriented service marketers follow up a service encounter with a handwritten note or a telephone call to check on customer satisfaction and to demonstrate continuing interest in the customer.

MAKING A VIRTUE OF INSEPARABILITY.   Services are typically produced by people and so the service is often indistinguishable from the person delivering it. This can have very negative effects. A pleasant and medically successful hospital stay can be fatally marred by a surly clerk demanding (not asking for) payment or the completion of even more forms on the last day of the hospitalization. Service encounters can be sabotaged by the museum guard who is unresponsive to a simple question, the teacher who is always suspicious of student excuses, the social worker who makes clients feel like they are ruining his or her day by mentioning problems, the librarian who makes it clear that interlibrary loans are "difficult," and even by the telephone operator who transfers a call and never checks to see that the calling party has reached someone who can help.

The basic cause of these attitudes is a lack of customer orientation. Key service personnel do not see themselves as being there to meet customer needs and wants. They put themselves and their organization's needs first and usually give the impression that they would prefer it if the customers would just go away so that they could get their jobs done. As an academic colleague once said somewhat facetiously: "this university would run a lot more efficiently and I could get a lot more of what I am paid to do done if only there weren't these damn students!"

The solution is *internal marketing*. The entire organization must come to realize that every encounter with a customer is what Jan Carlzon of Scandinavian Airlines calls "a moment of truth."[5] A moment of truth is any occasion on which a customer comes into contact with some aspect of the organization and has a chance to form an impression. As Albrecht and Zemke note in their book, *Service America! Doing Business in the New Economy,*

> The problem and the challenge, from this point of view, are that most moments of truth take place far beyond the immediate line of sight of the management. Since managers cannot be there to influence the quality of so many moments of truth, they must learn to manage them indirectly, that is, by creating a customer-oriented organization, a customer-friendly system as well as a work environment that reinforces the idea of putting the customer first.[6]

The authors then cite a number of what they call "shining moments" when an organization shows that it is truly customer oriented in its service delivery. Here are three:

1 A Memphis hospital has a doorman meet surgery patients at curbside, lead them to a special desk for "check-in," and has a bellman take the "guest" to their room. Only then does someone come by to have the guest fill out the necessary admissions records.

2 A policeman in Japan accompanied a tourist back to his motel to inspect the passport the tourist claimed to have forgotten. Having satisfied the legal necessities, the policeman went far out of his way to take the tourist to the restaurant he was originally seeking, introduced him to the restaurant manager, and only then went back to his business of policing.

3 A college in Florida handles all the registration for enrollees in its professional extension programs, sends them course outlines, and even buys their textbooks for them. They feel that busy executives do not have the time for such busywork and would attend a school that recognized that need.[7]

Exhibit 13–1 shows how the Walt Disney Organization conducts internal marketing.

Staffers who come into contact with customers are called "frontline people." It is not enough to make frontline people customer oriented, there must be customer-oriented systems in place to support them. One recurring problem is the customer experiencing insensitive behavior of well-meaning employees who are afraid to ignore organization policy in order to satisfy a customer. This leads to delays and ill will while the frontline staffer "checks with management" or says that "it is against company policy." Farsighted service marketers realize that this is counterproductive and establish a system that *empowers* their frontline people to take whatever action is needed to satisfy the customer as long

EXHIBIT 13-1

Internal Marketing at Walt Disney Enterprises

Service organizations—colleges, hospitals, social agencies, and others—are increasingly recognizing that their marketing mix consists not of four Ps but five: product, price, place, promotion, and people. And people may be the most important P. The organization's employees come in continuous contact with consumers and create good or bad impressions about the organization, as the case may be. Service organizations are eager to figure out how to produce a genuine customer orientation and service-mindedness in their employees.

Not many organizations have really figured out how to motivate their inside people (employees) to serve their outside people (customers). Consider the following things that the Disney organization does to market "positive customer attitudes" to its employees:

1 The personnel staff at Disney makes a special effort to welcome new job applicants and make a good impression on them. The initial impression is very important. Those who are hired are given clearly written instructions on what to expect—where to report, what to wear, and how long each training phase will take.

2 On the first day, new employees report to Disney University for an all-day orientation session. They sit four to a table, receive name tags, and enjoy coffee, juice, and pastry. The four new employees at each table are asked to get acquainted and then introduce each other. As a result, each new employee immediately knows three other people and feels part of a group.

3 During the next eight hours, the employees are introduced to the Disney philosophy and operations through the most modern audio-visual presentations. The new employees learn that they are in the entertainment business. They are "cast members" whose job it is to be enthusiastic, knowledgeable, and professional in serving Disney's "guests." Each division in the organization is described, and how these divisions relate to each other to produce the "show." They are then treated to a free lunch, and in the afternoon, the new employees are given a tour of the park and also shown the private recreational area set aside for the employees' exclusive use, consisting of a lake, recreation hall, picnic areas, boating and fishing, and a large library.

4 The next day, the new employees report to their assigned jobs, such as security hosts (policemen), transportation hosts (drivers), custodial hosts (street cleaners), or food and beverage hosts (restaurant workers). They will receive a few days of additional training before they go "on stage." When they really know their function, they receive their "theme costume" for that function and are ready to go on stage.

5 The new employees receive additional training on how to answer the scores of questions guests frequently ask about the park. When they don't have the answer, they can dial a special number where a cadre of switchboard operators armed with thick factbooks stands ready to answer any question.

6 The employees regularly receive an eight-page 8½" × 11" newspaper called *Eyes and Ears* that features all sorts of activities, employment opportunities, special benefits, educational offerings, and so on. Each issue contains a generous number of employee pictures, all of them smiling.

7 Each Disney manager spends a week each year in "cross-utilization," namely, giving up the desk and heading for the front line, such as taking tickets, selling popcorn, or loading or unloading rides. In this way, management stays in touch with the daily challenges of running the park and problems of maintaining quality service to satisfy the millions of people who visit the theme park yearly. All the managers and employees wear name badges and address each other on a first-name basis, regardless of rank.

8 All exiting employees receive a questionnaire to indicate how they felt about working for Disney, particularly any dissatisfactions they might have had. In this way, Disney's management can measure how good a job they are doing in producing employee satisfaction and ultimately customer satisfaction.

No wonder the Disney people have had such huge success in satisfying their "guests." Their exchange with employees makes the latter feel important and personally responsible for the "show." The employees' sense of "owning this organization," of being worthwhile members of a worthwhile organization, results in their satisfaction spilling over to the millions of visitors with whom they come in contact.

SOURCE: This is a summary of the major points found in N.W. Pope, "Mickey Mouse Marketing," *American Banker*, July 25, 1979; and "More Mickey Mouse Marketing," *American Banker*, September 12, 1979.

as the staffer believes it is in the organization's long-run best interests. This system requires that management accept misguided, but well-meaning, staff actions. However, the payoffs in customer satisfaction and long-term loyalty typically prove dramatic as for-profit marketers like American Express and Federal Express have long understood.

MANAGING VARIABILITY. Quality is the greatest concern of service marketers: how to deliver it and how do you keep it consistent. The major step is to develop a good personnel selection and training program. Airlines, banks, and hotels, for example, spend substantial sums of money to train their personnel to provide uniform and friendly service. Far too many nonprofit museums and hospitals rely on untrained volunteers and do very little to train their paid staffs to provide consistent high quality. They apparently do not appreciate how a few bad experiences can permanently damage a services provider's position. A second step is to routinize or even automate many parts of the service. A third step for controlling variability is to develop adequate customer satisfaction monitoring systems. The main tools are suggestions and complaint systems, customer surveys, and comparison shopping.[8]

MANAGING PERISHABILITY.   Service organizations are, in a sense, associations of individuals, facilities, and/or products brought together to perform services as customers demand them. They represent *organized capacities to serve.* These capacities can be as simple as a renowned educator sitting at the end of a log awaiting a student or as complex as a grand opera production of *Aïda* complete with elephants and camels awaiting opening night. These capacities are, on the one hand, wasted if demand is too low and, on the other, difficult to expand if demand is too high. Service managers must try to bring supply and demand into balance. Sasser has described several strategies for managing demand and supply.[9] On the demand side, the strategies include the following:

1   *Differential pricing* can be used to shift some demand from peak to off-peak periods. An example would be lower fares for riding buses in off-peak hours.
2   *Nonpeak demand can be developed* through marketing campaigns. The Miami Beach Chamber of Commerce has attempted to convince people to vacation in Miami Beach during the summer months.
3   *Complementary services* can be developed during peak time to provide diversions or alternatives to waiting customers. Physician's offices provide magazines for patients to read while waiting.
4   *Reservation systems* are a way to presell service, know how much service is needed, and reduce consumer waiting. Some hospitals, for example, assign patient beds by requiring physicians to make reservations.

On the supply side, these strategies may be used:

1   *Part-time employees* can be used to serve peak demand. Colleges add part-time teachers when enrollment goes up.
2   *Peak-time efficiency routines* can be introduced. Some computer centers do not permit large data sets to be loaded during peak periods.
3   *Consumer participation* in the tasks can be increased. New patients may be asked to fill out their own medical histories before seeing a physician during busy periods.
4   *Shared services* can be developed. Several hospitals can agree to shift patients among themselves, depending on load.
5   *Expandable facilities can be planned.* A nursing home can make arrangements with a nearby motel for extra beds during periods of excess demand.

HELPING CONSUMERS CONSUME.   Many services require the active participation of consumers. If consumers misuse the service or do not get as much benefit from it as they could, then (1) the service is de facto of lower quality than would otherwise be the case and (2) the chance of the consumer being dissatisfied is significantly greater. There are several approaches service marketers may adopt for this problem. However, they primarily focus on either changing the marketer or changing the customer.

The most manageable approach is for the marketer to adapt its own service as much as possible to the individual customer's ability to consume and appreciate it. Thus, a library designing an on-line computer-based information retrieval system may wish to design an idiotproof system with which everyone except the most computer-traumatized or inexperienced user can cope. Art museums could take a number of steps to make the experience that they and the customer *jointly produce* more meaningful:

- Study the types of visitors coming to the museum and what they are looking for. According to Andreasen, the types include *aesthetes,* those interested in the artistic merits of specific works; *historians,* those interested in where the work fits in the stream of art history; and *romantics,* those who want to know about the artist behind the work.[10] Visitors also differ in other respects. There are those who are willing to read the needed information and those who want to be talked to; those who will visit for a brief period and those who stay longer; and those who are visiting for the first time and those who are familiar with the museum.
- Provide separate suggested itineraries through the museum for each type of visitor.
- Provide guidebooks, wall posters, tape-recorded guides, and docent tours for the different types of visitors.

The alternative route is to try to teach the consumer to be a better consumer. This is routinely done in many nonprofit areas. Museums offer art appreciation classes to potential viewers. Symphonies offer before-concert lectures. Colleges offer how-to-study seminars for new students. There are other steps even these organizations could take. One goal would be to make service users' expectations more realistic. A major source of dissatisfaction on the part of many service customers is not inferior service but exaggerated expectations. Psychiatric patients often expect instant improvement for serious problems. Playgoers often expect not to be made uncomfortable. Students at many universities and extension courses expect instant job advancement and high salaries. Nonprofits should routinely ask themselves: What are potential customers being led to expect from this organization and can the organization deliver?

A second goal should be to take every opportunity to make consumers more discriminating. If the organization is proud of its offer mix and if it has effectively differentiated itself from its competitors, it should have little to fear from teaching consumers to be more discerning. Thus, charities could routinely hand out guides to evaluating charities, such as the December 1989 article in *Money* magazine on "New Guidelines for Giving."[11] Consultants, museum directors, and psychologists could have booklets available and give introductory "lectures" to new patients on "how to get the most from your consultant/museum/therapy." Nursing homes could teach their residents to hold high (but reasonable) standards. In all cases, a discriminating clientele cannot help but make a caring organization an even better provider of service.

A third approach is to think of customer contact as a continuing activity. Good service organizations do not focus on transactions as individual events, for example, as one-time sales. They see their task to be building long-term *relationships* with their customer base. A loyal customer may spend hundreds and thousands of dollars over a decade at a restaurant or clothing store. Recognizing this, good service marketers are quite willing to take short-term losses and make extra personalized "customer-training" efforts to build a solid relationship that will have a long-term payoff.

This position is sometimes taken to extremes. Danny Newman, former publicist for the Chicago Lyric Opera, has argued that performing arts organizations ought to *ignore* fickle individual customers and seek to presell virtually all seats for all performances to subscribers before the start of each season.[12] Newman says that selling all seats in advance would have three benefits:

1   Subscriptions would provide a secure financial platform for all activities.
2   Subscribers would guarantee a basic audience for even the most adventurous productions.
3   Marketing activities could be concentrated in one period of the year and costs thereby minimized.

Beginning in the early 1960s, Newman developed a "Dynamic Subscription Package" to build continuing relationships with a loyal group of target audience members who support the organization, grow with it, and learn to appreciate its special qualities. Many banks and department stores like Nordstrom's today pay the same degree of attention to building enduring customer relationships. They treat customers not as targets to be manipulated but as partners in satisfying service experiences.

SUMMARY

Its mix of offerings in many ways defines an organization and establishes its position against competition. While, traditionally, offerings are categorized as products or services, a broader definition focuses on the fact that, from the customer's standpoint, an offer is simply a set of potential positive and negative consequences (benefits and costs). Consequences can be delivered by products or services or by the customer's own actions (e.g., dieting or exercising). Many nonprofit organizations promote all three kinds of offerings.

Three levels of the concept of a product offering can be distinguished. The core product defines the needs the product is really meeting. The tangible product is the form in which the product exists. It is comprised of the product's features, styling, quality, packaging, and brand name. The augmented product consists of the tangible product and the additional services and benefits such as installation, after-sale service, delivery, credit, and warranty. As competition increases, organizations must carefully manage the length, width, and depth of their product offerings to compete.

Most nonprofit organizations are primarily in the service business. Services can be delivered by people, places, and objects or equipment. Services are especially difficult to manage because they are typically intangible, inseparable from the producer, variable in characteristics, perishable, and involve the customer in their production. Service marketers, therefore, must develop ways of making the intangible tangible such as using brand names and atmospherics.

Inseparability means that services are often synonymous with the people who deliver them. Service marketers must vigorously pursue internal marketing to ensure that key frontline people have a customer-first attitude and must have internal systems to empower frontline people to take the actions necessary to meet customer needs and wants.

Variability in service quality can be managed by good personnel selection and careful training along with as much routinization of the service itself as is possible without diminishing the service itself. Perishability requires attention to service demand and supply which can be altered to some extent through creative pricing, marketing campaigns, adjustment of personnel and facilities, and sharing services with other organizations during peak periods. Finally, customer involvement in service delivery can enhance demand and satisfaction if marketers design services so that they are as easy as possible to use and "train" customers themselves to be effective and appreciative coproducers.

QUESTIONS

1. Suggest ways in which a social work agency can make its various services more tangible.
2. What is the core, tangible, and augmented product offered by an organization promoting contraception in a developing country?
3. How could a performing arts center effectively use "branding" concepts from the private sector to make its services more tangible?
4. Describe the length, width, and depth of the line of offerings of a typical public library. Suggest ways in which the library could increase its offerings along each of these dimensions.
5. Government welfare agencies are well known for detailed rules and monitoring procedures that make it difficult for their staff members to be customer oriented. Outline a set of guidelines and an internal marketing program to empower these staffers to serve their customers better. Be sure to include plans for internal marketing to governing administrators and/or legislators who must approve any changes in established practice.

NOTES

1. See John B. Stewart, "Functional Features, Product Strategy," *Harvard Business Review*, March–April 1959, pp. 65–78.
2. Theodore Levitt, *The Marketing Mode* (New York: McGraw-Hill, 1969), p. 2.
3. For further details, see Philip Kotler, "Phasing Out Weak Products," *Harvard Business Review*, March–April 1965, pp. 107–118.
4. Philip Kotler, "Atmospherics as a Marketing Tool," *Journal of Retailing*, Winter 1973–1974, pp. 48–64.

5. Jan Carlzon, *Moments of Truth* (Boston: Ballinger, 1987).

6. Karl Albrecht and Ron Zemke, *Service America! Doing Business in the New Economy* (Homewood, Ill.: Dow Jones-Irwin, 1985), p. 27.

7. Ibid., pp. 123–128.

8. See, for example, G.M. Hostage, "Quality Control in a Service Business," *Harvard Business Review*, July–August 1975, pp. 98–106. Also James L. Heskett, *Managing in the Service Economy* (Boston: Harvard Business School Press, 1986).

9. Alan R. Andreasen, "Non-Profits: Check Your Attention to Customers," *Harvard Business Review*, May–June 1982, pp. 105–110.

10. Margaret T. Smith, "New Guidelines for Giving," *Money*, December 1989, pp. 141–151.

11. Danny Newman, *Subscribe Now!* (New York: Publishing Center for Cultural Resources, 1977).

14

Social Marketing

The Pawtucket Heart Health Program (PHHP) made extensive use of
social marketing techniques to bring about significant reductions in
community blood cholesterol levels. Program managers began by
analyzing audience characteristics and needs and carefully segmenting the
market. They then developed distinct strategies for each key segment
using a combination of marketing mix elements, including careful pricing
of self-help "Nutrition Kits"; extensive telemarketing and direct mail;
personal promotion in the form of screening, counseling, and referral
events (SCOREs); and print mass media and print media at worksites,
churches, and schools. Lefebvre and Flora report the following results:

> Briefly, 39 SCOREs were attended by 1,439 adults, 60% of whom were
> identified as having elevated blood cholesterol levels. Two months after the cam-
> paign, 72.3% of these persons had returned for a second measurement. Nearly 60%
> of this group had reduced their blood cholesterol level by an average of 29.1 mg/dl.
> More important than these short-term results has been the integration of the
> essential components of this campaign into on-going PHHP intervention activities.
> This marketing strategy has led to over 10,000 persons having had their blood
> cholesterol measured in the subsequent two years, all of whom have received
> information on how to help themselves make dietary changes to manage elevated
> levels, and many have subsequently been referred to their physician for more
> intensive treatment. Interestingly, a recent survey of local physician's attitudes and
> practice . . . found them to be more aggressive in initiating either drug or diet
> therapy [due in part to] patient requests for blood cholesterol measurements and/or
> dietary information.

Source: Developed from R. Craig Lefebvre and June A. Flora, "Social Marketing and Public
Health Intervention," *Health Education Quarterly*, Fall 1988, pp. 299–315.

One of the most dramatic developments of the late 1980s was the widening acceptance of *social marketing* among governmental agencies both in the United States and around the world. Social marketing has proven to be an immensely powerful tool for affecting massive behavior change. It has saved U.S. taxpayers over $20 billion in losses due to forest fires through the Smokey the Bear campaign. In the field of health care, social marketing has helped many communities and international agencies recruit blood donors to meet growing hospital and research needs, helped reduce infant mortality from diarrheal dehydration in Egypt and Honduras, contributed to major antismoking programs, and made family planning products and services more accessible than ever in Mexico, the Dominican Republic, Thailand, Ghana, and Bangladesh.

One example of the acceptance of social marketing is found at the U.S. Agency for International Development (USAID). From 1985 to 1990, USAID poured millions of dollars into programs attempting to improve the survival chances of children in selected developing countries. The program was labeled by USAID as "Communication for Child Survival." In 1989, the program was renewed for five years with a budget of over $30 million. It is now labeled "Communication and Marketing for Child Survival." This is a watershed development that is particularly remarkable given the hostility that social marketing has encountered in many public-sector agencies.

DEFINING SOCIAL MARKETING[1]

Despite wide evidence of success, many public policymakers and managers are still uncertain as to just what extent marketing should be encouraged and implemented outside its traditional economic boundaries. Unfortunately, consideration of the proper role of what has come to be called "social marketing" is hampered by the fact that there is great confusion about what the term really *means,* what social marketing *can* do, and what it *ought* to do. There is also a legitimate concern that, without careful training and monitoring, those adopting social marketing will employ some of the more unsavory persuasive strategies that have helped create economic successes of a number of socially dubious products and services. As with many powerful technologies, social marketing can be abused if its proper function and use is not clearly understood.

We make a distinction here between *generic marketing* and *social marketing.*

Generic Marketing

Social marketing is, in the first instance, simply the application of generic marketing to a specific class of problems. In this sense, it is similar to retail marketing, political marketing, or industrial marketing. Generic marketing can be defined in two ways, descriptively as merely another activity, like voting and learning, that members of a society do or prescriptively as something those members *ought to do* to achieve certain ends. It is the latter perspective that is appropriate here.

All marketers are in the profession of creating, building, and maintaining *exchanges*. For example, a customer pays $1.99 and gets a slice of pizza; a driver buckles up a seat belt and gets peace of mind; or a mother in Bangladesh attends a workshop on diarrhea management and learns how to save her children from dying of dehydration. Because exchanges only take place when a target audience member *takes an action*, the ultimate objective of generic marketing is to influence behavior.

This definition means that generic marketing – and, by extension, social marketing – is not designed ultimately either to educate or to change values or attitudes. It may seek to do so as *a means* of influencing behavior. However, if someone has as a final goal imparting information or knowledge, that person is in the education profession not marketing. Further, if someone has as a final goal changing attitudes or values, that person may be described as a propagandist, a lobbyist, or perhaps an artist, but not a marketer. While marketing may use the tools of the educator or the propagandist, its critical distinguishing feature is that its ultimate goal is to influence behavior (either changing it or keeping it the same in the face of other pressures).

Social Marketing

What then distinguishes social marketing from other types of marketing? Social marketing differs from other areas of marketing *only* with respect to the *objectives* of the marketer and his or her organization. Social marketing seeks to influence *social behaviors* not to benefit the marketer but *to benefit the target audience and the general society*. Social marketing programs, then, by definition are generic marketing programs carried out to change behaviors that are in the individual's or society's interests.

Social marketing can be carried out by anyone, individuals, informal groups or formal organizations. It can be carried out by nonprofits and for-profits. Its goal is not to market a product or service *per se* but to influence a social behavior (e.g. induce someone to stop smoking or drive 55 mph). Its sponsors simply wish to make the society a better place, not merely benefit themselves or their organization.

Finally, in stating that social marketing involves customer behavior that the marketer thinks is socially desirable, we make no judgments about whether in any given circumstances they are right. Sound marketing approaches and techniques can be used as easily by a Hitler or a Charles Manson as by a Mother Theresa or a Pope John. Our purpose is to show social behavior marketers how to do strategic marketing, not to debate whether they should use it in certain cases and not in others. Our hope is that by making social marketing technology available to everyone, no one side of an issue will have a greater advantage than any other side.[2]

THE DOMAIN OF SOCIAL MARKETING

Given these defining characteristics, it is clear that the outer bounds of social marketing's legitimate domain are *potentially* extremely broad. They comprise *any planned effort to influence any human behavior* where the change agent's motives are on balance more selfless than selfish. Further, since *anyone* can carry out social marketing not just organizations, it includes efforts ranging all the way from the personal and relatively trivial, such as a parent's attempt to get a teenager to clean up his or her room, all the way to the global and extremely important, such as the U.S. State Department's attempts to get the Soviet Union to sign a treaty limiting the deployment of intermediate ballistic missiles.

Social marketing can involve influencing individuals to use products or services such as condoms and vasectomies in contraceptive social marketing programs. But these are only means to the end of social behavior change, for example, in current attempts to influence how mothers treat infant diarrhea— when children are immunized—or how they are fed.

Social marketing can obviously involve sales and profits. Many social marketers, such as government organizations in developing countries selling oral rehydration packets, vitamin A capsules, or condoms are intending to serve ultimate behavior change objectives. Indeed, in early stages in the life of many social marketing organizations, the *majority* of its activities may involve fund-raising and sales campaigns that make the organization seem little different from a private-sector counterpart. The real test, of course, is where the organization is headed, not necessarily what it currently appears to focus on.

Thus, the domain of *potential applications* of social marketing is very broad. In practical terms, at any point the real potential domain is only where members of society will sanction its application. At the present time, for example, most private-sector physicians and many lawyers and even a few politicians do not feel it is "appropriate" for them to use marketing techniques. Some states still feel they should not have a lottery even if it is designed to benefit education or the state's underprivileged.[3]

To some extent, overcoming these reservations becomes a social marketing task itself. Only when social marketing is implemented where it has a clear differential advantage and implemented with the type of customer-centered philosophy, structure and systems outlined elsewhere in this book will it come to be seen in its proper role as one of many potentially effective social change techniques.

To understand what the conditions are for appropriate and effective use of social marketing, it is necessary to restate basic tenets from earlier chapters. Before proceeding, however, it is desirable to answer the objection that social behavior marketing provides Machiavellian guidance on how to get people to do what they do not want to do, or not do what they want to do—that is, it provides a means of social manipulation and control. In the first place, it is very difficult to change people's behavior with respect to issues that are important to them. Those who work face to face with individual clients and have their trust, such as psychiatrists, social workers, physicians, or relatives, know how difficult it is to change another person. It is even more difficult to change a whole group of people when the means are mass media ads that appear infrequently and are seen as coming from a biased source. Although social behavior marketing attempts to harness the insights of behavioral science and exchange theory to the task of social change, its power to bring about actual change, or bring it about in a reasonable amount of time, is very limited. The greater the target group's investment in a value or behavioral pattern, the more resistant it is to change. Social behavior marketing works best where the type of change is one people don't care about very much.

Distinctions Among Types of Social Behavior Change Programs

Social marketing aims to produce an optimal plan for bringing about a desired social change. The fact that the plan is optimal, however, does not guarantee that the target change will be achieved. It depends on how easy or difficult the targeted social change is. Without social marketing thinking, it may be that the desired social change has only a 10 percent chance of being achieved; the best social marketing plan may only increase this probability to 15 percent. In other words, some social changes are relatively easy to bring about, even without social marketing; others are supremely difficult to bring about, even with social marketing.

Three major dimensions determine the difficulty of successfully changing social behavior. In Chapter 4, we made the distinction between exchanges that were (1) low involvement or high involvement, (2) one-time or continuing, and (3) by individuals or groups. Examples of social behavior change programs in each of the six categories produced by these dimensions are indicated in Table 14-1.

Other things being equal, it is more difficult to change behaviors that are (1) high involvement, (2) group decisions, (3) continuing, or some combination of these. We shall discuss some of the problems of marketing one-time and continuous behavior changes.

One-Time Behavior Changes.   One-time behavior changes require that the target market comprehend something and take a specific action based on this comprehension. Action involves a cost to the actors. Even if their attitude toward the action is favorable, their carrying it out may be impeded by such factors as distance, time, expense, or plain inertia. For this reason, the marketer has to arrange factors that make it easy for target persons to carry out the one-time action.

Consider mass immunization campaigns. Medical teams in Africa visit villages in the hope of inoculating everyone. Over the years, medical teams have evolved a procedure to increase the number of villagers they attract. A marketing team is sent to each village a few weeks before the appearance of the medical

Table 14-1

A TAXONOMY OF SOCIAL BEHAVIOR CHANGE PROGRAMS

One-Time Behavior	Low Involvement	High Involvement
Individual	Donating money to a charity Registering to vote Signing up for Medicaid	Donating blood
Group	Voting for a change in a state constitution	Voting out restrictive membership rules in a club
Continuing Behavior		
Individual	Not smoking in elevators	Stopping smoking or drug intake Practicing family planning
Group	Driving 55 mph Driving on the right side of the road	Supporting the concept of an all-volunteer army

team. The marketers meet the village leaders to describe the importance and benefits of the program so that the leaders in turn will ask their people to cooperate. The marketers offer monetary or other incentives to the village leaders. They drive a sound truck around the village announcing the date and occasion. They promise rewards to those who show up. Posters are placed in various locations. The medical team arrives when scheduled and uses inoculation equipment that is relatively fast and painless. The whole effect is an orchestration of product, price, place, and promotion factors calculated to achieve the maximum possible turnout.

Another example in the mid-1960s involved Medicaid sign-ups. Medicare was enacted into law to provide medical benefits for the *elderly*. The following year, Medicaid was enacted into law to provide medical benefits for the *indigent and handicapped*. In the state of New York, persons and families earning under $6,000 were eligible for Medicaid. One year after Medicaid was enacted, only 1 million of the 3 million eligible persons in New York City were enrolled. A survey revealed three factors behind the low enrollment rate:

1 A widespread lack of knowledge of Medicaid and its benefits
2 Confusion of Medicaid with Medicare by elderly indigents who failed to realize the additional benefits available from Medicaid
3 A mistaken belief that one had to be literally on the welfare rolls to be eligible

The city of New York decided to launch a one-month campaign in June, 1967, to increase the number of eligible persons who signed up for Medicaid. The plan for the social marketing of Medicaid included the following elements:

1 The mayor declared the month of June as Medicaid Month.
2 Health educators in 30 health districts went into the community to organize public support. They enlisted the support of professional leaders, active lay leaders, informal leaders, volunteers from the police auxiliary, and persons from antipoverty programs.
3 Personnel and sound trucks appeared at busy locations on different days to answer questions.
4 Information tables were placed in three department stores in Brooklyn to reach shoppers who might be eligible for Medicaid.
5 Literature was distributed in the streets and through department stores, banks, post offices, supermarkets, and schools.
6 Publicity was placed in newspapers, radio, and television.
7 Car cards were placed in the city subway system.
8 Posters were distributed at hospital outpatient clinics, health centers, and antipoverty offices.

This campaign was so successful that it was extended into the month of July and in the two months, a total of 450,000 additional persons were enrolled in Medicaid.[4]

Continuing Behavior Change.   Getting individuals or groups to change their behavior permanently is harder than getting them to make one-shot action changes. People must unlearn old habits, learn new habits, and freeze the new pattern of behavior. In the area of birth control, for example, couples have to learn how to use new devices such as condoms or foaming tablets and get into the habit of using them regularly without anyone being around to help them or to reinforce the behavior. In the area of safer driving, drivers who have a tendency to drink heavily at social gatherings must learn either to drink less or to know when they are not fit to drive their own car. Various campaigns have been directed at problem drivers to condition them to be aware of the problem and the penalties and to delegate driving to "designated drivers."

LOW INVOLVEMENT CONTINUING BEHAVIOR CHANGE.   A good example of securing continuing group behavior change in a low-involvement area was the effort to get the Swedish motoring public to change their driving habits. This project is outlined in Exhibit 14-1.

EXHIBIT 14-1

Sweden Turns to the Right

At five o'clock in the morning of September 3, 1967, Sweden changed her rule of the road from driving on the left to driving on the right. For the people of Sweden—almost 8,000,000 of them—this meant that an old and extremely well learned pattern of behavior would have to be changed. From that time, 2,000,000 motor vehicles and 1,000,000 other vehicles would have to be driven on the right instead of on the left, and people would have to pass each other on the left instead of on the right. In addition they would have to learn how to find their way about in the large towns, where traffic engineers were taking the opportunity to make a thorough reorganization of traffic and to introduce, for example, many new one-way streets.

The reorganization meant that the whole population—and of course those who happened to be visiting Sweden at the time—would have to be supplied with information telling them that traffic was to be reorganized, when and how the reorganization was to be effected, what traffic rules would be in force afterwards, and what local changes had been made for the regulation of traffic. For two weeks before September 3, therefore, and after that date until the end of the year, an information campaign of seldom-experienced dimensions was put into action. All conceivable media were used in the campaign—between three and four TV programs a day; an average of two daily radio programs and more than ten trailers; a thirty-two-page brochure of which 7,900,000 copies were printed and which was distributed to every household in Sweden. The brochure was translated into nine languages and was directly distributed to aliens resident in Sweden. It was also issued in editions for the deaf, the blind, and other special groups.

Every pupil in Sweden's schools received study materials adapted to the various stages of education from kindergartens to higher secondary schools and other advanced types of schools. Special printed matter was also produced for other public institutions such as pensioners' homes, hospitals, and prisons. For weeks after the changeover, practically every poster site in the country was used, and along the highways reminder signs were set up every three to five kilometers.

An advertising campaign was carried on in all the 130 daily newspapers and in weeklies and trade papers, from the last weeks in August until November. Even comics of the "Donald Duck" type carried advertising with traffic information adapted to their readers. In addition radio, TV, and newspapers gave information about the changeover in their news. On September 4, facts about right-hand traffic took up one-third of column space in the dailies.

Advertising films were shown before the main feature in movie houses and a sound track reminded audiences of right-hand traffic before they left at the end of the show. Spectators were given similar reminders at sports contests and other events. Traffic information and notices of various kinds were also given on, for example, milk cartons, soft drinks, plastic cups, coffee cans, and department stores' carrier-bags. Private enterprise produced right-hand traffic games, men's underpants suitably marked with admonitions, and warning devices of the most diversified kinds for car drivers.

During the autumn of 1967, detailed analyses of the accident statistics showed that bicycle and moped accidents were at a relatively high figure during the first two weeks after the changeover, and also that head-on collisions were two to three times more than "normal" during the period from September to November. In both these cases, preventive measures were taken.

The conclusion that can be drawn from the course of developments after the changeover must reasonably be that it is possible to change the public's attitudes in traffic matters, that it is possible considerably to increase road users' traffic knowledge, and that it is possible to make a radical change in people's behavior in traffic.

SOURCE: "Getting all Swedish Drivers to Prepare for a Switch to the Right-Hand Side of the Road," condensed and reprinted from *Progress*, Vol. 53, no. 279 (Quarter, 1968), pp. 26–32. Reproduced with permission.

Change agents rely primarily on mass communication to influence permanent changes in low involvement behavior. In some cases, mass communication can be counterproductive. In the late sixties, when many young people were experimenting with hard drugs, advertising agencies, social agencies, and legislators felt that advertising could be a powerful weapon for discouraging hard drug usage among nonusers. Much money was funded privately and by the government, with donations of time by advertising agencies and media organizations. Fear appeals were first tried, followed by more informational advertising. Soon some people began to voice doubts about the good that this was doing. UN Secretary-General Kurt Waldheim, presenting a drug evaluation study to the UN, cautioned in 1972: "Special care must be exercised in this connection not to arouse undue curiosity and unwittingly encourage experimentation."[5] Antidrug messages, especially on television, reach a lot of young persons who may never have thought about drugs. These young persons do not necessarily perceive the message negatively and might in fact develop a strong curiosity about the subject. The worry is that this will be accompanied by the feeling that if the older generation is spending that much money to talk them out of something, there must be something good in it. They start discussing drugs with their friends and soon learn where to obtain illegal drugs, how to use them, and that their peers think they are not that dangerous if used carefully. Thus, mass advertising might provoke initial curiosity more than fear and lead the person into exploration and experimentation.[6] The main point is that nonprofit organizations often resort to advertising with insufficient knowledge of the audience or testing of the probable effects of their message upon the audience.[7] And they fail to create mechanisms that enable people to translate their motivation into appropriate actions.

HIGH INVOLVEMENT CONTINUING BEHAVIOR CHANGE.   The most difficult kind of behavior to change is that which first requires a major change in values. When values are highly resistant to change, many social behavior marketers prefer to use the law to coerce new behaviors even if the laws are not accompanied by efforts to change attitudes. The theory is that as people comply with the new law, forces will be set into motion that will produce the desired attitude change. Consider the 100 years of persuasive effort to get southern schools in the United States voluntarily to desegregate. All attempts to change racially prejudiced attitudes failed. These attitudes were not only ideological but practical in supporting the system of white supremacy in the South. Unable to wait any longer for an attitude change, the Supreme Court in 1954 declared that all schools had to be desegregated. In the years that followed, school districts and citizens were forced to comply with a law they did not like. Some resisted the court orders so that their behavior would be congruent with their attitudes. Others who complied gradually found their attitudes softening somewhat to come more into line with their behavior. The passage of a widely disliked law sets several forces in motion that may accelerate the adoption of the targeted attitude and behavior changes:

1   The new law helps the law's supporters gain new strength. They coalesce their forces and work harder for its implementation.

2 The new law stimulates more radical proposals, leading citizens to accept the original change in order to ward off the more radical proposals.

3 The new law creates sustained media attention and word-of-mouth discussion, which leads people to examine their ideas and values more carefully.

4 The new law elicits conformity on the part of citizens who believe laws are to be obeyed. Conformity eventually leads from mere compliance to acceptance through processes of dissonance reduction.

Thus, when it comes to changing continuing behavior in high involvement areas, the most effective means may be to pass laws requiring behavioral conformity, which set forces into motion that might accelerate the acceptance of new values. In this case, the social marketer's role is to build a climate favorable to the passage and acceptance of the new law.

PROCESS AND CONCEPTS

As noted throughout this book good social marketing begins with a philosophy deeply rooted in a customer or audience orientation. However, when developing specific programs and strategies based on this philosophy, a social marketer brings to bear central concepts and processes outlined elsewhere in this book that further differentiate their specific orientation. Among these are the following:

1. Exchange Is Accorded a Central Role. Marketing management involves influencing exchanges. Marketers conceive of decisions consumers make as choices among alternative behaviors that vary in the benefits and costs they will provide. For each alternative, the individual is contemplating giving up—that is, *exchanging*—costs for benefits. In social marketing situations, these exchanges are *complex, personal,* and *anticipatory*.

2. There Is a Willingness to Change the Offer. A customer-oriented social marketer, while convinced of the desirability of the behavior being promoted, is totally open to the possibility that many customers may not agree. The social marketer realizes that the behavior being promoted, the "offer," is not an objective reality but *what the customer thinks it is*. Changing the "offer" to the marketer then means changing these perceptions.

Sometimes the perceptions of reluctant or antagonistic customers are deadly accurate, and changing the offer requires that the marketer make fundamental, *real* changes. If seat belts really are uncomfortable and consumers are not just using this as an excuse for personal bravado, then seat belts must be redesigned. If oral rehydration solution (ORS) cannot safely be prepared by typical households in one-liter volumes, then ORS packets must be modified to accommodate the best local measure (e.g., a Coke or Pepsi bottle) available. Efforts to convince consumers that their perceptions are wrong will be ill considered.

There are also times when consumer perceptions do not reflect reality and it is the marketer's challenge to understand what has led to the misconception and how to alter it. Many mothers still feel ORS can induce vomiting so that two spoonfuls are enough for a small sick child.

It should be noted that good social marketers do not assume that it is the mother's ignorance or apathy that is "at fault" when she does not take action. They do not see their problem as just having to convince the target audience that they are wrong and that the behavior promoted is *really* highly desirable. Rather, they assume that it is more likely that the marketer has inadequately understood their target market's perceptions and their needs and wants. Mothers want to avoid any chance of vomiting, so marketers must make it clear that ORS must be given slowly with a spoon. Mothers believe two spoonfuls are enough because they've been told that ORS is a "medicine." If marketers "repositioned" it as a "tonic," perhaps this will change their understanding of the product and its benefits and, ultimately, their behavior. It is much easier for marketers to change their own behavior than try to change the target customer.[8]

3. There Is a Focus on Coordinated Programs.   Target customers fail to respond to a marketer's program because they see too few benefits or too many costs. Usually, the truth is a complex mixture. Effective marketing therefore requires a *coordinated* attack on *all* the major benefits and costs.

4. Market Research Is Given a Central Role.   Placing customer needs and wants at the center of marketing strategy puts a heavy reliance on marketing research. Good marketers recognize that such research must be carried out at the very start of the strategy development process to find out where target customers are "coming from" and then, as program elements are put in place (e.g., specific positioning platforms, packaging, advertising, and so forth), must continue to "check these out" with target audience members. Since the challenge in high-involvement behaviors is to influence *perceptions*, research must constantly check what those perceptions are and how they are being affected.

Simultaneously, marketers recognize the need for research to make sure other elements of the marketing mix are working well. This can mean audits of intermediaries to see that they are playing their roles, package testing to make sure products are easy to use, checks on the attitudes of significant outside "publics" to ensure they understand and support the program, and so on. Sophisticated social marketers frequently experiment with alternative strategies to learn which will be the most effective. Exhibit 14-2 describes an experiment by a Mexican family planning program to learn which was the best approach to promoting family planning within factories—working through traditional medical personnel in factory clinics or through volunteer workers who would promote family planning on their own. The volunteer promoters turned out to be both better at reaching workers and more cost effective.

5. There Is a Predilection for Segmentation.   Marketers who constantly keep attuned to their target audience are confronted again and again by the market's diversity. As a consequence, they assume markets almost always must be segmented with strategies fine-tuned to the needs and wants of each sub-

EXHIBIT 14-2

Conducting a Social Marketing Experiment

Although contraceptive prevalence is high along the Mexico-U.S. border, more Mexican-American women in the U.S. use family planning than do Mexican women in the Mexican border states. Since 65% of the maquiladora (assembly plant) labor force are young females, MIPFAC (Materno Infantil y de Planificación Familiar) a private, nonprofit, family planning organization in Ciudad Juárez, thought that a significant unmet need for family planning services existed among young workers at the border.

Two strategies were tested for providing services to factory workers. A clinic-based program used medical and paramedical personnel at the plant clinics to distribute methods in the factories. The promoter-based program drew upon factory workers to work as volunteer family planning promoters in the factory and distribute contraceptives. Training was offered to personnel involved in both interventions.

Data were collected on user characteristics, methods distributed, acceptability of services, and cost of service delivery.

The results indicated that the promoter program distributed 430.6 couple-years-of-protection (CYP) over the 18-month study period, compared with 264.7 CYP distributed by the clinic program. Additionally, the promoters were more successful in attracting male users; 18% of users in the promoter program were males, compared to 4% in the clinic program.

Promoters were more effective in reaching workers. Over the 18-month period, the promoters distributed an average of .74 CYP per worker, and clinic staff provided .39 CYP per worker. Although there were generally more promoters than clinic staff, the promoters provided almost twice as many CYP on a per capita basis to plant workers. Among the reasons thought to contribute to the promoters' more effective performance were more confidence with co-workers than with clinic staff and fewer workers per promoter.

There was also greater distribution in factories with low worker turnover. Among the 23 factories, the average monthly employee turnover was 8.5%. Among the group with less than 8.5% employee turnover, an average of 0.65 CYP per worker was distributed during the study; the group with high turnover accepted an average of .47 CYP per worker during the study. This statistically significant difference indicates that plants with low employee turnover may yield greater success in promoting family planning methods.

Workers want more information on family planning and sex education. Focus groups indicated that users in the factories have a need for more in-factory talks on family planning and sex education. Additionally, the males indicated that they felt more comfortable obtaining family planning methods from promoters than from clinic staff.

The promoter program was also more cost-effective. Because the promoter program involved more people and required more supervision, it was a marginally more expensive program to operate. However, the greater volume of CYP distributed by the promoters offset the additional cost, making the promoter strategy a more cost-effective means of providing family planning methods.

The promoter program cost $16.37 per CYP and the clinic program cost $20.29 per CYP. However, these costs are higher than found in most community-based distribution programs.

SOURCE: Adapted from: "MIPFAC: Family Planning Services Can Successfully Be Provided in the Work Place Through the Use of Promoters," *Alternatives*, March 1989, pp. 6, 9. Reproduced with permission.

population. Closeness to consumers also leads to recognition that traditional demographic approaches are seldom adequate to capture the rich diversity in target audience's needs, wants, life-styles, perceptions, and preferences.

6. There Is a Bottom-Line Orientation.   Good marketers are constantly mindful that their goal is to *influence behavior*. They also recognize that they have limited resources to do so. These two features give them a sometimes brutal yardstick against which to evaluate many of the things they and others would like to do: cost-effectiveness. They ask: Does this research study, this advertising campaign, or this cooperative project with another group help me do a better job of influencing behavior, and is it a good way to expend our limited economic, personnel, and intellectual resources? This bottom-line approach means constant attention to the *efficiency* and *effectiveness* of everything they do.

7. There Is a Commitment to Planning.   As part of their sense of responsibility for "the bottom line," good marketers believe very strongly in the need to take reasoned action. This encourages them to think systematically through major steps they undertake, both in determining long-range strategy and in making specific tactical decisions.

8. There Is a Willingness to Take "Reasoned Risks."   Marketers recognize that they are operating in a battleground for target audiences' minds. And, while they attempt to use research as much as possible to understand where those "minds" are now and/or how they might respond to a course of action under consideration, they recognize that minds are imperfectly knowable. This is especially so when one is dealing with important social behaviors about which consumers have complex, sometimes guilty feelings.

This recognition has two consequences. First, marketers realize that some proportion of their actions will fail. Good marketers are rarely immobilized by that prospect unlike those less accustomed to living with day-to-day risk. Marketers routinely take "reasoned risks" often incorporating some formal calculation of inherent risk into their decision-making processes.

Second, because they know their environment is in many ways unknowable or at least unpredictable, good marketers are by nature *experimental*. They do not always go ahead and make major irrevocable commitments to "one best strategy." When they do select a course of action, their bottom-line and research orientations make them vigilant for any signs of failure. And, because they have anticipated this risk, good marketers will have designed contingency plans.

DIFFERENCES IN SOCIAL MARKETING

We have argued above that generic marketing has the *potential* to bring a unique and proven approach to the challenges facing social change agencies. However, social marketing is not the same as generic marketing. If one is to understand marketing's potential, one must understand the principal ways in which generic and social marketing are different. Social marketers have the following responsibilities:

1. They Face Intense Public Scrutiny.   Since social marketers have as their goal the improvement of the target audience's or general society's welfare, it is typical that some form of formal or informal public scrutiny is accorded the social marketer's performance. This scrutiny may be by the government, a funding source, and/or the general public as represented by the press or academic researcher/critics. This scrutiny, among other effects, makes risk taking more difficult in social marketing and increases the importance of "politics" and "public relations" in the social marketing mix.

2. They Must Meet Extravagant Expectations.   In commercial markets, marketers are often given responsibility for improving market shares a few percentage points or launching a new product or brand that will yield to a firm a reasonable return on investment. In social marketing, the challenges may be for complete eradication of a problem or the universal adoption of some desirable behavior. Social marketers must spend at least some of their time *reducing* the expectations of key oversight publics.

3. They Are Often Asked to Influence Nonexistent Demand.   Many of the attitudes and behaviors social marketers are attempting to influence may be entirely new to their target audiences. Households who think that children come "naturally" or as "part of God's plan" need to learn that children are not inevitable. This must take place long before any marketing can be done about particular contraception methods, distribution points, and so on.

4. They Are Often Asked to Influence Negative Demand.   It is sometimes the case that social marketers must attempt to promote a behavior for which the target audience has a clear distaste. For example, driving 55 mph or wearing a seat belt is restricting to most people. Exercising is not anticipated positively by those who have never done it. Drug or alcohol addicts often are afraid to quit their habits. Conserving water, turning down the thermostat, and separating garbage for recycling are all "costly" behaviors that most consumers would rather avoid. Private-sector marketers are rarely challenged to promote a product or service that consumers consciously or unconsciously detest.

5. They Often Target Nonliterate Audiences.   Many social marketing programs take place in developing countries and/or with populations with limited reading skills. This restricts the kind of media and messages that can be used and creates major creative challenges for social marketers. In some markets, cartoon characters are used to achieve identification among nonliterate audiences (see Figure 14-1). Special problems are presented when complex information must be communicated.

6. They Must Understand Highly Sensitive Issues.   Most of the behaviors that social marketers are asked to influence are much more highly involving than most of those found in the private sector. Asking parents to begin to regulate family size or a rural mother to regularly weigh her child and expose the fact that her family has little food is much more serious than asking someone to buy a Toyota or new furniture. One consequence of this very high level of involvement is that it often makes it very hard for social marketers to carry out the customer research that they stress is essential to their approach.[9] One imaginative approach is described in Exhibit 14-3.

EXHIBIT 14-3

William Smith of the Academy for Educational Development on Conducting Delicate Research on Condom Usage

At the Academy for Educational Development, a nonprofit international assistance agency, marketing is a problem with cross-cultural dimensions. Being so distant from our target audience's daily experience (we work in African villages, Latin American suburbs, and crowded Asian cities) has forced us to rely on very "participatory" tactics. Traditional research in which target groups answer questions is being replaced by more active research involving audience segments in the actual design of materials.

Working with the Government of the Dominican Republic (D.R.) in the spring of 1989, our team was faced with helping female sex workers (FSWs) protect themselves and their clients from AIDS. Intercept interviews and street audits had suggested that these women already knew about condoms, carried condoms with them regularly, but complained that condoms were unreliable and often broke. We didn't know if these were exaggerated rumors, product defects, or poor usage.

We put together a research process that tested each hypothesis. The toughest job was measuring condom use skills—do FSWs know how to use condoms properly? Using a rubber dildo as a surrogate, we asked 91 women to place and remove a condom just the way they did in real life. Two surprises! First, 69 percent of the women unrolled the condom like they unroll a stocking while placing it over the dildo; needless stretching, stress, and in some cases small tears from their long fingernails were common. Surprise two. . . . women reported over and over again, *"we don't put condoms on the man—that's his job."* Further interviews showed that many of these women felt insecure talking about or touching condoms. We noticed that the more at ease a woman felt with the condom the more clever and willing she seemed to be in convincing her partner to use one. Conclusion: most FSWs don't put condoms on men in the D.R., but familiarity with condoms, particularly specific condom skills might give them added confidence to persuade men to use condoms properly. But how could we help increase confidence on a scale large enough to make a difference?

FIGURE 14-1

Using Cartoon Figures for Instruction Booklets

SOURCE: SOMARC (Social Marketing for Change). Reproduced with permission.

> We turned to participatory research. We organized several design groups of female sex workers, brought in a quick-sketch artist, and posed the question — *what will help you convince your clients to use condoms?* **Our** idea was a condom insert. But the women quickly nixed that idea. . . . *"it's too dark, and the men are in a hurry. . . . they're not going to read a condom insert. We need a wall sticker maybe — but it's got to be good looking and realistic."* Hours of working with the women, discussing each facial expression, article of clothing, and background element on the sticker paid off.
>
> Building on segmentation needs we were pleased when the women suggested creating modifications in the stickers for two different kinds of FSWs. In one wall sticker they created the man meets a women at a house and leaves her at the door — in the other, a couple meets on the street, goes to a house, and leaves together. These represent two very different kinds of FSW segments (brothel versus street walker) which the women insisted needed separate visual identities.
>
> The contribution of FSWs to the program continues as we now test where to distribute and place the stickers for maximum effectiveness.

SOURCE: William Smith, Executive Vice-president, Academy for Educational Development, private correspondence, December 1989.

7. The Behaviors to Be Influenced Often Have Invisible Benefits.   Whereas in the private sector, it is usually relatively clear what benefits one is likely to get with a Hilton Hotel room or a new Xerox machine, social marketers are often encouraging behaviors where *nothing happens.* Immunization is supposed to prevent disease "in the future." Individuals with high blood pressure are told it will be lowered if only they take their pills. Women are promised that taking a birth control pill means that a baby will not come. Mothers are told that ORS will prevent dehydration, a relationship many do not comprehend. The trouble is that the consumer has difficulty knowing whether the behavior worked! Often the consumer who agrees to the behavior has the nagging feeling that the same outcome would have occurred if they *hadn't* taken the recommended course of action. It is much harder to market behaviors without visible consequences than behaviors with them.

8. The Behaviors to Be Influenced Often Have Benefits Only to Third Parties. Some behaviors advocated by social marketers have payoffs for third parties such as poor people or society in general and not to the person undertaking the behavior. This is the case, for example, for energy conservation and obedience to speed laws. In these cases, most individuals consider slowing down or turning down the heat to be personal inconveniences, but many will still do so because they feel it is in the society's interests. It is much more difficult to motivate people to take actions where they do not benefit (even invisibly) than when they or their immediate families are not the direct beneficiary.

9. The Behaviors Often Involve Self-rewards.   As noted in the previous chapter, marketers of products and services have major control over the benefits offered their consumers. They can manipulate the qualities of their offerings and change the benefit bundles they provide. However, in social marketing, managers often must try to encourage behaviors like dieting or exercise where the marketer can only hold out promises. It is the consumers' own actions that ultimately generate the benefits. Thus, the nature and quality of those benefits are largely out of the marketer's control and very difficult to manipulate.

10. The Behaviors Often Involve Intangibles That Are Difficult to Portray. Because the consequences of social behavior change often are invisible, long term, self-generated, and/or apply only to others, they are much more difficult to portray in promotional messages. Marketers must be highly creative to develop advertising indicating the benefits to families and the country of family planning or growth monitoring. Because symbols in communications become highly central to success, there is often the risk of sending the wrong signals, as when rural consumers in developing countries are alienated by promotions that seem too "western."

11. Long-Term Changes Are Central. Because many of the proposed behavior changes are highly involving and/or entail changing individuals from negative to positive demand, the process for achieving behavior change can take a very long time. This will be because (1) often very large amounts of basic information will have to be communicated, (2) basic values will have to be changed, and (3) a great many outside opinion leaders and/or support agencies will have to be "brought on board." For example, to create widespread use of oral rehydration therapy (ORT), target consumers must learn that dehydration per se is life-threatening, that some "modern" remedies are better than some folk remedies and can be trusted, and that packaged, branded products are safe and reliable. Simultaneously, physicians, pharmacists, and public health workers must be educated about the problem and given/sold supplies to distribute. Marketers used to shorter-term objectives such as found in consumer packaged goods markets can find the extent of complications and length of time involved in social marketing very frustrating.

12. There Are Fewer Opportunities to Modify Offerings. If businesspeople or consumers want a faster, more flexible computer, Apple will invent a better MacIntosh. If a commercial marketer cannot satisfy a customer with one product, he or she simply creates another. But if women want a diarrhea remedy that stops the diarrhea as well as prevents dehydration, it does not exist. Years of research are needed to develop such a product. The responsiveness of many social marketers to consumer demand is limited by science. Products such as ORS, which meets important public health criteria for effectiveness, must be "marketed" despite inherent disadvantages or obstacles from the consumer's point of view.

13. There Are Severely Limited Budgets. Traditional marketers are used to working with relatively generous budgets to meet a given challenge (although they do not always think so) or to being able to convince superiors of the justice of enlarged budgets and the need to take economic risks to achieve clearly defined goals. Social marketers typically have severely restricted budgets, in part because there is not enough to go around and in part because of an implicit understanding that a project that is too well funded is somehow not being frugal with donated or taxpayers' money. As a consequence, social marketers must spend much time and effort *leveraging* their meager budgets by adding the assistance of distributors, advertising agencies, broadcast or print media, business firms, unions, and so forth to carry out their programs.

14. Social Marketers Need to Work with Those with a Suspicion of Marketing. Social marketers almost always work with those trained in other disciplines. It is not uncommon for such individuals to have a mistrust of marketing and, often, of what they see (negatively) as the "business mentality" in general.

RELATIONSHIP TO OTHER DISCIPLINES

The tools that social marketers use to achieve their ends are adapted from a wide range of other social science disciplines. One way of conceiving social marketing is as *applied social science* in the same sense that engineering may be considered applied physics. Among the many fields from which social marketing adopts its tools, four have been found to be particularly helpful. These are social anthropology, education, mass communications, and behavioral psychology. Each of these disciplines has a specific role to play at different stages of the social marketing process.

Social Anthropology

As suggested throughout this book, the hallmark of a modern social marketing program is that it is fully centered on a clear understanding of the customers it must influence. In most conventional economic transactions, the level of subtlety this understanding must achieve is limited to behaviors that are relatively inconsequential. This is decidedly not the case in social marketing where one often seeks to change very fundamental values, beliefs, and patterns of family and social interaction. The level of understanding that one must achieve to bring these about must be exceptionally deep and discriminating. The concepts and tools of social anthropology are particularly valuable in achieving this more profound level of understanding.

Social anthropologists can help social marketers to anticipate the resistances they will face and to tailor programs as closely as possible to the customs, norms, and values of the culture or subculture they seek to influence.[10] The insights of the trained social anthropologist can also help social marketers in the design of effective programs in other ways by

1   Helping to identify likely "early adopters" of specific new behaviors.
2   Learning how the behavior change can best be constructed to maximize adop-

tion (as when oral rehydration programs in The Gambia were designed around the use of readily available soft drink bottles and bottle caps).

3 Showing what words, phrases, and images are appropriate to describe the behavior change so that its benefits are clearly understood and the change advocated is as non-threatening as possible.

4 Helping to select and train change agents who can be most empathetic and effective in a given "foreign" culture.

Education and Mass Communication

Once the cultural context is understood in depth, the next two tasks facing the social marketer involve (1) creating a supportive climate of values and beliefs that make it "O.K." for *individuals* to change behavior and (2) actually to change the behavior of specific individuals and households in specific ways. These tasks can be seen as overcoming four problems:

1 The new behavior must be seen as socially desirable ("for people like us"); this is *the value-change problem.*

2 The new behavior must be seen as personally desirable ("for our family"); this is *the motivation problem.*

3 The new behavior must be understood; this is *the education problem.*

4 The new behavior must be practiced (i.e., begun and repeated); this is *the behavior modification problem.*

Mass communications and education techniques are particularly relevant to the first three of these problems. Mass communication principles can be used to inculcate new values and show large numbers of target consumers how the new behavior can improve their lives or the lives of their children. Mass media, such as radio and simple posters, can be used to modify the general climate and to explain and legitimize the new behavior. In many developing countries, a major accomplishment of the public advertising campaigns in contraceptive social marketing programs has been to demythologize contraception and to make it "O.K." for couples, teachers, and public figures to talk about it and about individual contraceptive methods. Until this is accomplished, any social marketing efforts devoted to *personal* motivation and behavior change will prove largely fruitless.

Mass communication and education can also be helpful in the motivation phase if marketers choose to focus on a *persuasion* strategy of behavior change. This approach rests upon the assumption that the best (perhaps, only) way to get someone to change behavior in the long run is to convince them that this is a good thing to do. This obviously requires that, for example, mothers (1) understand the role vitamins play in their children's diet or how immunization helps prevent disease (an education problem), (2) agree that the new behavior is something that is good to do (a motivation problem), and (3) know where to go and what to do actually to begin the new practice (another education problem).

The assumption here is that a properly informed consumer will act in his or her (or the child's) best interests.

If the persuasion approach is adopted, mass communication and education concepts can help to

1   Develop memorable themes for promotion campaigns.
2   Choose spokespeople for mass education and advertising campaigns.
3   Discover and employ the best channels of communication (usually in combination) to reach the target audience (see Figure 14-2).
4   Develop curricular materials, including effective audiovisual aids, for classroom and lecture presentations.
5   Develop instructive and motivating presentations for face-to-face "sales" presentations.

Behavioral Analysis

The major alternative to the persuasion approach may be called the *behavioral modification* approach. This approach is based upon the assumption that people act in certain ways because they learn to appreciate the rewards such actions produce. To secure behavior change from this perspective, then, requires that the social marketer understand the behavior-reward systems to be modified and then restructure these systems to bring about the desired new behaviors. Under the behavior modification approach, little attention is paid to convincing people that the new actions are good things. Instead, the focus is on getting people started on the behavior by some means or other and then ensuring effective *reinforcement* of desired behavior. (See also Chapter 18.)[11]

In Honduras, behavioral reinforcement was considered crucial to the success of a tuberculosis treatment program. It was found that many patients were stopping treatment because their families and communities were not supportive and, in fact, treated patients as outcasts. As a result, the social marketing program was designed in part to teach family members about tuberculosis and about their crucial role in encouraging the patient to complete the necessary treatment. At the same time, radio was used to praise tuberculosis patients who had completed their treatments.[12]

Marketing's Coordinating Role

As an eclectic, applied discipline, marketing seeks to employ whatever tools are most appropriate to a given change issue. Social marketers have no vested interest in any one of the four approaches described above. They blend anthropology, education, mass communication, and behavior modification approaches as appropriate, usually shifting both their content and role as the campaign progresses. Social marketers' commitment to market research assures that there is continual, careful monitoring of each program element. Particular attention is paid to making program adjustments, both major and minor, in the relative

FIGURE 14-2

Using Print and Radio in Developing Countries

SOURCE: Academy for Educational Development. Reproduced with permission.

emphasis on persuasion versus behavior modification strategies as the campaign progresses.

CONCLUSIONS AND RECOMMENDATIONS

Social marketing can be extremely effective. For example, a recent review of seven field programs in developing countries shows just how effective it can be in improving child survival:

- In Honduras after two years of broadcasting specific messages, 60 percent of rural women interviewed had used the government's new oral rehydration salts and some 35 percent of all cases had been treated with oral therapy.
- In The Gambia after two years, 70 percent of rural women interviewed had correctly learned how to mix a new sugar, salt, and water rehydration solution, and home treatment of diarrhea rose from 17 percent to 50 percent of cases.
- In Egypt the percentage of women who correctly mixed the government's new oral rehydration solution rose from 25 percent in 1983 to 60 percent in 1984. A study of death registrations in Alexandria suggested that during the diarrheal season, over-all mortality in children under one year dropped by about 30 percent between 1982 and 1984.
- In Bangladesh 1.3 million households were taught to prepare and use oral rehydration solution in a two and one-half-year period. The program evaluation showed that 90 percent of the women interviewed remembered the ORS lessons up to six months after the household visit.
- In Colombia some 800,000 children were immunized during a single three-day massive campaign.
- In Indonesia the Nutrition Communication and Behavior Change Project showed that by 24 months of age, 40 percent of the project infants were better nourished than infants in the comparison group.
- In Swaziland clinic data show that after only three months of a communications campaign, mothers reporting use of ORS made in the home rose from 43 percent to 60 percent.[13]

Unfortunately, as noted at the outset, the prospect of applying generic marketing to social problems is often met with mixed emotions and usually with a certain amount of suspicion by those who must sponsor or carry out such programs. This is partly the result of a misunderstanding of what social marketing is and is not and partly as a result of evaluating it on the basis of how it has been done, not on how it *should* be done. For social marketing to be effective, its practitioners must adhere to a number of important principles. In many cases, this may require major changes in the way organizations think, are structured, and carry out their day-to-day activities.

The major requirements for a sound social marketing program are the following:

1   Those managing and overseeing the marketing program must understand fully and accept deeply the *customer-oriented approach* to marketing. In part, this implies constant vigilance for telltale signs of relapse into a "selling" or "product" orientation.

2 Managers in the social marketing program must have extensive training in modern marketing methods and/or have at their disposal advisory councils or consultants who will input the needed generic marketing know-how.

3 Information systems must be put in place to

  a Provide extensive information on target customers for (i) strategic planning, (ii) pretesting marketing programs and tactics, and (iii) posttesting implemented programs.

  b Track program costs *and* performance over time frequently enough to permit (i) ongoing assessment of overall success or failure and (ii) rapid adjustment of program elements in the face of either poor or demonstrably superior performance.

  c Track competitors' strategies and tactics (where relevant) to permit rapid response to changes in this uncontrollable aspect of the marketplace.

4 Recognition must be constantly given to the need to market to *all* publics including intermediaries, staff, crucial opinion leaders and outside advisors and facilitators (e.g., the media).

5 Every effort must be made to recognize and defuse any "culture conflict" between those with a "pure" service orientation and those with a corporate mentality inside the organization.

6 Finally, while oversight should be minimized to the extent that it improperly interferes with a marketer's legitimate efforts to operate efficiently, effectively, and with appropriate risk taking, a mechanism must be put into place to ensure that the programs are truly *social* marketing, that is, that their long-run objectives are, in fact and in deed, selfless.

SUSTAINABILITY AND INSTITUTIONALIZATION

A large majority of social marketing programs, particularly those in developing countries, are temporary in nature. They are often heavily subsidized by "outside" organizations such as the U.S. Agency for International Development or the World Bank and rely extensively on consulting help from specialists, usually from the United States. As a consequence, both those funding social marketing programs and those who manage them are increasingly concerned about two issues, *sustainability* and *institutionalization*.

Sustainability refers to maintaining the behavior change the social marketers are seeking to influence. It is often *relatively* easy to get a target consumer to begin a behavior change process, such as stopping smoking, wearing a seat belt, or practicing contraception. But, as noted earlier, many of the behaviors to be influenced (like these) are continuing behaviors. It has been estimated that 70 to 80 percent of those who quit smoking go back. As a consequence, marketers have become much more sensitive to approaches that will increase the probability that the changes are sustainable. William Smith of the Academy for Educational Development suggests a number of "slogans" he believes can guide efforts at sustainability.[14] For child survival behavior changes, they are

> *"Make It Rewarding in Their Terms."* Give people something they really want; don't fool yourself about what they "should" want.
> *"Make It Easy to Succeed."* Make everything about it easy—easy to open, easy to find, easy to use, easy to understand.

"Catch People Doing Things Right." Look for ways to reward success. Train health care workers to give mothers a pat on the back.

"Make It Communal." Make it part of the local fabric of life—normal, respectable. Tie it to broader values, the family, and community.

"Keep Pace with the Audience." Audiences change. They often leave us behind. Don't work on awareness when they're already aware and need greater access or new benefits.

"Keep the Safety Net Intact." Your distributors, salesforce, and health educators are your safety net. Don't let them down. Keep them motivated and informed.

"Monitor the Whole Marketing Mix." Sustainability means people want it, but they also must be able to find it, afford it, and use it. All four elements of the marketing mix are needed so they must all be monitored regularly to avoid mistakes.

"Be Prepared for the Long Haul." Make people aware that there are few short cuts to sustained behavior change. Be prepared for long-term commitment.

Institutionalization refers to the task of inducing "local" organizations to take over the social marketing process itself so that, when outside financial and intellectual support is no longer forthcoming, the project neither loses momentum nor expires completely. Thus, in most social marketing programs, conscientious steps are taken to train local staff in critical marketing skills such as strategic planning, marketing research, recruiting and training salesforces, and developing effective advertising. Turnkey systems are developed, handbooks written, and seminars held all to the end of making outsiders superfluous.

Institutionalization is a frustrating process in part because of inertia and in part because of local staff fears of taking on risks and responsibilities. This is particularly the case where the local coordinating agency is a government department. As a consequence, in some programs, alternative efforts are made to induce local private-sector marketers to substitute for the outside skills or to take over some or all of the social marketing activities directly. When it has been feasible, these steps have generally proved highly effective.

William Smith of AED has several slogans to guide the institutionalization process as well.[15] For health care programs, these are

"Fight the Big Battles." Keep a policy perspective. Work for the big changes in staffing, budgets, norms. Don't fight over things that are short term.

"Build Bridges to the Future." Invest in training, curricula, and institutions that train young people. Don't ignore the long-term payoff for short-term victories.

"Show that it works." Demonstrate clear results in terms physicians and public health professionals understand.

"Don't Let the Organization Chart Get in the Way." Work from both ends; build friends and supporters at all levels at the same time.

"Psych Out the Local Communication System." Tie into the real way information moves around an institution. Find out who is listened to and how they communicate, then follow their lead.

"Write the Dictionary Together." Every new movement has a dictionary—a set of key words that helps define it. Write those words with your counterparts—don't impose vocabulary—give them the ownership.

"Keep it Simple." If you can't explain it in a sentence, it's too complicated. Keep the big ideas few, simple, and straightforward.

"Don't Stand Out in the Crowd." Let the program speak for itself. Don't establish a separate identity and garner personal credit.

"Make the Institution a Solid Hero." Publicize their success. Make success credible by giving credentials to the winners. Build a solid basis of seriousness (courses, degrees, titles, budgets) under the visible trappings of success.

"Pay Attention to the Wounded." Every new idea produces a cadre of wounded people who don't agree or understand, or who feel threatened. Don't dismiss them—keep working to persuade the toughest cases, the resisters. Try to understand their point of view.

SUMMARY

Social marketing is one of the fastest-growing sectors of nonprofit marketing. Social marketing is the application of generic marketing to a specific class of problems where the object of the marketer is to change social behavior primarily to benefit the target audience and the general society. Social marketing can seek to influence behavior that is low or high involvement, individual or group, and one time or continuing. Continuing high-involvement behavior of groups or individuals is the most difficult to influence and often requires legal measures to achieve any major, long-term effect.

Good social marketers accord exchange a central role in their planning, are willing to change their offer (or consumer perceptions of it), seek to develop coordinated programs, make extensive use of marketing research, segment their markets, have a "bottom-line" orientation, are committed to planning, and are willing to take reasoned risks. Social marketing differs from generic marketing in that it is subject to public scrutiny and extravagant expectations and often must seek to influence nonexistent or negative demand of nonliterate target audiences. They deal with sensitive, hard-to-research issues, invisible benefits or benefits to third parties that are difficult to portray and that are supposed to lead to long-term change. Social marketers, however, have less freedom to change their offerings, more limited budgets, and need to work with others who are often suspicious of marketing.

Social marketers make use of other disciplines, particularly social anthropology, education and mass communication, and behavioral analysis. Marketing is accorded the coordinating role.

While social marketing can now document a significant number of successes, social marketers have recently turned their attention to the problems of sustaining the behavior they have attempted to influence and of institutionalizing the process of social marketing itself.

QUESTIONS

1. Many target consumers in social marketing are not literate. What restrictions does this place on each element of the marketing mix other than advertising?

2. Table 14-1 suggests that some social behavior changes, such as passage of new laws, are really made at the group level. Is this a useful distinction or is all behavior really influenced at the individual level?

3. How would the marketing strategy for a behavior with negative demand differ from the strategy for one with merely nonexistent demand? Use examples in each case.

4. How can social marketers convince individuals to take actions where the benefits are almost exclusively to third parties? Give three examples.

5. Assuming that almost all the marketing know-how for a social marketing program in a developing country is provided by foreign consultants. Assume, further, that the country presently implements much of the social marketing program through its Ministry of Health with no help from the private sector. How would you go about setting priorities for institutionalizing the foreign know-how within the country?

NOTES

1. Material in this section is drawn from Alan R. Andreasen, "Social Marketing and Child Survival," working paper, Academy for Educational Development, Washington, D.C., 1989.

2. For a discussion of ethical issues posed by social marketing, see Gene R. Laszniak, Robert F. Lusch, and Patrick Murphy, "Social Marketing: Its Ethical Dimensions," *Journal of Marketing*, Spring 1979, pp. 29–36. See also Elizabeth C. Hirschman, "Marketing as an Agent of Change in Subsistence Cultures: Some Dysfunctional Consumption Consequences," in Richard J. Lutz, ed., *Advances in Consumer Research*, Vol. 13 (Provo, Utah: Association for Consumer Research, 1986), pp. 99–104.

3. Charles T. Clotfelter and Philip J. Cook, "The Unseemly 'Hard Sell' of Lotteries," *The New York Times*, August 20, 1987, p. 21.

4. Raymond S. Alexander and Simon Podair, "Educating New York City Residents to Benefits of Medicaid," *Public Health Reports*, September 1969, pp. 767–772.

5. "Wrong Publicity May Push Drug Use: UN Chief," *Chicago Sun-Times*, May 8, 1972, p. 30.

6. See "Drug Ed a Bummer," *Behavior Today*, November 13, 1972, p. 2.

7. See Michael L. Ray, Scott Ward, and Gerald Lesser, *Experimentation to Improve Pretesting of Drug Abuse Education and Information Campaigns: A Summary* (Cambridge, Mass.: Marketing Science Institute, September 1973).

8. Mark R. Rasmuson, Renata E. Seidel, William A. Smith, and Elizabeth Mills Booth, *Communication for Child Survival* (Washington, D.C.: Academy for Educational Development, June 1988).

9. N. Ferencic, "Guidelines for Carrying Out In-Depth Interviews about Health in Developing Countries," Working Paper #107, Annenberg School of Communications, University of Pennsylvania, 1989.

10. See, for example, *Anthropological Perspectives on AIDS in Africa: Priorities for Intervention and Research* (Research Triangle Park, N.C.: AIDSTECH Project, January 1988), and Claire Monod Cassidy, Robert W. Porter, and Douglas Feldman, "Ethnographic Survey of Nonpenetrative Sexual Activity," working paper, AIDSCOM Project, Academy for Educational Development, 1989.

11. Albert Bandura, *Principles of Behavior Modification* (New York: Holt, Rinehart, and Winston, 1969). Also B. Springer, T. Brown, and P.K. Duncan, "Current Measurement in Applied Behavioral Analysis," *The Behavior Analyst*, Vol. 4 (1981), pp. 19–31.

12. Carl Kendall, Dennis Foote, and Reynaldo Martorell, "Anthropology, Communications, and Health: The Mass Media and Health Practices Program in Honduras," *Human Organization*, Vol. 42, no. 4 (Winter 1983), pp. 353–360.

13. HealthCom, *A Consumer Strategy for Health, Nutrition, and Population* (Washington, D.C.: Academy for Educational Development, n.d.).

14. *Communication and Marketing for Child Survival* (Washington, D.C.: Academy for Educational Development, August 8, 1989), p. 5.

15. Ibid.

15

Developing and Launching New Offerings

Like many other local councils of the Boy Scouts of America, the Western Los Angeles County Council is faced with a rapidly changing target population. Los Angeles is undergoing dramatic shifts in its racial and ethnic composition. Like the rest of America, it is also subject to major changes in family structures and in the working habits of adult Americans. These changes have put pressures on the Boy Scouts to come up with innovative programs to reach out to new and untapped groups.

In-school Scouting is one such innovative program. It was designed by the Boy Scouts of America and approved by the Los Angeles Unified School District to provide the benefits of scouting to "hard-to-serve" youth. Scout meetings are held in the classroom and focus on scouting activities agreed to by the Scouting Leader and the local teacher and principal. Among the programs themes promoted in 1989 were: career awareness; community awareness; citizenship, law, and justice; environment and ecology; and communications.

The In-school Scouting Program began in 1983 serving 2,617 youths. By 1989, membership had almost doubled to an estimated 5,000 cubs and scouts. This success led the Western Los Angeles County Council to expand the program with three new offerings:

1 The Afterschool Program is designed to involve boys in activities out-of-doors to earn scouting advancement.
2 The Handicap Program is for special children who in the past have not had the chance to benefit from scouting or to attend scouting camps.
3 The Latchkey Program is designed as a constructive and challenging alternative

for children who would otherwise have to remain at home or on the streets while their parents are working.

All three new programs both advance the Boy Scouts' marketing objectives and meet real community needs.

As we have indicated throughout this volume, the market environment facing nonprofits in the 1990s is one marked by extremely aggressive competition in a large number of sectors, including health care, charitable contributions, and education. This increased competition means that nonprofits continually run the risk that their existing offer mix will become obsolete—or at least suboptimal. For a vibrant organization to remain on top of its market, it must produce a continuing stream of new offerings simply to "stay in place." Producing such new offerings is even more critical if the organization wishes to grow.

New offerings, of course, can come about by chance insight, the "eureka" of discovery. But a well-managed organization cannot survive merely on chance or insight. New offerings must *continually* be generated. This requires that a *system* be put in place for developing and launching new offerings. This is the focus of this chapter. We shall describe how one systematically goes about generating, evaluating, and bringing to market new ideas and then distributes, promotes, and (sometimes) modifies them through the introductory and growth phases of their offer life cycles.

OFFER DEVELOPMENT— A PROBLEM OF STRATEGIC PLANNING

The choice of offer development strategies is one of the most important that any manager faces. What an organization offers very much determines what the organization actually is and how it is seen by its customers, competitors, staff, volunteers, and the general public. Choices of new offerings will significantly affect the future of every organization and, therefore, must be carefully thought through and not left to chance or personal preferences.

The nonprofit organization has available to it nine basic growth strategies (see Table 15-1). These strategies differ by the extent to which the marketer wishes to emphasize development of markets or offerings. First, the organization can decide to focus on its existing offerings and existing markets (cell 1). For this strategy, it can choose among three substrategies. It can seek to grow by more actively penetrating its existing market either through market expansion or through inducing patronage-switching by those already in the market. It can decide not to grow significantly, but become more efficient at marketing to its present clients. Or it can choose to maintain the status quo. While it may seem

Table 15-1

OFFER STRATEGY OPTIONS FOR NONPROFIT ORGANIZATIONS

	Existing Offerings	*New Offerings:* *Similar*	*New Offerings:* *Dissimilar*

Existing markets	1. a. Market penetration
	    b. Cost reduction
	    c. Share maintenance
		4. Offer extension	7. Offer development

New markets: Similar	2. Market extension	5. Continuous diversification	8. Offer diversification
New markets: Dissimilar	3. Market development	6. Market diversification	9. Radical diversification

that neither of the last two strategic postures would appeal to many organizations, there are two situations in which they make sense:

- *Declining markets.* If the market demand is declining, as in the need for funding for polio research and treatment, the marketer might want to treat the program as a "cash cow," pull out resources, or become more efficient, thus producing a surplus to be used elsewhere.
- *New competition.* A market leader always faces possible challenges from new competitors. Thus, a major hospital may consider it a great success if it can simply maintain its present level of emergency room volume after a new emergency care center enters the market.

The second posture the organization can take is to seek out new markets for its existing offerings (cells 2 and 3). Firms can add market segments that are similar to their present markets, as when contraceptive social marketers seek to take programs that worked in Bangladesh and introduce them in nearby countries like India or Nepal (cell 2, market extension). More daring and therefore more challenging would be an attempt to adapt contraceptive programs to more dissimilar markets such as West or East Africa, Tibet, or aboriginal tribes in New Guinea (cell 3, market development).

Carrying out these strategies does not require major changes in the organization's offerings. Rather, it requires more attention to other marketing mix variables like advertising, distribution channels, personal selling, and price and cost management. It can also involve minor changes in the offer such as packaging changes, redesign of features, and so on.

In this chapter, our attention turns to the six remaining strategies suggested in Table 15–1 that involve new offerings. The nonprofit organization can add new offerings that are relatively similar or relatively dissimilar to their present offerings. In either case, they can focus on existing markets (cells 4 and 7), similar new markets (cells 5 and 8), or dissimilar new markets (cells 6 and 9). Clearly, the riskiest stance of all is cell 9, where entirely new offerings (especially offerings new to the world) are brought to radically different markets. Getting very young children to learn to read by speaking into a voice-reading computer would be an example of such a venture. A system of this type has been explored by Educational Development Associates of Newton, Massachusetts.

One organization that has explored offerings in all six of the new offering cells in Table 15–1 is Population Development Associates (PDA), Thailand's major contraceptive social marketing organization:

1 *Offer Extension (cell 4).* PDA has added new *types* of contraceptives (that is, new oral pill formulations) to serve its existing customer markets.
2 *Offer Development (cell 7).* It has made syringes, aspirin, and other noncontraceptive products available to villagers in the homes of its village contraceptive distributors and change agents.
3 *Continuous Diversification (cell 5).* PDA has added noncontraceptive health care services in its family planning clinics, to which any person can come.
4 *Offer Diversification (cell 8).* PDA began helping households in the villages it serves with procedures and funding for building much needed water tanks for storing rain water.
5 *Market Diversification (cell 6).* PDA has developed a program for providing health tests in schools and hospitals, using excess capacity among its full-time medical staff.
6 *Radical Diversification (cell 9).* PDA has taken advantage of serendipitous circumstances and has attempted to market Czechoslovakian tractors through its rural field offices and to manage a small tourist resort in a remote province of Thailand.

These new ventures are the result of the natural enthusiasm of young organizations still in their growth phase. The remainder of this chapter will concern itself with the question of how a *mature* nonprofit organization ought to develop new offerings.

Every nonprofit sector contains organizations that can be called "innovators." However, a will to innovate is not enough. Many organizations launch new services that fail.

A 300-bed hospital in southern Illinois got the bright idea of establishing an Adult Day Care Program as a solution to its underutilized space. It designed a whole floor to serve senior citizens who required personal care and services in an ambulatory setting during the day, but who would return home each evening. The cost was $16 a day to the patient's family, and transportation was to be provided or paid for by the patient's family. About the only research that was done on this concept was to note that a lot of elderly people lived within a 3-mile radius. The Adult Day Care Center was opened with a capacity to handle 30 patients. Only 2 signed up!

There are many reasons why this and similar new programs can fail:

1 A top administrator pushes the idea through in spite of the lack of supporting evidence.
2 There are poor organizational systems for evaluating and implementing ideas

for new offerings (poor criteria, poor procedures, poor coordination of departments).

3 There is poor market size measurement, forecasting, and market research.
4 There is poor marketing planning, that is, poor positioning, poor segmentation, underbudgeting, and overpricing.
5 The distinctiveness of the offer or of consumer benefits is not sufficiently clear.
6 The offer is poorly designed.
7 Development costs are unexpectedly high.
8 The competitive response is unexpectedly intense.
9 Promotion is inadequate.

In the sections to follow, we shall describe processes and tools to overcome these problems.

A PROCESS FOR DEVELOPING NEW OFFERINGS

New offerings should not be left to whim or chance. An organization that wishes to be entrepreneurial must set up systems that will develop and launch successful new offerings. There is an effective methodology for introducing new offerings which, while it does not guarantee success, usually raises the probability of success. Figure 15–1 shows the overall steps involved in new product development. These steps are described in the following sections.

Idea Generation

Organizations differ in their need for new ideas. Some organizations are quite busy carrying out their current activities and do not need new things to do. A social security office, for example, is mandated to carry out certain procedures and is not interested, or even legally able, to consider undertaking new ventures not related to its main business. Other organizations need one or two big new

FIGURE 15-1

Major Stages in New-Product Development

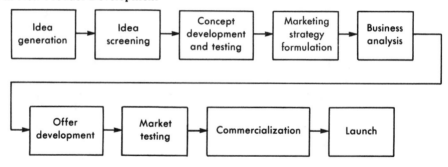

ideas because their main business is taking a turn for the worse. In the early 1970s, the March of Dimes had to come up with an entirely new focus when polio was effectively controlled. Still other organizations need several new ideas simply to keep up with the changing environment. Colleges, for example, need to consider new courses and programs to meet the changing interests of the public. Similarly, the YMCA needs to develop new programs as interest in some of its existing programs fades.

The idea generation stage is most relevant to organizations that need one or more ideas to maintain or expand their services. Indeed, it is our position that, given the high failure rate of many new ideas, the more ideas an organization generates—and the more diverse they are—the more chance there will be of finding *successful* ideas. Ideas can occur spontaneously from the following "natural" sources:

- Personal inspiration of one or more members of the organization.
- Serendipitous stimuli from the environment—for example, learning of a new idea from a competitor or in discussion with nonprofit managers from other parts of the country or the world.
- Client requests for new offerings or modification of existing offerings.

Such sources have two major shortcomings. First, relying on them requires a chance combination of an idea appearing *and* management's alertness in recognizing it. Reliance on these approaches may be acceptable for a fledgling nonprofit with a limited budget. However, they are definitely not the type of approaches a mature nonprofit organization ought to adopt. These casual approaches have a second problem. As noted by Crompton: "There is a great deal of evidence which suggests that many efforts to produce new programs which meet client needs are incestuous. That is, there is a tendency to reach for prior experiences, prior approaches, or moderate distortions of old answers, as opposed to really searching for new ideas. We become victimized by habit."[1]

If an organization is to be both systematic and creative in its idea generation, four steps must be taken:

1 A *commitment* must be made routinely and formally to seek new ideas.
2 *Responsibility* for this task must be specifically assigned to someone or some group.
3 A *procedure* must be put in place for *systematically* seeking new ideas.
4 The procedure must contain a *creative* component if truly new ideas are sought.

Procedures for Gathering New Ideas.　Establishing an idea generation *procedure* involves the organization in outlining all possible sources for new ideas and then a strategy for generating or collecting ideas routinely from each source. Major sources and procedures for mining them are listed here:

1 *Similar organizations*
   a A jointly funded *clearinghouse* could be established to share new ideas.

    b   Routine visits or telephone conversations with similar organizations on *specific dates* (for example, the first week of every February and every July) should be scheduled.

2 *Competitors*

    a   If the competitor has publicly traded stock, a few shares should be purchased to acquire regular reports that may indicate their development ideas.

    b   If board meetings are open to the public, someone should be assigned to attend them.

3 *Journals, newspapers, magazines*

    a   Potential sources of ideas should be identified, subscriptions acquired, and someone (or several people) assigned to peruse these sources routinely.

    b   A clipping service can be subscribed to.

    c   A librarian can be hired and assigned these tasks.

    d   A computer-based information retrieval system can be subscribed to.

4 *Conferences, trade shows, lectures*

    a   People should be routinely assigned to attend important gatherings to collect ideas and useful literature.

5 *Customers and middlemen*

    a   The organization should *solicit* final customers and distributors for their ideas rather than wait until they spontaneously offer them. Many organizations obtain most of their best new ideas by soliciting or actively listening to customers.[2]

6 *Employees and staff*

    a   The organization should *solicit* employees for suggestions and reward them monetarily or in some other way when these ideas are fruitful.

Specific dates should be set for carrying out each of the above information-gathering techniques. Further, a formal reporting and assessment mechanism should be developed to assure that each idea will be formally considered. Finally, the system should be *unblocked*. Lower-level managers should not be able to sabotage the idea generation process by labeling ideas as "too outrageous" or "not really appropriate for us right now." Such judgments must be top management's.

One technique for improving the likelihood that new ideas will emerge is to assign responsibilities to someone who might be called an *idea manager*.[3] The idea manager would serve as a receiving station for the good ideas spotted by others. He or she would do a preliminary analysis and evaluation of the ideas that flow in and make an effort to identify the really good ones, those that help the target customers and the organization. Finally, the idea manager would shepherd new ideas through the organization and serve as their champion.

The idea manager function *should be assigned to someone who has some power and stature in the organization.* Two good candidates are the managers of strategic planning and marketing. Both managers must produce new ideas that will ensure a future for their institution. It is essential, however, that the nonprofit organization's president "buy" the idea of assigning idea management to one of these people.

Procedures for Stimulating Creativity.   The above techniques involve either routinely scanning or prodding various systems for ideas. This will yield a high proportion of at least modest ideas or extensions of existing approaches. If an organization seeks "breakthrough-quality" ideas, it can apply a number of proven techniques. Some techniques can be used by individuals; most are best done in groups where members can spark ideas off each other.[4]

Attribute Listing.   Here, the major attributes of the product, service or idea are listed and then each attribute is scrutinized to see if it can be adapted, minified, magnified, substituted, rearranged, reversed, or combined. The traditional approach to borrowing a book from a library, for example, involves (1) going to the library, (2) looking up the book in the card catalogue, (3) going to the shelf to obtain the book, (4) taking it to a central counter, (5) having the book stamped and the borrowing details recorded, (6) taking the book home, and (7) bringing it back to the library when the borrower is finished. The idea-generating process would involve trying to think of new ways to accomplish each of the seven steps to produce greater "sales." Step 1, for example, could be done by using a telephone or the mail, by using a computer terminal, by bringing the "library" to the borrower's home or neighborhood in a mobile van, by hiring a courier to bring the book for a fee, or by asking the librarian to copy the necessary pages and mail them to the borrower. Then one would proceed to steps 2 and 3, imagining innovative ways to look up and retrieve the book, including voice-activated computer systems and the use of automatic conveyor belts, or even robots.[5]

Forced Relationships.   Here, several objects or elements are listed and each is considered in relation to the other. Thus, a library's list might include children's storytelling hours, card catalogues, and reference books. An analysis of possible relationships might suggest stories to be told to children to teach them indirectly what reference books are and how the library's catalogue can help find them.

Problem Analysis.   Here consumers are asked about problems they encounter in making a particular exchange. Each problem can be the source of new ideas. Library patrons, for example, could express frustration at sometimes having to wait a long time to check out a book. The librarian might think of installing some form of amusement—for example, a computer game, an interesting exhibit, or closed-circuit television—to distract patrons while waiting.

Brainstorming.   Probably the best known technique for forcing creativity, brainstorming, involves putting six to eight people, preferably of diverse backgrounds, together in a room and giving them a very broad problem mandate. They are told (1) to come up with as many solutions as possible; (2) that the wilder the solutions, the better; and (3) that nobody is to evaluate—most particularly, criticize—*any idea at this stage.* The objective is to place the participants in a nonthreatening environment where they can let their imaginations soar as they use each other's input to suggest new and (one hopes) increasingly creative solutions. William J.J. Gordon suggests that it is sometimes useful to make the topic as broad as possible, such as, "How can the library match people and ideas?" and only later in the session, as in focus groups, narrow it to specific issues, such as, "How can a library use its limited budget to have the most reference material available for the most users?"[6]

Idea Screening

Once the idea-generating system has accumulated a significant array of ideas, some of them patently outlandish, some attempt must be made to winnow the set to the most promising ideas. The purpose of idea screening is to take a preliminary look at the new ideas and eliminate those that do not warrant further attention. There is some chance that screening might result in an excellent idea being prematurely dropped (a drop error). What might be worse, however, is accepting a bad idea for further development (a go error) as a result of not screening. Each idea that is developed takes substantial management time and money. The purpose of screening is, therefore, to eliminate all but the most promising ideas.

As an example, in the early 1970s, De Paul University was looking for ideas for new programs to expand its educational services in the greater Chicago area. Among the new program ideas were (1) a new program of women's studies, (2) a new program of black studies, (3) a school of dentistry, (4) a new adult degree program, and (5) a weekend executive master's degree program in business. De Paul did not have the resources to launch more than one of these new programs, and so it needed a way to identify the most attractive program.

Several steps are necessary to ensure effective idea screening for an organization like De Paul:

1 A formal screening committee should be established to evaluate new ideas. The committee should include representatives of each key functional department that has expertise that bears on one or more of the proposed undertakings.
2 Regular meetings should be scheduled to evaluate new ideas.
3 Criteria should be developed against which the ideas are to be evaluated. The criteria would be consistently applied over many evaluation sessions. Examples of such criteria include the following:
    a Size of potential target audience
    b Size of financial investment necessary
    c Probable demand on management's time and energy
    d Newness of the idea to the target audience and organization
    e Consequences for the organization's desired public image
    f Extent of probable competition
    g Likelihood of outside funding assistance
    h "Downside" consequences if venture fails.
4 Weights for the criteria should be developed prior to *each* evaluation session. These weights should be set by top management since they will directly affect

where the organization wishes to go in the future. Giving a heavy weight to "newness of idea to the organization" (a negative trait), for example, inevitably means that the organization will accept more ideas nearer to its present offerings. Alternatively, giving a low weight to this factor implies that the organization is more likely to undertake relatively bold innovations.

5 Prior to the committee evaluation meeting, one or more staff members should prepare briefs on each idea as a basis for group discussion. Each brief should present data that are relevant to each of the major criteria.

6 The group should meet and discuss each idea. Afterwards, they should rate each idea either individually or collectively on each criterion. (A form should be devised for this purpose.) Each evaluator (or the group as a whole) should also indicate how confident he or she is of the rating on each criterion.

7 A weighted value rating for each new idea should be computed along with a weighted certainty rating.

8 Candidate ideas should then be arranged by value and certainty ratings, as illustrated in Figure 15–2.

9 The best ideas should be moved on to the next stage. These choices will involve management trade-offs between value and certainty ratings. These trade-offs are shown by the F equivalence curves in Figure 15–2. Thus F_1 shows that management feels that a new venture with a value rating of 50 and a certainty rating of 25 is just as acceptable as an idea with a value rating of 25 and a certainty rating of 50. Management would then decide how many projects it would fund by using F_1, F_2, and so on, as the feasible frontier. If it chose F_5, for example, management would only consider the adult degree program; if it chose the more generous frontier F_3, it would also consider the executive MBA and the school of dentistry.[7]

FIGURE 15-2

Hypothetical Array of New Programs for De Paul University

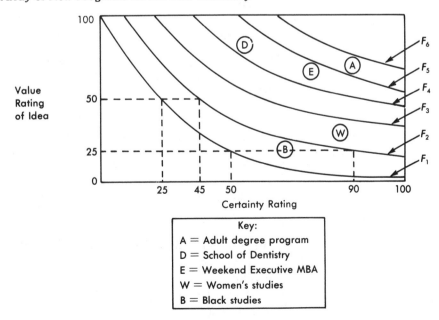

Concept Development and Testing

Those ideas that survive screening must undergo further development into full concepts. It is important to distinguish between an idea, a concept, and an image. An *idea* is something the organization can see itself offering to the market. The idea must be developed into a *concept* that is an elaborated version of the idea expressed in meaningful consumer terms. An *image* is the particular picture that consumers acquire of an actual or potential innovation.

Concept Development.   As a result of screening the various new program ideas, De Paul University decided the best one was a new adult degree program.[8] This is an offer *idea*. De Paul's task was to turn this idea into an appealing concept. Every idea can be turned into several concepts, not all of them equally attractive. Among the concepts that might be created around this idea are

- Concept 1. An evening program with a liberal arts orientation, mostly required courses, and no credit for past experience.
- Concept 2. An evening program with a career development orientation, much latitude in the courses that could be taken, and credit for past experience.
- Concept 3. An evening program with a general education orientation for people over 50 years of age who want a bachelor's degree.

Clearly, one idea can give rise to a number of alternative concepts.

Concept Testing.   Concept testing calls for gathering the reactions of target consumers to each concept. Each concept should be presented in written form in enough detail to allow the respondent to understand it and express his or her level of interest. Here is an example of concept 2 in more elaborate form:

> An evening program, called the School for New Learning, with a career development orientation and much latitude in the courses that can be taken. The program would be open to persons over 24 years of age, lead to a bachelor's degree, give course credit for past experiences and skills that the individual has acquired, give only pass-fail grades, and involve a "learning contract" between the student and the school.

Target consumers are identified and interviewed about their reactions to this concept. One approach is to use questions like those in Table 15–2. The last question in Table 15–2, for example, assesses the consumer's *intention to act* and usually reads: "Would you definitely, probably, probably not, definitely not enroll in this program?" Suppose that 10 percent of the target consumers said "definitely will enroll" and another 5 percent said "probably will enroll." De Paul would apply these percentages (or slightly lower ones) to the corresponding size of the target market to estimate whether the estimated number of enrollees would be sufficient. Even then, the estimate is at best tentative because people often do not carry out their stated intentions. Nevertheless, by ranking the alternative concepts with target consumers in this way, De Paul would learn which concept has the best market potential.

Table 15-2

MAJOR QUESTIONS IN A CONCEPT TEST FOR A NEW
EDUCATIONAL PROGRAM

1. Is the concept of this adult degree evening program with its various features clear to you?
2. What do you see as reasons why you might enroll in this program?
3. What expectations would you have about the program's quality?
4. Does this program meet a real need of yours?
5. What improvements can you suggest in various features of this program?
6. Who would be involved in your decision about whether to enroll in this program?
7. How do you feel about the tuition cost of this program?
8. What competitive programs come to mind and which appeal to you the most?
9. Would you enroll in this program?

An alternative approach would involve the technique of conjoint analysis described in Chapter 4. Suppose De Paul identified key dimensions of the program offer and levels of each as follows:

1 Orientation: (a) liberal arts, (b) general education, (c) career development
2 Credit for past experience: (a) yes, (b) no
3 Student body: (a) mostly under 35, (b) mostly 35 to 50, (c) mostly over 50
4 Cost per semester: (a) $800, (b) $950, (c) $1,200
5 Nightly attendance per week: (a) 4-5 times, (b) 2-3 times, (c) once.

The target audience could then be offered combinations of these dimensions described in some detail as a large number of potential program offerings (that is, concepts) and asked to rank them. This technique would then not only suggest which alternative is rated highest overall, but would indicate the implicit weights the target audience was assigning to each dimension.

Marketing Strategy Formulation

Once a concept has been chosen, the organization should develop a preliminary outline of the marketing strategy it would use to introduce the new program to the target audience. This is necessary so that the full revenue and cost implications of the new program can be evaluated in the next stage of business analysis.

The core marketing strategy should be spelled out in a statement consisting of three parts. The first part describes the size, structure, and behavior of the target market, the intended positioning of the new offering in this market, and the volume and impact goals for the first few years. For De Paul, this might be as follows:

The target market is adults over age 24 living in the greater Chicago area who have never obtained a bachelor's degree but have the skills and motivation to seek one. This program will be differentiated from other programs by offering course credit for relevant past experience, as well as in its career development emphasis. The school will seek a first-year enrollment of 60 students with a net loss not to exceed $100,000. The second year will aim for an enrollment of 100 persons and a net income of at least $20,000.

The second part of the marketing strategy statement outlines the offering's intended price (if any), distribution strategy, and marketing budget for the first year.

> The new program will be offered at the downtown location of De Paul University. All courses will take place once a week in the evening from 6:00 to 9:00 P.M. Tuition will be $500 per course. The first year's promotion budget will be $80,000, $50,000 of which will be spent on advertising materials and media and the remainder on personal contact activities. Another $10,000 will be spent on marketing research to analyze and monitor the market.

The third part of the marketing strategy statement describes the intended long-run goals and marketing mix strategy over time:

> The university ultimately hopes to achieve a steady enrollment of 400 students in this degree program. When it is built up to this level, a permanent administration will be appointed. Tuition will be raised each year in line with the rate of inflation. The promotion budget will stay at a steady level of $50,000. Marketing research will be budgeted at $10,000 annually. The long-run target income level for this program is $100,000 a year, and the money will be used to support other programs that are not self-paying.

Business Analysis

As soon as a satisfactory offer concept and marketing strategy have been developed, the organization is in a position to do a hardheaded business analysis of the attractiveness of the proposal. De Paul, for example, must estimate the possible revenues and costs of the program for different possible enrollment levels. *Break-even analysis* is the most frequently used tool in this connection. Suppose De Paul learns that it needs an enrollment of 260 students to break even. If De Paul manages to attract more than 260 students, this program will produce a net income that could be used to support other programs; if there is a student shortfall, De Paul will lose money on this new program.

Offer Development

If the organization is satisfied that the concept is financially viable, it can begin giving the program concept concrete form. The person in charge of the concept can begin to develop brochures, schedules, ads, sales plans, and other materials to implement the program. Each of the developed materials should be *consumer tested* before being printed and issued. A sample of prospects in the target audience, for example, might be asked to respond to a mock-up of the brochure describing the new program. This usually results in very valuable suggestions leading to an improved brochure.

Market Testing

When the organization is satisfied with the initial materials and schedules, it can set up a market test to see if the concept is really going to be successful. Market testing is the stage at which the offer and marketing program are introduced into an authentic consumer setting to learn how many consumers are really interested in the program. Thus, De Paul University might decide to mail 10,000 brochures to strong prospects in the Chicago area during the month of April to see whether at least 30 students can be attracted. If more than 30 students sign up, the market test will be regarded as successful and full-scale promotion can be launched. Otherwise the program can be reformulated or dropped.

Test markets are the ultimate form of testing the target market's reaction to a new product. The organization can use two or more sites to measure the new program's viability without installing it wholesale throughout the system. The market test can serve an important second function—determining which of several alternative marketing strategies is best. Suppose that the State University of New York (SUNY) was considering the same new program as De Paul. SUNY consists of 64 campuses, not just one campus. SUNY could develop the concept and test it at one of the campuses to see how well it works, or it could test it at several campuses. One campus could emphasize direct mail to alumni, a second could purchase a mailing list of nonalumni who might be interested, a third could use primarily local newspaper ads, and a fourth could advertise in regional editions of national magazines like *Time* or *Newsweek.* As a result, SUNY could develop valuable insights into the cost effectiveness of different promotional approaches. If the new program proved successful in one or all of the test markets, it could then be launched at other campuses where appropriate.

Commercialization

Commercialization is the set of activities undertaken following the test market's "go" recommendation to actually bring the new offering to market. The first step is to make four crucial decisions about the launch (although not all four will apply in every case).

1   *When* to launch. Factors to consider are (a) whether there is a need to first phase out an old program (for example, use up existing supplies of a product), (b) whether there is a seasonal peak time for introducing the item (for example, a new museum for children at the start of summer or a drunk-driving program just before the Christmas holidays, (c) whether further work on the offer could profitably be carried out, and (d) whether there is any risk that important rivals will reach the market first (or otherwise compromise favorable launch circumstances).

2 *Where* to launch. If the offer is potentially to be marketed in a wide geographic area, the organization must decide whether to tackle the whole market at once or to start slowly, rolling out the offer on a market-by-market basis. A social service program, for example, could be aimed at the entire city or state or tried out neighborhood by neighborhood. The "whole market" approach has the advantages of scale economies, of preempting competitors, and of achieving significant advertising and public relations impact. It does, however, assume that the program has pretty well been finalized and that its chances of ultimate success are excellent. The advantages of the roll-out introduction, which can well compensate for its slower speed and greater total cost, are that (a) one can learn as one goes, and (b) if optimistic projections are not realized, the project can be aborted or "sent back to the drawing boards" at lower economic cost and with less embarrassment to the organization.

3 *To whom* to aim the launch. Even in a local roll-out, the program manager must decide whether to aim at all eventual consumers or to focus at first on (a) those most likely to respond to the offer, (b) those most likely to have an important leadership role for others, or (c) both of these groups.

4 *How* to launch. Tactical decisions must be made about how to achieve the maximum impact at launch date and thereafter. Included are decisions about teaser ads, degree of secrecy, amount and type of media coverage, and so on.

A second step in the commercialization process is to assign responsibility for the launch and introductory period to some individual or group. Here, management must decide whether to have a separate venture management group (or individual) for the new offer, a separate new venture *department* to launch *all* new ventures, or to fold the new venture in with the responsibilities of an existing individual or sales department.

The last step is to set up a formal scheduling procedure to ensure that all the needed tasks are (1) done in the right order, (2) done on schedule, and (3) done at the least possible cost. There are a number of valuable scheduling tools, such as PERT, CPM, and so on, for this task.[9] Most of them provide (1) directions for individuals who must accomplish each step, (2) a forecast of probable launch dates, (3) the critical series of steps (called *the critical path*) whose delay will mean postponing the launch date, (4) a monitoring tool with checkpoints to ensure that the process is on schedule, and (5) a decision-making capability that would permit the launch manager to decide which activities along the critical path to speed up if the project falls behind schedule. An example of a planning system for the introduction of two new contraceptive products in Jamaica is given in Figure 15–3.

LAUNCHING THE NEW OFFERING

Once an offering has passed through the commercialization stage of the development process described in the previous chapter, it must be launched and managed carefully. The performance of a new offering launched into the marketplace typically follows an S-shaped pattern over a period known as the *offer*

FIGURE 15-3

Flow Chart for Introduction of Low-Dose Oral and Ultra-Thin Condom Jamaica Family Planning Project, September 26, 1983

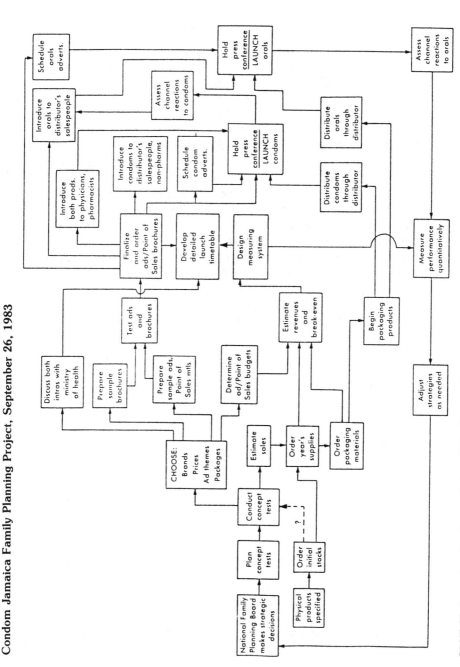

SOURCE: Reproduced with permission of The Futures Group.

life cycle (OLC) (Figure 15–4). The S-shaped curve is marked by the following four stages:

1 *Introduction* is a period of slow growth as the offering is introduced in the market.
2 *Growth* is a period of rapid market acceptance.
3 *Maturity* is a period of slowdown in growth because the offering has achieved acceptance by most of the potential buyers.
4 *Decline* is the period when performance shows a strong downward drift.

The offer life cycle concept can be defined further according to whether it describes an offer *class* (mental health service), an offer *form* (psychoanalysis), or a *brand* (Menninger Clinic). The OLC concept has a different degree of applicability in each case. Offer classes have the longest life cycles. The performance of many offer classes can be expected to continue in the mature stage for an indefinite duration. Thus, "mental health service" began centuries ago with organized religion and can be expected to continue in the mature state for an indefinite duration. Offer forms, on the other hand, tend to exhibit more standard OLC histories than offer classes. Thus, mental health services are dispensed in such forms as psychoanalysis, bioenergetics, group therapy, and so on, some of which are beginning to show signs of maturity, while others, such as "rolfing," may well be in their decline stage. As for brands, they are the most likely to have finite histories. Thus, the Menninger Clinic is a well-known

FIGURE 15-4

Typical S-Shaped Offer Life Cycle

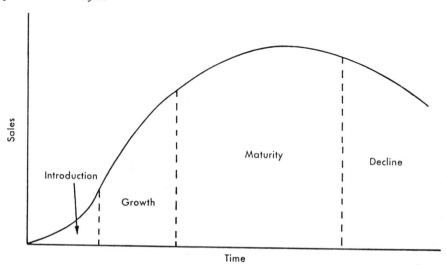

psychoanalytically oriented clinic that had a period of rapid growth and is now mature. It will pass out of existence eventually, like most brands and institutions.

Not all offerings exhibit an S-shaped life cycle. Three other common patterns are

1 *Scalloped pattern.* (Figure 15–5A.) In this case, the offer during the mature stage suddenly breaks into a new life cycle. The new life is triggered by modifications, new uses, new users, changing tastes, or other factors. The market for psychotherapy, for example, reached maturity at one point, and then the emergence of group therapy gave it a whole new market. At the brand level, interest in the March of Dimes was waning until the organization shifted its focus to birth defects.

2 *Cyclical pattern.* (Figure 15–5B.) The performance of some offerings shows a cyclical pattern. Engineering schools, for example, go through alternating periods of high enrollment and low enrollment, reflecting changes in demand and supply in the marketplace. Preferences for political parties also seem to follow this pattern. The decline stage is not a time to eliminate the offer, but to maintain as much of it as possible, waiting for the next up cycle.

3 *Fad pattern.* (Figure 15–5C.) Here, a new offer comes on the market, attracts quick attention, is adopted with great zeal, peaks early, and declines rapidly. The acceptance cycle is short and the offer tends to attract only a limited following of people who are looking for excitement or diversion. Some art and therapy forms exhibit the pattern of a fad.

While the fact that offers have life cycles may at first seem like just common sense, it turns out to be a very useful strategic planning device because it alerts management to the fact that they need to adjust the focus of their marketing thinking depending on the OLC stage they currently are in. The next part of this chapter describes marketing strategies for the introduction and growth stages.

FIGURE 15-5

Three Anomalous Product Life Cycle Patterns

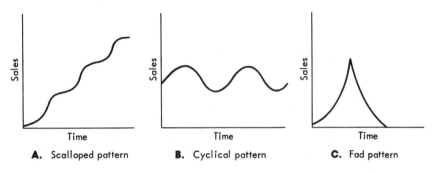

A. Scalloped pattern   B. Cyclical pattern   C. Fad pattern

FIGURE 15-6

Trial and Repeat Behavior Over the Offer Life Cycle

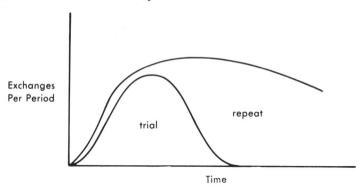

INTRODUCTION AND GROWTH STAGES

One way to characterize the changes sought by all marketers is to distinguish between first-time and repeat acceptance of the marketer's offering. Obviously, the strategic problems of getting people to take an action initially are very different from those of getting them to repeat or continue a given behavior. Thus, getting someone to give blood the first time, begin contraception, or even vote Democratic for the first time can be very difficult. Once over this hurdle, the marketing task is infinitely easier, especially if the initial experience is satisfying.

Following this line of reasoning, the offer life cycle can be divided into the two parts shown in Figure 15-6. For some nonprofit offerings, the OLC may *only* involve first-time use. Thus, a male only needs to have one vasectomy; there (usually) is no need to repeat the operation. This however, is relatively rare. Most strategies involve trial followed by repeat exchanges. Repeat exchanges may differ, however, as to whether we mean *repeating* an action like giving blood or attending an opera or whether we mean *continuing* a newly adopted behavior pattern like not smoking.

Innovation Adoption

Many social science disciplines have studied the process by which target audiences begin something new. Cultural anthropologists have researched how ancient cultures adopted new metals, new pot-glazing techniques, and new crops. Rural sociologists have studied how farmers have adopted new fertilizing and farm management practices and new types of seeds. Economists have investigated how firms adopt new manufacturing technologies like oxygen lancing in steel making, while educators have studied the dynamics of adopting teaching innovations, such as the "new math" or "new English." Social psychologists have studied the processes by which individuals acquire smoking, drug, and drinking addictions. And marketers, of course, have long studied new product adoptions.

The findings from these studies can help nonprofit managers understand how to induce first-time behaviors. First, they provide insight into the characteristics of those who adopt an innovation at different points during its introduction, growth, and maturity phases and into the interactions among these characteristics. Second, they describe the typical stages that individuals go through to adopt a given innovation. Finally, they identify the characteristics of offerings that will be relatively easy to introduce as compared to those that will not.

Finding Potential Innovators

The earliest approach used by marketers to launch a new offering was a *mass market approach*. A hospital, for example, might start a first aid course and try to attract everyone to take it. A mass market approach, however, has two drawbacks: (1) it requires heavy marketing expenditures, and (2) it involves a substantial number of wasted exposures to nonpotential and low-potential customers. These drawbacks led to a second approach, *target marketing*, in which the offer is directed to the groups that are likely to be most interested. This makes sense, provided that strong prospects are identifiable. But even within strong prospect groups, persons differ in how much interest they show in new ideas and in how fast they can be drawn into trying them. Certain persons are early adopters, and the marketer of an innovation ought to direct marketing efforts to them. *Innovation-adoption theory* holds that

1 Persons within a target market differ in the amount of time that passes between their exposure to a new offering and their trial of it.
2 Early adopters are likely to share some traits that differentiate them from late adopters.
3 There exist efficient media for reaching early-adopter types.
4 Early-adopter types are likely to be high on opinion leadership and therefore helpful in "advertising" the new offer to potential buyers.

The differences among individuals in their response to new ideas is called their *innovativeness*. Specifically, innovativeness is the degree to which an individual is relatively earlier in adopting new ideas than the other members of his or her social system. On the basis of their innovativeness, individuals can be classified into different *adopter categories*. In each product area, there are apt to be "consumption pioneers" and early adopters. Some women are the first to adopt new clothing fashions or new appliances, such as the microwave oven, some doctors are the first to prescribe new medicines,[10] and some farmers are the first to adopt new farming methods.[11]

Other individuals, however, tend to adopt innovations much later. This has led to a classification of people into the adopter categories shown in Figure 15–7.

FIGURE 15-7

**Adopter Categorization
on the Basis of Relative Time of Adoption of Innovations**

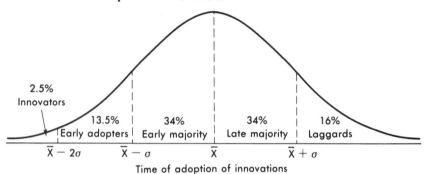

The adoption process is represented as following a normal (or near normal) distribution when plotted over time. After a slow start, an increasing number of people adopt the innovation, the number reaches a peak, and then it diminishes as fewer persons remain in the nonadopter category.

Convenient breaks in the distribution are used to establish adopter categories. Thus innovators are defined as the first $2^{1}/_{2}$ percent of the individuals to adopt a new idea; the early adopters are the next $13^{1}/_{2}$ percent who adopt the new idea, and so forth.

Rogers has characterized the five adopter groups in terms of their central values.[12] The dominant value of innovators is *venturesomeness*; they like to try new ideas, even at some risk, and are cosmopolitan in orientation. The dominant value of early adopters is *respect*; they enjoy a position in the community as opinion leaders and adopt new ideas early with an eye to whether the adoption will enhance their status as trendsetters. The dominant value of the early majority is *deliberateness*; these people like to adopt new ideas before the average member of the social system, although they are rarely leaders. Indeed, this group more often comprises the followers who pay attention to the advice given or the example set by the opinion leaders who preceded them. The dominant value of the late majority is *skepticism*; they do not adopt an innovation until the weight of majority opinion seems to legitimize its utility. They typically pay little attention to the opinion leaders, relying more on market cues of general acceptance. Finally, the dominant value of the laggards is *tradition*; they are suspicious of any changes, and adopt the innovation only because it has now taken on a measure of tradition itself.

Rogers has characterized the earlier adopters as follows:

> The relatively earlier adopters in a social system tend to be younger in age, have higher social status, a more favorable financial position, more specialized operations, and a different type of mental ability from later adopters. Earlier adopters utilize information sources that are more impersonal and cosmopolite

than later adopters and that are in closer contact with the origin of new ideas. Earlier adopters utilize a greater number of different information sources than do later adopters. The social relationships of earlier adopters are more cosmopolite than for later adopters, and earlier adopters have more opinion leadership.[13]

These findings have obvious implications for the kind of strategy one should adopt as one moves through the introductory and growth phases.

Innovators.   This group enters the market during the introductory phase of the OLC. The marketer can largely ignore the group, however, for three reasons. First, they are a relatively small group. Second, because of their venturesomeness, they are likely to discover the innovation even without the marketer's help. Finally, they have little or no influence on those who follow later. Since the early adopters and early majority tend to look upon the innovators as "try-anything-once" oddballs, the marketer runs a severe risk of cutting off further adoption by identifying too closely with this group.

Early Adopters.   Early adopters are the key to the success of most innovations. If one does not win them over, the introductory period will be prolonged, or the innovation may totally fail. Thus, an important first step in any marketing program involving an innovation is to identify the opinion leaders. Unfortunately, opinion leadership is not a generalized trait. Particular consumers or households may be innovators in one area but not in another. The fraternity or sorority fashion leader may not be the first to give blood or attend the latest movies. Furthermore, the notion that innovations "trickle down" from the upper to the lower classes has been found to have limited application. Past research has shown that opinion leaders are not necessarily the elite of a society; they can be found in all social strata. On the other hand, there is some evidence that the same opinion leaders may be found for *similar* innovations. Thus, the early adopters of protective car seats for their babies might be good prospects as opinion leaders supporting airbag legislation. Yet, these assumptions should be tested. Three approaches to identifying opinion leaders are possible:[14]

- *Self-reporting.* Individuals can be directly asked whether they would classify themselves as opinion leaders either in general or in ways related to the innovation in question.
- *Reputational.* Individuals may be asked to identify others to whom they might go for information or advice in this particular category. They can be asked to describe the most salient characteristic of these significant others.
- *Sociometric.* The researcher could directly map the interaction among members of a population and use this to determine the most influential members. Thus, Coleman, Katz, and Menzel found that by asking physicians in a particular community whom they would contact (a) to refer a patient, (b) to secure advice on a medical problem, and (c) to socialize with, they could rather accurately predict who would be the early adopters of a new drug and who would be likely to follow them when they did.[15]

Early Majority.   Some time will elapse before the marketer's strategy of attracting opinion leaders has its effect. The marketer should then make it clear to the early majority that the opinion leaders have already adopted—and, therefore, legitimized—the innovation. This can be accomplished by testimonials, editorials, and news and feature items. A good example of the use of opinion leadership has been the role of former First Lady Betty Ford in trying to get others to follow her lead in detection of breast cancer and in the treatment of drug abuse.

The Late Majority and Laggards.   Once the early majority has been heavily penetrated, tactics should shift from securing trial to emphasizing repeat behavior. This is desirable on two grounds. First, if a good trial rate has been achieved, competitors will enter the market and attention will shift to providing superior offers. Second, the emergence of more suppliers and offers will send a clear signal to the late majority that the innovation is accepted. By changing a campaign that says "try this" to one that says "try ours, not theirs," the marketer can make the late majority realize that the innovation is no longer risky. Whether such tactics will have an effect on the laggards is unclear.

Stages in the Innovation Adoption Process

Rogers and Shoemaker[16] have identified four steps that individuals typically go through in adopting some new pattern of behavior:

1   *Knowledge.* First, the target consumer must (a) become aware of the innovation and (b) learn enough about it to deduce that it has some relevance to his or her needs, wants, and life-style.
2   *Persuasion.* Next, the target consumer must move from simple awareness and vague interest to being motivated to take action. This is primarily a matter of attitude change, although it is also possible that a behavioral response could be achieved through *incentivization* or *coercion* with relatively little attitude change.
3   *Decision.* At some point, the target consumer thinks through the probable consequences of the proposed behavior change and makes a decision to adopt or reject it. This stage might well involve a vicarious or personal trial. Thus, a person suffering from hypertension might reduce salt intake for a few days or quiz others who have tried this approach.
4   *Confirmation.* After the initial decision, it is hoped that the target consumer will continue the behavior. This can be a major problem for social change agents. For example, over seventy percent of smoking quitters resume the habit within a year. In the case of seat belts, Lovelock and Weinberg showed that seat belt usage rose and then fell after mandatory seat belt usage legislation was enacted in British Columbia, Canada:[17]

	Percentage Using Seat Belts	
	Drivers	*Passengers*
Before announcement of legislation	29	24
Immediately after legislation	72	66
Sixteen months after legislation	54	43

The value of the Rogers-Shoemaker adoption model is threefold. First, it points out that there is a *sequence* of tasks necessary to move a given target segment to adopt. Thus, early messages must create awareness and interest, subsequent messages must persuade, and later messages must secure and reinforce decisions.

Second, it provides a monitoring framework to help identify reasons for a slow rate of acceptance. Thus, if research on quitting smoking shows that many smokers are blocked at the decision stage, persuasion attempts are no longer necessary, and effort should focus on inducing a decision.

Finally, the model can be used to develop a segmentation strategy. Suppose that research has identified three target segments for a new health program: males working in blue-collar jobs, pregnant women, and senior citizens. Suppose that target audience members have reached the stages of the adoption process listed in Table 15-3. Obviously, strategies aimed at a blue-collar male sample should seek to produce decisions. As for pregnant women, some messages should create greater interest in the health program; other messages should reinforce the behavior of those who have already acted. (Further research differentiating these two subpopulations could lead to finer tuning of strategy.) Finally, the majority of senior citizens are not being reached by current messages. New messages, better execution, or better media are warranted.

Innovation Characteristics

The innovation's characteristics will affect the rate of adoption. Five characteristics have an especially important influence on the adoption rate. The first is the innovation's *relative advantage,* the degree to which it is perceived to be superior to previous ideas. The greater the perceived relative advantage (higher quality, lower cost, and so on), the more quickly the innovation will be adopted. Thus, a five-day smoking cessation program that has a 35 percent initial success rate will

Table 15-3

DISTRIBUTION OF TARGET AUDIENCE MEMBERS ACROSS ADOPTION CATEGORIES

Stages of Adoption Process	Blue-Collar Male	Pregnant Women	Senior Citizens
No awareness	4%	12%	53%
Knowledge	26	51	35
Persuasion	61	14	6
Decision	2	23	4
Confirmation	7	0	2
	100%	100%	100%

be adopted faster than a three-month program that has 20 percent initial success rate—even though both programs may have the same *long-term* effectiveness.

The second characteristic is the innovation's *compatibility*, the degree to which it is consistent with the values and experiences of the individuals in the target social system. Thus, persuading Moslem women to practice birth control when they believe that their number of children is "in God's hands" will take more time than persuading them to boil water before drinking it, because the latter has no religious significance.

In the first year it attempted to establish opera in Los Angeles, the Los Angeles Music Center Opera organization portrayed a popular movie star, Dudley Moore, dressed in a modern suit on its promotional materials rather than traditional scenes from older operas (see Figure 15–8). This strategy makes opera attendance more compatible with Los Angeles's contemporary life-styles and its identification with the movie industry.

The third characteristic is the innovation's *complexity*, the degree to which it is relatively difficult to understand or use. More complex innovations take a longer time to diffuse, other things being equal. Condoms, for example, are easier to introduce in a given country than intrauterine devices (IUDs).

The fourth characteristic is the innovation's *divisibility*, the degree to which is may be tried on a limited basis. The evidence of many studies indicates that divisibility helps increase adoption. Thus, a severely hypertensive person will be more ready to adopt a salt-restricted diet than corrective heart surgery, since the latter is an all-or-nothing proposition.

The fifth characteristic is the innovation's *communicability*, the degree to which the intended results are observable or describable to others. Innovations whose advantages are more observable will diffuse faster in the social system. Thus, obese people will adopt new eating and exercise habits faster than hypertensives because the former will observe their weight loss, whereas hypertensives will not observe any changes unless they use a blood pressure gauge.

The marketing strategist should research how any proposed innovation is perceived by the target market in terms of these five characteristics before developing the marketing plan. Preliminary studies of the potential for injectable, longer-term contraceptives in developing countries, for example, have brought to light the following characteristics:

1   *Relative advantage.* Three advantages are clear. First, the technique puts less of a burden on the woman in terms of memory and possible interference with sex (real or perceived). Second, it is a technique that can be adopted easily and in private. Thus, it permits women to secure protection without their parents, friends, and sometimes their husbands or boyfriends knowing about it. Third, depending on the formulation, protection from one injection lasts one to three months.

2   *Compatibility.* Women are used to taking injections for other purposes so that the concept is not as "strange" as the IUD.

3   *Complexity.* There is an understandable problem for women in that the physical side effects are diverse and sometimes quite pronounced in early months. The problem is also complex for physicians because the U.S. Food and Drug Admin-

FIGURE 15-8

Brochure for 1987–1988 Season
of the Los Angeles Music Center Opera

135 North Grand Avenue
Los Angeles, California 90012

Five Performances Only!

A MIDSUMMER NIGHT'S DREAM
by Benjamin Britten

Conducted by **Robert Duerr**
Directed by **Gordon Davidson**
Sets by **Douglas W. Schmidt**
Costumes by **Lewis Brown**
Los Angeles Chamber Orchestra

CAST:
Jeffrey Gall: Oberon
Virginia Sublett: Tytania
John Allee: Puck
Peter Van Derick: Theseus
Stephanie Vlahos: Hippolyta
Jonathan Mack: Lysander
Rodney Gilfry: Demetrius
Alice Baker: Hermia
Angelique Burzynski: Helena
Michael Gallup: Bottom
Heinz Blankenburg: Quince
Stephen Plummer: Snout
John Atkins: Starveling
Greg Fedderly: Flute
Peter Atherton: Snug

Eleven Performances Only!

THE MIKADO
by W.S. Gilbert and Arthur Sullivan

Conducted by **Robert Duerr**
Directed by **Jonathan Miller**
Sets by **Stefanos Lazaridis**
Costumes by **Sue Blane**
Los Angeles Chamber Orchestra

CAST:
Dudley Moore: Ko-Ko
Michael Smith: Nanki-Poo
Donald Adams: Pooh-Bah
Dale Wendel: Yum-Yum
Kenneth Cox: Mikado
Marvellee Cariaga: Katisha
Suzanna Guzman: Peep-Bo
Stephanie Vlahos: Pitti-Sing
Michael Gallup: Pish-Tush

istration has banned the product because of a small risk that it might produce breast cancer. Doctors face a tough ethical choice between endangering the mother due to the product and endangering her health from too frequent pregnancies.

4 *Divisibility*. Divisibility exists because the product can be stopped and another technique substituted. Several months have to elapse, however, before the woman can become pregnant again.

5 *Communicability*. The product's effectiveness in preventing pregnancies can be easily communicated. There are problems at the confirmation stage in convincing women that the strong side effects are not serious and will disappear soon.

After learning how the innovation is perceived by the target audience, the marketer can then proceed to make the innovation relatively more advantageous, more compatible, more divisible, less complex, and more communicable.

SUMMARY

To be successful in today's nonprofit environment, organizations must learn to effectively and efficiently develop and launch new offerings. These may involve new or existing offerings in combination with new or existing markets. Extensions into new offerings or markets may involve undertakings that are similar or dissimilar to present marketing programs.

To be successful in developing new offerings, the organization must be both creative and systematic. The first stage of the process is to generate ideas for new offerings. This can involve careful searching of available information or attempts to create new ideas through a variety of artificial idea-generation techniques. Once the ideas have been produced, it becomes necessary to screen them to eliminate those that do not meet established organization goals.

The next stage involves elaborating the idea into a concrete concept that can be subjected to formal testing. The concept, if successful, must then generate a specific marketing strategy which, in turn, must survive a rigorous business analysis. The final stages of the development process then involve specific offer development and market testing, followed by a carefully orchestrated and timed commercialization process. Critical path techniques may be used to assure that the project meets any crucial timing and cost objectives.

New offerings follow an S-shaped pattern over their life cycle. They move through introductory, growth, maturity, and decline stages. The strategic issues facing the nonprofit marketing manager differ across these stages.

In the introductory and growth stages, the manager must first be concerned with securing trials of the new offering. Five customer groups may be identified on the basis of when they are likely to enter the innovation adoption process. First are the innovators, who will try almost anything that is new and who are often considered odd by the rest of the population. They can usually be ignored by the new offer manager. The second group, the early adopters, cannot be ignored because they are the opinion leaders who influence the next large group, the early majority. The late majority, which enters next, pays less attention to others in making their decisions to adopt and must be convinced that the new offering is not a fad. The last group, the laggards, can typically also be ignored because they are very tradition oriented and very slow to try anything new.

There is a clear set of stages through which anyone goes in adopting an innovation, from knowledge to persuasion to decision and confirmation. Innovations that have significant relative advantages over old approaches, that are compatible with the culture, and that are not complex and can be communicated easily and tried out before full adoption will diffuse faster than other innovations.

QUESTIONS

1. List the attributes of the experience of visiting an art museum. How could these attributes be adapted, minified, magnified, substituted, rearranged, reversed, and/or combined to create new offerings?

2. Form groups of eight people. Conduct a "brainstorming" session to generate new marketing programs to tackle the crack cocaine problem.

3. Outline the criteria that a children's museum should use at the idea screening stage of the offer development process. Assume that someone has proposed the idea that the museum spend $40,000 to produce three one-hour TV programs for cable TV–taking viewers on "video visits" to various parts of the museum. Evaluate this idea against the criteria you have established.

4. Create examples of future offer strategies for a small town hospital using the matrix outlined in Table 15–1.

5. Assume that you and a friend are thinking about taking a two-week vacation in an Eastern European country next year. You have never been outside your homeland up to the present. Draw a flowchart of the steps involved in undertaking this innovative activity. Indicate the critical path on the flowchart.

6. List five innovations that hospitals have offered in the last five years. Rate each as to its relative advantage, complexity, compatibility, divisibility, and communicability.

7. How would direct-mail promotions for a hospital's new holistic preventive health program be aimed at (a) innovators, (b) early adopters, and (c) early majority? How will the hospital know when to send mailings to each group?

NOTES

1. John Crompton, "Developing New Recreation and Park Programs," *Recreation Canada*, July 1983, p. 29.

2. Eric A. von Hippel, "Users as Innovators," *Technology Review*, January 1978, pp. 3–11.

3. Philip Kotler, "Idea Management: A Way to Increase Health Services' Marketing Effectiveness," presentation to Academy of Health Services Marketing, Las Vegas, Nevada, March 11, 1985.

4. For a useful discussion of creativity techniques, see Sidney J. Parnes and Harold F. Harding, eds., *Source Book for Creative Thinking* (New York: Scribners, 1962).

5. See Alex F. Osborn, *Applied Imagination*, 3rd ed. (New York: Scribners, 1963), pp. 286–287.

6. Ibid., p. 156.

7. See also Barry M. Richman, "A Rating Scale for Product Innovation," *Business Horizons*, Summer 1962, pp. 37–44; and John T. O'Meara, Jr., "Selecting Profitable Products," *Harvard Business Review*, January–February 1961, pp. 83–89.

8. "De Paul's New Study Plan," *Chicago Tribune*, January 6, 1974.

9. For example, see Yoram J. Wind, *Product Policy: Concepts, Methods and Strategy* (Reading, Mass.: Addison-Wesley, 1982), pp. 237–239; also, Glenn L. Urban and John Hauser, *Design and Marketing of New Products* (Englewood Cliffs, N.J.: Prentice-Hall, 1980), p. 469.

10. See James Coleman, Elihu Katz, and Herbert Menzel, "The Diffusion of an Innovation Among Physicians," *Sociometry*, December 1957, pp. 253–270.

11. See J. Bohlen and G. Beal, *How Farm People Accept New Ideas*, Special Report No. 15 (Ames: Iowa State College Agricultural Extension Service, November 1955).

12. Everett M. Rogers, *Diffusion of Innovations* (New York: Free Press, 1962).

13. Ibid., p. 192.

14. Everett M. Rogers and David G. Cartano, "Methods of Measuring Opinion Leadership," *Public Opinion Quarterly*, Fall 1962, pp. 43–45; and George Booker and Michael J. Houston, "An Evaluation of Measures of Opinion Leadership," in Kenneth L. Bernhardt, ed., *Marketing 1776–1976 and Beyond* (Chicago: American Marketing Association, 1976), pp. 562–564.

15. Coleman, Katz, and Menzel, "Diffusion of Innovation."

16. Everett M. Rogers with F. Floyd Shoemaker, *Communication of Innovations* (New York: Free Press, 1971).

17. Ibid.

16

Managing Perceived Costs

Pricing a hospital product or service should be based on the market value instead of product cost.

Riverside HotelCare was established in April 1987 to provide overnight accommodations for Riverside patients and their families. The program is a joint venture between Riverside and the Parke University Hotel.

The initial nightly rate was set at $55, based on a consulting firm's research of rates charged by full-service hotels combined with [costs of providing] transportation and social work counseling.

After four months, however, the program had an average monthly use rate of only 2-8 guests instead of the projected 21 guests per night. To determine why, the marketing and medical staff marketing departments conducted research in the form of a competitive analysis, pricing analysis, and review of an [earlier] external market research study.

[In the earlier study, a] national CPA firm [had] reviewed the possible development of an overnight lodging facility on the hospital campus. In this survey and analysis, 72% of the respondents indicated that the maximum rate they would pay for an overnight lodging facility in Riverside's vicinity would be $35 or less. About 39% were only willing to pay up to $30 for overnight accommodations.

The study recommended that the room rate for 1987 should be $35.75, with a projected occupancy rate of 72%.

Following a price reduction to $36, the use rate of the program increased from 114 nights in August 1987 to 243 nights in January 1988 with no additional marketing activity.

Source: Adapted from Donna A. Newman and Terrance M. Tucker, "Research Shows Hospital Best Pricing Strategy," *Marketing News*, Vol. 22, no. 18, August 29, 1988, p. 16. Published by the American Marketing Association, Chicago, Ill. Reproduced with permission.

Our view of the marketing task is that it starts with consumers and their perceptions of the costs and benefits to be derived from undertaking the behavior the marketer wants. In the preceding three chapters, we considered some of the tactics a manager might use to increase the real and perceived benefits that flow from a product, service, or social behavior. In the present chapter, we look at the other side of the exchange equation, its costs. The reader will note that we said "costs," not "cost." This distinction is crucial to the manager's understanding of this component of the marketing task.

THE NATURE AND ROLE OF COSTS

Consumers balance the expected benefits from an action against the expected costs. Money payment might be only one of these costs or sacrifices—a price in the traditional economic sense. Consider the case of a woman who is deciding whether to go to a doctor's office to have a breast examination because she has a history of breast cancer in her family. She has been exposed to social behavior marketing urging her to have regular examinations and to learn self-examination techniques. The visit to the doctor will cost her money. She will have to pay the doctor (or make a co-payment along with her insurance company). If she is an hourly worker and has no automobile, she will have to pay money for transportation and lose perhaps three hours of wages. If she is at home with a young child and drives, she may have to pay for a baby-sitter, an expressway toll, gasoline, and a parking fee.

Getting to and from the doctor involves nonmonetary costs in terms of physical energy or effort. For many, this may not be an important cost. For an elderly person, however, such a cost can be very dramatic. Then there are a number of psychic costs, including

- Awkwardness at having to ask for time off from work.
- Embarrassment at having to explain to coworkers where you are going (or lying to them).
- Aggravation at having to find a taxi and find one quickly so as not to wait long (or, if she drives, aggravation at traffic delays and wasting time looking for a parking space).
- Worry that the doctor will be late in seeing her.
- Embarrassment at having her breasts examined.
- Fear that the examination might hurt (for example, if a biopsy has to be done).
- Fear that something will be found.
- Worries that, if something is found, treatment will be costly, consume even more time, and be painful.
- Worries that treatment might involve breast removal, which can cause "disfigurement," problems for her marriage, and embarrassment with her husband, children, and friends.

All of these "perceived costs" will run through her mind. A marketer who focuses primarily on promoting the *benefits* of having a periodic breast examination will probably fail to motivate many women. Many women know the benefits. It is the vast array of perceived costs that keep them from completing the action the marketer wants. In a great many of the exchanges a nonprofit marketer seeks, managing the perceived costs is often much more important than managing the benefits. Furthermore, the nominal *money* price tag on the exchange may be the least important of the perceived costs the consumer is concerned about; in social behavior exchanges there usually is no price tag at all. We define perceived costs as follows:

> A **perceived cost** is any expected negative outcome of a proposed exchange perceived by a target consumer.

The Duality of Costs

In an exchange, what is a benefit for one side of the exchange is typically a cost for the other. Thus, a marketer who provides benefits to the consumer in the form of high quality service, nice surroundings, and a satisfaction guarantee does so at a cost to the marketer's own organization. These are the economic costs *the marketer* has to pay. On the other hand, a consumer paying money in exchange for these benefits provides a benefit for the marketer. Therefore, where an exchange involves a money price tag, the marketer is faced with an odd dilemma. There are many nonmoney costs the marketer will work hard to *minimize* so as to secure more exchanges. At the same time, there is at least one cost (the economic price) the marketer would like to *maximize* so the organization can stay in business and grow. To complicate matters even further, there may be occasions when the marketer may not want to minimize nonmoney costs and, indeed, may want to *increase* them. Often a marketer wishes to increase a nonmoney cost because the marketer will enjoy economic savings, which, in turn, will mean more profits from the exchange that could be used to reduce costs elsewhere or permit lower prices overall. Thus, a transit authority may reduce the frequency of its service in a high-income area (thus increasing waiting time and frustration for this market) so as to provide more service in a low-income area, invest in a subway system, or reduce the subsidy required from city or county revenues. Or, a hospital may require a patient to walk in for simple outpatient surgery and bear some of the physical, economic, and psychic costs of managing his or her own convalescence in order to keep all patients' out-of-pocket costs as low as possible.

COSTS MANAGEMENT

This dual nature of cost management presents a delicate problem for the non-profit marketer. An optimal cost management strategy from the marketer's standpoint is one that maximizes the number of exchanges (or revenue) for a given cost to the marketers. How can such a strategy be developed? The marketer must begin by researching consumer perceptions of the costs they must pay. Otherwise, marketers may miss crucial but subtle barriers affecting particular consumer segments. Consider the following examples:

- The National Cancer Institute only realized within the last 20 years that a perceived cost keeping many people from trying to quit smoking was the fear of failure.
- In rural villages in many countries, women who personally want to practice contraception do not do so because all the methods they know require that someone (or many people) become aware of their behavior.
- Some potential attenders of symphony concerts won't go because they believe they have to "dress up."
- Many elderly people do not attend theater in downtown areas because they believe they will be mugged or robbed.
- Many elderly people will not accept nursing home care because this involves admitting that they are old.
- Many alcoholics avoid treatment because they don't want to admit to themselves that they are alcoholics.
- Some males do not take medication for high blood pressure because they believe it will make them sterile or impotent.
- Many uneducated women do not use IUDs because they believe that (1) an unexpected baby could be born with the IUD embedded in its body, or (2) the IUD will work its way up through the woman's body, causing all sorts of unimaginable problems.
- Some organizations won't hire consultants because to do so would be an admission that they lack certain competences.
- Sanitary water systems are resisted in some villages because they disrupt established social intercourse systems (for example, the twice-daily congregation at the village well).
- Many potential theater, ballet, opera, and symphony attenders avoid going because they don't want to feel ignorant about what's being presented.

Once these costs are understood, the marketer can consider the following questions:

1 Are there strategies that can be used to reduce the perceived costs?
2 What is the cost to the marketer of reducing a perceived cost to the customer?
3 What is the probable responsiveness of the consumer to given levels of perceived cost reduction expenditure by the marketer?

We shall consider how marketers can answer these questions from a theoretical and then a practical perspective.

A Theoretical Approach

The traditional microeconomic pricing model presents a useful theoretical framework for thinking about these cost issues. Consider the hypothetical case presented in Figure 16–1A. The horizontal axis represents the number of exchanges

FIGURE 16-1

Models for Optimizing Price Reduction for Consumer

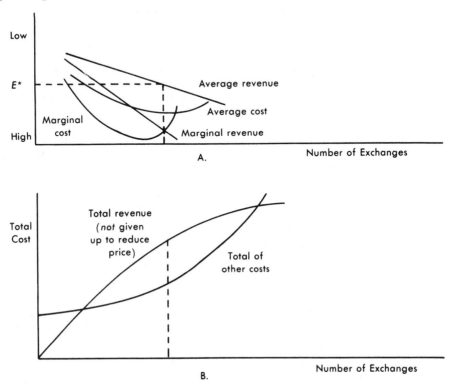

A.

B.

(or sales). The vertical axis represents both revenue and cost per unit of exchange to the marketer. In the typical for-profit case, the vertical axis would represent price and cost per unit. Each step moving *down* the vertical axis represents something given up by the marketer (that is, the difference between the current price and the amount the marketer could have obtained at the next highest price). On the other hand, reducing prices lowers the cost to consumers, and this should generate more exchanges (sales). Conversely, a step *up* the vertical axis means more retained revenue per unit to the marketer. This revenue, in a sense, is taken away from the customer (that is, the cost to the consumer is increased, as is the benefit to the marketer), thus lowering sales.

The problem for the marketer, then, is to choose the optimal balance between what the marketer receives and what burdens are put on customers (for example, the economic, social, or psychological "costs" he or she must pay). Two of the curves presented in Figure 16–1A suggest a solution. The four curves may be defined from the marketer's perspective as follows:

> **Average revenue** is the average return to the marketer for each unit of exchange (where this exchange involves the sale of goods or services, average

revenue equals price; it is equivalent to the total revenue divided by the number of units exchanged).

Average cost is the average amount the marketer spends to create a unit of exchange (for goods or services, this would be the average dollar cost per unit; it is equivalent to the total cost divided by the number of units exchanged).

Marginal revenue is, at each volume level, the amount of revenue the marketer gained by creating the last unit of exchange (it is equivalent to total revenue at the given level of volume minus total revenue at one unit less volume).

Marginal cost is, at each level of volume, the amount of cost the marketer would incur in creating the last unit of exchange (it is equivalent to total cost at the given level of volume minus total cost at one unit less volume).

Note that at low volume levels, marginal revenue exceeds marginal cost. As long as this is the case, the marketer is correct in encouraging increased units of exchange (presumably by lowering the perceived costs to the consumer and, of course, increasing the marketer's own expenditures). That is, each unit added brings in more revenue than it costs to create it. On the other hand, at high levels of exchange (to the right in Figure 16–1A), the opposite is true—creating additional units is a mistake if marginal cost exceeds marginal revenue.

Clearly, then, the optimal price to impose on one's customers is the one that will generate the volume level where marginal cost just equals marginal revenue. This point, marked E^*, is also where total revenue exceeds total costs by the widest amount, as shown in Figure 16–1B.

Unfortunately, this theoretical approach is difficult to implement in practice because it is hard to estimate the response function (average revenue curve). (It is easier to estimate the cost functions.) There are four possible estimation approaches:

1 *Historical analysis.* The marketer observes the amount of exchanges that did take place at different levels of the particular price. This approach requires that there be enough variation in the price variable (across time or across markets) to permit analysis and that all other factors are constant or that their differentiated effects can be "removed" from the analysis.
2 *Experimental analysis.* The marketer systematically manipulates the price and watches what happens to the number of exchanges.
3 *Intentions research.* The marketer asks potential consumers how likely they are to undertake the exchange at various price levels.
4 *Subjective estimation.* The manager or other experts make their best guess as to the shape of the response curve.

Practical Management of the Cost Bundle

The difficulty of precisely estimating the revenue response function should not discourage the marketer. If there is a single clearly important cost that drives consumer demand (for example, money price), then a formal analysis of the single response curve may well be justified. As noted in Chapter 4, consumer responses to offers, however, are usually a reaction to a *bundle* of costs (and, of course, a bundle of benefits). The problem in managing *costs* rather than *a cost* (singular) is to figure out *which* of many costs to reduce and *how much* to reduce them. For these decisions, the marketing manager needs to know *relative responses.* That is, for a given amount of the marketer's expenditure, which cost or costs should be impacted to yield the largest net gain in the number of exchanges.

Suppose a clinic is considering reducing one of several customer costs. Suppose further that preliminary research indicates that four nonmoney costs keep potential patients from coming in more often (for example, for checkups) or drives them to other clinics or doctors. These costs are

- Parking costs and the accompanying frustrations.
- Waiting time in the office.
- Inconvenience in filling out forms (for example, for insurance).
- The general unpleasant experience of waiting in unattractive facilities.

The marketer should first determine ways to reduce each cost. Assume that the marketer can spend increments of $5,000 to bring about improvements in each area. For $5,000 to be spent on improving appearances, for example, the waiting and other rooms could be painted and new curtains installed. For $10,000, the clinic could acquire new waiting room furniture. Fifteen thousand dollars would also allow recarpeting. And so on. What the marketer now needs is a set of response functions for each of the four areas where costs can be reduced, as in Figure 16–2.

FIGURE 16-2

Responses to Expenditures on Reducing Consumer Costs

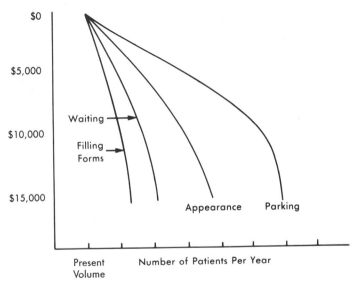

As we can see, the best place to put the first $5,000 is toward improving parking. This yields the largest gain in exchanges. The next $5,000 should also go for parking. At that point, assuming that the cost functions are independent, a further $5,000 should be spent on appearance. Given that the marketer can estimate the economic value of the extra exchanges generated by each expenditure increment beyond those indicated in Figure 16-2, he or she can expend $5,000 amounts until the gain in value from the added number of patients is no greater than the last expenditure.

The level of precision the marketer needs for this task is not great. It may be adequate simply to secure intentions data from a representative sample of current and past clinic customers.

Setting Money Prices

Since a major determinant of the demand for many of the offerings of nonprofit organizations is money price, we shall devote more attention to this part of the bundle. Money prices are placed on a great range of goods and services and go by various names:

> Money price is all around us. You pay RENT for your apartment, TUITION for your education, and a FEE to your physician or dentist. The airline, railway, taxi and bus companies charge you a FARE. The local utilities call their price a RATE, and the local bank charges you INTEREST for the money you borrow. The price for driving your car on Florida's Sunshine Parkway is a TOLL, and the company that insures your car charges you a PREMIUM. The guest lecturer charges an HONORARIUM to tell you about a government official who took a BRIBE to help a shady character steal DUES collected by a trade association. Neighborhood associations to which you belong may make a special ASSESSMENT to pay unusual expenses. Your regular lawyer may ask for a RETAINER to cover her services. The "price" of an executive is a SALARY; the price of a salesperson may be a COMMISSION; and the price of a worker is a WAGE. Finally, although economists would disagree, many of us feel that INCOME TAXES are the price we pay for the privilege of making money!
>
> In addition, price for products comes in several varieties. *List price* refers to the stated price of the product or service. *Actual price* may be greater or smaller, depending upon the presence of a *premium* or *discount*. Discounts can be extended to special groups such as seniors and students. If the buyers finance the purchase, they will be interested in the *credit* terms, that is, the monthly cost and time period of payments. Finally, the actual price might include additional charges representing *delivery, taxes,* and so on. All these elements can be varied as part of a pricing strategy.[1]

In handling the complex issues in money pricing, an organization should proceed through three stages. First, it should determine the *pricing objective,* whether it is to maximize profit, usage, fairness, or some other objective. Second, it should determine the *pricing strategy,* whether it should be cost based, demand based, or competition based. Third, it should determine when and whether a *price change* is warranted and how to implement it.

SETTING THE PRICING OBJECTIVES

The first thing an organization must decide in developing a price or pricing policy is the objectives that it wants to achieve. Often the objectives are in conflict, and a choice must be made. Consider the following statement made by a camp director: "I want to keep my camp tuition fees as low as possible to enable more people to enjoy a summer camping experience, but I also must keep the price high enough to ensure that the camp will not lose money in the long run."[2] In this case, the camp director is in conflict over the two opposing goals of *audience size maximization* and *cost recovery maximization.*

However, these are only two of several possibilities. Five different pricing objectives can be distinguished: surplus maximization, cost recovery, market size maximization, social equity, and market disincentivization. Returning to the camp illustration, the camp may aim for surplus maximization on conferences, full cost recovery on weekend retreats, market size maximization for its summer camp program, and lower prices for all events for low-income families.

Surplus Maximization

One would think that nonprofit organizations never use the principle of profit or surplus maximization. This is not so. There are many situations in which a nonprofit organization will want to set its price to yield the largest possible surplus. Thus, a charity organization will set the price for attending a major benefit dinner with the objective of maximizing its receipts over its costs. A university whose faculty has developed patented inventions will price these inventions to maximize its profits.

Surplus-maximizing pricing requires the organization to estimate two functions, the response (demand) function and the cost function. These two functions are sufficient for deriving the theoretical best price. The demand function describes the expected quantity demanded per period (Q) at various prices (P) that might be charged. Suppose the firm is able to determine through demand analysis that its demand equation is

$$Q = 1,000 - 4P \tag{16-1}$$

This says that demand is forecasted to be at most 1,000 units (i.e., $P = 0$), and for every \$1 increase in price, there will be four fewer units sold. Thus, the number of units purchased at a price of, say, \$150, would be 400 units [$Q = 1,000 - 4(150)$].

The cost function describes the expected total cost (C) for various quantities per period (Q) that might be produced. Suppose the company derived the following cost equation for its product:

$$C = 6,000 + 50Q \tag{16-2}$$

With the preceding demand and cost equation, the organization is in a position to determine the surplus maximization price. Two more equations are needed, both definitional in nature. First, total revenue (R) is equal to price times quantity sold:

$$R = PQ \tag{16-3}$$

Second, total surplus ($) is the difference between total revenue and total cost:

$$\$ = R - C \tag{16-4}$$

With these four equations, the organization is in a position to find the surplus maximizing price. The surplus equation (16–4) can be turned into a pure function of the price charged:

$$
\begin{aligned}
\$ &= R - C \\
\$ &= PQ - C \\
\$ &= PQ - (6{,}000 + 50Q) \\
\$ &= P(1{,}000 - 4P) - 6{,}000 - 50(1{,}000 - 4P) \\
\$ &= -56{,}000 + 1{,}200P - 4P^2
\end{aligned}
\tag{16-5}
$$

Equation 16–5 shows total surplus expressed as a function of the price that will be charged. The surplus maximizing price can be found in one of two ways. The researcher could use trial and error, trying out different prices to determine the shape of the profit function and the location of the maximum price. The surplus function turns out to be a parabola or hatlike figure and surplus reaches its highest point ($34,000) at a price of $150. At this price, the organization sells 400 units that produce a total revenue of $60,000.

This model for finding the surplus maximizing price, in spite of its theoretical elegance, is subject to five practical limitations:

1   The model shows how to find the price that maximizes short-run surplus rather than long-run surplus. There may be a trade-off between short-run and long-run surplus maximization, as when clients get angry at high prices they must pay in the short run (e.g., for a special opera) and eventually switch to other sellers (e.g., go to the theater in future).

2   There are other parties to consider in setting a price. The model only considers the ultimate consumer's response to alternative prices. Other groups that may respond are competitors, suppliers, intermediaries, and the general public. A high price might lead competitors to raise their price, in which case the demand would be different from that suggested by the demand function if it assumed no competitive reaction. Various suppliers, employees, banks, and raw material producers may take the price to reflect the organization's ability to pay and may raise their prices accordingly, in which case the cost function would be different from that assumed with no supplier reaction. Intermediaries who handle the product may have some strong feelings about the proper price. Finally, the

general public might complain about the organization if its price appears to be too high.

3   The government, acting in the interests of the public, might establish a price ceiling, and this may exclude the surplus maximizing price.

4   This pricing model assumes that price can be set independently of the other elements in the marketing mix. But the other elements of the marketing mix affect demand and must be part of the demand function in searching for the optimal price. Thus, a ballet company can charge a higher price if it advertises extensively and builds up consumer interest.

5   This pricing model assumes that the demand and cost functions can be accurately estimated. In the case of a new service, there will be no experience upon which to base these estimates. Unless data are available on a similar service, estimates are likely to be highly subjective. Because the demand and cost equations are estimated with an unknown degree of error, the criterion of maximizing surplus may have to be replaced with the criterion of maximizing *expected* surplus where various demand levels for each price are weighted by their likelihood of occurrence. In any situation of risk and uncertainty, the pricing decision maker will want to see how sensitive the theoretically calculated optimal price is to alternative estimates of the demand and cost functions.

Cost Recovery

Many nonprofit organizations seek a price that would help them recover a "reasonable" part of their costs. This is the idea behind the pricing of toll roads, postal services, and public mass transit services. Although the organizations could conceivably charge higher prices and increase their revenue (because of their monopolistic position), they do not want to incite an adverse reaction from the public or legislature.

How much cost should the organization try to recover through its pricing? Some organizations—such as universities and public mass transit organizations—aim at recovery of their operating costs. This would not provide money for expansion; they would have to rely on gifts or bond issues to raise the needed capital. Other organizations aim for *full cost recovery*, because they cannot rely on raising sufficient funds from other sources.

Market Size Maximization

Some nonprofit organizations—public libraries and museums, for example—want to maximize the total number of users of their service. These organizations feel that the users and society profit from their services. In this case, a zero price will attract the greatest number of users. Even here there can be exceptions. Consider the following situation:[3]

> Family planners in India initially believed the distribution of free contraceptives would lead to the greatest level of usage. However, they discovered two flaws in the reasoning. Some potential consumers interpreted the zero price to signify low quality and avoided the free brand. In addition, many retailers would not carry

it or display it prominently because it did not yield them profit, with the result that fewer units were ultimately available to consumers.

In most situations, a low price normally stimulates higher usage *and* may produce more revenue in the long run. Weinberg advocates that theaters should set low ticket prices because this attracts a larger audience, many of whom would eventually make donations to the theaters that would more than make up for the lower ticket prices.[4]

Social Equity

Organizations may wish to price their services in a way that contributes to social equity. In a study of who pays for library services, Weaver and Weaver concluded that "public libraries actually distribute income from the poorest to the more affluent strata of the community."[5]

One of the principal arguments leading to this conclusion is that because the poor rarely use the public library and because public libraries are often supported out of general tax revenues, the poor are paying for the nonpoor's libraries. Admittedly, there are other situations, such as city parks and welfare services, where the reverse is true. Our concepts of social equity hold that, wherever possible, public (and by extension, nonprofit) services should not operate to transfer wealth from the poor to the rich. In the public library case, the goal of social equity might be achieved by charging users for library services, perhaps charging even more for services (such as videocassette rentals) that the upper classes use relatively more often.

Market Disincentivization

Pricing might be undertaken for the objective of discouraging as many people as possible from purchasing a particular product or service. There are many reasons an organization might want to do this. It might consider the product to be bad for people; it might want to discourage people from overtaxing a facility; it might be trying to ration demand to solve a temporary shortage; or it might want to discourage certain classes of buyers.

The purpose of the high government tax on cigarettes and liquor is to discourage the use of these products. But the price is never raised high enough because the government has come to rely on the substantial revenue produced by these taxes. A tax that is truly disincentivizing would yield the government no revenue and possibly create a large black market.

The Golden Gate Authority of San Francisco resorted to disincentive pricing when it learned that the famous bridge structure was overtaxed with traffic. A motorist was charged according to how many passengers were in the car, with the highest fee charged to cars with only the driver. This led to the formation of more driving car pools, although not as many as the authority had hoped.

Public mass transit companies have considered using disincentive pricing to discourage commuting during rush hours. These companies are in a weak financial situation because they have to finance the purchase of enough equipment to cover needs during the rush hours while the equipment sits idle the rest of the time. The pricing possibilities include raising the fare during rush hours or offering a lower fare at off hours.

The emergence of shortages of gasoline, natural gas, and electrical energy from time to time increases the interest of organizations in disincentive pricing. The theoretical pricing model described earlier can be used to find the price that would achieve a specified reduction in usage.

CHOOSING A PRICING STRATEGY

After the organization has defined its pricing objective, it can consider the appropriate strategy for setting a specific price. Pricing strategies tend to be cost oriented, demand oriented, or competition oriented.

Cost-Oriented Pricing

Cost-oriented pricing refers to setting prices largely on the basis of costs, either marginal costs or total costs including overhead. Two examples are markup pricing and cost-plus pricing. They are similar in that the price is determined by adding some fixed percentage to the unit cost. *Markup pricing* is commonly found in the retail trades where the retailer adds predetermined but different markups to various goods. Museum gift shops use markup pricing in pricing their various items. *Cost-plus pricing* is used to describe the pricing of jobs that are nonroutine and difficult to "cost" in advance, such as some kinds of marketing research.

Nonprofit organizations vary in where they peg their price in relation to their costs. The American Red Cross charges a price for its blood that covers the "irreducible cost of recruiting, processing, collecting, and distributing the blood to the hospitals." On the other hand, several nonprofit organizations have historically charged less than their costs (called cost-minus pricing). Tuitions at private colleges and ticket prices for symphony orchestras often cover less than 50 percent of the total cost of these services; the remaining costs are covered by donations and interest on endowment funds.

The most popular form of cost-oriented pricing uses *break-even analysis*. The purpose of break-even analysis is to determine, for any proposed price, how many units of an item would have to be sold to cover fully the costs; this is known as the *break-even volume*. To illustrate, the director of a summer camp wants to set a tuition for an eight-week summer session that would cover the total costs of operating the camp. Suppose the fixed costs of the camp—real estate taxes, interest charges, physical property, insurance, building mainte-nance, vehicle expense, and so on—are $200,000. This is shown on the break-even chart in Figure 16–3 as a horizontal line at the level of $200,000. The variable cost for serving each camper—food, handicraft supplies, camper insurance, and so on—is $500 per camper. This is shown on the total cost line, starting at $200,000 and rising $500 for each camper. Finally, the camp director initially considers charging $1,000 tuition per camper. This is shown on the total revenue line, which begins at $0 and rises $1,000 per camper. The number of campers needed to break even is determined by the intersection of the total revenue and the total cost curves, here 400 campers. If the camp fails to attract at least 400 campers at $1,000 each, it will suffer a loss varying with the number of campers attracted. If the camp attracts more than 400 campers at $1,000 each, it will generate profits. The camp director's task is to estimate whether it will be easy or difficult to attract 400 campers at a tuition of $1,000.

The break-even volume can be readily calculated for any proposed price by using the following formula:

$$\text{Break-even volume} = \frac{\text{fixed cost}}{\text{price} - \text{variable cost}} \qquad (16\text{-}6)$$

Using the numbers in the previous example, we get

$$\text{Break-even volume} = \frac{\$200,000}{\$1,000 - \$500} = 400$$

On the other hand, if the camp director thought of charging $700 tuition,

FIGURE 16-3

Illustration of Breakeven Analysis

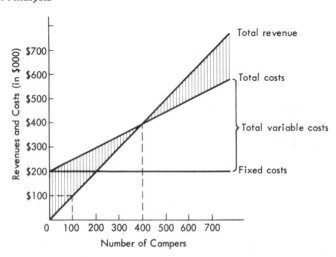

equation (16–6) indicates that he would have to attract 1,000 campers to break even.

Suppose the camp has a capacity to handle 1,000 campers and the camp director would like to attract that number. He can try to estimate a demand curve showing how many campers would be attracted at each price. Figure 16–4 shows the estimated demand curve. Accordingly, the $1,000 tuition would succeed in attracting 400 campers and allow the camp to break even. But the $700 tuition would attract only 800 campers, not 1,000 campers, and result in a loss. The camp director may decide to bear the loss, making it up through fund-raising, in order to attract 800 campers. If he wants to attract 1,000 campers, a $550 tuition would be required according to Figure 16–4, thus creating an even larger loss.

Cost-oriented pricing is popular for a number of reasons. First, there is generally less uncertainty about costs than about demand. By basing the price on cost, the seller simplifies the pricing task considerably; there is no need to make frequent adjustments as demand conditions change. Cost-plus pricing is also easier to implement for organizations that have a great many items to price, such as museum bookstores or Boy Scout equipment centers. Second, when all organizations in the industry use this pricing approach, their prices are similar if their costs and markups are similar. Price competition is therefore minimized, which would not be the case if competitors paid attention to demand variations. Third, there is the feeling that cost-markup pricing is socially fairer to buyers and sellers. Sellers do not take advantage of buyers when the demand becomes acute, yet sellers earn a fair return on their investment. It is also seen as socially fair when different prices must be charged to different users, i.e., everyone pays 20 percent over costs. Thus the popularity of cost-oriented pricing rests on its administrative simplicity, competitive harmony, and social fairness.

FIGURE 16-4

Estimated Demand Curve for a Summer Camp

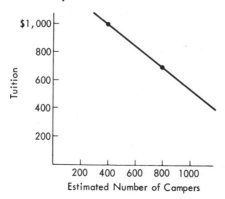

Demand-Oriented Pricing

The problem with cost-oriented pricing is that it ignores how valuable the offering is to target customers. Demand-oriented pricing looks at the condition of demand rather than the level of costs to set the price. Demand-oriented sellers estimate how much value buyers see in the market offer, and they price accordingly. Thus, a fine arts organization might set a ticket price of $50 for an Isaac Stern concert and $15 for a violin concert by a less well-known performer. The premise is that price should reflect the *perceived value* in the consumer's head. A corollary is that an organization should invest in building up the perceived value of the offer if it wants to charge a higher price. Thus, a private college that builds a reputation for excellence in teaching and research can charge a higher tuition than can an average private college.

A common form of demand-oriented pricing is price discrimination, in which a particular product is sold at two or more prices. Price discrimination takes various forms. Pricing that discriminates on a customer basis occurs when a museum charges a lower price to students than to the general public. Pricing that discriminates on a product-version basis occurs when the U.S. Postal Service charges more for registered mail than for unregistered mail. Pricing that discriminates on a place basis occurs when a symphony charges more for front-row seats than back-row seats. Pricing that discriminates on a time basis occurs when a public golf course charges higher greens fees on weekends than on weekdays. Another example is when high prices are charged for a new product or service when it is first introduced. This is called *skimming pricing* and is practiced when performing arts organizations charge higher prices on opening night.

For price discrimination to work, certain conditions must exist.[6] First, the market must be segmentable, and the segments must show different intensities of demand. Second, there should be no chance that the members of the segment paying the lower price could turn around and resell the product to the segment paying the higher price. Third, there should be little chance that competitors will undersell the firm in the segment being charged the higher price. Finally, the cost of segmenting and policing the market should not exceed the extra revenue derived from price discrimination.

Competition-Oriented Pricing

When an organization sets its prices chiefly on the basis of what its competitors are charging, its pricing policy can be described as competition oriented. It may choose to charge the same as competition, a higher price, or a lower price. The distinguishing characteristic is that the organization does *not* seek to maintain a rigid relation between its price and its own costs or demand. Its own costs or demand may change, but the organization maintains its price because competitors maintain their prices. Conversely, the same organization will change its prices when competitors change theirs, even if its own costs or demand have not altered.

The most popular type of competition-oriented pricing occurs when an organization tries to keep its price at the average level charged by the industry. Called *going-rate* or *imitative pricing,* it is popular for several reasons. Where costs are difficult to measure, it is felt that the going price represents the collective wisdom of the industry concerning the price that would yield a fair return. It is also felt that conforming to a going price would be least disruptive of industry harmony. The difficulty of knowing how buyers and competitors would react to price differentials is still another reason for this pricing.

Going-rate pricing primarily characterizes pricing practice in homogeneous product or service markets. The organization selling a homogeneous product has little choice about the setting of its price. Daring to charge more than the going rate would attract virtually no customers. Deciding to charge less is unnecessary either because the organization can sell its current output at the going price or because it fears that competitors will cut their prices too.

In markets characterized by *product differentiation,* organizations have more latitude in their price decision. Product differences serve to desensitize the buyer to existing price differentials. Organizations such as private universities try to establish themselves in a pricing zone with respect to their competitors, assuming the role of a high-tuition university, a medium-tuition university, or a low-tuition university. Their product and marketing programs are made compatible with competitors in this chosen pricing zone. They respond to competitive changes in price to maintain their pricing zone.

CHANGING THE PRICE

Pricing is challenging when the organization is thinking about initiating a price change. The organization may be considering a *price reduction* to stimulate demand, to take advantage of lower costs, or to gain on weaker competitors. Or it may be considering a *price increase* in order to take advantage of strong demand or to pass on higher costs. Whether the price is to be moved up or down, the action will affect buyers, competitors, distributors, and suppliers, and can attract the interest of government as well. The success of the move depends on how the parties respond. Yet their responses are among the most difficult things to predict. Thus, a contemplated price change carries great risks. Here we will examine methods of estimating probable customer reactions to price changes.

Price Elasticity of Demand

The traditional analysis of buyers' reactions to price change is based on the assumption that all buyers learn of the price change and take it at face value. The magnitude of their response to the price change is described by the concept of *price elasticity of demand.* This term refers to the ratio of the percentage change in demand (quantity sold per period) to the percentage change in price.[7] A price elasticity of −1 means that sales rise (fall) by the same percentage as price falls (rises). In this case, total revenue is left unaffected. A price elasticity greater than −1 means that sales rise (fall) by more than price falls (rises) in percentage terms. A price elasticity lower than −1 means that sales rise (fall) by less than price falls (rises) in percentage terms.

Price elasticity of demand allows more precise answers to the question of whether the organization's price is too high or too low. For example, suppose the price elasticity for tolls on the Massachusetts Turnpike is −1/2. This means that the Massachusetts Turnpike could raise the present toll and increase its total revenue. A 1 percent increase in the toll will lead to only a 1/2 percent decline in usage. If, on the other hand, the price elasticity of the Massachusetts Turnpike is −2, it could increase its total revenue by lowering the toll. This is why it is critical to measure price elasticity.

In practice, price elasticity is extremely difficult to measure. There are definitional as well as statistical hurdles. Definitionally, price elasticity is not an absolute characteristic of the demand facing a seller, but a conditional one. Price elasticity depends on the magnitude of the contemplated price change. It may be negligible with a small price change and substantial with a large price change. Price elasticity also varies with the original price level. A 20 cent increase over a current price of $1 may exhibit quite a different elasticity than a 40 cent increase over a current price of $2. Finally, long-run price elasticity is apt to be different from short-run elasticity. Buyers may have to stick with the seller immediately after a price increase because choosing a new seller takes time, but they eventually stop purchasing from him or her. In this case, demand is more elastic in the long run than in the short run. Or the reverse might happen; buyers drop a seller in anger after he or she increases prices but then return later. The significance of this distinction between short-run and long-run elasticity is that sellers might not know how wise their price change is for a while.

Promotional Pricing

Often a nonprofit organization will maintain its list price but introduce "price specials" in order to stimulate increased buying. Promotional pricing can take many forms. Consider a theater performing group that wants to attract a larger audience to its performances. Here are some promotional pricing options:

1   The theater group can promote a series subscription that represents a savings over buying individual tickets to all of the performances. A popular way to express the savings is "See five plays for the price of four." Newman strongly favors discounts for subscription series on the grounds that the savings are a prime motivator for buying a subscription.[8] But Ryans and Weinberg, in a survey of subscription buyers for the American Conservatory Theater (ACT) in

San Francisco, found that subscribers reported that the main reason for buying subscription series was not the savings but to make sure they went to the theater more often and were assured of a good seat. ACT abandoned the discount in the next season with no palpable impact on subscription sales.[9]

2   The theater group can offer an "early bird" discount on the series subscription to those subscribing up to two months in advance of the first performance.

3   The theater group can offer second tickets at half price. Andreasen and Belk found potential theatergoers reacting extremely favorably to this proposal, reacting even more positively than to percentage discounts ("40% off") that were better bargains.[10] It apparently taps into the notion of bringing a friend or a date to the theater.

4   The theater group can offer unsold tickets at half price on the day of the performance. This method is used successfully by the ticket kiosks in New York City, Washington, D.C., Boston, London, and San Francisco. The theater gets not only the extra seat revenue it would have lost, but also the revenue from the sale of drinks and candy during intermission.[11]

SUMMARY

Nonprofit marketers seek to influence exchanges. From the target consumer's perspective, these exchanges involve trading bundles of benefits for bundles of costs. Costs are the prices the customers perceive they must pay to participate. They can be monetary, nonmonetary, or mixed. Nonmonetary costs include psychic pain, the need to change old habits or ideas, expenditures of time and energy, and dislocations of social arrangements.

The nonprofit manager has a dual task in managing these costs. Some costs must be kept reasonably high to assure continuing revenues to the organization. Other costs must be reduced as much as possible to lower barriers to customer action. Since it will cost the organization to reduce each of these costs, it needs to know the relative responsiveness of target customers to each of these reductions.

In developing a strategy for monetary prices, the organization must first establish objectives. It could seek surplus maximization, cost recovery, market size maximization, social equity, or market disincentivization. Its specific strategy to meet these objectives may be primarily cost oriented, demand oriented, or competition oriented. Organizations that are planning to change an existing price should take into account the price elasticity of demand and perceptual factors in the target audience's response.

QUESTIONS

1.   List all of the monetary and nonmonetary costs a married 42-year-old executive with two children under age 12 would consider when thinking of enrolling in a ten-week night course on advanced computer software for business at a local university. How could each of these costs be reduced?

2. A contraceptive social marketer in Thailand markets oral pills, condoms, abortions, and pregnancy counseling. How can it develop a pricing strategy for this "product line" that will achieve social equity?

3. Describe an experiment a legitimate theater might run to test the effects on demand of reducing three different kinds of costs. Include at least one nonmonetary cost.

4. List the advantages and disadvantages to a nonprofit hospital in a small town of following a cost-plus, demand-based, or competitive pricing strategy.

5. How should the YMCA marketing director respond to the decision by three major competing local fitness centers to reduce the cost of their first ten visits by 50 percent? The centers price their program at a 25 percent premium (on average) above the Y. The marketing director of the YMCA estimates that the Y has a 40 percent share of the local fitness center market but it is just breaking even.

NOTES

1. David J. Schwartz, *Marketing Today: A Basic Approach*, 3rd ed. (New York: Harcourt Brace Jovanovich, 1981), p. 271.

2. Quoted from an article by Ben F. Doddridge, "Toward the Development of a Practical Approach for a Solution of the Pricing Dilemma," *Christian Camping International*, January–February 1978, pp. 19–22.

3. See T.R.L. Black and John Farley, "Retailers in Social Program Strategy: The Case of Family Planning," *Columbia Journal of World Business*, Winter 1977, pp. 33–43.

4. Charles Weinberg, "Marketing Mix Decision Rules for Nonprofit Organizations," in Jagdish Sheth, ed., *Research in Marketing*, Vol. 3 (Greenwich, Conn.: JAI Press, 1980), pp. 191–234.

5. Frederick S. Weaver and Serena A. Weaver, "For Public Libraries the Poor Pay More," *Library Journal*, February 1, 1979, pp. 325–355.

6. See George Stigler, *The Theory of Price*, rev. ed. (New York: Macmillan, 1952), p. 215 ff.

7. In symbols,

$$Eqp = \frac{(Q_1 - Q_0)/^{1/2}(Q_0 + Q_1)}{(P_1 - P_0)/^{1/2}(P_0 + P_1)}$$

where

Eqp = elasticity of quantity sold with respect to a change in price
Q_0, Q_1 = quantity sold per period before and after price change
P_0, P_1 = old and new price

8. Danny Newman, *Subscribe Now!* (New York: Publishing Center for Cultural Resources, 1977).

9. Adrian B. Ryans and Charles B. Weinberg, "Consumer Dynamics in Nonprofit Organizations," *Journal of Consumer Research*, September 1978, pp. 89–95.

10. Alan R. Andreasen and Russell W. Belk, "Consumer Response to Arts Offerings: A Study of Theater and Symphony in Four Southern Cities," in Edward McCracken, ed., *Research in the Arts* (Baltimore: Walters Art Gallery, 1979), pp. 13–19.

11. "New York City Opera Rolls Back Prices," *The Cultural Post*, Vol. 7, March–April 1982, p. 9.

17

Managing
the Marketing Channel

Although child survival products such as oral rehydration solution (ORS) are usually part of public health promotions and are available at public health centers, sometimes these centers are not accessible enough or popular enough with local audiences to be effective as the only "place" where products are available.

In Egypt and Indonesia, audience research determined that pharmacies were important sources of both medicine and information to large portions of the population. Program planners therefore decided to promote retail sales of ORS, while also making it available at health centers. Pharmacists received special training in diarrheal disease management so that they could provide correct information to consumers whenever they distributed the packets. In Honduras, a program is underway to involve private pharmaceutical companies in the production and distribution of ORS through *pulperias,* or small general stores in rural areas. It is anticipated that these outlets will be the most popular with the rural population, and that the volume of ORS sold will satisfy private firms.

In Malawi, where malaria accounts for at least ten percent of hospital deaths, chloroquine has been available at both health centers and retail stores. But neither kind of outlet was accessible enough to most people. Program planners wondered whether they could "create" a new "place" for chloroquine distribution. Since traditional birth attendants (TBAs) are respected and active in most rural areas, planners decided to conduct a pilot study to train a group of them to distribute chloroquine and to instruct mothers in its use and in preventive measures which can be taken around the home, such as burning of cow dung and elimination of mosquito breeding sites. Results showed the TBAs would be highly effective in this role.

Source: Mark R. Rasmuson, Renata E. Seidel, William A. Smith, and Elizabeth Mills Booth, *Communication for Child Survival* (Washington, D.C.: Academy for Educational Development, June 1988), p. 11. Reproduced with permission.

For an exchange to take place, marketers must be able to make contact directly or indirectly with their target customers. In the case of products, this means among other things that the goods must be physically delivered. For services, it means making the service available when and where the consumer can utilize it. And for social behaviors, it means having a communications vehicle to directly contact target consumers. All of these involve bringing the marketer and the consumer together to complete the transaction. The marketer's task is to create *time and place utility* for the customer.

THE NATURE AND ROLE
OF CHANNEL DECISIONS

We shall refer to the aspects of an organization's marketing strategy that deal with creating time and place utilities as channel decisions. We define a channel as follows:

> A **channel** is a conduit for bringing together a marketer and a target customer at some place and time for the purpose of facilitating a transaction.

Among the channels a marketer can use are

- Specific buildings—stores, offices, clinics, and showrooms
- Salespeople—paid or volunteer
- Independent intermediaries, such as wholesalers and retailers
- Telephones
- Advertising media
- Direct mail

An example of the set of channels in one industry is given in Exhibit 17–1.

Careful planning of channel strategy can have important positive payoffs. Nonprofit organizations are typically deficient in resources, both financial and personnel. They usually need the help of other individuals and organizations to bring their offerings to the public. The careful use of independent channels can

EXHIBIT 17-1

The Health Care Delivery System of the United States

Health care delivery systems are institutions that deliver preventative and curative health services to the public. In the past, Americans obtained health care services in two ways: by visiting a private physician or an emergency room of a local hospital. Some consumers sought out their pharmacists for advice on minor problems such as the common cold.

Today's health care services are available through several channels.

1 *Health maintenance organizations.* A growing number of people obtain their medical care through health maintenance organizations. By joining and paying a monthly fee, they can see staff doctors at any time and also get their hospitalization cost covered.

2 *Neighborhood health clinics.* Consumers in poorer neighborhoods often go to neighborhood health clinics for help. The clinic charges no fee or a low fee and has doctors ready to examine sick patients. The clinic is supported by public money, private money, or both.

3 *Hospital-based ambulatory care units.* Many hospitals have opened clinics in shopping areas or apartment buildings where people pay a fee for service. Since some of these patients need hospital care, these clinics serve as feeder operations to the hospital.

4 *Group practices.* The vast majority of physicians now belong to private group practices, which give them the opportunity to structure their hours better and gain the advantages of having expert colleagues. Patients pay a fee for service every time they visit their physician.

5 *Freestanding specialized service units.* Consumers can directly obtain specific services such as X rays, blood tests, and minor surgery in specialized units set up for these purposes. They pay fees that in most cases are reimbursed by their health insurance plans.

make marketing programs more *efficient* by sharing costs, achieving economies of scale, and so on, and make them more *effective* by leveraging meager resources, small staffs, cramped facilities, and so on. The National Cancer Institute's antismoking program, for example, was able to have a significant impact with a relatively small budget by enlisting the help of physicians to distribute how-to-quit materials and to carry out "personal selling" with patients who had a history of smoking. NCI was able to obtain the same kind of leveraging for their breast self-examination program by securing the help of major corporations to serve as intermediaries for their awareness and training programs.

While potentially very helpful, independent channel members can sometimes hurt an otherwise effective program. Here is a telling example:

In 1976, the Treasury decided to reintroduce the Jefferson $2 bill to save on costs of printing and transporting $1 bills. Treasury officials estimated that if one-half of the 1.6 billion $1 bills in circulation were replaced with $2 bills, the country would save $35 million in printing costs within a five-year period. The Treasury commissioned a Harvard Business School survey to see if the public, banks, and retailers would use the new $2 bill. The survey discovered some negative attitudes, but believed that these could be overcome by a substantial advertising campaign. When the $2 bill was introduced, it met with great resistance from merchants as well as consumers. Merchants felt they needed another slot in their cash registers or else the $2 bill would be confused with the $20 bills. Merchants also expressed fears that if they pushed the new bills on to consumers, many would not want them and so the merchants would lose patronage. Banks were also reluctant to push the bills, claiming the merchants did not want them and that they could be confused with $20 bills. The Treasury, which had planned to spend $300,000 advertising the $2 bill, dropped the idea because of the expense. A Federal Reserve official said, "They could have test-marketed the bill in two big cities for a year, found out their problems, and applied the information to marketing bills in the rest of the country."[1]

If the Treasury had put more effort in advance into studying the perceptions, needs, and wants of these crucial intermediaries (rather than focusing most of their market research on the individual consumers), they could have developed more effective strategies for this crucial intermediary market. With hindsight, it seems clear that a subtle combination of education, persuasion, and a touch of political pressure would have removed the bottlenecks that eventually throttled the entire program.

Some nonprofit organizations are not fully aware of their channel problems and possibilities. Organized religion, for example, can be thought of as operating a religious service distribution system. Consider the following example of the Evangelical Covenant Church of America.

> The central church office can be seen as the *manufacturer* or originator of the church's products; the regional offices throughout the country can be viewed as the *wholesaler;* and the individual churches, such as Faith Evangelical Covenant Church in Wheaton, might be viewed as the *retail outlets* for the church's services and products. As a "retailer" of the Evangelical Covenant Church of America's services and products, Faith Covenant Church is the part of the organization that comes face to face with the customer or members of the church and potential members. It is the individual "outlet" that can perform many of the critical functions needed to maintain members of the church and in fact, to increase its membership rolls.[2]

A host of other organizations face the problem of locating a set of facilities to serve optimally a spatially distributed population. This can be characterized in the following terms:

> Hospitals must be located . . . to serve the people with complete medical care, and we must build schools close to the children who have to learn. Fire stations must be located to give rapid access to potential conflagrations, and voting booths must be placed so that people can cast their ballots without expending unreasonable amounts of time, effort, or money to reach the polling stations. Many of our states face the problem of locating branch campuses to serve a burgeoning and increasingly well-educated population. In the cities we must create and locate

playgrounds for the children. Many overpopulated countries must assign birth control clinics to reach the people with contraceptive and family planning information.[3]

CHANNEL STRATEGY

All marketers need conduits to their target consumers, and consumers need access to the marketer's services. The kinds of channels a marketer might use will vary depending on whether goods, services, or communications are the major flows within the channel. There are a number of strategic problems, however, that apply to all channel decisions:

1 *Quality of service.* The nonprofit must decide how much place and time utility to offer as part of its offer mix.
2 *Direct versus indirect marketing.* The nonprofit must decide whether to carry out channel activities within its own organization, and if so, which ones.
3 *Length and breadth of channel structure.* The nonprofit must decide on (a) the number of levels to be interposed between the production of the offer and its exchange with consumers (length decisions) and (b) the total number of different channels or the number of elements to be included at each level of the channel (breadth decisions).
4 *Allocation of functions.* The nonprofit needs to decide who will handle the several channel flows (for example, information, goods, and money) in the channel.
5 *Recruiting channel members.* The nonprofit needs to know how to recruit and help motivate channel members.
6 *Coordination and control.* The nonprofit must develop systems for coordinating and controlling various channel members in the system.[4]

In considering these complex issues, we will use *efficiency* and *effectiveness* as our principal criteria. We define these as follows:

Efficiency is the extent to which a system achieves a given level of performance at the least possible cost in financial, time, and personnel resources or achieves the maximum performance for a given level of resource cost.

Effectiveness is the extent to which a system achieves its objectives.

Quality of Customer Service

The first decision the marketer has to make is to determine the level and quality of service to offer to the target market. Each organization can visualize a maximum level of service that could be offered. Here are some examples:

• A public welfare department must distribute thousands of checks a year to people on public relief. The maximum level of service would be to mail checks daily to their homes or even to deliver the checks personally to avoid mail theft.

- A public library could render the maximum amount of service if it stood ready to receive calls for books and to deliver them within a few hours to the person's home.
- A city health department could dispatch doctors to the homes of sick patients upon call.
- A university could send a lecturer to any home or site upon request.

These solutions are oriented toward maximum consumer convenience. They are not practical because consumers would probably not pay for the extra convenience and the supplying organization could not afford the cost. Organizations have to find solutions that offer less consumer convenience in order to keep down the cost of distribution. Libraries and health departments, for example, can bring down their costs by offering their services in only a few locations and leaving the cost of travel to the consumers. They can cut down their costs still further by running an efficient organization in which waiting time is borne mainly by customers instead of becoming idle time borne by the staff. If a health clinic had five doctors instead of ten, the doctors would be continuously busy while the patients would absorb the cost of waiting. Finally, they could reduce their costs by using other media for delivery such as when a university offers interactive TV lectures on pay cable for those who wish to pay for it. Thus, we see that organizations must begin their channel planning with a concept of the level and quality of place utility they will offer.

A second issue that determines the quality of service is the design of the channel facilities. Nonprofit organizations have to make decisions on the "look" of their facilities, because the look can affect customers' attitudes and behavior and their level of satisfaction. Consider how the "atmosphere" of a hospital can affect patients. Many older hospitals have an institutional look, with long narrow corridors, drab wall colors, and badly worn furniture, all of which contribute a depressed feeling to patients who are already depressed about their own condition. Newer hospitals are designed with colors, textures, furnishings, and layouts that reinforce positive patient feelings. They have circular or rectangular layouts with the nursing station in the center, permitting nurses to monitor patients better. Single-care units are replacing the traditional semiprivate rooms, based on the overwhelming preference for single-care units by both patients and physicians.

One of the most dramatic changeovers in atmosphere has occurred in abortion clinics.[5] When abortions were performed illegally, women would enter a depressing office with a single table on which the abortion would be performed. The sight of the office contributed to the patient's feeling of risk and sense of guilt and shame. Today's abortion clinics resemble normal doctor's offices with a comfortable waiting room and a competent receptionist who shows great understanding in dealing with the patient's needs and fears. The patient feels that she is being professionally supported in this difficult moment in her life.

Marketing planners in the future will use atmospherics as consciously and skillfully as they now use price, advertising, personal selling, public relations, and other tools of marketing. *Atmospherics* describes the conscious designing of the place of delivery to create or reinforce specific effects on buyers, such as feelings of well-being, safety, intimacy, or awe.[6]

An organization that is designing a service facility for the first time faces four major design decisions. Suppose a city wishes to build a public art museum. The four decisions are as follows:

1 *What should the building look like on the outside?* The building can look like a Greek temple (as many museums have looked in the past), a villa, a glass skyscraper, or another genre. It can look awe inspiring, ordinary, or intimate. The decision will be influenced by the type of art collection and the message that the museum wants to convey about art in general.

2 *What should be the functional and flow characteristics of the building?* The planners have to consider whether the museum should consist of a few large rooms or many small ones. (Many compromise by having large rooms with many movable walls.) They also have to consider whether the major exhibits and best known artworks should be located near the entrance or at the other end of the building. The rooms and corridors must be designed in a way to handle capacity crowds so that people do not have to wait in long lines and experience congestion.

3 *What should the museum feel like on the inside?* Every building conveys a feeling, whether intended or unplanned. The planners have to consider whether the museum should feel awesome and somber, bright and modern, or warm and intimate. Each feeling will have a different effect on the visitors and their overall satisfaction with the museum.

4 *What materials would best support the desired feeling of the building?* The feeling of a building is conveyed by visual cues (color, brightness, size, shapes), aural cues (volume, pitch), olfactory cues (scent, freshness), and tactile cues (softness, smoothness, temperature). The museum's planners have to choose colors, fabrics, and furnishings that create or reinforce the desired feeling.

The same questions arise for other facilities such as a post office, social service agency, unemployment office, college science building, city police station, and so on. Each facility will have a look that may add or detract from consumer satisfaction and employee performance. The latter point deserves special emphasis. Since the employees work in the facility all day long, the facility should be designed to support them in performing their work with ease and cheerfulness. Granted, many nonprofit organizations are financially weak and cannot afford the facilities that would be desired in principle. But the organization should use the premises as a means of marketing to its employees and customers. It must pay attention to small details of the present facility and take even minor steps to improve the comfort or effectiveness of the facility. Every facility conveys something to the users about the service provider's attitudes toward them. It has been argued that a major reason for the ineffectiveness of YMCAs in attracting fitness-conscious consumers has been the antiquated and excessively spartan facilities they have in many locations.

Direct Versus Indirect Channels

Other things being equal, organizations normally prefer to deal with their consumers directly and not use intermediaries. There are a number of advantages to such an approach:

1 Any revenue from the transaction does not have to be shared with other organizations or individuals.
2 All channel activities are controlled by the marketer.
3 Direct contact with customers provides the marketer with a better understanding of their needs and wants.
4 Direct contact with customers means quicker awareness of any problems with programs and products.
5 Responses to changes in the marketplace (for example, to new competitor initiatives) can be more rapid.
6 Opportunities for experimentation with alternative ways of reaching consumers are available.
7 More attention can be given to the marketer's offering than would be possible if it were only one of many carried by intermediaries.
8 Strategies aimed at various consumer segments can be precisely tailored.

Given all of these advantages, why would an organization give up control at all? One reason we have already noted is that many organizations lack the financial resources to carry out a full program of direct marketing themselves.

Even if an organization has the funds to build its own channel to the final markets, it might not be able to do so as cheaply as through using an existing system. The cost of distributing contraceptives throughout India is low because the intermediaries carry many other products that share in the cost of the distribution network. In a one-product distribution system, all the cost would be borne by that product.

Nor should the organization build its own distribution system if it can put its funds to better use. Thus, the number of births averted might be higher if the Indian government spent its funds to advertise family planning nationwide rather than using all its money to set up its own distribution systems.

The case for using intermediaries often rests on their superior efficiency and effectiveness in the performance of basic marketing tasks and functions. Marketing intermediaries, through their experience, specialization, contacts, and scale, offer the producing organization more than it can usually achieve on its own.

Length Versus Breadth

Once a nonprofit decides that it would be efficient to use intermediaries, decisions must be made as to how many levels to have and how many units to have at each level. These are often referred to as length and breadth decisions, and they usually are not independent decisions. Consider first the breadth decision.

The organization that decides to use retailers for its service rather than directly deliver it to consumers has the further decision of how many retail outlets to operate. The most economical decision is to open a single outlet. By having one large library in a major city, duplication of books, staff, and building costs are avoided. Citizens gain in that they will find an extensive collection of books. They pay the price, however, of having to travel a longer distance. A system consisting of many library branches would attract more users. Most major cities compromise by building a central library and several branch libraries for the convenience of consumers. Some go further and operate bookmobiles, which are mobile libraries that park in different neighborhoods on different days and make books available to consumers.

The cost of running a state university is normally minimized by operating a single campus. Years ago, the University of California was located in Berkeley, California, and the University of Wisconsin was located in Madison, Wisconsin. Gradually these universities opened additional branches, partly to offer more convenience to residents in other parts of the state and partly to keep a single campus from becoming overly large and impersonal. Today the State University of New York (SUNY) operates 64 campuses! Once these universities decided to distribute their offerings throughout the state, they encountered all the classic distribution decisions faced by business firms: how many branch locations to establish, how large should they be, where should they be located, and what specialization should take place at each branch.

At the retail level, breadth decisions are often dictated by consumers. Certain offerings must be mass distributed because consumers will not go out of their way to acquire them. These offerings are called *convenience goods*. In retailing, they usually involve offerings that are not particularly distinctive. For example, men will normally not go far out of their way to acquire condoms for birth control. Similarly, messages designed to change social behavior must be broadly distributed. Consumers do not seek out messages about 55-mile-per-hour speed limits or the use of seat belts. Many target consumers actively avoid channels that might influence them in ways in which they do not really want to be influenced. Alcohol and drug addicts may stop visiting doctors or attending church for fear of inadvertently encountering social marketing messages designed to change their behavior. Marketers must be persistent and innovative to reach these aversive consumers in many locations.

Where some offers and messages must be made very convenient for consumers, other offers may be such that consumers will undertake some effort to find and evaluate them. In retailing, these are referred to as *shopping goods*, since consumers believe they would gain something by looking around. Thus, consumers will go a moderate distance to secure the best emergency care service or smoking-cessation clinic. They will go some distance to see a good museum or watch a good play. In such cases, channel breadth becomes less important.

The final class of offerings is usually referred to as *specialty goods*. These are offers that consumers find so special that they will make a strong effort to seek them out. Further, these offers are perceived to be sufficiently unique that consumers will typically not accept substitutes. This status of being a specialty offering is one that many nonprofit marketers covet. The Mayo Clinic, for example, is clearly a "specialty institution" for well-off consumers with unusual afflictions. A number of traveling art exhibits have proved to be "specialty goods" consumers would go long distances and endure long lines to see. Harvard does not need branch campuses because students consider it a special privilege to study there. On the other hand, the State University of New York (SUNY) needs many branch campuses because students will not travel very far to attend a SUNY institution when nearby substitutes are available.

If a nonprofit organization determines that its customers require a broad distribution system, the next channel strategy question is, "How long should the channel be?" For nonprofits that manufacture a product (like the Sierra Club or the U.S. Treasury), two-, three-, and four-level channels are possible, as suggested in Figure 17–1. In general, the *broader* the distribution at the retail level, the *longer* the channel has to be. That is, if a nonprofit marketer wanted only *exclusive distribution* in a few major locations, a two-step channel (manufacturer to retailer to consumer) would be perfectly adequate. On the other hand, if a *selective distribution* system is chosen, with, say, half a dozen retailers handling the manufacturer's line in each of the largest 250 Standard Metropolitan Statistical Areas in the United States, then several regional wholesalers may be needed to provide coverage. And, if the manufacturer wishes to have *mass distribution* in every nook and cranny of the country, then a manufacturer's representative may be needed to contact the hundreds of wholesalers required to service such a broad market.

Finally, note that strategic decisions about the length and breadth of a channel and whether the channel should be owned by the nonprofit marketer are independent decisions. That is, a marketer could choose a three-tiered system but set up its own wholesaling functions. This tactic would be known as *forward integration*. An environmental lobbying organization that produced its own books and calendars, for example, initially could use wholesalers to market them to recreation areas, book chains, university bookstores, and the like. But later, it could decide that recreation areas were underserved and that it could do better by handling its own product lines and even those of other manufacturers seeking better representation in recreation areas.

Nonprofit organizations can also undertake *backward integration*. Nonprofits such as museums and hospitals have active retail operations for which they contract with one or more wholesalers for merchandise. Many service-based nonprofits, such as nursing homes and religious organizations, acquire substantial amounts of supplies from wholesalers to carry out their operations. Some of these organizations could use available investment capital to integrate backwards in their channel by buying out or setting up a wholesale operation of their own, possibly serving other outlets as well. Again, the prime consideration in such a move should be whether it would result in important efficiencies, better service, or new revenues.

FIGURE 17-1

**Alternative Channel Structures
for a Hypothetical Nonprofit Manufacturer**

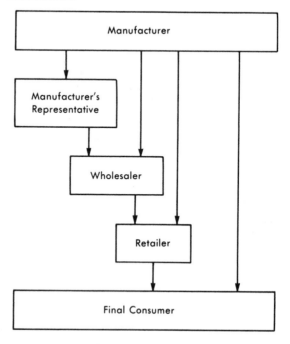

Allocations of Functions

Channels exist to perform a number of functions. Consider the distribution channel for an environmental organization's books. For transactions to take place, the following functions would typically have to be performed:

1 *Physical transportation* of the books from the manufacturer to point of sale.
2 *Financing* of the various transactions between channel members, including the final customer.
3 *Transfer of title* from the manufacturer through to the consumer.
4 *Physical storage* of books at different channel levels.
5 *Determining elements of the offer*, including price, channel discounts, packaging, and so forth.
6 *Communicating* with others about the availability and terms of the offering.
7 *Conducting market research* to learn what consumers want and whether they are satisfied with the present offering.
8 *Providing after-sale service*, such as repairing or replacing damaged merchandise.

Assuming a three-step channel involving a manufacturer, wholesaler, retailer, and final consumer, several alternative allocations of these functions are possible. The standard allocation of functions would be as follows. The manufacturer would determine all pricing and design issues. Books would be delivered to the wholesaler, who delivers to the retailer, to whom the consumer comes to browse and purchase. Each intermediary would take title as the merchandise is received, and each would hold some inventory. The manufacturer would carry out some advertising to retailers and wholesalers, and sometimes, in cooperation with the retailer, to final consumers. The book publisher might also have salespeople who would travel to selected retail outlets promoting books and securing orders to be passed on to the wholesalers. "Market research" could be conducted by the retailers, mostly by observing and talking with book buyers. The retailer would pass the information back, either through the wholesaler to the manufacturer or directly to the manufacturer's salespeople. After-sale exchanges and replacements would be handled by the retailer.

But a number of alternative allocations are possible:

1 The manufacturer could retain title to the goods until they are sold to final consumers. This approach, called consignment selling, would put the entire risk of losses of unsold books with the manufacturer. On the other hand, by retaining ownership, the manufacturer could be assured that the retailer (or wholesaler) would not price the books lower or higher than the manufacturer believed was ideal.
2 The wholesaler could not hold inventory except to service its smallest retail customers. These wholesalers would take title, but the goods destined for large retailers would stay at the manufacturer's until the retailers placed an order.
3 Retailers could carry only a browsing copy. Orders would be sent to the manufacturer, who would ship directly by mail to consumers.
4 The manufacturer could delegate pricing and promotion decisions to wholesalers, who are closer to their markets and better able to tailor the offer to each particular marketplace.
5 The manufacturer might decide that the books are receiving inadequate attention at the retail level and station its own salespeople in larger retail outlets to communicate with customers, secure feedback and sell merchandise directly.

Each of these rearrangements could potentially improve the overall system's efficiency or effectiveness. Consider the second example above, in which the manufacturer shipped directly to the retailer. This could increase *efficiency* if (1) the manufacturer's carrying costs (for example, warehouse rental and interest on working capital) were lower than wholesaler's, (2) the manufacturer could more precisely predict consumer demand and smooth out production runs, and (3) the wholesalers would have no returns of unsold books (only retailers would have returns), so total inventory at any time in the system would be less and the costs of the actual paperwork and shipping of returns would be lower. The move could also improve *effectiveness* if (1) these cost savings permitted a reduction in prices to consumers that brought sales closer to desired levels, and (2) closer contact with retailers more quickly revealed spurts or declines in sales to final consumers, allowing faster manufacturer response (for example, price cuts) to changes in demand or new competitors' strategies.

ATTRACTING CHANNEL RESOURCES

Most nonprofits lack the resources to carry out many of the programs they are mandated to put in place. Thus, they must attract the help of others. In some cases, the problem is how to create channels that do not yet exist. Often this means getting other organizations to help out, as occurred when the American College of Physicians helped with the National Cancer Institute's (NCI) anti-smoking program; AT&T, Alcoa, Xerox, Pillsbury, and Honeywell contributed significantly to NCI's smoking and breast cancer programs; and FAFCO Solar Heating Systems helped distribute a brochure for the President's Council on Physical Fitness and Sports (see Figure 17–2).

Securing corporate sponsorship of programs in the workplace can be particularly effective, especially with respect to health care issues. As Novelli and Ziska point out, "The worksite, where millions of Americans spend roughly one-third of their average day, may be the most promising environment for health behavior change." They note that Kimberley-Clark and Metropolitan Life Insurance both maintain extensive health promotion programs for their staff. Metropolitan's program includes nutrition education and special cafeteria meals as well as fitness, smoking-cessation, breast self-examination, and stress management programs. The director of Metropolitan's Center for Health Help offers the company's rationale for such programs: "People are our company's single biggest asset. It makes good business sense to invest wisely in our employees' good health."[7] New York Telephone claims that its health promotion programs saved it a minimum of $2.7 million in 1981, not considering the possible benefits of more positive employee attitudes and feelings.[8] Many companies would respond very favorably to the kinds of promotions indicated in Figures 17–3 and 17–4.

Nonprofits can secure help by showing that the cooperating organizations can benefit in two ways. First, their participation can improve *public goodwill.* Many consumers, for example, feel more favorable toward the 7-Eleven convenience store chain for helping out with the annual Muscular Dystrophy campaign. Many businesses are impressed with advertising agencies that contribute free help to public service campaigns for the Advertising Council.

Second, their participation can confer *political advantages.* This was clearly a major incentive for five multinational marketers of consumer nondurables who were willing to help the government of India in the early stages of its Nirodh contraceptive marketing program. A major problem for any contraceptive program in a developing country is distributing the product in the most distant regions of the market. The fact that marketers like Unilever and Brooke Bond Tea Company had extensive networks of trucks and peddlers on horseback reaching these remote areas provided major leverage for the Indian program. These foreign-owned companies rely on the government for their import licenses and other assistance. This was undoubtedly in their minds when they agreed to assist the government in its Nirodh program.

FIGURE 17-2

Private-Sector Distribution of a Nonprofit Marketer's Offer

SOURCE: With permission of FAFCO, Inc.

There are many examples of *goodwill-based* private-sector assistance in carrying out nonprofit programs. Examples include the following:

- Major corporations permit payroll deductions for charitable contributions, which provide a significant proportion of United Way's annual collections of more than $3 billion.
- Various media companies contribute substantial amounts of free time and space for public service announcements.
- General Motors has contributed to the seat belt usage drive by offering a $10,000 insurance payout to the beneficiary of anyone killed in a G.M. car while wearing a seat belt.

FIGURE 17-3

Advertisement Asking for Private-Sector Support

SOURCE: Porter/Novelli.
Reprinted with permission.

- Many small retail stores are willing to display containers soliciting donations for charities such as the Kiwanis Club.
- Several milk companies have been putting photographs of lost children on their milk cartons, and selected utilities send out such pictures with their monthly bills.

In late 1985, E.F. Hutton agreed to prepare in-house ads for the American Red Cross's emergency disaster relief campaign. It spent an additional $500,000 on

FIGURE 17-4

Advertisement Asking for Private-Sector Support

SOURCE: Porter/Novelli. Reprinted with permission.

placement of the ads on ABC's "Monday Night Football" and in 85 newspapers. Seven thousand Hutton brokers and corporate officers also made telephone solicitations just before the Christmas holidays. *Advertising Age* suggests that Hutton's motives may be mixed: "The effort should add some luster to Hutton's image as the company continues to feel aftershocks of its check float problems."[9]

Alternative possibilities for using intermediaries to promote mass transit systems are outlined in Exhibit 17-2.

EXHIBIT 17-2

Using Intermediaries to Promote Mass Transit

Robert Prowda of the Portland, Oregon, Transit System has listed a wide range of possibilities that have been tried or proposed for securing intermediary help in promoting mass transit. He grouped these into three categories: fare or service subsidies, cooperative promotional, and institutional.

A. Fare or Service Subsidies

1   Employers purchase tickets or passes and sell them at a discount to employees. In the mid-1980s Southern California Rapid Transit District sold 5,100 passes per month to 20 major employers in the Los Angeles area under such a program.

2   A shopping center, city, or merchants' association may subsidize fares for shoppers coming to their markets. In 1984, for example, SCRTD sold 53,000 tokens to the city of Downey to encourage shopping in their city.

3   Level-of-use guarantees can be made by employers in several cities for special schedules and routes to bring workers to their offices and factories.

4   Sponsors of special recreation, sporting, and cultural events can provide fare subsidies and cooperation on promotion for special transit service to their events.

5   A company or group may subsidize a bus or the entire transit system for a day, night, or weekend for the publicity or advertising benefits. In Champaign, Illinois, a local supermarket chain subsidized a "generic bus." In another American city, a firm has subsidized all transit fares on New Year's Eve to reduce accidents.

6   Firms or organizations can erect bus shelters or transit information displays on their property or provide space for a park-and-ride lot.

B. Cooperative Promotion

1   Employers can sponsor contests, drawings, and the like in which the prizes are passes or reduced fares on public transit.

2   Radio stations can sponsor contests for listeners offering public transit prizes.

3   The Southern California RTD has programs for distributing discount coupons on buses good at selected Pizza Hut and El Pollo Loco locations in Los Angeles.

C. Institutional

1   Efforts can be made to change public incentives to ride the transit system. The Duluth Transit Authority has proposed that bus riders receive a credit on their Minnesota income tax.

2 The Massachusetts Bay Transportation Authority obtained an agreement with the state insurance commission for transit users to receive a 10 percent reduction on their automobile insurance.

3 State agencies reimbursing citizens for any transportation costs could be encouraged to include bus transit. It was discovered, for example, that the state of Oregon was paying jurors 15 cents a mile for auto travel but nothing for use of public transit.

4 If work contracts provide parking subsidies for employees, they should also include subsidies for public transit.

SOURCE: Adapted from Robert M. Prowda, "Leveraging Marketing Efforts Through Third Parties," in Richard K. Robinson and Christopher H. Lovelock, eds., *Marketing Public Transportation* (Chicago: American Marketing Association, 1981), pp. 81–86.

ACHIEVING COORDINATION AND CONTROL

Whether a nonprofit marketer is the "captain" of a channel system or a member of someone else's system, a crucial set of issues involves the day-to-day management of the system. In a mature marketing system, it is usually extremely important not only to have the right intermediaries performing the right function, but to make sure that they are carrying out those functions *when* and exactly in the *form* that is in the best interests of the overall system.

For many reasons, coordination and cooperation is difficult to achieve in nonprofit organizations. Among the impediments are the following:

- Competition for limited funds from either federal sources or third-sector agencies like the United Way may make organizations reluctant to help out present or possible future rivals. Cooperation may be viewed as helping another agency grow, possibly at the expense of one's own agency.
- The insecurities of nonprofit leaders or staff may lead to the perception of cooperation as potential meddling, as a waste of time, or as a distraction from an insecure job.
- Territoriality can be a problem if one agency is unwilling to be subservient to another in an area in which the first agency believes it should be in charge.
- Differences in goals and values can often be a very serious problem when marketing "rears its ugly head." Those who have a social service orientation may feel that involvement with another agency that is an aggressive marketer will be "unprofessional" or will otherwise taint the potential channel member.
- Excessive time and energy costs may occur. If the channel is not well managed, much time might be spent in meeting, planning, and "coordinating." Besides delaying action, this can drive away more action-oriented participants. It has discouraged more than one private-sector marketer from cooperating in a nonprofit program.
- Personality clashes are not unusual. Early in their organizational life cycle, many nonprofits are small and dominated by strong-willed, charismatic executives. In the struggling years of the enterprise, rivalries with other equally strong-willed leaders may develop. These can be very acrimonious and for many years stand in the way of needed cooperation.

The Basic Problem[10]

The fundamental difficulty in achieving coordination and control is that another, separate organization with different perceptions, goals, and skills must undertake tasks that will help the organization achieve its goals. Yet the "channels cooperation problem" is not really different from the problem involved in marketing to final consumers. The problem is still one of *achieving exchanges with target markets*, in this case, key intermediaries. As such, the steps involved in developing an effective intermediary marketing strategy are clear:

1   Identify all potential intermediary segments.
2   Evaluate potential segments and select the best subset for detailed investigation.
3   Identify the basic needs and wants of these target intermediaries.
4   Ascertain their current perceptions of the organization as to the *costs* and *benefits* of compliance as well as noncompliance in the proposed exchanges.
5   Develop strategies to increase the perceived benefits and reduce the perceived costs of participation.
6   Evaluate the probable costs and payoffs of each strategy and select, for the given planning period, those that will best achieve the organization's objectives.
7   Determine optimal strategies for *maintaining* the desired relationships.

Implicit in this approach are a number of marketing principles that we have already emphasized:

● The best marketing strategy *begins with the customer* (the intermediary) rather than the organization.
● It is the target customer's needs, wants, and perceptions that are crucial to success, not those of the organization.
● Since these needs, wants, and perceptions are subjective phenomena, the marketer cannot *know* them and so must resort to formal or informal research to ascertain them.
● The number of exchanges *increases* if and only if the cost/benefit ratios perceived by selected target audiences are *changed* in a favorable direction.
● Since *change* in cost/benefit ratios is crucial, the key research issue is how will target audience perceptions *change* as a result of alternative marketing strategy choices?
● Strategies must be developed not only to create first-time trials, but also to ensure *continued* usage by trial participants, to *increase* usage by present or trial participants, or both.
● Finally, the selection of optimum short- and long-run strategies is not merely a matter of increasing *effectiveness* in creating exchanges, the selection must also take into account the costs to the organization of creating exchanges (the *efficiency* issue).

Strategies for Involving Intermediaries

The ability to make the channel dependent on the marketer indicates that influence has been exerted. The influence potential rests on some form of power. French and Raven have identified seven sources of such power.[11] Each is a *perceived* source of power. To be effective, power never need actually be exerted nor even mentioned (a mob loan enforcer need never *really* break any arms or legs or even *suggest* this to achieve a 100 percent repayment rate). The following are examples of each type of power in nonprofit marketing.

1 *Reward power:* The ability to offer *rewards.* The Public Broadcasting System can allow corporate sponsors of PBS programs to present "commercials" at the beginning and end of prestigious productions. Weight Watchers and Alcoholics Anonymous can permit successful dieters or abstainers to brag about their accomplishments in public. Federal agencies secure cooperation from local counterparts by suggesting that future contracts or grants will be funded or refunded. Charities can provide considerable favorable publicity to cooperating businesses and other organizations.

2 *Coercive power:* The ability to impose punishments. Both public and private universities can be threatened with loss of federal grants if they do not meet Department of Education guidelines as to minority and female hiring. Corporations continuing to pollute the air or water can be threatened by governmental and private groups with significant adverse publicity about their "antisocietal" actions (or *in*actions).

3 *Legal legitimate power:* The ability legally to require desired behaviors. Government contracts can impose requirements for nondiscriminatory behavior on the part of contractors. Contracts for various social change programs can require specific performances, including, for example, evaluation studies at their conclusion (marketing research or a marketing audit).

4 *Traditional legitimate power:* The socially accepted (but not yet legal) ability to require desired behaviors. Although volunteer workers are not contractually bound to the organizations they serve, the latter can dictate dress codes, sales presentations, and sometimes timing and place of work. Contractors in government programs may not be *required* to permit inspection of their programs, but aspects of those programs that don't involve "trade secrets" are generally considered to be open to funders' observations and even participation. Corporations today can be made to feel that local and state officials, by virtue of permitting operations in a given community, have the "right" to dictate certain socially responsible behaviors (specific kinds of waste treatment, job training, and so forth).

5 *Expert power:* The ability to provide expert assistance or guidance. Local chapters of voluntary agencies such as the United Way or the Republican Party can be made to acquiesce to the marketing recommendations of their national organizations because of the latter's presumed greater sophistication. Research contractors new to a topic area can be encouraged to permit heavy editorial guidance for reports aimed at unfamiliar target audiences.

6 *Referent power:* The ability to offer association with a prestigious program or institution. Many liquor manufacturers and beer distributors offer goods and services and/or funding for charitable events because this increases their goodwill. Commercial researchers may agree to carry out specific methodologies because they wish to include work for a prestigious sponsor in their organizational brochures.

7 *Informational power:* The ability to offer information that will help the target organization achieve its goals. This differs from expert assistance in that no superiority in skills is implied. Thus, the Office of Cancer Communications can offer participating physicians informational kits containing antismoking office posters, pamphlets to give to patients who wish to quit, and so on. Various public service agencies can provide cooperating television stations with com-

mercials, announcements, speakers, or educational films to help the stations meet the requirement that they devote a given percentage of their weekly air time to so-called public service announcements (PSAs).

Kasulis and Spekman have suggested that coercive power yields the lowest level of long-run compliance since this relationship often fosters conflict within the channel.[12] On the other hand, legal legitimate power is more effective because it may be internalized to some degree. Referent power is less effective than expert power in achieving long-run identification because the former is subject to the vagaries of peer and public opinion, which is to some degree outside the marketer's control. Finally, traditional legitimate power is less effective than informational power in achieving internalization since the latter, by definition, means that participation in the marketer's program fits closely with the intermediary's goals.

Developing Intermediary Coordination Strategies

The nonprofit marketer seeks to choose influence strategies that will secure intermediary participation and cooperation in particular programs. The choice should be based on an analysis of the marketer's power bases. While the choice often yields a mixed strategy, the options can be grouped into three broad strategic categories. These categories can be described as follows:

1   *Requiring* intermediary cooperation through the use of coercive, traditional legitimate, and legal legitimate power, often in the framework of specific contracts.
2   *Rewarding* intermediary cooperation through the manipulation of reward or referent power.
3   *Persuading* intermediaries to cooperate through the use of expert and informational power (although persuasion, in a sense, is implicit in *all* of these alternatives).

Requiring Cooperation.   Requiring cooperation is a common form of channel control in both the private and public sectors. It is carried out through the use of formal contracts, which specify in greater or lesser degree the rights and duties of each party. These contracts can cover specific functions, as when an advertising agency agrees to provide copy and execution for a series of ads, place the ads in media, and perhaps evaluate the advertising's effects.

> In Bergen County, New Jersey, the state Division of Youth and Family Services (DYFS) handles responsibilities for group counseling and foster day-care services but contracts out half of its services to private medical practitioners and community-based organizations. For example, in cases involving child abuse, emotional neglect, or sexual molestation, it uses the Family Life Center, a hospital-based therapeutic agency. The Family Life Center (FLC) is compensated on a per case basis as specified in the contract. DYFS maintains overall case responsibility as it is legally mandated to do. Operational decisions such as treatment method (individual, family, or group) are left to FLC. DYFS assigns a caseworker to each case, who attends FLC case conferences. DYFS has the final say as to whether and when a case is terminated, although it seeks the advice of FLC therapists.[13]

Such contracts can be very beneficial to the nonprofit because it gains the skills and economies of others while having the contract power to insist on performance. An issue here is how tightly to word the contract. In the private sector, contracts are usually very specific and carefully monitored. In the nonprofit sector, contracts sometimes involve voluntary assistance by the contractee at or below market prices. In such cases, the temptation is to write the contract loosely so that the partly volunteer subcontractor (for example, a research or advertising agency or a broadcasting medium) is not "offended" by "meddling" in their delegated area of responsibility. This loose wording is generally unsatisfactory to both sides. Subcontractors may not know what is expected of them. They may exaggerate their independence and feel abused when the contractor tries to impose its will upon them. The contractor, on the other hand, may feel that it has no clear grounds for making criticisms and that it has lost control of the subcontracted operation. And, of course, if legitimate disputes do arise, the ensuing bickering can destroy a channel relationship that may be the *only* way for a nonprofit contractor to get its job done.

A channel control technique that has become increasingly common in the private sector is *franchising.* For years, there have been territorial agreements in the automobile and beverage industries whereby the number of dealers in an area is regulated. In return for this local partial monopoly, the franchisee is expected to meet certain performance standards (for example, quotas) and to carry on the enterprise in a particular fashion (for example, use certain signs, charge certain prices, engage in so much cooperative advertising, and so on). Recent growth, however, has been in franchise systems with much stronger central control. In the McDonald's, Burger King, Midas Muffler, and other chain franchises, virtually the entire operation of the franchise may be specified by the franchisor down to the size of the dollop of catsup to go on a hamburger or the number of straws in a soft drink. Usually, the franchise is based upon some distinctive trade name or style such that the franchisee is willing to pay for both the expertise and the extra marketplace competitive edge.

In Egypt, the franchise concept has been proposed as a way of standardizing family planning clinics and upgrading their image in the minds of target consumers. The Family of the Future (FOF) social marketing organization has been building a reputation as an efficient and effective marketer of contraceptive products. It has begun four successful clinics of its own. By contrast, other clinics in Egypt, especially in the more rural areas, are in very poor condition, are poorly managed, and suffer very low reputations. It has been proposed that FOF take over the *management* of these clinics and possibly franchise its name to other clinics that are currently private as a way of securing more coverage and higher, more standardized quality of services. To the extent that such a network could be established, national advertising could be used to make the franchise name attractive to other private clinics or new investors.

The contractual approach ultimately relies on legal authority and the potential imposition of penalties as a means of achieving the nonprofit marketer's ends. As long as the terms are carefully described, are fair to both sides, and there is a sense of shared responsibility for desired social outcomes, a contractual approach can work well, and the use of formal power by the contractor need only be a subtle background issue. On the other hand, if the contractual relationship is unclear and the interaction between the parties discordant, power may be used by the contractor to coerce the contractee into performing the needed channel functions. To the extent that such formal coercive power has to be used, the long-term potential for the channel relationship is not promising.

Rewarding and Persuading Cooperation.   Rather than base channel cooperation on negative incentives, many organizations simply make it worthwhile for others to help them out. They offer specific economic rewards such as commissions or noneconomic rewards such as increased prestige through cooperating with a major social program. In both cases, extensive persuasion may still be needed to convince potential target intermediaries that cooperation will benefit both parties.

SUMMARY

Exchanges require that offers be made available at a particular time and in a particular place. Often, this requires the services of other agencies (who can provide warehouse and transportation facilities) and careful coordination of complex interacting systems. While channels may simply be means to facilitate consumers' time and place utilities, they have the potential to either significantly augment or effectively sabotage carefully designed marketing programs.

To achieve an effective and efficient channel strategy, the nonprofit marketer must decide what quality of service to offer and whether marketing will be direct or indirect. Then, the marketer must determine the length and breadth of the channel, recruit channel members, and assign functions. Finally, the marketer should put systems for effective coordination and control among the channel members in place.

Coordination and control are best achieved by judicious use of the power potentially available to the nonprofit marketer. This power can be based on rewards, coercion, law, social norms, expertise, prestige, or control of critical information. In general, power strategies that rely on simple compliance on the part of intermediaries (for example, those based on coercion or the law) are less effective in the long run than strategies that encourage intermediaries to identify with and internalize the nonprofit organization's goals.

QUESTIONS

1.   What are the kinds of power that the United Way of America could use to

get local United Ways to carry out at least three surveys in major workplaces in each of the next four years? Give examples in as many of the seven power categories mentioned in this chapter as possible.

2. What assistance from intermediaries could the U.S. Agency for International Development secure in a developing country to assist in a marketing program to get more children immunized against major communicable diseases?

3. An art museum in a medium-sized city has decided to produce a limited number of moderately priced art books ($25 to $50 each). What factors should it consider in deciding whether to use a broad or a deep distribution strategy?

4. When nonprofits use for-profit distributors in developing countries, the latter often seek ways to make the distribution effort more efficient. Nonprofits are typically suspicious of such efforts, fearing that they will compromise the effectiveness of their programs. What rules could they establish to maintain program effectiveness while permitting the for-profits to seek greater efficiency?

5. Federal government agencies like the National Cancer Institute often cooperate with major corporations to carry out programs. How could corporations sabotage unintentionally such programs (not just fail to pursue them)?

NOTES

1. Michael B. Anspaugh, "Americans Continue to Ignore the $2 Bill," *Flint Journal*, November 7, 1978, reprinted in Christopher H. Lovelock and Charles B. Weinberg, eds., *Readings in Public and Nonprofit Marketing* (Palo Alto, Calif.: Scientific Press, 1978), pp. 222–223; and "Numismatic Ms.," *Time*, July 9, 1979, p. 54.

2. Quoted from an unpublished term paper on the Faith Covenant Church of Wheaton written by Mark F. Pufundt at Northwestern University, 1980.

3. Ronald Abler, John S. Adams, and Peter Gould, *Spatial Organization* (Englewood Cliffs, N.J.: Prentice-Hall, 1971), pp. 531–532.

4. An excellent introduction to these issues is found in Louis W. Stern and Adel I. Ansary, *Marketing Channels*, 2nd ed. (Englewood Cliffs, N.J.: Prentice-Hall, 1982).

5. Donald W. Ball, "An Abortion Clinic Ethnography," in William J. Filstead, ed., *Qualitative Methodology* (Chicago: Markham, 1970).

6. For more details, see Philip Kotler, "Atmospherics as a Marketing Tool," *Journal of Retailing*, Winter 1973–1974, pp. 48–64.

7. This and the Novelli and Ziska quote are from William D. Novelli and Deborah Ziska, "Health Promotion in the Workplace: An Overview," *Health Education Quarterly*, Vol. 9, Special Supplement, 1982, pp. 20–26.

8. "Health Program Savings Cited," *American Medical News*, September 4, 1981.

9. Brian Moran, "Hutton Aids Red Cross Plea," *Advertising Age*, December 9, 1985, p. 67.

10. The material in the following section is adapted from Alan R. Andreasen, "A Power Potential Approach to Middlemen Strategies in Social Marketing," *European Journal of Marketing*, Vol. 18, no. 4 (1984), pp. 56–71.

11. John R. French and Bertram Raven, "The Bases of Social Power," in D. Cartwright, ed., *Studies in Social Power* (Ann Arbor: University of Michigan Press, 1959).

12. Jack Kasulis and Robert Spekman, "A Framework for the Use of Power," *European Journal of Marketing*, October 1980, pp. 70–78.

13. Adell P. Fine and Seymour H. Fine, "Distribution Channels in Marketing Social Work," *Social Casework*, Vol. 67, April 1986, p. 231.

18

Formulating
Communications Strategies

The "sponsors" of child survival programs are sometimes movie stars, sometimes the wives of presidents, sometimes rock singers—but not always. Sometimes they aren't even real, and sometimes they aren't even human.

- Dr. Salustiano (or Dr. Healthy) was a deep-voiced fictional radio character in Honduras with a homey image. The caring voice of the actor who played Dr. Salustiano made him an instant hit. Within a year, local pharmaceutical firms used the same actor to promote their drugs. After a lull in the campaign, the director general of health held a press conference and a reporter asked, "When will the Ministry of Health reinstate Dr. Salustiano?" The director general replied casually, "Oh, someday he'll come back." But the reporter responded, "Dr. Salustiano is an important figure in Honduras and the public demands that he return to give us helpful advice."

- *La bolsa*, according to traditional Honduran beliefs, is a bag which rests in the lower middle abdomen and contains worms. When a person eats greasy or spoiled foods, the worms leave their bag and cause diarrhea. There is no medical foundation for this belief, and the Ministry of Health did not want it encouraged. Communication specialists decided to make use of the local belief in a comic way, without ridiculing it. Lombricio and Lombrolfo, two charming worms, were introduced in a radio spot in which they talked to each other about life in the bag. They described the things they hate most: clean food, boiled water, and so forth. The Ministry of Health was satisfied. The audience loved them.

Source: Mark R. Rasmuson, Renata E. Seidel, William A. Smith, Elizabeth Mills Booth, *Communication for Child Survival* (Washington, D.C.: Academy for Educational Development, June 1988), p. 47. Reproduced with permission.

In Chapter 1, we defined marketing as a philosophy, process, and set of strategies and tactics for influencing behavior—either changing behavior or preventing it from changing (for example, keeping teenagers from taking up smoking). In the immediately preceding chapters, we considered the offer, price, and place components of the marketing mix and saw that these components must be in place before any program can be successful. We have also seen that these components can influence behaviors directly by providing incentives for action or reducing disincentives. But in the vast majority of nonprofit marketing strategies, influencing behavior is largely a matter of *communication*. It is a matter of *informing* target audiences about the alternatives for action, the positive consequences of choosing a particular one, and the motivations for acting (and often *continuing* to act) in a particular way.

Communication is not something that nonprofits can ignore. Everything about an organization—its products, employees, facilities, and actions—communicates something. Each organization must examine its communication style, needs, and opportunities and develop a communication program that is influential and cost effective. The organization's communications responsibilities go beyond communicating to target consumers. The organization must communicate effectively with external publics such as the press, government agencies, and the financial community. It must communicate effectively with its internal publics, particularly its board members, middle management, and professional and clerical employees as well as any volunteers it uses. The organization must know how to communicate about itself to various groups in order to gain their support and goodwill.

An organization may use a great many communications vehicles to inform and motivate target publics. These include

- Space and time advertising
- Loudspeaker advertising
- Mailings
- Speeches
- Sales presentations
- Demonstrations
- Word of mouth
- Posters and show cards
- Point-of-sales displays
- Sales literature
- Catalogs
- Films
- Trade exhibits
- Sales conferences
- Packaging
- Packaging inserts
- House-organ publications
- Offer publicity
- Corporate publicity
- Corporate identification programs
- Endorsements
- Special events
- Promotional giveaways

However, decisions on which of these vehicles to use, when to use them and how must follow from a clear understanding of the communications process.

THE COMMUNICATIONS PROCESS

Any communication process involves a message *sender* and a message *receiver* (a target audience). The sender has an *intended message*, but whether the *received message* is in most respects identical to it is determined by the extent to which the communications process is relatively noise free and the sender and receiver share the same *cultural codes*. This process is outlined in Figure 18-1.

A *sender* (the Los Angeles Philharmonic, for example) formulates an *intended message* ("A new conductor, Esa-Pekka Salonen, brings fresh, new excitement to Los Angeles Philharmonic concerts"). The *encoder* (an advertising agency) translates this intended message into an *encoded message* (a picture of an energetic Esa-Pekka Salonen, a headline: "Musical Excitement Comes to L.A.," and four paragraphs describing Salonen's past connections with Los Angeles and his rave reviews as guest conductor of the Los Angeles Philharmonic. The paragraphs also describe the diversity of his background and his own thoughts on his plans for Los Angeles).

This message gets transmitted through such *media* as regional editions of *Time* and *Newsweek* magazines, which the ad agency believes will add an aura of "seriousness" to the encoded message. The *decoders* may be a young couple glancing at a magazine in a doctor's office, discussing between themselves the direct and implied content of the ad ("Gee, he seems awfully young. I wonder if he is one of those 'with-it' kids who loves Philip Glass but can't cope with

FIGURE 18-1

Elements in the Communication Process

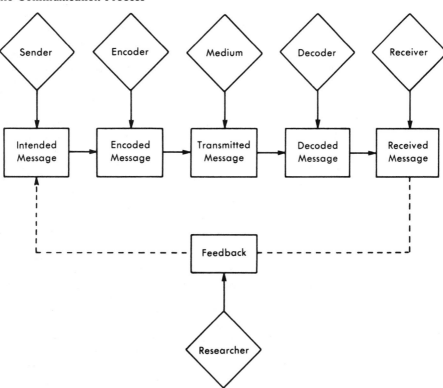

Mahler or handle a mature, demanding orchestra.") Finally, each *receiver* member of the couple retains traces of the memorable parts of the message and associations (for example, Salonen's age and his quotes about Los Angeles), which can be assessed by a market *researcher* checking for *feedback* in a posttest telephone survey.

In many actual situations, the roles portrayed in Figure 18-1 may be combined. For example, there can be two-party communication involving (1) the sender-encoder-medium-researcher and (2) the decoder-receiver. This would be the case in many kinds of personal selling situations. The salesperson would decide what message to get across, encode it into a "sales pitch," transmit it verbally, and watch for or inquire about the customer's response. The customer would decode the salesperson's sales pitch and store whatever was personally meaningful in it.

Even in this relatively simple two-party situation, a number of kinds of "noise" can creep in:

1 *Encoding*. The salesperson may choose the wrong wording to convey key concepts. A donor solicitation specialist for a nonprofit foundation, for example, may intend to make it clear that the donor can be anonymous, but by making frequent references to *possible* forms of recognition, leave the overall impression that the donor cannot escape publicity.

2 *Transmitting*. Vocal inflections or body language in the delivery of the message can change its meaning. For example, if a person seeking a donation for a hospital adopts too "serious" a tone of voice when speaking about the scientific quality of the research work being done at the hospital, he or she may unintentionally convey the impression that the scientists are pessimistic about possible outcomes. In another example, if a flip chart is used to outline the possible types of funding sought and possible uses of those funds, the speed with which pages of the chart are physically "flipped" may unintentionally tell a potential donor which areas the hospital *really* thinks are important.

3 *Decoding*. The target audience can mishear what is said. A 70 percent success rate for a health care facility may be heard as 17 percent. A distracted decoder may miss important benefits. The meaning given to heard statements can also vary greatly, depending on what experiences the decoder brings to the message.[1] A potential donor with queasy personal reactions to the sight of blood may not really "see" flip chart pictures or slides showing or implying "bloody" events. A racially prejudiced potential donor may "decide" that an agency is not well run if "too many" staff blacks or Hispanics are portrayed. The target audience member may not like the salesperson and so tend to discount his or her opinions or assertions.

4 *Researching*. Salespeople vary greatly in their ability to read the responses of target customers. Indeed, as noted in Chapter 21, an important characteristic of a good salesperson is "empathy," the ability to put oneself in another's shoes. Thus, noise is added to the communications process if the salesperson interprets a potential donor's silence as signaling a lack of interest when it actually means that the donor is reflecting carefully on the merits of a proposal. Alternatively, a salesperson might decide that the cause of a potential donor's indifference is stinginess when in fact it is caused by the donor's irritation at the salesperson's manner of presentation. Finally, it is possible that the target consumer may encode his or her own feelings with some distortion. Indeed,

feedback is really another communications process with the target consumer as the sender and the marketing organization as the receiver.

Of course, in a great many communications situations, the process involves several agencies or individuals acting in one or more of the roles indicated in Figure 18-1. In these cases, the potential for "noise" is enhanced:

1 *Encoding*. Salespeople may be designated as agents for communicating top management's sense of mission for the hospital—and can get the message wrong or distort it. Alternatively, an advertising agency or public relations firm may be given the task of encoding the organization's *intended* message but may produce words or images that distort or inflate management's intentions. Thus, too-slick graphics or a "with it" ad layout for a symphony orchestra may suggest that the orchestra is not a solid, well-trained ensemble or that its repertoire is too avant-garde for most tastes. Every time another player is added to the communication process, he or she brings to it his or her own interests, values, goals, and perceptions. Some advertising or public relations agencies direct their messages at least partly towards their fellow advertising or PR colleagues. Sometimes their main goal seems to be to attempt to dazzle their peers with the style and drama of a message's "encoding." The advertising community is replete with stories of award-winning campaigns (such as Alka Selzer's "spicy meatball" ads of the 1970s) that were later abandoned by the advertiser because they were ineffective in generating sales.

2 *Transmitting*. The vehicle through which you say something can enhance or distort a message. Many advertisers believe that putting an ad in a particular medium (for example, *The New Yorker* or *Town and Country*) adds a sense of "class" to their presentation. Or they may choose a spokesperson (a Cliff Robertson, Barbara Bush, or Bill Cosby) who will bring his or her own prestige or charisma to the nonprofit agency's message. But sometimes the spokesperson can be inappropriate, can be seen as "doing it for the money" or as having little in common with the target audience.

   Certain media can be inappropriate. Radio ads on a rock station may be wrong for a "serious" hospital, and a classical music station may be wrong for a hospital trying to position itself as being "for everyone." Print ads in *Playboy* may get high readership but convey the wrong impression about a clinic's exercise therapy program. A symphony that wants to seem less elite should avoid *U.S. News and World Report*, while a political candidate might find this magazine a very appropriate vehicle for adding to his or her "stature."

3 *Decoding*. Depending on how they are viewed by potential customers, channel members and their agents may serve as decoders for consumers. Thus, a physician may be asked by a patient to interpret the latest publicity release on smoking or high blood pressure or by a young woman to explain what a new low-dose contraceptive pill will really do for her (or *to* her, in the case of side effects). In a similar fashion, newspaper or TV critics may "decode" a symphony or theater's offering. The Consumers Union may evaluate products, services, and even advertising themes. Reporters and political analysts play the same role for voters. In all of these cases, what the marketer wants to say may take on very different meaning once it is filtered through these "helpful" role players.

4 *Researching*. Outside agencies can be hired by the marketer to assess directly the target audience's present moods, opinions, or specific responses to the marketer's messages. To the extent that this intervention involves the perceptions,

judgments, empathy, *and* communications skills of these other agents, there is significant potential for distortion.

Most problematic is the case where "independent" third parties take on the role of providing feedback to the marketer. Examples would include the self-appointed spokesperson for the oppressed who tells marketers "the truth" about how the group has been mistreated and the opinion polls from trade associations that tell the government how the public is reacting to particular ongoing programs or new proposals. On the other hand, there are also many respected associations that offer accurate feedback about what their members think and feel as well as thoughtful newspaper, magazine, and television commentators who are well attuned to the public opinions of special subgroups.

Strategic Implications

The major implication of this view of the communication process is that in any given situation the probability is very high that the *received message* will be different from the *intended message*. Two corollaries of this conclusion are:

1 The more role players there are in the communications process, the greater the chance for distortion.
2 The less control the marketer has over the role players in the communications process, the greater the chance for distortion.

This has several implications for marketing strategy:

1 The nonprofit communicator should *never* assume that the target audience is "receiving" what the communicator thinks is being "sent."
2 If communication strategy is to be improved, it is essential that the marketer know what is being received.
3 If knowing what is received is crucial, careful attention must be paid to the quality of the *feedback* link in the system.
4 If quality feedback is desired, the marketer should carefully control the feedback process, at the very least conducting formal research before or after the message is transmitted.
5 If formal feedback research is carried out before the launch of the message or a message campaign, pretesting should simulate the *entire* communication process. For example, if a program of patient hypertension education is to be conducted by slide presentations and brochures that physicians pass along to patients, simply testing physicians' responses or patients' responses to the materials alone would be inadequate. The marketer must test *both* steps in either a laboratory or a test market setting to see (a) how the physicians perceive the materials, (b) how often and with what advice they pass them on to the patients, and (c) how patients decode and store what the physicians tell them.
6 If communications are distorted at the receiving end, it is important to trace the source of the distortion to its roots. In the preceding example, the hypertension message could be inaccurately received because:
   a it was poorly encoded by the marketer in the first place (that is, the brochures and slides were poorly designed);

    b   it was well encoded, but physicians often added their own embellishments, verbal cues, or body language, which changed the content; and/or

    c   the typical receiver was sufficiently misinformed about the disease *before* hearing the message that parts that seemed frightening were simply not "heard" at any important level.

The changes needed in the communications program would vary significantly depending on which of these problems was the primary source of message noise.

7   If a message *must* be received undistorted (for example, instructions about what a mother should do when her child is in a life-threatening situation), and it must be the same for all targeted customers, perfectly clear written communications directly delivered to the consumer are obviously superior.

8   On the other hand, if a message must be carefully adjusted to individual consumers (for example, how a person should change personal diet and exercise patterns), then a flexible, personally delivered message strategy is preferable because of its potential for ongoing feedback. (The one proviso here is that the personal salesperson be one who is naturally empathetic or is carefully trained in *undistorted listening* techniques.)

MAJOR STEPS IN DEVELOPING EFFECTIVE COMMUNICATIONS

We shall now consider the major steps in developing effective persuasion communications. The steps include (1) setting communication objectives, (2) generating possible messages, (3) overcoming selective attention, (4) overcoming perceptual distortion, (5) choosing a medium, and (6) evaluating and selecting messages. We turn later to the possibilities of modifying behavior directly.

Setting Communication Objectives

The first step calls for the marketer to define carefully the objective or objectives of the communications program. Possible objectives include

  1 Making target consumers aware of a product, service, or social behavior.

  2 Educating consumers about the offer or changes in the offer.

  3 Changing beliefs about the negative and positive consequences of taking a particular action.

  4 Changing the relative importance of particular consequences.

  5 Enlisting the support of intermediary agencies (for example, securing shelf space).

  6 Recruiting, motivating, or rewarding employees or volunteers.

  7 Changing perceptions about the sponsoring organization.

  8 Influencing governing agencies, review boards, commissions, and the like.

  9 Preventing discontinuation of behaviors.

10 "Proving" superiority over competitors.

11 Combating injurious rumors.

12 Influencing funding agencies.

Generating Possible Messages

Once the nonprofit marketer has determined a broad objective or set of objectives for the communications program, the next step is to encode it in *specific* messages. Message generation involves developing a number of alternative messages (appeals, themes, motifs, ideas) from which the best one can be chosen.

Messages can be generated in a number of ways. One approach is to talk with members of the target market and other influential parties to determine how they see the product or service, talk about it, and express their desires about it. A second approach is to hold a brainstorming meeting with key personnel in the organization to generate several ideas. A third method is to use some formal deductive framework to tease out possible advertising messages. We will discuss three deductive frameworks.

Rational, Emotional, Moral Framework.   One framework identifies three types of messages that can be generated: rational, emotional, and moral.

1   *Rational messages* aim at passing on information, serving the audience's self-interest, or both. They attempt to show that the service will yield the expected functional benefits. Examples would be messages discussing a service's quality, economy, value, or performance.

2   *Emotional messages* are designed to stir up some negative or positive emotion that will motivate the desired behavior. Communicators have worked with fear, guilt, and shame appeals, especially in connection with getting people to start doing things they should do (for example, brush their teeth, have an annual health checkup) or stop doing things they shouldn't do (for example, smoke, overimbibe, abuse drugs, overeat, or bring illegal fruit across the border). (See Figure 18-2.) Advertisers have found that fear appeals work up to a point, but if there is too much fear the audience will ignore the message.[2] Communicators have also used positive emotional appeals such as love, humor, pride, and joy. Evidence has not, however, established that a humorous message, for example, is necessarily more effective than a straight version of the same message.

3   *Moral messages* are directed to the audience's sense of what is right and proper. They are often used in messages exhorting people to support such social causes as a cleaner environment, better race relations, equal rights for women, and aiding the disadvantaged. An example is the March of Dimes appeal: "God made you whole. Give to help those He didn't." Moral appeals are less often used in connection with everyday products.

Reward/Situation Framework.   Maloney proposed another deductive framework. He suggested that buyers may expect any of four types of reward from an offering: a *rational, sensory, social,* or *ego satisfaction* reward. And they may visualize these rewards from *results-of-use experience, product-or-service-in-use experience,* or *incidental-to-use experience*. Crossing the 4 types of rewards with the 3 types of situations generates 12 types of advertising messages.[3] (See Table 18-1.)

Attitude Change Theory Framework.   A third way to generate possible

FIGURE 18-2

Example of "Shame" Appeal

SOURCE: Foote Cone & Belding, Chicago, IL. Reproduced with permission.

messages is to work through an attitude change framework. Consider the communications problem of the marketing director of St. Anthony's Hospital, Axel Arneson, who is seeking to persuade a specific physician, Dr. Laura Goldman, to admit more of her patients to the hospital's oncology ward instead of to a competitor, the Downtown Medical Center. Suppose that from conversations with Dr. Goldman, Mr. Arneson has determined that there are four key consequences that Dr. Goldman considers when deciding where to admit a patient. These consequences are:

1 The extent to which the nursing staff is well trained enough to competently administer Dr. Goldman's treatment plan and to make sensible judgments on occasions when the plan doesn't apply and Dr. Goldman is unavailable for consultation.
2 The extent to which other physicians affiliated with the hospital (especially those in oncology) can provide good advice and share in patient treatment.
3 The extent to which Dr. Goldman will have access to the latest testing and treatment equipment and other patient care facilities.
4 The extent to which Dr. Goldman will have her wishes respected and carried out regarding admissions, treatment, office space, fees, and billing.

Mr. Arneson has estimated her beliefs about the likelihood of achieving these consequences from each of the rival hospitals as follows:

	St. Anthony's	Dowtown Medical Center
Good nursing care	.8	.7
Access to knowledgeable colleagues	.9	.6
Access to best facilities	.5	.7
Have my wishes respected	.4	.8

From his conversation, Mr. Arneson judges that Dr. Goldman gives weightings of 20 percent, 30 percent, 30 percent, and 20 percent, respectively to the four consequences. Mr. Arneson further believes that Dr. Goldman's attitude toward the two institutions is very similar to those of a sizable contingent of other physicians in the area. Finally, Mr. Arneson believes that his hospital's low ratings on the "facilities" and "respect" consequences stem from the relative age and overcrowded appearance of his physical plant.

Now let's apply the attitude framework to Mr. Arneson's problem. Given the definition of attitude in Chapter 4 as an overall evaluation of the consequences of taking action, attitudes can be changed in three ways:

• Changing the importance of one or more consequences
• Changing beliefs about one or more consequences
• Adding new (presumably positive) consequences

CHANGING IMPORTANCE WEIGHTS.   The first possibility open to Mr. Arneson is to attempt to change the importance weightings that Dr. Goldman and those like her attach to the four consequences. Thus, he might attempt to increase the weighting given to "access to knowledgeable colleagues" (on which his hospital scores well) and reduce that given to "access to best facilities" by arguing as follows:

Table 18-1

EXAMPLE OF REWARDS/SITUATIONS MESSAGES FOR A
HOSPITAL OBSTETRICS PROGRAM

	Situations		
Rewards	*Results-of-Use*	*Product-or-Service-in-Use*	*Incidental-to-Use*
Rational	You pay less at our hospital.	You make the major decisions about the birth at our hospital.	We bill your insurance company directly.
Sensory	We videotape the birth so you can relive the wonder of the birth.	Husbands share the emotions of the birth.	We have great food and wine.
Social	Husbands and wives will feel they shared something important.	Husbands can help in the delivery.	We allow your children to visit.
Ego Satisfaction	You will be assured that you have given your new baby the best start on life.	First-time mothers will feel really in control of our program.	You can tell your friends you were among the first to use our new service.

"Many physicians think that the kind of hospital they want to work in is the one with the very best equipment and testing facilities. We know that's important. But the best equipment is only as good as the people who make it work and who help draw the most from its results. It is one thing to have the latest CAT scanner, quite another to be around colleagues who know just when to use it and how to wring the last ounce of meaning out of its readouts. We think that is *really* the kind of institution you want to be affiliated with, one that has the most up-to-date facilities but, even more, that has the staff and colleagues who are on the leading edge of research and diagnoses using these new technical wonders."

Notice that this attempt at attitude change made no mention of St. Anthony's or its rivals. Mr. Arneson knew that St. Anthony's scored well on "knowledgeable colleagues" and not so well on "facilities." He knows that if he can switch the weightings from 30 to 40 percent on "colleagues" and 30 to 20 percent on "facilities," St. Anthony's would be the favored institution, not Downtown Medical Center.

CHANGING BELIEFS.   Should Arneson decide that changing the weightings is too difficult or too risky to attempt, he has another option, trying to change beliefs. Here, he can make use of suggestive social science frameworks, such as dissonance and assimilation/contrast theories.

Dissonance theory. One characteristic of human beings is that we prefer order and meaning. We like things to fit well together. We don't take kindly to messages that run counter to our present cognitions. When we encounter such dissonant messages, if the issue is involving, we will attempt to reassert order in our cognitive structure, our view of the world. That is, we will attempt to restore consonance.[4] We adopt several strategies to cope with dissonance.

Suppose that Dr. Goldman heard a rumor that several Downtown Medical internists and laboratory technicians had serious drug abuse problems. This would be dissonant with her view that Downtown had reasonably good colleagues (and, of course, with any interest in sending her patients there). Dr. Goldman could restore consonance in several ways:

1 *Denial.* She could convince herself that the rumors "couldn't be true" (for example, that they were the work of "enemies" of DMC).
2 *Search for disconfirmation.* She could seek information from administrators at DMC that would counter the rumors.
3 *Reduce the importance of the issue.* We can all live with some amount of dissonance provided it isn't perceived to be related to an issue in which we are highly involved. Thus, Dr. Goldman might decide that although the rumor may be true, it isn't really a very serious matter because (a) the people in question probably don't work in highly technical areas like hers, (b) even if they did, she could personally spot them and avoid them, (c) hospital administrators would certainly take care of the problem; or (d) even if the problem can't be entirely dealt with, it would be no better anywhere else (for example, at St. Anthony's).
4 *Change prior beliefs.* Dr. Goldman may judge the rumors to be true and change her belief about DMC's staff and her own decision to send patients there.

The last mentioned is, of course, an instance of *changed beliefs*. It is a case in which new information caused a negative result from DMC's standpoint but a positive one where St. Anthony's is concerned. While one would not expect Mr. Arneson to resort to spreading unsubstantiated rumors about a rival institution, one can see that the introduction of dissonant information can change beliefs. Thus, Mr. Arneson could seek to offer facts about St. Anthony's or about Downtown Medical Center that he believed Dr. Goldman would find dissonant. It is crucial that the facts chosen (1) be so convincing that they could not easily be denied, (2) concern some highly involving area not likely to be minimized by Dr. Goldman, and (3) be difficult to counter by other facts.

Assimilation/contrast theory. A danger that Mr. Arneson risks in presenting potential dissonant information is that it may fail a plausibility test even before Dr. Goldman considers it. Sherif and Sherif, have proposed that each individual has a position on a given belief dimension.[5] Thus, we noted that Dr. Goldman's best estimate of the likelihood that she will receive respectful treatment at St. Anthony's is currently .4. If one were to probe Dr. Goldman's beliefs further, we might discover that given additional information she might revise this probability downward as low as .2 or upward as high as .7. Sherif, Sherif, and

Nebergill refer to this range as Dr. Goldman's *latitude of acceptance*. By contrast, if for some reason Mr. Arneson tried to maximize Dr. Goldman's dissonance by suggesting that the true probability would be .9 or 1.0 (in sharpest contrast with .4), Dr. Goldman would just find the assertion implausible. In such a case, dissonance would not occur and no attitude change would ensue. The region in which implausible statements would fall is labeled by the Sherifs as the *latitude of rejection*. (Beliefs falling into neither range are said to be in the *latitude of indifference*.)

To get the maximum attitude change, the Sherifs would recommend that Mr. Arneson try to bring information to bear that would seem likely to bring Dr. Goldman's belief to the .7 level. Thus, he should *not* promise her a large, immaculately furnished office and instant response to requests for laboratory tests. Rather, he should indicate, for example, that she would have a recently redecorated, if modest-sized, office equal to that of other senior staff members and that her laboratory requests would be given rapid attention as befits a senior staffer (providing she was judicious in the number of rush requests). That is, he should suggest that the "respect" and "facilities" consequences of affiliating with St. Anthony's would be at the believable level of .7 rather than the unbelievable 1.0 level. In general, as suggested in Figure 18-3, it is best to bring individuals to the farthest and most desirable point *within* their latitude of acceptance. Further, the theory suggests that, as the target audience adjusts to this new belief, their latitude of acceptance will also shift and new communication strategies can be

FIGURE 18-3

Hypothetical Beliefs of Two Individuals about the Consequences of Increased Pollution Control on Business

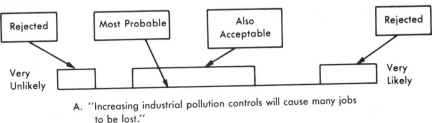

A. "Increasing industrial pollution controls will cause many jobs to be lost."

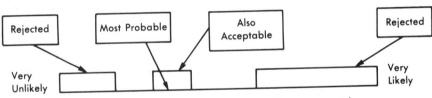

B. "Increasing industrial pollution controls will cause many jobs to be lost."

designed to move them even further along. By this process, they may eventually be brought to the point advocated by the dissonance theorists in the first case.

Of course, not everyone will have either the same beginning beliefs or the same range of acceptable positions. Indeed, one measure of the firmness of a person's beliefs is the ratio of the latitude of acceptance to the latitude of rejection. The individual in Figure 18-3A is clearly much more fixed in beliefs than the individual in Figure 18-3B. The former is described as being much more *dogmatic* or narrow minded.

ADDING CONSEQUENCES.   A third alternative available to Mr. Arneson is to add one or more new, positive beliefs. Indeed, this is a common strategy in the profit sector for differentiating a brand in a highly competitive market environment or rescusitating a brand in the decline phase of its life cycle. Potential customers are told about a new consequence of using the product or service or engaging in a behavior. Sometimes, these new consequences only require imagination and not a fundamental change in the offering. Thus, a marketer may point out to those not swayed by arguments about the positive health consequences of participating in a stop-smoking clinic that participation may also lead to making new friends. Or new parents may be encouraged to use a library not only for information about parenting, but also to learn about library services that their new child could appreciate or learn to use, such as weekly storytelling hours or children's record rentals.

Sometimes, however, the marketer may wish to change the offer fundamentally or marginally by adding one or more new consequences. This, of course, is the intended effect when marketers offer premiums or bonuses for purchases or attendance. Thus, a symphony orchestra could entice more new attenders by having the conductor or soloist on a particular evening agree to autograph album covers before a performance. Or the Peace Corps could offer to photograph participants in the field and to write reference letters to impress future employers.

In Mr. Arneson's case, he may discover "perks" that might appeal to Dr. Goldman. This could be an augmentation to the basic offering such as a special parking location, an advanced dictation system for patient reports, or first perusal of the library's copies of key journals in her field. Alternatively (or in addition), Mr. Arneson may simply point out additional existing features of St. Anthony's and its staff, such as the publication record of attending physicians, which would indicate that both typing facilities and knowledgeable colleagues would be available for whatever writing ambitions Dr. Goldman might harbor.

Assuming that Mr. Arneson wishes to improve Dr. Goldman's belief about the "respect" consequences of sending her patients to St. Anthony's, he can only do so moderately. There are other problems he must also overcome. These are customers' tendencies to attend to messages selectively and to distort perceptually what they see.

Overcoming Selective Attention

Mr. Arneson must recognize that people are constantly bombarded with promotional messages. Some estimates suggest that we are exposed to as many as 1,400 messages in a day. But, of course, we perceive far fewer. We selectively attend to the information environment around us. This is often called "the cocktail party effect."[6] It helps us simplify and manage our lives. We attend to subjects, themes, or images that interest us and ignore others that don't. Thus, older people will notice ads for extended vacations. Hypochondriacs catch ads for over-the-counter drugs and business people seldom ignore computer ads.

On the other hand, we tend to avoid messages that don't interest us or that in some way frighten us. This is a particular problem with fear appeals. Many nonprofit organizations involved in social or health issues find it tempting to use fear appeals (see Figure 18-4). For example, the Metropolitan Energy Council, a group of New York fuel dealers, tried to compete with gas suppliers with an ad in *The New York Times* that depicted a young mother saying: "Gas comes from a big utility. They don't know my family. If you need prompt service from them, you have to say, 'I smell gas.' That's what scares me most. I think gas heat is dangerous . . . too dangerous for my home, my kids."[7]

Fear is not always effective. Researchers in Ontario, Canada, reviewed past studies of seat belt usage and determined that an appeal based on the fear of being injured *but not killed* in a car crash could be potentially quite powerful. A test set of six messages was constructed (see Table 18-2) and run 943 times over nine consecutive months on one cable network of a dual cable system in Ontario. Seat belt usage of a random sample of drivers was unobtrusively observed before, during, and after the study by using license plates to learn which cable network each driver was exposed to. After correcting for the effects of weather (seat belts are less often used with bulky clothes in Canadian winters), the researchers concluded that the television campaign was a failure and that only coercion would work, either laws or mandatory passive restraint systems like air bags or automatic seat belting systems.[8]

The researchers may have been too pessimistic about persuasive approaches using fear in general. The level of invoked fear may have been too great! Ray and Wilkie point out that fear can have both motivating and inhibiting effects.[9] Fear has the potential to motivate use *if* we (1) attend to the message and (2) are scared by it. But the greater the fear level, the more our selective attention mechanisms will be invoked, and the fear appeal will never get the *chance* to motivate us. Thus, Ray and Wilkie argue that fear effects may well be curvilinear and the ideal level may be "moderate." The ideal level will also vary by topic and individual involvement. Those who wish to use fear, therefore, must pretest their message to assess just what amount of fear is optimal in their particular setting or for a particular audience. Burnett and Wilkes, for example, found that while high-fear appeals were more effective in changing attitudes

FIGURE 18-4

USING IT WON'T KILL YOU. NOT USING IT MIGHT.

Maybe you don't like using condoms. But if you're going to have sex, a latex condom with a spermicide is your best protection against the AIDS virus.

Use them every time, from start to finish, according to the manufacturers' directions. Because no one has ever been cured of AIDS. More than 40,000 Americans have already died from it.

And even if you don't like condoms, using them is definitely better than that.

HELP STOP AIDS. USE A CONDOM.

 AMERICAN FOUNDATION FOR AIDS RESEARCH   Ad Council   A Public Service of This Publication & The Advertising Council   NATIONAL AIDS NETWORK

Photo: Jerry Friedman   © 1988, The Ad Council.

AIDS CAMPAIGN
NEWSPAPER AD NO. AIDS-88-1382—2 COL.
TABLOID SIZE (9⅜" x 14") AD NO. AIDS-88-1381

SOURCE: The Advertising Council. Reproduced with permission.

Table 18-2

EXAMPLES OF FEAR APPEALS
IN A SEAT BELT USAGE CAMPAIGN

1. A father is shown lifting his teenaged son from a wheelchair into a car. As they ride along, safety belts obviously fastened, the father's thoughts are voiced off camera intermixed with the son's on-camera expressions of excitement at going to a football game. The father expresses guilt for not having encouraged his son to use safety belts before the crash in which he was injured. An analogy to the protection that the son wore when he played football is drawn.

2. A teenaged girl is shown sitting in a rocking chair looking out a window. She says, "I'm not sick or anything. I could go out more but since the car crash, I just don't . . . The crash wasn't Dad's fault. I go for walks with my father after dark . . . that way I don't get, you know, stared at." She turns enough to reveal a large scar on what was the hidden side of her face. She continues, "It doesn't hurt anymore." An announcer says off camera, "Car crashes kill two ways: right away and little by little. Wear your safety belts and live!"

3. A woman whose face cannot be seen is shown in front of a mirror applying makeup. A full-face picture on her dressing table shows her as a beautiful woman. Her husband enters the scene and suggests that they go to a party. She asks him not to look at her without makeup as she turns to reveal a scarred face. An off-camera announcer describes a crash in which the wife was driving slowly and carefully. The announcer continues, as the picture on the table is shown, "Terry would still look like this if she had been wearing seat belts." Safety belts are shown through a shattered windshield. Announcer: "It's much easier to wear safety belts than to hear your husband say, 'Honey, I love you anyway.' "

4. A father and mother are shown riding in the front seat of a car, their eight-year-old daughter seated between them. The father must brake hard to avoid another car entering from a side road. The daughter bumps her head as she is thrown into the dashboard and begins to cry. A policeman walks up to the car and the father angrily says: "Did you see what that guy just did? That jerk. I had to jam on my brakes. My little girl hit her head." The policeman asks the father why the child wasn't wearing safety belts. Over the father's protestations about the other driver, the policeman emphasizes the father's responsibility to protect his child. The scene closes with the policeman walking away saying "When are people gonna learn?" and the announcer following with "It doesn't take brains to wear safety belts. But it sure is stupid not to."

5. Two physicians and a nurse are shown ordering coffee. The nurse asks: "Trouble?" A doctor replies: "Another guy driving home not wearing his safety belts." Nurse: "Gonna live?" Doctor: "Guess you could call it living." Nurse: "You've had a lot of car crash cases lately." Doctor: "Yeah, and I'm getting sick of it. They've got safety belts in the cars. Why . . . why in the name of God don't they put 'em on?" Waitress: "Do safety belts really make a difference?" The doctor shows her how a thermometer case can be hit and the thermometer inside not broken, but it shatters when hit out of the case. The waitress expresses further doubt and the doctor says: "How many times do you have to tell 'em?"

6. A car is shown in a driveway. From a puff of smoke steps a witch who announces: "Ha, ha, ha. I'm the Wicked Car Witch. Your Mommy and Daddy cannot see me but I make them drive without their safety belts. That's how they get hurt in car crashes." The mother gets into the car and the witch hides some belts in the seat and tangles others. A Good Car Fairy appears and says: "Children! I am the Good

Car Fairy. When your Mommy and Daddy get in the car, say 'Mommy! Daddy! If you love me, wear your safety belts!' " The Wicked Witch and the Good Fairy argue as the father enters the car. A little girl calls from the porch: "Mommy! Daddy! Wear your safety belts." The parents fasten the belts, the Wicked Witch disappears in a puff of smoke, and the Good Fairy again admonishes the children to urge their parents to demonstrate their love by wearing their safety belts.

SOURCE: Leon S. Robertson, Albert B. Kelley, Brian O'Neill, Charles W. Wixom, Richard S. Eiswirth, and William Haddon, Jr., "A Controlled Study of the Effect of Television Messages on Safety Belt Use," *American Journal of Public Health,* Vol. 64, November 1974, p. 1074. Reprinted with permission of the American Public Health Association.

toward a health maintenance organization (HMO) than low-, medium-, or no-fear approaches, this result held only for three segments: older blue-collar whites, older blue-collar blacks, and older liberals.[10]

The existence of the selective attention phenomenon should alert Mr. Arneson to the possibility that Dr. Goldman may simply not hear what he says or see what he might send her in the mail. If she has determined that she is simply not interested in St. Anthony's, she may not really notice his messages. He may need to invoke some unusual or humorous pretext to introduce the topic, perhaps catching her off guard. If he has a potentially scary piece of information about Downtown Medical, he should first consider whether it may be too fear provoking for Dr. Goldman to pay attention.

Message Execution

Overcoming the selective attention problem is the responsibility of the creative specialists on the nonprofit communication team (in-house or at the advertising or public relations agency). These specialists have several variables at their command in designing an effective message. They need to find a *style, tone, wording, order,* and *format* to make the message effective.

Any message can be put across in different *execution styles.* Suppose the YMCAs around the country are planning to launch an early-morning jogging program (6:30 A.M.) and want to develop a 30-second television commercial to motivate people to sign up for this program. Here are some major advertising execution styles they can consider:

1   *Slice-of-life.* A husband says to his tired wife that she might enjoy jogging at the Y in the early morning. She agrees, and the next frame shows her coming home at 7:45 A.M. feeling refreshed and invigorated.
2   *Life-style.* A thirty-year-old man pops out of bed when his alarm rings at 6:00 A.M., races to the bathroom, races to the closet, races to his car, races to the Y, and then starts racing with his companions with a "big kid" look on his face.
3   *Fantasy.* A jogger runs along a path and suddenly imagines seeing her friends on the sidelines cheering her on.
4   *Mood.* A jogger runs in a residential neighborhood on a beautiful spring day, passing nice homes, noticing flowers beginning to bloom and neighbors waving

to him. This ad creates a mood of beauty and harmony between the jogger and his world.

5 *Musical*. Four young joggers run side by side wearing YMCA T-shirts. A specially written pulsating rock melody fills the background.

6 *Personality symbol*. A well-known sports hero is shown jogging at the Y with a smile on her face.

7 *Technical expertise*. Several Y athletic directors are shown discussing the best time, place, and running style that will give the greatest benefit to joggers. (For an example of a technical expert dealing with water safety, see Figure 18-5.)

8 *Scientific evidence*. A physician tells about a study of two matched groups of men, one following a jogging program and the other not, and the greater health and energy felt by the jogging group after a few weeks.

9 *Testimonial evidence*. The ad shows three members of the Y jogging group telling how beneficial the program has been.

The communicator must also choose a *tone* for the message. The message could be deadly serious (as in an antismoking ad), chatty (as in a message on weight control), humorous (as in a zoo ad), and so on. The tone must be appropriate to the target audience and target response desired.

Words that are memorable and attention getting must be found. This is nowhere more apparent than in the development of headlines and slogans to lead the reader into the message. There are six basic types of headlines:

- *news* ("United Way Offers New Giving Options")
- *questions* ("How Many Calories in this Health Shake?")
- *narrative* ("In the 1989 San Francisco Earthquake, the Middle Classes Became the American Red Cross's Newest Homeless Victims")
- *command* ("Save Water – Shower with a Friend")
- *1-2-3 ways* ("12 ways to Enjoy the High Cs at the Long Beach Opera")
- *how-what-why* ("You Can't Get AIDS from a Door Knob, a Public Swimming Pool, or a Handshake").

A symphony orchestra such as the Toronto Symphony Orchestra (TSO) might develop headlines for season ticket mailings using each of these styles:

1 *News*: "The TSO's new conductor has received rave reviews from international music critics. Just listen to these glowing reports . . . "

2 *Questions*: "Why are this famous football player . . . this executive secretary . . . and this 25-year-old rock star attending a TSO concert?"

3 *Narrative*: "At the flash of the downbeat, the orchestra was galvanized into a dynamic performance of the Carmen Suite and I found my head spinning in wonderment."

4 *Command*: "You've always said you wanted to 'get into' classical music. Well, do it now while our season ticket discounts make it so easy."

5 *1-2-3 Ways*: "Our 17 combinations of season concert packages let you design a music season to *your* taste and *your* schedule."

6 *How-what-why*: "Designing your very own music season is as easy as connecting the dots when you were a kid. Let us show you the way."

FIGURE 18-5

Using a Technical Expert

DIVING SAFETY

Presented by the National Swimming Pool Foundation

:30 Second PSA

(Background sounds)

"Jamie, Jamie!" Learning how to dive the right way. . .

can prevent a serious injury.

I'm Greg Louganis and I'd like to pass along these tips.

Always know the depth of the water before you dive...

don't dive deep, plan your dive path...

keep your hands in front of your face at all times.

And don't clown around or showboat. They cause more accidents than anything.

Diving is a great sport...let's do it right!

SOURCE: Porter/Novelli. Reprinted with permission.

Once the headline and the themes are determined, the communicator must consider the ordering of the ideas. There are three issues: conclusion drawing, one- or two-sided arguments, and order of presentation.

The first is the question of *conclusion drawing*, the extent to which the ad should draw a definite conclusion for the audience, such as telling them to give five hours a week to volunteering. Experimental research seems to indicate that explicit conclusion drawing is more persuasive than leaving it to the audience to draw their own conclusions. There are exceptions, however, such as when the communicator is seen as untrustworthy or the audience is highly intelligent and annoyed at the attempt to influence them.

The second issue is the question of the *one-* or *two-sided argument* — that is, whether the message will be more effective if one side or both sides of the argument are presented. Two-sided arguments are of two types. First, there is the approach that admits that the offering has some defects. The classic example of this approach is the early series of ads for the Volkswagen Beetle that admitted it was homely and that it didn't change its looks every model year, but that otherwise it was a marvelously sensible purchase! In the nonprofit sector, there are many situations in which the target audience will *know* there is a negative side to a requested behavior:

- Potential blood donors *know* the needle will hurt and that they may feel a little faint.
- Alcoholics, smokers, and drug addicts *know* that quitting or cutting down will be agonizing and require very strong willpower.
- Older persons *know* that investigating a retirement home means admitting negative things about their own competence.
- Young people *know* that not drinking or smoking in some cases may subject them to the teasing of friends and classmates.
- Symphony, theater, and museum goers *know* that a great many of the events they could attend will have elements they don't understand.

A two-sided message would recognize these counterarguments.

The other kind of two-sided argument recognizes the fact that there are other alternatives. The burger and cola "wars" are message campaigns fully recognizing that there are tough competitors "out there." In the nonprofit sector, there are many parallel situations:

- Going to the theater or symphony means not going to a movie or nightclub or just staying home to watch TV.
- Having a medical checkup or practicing breast self-examination means giving up the "bliss of ignorance."
- Giving to the United Way may mean not giving to the American Cancer Society or a university's alumni fund.
- Choosing UCLA means not choosing Stanford, Northwestern, and Harvard.
- Choosing to vacation in Jamaica or Southeast Asia means not vacationing in Sun Valley or Paris.
- Practicing birth control means not having the potential long run economic benefits of another income-producer and immediate psychic pleasures of an additional child.

One-sided presentations are common in both the profit and nonprofit sectors. They are often synonymous with what many would call a "hard-sell" approach. Yet social science research suggests that one-sided approaches may be relatively more effective in three situations: (1) when the audience is less educated, (2) when the audience already favors the message's central proposition, and (3) when the audience is not likely to be exposed later to counter-propaganda. Two-sided messages are said to be more effective when the opposite is true.

There is another, perhaps more compelling factor that should influence whether two-sided messages are used: it is the degree of the audience's involvement in the behavior that the marketer is attempting to influence. In general, we would argue the following: the higher the audience's involvement in the behavior, the more frequently the nonprofit marketer should use two-sided messages.

There are several reasons for this. In high-involvement situations, target audience members are more likely to

- be very concerned about the *costs* of the behavior (see Chapter 16).
- be opposed to the action advocated, if it means change.
- be aware of very attractive alternatives.

In high-involvement situations, the target audience will engage in extensive internal cognitive activity which will include considering costs and alternatives. They will engage in an extensive external search that will make available to them the "other side" of the argument. The marketer should seize the initiative and deal with the other side of the issue rather than leave it to the individual or to competitors. A useful concept in this regard is what is called *inoculation theory*. If a communicator knows that a target audience member will *later* be exposed to counterpropaganda (the "other side"), a more favorable outcome will be achieved if the marketer deals with the counterarguments in advance, in effect "inoculating" the target audience against the later influence attempts.

Finally, it must be reemphasized that in situations in which a two-sided strategy would be appropriate, the nonprofit communicator must go to great lengths to understand what *the target audience* perceives to be the key costs of the behavior and what *they* consider to be the reasonable alternatives. Only with a solid research base can an effective two-sided strategy be developed.

In the case of St. Anthony's Hospital, Mr. Arneson should recognize that Dr. Goldman will be exposed to counterpropaganda from DMC at some later point. Thus, the two-sided inoculation concept indicates that Arneson must say things like "I know you'll hear people say that St. Anthony's is overcrowded. Let me set the record straight right now." If at all possible, Arneson should seek to have Dr. Goldman agree with St. Anthony's arguments. Internalizing a position makes it more likely that an individual will adhere to it even after other information is received.

A third issue for the marketer in cases where several ideas are to be conveyed is the best *order of presentation*. Social scientists have found that, other things being equal, people tend to remember the items in a message stream presented first (the primacy effect) and last (the recency effect). There are arguments for putting one's strongest statements in either position. Where one is using a two-sided message, the case is more complex. However, the following approach appears reasonable:[11]

1   If the audience is likely to attend to the message under most circumstances (that is, not filter it out), it is probably best to place the message about the "other side" in the middle of the message where it is more likely to be forgotten and the arguments for one's own position in the first and last positions.

2   If the audience is opposed to the message and likely to screen it out, then beginning with the other side of the issue or with the other alternative may disarm the audience into "hearing" the marketer's message. Thus, a symphony marketer might say, "A night at home with the family watching TV by a warm fire would be great this winter. But the Toronto Symphony Orchestra has some good reasons for you to consider other pleasures."

Format elements can make a difference in an ad's impact, as well as in its cost. If the message is to be carried in a print ad, the communicator has to develop the elements of headline, copy, illustration, and color. Advertisers are adept at using such attention-getting devices as *novelty, contrast, arresting pictures,* and *movement.* Large ads, for example, gain more attention, and so do four-color ads, and this must be weighed against their higher costs. If the message is to be carried over the radio, the communicator carefully has to choose words, voice qualities (speech rate, rhythm, pitch, articulation), and vocalizations (pauses, sighs, yawns). If the message is to be carried on television or given in person, then all of these elements plus body language (nonverbal cues) have to be planned. Presenters have to pay attention to their facial expressions, gestures, dress, posture, and hairstyle.

Overcoming Perceptual Distortion

As we have already noted, individuals have a substantial background of experiences, categorization schemes, prejudices, associations, needs, wants, and fears that can markedly affect what they "see" or "hear" in the message. Thus, poor children will draw foreign coins that they have seen larger than will children who are economically better off. Pessimists will see half-empty glasses, optimists half-full ones.

This potential for distortion can work to the communicator's advantage. Messages can be relatively economical in what they say by using associations that they know people will bring to a symbol, a word, or an example. For example, readers need to see only *one* of the following symbols depicted in an ad to know that a restaurant is *not* a fast-food outlet; a tablecloth, flowers on the table, silverware, a waiter taking an order, candles or subdued lighting, upholstered chairs, wine glasses, or china. Someone sipping wine is assumed to be of a higher social class than someone who has a beer mug. Someone with glasses is supposed to be smarter than someone without them. Colors have symbolism. In the United States, white is pure, gold is rich, blue is soothing, pastels are "modern," and so on.[12]

Symbolism, however, varies significantly both within and across cultures. In Norway, an advertisement showing a female flight attendant fluffing a pillow and offering a brandy to a tired businessman was considered offensive to the consumer ombudsman as depicting women as merely servants to men.[13] The airline company, Singapore Airlines viewed the scene very differently, of course, since their cultural norms were very different. Similarly, showing wives making the decisions about the couple's social life would be perfectly appropriate in upper-class white American social settings but less appropriate in many immigrant groups.

Symbols can help or hurt communicators. The problem, of course, is to choose the right symbols and to be assured that your audience sees them as you do. Mr. Arneson may make an important mistake by assuming, for example, that Dr. Goldman would associate formica furnishings with high-quality office decor. While Mr. Arneson should carefully plan his choice of associations, one advantage of personal communication is that a sensitive communicator can secure feedback on how the message is actually perceived and fine-tune it so that it is perceived as intended.

Even if a message is perceived in an appropriate fashion, this does not guarantee that it will be retained or, more importantly, recalled at the moment it is "needed" to influence a particular behavior. One technique to reduce this possibility is, of course, repetition. Krugman and others have suggested that up to three repetitions will improve the probability of retention under high-involvement conditions.[14] Thus, Mr. Arneson might mention the hospital's superior accounting and scheduling services several times in a conversation or over a series of conversations to increase the likelihood that the information will be permanently retained. Another technique is to link the new information to existing cognitions. Individuals are more likely to recall things that they can assimilate well.

Choosing a Medium

The message the marketer decides to use will be transmitted to the target consumer through some medium or a combination of media. The medium chosen can be *personal*, as when the organization's own salesperson is used, or *impersonal*, as when a poster, a brochure, a magazine or newspaper advertisement, a product container, a shopping bag, or the side of a truck is used. The medium can be perceived by the customer as an *advocate* for the offering or as *independent*. Thus, there are four possibilities, as suggested in Table 18-3.

We consider the use of conventional advocate media in the following two chapters. We turn to the possibilities of using independent media–to the extent that they can be influenced–in Chapter 21. Here, we consider the problem of choosing spokespeople.

In many situations involving either paid or unpaid advocacy of a nonprofit organization and its product, service, or cause, the marketing manager will wish to use some person to deliver the message. Whom to choose and what to have the person say are crucial questions. *Balance theory* is useful here.

Balance theory starts with a fundamental assumption similar to that of

Table 18-3

ALTERNATIVE MEDIA

	Personal	*Impersonal*
Advocate	Salesperson Political supporter "Friend of the Arts"	Brochure Advertisement Billboard
Independent	Newscaster Independent researcher Noted physician	*The Wall Street Journal* Government Study *Consumer Reports*

dissonance theory, that is, that individuals like to have balance in their cognitive structures. They like things to "fit." And when they come across a piece of information that is not consistent with their present cognitions, they exert some effort to restore balance. The level of effort is proportional to the degree of imbalance and the importance of the subject. For example, executives of Coca-Cola in mid–1985 were convinced that New Coke would be a successful substitute for Old Coke. The evidence to the contrary that emerged after the introduction presumably took a long time to sink in, in part because it was so different from what management expected and because the subject was so important to them. Presumably, the readers of this book did not find the less-than-spectacular initial introduction of New Coke so difficult to accept.

Balance theory helps explain the problem facing the marketing manager in choosing a spokesperson. Consider the diagram in Figure 18-6. Here we see a situation in which the marketer wishes to use a spokesperson (S) to advocate a behavior (B) to a target consumer (T). (The target, of course, could be a corporation, a political body, or the nonprofit's own employees.)

The three sides of the triangle in Figure 18-6 can be seen as having algebraic signs—plus or minus. The system is in balance whenever the multiplication of the signs is *positive*. Thus, if the target hated the spokesperson or did not wish to perform the behavior the spokesperson advocated, the system would be in balance, just as it would be if the target's views of the three links were all positive. (Remember that the signs are all in the target consumer's head. This is where the spokesperson will "do battle.")

If the system is out of balance and the issue is important enough to the target consumer, he or she will seek to restore balance. Presumably, change will take place at the weakest link of the system portrayed in Figure 18-6. In the typical case, the target consumer is presented with a spokesperson's message advocating a behavior that the target does not wish to perform. For example, a teenager hears a message discouraging marijuana use, which he or she likes or feels the need to engage in because of peer pressure. In such cases, the T-B link is negative and the S-B link is positive. Now, suppose further that, as the nonprofit marketer hopes, the T-S link is positive. What will happen? Obviously, there are four possibilities:

FIGURE 18-6

Hypothetical Balance Theory Diagram

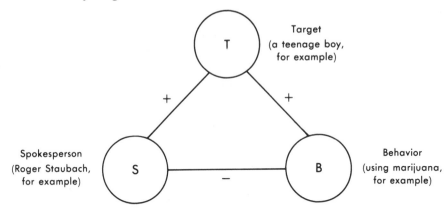

1 The target changes his or her attitude toward the advocated behavior. The target says, "I guess that person is right, I should give up the behavior." T-B becomes positive.
2 The target changes his or her attitude toward the spokesperson. The target says, in effect, "I guess I was wrong about the person. How can he be against such a great behavior?" T-S becomes negative.
3 The target distorts his or her perception of what the spokesperson is saying. The target says, in effect, "That person really mustn't mean that. He must have been paid a lot to say that." S-B becomes negative.
4 The target simply diminishes the importance of the issue ("Oh, it's no big deal!") and lives with the imbalance.

Obviously, the marketer wishes the first outcome to take place. The obvious solution, as advocated by Figure 18-6, is to make sure that the T-B link is the *weakest* in the system. Therefore, to make sure that the T-S link is as strong as possible, the nonprofit marketer must be very careful in the selection of spokespersons. It is critical that the spokesperson have as strong a positive connection with the target consumer as possible.

Spokespersons tend to be viewed positively for one of two reasons.[15] First, they may be respected as *credible experts* on a particular topic. This would be the case where a teenage former drug user or a noted medical expert is the spokesperson for the advocated behavior. The other case is where the person is not an expert but is considered by the target audience to be highly *trustworthy*. Thus, the nonprofit might use Roger Staubach or Tom Brokaw to advocate a drug-free life. The target may reason that although the spokesperson doesn't necessarily know anything about the subject, he or she can be counted on to tell the truth or advise one wisely. Betty Ford, when speaking about drugs, is presumably both a credible and a trustworthy person.

Choosing the ideal spokesperson is not easy. Of course, the appropriate choice will depend on both the topic and the issue. One possibility is to hedge one's bets by using multiple spokespeople as has the Boy Scouts of America. In all cases, it is important that the nonprofit marketer research the credibility and trustworthiness of the proposed spokespersons with the target audience. It is seldom a good idea to use someone who is very famous but who may seem to be so lacking in expertness that his or her credibility is low.

Once the spokesperson is chosen, the last link, S-B, must also be constructed as firmly as possible. Half the battle will be won if the right spokesperson is chosen. Still, alternative messages must be carefully pretested to ensure that there is little possibility that the target audience could believe that the spokesperson somehow really didn't mean it.

Message Evaluation and Selection

Now the marketer must select the best message from the set of alternatives. This calls for evaluation criteria. Twedt has suggested that contending messages be rated on three scales: *desirability, exclusiveness,* and *believability*.[16] He believes that the communication potency of a message is the product of these three factors because if any of the three has a low rating, the message's communication potency is greatly reduced.

The message must first say something desirable or interesting about the product or behavior. This is not enough, however, since many competitors may be making the same claim. Therefore the message must also say something exclusive or distinctive that does not apply to every alternative. Finally, the message must be believable or provable. By asking consumers to rate different messages on desirability, exclusiveness, and believability, these messages can be evaluated for their communication potency.

For example, the March of Dimes was searching for an advertising theme to raise money for its fight against birth defects.[17] A brainstorming session led to over 20 possible messages. A group of young parents were asked to rate each message for interest, distinctiveness, and believability, assigning up to 100 points for each. The message "Seven hundred children are born each day with a birth defect," for example, scored 70, 60, and 80 on interest distinctiveness and believability, while "your next baby could be born with a birth defect" scored 58, 50 and 70 (see Figure 18-7). The first message outperforms the second and would be preferred for advertising purposes. The best overall message was "The March of Dimes has given you: polio vaccine, German measles vaccine, 110 birth defects' counseling centers" (70, 80, and 90).

MODIFYING BEHAVIOR DIRECTLY

The approaches offered for communications strategies to this point have been based on a model of the attitude-behavior relationship that assumes that attitude change must be obtained *before* behavior change. Indeed, the traditional persuasion approach required that attitudes be changed in order for behavior to

FIGURE 18-7

Advertising Message Evaluation

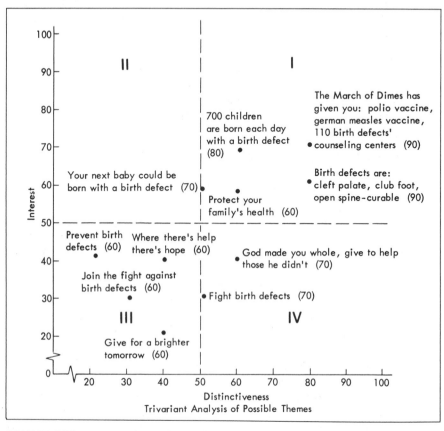

SOURCE: William A. Mindak and H. Malcolm Bybee, "Marketing's Application to Fund Raising," *Journal of Marketing,* July 1971, pp. 13–18.

change. This position has been challenged by a number of scientists on both theoretical and empirical grounds. They argue that we often adjust our attitudes to fit our behavior rather than vice versa. We observed in the Ontario seat belt study that it is often very difficult to get behavior to change by first changing beliefs. This is more true the more involved the individual is in the behavior to be changed, that is, the more central the behavior is to the person's self-concept. Thus, a teenager who believes smoking is "absolutely necessary" to the image of a self-possessed young person may be virtually impermeable to attitude-change-based persuasion strategies. Or the older person who sees herself as perfectly self-sufficient may selectively screen out or distort any messages attempting to lead her to enter a "retirement home" or to have professional helpers routinely come to her home.

In such circumstances, a more cost-effective communication strategy may be to seek behavior change directly rather than worrying about attitude change at all. One approach is through legal sanctions, although this has had mixed results.[18] Another approach is known variously as *instrumental conditioning* or *behavioral modification* and is most closely associated with the name of B.F. Skinner.[19]

The approach is grounded in the view of consumer behavior that we have used throughout this volume. We have argued that consumers take particular courses of action because of the anticipated consequences. The persuasion approach to behavior change seeks to modify consumer's *anticipations* about possible consequences. Behavior modification attempts *to modify the consequences themselves*. By teaching the target individual that a particular action will lead to a desired reward, the probability of the action is increased. Thus, if a consumer finds an unanticipated coupon at the bottom of a box of cereal or jar of instant coffee, behavior modification theory predicts that the chances are increased that the consumer will buy the product again. The coupons in this case are referred to as *reinforcers*. Cracker Jack has successfully used modest prizes for years as just such reinforcers.

There are many kinds of reinforcers, including

- *Economic*: Coupons, trading stamps, prizes, rebates, chances in a contest, free goods.
- *Social*: Praise, commendation, affection, conversation, attention.
- *Other*: Food, candy, feedback on achievement.

Social scientists have documented that children who are given more attention and praise after eating unfamiliar food are more likely to repeat this behavior (and subsequently to "like" the foods) than those who are not. Simple feedback on household energy consumption has led to a reduction in energy use. Reductions in home oil usage, for example, were induced by rewarding householders with a window sticker saying "We Are Saving Oil."

A great many companies have used economic incentives to get their employees to take better care of their health. At Johnson & Johnson, for example, employees could earn "Live-for-Life Dollars" to be exchanged for sweat suits, socks, or fire extinguishers for attending smoking or stress workshops, exercising for 20 minutes, wearing seat belts, or installing home smoke detectors. Intermatic, Inc. gave employees who quit cigarettes for a year a trip for two to Las Vegas. Hospital Corporation of America paid workers 24 cents for each mile walked or run, each quarter mile swum, or each 4 miles bicycled. The government of Bellevue, Washington, and firms like the Berol Corporation and King Broadcasting in Seattle gave rewards negatively related to the amount of health insurance claims an employee files. Speedcall Corporation gave a $7 bonus for each week an employee didn't smoke on the job. In four years, the number of smokers in the company fell 65 percent and the number of health insurance claims by quitters fell 50 percent.[20]

Examples of incentives and disincentives that have been used around the world to promote smaller families are reported in Exhibit 18-1.

EXHIBIT 18-1

Worldwide Small Family Incentives and Disincentives

1 Villages in Indonesia are passing resolutions to have not more than two children per family. Each year, the provincial governors award certificates of acclamation to those villages that have been successful in achieving the two-child goal.

2 In China, a collective decision is made at the community level as to who will have children during a specific year. Parents are encouraged, often through peer pressure, to have only one child.

3 In Korea, Mothers Clubs are formed to give support to couples who have one and two children. The clubs have given health, education, and financial assistance to those members who are committed to small families.

4 In Bangladesh and India, Green Cards are being issued to couples who have only one or two children. The cards give the holder priority health and educational opportunities.

5 In Taiwan, family planning field workers are asking couples to register their intent to have a child. The government is better able to provide for the educational, health, and social services for those communities where all births are planned and wanted.

6 In Singapore, couples with three or more children are taxed more, are not eligible for governmental housing, and the third child cannot go to the same school as his or her siblings.

7 In some religious ceremonies, couples are being asked to decide on how many children they want and when they want them. Some marriage vows include commitments to having only one or two children.

8 In Thailand and Indonesia, community awards that help employ women are being given by banks and cooperatives when the prevalence of contraceptive use leads to a level of reproduction that keeps the population from growing.

9 In Indonesia, successful family planners are given awards by President Suharto. These awards give the bearer status within the community. Awards are also given to those individuals who come up with the most innovative incentive and disincentive proposals.

10 In some Chinese villages "Certificates of Praise" are placed on the doors of couples who have only one child.

11 In Kerala State, India, nonpregnant women receive money deposits every six months. After three years, they can withdraw the funds.

12 In Gujarat, India, a bag of cement is given to the village councils for every vasectomy performed in the villages.

SOURCE: Robert W. Gillespie, *A Review of Incentives and Disincentives in Developing Countries*. Working paper, Population Communications, Inc., Pasadena, California, November 1985. Reproduced with permission.

There is some controversy about what patterns of reinforcement should be used. In general, *constant reinforcement* (rewarding every instance of the desired behavior) yields the fastest rate of learning but also the fastest extinction of the behavior when the reinforcements are stopped. On the other hand, *random reinforcement* yields slower rates of initial learning but also slower extinction. The reasons offered for this finding are that during the reinforcement period, the subject is initially not sure which behavior (if any) is being rewarded. This accounts for the slower rate of initial learning. Then, when rewards *are* linked to the behavior, the subject must interpolate his or her own rewards on those occasions when the externally manipulated rewards are absent.

In a study, Deslauriers and Everett found that offering ten-cent tokens to bus riders had a positive effect on bus usage. However, they found that variable reinforcement (every third passenger) was just as effective as continuing reinforcement and, of course, much more economical.[21]

For this type of behavioral modification to work, certain simple conditions must be present:

1   The desired behavior must be under the individual's control (thus, it is not particularly effective with physical drug dependency).
2   There must be a clear link between the behavior and the reinforcement although this need not always be apparent to the subject; the closer the reward is in time to the behavior, the greater the effect (thus, praising someone two days after a desired behavior – for example, cutting out certain smoking occasions – is less effective than immediate praise).
3   The reinforcer must constitute a reward for the individual (thus, praise from a feared autocratic school teacher would not be as reinforcing for a schoolchild as praise from a peer).

Shaping

The approach just described presumes that there is a specific behavior that is rewarded and that the probability of its recurrence is affected by the manipulation of reinforcements. There are some behavioral outcomes that can be approached, not in one step, but by successive approximations. This is known as "shaping" behavior. Shaping can take place directly by the manipulation of rewards or indirectly by *modeling* the desired behavior either in person (e.g., in demonstration seminars) or through the media. Marketers using the media, however, lack direct feedback from the people they are trying to influence. Thus, they need research to learn whether they are having the effects they desire. Exhibit 18-2 shows how the Academy for Educational Development learned that it was modeling the wrong immunization behavior.

One of the areas in which shaping is used as a behavior change technique is in securing smoking cessation. The ultimate goal of complete cessation is set initially and the smoker is asked to observe his or her own smoking behavior, noting two things; the occasions on which a cigarette is smoked, and the relative

EXHIBIT 18-2

William Smith of the Academy for Educational Development on Modeling Immunization Behavior in Ecuador

The Academy for Educational Development works with governments around the world helping develop social marketing strategies to save infants from diarrhea, protect adults from AIDS, and help couples space their children. Immunization of children is a big priority and the problem in many developing countries is that mothers just don't realize or believe that more than one shot is needed to protect their child fully from polio, diphtheria, or tetanus.

Working in Ecuador from 1985 to 1988, AED staff helped the government's massive program of immunization draw thousands of women for their child's first shot. But by the end of year 1, most children over one year old were still not fully immunized (three shots plus one for measles was needed).

The campaign had popularized two children, the PREMI kids, as the major theme (see Figure 18-8). Focus groups and intercepts conducted after phases 1 and 2 of the campaign discovered the kids looked 2 to 3 years old to most mothers. We'd found the problem! The campaign's biggest visual cue modeled the wrong behavior.

The answer was a birth in the family. The PREMI kids had a baby brother, Carlitos, (see Figure 18-9), who became the hook to tie all our messages to *"get your Carlitos"* immunized by age one. A special gold star was added to a diploma women received if their child was immunized by age one (see Figure 18-10). A *"crystal bell"* radio and TV campaign was tied into the Carlitos program to remind mothers each week, at the sound of the bell, "ask yourself—does your child need his next shot?"

Research, the right cues, and simple incentives made a difference. Full immunization coverage rose from 14 percent to 32 percent over the course of the program. Carlitos became widely known, and the certificate with a gold star became a prized possession.

SOURCE: William Smith, Senior Vice-president, Academy for Educational Development, private correspondence, December 1989.

importance of the smoking behavior on each occasion. The smoker then determines his or her own schedule of cutting down (shaping) the smoking behavior. The smoker starts by eliminating the least important smoking occasions and then works up to the most important. Smokers are trained to either reward themselves directly or to report their successes to a smoking cessation group or an individual therapist for attention, praise, and affectional reinforcement.

FIGURE 18-8

Record Jacket Showing Original PREMI Kids in Ecuador

SOURCE: Academy for Educational Development HEALTHCOM Project
(U.S. Agency for International Development), and PREMI/INNFA,
Ministry of Health, Government of Ecuador. Reproduced with permission.

    Several variations on personal reinforcement have been devised. One
technique is simply selecting a desired reward (for example, a weekend vacation, dinner in a fancy restaurant, or a manicure) after a certain number of
behavior change "points" have been accumulated. Another approach is to set
aside a significant sum of money to go to a disliked organization or cause (for

FIGURE 18-9

Revised PREMI Kids in Ecuador with Sticker

SOURCE: Academy for Educational Development
HEALTHCOM Project (U.S. Agency for International
Development), and PREMI/INNFA, Ministry of Health,
Government of Ecuador. Reproduced with permission.

example, a pro- or antiabortion group, the Ku Klux Klan, or the Communist party). Then a specific amount of money may be withdrawn from the amount set aside with the passage of each milestone.

Two variations on the concept of shaping behavior are the so-called "foot-in-the-door" and "door-in-the-face" techniques.

The Foot-in-the-Door Technique.   The "foot-in-the-door" technique is based on a finding that if you can get target audience members to take a small step in a desired direction, they are much more likely to take a major step later. This effect is explainable by self-perception theory, which says that we all tend to behave in ways that we feel are consistent with our views of ourselves. What is alleged to happen in the foot-in-the-door situation is that compliance with the initial modest request changes target persons' self-perceptions. They now see themselves as "the kind of person" who helps out in these situations. This makes them much more likely to comply with a later, more demanding request.

Scott tested this foot-in-the-door technique in the context of a recycling

FIGURE 18-10

Reward Incentive for Ecuadorian Immunization Program

SOURCE: Academy for Educational Development HEALTHCOM Project (U.S. Agency for International Development), and PREMI/INNFA, Ministry of Health, Government of Ecuador. Reproduced with permission.

campaign.[22] Residents were assigned experimentally to different treatment conditions, and all but one group was asked to place a small sign in their windows promoting recycling. Some were given small incentives ($1.00 or $3.00) to take the initial small step. These incentives had no effect on whether a person complied with the initial request.

Two weeks later, *all* subjects were asked to perform a more substantial helping behavior. Half were asked to address 25 envelopes to be used in the recycling campaign and half were asked to address 75 envelopes. Those who received no incentive but did place the sign in the window were four times as likely to agree to a request to address 25 envelopes as were those who were not asked to display the sign. Further, when the first behavior was prompted by financial rewards, the rate of behavioral compliance to the second request declined. This is consistent with self-perception theory, which would suggest that, in the latter cases, individuals would be saying to themselves (at least in part), "I helped with the sign because I could use the reward. I perceive myself as someone who does things for a reward. I didn't get a reward the second time." Those who got no reward would be assumed to ask themselves, "Why did I help out? It wasn't for money. It must be because I am someone who helps out in this cause." It should be noted that the findings for the larger request are in the expected direction but are not statistically significant. This led Scott to conclude that the foot-in-the-door technique will work when:

- The behavior is not too large. In practice this would not appear to be a serious restriction. Rather, it indicates that change may be achieved through a series of foot-in-the-door operations, each requiring a larger change in behavior than the one before (that is, shaping). What constitutes a "large" behavior, of course, may depend on a number of factors, including the nature of the task itself.
- The requests are made in person. Mere repetition of contact did not affect subsequent behavior (that is, those who did not comply with the initial requests were no more likely to comply with the second request than control subjects); thus, personal communication may be needed to ensure initial compliance. Some initial evidence exists, however, which suggests that foot-in-the-door and other attribution-based messages may be more effective than traditional persuasive appeals in mass communication settings where personal contact is not possible.[23]

Mr. Arneson might wish to try the foot-in-the-door technique. He could suggest to Dr. Goldman that she "try-out" St. Anthony's by sending two outpatients for some particular test. The hope would be that Dr. Goldman would begin to perceive herself "as someone who sends patients to St. Anthony's." As Scott suggests, it may be necessary to gradually increase the suggested behaviors before Dr. Goldman would send *all* of her patients there.

The Door-in-the-Face Technique.   This technique is just the opposite of foot-in-the-door, but, surprisingly, it is based on the same theory. The door-in-the-face technique requires that the communicator begin with an *initial* request that is so large that it is sure to be turned down. Assuming that the behavior involves a socially desirable end, it may be expected that when a later, more modest request is made, the target audience member who had earlier slammed the door "in the face" of the requester will say "I'm not the kind of person who is unwilling to help with these causes. I should change my behavior to fit my self-perception. I'll help out this time." Empirical research using this technique has yielded mixed results.[24]

In Mr. Arneson's case, the "door-in-the-face" technique might suggest first asking Dr. Goldman to assign all her patients to St. Anthony's and then, after this is refused, asking her to assign a few patients initially.

SUMMARY

Every contact a nonprofit has with its many publics directly or indirectly is an occasion for influence. These contacts may be carried out by many different departments or people using diverse vehicles ranging all the way from standard paid and unpaid media to package designs, corporate publicity releases, personal sales presentations, and even promotional "gimmicks" like shopping bags and T-shirts. The chapters to follow will consider detailed influence strategies involving advertising, sales promotion, public relations, and personal selling. For programs to be effective, however, they must be grounded in a clear understanding of influence processes.

Influence typically involves persuasion. This requires the preparation and transmittal of specific messages. Messages must be encoded by the marketer, communicated through media, and then decoded by the receiver. At each of these stages, considerable noise can be introduced into the communications process such that the accumulated effect of the received message is very different from what was intended. In general, the more parties involved in the communications system and the less control the marketer has over them, the greater the chance for miscommunication. Marketers use formal and informal feedback to track these effects. Where communication is face to face, feedback can be easily obtained. Where it is not, as in media campaigns, pre- and posttests of message strategies must always be carried out.

Six steps are involved in developing effective messages. First, the communication objectives must be determined. Second, messages must be generated. These can be rational, emotional, or moral, or they can be generated from a rewards/situations framework. Third, thought must be given to how these communications can overcome consumers' tendencies to selectively expose themselves or attend to messages in which they are interested. The style, tone, wording, order, and format of the messages are all critical to getting a message noticed. Fourth, thought must be given to constructing the communications to overcome perceptual distortion, the tendency to add to and reinterpret what is actually in the message based on the audience member's own past experience, motives, and biases. Fifth, a medium must be chosen to convey the message to achieve maximum impact. Often, in the nonprofit sector, this means choosing a spokesperson. If a spokesperson is used, the marketer must assure that he or she is credible and trustworthy and that their message is so clear that it cannot be distorted by a target audience. Sixth, the marketers must evaluate all the possible messages and select the ones that are most desirable, exclusive, and believable.

The marketer must recognize that strategies to influence behavior need not rely only on persuasion; that is, on first changing cognitions in order to change behavior. Other strategies, such as behavior modification, can simply manipulate rewards. These strategies (such as shaping and the foot-in-the-door and door-in-the-face techniques) rely on a different model, in which it is assumed that changing behavior is an adequate goal in itself and that, once behavior is changed, attitudes and other cognitions may also change.

QUESTIONS

1. The National Cancer Institute wishes to tell pregnant women that smoking can injure their fetuses. Focus group interviews show that members of the target audience frequently misunderstand what NCI is telling them. What are some possible explanations for this?

2. How could the National Cancer Institute design warnings on cigarette packages to get past smokers' selective attention bias against the messages?

3. Who would be good spokespeople for family planning programs in the United States, and why? How would you go about learning who the best spokespeople would be in a foreign country and whether spokespeople would be effective at all?

4. List the communications goals that a rapid transit district in a medium-sized community might have for an annual strategic plan.

5. Suggest how a headline to introduce a new children's wing at a library might be written using each of the nine execution styles outlined in this chapter.

6. How could behavior modification techniques be used to get college students to become more active recruiters of future college enrollees from their hometowns?

NOTES

1. See, for example, Peter L. Wright, "The Cognitive Processes Mediating Acceptance of Advertising," *Journal of Marketing Research*, February 1973, pp. 53–62.

2. See Michael L. Ray and William L. Wilkie, "Fear, The Potential of an Appeal Neglected by Marketing," *Journal of Marketing*, January 1970, pp. 55–56; and Brian Sternthal and C. Samuel Craig, "Fear Appeals Revisited and Revised," *Journal of Consumer Research*, December 1974, pp. 22–34.

3. See John C. Maloney, "Marketing Decisions and Attitude Research," in George L

Baker, Jr., ed., *Effecting Marketing Coordination* (Chicago: American Marketing Association, 1961).

4. The classic work in this field is Leon Festinger, *A Theory of Cognitive Dissonance* (Evanston, Ill.: Row, Peterson, 1957). See also J.W. Brehm and A.R. Cohen, *Explorations in Cognitive Dissonance* (New York: John Wiley, 1962). For an example showing consumers' willingness to live with dissonance in a nonprofit context, see M.T. O'Keefe, "The Anti-Smoking Commercials: A Study of Television's Impact on Behavior," *Public Opinion Quarterly*, 1971, pp. 242–248.

5. Carolyn W. Sherif, Muzafer Sherif, and Ronald Nebergill, *Attitude and Attitude Change* (New Haven, Conn.: Yale University Press, 1961).

6. See J.T. Bertrand, "Selective Avoidance on Health Topics: A Field Test," *Communications Research*, July 1979, pp. 271–294. Also, Wolfgang Schaefer, "Selective Perception in Operation," *Journal of Advertising Research*, February 1979, pp. 59–60.

7. "Death Turns Up the Thermostat," *Newsweek*, October 15, 1984.

8. Leon S. Robertson, Albert G. Kelley, Brian O'Neill, Charles W. Wixom, Richard S. Eiswirth, and William Haddon, Jr., "A Controlled Study of the Effect of Television Messages on Safety Belt Use," *American Journal of Public Health*, November, 1974, p. 1070 ff.

9. Ray and Wilkie, "Fear: The Potential."

10. John J. Burnett and Robert E. Wilkes, "Fear Appeals to Segments Only," *Journal of Advertising Research*, Vol. 20, no. 5, October 1980, pp. 21–24.

11. There is some debate over order effects with two-sided messages. See James F. Engel and Roger Blackwell, *Consumer Behavior*, 4th ed. (Chicago: Dryden Press, 1982), pp. 479–481.

12. Edward T. Hall, *The Silent Language* (Garden City, N.J.: Doubleday, 1973).

13. John Karevoll, "Singapore Girl Nixed in Norway," *Advertising Age*, March 23, 1981, pp. m-2-3.

14. Herbert E. Krugman, "Why Three Exposures May Be Enough," *Journal of Advertising Research*, December 1972, pp. 11–15.

15. See Brian Sternthal, R.R. Dholakia, and Clark Leavitt, "The Persuasive Effect of Source Credibility: Test of Cognitive Response," *Journal of Consumer Research*, Vol. 4, (1978), pp. 252–260; and C. Samual Craig and John M. McCann, "Assessing Communications Effects on Energy Conservation," *Journal of Consumer Research*, Vol. 5, September 1978, pp. 82–88.

16. Dik Warren Twedt, "How to Plan New Products, Improve Old Ones, and Create Better Advertising," *Journal of Marketing*, January 1969, pp. 53–57.

17. See William A. Mindak and H. Malcolm Bybee, "Marketing's Application to Fund Raising," *Journal of Marketing*, July 1971, pp. 13–18.

18. See, for example, Stanley I. Ornstein and Dominique M. Hanssens, "Alcohol Control Laws and the Consumption of Distilled Spirits and Beer," *Journal of Consumer Research*, Vol. 12, no. 2, September, 1985, pp. 200–213.

19. Michael Rothschild and William C. Gaidis, "Behavioral Learning Theory: Its Relevance to Marketing and Promotions," *Journal of Marketing*, Spring 1981, pp. 70–78.

20. "Giving Goodies to the Good," *Time*, November 18, 1985, p. 98.

21. Brian C. Deslauriers and Peter B. Everett, "Effects of Intermittent and Continuing Token Reinforcement on Bus Ridership," *Journal of Applied Psychology*, Vol. 62, no. 4, 1977, pp. 369–375.

22. Carol A. Scott, "Modifying Socially-Conscious Behavior: The Foot-In-The-Door Technique," *Journal of Consumer Research*, 1977, pp. 156–164.

23. Although the foot-in-the-door approach appears promising here, two researchers were unsuccessful in applying it to blood donations behavior; see R.B. Cialdini and K. Assam, "Test of a Concession Procedure for Inducing Verbal, Behavioral, and Further Compliance with a Request to Give Blood," *Journal of Applied Psychology*, 1976, pp. 295–300.

24. Peter H. Reingen, "On Inducing Compliance with Requests," *Journal of Consumer Research*, September 1978, pp. 96–102; John Morwen and Robert Cialdini, "On Implementing Door-in-the-Face Compliance Techniques in a Business Context," *Journal of Marketing Research*, May 1980, pp. 253–258.

19

Managing Advertising and Sales Promotion

Dan Rooney, owner of the Pittsburgh Steelers, perhaps best described the United Way/NFL relationship. Paraphrasing his father's famous comment on winning, Rooney said, "Success is a matter of chemistry. It's not enough to have a good cause, good people, or good luck. You have to have all three and the wisdom to know how to use them."

Over the past 15 years, all the elements that contribute to the winning formula were in abundance with respect to the United Way/NFL relationship. The largest and longest-running public service campaign in the nation has been the result. As United Way of America President William Aramony put it, "United Way has been in business now for 102 years. The most productive years have been the last 15—during our partnership with the National Football League."

This winning combination came about in 1973 when Aramony and Mario Pellegrini, who was then president of United Way Productions for United Way of America, called on NFL Commissioner Pete Rozelle and NFL director of communications Joe Browne.

The purpose of the call was to interest the NFL in donating the 60 seconds of airtime it had under the terms of its network contracts and to use the time to promote United Way during game telecasts.

"The dynamic Mr. Aramony came prepared to go all out in selling us his idea of a partnership," recalls Pete Rozelle. "But he only had to sell at about the 10 percent level. We immediately grasped the benefits in what he wanted to do. His plan made more sense to us than using that 60 seconds to promote NFL ticket sales or sell team t-shirts."

Given Rozelle and Browne's desire to work with United Way, and the generosity of NFL team owners in contributing the time, Mario Pellegrini began writing, directing, and producing the spots.

The arrangement called for the NFL to select the players—or other members of the NFL family such as coaches, team owners, game officials, and front office personnel—who would volunteer their time to appear in the spots.

During football season, the United Way/NFL spots reach approximately 80 million viewers per week with an estimated value of $45 million in contributed airtime. The series shows the power of people helping people as members of the NFL family share their private lives with the nation. "To date we've done over 500 spots," says Pellegrini. "There is no area of human need we haven't touched."

"These TV moments take the helmets and shoulder pads off our players and show them to be good citizens," says Browne. "Since we began the spots in 1974, United Way contributions have moved from $800 million to $2.8 billion. We'd like to think we've helped."

"Helped" is hardly the word. "The NFL's support stands out above all others," says Aramony. "The contribution of TV time and the resulting visibility to United Way make this the most far-reaching gift we receive."

Source: "The NFL and the United Way: A Winning Combination," *Community,* Summer 1989. Reproduced with permission.

The nonprofit marketer has a large number of tools available for carrying a message to a target audience. There are five main tools, and each differs in the coding and encoding problems suggested earlier in Figure 18-1 it presents to managers.[1]

- *Paid Advertising: Any paid form of nonpersonal presentation and promotion of an offer by an identified sponsor through a formal communications medium.* Paid advertising permits total control over encoded message content and over the nature of the medium, plus substantial control of the scheduling of the message (and therefore its specific environment). On the other hand, paid advertising permits no control over message decoding by the audience and little (or, at best, lagged) feedback on the received message.

- *Unpaid (public service) advertising: Any form of advertising in which space or time for the placement of the advertisement is free.* Marketer control is similar to that with paid advertising except that there is very little control over the scheduling of the message. Many public service radio or television advertisements appear after midnight or on Sunday mornings when the audience is small and the media have unsold spots.

- *Sales promotion: Short-term incentives to encourage purchase or sales of a product or service or the performance of a behavior.* Marketer control is substantial, although the decoding of specific promotions by the receiver is not controllable.

- *Publicity: Nonpersonal stimulation of demand for an offering by securing the reporting of commercially significant news about the offer in a published medium or on radio, television, or the stage that is not paid for by the sponsor.* Here, the marketer's control over message encoding and the medium varies depending on whether journalists will use and revise the message. Some feedback is possible from journalists or from selected target audiences.
- *Personal selling: Oral presentation of information about an offering in a conversation with one or more prospective target audience members for the purpose of securing a desired transaction.* In personal selling, the organization has less control over encoding, that is, what the salesperson actually says. The salesperson, however, has excellent opportunities to secure feedback on how the message is being received.

In this chapter, we will consider specific issues relevant to advertising and sales promotion. The next two chapters will deal with public relations and personal selling, respectively.

ADVERTISING

Advertising consists of nonpersonal forms of communication conducted through paid media under clear sponsorship. It involves such varied media as magazines and newspapers, radio and television, outdoor media (posters, signs, and skywriting), novelties (matchboxes, calendars), cards (car, bus), catalogues, directories and references, programs and menus, circulars, and direct mail. It can be carried out for such diverse purposes as long-term buildup of the organization's name (institutional advertising); long-term buildup of a particular product (product advertising) or brand (brand advertising); information dissemination about a sale, service, or event (classified advertising); announcement of a special sale (sales advertising); and so on.

Total advertising in the United States was estimated to be $118 billion in 1988. It was also estimated that, of the U.S. total, 56 percent comprised national advertising and 44 percent local.[2] Advertising is coming into increasing use by nonprofit organizations public and private. The major categories of nonprofit organization advertising are as follows:

1 *Political advertising.* Political advertising has skyrocketed in recent elections. Political television advertising expenditures alone in the 1988 U.S. presidential election were $227.9 million, up 48 percent over the 1984 election.[3]
2 *Social cause advertising.* For many years, the Advertising Council, Inc., a nonprofit organization financed by American industry, has used advertising to promote social causes such as brotherhood, safe driving, aid to education, religious faith, forest fire prevention, and so on. It accepts a number of causes each year and solicits donated services from advertising agencies and media to prepare and broadcast this advertising. The estimated value of the space and time for this advertising was $1.2 billion in 1989. It tends to avoid controversial causes. Social cause organizations such as ecology groups, family planners, and

people with AIDS have also stepped up their advertising budgets to get their messages out to the public.[4]

3 *Charitable advertising.* Charitable advertising is specifically directed toward raising donations on a regular or emergency basis; the money is used to help the needy, unfortunate, or sick. Examples include the paid or donated advertising done by the Red Cross, United Way, Easter Seal Society, and so on.

4 *Government advertising.* Various government units are frequent advertisers. Municipalities, states and counties spend considerable sums to attract new residents, tourists, and industrial developers. Park and recreation departments advertise outdoor recreational facilities. Police departments issue messages to the general public on safety issues. The federal government has used paid advertising to sell products (U.S. postage stamps), services (Amtrak train travel), and ideas (energy conservation). Its largest advertising expenditures are on military recruitment; it budgeted $185 million on military recruiting in 1988.[5]

5 *Private nonprofit advertising.* Colleges, museums, symphonies, hospitals, and religious organizations all have strong communication programs and develop annual reports, direct mailings, classified ads, broadcast messages, and other forms of advertising. Various professionals whose ethical codes formerly banned advertising–social workers, psychologists, and so on–have been free to advertise ever since the Federal Trade Commission ruled that the American Medical Association could not prevent physician members from advertising.

6 *Association advertising.* Professional and trade associations have substantially increased their use of paid advertising. The American Bankers Association, the American Dental Association, and the National Association of Realtors spend several million dollars annually on television and print advertising. Their objective is to improve their public image and also the public's knowledge of their services. Public service advertising programs have recently been undertaken by associations representing lawyers, accountants, engineers, and nurses.

In developing an advertising program, marketing management must make five major decisions (see Figure 19-1). We considered message issues in the preceding chapter and will discuss the remaining four decisions in the following sections.

FIGURE 19-1

Major Decisions in Advertising Management

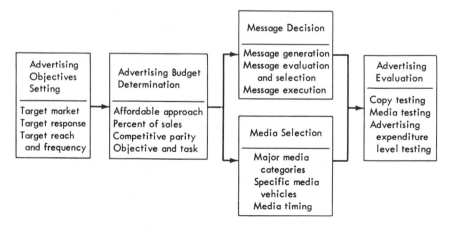

SETTING ADVERTISING OBJECTIVES

Before an advertising program and budget can be developed, advertising objectives must be set. These objectives must flow from prior decision making on the target market, market positioning, and marketing mix. The marketing strategy defines advertising's job in the total marketing mix.

Developing advertising objectives calls for defining the target market, target response, and target reach and frequency.

Target Market Selection

A marketing communicator must start with a clear target audience in mind. The audience may be potential buyers of the organization's services, current users, deciders, or influencers. The audience may consist of individuals, groups, particular publics, or the general public. The target audience has a crucial influence on the communicator's decisions on *what* to say, *how* to say it, *when* to say it, *where* to say it, and *who* should say it.

Consider this in terms of a small private college in Iowa called Pottsville. Suppose it is seeking applicants from Nebraska, and it estimates that there are 30,000 graduating high school seniors in Nebraska who might be interested in Pottsville College. The college must decide whether to aim its communications primarily at high school counselors in Nebraska high schools or at the high school students themselves. Beyond this, it may want to develop communications to reach parents and other people who are influential in the college decision process. Each target market would warrant a different advertising campaign.

Target Response

Once the target audience is identified, the marketing communicator must define the target response that is sought. The ultimate response, of course, is behavior. But in highly involving and infrequent decisions, behavior is the end result of a consumer decision-making process. The marketing communicator needs to know the current state of the decision process of the target audience and which state it should be moved to next.

Any member of the target audience may be in any one of six stages of the decision process with respect to the service or organization. These stages— *awareness, knowledge, liking, preference, conviction, action*—are described in the following paragraphs.[6]

1 *Awareness.* The first thing to establish is how aware the target audience is of the desired behavior. The audience may be completely unaware of the behavior or of the products and services it involves or may know one or two things about them. If most of the audience is unaware, the communicator's task is to build awareness, perhaps just name recognition. This calls for simple messages such

as repeating the name. Even then, building awareness takes time. If Pottsville College has no name recognition among high school seniors in Nebraska, the college might set as its objective making 70 percent of these students aware of Pottsville's name within one year.

2   *Knowledge.* The target audience may be aware of the behavior or associated objects and services but may not know much about them. In this case the communicator's goal is to transmit some key information. Thus, Pottsville College may want its target audience to know that it is a private four-year college in eastern Iowa that has distinguished programs in ornithology and thanatology. Following its advertising campaign, Pottsville can sample the target audience to measure whether they have little, some, or much knowledge of Pottsville College and to assess the content of their knowledge. The particular set of beliefs that makes up the audience's picture of an object is called the *image.* Organizations must periodically assess their public images as a basis for developing communication objectives.

3   *Liking.* If the target audience members know about the behavior, the next question is, how do they feel about it? We can imagine a scale covering a range of responses such as *dislike very much, dislike somewhat, indifferent, like somewhat,* and *like very much.* If the audience has an unfavorable view of attending Pottsville College, the communicator has to find out why and then develop a communications program to build up favorable feelings. If the unfavorable view is rooted in real inadequacies of the college, then a communications campaign would not do the job. The college would have to first improve and then communicate its quality. Good marketing requires that the "product" element of the marketing mix be firmly in place before promotion is begun.

4   *Preference.* The target audience may like the desired behavior but may not prefer it over others. It may be one of several acceptable behaviors. In this case the communicator's job is to build consumer preference. The communicator will have to tout its quality, value, performance, and other attributes. The communicator can check on the success of the campaign by subsequently surveying the audience to see if their preference has grown stronger.

5   *Conviction.* A target audience may prefer a particular behavior but may not develop a conviction about carrying it out. Thus, some high school seniors may prefer Pottsville to other colleges but may not be sure they want to go to college. The communicator's job is to build conviction that going to college is the right thing to do.

6   *Action.* Some target audience members may have conviction but not act. They may be waiting for additional information, plan to act later, and so on. In this situation, a communicator must lead the consumer to take the final step, which, in a purchase situation, is called "closing the sale." Among the action-producing devices are offering a low price if the behavior is undertaken now, offering a premium, offering an opportunity to try the behavior on a limited basis, and indicating that the opportunity will soon become unavailable.

This model assumes that buyers pass through a hierarchy of states on the way to the behavior. The communicator's task is to identify the stage that most of the target audience is in and develop a communication message or campaign that will move them to the next stage. It would be nice if one message could move the audience through all stages, but this rarely happens. Most communicators seek a cost-effective communication approach to move the target audience one stage at a time. The critical thing is to know where the main audience is and what the next feasible stage is.

A variation of this hierarchical model was elaborated recently in a proposed social marketing approach for the Egyptian government's family planning program. It was suggested that a totally uninformed man or woman would have to pass through 11 steps to adopt the behavior that the Egyptian government seeks—*continuous correct use* of some effective family planning method. The steps constitute a *contraceptive social behavior change model* and are outlined in Figure 19-2. The 11 steps are grouped into five broad sets of tasks for management:

FIGURE 19-2

Contraceptive Social Behavior Change Model

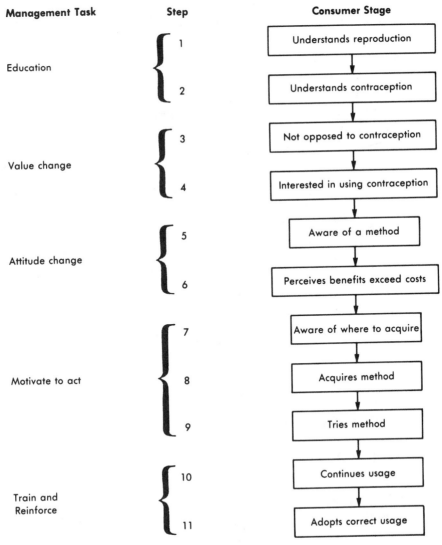

1 *Basic education.* To become a family planner, an individual must have some rudimentary understanding of the nature of reproduction and contraception.
2 *Value change.* The individual must believe that family planning is an *acceptable* practice. Furthermore, the individual must come to see that family planning is something potentially relevant to his or her own life. These steps may require modification of religious or moral values and a breaking away from the influences of family, peers, village elders, and other significant figures in the individual's community.
3 *Attitude change.* The individual must learn of the existence of at least one specific method and believe that the benefits of using it exceed the costs.
4 *Motivation to act.* The individual must have access to and learn where and how to acquire the preferred method. Furthermore, the individual must be propelled to try the method.
5 *Training and reinforcement.* Once the consumer undertakes a trial of a method, the process is almost completed. At that point, the individual must know proper usage and be sufficiently satisfied to continue using contraceptive methods.

A key feature of this contraceptive social behavior change model is that each target consumer can be categorized as being at one of the 11 steps at any point in time. The fact that target consumers can be assigned to unique stages in this process has several uses:

1 The model can be used to measure the overall progress of a program within a country or to compare one country to another.
2 It can be used to segment the market into groups requiring different messages.
3 It can be used to set communication goals, such as moving 100,000 households from stage 2 to stage 3.

The hierarchical model leads to many specific communications objectives for advertising. Colley distinguished 52 possible advertising objectives in his *Defining Advertising Goals for Measured Advertising Results* (DAGMAR). The various advertising objectives can be categorized on the basis of whether their aim is to inform, persuade, or remind.[7]

It should also be noted that not every marketing objective involves building demand. Sometimes nonprofits have to demarket a product or service, as was the case at Orange County Airport in 1984. (See Exhibit 19-1).

Target Reach and Frequency

The third objective a nonprofit manager must set is the optimal *target reach and frequency* of the advertising. Funds for advertising are rarely so abundant that everyone in the target audience can be reached, and reached with sufficient frequency. Marketing management must decide what percentage of the audience to reach with what exposure frequency per period. Pottsville College, for example, might decide to use local newspapers and buy 20,000 advertising

EXHIBIT 19-1

Demarketing John Wayne Airport

It is an odd assignment by any standard. The advertiser wishes to discourage customers and refer them to a competitor.

The advertiser in this case is Orange County's John Wayne International Airport. Stretched to capacity and unable to expand, the beleaguered commercial airport has hired an agency to help it steer some of the local airline passengers to nearby Ontario International Airport in Los Angeles County. Also a self-supporting public facility, Ontario Airport says it welcomes growth but it is concerned that a vigorous ad campaign simply will transfer the overcrowding problem over the county line.

Basso & Associates, Newport Beach, won a contract last summer to develop the creative concept for an overall awareness program to urge residents of the northeast quadrant of Orange County to consider using Ontario rather than John Wayne.

Basso's recommendation, awaiting approval from a special Orange County Airport task force, calls for a comprehensive $150,000 to $300,000 radio, print, and outdoor campaign.

If the recommendation meets with the approval of both the airport commission and the county board of supervisors, agencies will bid on the execution of the recommendation.

As the only commercial airport in Orange County, John Wayne has suffered from overcrowding since its terminal building was dedicated in the late 1960s. It now accommodates about 10 million passengers annually. Residents in nearby Newport Beach—directly under the airport's flight path—have blocked an increase in the number of commercial flights allowed to enter or leave the airport. They are also unwilling to have the airport extend its hours.

Twenty-five miles away in Los Angeles County, Ontario International Airport, which was acquired by the County in 1967, handles about 3 million passengers annually, although the facility was designed ultimately to accommodate 12 million.

While Ontario Airport has no plans to combat John Wayne Airport's advertising campaign if it passes the various boards, it has adopted a policy of "noncooperation," according to a spokesman.

"We'd rather see slow, steady growth," the spokesman said. "We don't want to see ourselves as a convenient area for Orange County's spillover."

SOURCE: Cleveland Horton, "John Wayne Airport Steers Traffic to Reluctant Rival." Reprinted with permission from *Advertising Age*, November 5, 1984, p. 72w. Copyright 1984 by Crain Communications, Inc.

exposures. This leaves a wide choice available concerning target reach and frequency. Pottsville could place one advertisement in one paper in a large city and reach 20,000 different students, or it could place two different ads a week apart in five smaller papers and reach 10,000 students twice, and so on. The issue is how many exposures are needed to create the desired response, given the market's state of readiness. One exposure could be enough to convert students from being unaware to being aware. It would not be enough to convert students from awareness to preference.

ADVERTISING BUDGET DETERMINATION

We assume that Pottsville College is using the preferred objective-and-task approach to setting advertising budgets (see Chapter 12). Suppose that Pottsville wants to place two ads in five papers to reach 10,000 students twice. The gross number of exposures would be 20,000. Suppose the average ad in each paper costs $2,000 and design costs for the two ads were $5,000, Pottsville will need a rough advertising budget of $25,000.

In addition to estimating the total size of the required advertising budget, a determination must be made of how the budget should be allocated over different market segments, geographical areas, and time periods. In practice, advertising budgets are allocated to segments of demand according to their respective populations or sales levels or in accordance with some other indicator of market potential. It is common to spend twice as much advertising money in segment B as in segment A if segment B has twice the level of some indicator of market potential. In principle, the budget should be allocated to different segments according to their expected marginal response to advertising. A budget is well allocated when it is not possible to shift dollars from one segment to another and increase total market response.

MEDIA SELECTION

Once the advertising budget is set for a given market segment, region, and time period, the next step is to allocate this budget across media categories and vehicles. Presumably some thought will already have been given to this problem, since the selection of a target segment inevitably leads to the use of media to which the segment is most frequently exposed. Also, the media considered will affect one's thinking about the size of the overall budget; a television campaign is much more costly than a radio campaign. Finally, the media affect the kind of messages one can use.

There are three basic steps in the media selection process: choosing among major media categories, choosing among specific media vehicles, and timing.

Choosing Among Major Media Categories

The first step calls for allocating the advertising budget to the major *media categories*. These categories must be examined for their capacity to deliver reach, frequency, and impact. In order of their advertising volume, they are newspapers, television, direct mail, radio, magazines, and outdoor. Marketers choose among these major media categories by considering the following variables:

1 *Target audience media habits.* For example, radio and television are the most effective media for reaching teenagers.

2 *Product or service.* Media categories have different potentialities for demonstration, visualization, explanation, believability, and color. Television, for example, is the most effective medium for demonstrating how a product or service works or for creating an emotional effect (see Figure 19-3), while magazines are ideal for accurately reproducing the appearance of food products or home decorating ideas.

3 *Message.* A message announcing an emergency blood drive tomorrow requires radio, newspapers or posters. A message containing a great deal of technical data might require specialized magazines or direct mailings. Messages that would benefit from consumers adding their own images and fantasies might be most effective on the radio.

4 *Cost.* Television is very expensive, and newspaper advertising is inexpensive. What counts, of course, if the cost per thousand exposures rather than the total cost. In developing countries, posters are often highly cost effective.

Recently, SOMARC (Social Marketing for Change) has summarized the advantages and disadvantages of the major media (see Table 19-1).

On the basis of these characteristics, the marketer has to decide how to allocate the given budget to the major media categories. The U.S. Army Recruiting Command, for example, might decide to allocate $14 million to evening television spots, $4 million to male-oriented magazines, and $2 million to daily newspapers.

Selecting Specific Media Vehicles

The next step is to choose the specific media vehicles within each media category that would produce the desired response in the most cost-effective way. Consider the category of male-oriented magazines, which includes *Playboy, Home Mechanics, Esquire, Motorcycle,* and so on. The media planner turns to several volumes put out by Standard Rate and Data that provide circulation and cost data for different ad sizes, color options, ad positions, and quantities of insertions. Beyond this, the media planner evaluates the different magazines on qualitative characteristics such as credibility, prestige, availability of geographical or occupational editions, reproduction quality, editorial climate, lead time, and psychological impact. The media planner makes a final judgment as to which specific vehicles will deliver the best reach, frequency, and impact for the money.

Media planners normally calculate the *cost per thousand persons* reached by a particular vehicle. Suppose the marketing manager of a Los Angeles charitable organization is considering advertising in either the Los Angeles regional edition of *Time* magazine or *Los Angeles* magazine. In 1988, a one-page four-color ad in

FIGURE 19-3

Use of Television to Address an Emotional Issue

It brings out the best in all of us.™

United Way

TV PUBLIC SERVICE SPOTS

"ABC'S"

CNUW9130 30 SECONDS

(MUSIC UNDER)
TEACHER: Everyone makes mistakes, Matthew.

(CHILDREN'S LAUGHTER)

(CHILDREN'S LAUGHTER)

Don't pay any attention to the other children.

(CHILDREN'S LAUGHTER)

(CHILDREN'S LAUGHTER)

ANNCR: (VO) For this bright six year old, the ABC's have never been as simple as ABC.

(CHILDREN'S LAUGHTER)

(CHILDREN'S LAUGHTER)

United Way
It brings out the best in all of us.

Where do you go when you're different from the other kids? He got help at a center for learning disabilities.

They got help from the United Way. All because the United Way got help from you.

The United Way. It brings out the best in all of us.

Volunteer Advertising Agency: Lowe Marschalk, Inc.
Volunteer Coordinator: Norman Levy, The Procter & Gamble Company.

289

Table 19-1

STRENGTHS AND WEAKNESSES OF ALTERNATIVE MEDIA
FOR NONPROFITS

Strengths	*Weaknesses*
TELEVISION	
High Impact	High production costs
Audience selectivity	Uneven delivery by market
Schedule when needed	Upfront commitments required
Fast awareness	
Sponsorship availabilities	
Merchandising possible	
RADIO	
Low cost per contact	Nonintrusive medium
Audience selectivity	Audience per spot small
Schedule when needed	No visual impact
Length can vary	High total cost for good reach
Personalities available	Clutter within spot markets
Tailor weight to market	
MAGAZINES	
Audience selectivity	Long lead time needed
Editorial association	Readership accumulates slowly
Long life	Uneven delivery by market
Large audience per insert	Cost premiums for regional or demographic
Excellent color	editions
Minimal waste	
Merchandising possible	
NEWSPAPERS	
Large audience	Difficult to target narrowly
Immediate reach	Highest waste
Short lead time	High cost for national use
Market flexibility	Minimum positioning control
Good upscale coverage	Cluttered
POSTERS, BILLBOARDS	
High reach	No depth of message
High frequency of exposure	High cost for national use
Minimal waste	Best positions already taken
Can localize	No audience selectivity
Immediate registration	Poor coverage in some areas
Flexible scheduling	Minimum one-month purchase

SOURCE: *A Program Manager's Guide to Media Planning* (Washington, D.C.: SOMARC, The Futures
Group, no date). Reproduced with permission.

Time magazine cost $14,397 and in *Los Angeles*, $10,210. While *Los Angeles* is less
expensive, it has a circulation of only 172,000 while *Time* reaches 272,000. On a
cost-per-thousand basis, *Time* is the better buy at $52.93 per thousand compared
to $59.36 for *Los Angeles*. Costs for other potential vehicles, including television
and radio, could be calculated in the same way.

The media planner would then adjust these figures for impact. One simple procedure would be to assign an impact score of 1.0 for the best vehicle and values from 0 to 1 for the remainder. Each vehicle's cost per thousand would then be divided by the impact index to yield an impact-adjusted cost per thousand which would then guide media allocation. Where these allocation decisions are made repeatedly (as in an advertising agency), it is usually desirable to computerize the process.

Direct Mail

A medium increasingly being used by nonprofits, particularly arts and health care organizations and charities, is direct mail. Novelli has suggested that direct mail has seven important advantages for nonprofit marketers:[8]

1 It tends to be very focused: it can achieve maximum impact on a specific target market.
2 It can be private and confidential, a major advantage for charities and programs dealing with venereal disease, child abuse, and family planning.
3 Purchase of direct-mail services is not forbidden to government agencies, whereas purchase of broadcast, newspaper, magazine, outdoor, and other media sometimes is forbidden.
4 Cost per contact and cost per response can often be very low, which is an important appeal to impoverished nonprofits.
5 Results are quite often clearly measurable, and this can help make nonprofit marketing programs more accountable. The American Heart Association may not know their effect on cholesterol levels, but they can calculate how many responded to a specific mail promotion of a low-cholesterol cookbook and what cost they incurred per inquiry.
6 Small-scale tests of proposed strategies are very feasible with direct mail. In fact, direct mail is an ideal field-test vehicle. A number of marketing factors can be varied over several mailings and the results compared to baseline measures. In tests of other media, it is often difficult to link a specific surge in sales to, say, a flight of radio advertisements. By contrast, if more cookbook requests come in from those who receive a mailing with a message about cholesterol involving a medium level of fear than from those who get a high-fear or low-fear treatment, it is hard not to conclude that a medium-fear message works best.
7 The effectiveness of direct mail can be assessed directly in terms of *behavior* (for example, orders, requests, and inquiries), whereas other media assessments usually require attitude and awareness indicators which are fraught with measurement problems.

There are several steps in establishing a strategically effective mail-order operation.

1 *Determine the objectives* of mail-order programs carefully in advance. Is the program to produce sales, create awareness, change attitudes, or make contacts to be followed up through other media? In some cases, a phased strategy is appropriate in which earlier mailers are used to develop awareness and later mailers for direct action.

2 *Determine the target audience.* Some groups are more responsive to direct mail than others. According to Herb Bell of NLT Computer Services Corporation, charities should target "women, 49 to 79 years old, as they are more likely to be touched by emotional appeals and more likely to have disposable income. Women usually open the mail and pay the bills. Older women are less likely to be supporting children. They are looking for meaningful ways to perpetuate themselves through charity."[9]

3 *Develop mail lists.* Outside services can be the source of highly tailored prospect lists defined by schooling; occupation; area of the country; socioeconomic status of the neighborhood; ownership of certain credit cards; patronage of particular products, services, or outlets; and so on. Whenever time permits, new rented lists should be tested with small mailings to see if they are productive before a budget is committed to an unknown target list. The best lists, however, are always those containing the addresses of people with whom the organization *already* has some form of contact. Thus, one's best prospects are those who have responded to past mailings, who have made inquiries in some other fashion, or who are past or present supporters of the organization.

4 *Develop effective copy.* Investment in effective graphics and compelling messages is seldom wasted. Direct mail pieces are meeting more and more competition every day in the "mail box arena," and one needs powerful messages and compelling visual images to stand out. Attention must be paid to envelope design (to get the message exposed), the cover letter (to get it read), and motivational themes (to get it acted on). Many mailings fail because they are not consciously directed toward stimulating responses.

5 *Pretest each mailer.* This can be done inexpensively and, if sample target audience members are used, can both indicate probable successes and point up potential problems.

6 *Schedule mailings carefully.* Some mailings have predetermined timings (for example, for particular events). In those cases, the mailing should arrive just as the evaluation stage of consumer decision making is taking place. Thus, mailings for arts events are best sent six to eight weeks before the event. They are seldom effective in the last week unless targeted to an impulse-purchase audience. When the timing of mailings is discretionary, the marketer should carefully test different patterns, for example, with mailings bunched together in *flights* or spread out over time.

7 *Use responses as feedback.* The savvy direct mailer learns from each mailing what works or doesn't work in the mailing design itself. If a systematic program of experimentation is used over the years, much can be learned about effective tactics for particular audiences. Mail responses can also tell something about the responder. As Tom McCabe of International Marketing Group notes: "You know exactly who responds and why. . . . Every time someone responds to a mailing, you learn something about that person. Direct marketing is very efficient because eventually you will be able to know what kind of return to expect on every marketing dollar you spend."[10]

Deciding on Media Timing

The third step in media selection is *timing.* It breaks down into a macro problem and a micro problem. The macro problem is that of *cyclical* or *seasonal timing.* For most products and services, audience size and interest vary at different times of the year. There is not much interest in Senator X until his reelection comes up or much interest in university affairs during the summer. Most marketers do not advertise when there is little interest, spending the bulk of their advertising budgets just as natural interest in the product or service class begins to increase and when it peaks. Counterseasonal or counter-cyclical advertising is still rare in practice.

The other problem is more of a micro problem, that of the *short-run timing* of advertising. How should advertising be spaced during a short period of, say, one week? Consider three possible patterns. The first is called *burst advertising* and consists of concentrating all the exposures in a very short period of time, say all in one day. Presumably, this will attract maximum attention and interest, and if recall is good, the effect will last for a while. The second pattern is *continuous advertising,* in which the exposures appear evenly throughout the period. This may be most effective when the audience buys or uses the product frequently and needs to be continuously reminded. The third pattern is *intermittent advertising,* in which intermittent small bursts of advertising appear with no advertising in between. This pattern is able to create a little more attention than continuous advertising, yet it has some of the reminder advantage of continuous advertising.

Timing decisions should take three factors into consideration. *Audience turnover* is the rate at which the target audience changes between two periods. The greater the turnover, the more continuous the advertising should be. *Behavior frequency* is the number of times the target audience takes the action one is trying to influence (for example, smoking, not wearing seat belts). The more frequent the behavior, the more the advertising should be continuous. The *forgetting rate* is the rate at which a given message will be forgotten or a given behavior change extinguished. Again, the faster the forgetting, the more continuous the advertising should be.

A related issue is the sequencing of various types of advertising in an overall strategic program. An example of such a program is shown in Exhibit 19-2.

ADVERTISING EVALUATION

The final step in the effective use of advertising is *advertising evaluation.* The most important components are copy testing, media testing, and expenditure-level testing.

Copy testing can occur both before an ad is put into actual media (copy pretesting) and after it has been printed or broadcast (copy posttesting). The purpose of *ad pretesting* is to make improvements in the advertising copy to the fullest extent prior to its release. There are several methods of ad pretesting:

   1 *Comprehension testing.* A critical prerequisite for any advertisement is that it be comprehensible. This can be a major problem when dealing with less educated or even illiterate audiences. When words are used in the advertisement, a

EXHIBIT 19-2

Sequenced Strategy at Royce Hall

The performing arts program at UCLA's Royce Hall has been highly successful because it attracts high-quality performers. Recent attendance has been further enhanced by the careful development of well-thought-out marketing strategies. One feature is the careful *sequencing* of communications for each season. In a recent year, it carried out the following eight steps:

1 First, announcements were sent to past program subscribers to give them first chance at the best seats for season subscriptions and, not incidentally, to make them feel that they were receiving special attention.

2 After a suitable delay, full-page advertisements in local papers announced the entire program to the general public and solicited season ticket subscriptions.

3 Once season ticket subscription orders plateaued, single ticket availability was announced to past subscribers by mail and then to the general public.

4 At this point, attention was shifted to recapturing past season ticket subscribers who had not renewed through relatively high-cost telephone marketing (telemarketing).

5 Just before the season started, mailers were sent to subscribers, non-subscribers, and others, and newspaper ads were placed reintroducing the fall portion of the schedule.

6 Radio ads, both paid and public service, and quarter-page newspaper ads then promoted the first (and each subsequent) performance.

7 Flyers were sent to those who subscribed to or bought single tickets for one specific series promoting *other* similar events in which they might be interested.

8 Finally, on the night of the performances, posters were hung on campus, and ads were placed in programs promoting related events, presumably catching concertgoers at the moment when they are most in the spirit of "going out to the theater."

marketing staff member can apply one or more readability formulas to predict comprehension. These formulas measure the length of sentences and the number of polysyllabic words. One popular measure called SMOG has been used by the Office of Cancer Communications of the National Cancer Institute to test public and patient education health materials.

2 *Mailed questionnaires.* Here a panel of target consumers or of advertising experts is mailed a set of alternative ads and fills out rating questionnaires. Sometimes a single question is raised, such as "Which of these ads do you think would influence you most to buy the service?" Or a more elaborate form consisting of several rating scales may be used, such as the one shown in Table 19-2. Here the person evaluates the ad's attention strength, read-through strength, cognitive strength, affective strength, and behavioral strength, assigning a number of

Table 19-2

RATING SHEET FOR ADS

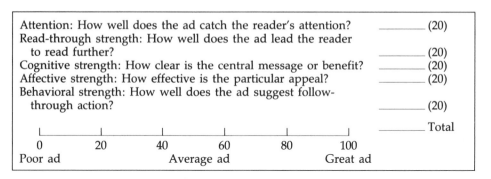

Attention: How well does the ad catch the reader's attention?   _____ (20)
Read-through strength: How well does the ad lead the reader
   to read further?   _____ (20)
Cognitive strength: How clear is the central message or benefit?   _____ (20)
Affective strength: How effective is the particular appeal?   _____ (20)
Behavioral strength: How well does the ad suggest follow-
   through action?   _____ (20)

                                                                           _____ Total

points (up to a maximum) in each case. The underlying theory is that an effective ad must score high on all these properties if it is ultimately to stimulate buying action. Too often ads are evaluated only for their attention-getting or comprehension-creating abilities. At the same time, direct rating methods are judgmental and less reliable than harder evidence of an ad's actual impact on target consumers. Direct rating scales help primarily to screen out poor ads rather than to identify great ads.

3 *Portfolio recall tests.* Here respondents are asked to read a portfolio of ads. After putting them down, the respondents are asked to recall the ads they saw—unaided or aided by the interviewer—and to describe as much as they can about each ad. The results are taken to indicate an ad's ability to stand out and its intended message's ability to be understood.

4 *Physiological tests.* Some researchers assess the potential effect of an ad by measuring physiological reactions—heartbeat, blood pressure, pupil dilation, perspiration—using such equipment as galvanometers, tachistoscopes, and pupil dilation–measuring equipment. These physiological tests at best measure the attention-getting and arousing power of an ad rather than any particular cognition or emotion that the ad might produce.

5 *Focus-group interviews.* Since advertisements are often viewed in a group setting, pretests with groups can often indicate both how a message is perceived and how it might be passed along. As noted in Chapter 7, the focus-group technique also has the advantages that (a) its synergism can generate more reactions than a one-on-one session, (b) it is more efficient in that it gathers data from 6 to 12 people at once, and (c) it can yield data relatively quickly.

There are three popular *ad posttesting methods,* whose purpose is to assess if the desired impact is achieved after transmission or what the possible ad weaknesses are:

1 *Recall tests.* These involve finding persons who are regular users of the media vehicle and asking them to recall advertisers and products contained in the issue under study. They are asked to recall or play back everything they can remember. The administrator may or may not aid them in their recall. Recall scores are prepared on the basis of their responses and used to indicate the ad's power to be noted and remembered.

2 *Recognition tests.* Recognition tests call for sampling the readers of a given issue of the vehicle, say a magazine, and asking them to point out what they recognize having seen or read before. In one such technique, Daniel Starch computes three different readership scores:

- *Noted.* The percentage of readers of the magazine who say they had previously seen the advertisement in the particular magazine.
- *Seen/associated.* The percentage of readers who say they have seen or read any part of the ad that clearly indicates the names of the product (or service) of the advertiser.
- *Read most.* The percentage of readers who not only looked at the advertisement, but who say that they read more than half of the total written material in the ad.

The Starch organization also furnishes Adnorms—that is, average scores for each product or service class for the year—and separate scores for men and women for each magazine, to enable advertisers to evaluate their ads over time and in relation to competitors' ads.

3 *Direct response.* The preceding techniques measure *cognitive outcomes* of advertising. But favorable cognitive outcomes may not translate into *behavioral* outcomes! Behavioral responses can be solicited by a message, however, and the results directly measured. The effectiveness of alternative messages or media in influencing behavior can be tracked as follows:

- Placing mailback coupons with a code number or P.O. box in the advertisement that varies by message and medium.
- Asking target audience members to mention or bring in an advertisement in order to receive special treatment (for example, a price discount or free parking).
- Setting up an 800 number and asking individuals to call for further information (on which occasion they can be asked where they saw the ad, what they remember, and so on).
- Staggering the placement of ads so that this week's attendance or sales can be attributed to ad A while next week's can be attributed to ad B. This is also an effective method for assessing alternative expenditure levels.

As mentioned in Chapter 7, marketers can learn a great deal about the effectiveness of alternative message and media strategies by designing experiments coupled with careful posttest measures and accumulating their insights over time.

SALES PROMOTION

In the private sector, sales promotion has supplanted media advertising as the major communications and persuasion technique among consumer goods marketers. Sales promotion comprises a wide variety of tactical promotional tools of a short-term incentive nature designed to stimulate earlier or stronger target market response. These tools can be subclassified into tools for *consumer promotion* (for example, samples, coupons, money refund offers, prices off, gifts, contests, trading stamps, demonstrations), *intermediary promotion* (for example, free goods, merchandise allowances, cooperative advertising, push money, dealer sales contests), and *sales force promotions* (for example, bonuses, contests, sales rallies). While usually used to stimulate *sales* of goods and services, promotion tools can also be designed to affect social behaviors such as blood donations, applying to college, joining the armed forces, and so on.

Sales promotion tools are used by a large variety of nonprofit organizations. Some colleges in recent years have offered finder's fees, sponsored all-expense-paid college weekends for high school counselors and prospective students, and so on. Some hospitals have sponsored filet mignon candlelight dinners for new mothers, televised bingo games for patients, and provided country club memberships for new doctors joining their staff. And family planners in many parts of the world have offered incentives—transistor radios, cookware, costume jewelry, free bank accounts, and so on—to potential adopters of birth control measures.

No single purpose can be ascribed to sales promotion tools, since they are so varied in form. Overall, sales promotion tools make three contributions: (1) *communication*—they gain attention and usually provide information that will, it is hoped, lead to trying the product; (2) *incentive*—they incorporate some concession, inducement, or contribution that is designed to represent value to the receiver; and (3) *invitation*—they include a distinct invitation to engage in the transaction now.

We will define an *incentive* as *something of financial or symbolic value added to an offer to encourage some overt behavioral response.*[11] The decision by an organization to use incentives as part of its promotional plan calls for six distinct steps.

The first step is to specify *the objective* for which the incentive is undertaken. Three objectives can be distinguished. Sometimes incentives are offered to create an immediate behavioral response because the organization has excess capacity or inventory. A local YMCA lacking sufficient enrollment may offer a low-cost trial membership plan. Incentives may also be offered to promote trial of a product or service by groups that normally would not try it. Thus, a museum might give away free art posters to adolescents attending a new exhibit. Finally, incentives may be offered to win goodwill toward the organization, as when an organization offers to match its employees' contributions to a particular charity.

The second step is to specify the *recipient* of the incentive—that is, whether incentives will go to consumers, suppliers, or sales agents. Incentives to promote vasectomies, for example, may be offered to the consumer, to the doctor, or to the canvasser who recruits prospects. At one time, canvassers for vasectomies in India received such incentives to find prospects that they brought in men who were too young to know better and men who were too old for it to matter!

The third step is to determine the *inclusiveness of the incentive*—that is, whether it will be offered to individuals or to the groups to which the target individuals belong. Most incentives are offered to individuals for their direct benefit. The case of an incentive that is offered to a group is exemplified in communities that offer to provide free blood to all persons in the community if 4 percent or more of the community's residents make blood donations. Another is the case in Thailand where villages get economic development money in proportion to the extent that the village as a whole practices family planning.

The fourth step is to determine the *form of the incentive*—that is, whether it will consist of money or items of nonmonetary value, such as food, free education, health care, lottery tickets, or old age security. The form of the incentive must be carefully researched because its nuances may offend the target group. Although cash is a very tangible incentive, for example, it may be viewed as a corrupt consideration if it is used to influence decisions on how many children to have. An offer of better housing may be received more favorably.

The fifth step is to determine the *amount of incentive*. Too small an incentive is ineffective and an overly large one is wasteful. If the incentive is nongraduated, the amount may seem too small for those in higher income brackets and too much for those in lower income brackets. This has led to interest in graduated incentives whereby the amount offered varies with the consumer's economic circumstances or interest in the offer. Public television stations, for example, vary the premiums offered based on how much one gives.

The sixth step is the *time of payment of the incentives*. Most incentives are paid immediately upon the adoption of the target behavior. Thus, in the family planning area, the adoption of sterilization is usually immediately followed by payment. But the agreement to use birth control pills may not be rewarded except on the basis of results each year.

In summary, incentives are an important means of promotion but they require research and analysis. Commercial companies tend to learn over time which incentives work best and what amounts and timing are optimal. As noted in Chapter 18, several propositions are emerging about incentives and their effective use. Knowledge is also accumulating on the effectiveness of incentives in other health-related areas, such as nutrition, immunization, and self-medication practice. The outlook is for increasing use of incentives in social and organizational marketing.

SUMMARY

Advertising, nonpersonal communication conducted through paid media under clear sponsorship, must be planned strategically like any other element of the marketing mix. Objectives must be set, budgets determined, messages defined, media selected, and a system of evaluation established.

Advertising objectives must fit with prior decisions about the target market, offer positioning, and the nature of the remainder of the marketing mix. It must be clear what response from the target audience is sought. Typically, the response is movement forward through six stages: awareness, knowledge, liking, preference, conviction, and action.

Budgets can be set by affordable, percent-of-sales, or competitive methods, but the objective-and-task method is best. Budgets must be both set in total and allocated among different market segments, geographical areas, and time periods. Budgets must also be allocated across media categories and to specific media vehicles. Choices here depend on the marketer's objectives, the intended target audience, the planned message, and media costs.

Managers must also decide on media timing. Ads should be scheduled seasonally or cyclically to parallel changes in audience interest. Within seasons, decisions must be made on short-run timing. The major options are to advertise continuously, intermittently, or in preplanned bursts. These choices should be based on audience turnover, the frequency of the behavior to be influenced, and forgetting rates.

Evaluation schemes involve pretesting and posttesting advertising. Pretesting can incorporate comprehension studies, mailed questionnaires, portfolio recall tests, physiological tests, focus-group interviews, or self-administered questionnaires. Posttests are usually based on recall, recognition, or some direct behavioral response such as inquiries or sales.

Sales promotion involves a wide range of incentives designed to have short-term effects on specific behaviors of consumers, intermediaries, or the sales force. Sales promotion incentives can impel immediate action but there must be careful planning of objectives, recipient, inclusiveness, and form, amount and time of payment.

QUESTIONS

1. Assume a marketer seeking to increase the practice of "safe sex" among teenagers was considering running (a) three ads each in four national teen magazines at a cost of $45,000 per ad or (b) two 30-second ads on TV in five major metropolitan areas at a cost of $12,000 for each ad in each city. The estimated audiences for each teen magazine is 12,000 and is 10,000 for the average teen program in each of the five cities. The total annual budget is $1 million and would pay for production costs for either approach. How should the marketer proceed to choose between the two approaches? What additional information should be gathered?

2. How should the ads in Question 1 be timed over a target year?

3. Develop a behavior change model similar to that in Figure 19-2 setting out the steps necessary to move someone from lack of awareness of the need for practicing "safe sex" to becoming a regular adopter of such behavior. How would this model guide a promotion strategy?

4. Assuming that you were asked to prepare a series of direct-mail pieces to be sent to students in a local college promoting an upcoming blood drive, set overall objectives for this program and indicate how these would vary by segments within the college community. How would you pretest the mes-

sages and the form of the direct-mail pieces to be used to achieve your objectives?

5. List ten incentives that might be used to induce college students to give blood. Evaluate these incentives from a cost/benefit standpoint paying particular attention to their ability to induce both initial and repeat donation behavior.

NOTES

1. These definitions, with the exception of the one for sales promotion, came from *Marketing Definitions: A Glossary of Marketing Terms* (Chicago: American Marketing Association, 1960).

2. "100 Leading National Advertisers," *Advertising Age,* September 27, 1989, p. 8.

3. "Political Advertising Sets New Record," *Adweek,* February 20, 1989.

4. See John A. Zeigler, "Social Change Through Issue Advertising," *Sociological Inquiry,* Winter 1970, pp. 159–165.

5. Janet Meyers, "Pentagon to Cut Ad Ammunition?" *Advertising Age,* December 18, 1989, p. 3.

6. There are several models of buyer readiness states. See, for example, Robert J. Lavidge and Gary A. Steiner, "A Model for Predictive Measurements of Advertising Effectiveness," *Journal of Marketing,* October 1961, pp. 59–62. For another approach, see Geraldine Fennell, "Persuasion as Behavioral Science in Business and Nonbusiness Contexts," in Russell W. Belk, ed., *Advances in Nonprofit Marketing,* Vol. 1 (Greenwich, Conn.: JAI Press, 1985), pp. 95–160.

7. See Russell H. Colley, *Defining Advertising Goals for Measured Advertising Results* (New York: Association of National Advertisers, 1961).

8. William D. Novelli, "Social Issues and Direct Marketing: What's the Connection?" presentation to the Annual Conference of the Direct Mail/Marketing Association, Los Angeles, Calif., March 12, 1981.

9. Belinda Hulin-Salkin, "Strategies of Charities," *Advertising Age,* January 19, 1981, pp. 528–531.

10. Ibid., p. 529.

11. This definition and the following discussion rely largely on two sources: Edward Pohlman, *Incentives and Compensation in Birth Planning* (Chapel Hill: Carolina Population Center, University of North Carolina, 1971); and Everett M. Rogers, "Effects of Incentives on the Diffusion of Innovations: The Case of Family Planning in Asia," a chapter in Gerald Zaltman, ed., *Processes and Phenomena of Social Change* (New York: John Wiley, 1973).

20

Managing Public Relations

Small charities and other nonprofit organizations have great difficulty getting the world to pay attention to them. They compete with hundreds of other organizations clamoring for newspaper space and air time for their equally-important stories and events. Small organizations all too often get lost in the deluge of public relations material that reach media gatekeepers every working day.

The fate of being just one more (small) player in a public relations mob scene can sometimes be overcome through clever graphics and a compelling story. However, one of the surest ways to a higher profile is to have a celebrity spokesperson. The large nonprofits and charities have known this for a long time. The Muscular Dystrophy Association gets great mileage out of its association with Jerry Lewis. Farm Aid is identified with Willie Nelson and the United Way uses many local NFL football players to get across the message that it cares.

Finding a champion can be difficult. However, a new nonprofit organization, called the Celebrity Outreach Foundation, may help solve the problem. The foundation has been set up to assist organizations with budgets less than $2 million. It maintains a list of 2,500 celebrities and attempts to match them to organizations needing help with an event, a public service announcement, or general public support. Some celebrities participate because they believe in the particular cause or simply because they, too, could use the exposure.

The Celebrity Outreach Foundation began in California. However, by 1990, it was receiving 20 percent of its requests for help from outside the state. In 1990, the U.S. Census Bureau sought the Foundation's help in securing cooperation for their enumerators on the part of Latinos, Blacks, and Native Americans.

Source: See also Julie Wheelock, "Nonprofit Group Puts Charities in Touch with 'Cause Celebrities,' " *Los Angeles Times*, December 26, 1989, p. E8.

To achieve their strategic objectives, organizations must influence the behavior of a great many publics. The behaviors they seek are of three types: responses, participation, and support. *Responses* are sought from consumers, donors, suppliers, and intermediaries and are the responsibility of the marketing and/or fund-raising departments (although others such as the CEO may be involved from time to time). *Participation* is sought from management, staff, volunteers, and the board of directors and is usually the responsibility of the personnel function.

Direct responses and participation typically involve specific explicit exchanges: services for fees, publicity for donations, salary for staffing. *Support*, however, is different in that it often means a lack of response (i.e., tolerance) on the part of important publics such as regulators, social critics, or civic officials as well as direct or indirect expressions of good wishes on the part of the media, other nonprofits, and the general public. Responsibility for achieving support in more sophisticated organizations is typically lodged with the public relations manager.

The *public relations manager* is usually responsible for maintaining and enhancing the reputation of the organization among key publics. While the principal focus of this effort is on support publics, it is quite clearly recognized that an organization's image has important effects on its own employees, its donors and volunteers, and its clients. By employing a public relations manager, the organization can gain several advantages: (1) better anticipation of potential problems, (2) better handling of these problems, (3) consistent public-oriented policies and strategies, and (4) more professional written and oral communications.

The public relations function can be accorded high or low influence in the organization, depending on the board's and chief executive officer's attitude toward the function. In some organizations, the public relations manager is a vice-president and sits in on all meetings involving information and actions that might affect public perceptions of the organization. He or she not only puts out fires but also counsels management on actions that will avoid starting fires. In other organizations, public relations is a middle-management function charged with getting out publications and handling news and special events. The public relations people are not involved in policy or strategy formulation, only in tactics.

The recent emergence of marketing as a "hot topic" in nonprofit circles has raised a major question in the minds of chief administrators and public relations managers as to the relationship between marketing and public relations in a nonprofit organization. Clearly, the two functions work well together in business firms with marketing focusing on the development of plans to market the company s products to consumers, while public relations takes care of relations with other publics. In nonprofit organizations, the relationship between the public relations and marketing departments has been marked by tension and lack of clearly defined areas of responsibility. The tension is mainly a historical artifact. In many institutions, the public relations function was already well established when marketing was introduced. In such cases, three factors tended to create friction between the two areas. First, the marketing department was often assigned functions that were "taken away" from public relations. Second, public relations directors often felt that they should have been given the new, often more prestigious and better-paying position of marketing director in the new organization. Third, many public relations executives felt that marketing ought properly to be a division within their department or that marketing as a separate function was not needed at all.

These frictions were often exacerbated by lack of clearly specified separate roles for the two functions and a clear understanding of how they were to be coordinated with each other. Both are boundary functions concerned with achieving certain results with various internal and external publics. Are the two functions redundant? Is one more important or comprehensive than the other? Do they play equal but different roles?

This chapter advances the thesis that public relations is most effective when viewed and conducted as part of the marketing mix being used by the organization to pursue its marketing objectives. We will look at the following questions:

1 How did the public relations function evolve?
2 What is the relation between public relations and marketing in nonprofit organizations?
3 How should the public relations function be carried out?

THE HISTORICAL EVOLUTION
OF PUBLIC RELATIONS

Public relations, like marketing, is a relatively new corporate function, although its roots go back into ancient history.[1] Corporate public relations first emerged in the late nineteenth century and passed through the five stages shown in Figure 20-1. In the first stage, corporations established a *contact* function to influence legislators and newspapers to support positions favorable to business. The legislative contact function became known as *lobbying,* and the newspaper contact function became known as *press agentry.* George Westinghouse is credited with formally establishing public relations when he hired two men in 1889 to fight the advocates of direct current electricity and to promote instead alternating current.[2]

The next stage occurred when companies began to recognize the positive value of planned *publicity* in creating customer interest in the company and its products. Publicity entailed finding or creating events, preparing company- or product-slanted news stories, and trying to interest the press in using them. Companies recognized that special skills are needed to develop publicity and began to add publicists to their ranks.

Somewhat later, public relations practitioners began to recognize the value of conducting *research* into public opinion prior to developing and launching public relations campaigns. The emerging sciences of public opinion measurement and mass communication theory permitted more sophistication in the conduct of public relations. Forward-looking firms added specialists who could research public opinion.

These functions—contact, publicity, and research—were uncoordinated in the typical firm. The organization's lobbyists had little to do with the organization's publicists and the publicists had little to do with the researchers. This led finally to the concept of a *public relations department*, which integrated the work going on to cultivate the goodwill of the company's different publics. In larger organizations, public relations departments grew to encompass subspecialties to deal with each public (stockholders, neighbors, employees, customers, government agencies) and each tool (publications, press relations, research, and so on).

The establishment of a public relations department did not ensure that the organization as a whole acted like a *public-oriented company*. The vice-president of public relations had limited influence over other departments and needed the backing of top management to press for public-oriented actions by all departments. Organizations were facing growing challenges in the form of consumerism, environmentalism, energy conservation, inflation, shortages, employment discrimination, and safety. Public relations people wanted a more active role in counseling the organization and its departments on how to act as public citizens. PR practitioners emphasize that their job is not just to produce "good words" but to produce "good deeds followed by good words." Unless they can get the organization to act like a good citizen, good words alone will not be enough.

FIGURE 20-1

Historical Evolution of Public Relations

THE RELATIONSHIP BETWEEN PUBLIC RELATIONS AND MARKETING

Public relations is often confused with one of its subfunctions, such as press agentry, company publications, lobbying, fire fighting, and so forth. Yet it is a more inclusive concept. The most frequently quoted definition of PR is the following:

> **Public relations** is the management function that evaluates the attitudes of important publics, identifies the policies and procedures of an individual or an organization with the public interest, and executes a program of action to earn understanding and acceptance by these publics.[3]

Sometimes a short definition is given, which says that PR stands for *performance* (P) plus *recognition* (R).

We see the following differences between public relations and marketing:

1   Public relations is primarily a communication tool, whereas marketing also includes need assessment, product development, pricing, and distribution.
2   Public relations seeks to influence attitudes, whereas marketing tries to influence specific behaviors, such as purchasing, joining, voting, donating, and so on.
3   Public relations does not define the goals of the organization, whereas marketing is intimately involved in defining the business's mission, customers, and services.

On the other hand, the mission of public relations is one that can benefit from the kind of strategic marketing planning that we have stressed throughout this book. For the public relations function, we have simplified the strategic planning process to the seven steps outlined in Figure 20–2.

THE PUBLIC RELATIONS STRATEGIC PLANNING PROCESS

We cannot emphasize strongly enough the need for careful long-range and annual planning of the public relations function. It has been our experience that in many organizations, public relations is mainly (or *only*) *reactive*. It gets out press releases as needed, fights "brush fires" as they emerge, and copes with individual and group complaints. This reactive stance has many negative consequences:

1   The environment rather than the organization sets the public relations agenda.
2   The organization's image is defined only by its response to special situations rather than by the creation of a set of carefully designed messages over a long period of time.
3   The organization's responses to crises are not guided by a long-term strategy.

FIGURE 20-2

The Public Relations Strategic Planning Process

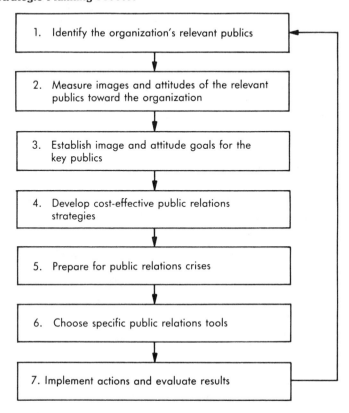

1. Identify the organization's relevant publics

2. Measure images and attitudes of the relevant publics toward the organization

3. Establish image and attitude goals for the key publics

4. Develop cost-effective public relations strategies

5. Prepare for public relations crises

6. Choose specific public relations tools

7. Implement actions and evaluate results

The *active* public relations stance avoids these problems and assures that the organization has control over how others see it. We now examine the seven steps in the public relations planning cycle necessary to implement such a *strategic* approach. (See Figure 20–2.) We shall return to the problems of crisis management shortly.

Identify the Organization's Relevant Publics

An organization would like to have the goodwill of every public that is affected by or affects it. Given limited public relations resources, however, the organization will have to concentrate more of its attention on some publics than others. An organization has primary, secondary, and tertiary publics.

An organization's primary publics are those that it relates to actively and continuously, such as clients, employees, directors, and the general community. Secondary publics are those it must monitor and relate to less frequently but on a fairly continuous basis—suppliers, agents, government officials, and competitors. Tertiary groups include various membership groups such as unions, churches, clubs, and associations that seek advantages for their own members and various social action groups and charities that seek to help others. Each of these tertiary groups can present opportunities and challenges to a specific nonprofit organization from time to time.

The various publics are related not only to the organization, but also to each other in many important ways. A particular public may have great influence on other publics. Consider a college whose students are highly satisfied. Their enthusiasm will be transmitted to their parents and to friends back home who might be potential students. Their enthusiasm will have a reinforcing effect on the faculty, who will feel that their teaching is effective. Their enthusiasm will affect the future level of support they give to the school as alumni. Thus, the satisfaction felt by students will influence the attitudes and behavior of other university publics. These dynamics are outlined in Figure 20–3.

Measure Images and Attitudes
of the Relevant Publics

Once the organization has identified its key publics, it needs to find out how each public thinks and feels about the organization. Management will have some ideas of each public's attitude simply through its regular contacts with that public. But impressions based on casual contact cannot necessarily be trusted. At one time, a college wanted to rent its stadium facilities to a professional football team for five Sundays as a way of raising more revenue. The college's administrators thought that most local residents and city council members would approve. When it sought a favorable city council vote, however, a group of local citizens attacked the college, calling it insensitive and arrogant. They complained that the football crowd would use up parking spaces, leave litter, walk on lawns, and be rowdy. A large number of citizens, including city council

FIGURE 20-3

Dynamic Relations between a University and Its Publics

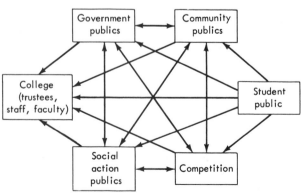

members, revealed deep-seated hostile attitudes toward the college that only needed an issue to flare up. Even in this case, the college's administration dismissed the community spokesman as a minority voice. Needless to say, the vote went against the college, to its surprise.

To know a public's attitudes well enough to use them as a solid basis for its strategic planning, the organization needs to undertake some formal marketing research. A good start is to organize focus groups of publics annually to probe their knowledge and feelings about the organization. While the observations of these focus groups are not necessarily representative, they normally contribute perspectives and raise interesting questions that the organization will want to explore more systematically. Most importantly, they will alert management to key problems as they emerge. Eventually, the organization may find it worthwhile to conduct formal field surveys on a regular basis. It can track awareness, knowledge, interest, and attitudes toward the organization. Exhibit 20–1 describes the highlights of a public opinion survey conducted for the American Red Cross.

Establish Image and Attitude Goals for Key Publics

By periodically researching its key publics, the organization develops hard data on how these publics view the organization. To translate this information into a strategic plan, the organization must evaluate each key public in terms of the probability that they have a negative attitude toward the organization and the degree of impact they can have on the organization if they act on their negative attitude.

Suppose the public relations manager for a hospital rates 20 key publics in terms of these two factors. (See Table 20–1.) She concludes that there are 5 groups that have a *high* probability of being unfavorably disposed toward the hospital in the next year (bottom row). However, the competitive nature of the hospital market and the relatively weak position of unions in this particular state have led her to conclude that the negative reactions of two publics, competitors and labor unions, will have little impact on the hospital. Local politicians are seen as hostile, but no legislation is presently pending. If politicians do decide to act, however, they can be troublesome, so the hospital must pay some attention to them. Technicians and insurers (lower right corner) are a more serious problem. Technicians are upset about the hospital's recent decision not to buy certain state-of-the-art equipment to replace older equipment. Insurers are rankled by the hospital's antiquated billing procedures and higher-than-average charges for certain exotic surgical procedures. Both groups should receive considerable attention in the upcoming year.

Physicians, patients, and media should also receive close attention. Although the probability of negative reaction from these groups is only medium, they can have a major impact on the organization. All are concerned about a

EXHIBIT 20-1

Public Opinion Research for the American Red Cross

The public opinion polling firm of Louis Harris conducts periodic surveys of public opinion toward the American Red Cross. Here is a sample of the questions asked in the 1976 survey.

What Does the Public Know About Red Cross Services?

1 What comes to mind first when you hear the words "American Red Cross?"
2 What other kinds of activities is the Red Cross engaged in?
3 For each activity, please say which statement on the list describes how important you feel that activity is (extremely important, very important, quite important, rather important, not too important, not at all important).
4 For each activity, please mention which one or more organizations provide that service.
5 Which one of these activities do you think the American Red Cross spends the most money on?

How Important Is the Work of the Red Cross and How Well Does It Do Its Job?

1 These organizations serve the American community. Which one do you personally feel does the *most* important work? Which does the *next* most important work? Which does the *third* most important work?
2 For each organization, would you say its performance is extremely good, very good, good, just fair, or poor?
3 Is there anything you don't especially like about the American Red Cross?

Where Does the Red Cross Get Its Funds?

1 Do any of the United Way contributions get distributed to the American Red Cross or not?
2 If yes, about what percent of the money raised by the United Way would you guess *is* distributed by it to the American Red Cross?
3 Which one of these statements best describes your feeling about the amount of money the Red Cross has available? It has more than it really needs. It has enough money to do the job. It doesn't have quite enough money to do its job. It has a serious lack of funds. Not sure.

The 1976 poll yielded a number of important findings: (1) The Red Cross is perceived almost exclusively as a disaster relief organization, its other services being less well known. (2) There is a vague antipathy toward the Red Cross. (3) Red Cross performance is perceived to be not as good as that of other organizations. (4) Perception of Red Cross need for funds is relatively low.

SOURCE: 1976 National Public Opinion Research Concerning the American National Red Cross.

Table 20-1

A PORTFOLIO OF PUBLICS FOR ST. ANTHONY'S HOSPITAL

Probability of Negative Reaction	*Potential Impact*		
	Low	*Medium*	*High*
Low	Suppliers	Nursing Schools Volunteers	Board Nurses Regional Health Agency Charities
Medium	General Public Nonmedical Staff	Medical Schools Research Foundations	Physicians TV/Radio Newspapers Patients
High	Competitors Labor Unions	Local Politicians	Technicians Insurers

recent scandal at the hospital in which two physicians were discovered abusing drugs. The same issue has caused a potential problem for the other groups in the medium-probability, medium- and high-impact cells of the matrix. Informal soundings indicate that all six publics in these two cells are concerned about the hospital's medical staff and control systems. Medical schools and research foundations must be satisfied, since negative attitudes on the part of these publics have the potential for affecting future recruitment of physicians and winning of research grants. The upper right cell is a discretionary target. Some attention may be devoted to the board, nurses, regional health agencies, and charitable organizations. Their interests and concerns, however, might be met by programs directed at other target publics.

As for the three remaining cells of the matrix, the analysis suggests that the public relations manager can pay relatively little attention to suppliers, nursing schools, volunteers, the general public, and nonmedical staff in the upcoming year. She should continue, however, to monitor their attitudes over the year to make sure that her initial assessment of a favorable attitude is correct and that they do not "migrate" to other, more potentially damaging cells.

Once the public relations manager has determined the amount of effort to direct to each key public in the matrix, specific communication goals must be set for each segment. The manager might set a goal, for example, that "90 percent of TV and radio news directors and city newspaper editors within a 50-mile radius of the hospital should know within six months the full details of the hospital's internal policing system. Seventy-five percent should have full confidence in the hospital by the end of that period." These specific goals naturally suggest the means for their achievement and indicate what results should be measured later to evaluate the success of the strategic plan.

Develop Cost Effective PR Strategies

An organization usually has many options in trying to improve the attitudes of a particular public. Its first task is to understand why negative attitudes have arisen so that the causal factors can be appropriately addressed. Consider the case of the college that found it had weak community support when it wanted to rent its stadium to a professional football team. In digging deeper into the negative citizen attitudes, the college discovered that many citizens harbored a history of resentment against the college for reasons including (1) the college never consults citizen groups before taking actions, (2) the college discriminates against local high school students, preferring to draw students from other parts of the country, (3) the college does not actively inform the local community about campus events and programs, and (4) the college owns local property that goes tax free and thereby raises the taxes of the citizens. Essentially, the community feels neglected and exploited by the college.

The diagnosis suggests that the college needs to change its ways and establish stronger ties with the community. It needs to develop a *community relations program* as part of its public relations strategy. Here are some of the steps it might take:

1 Identify the local opinion leaders (prominent business people, news editors, city council members, heads of civic organizations, school officials) and build better relationships by inviting them to campus events, consulting with them on college issues that will affect the community, and sponsoring luncheons and dinners.
2 Encourage the college's faculty and staff to join local organizations and participate in community campaigns such as the United Way and American Red Cross Blood Bank programs.
3 Develop a speakers' bureau to provide speakers to local groups such as the Kiwanis, Rotary, and so on.
4 Make the college's facilities and programs more available to the community. Classrooms and halls can be offered to local organizations for meetings.
5 Arrange open houses and campus tours for the local community.
6 Participate in community special events such as parades, holiday observances, and so on.
7 Establish an advisory board of community leaders to act as a sounding board for issues facing the college and the community.

Each project involves money and time. The organization will need to estimate the amount of expected attitude improvement for each project to arrive at the best mix of cost-effective actions.

Prepare for Public Relations Crises

Every nonprofit organization more than a few years old has "horror stories" of organizational oversights, executive improprieties, volunteer excesses, and so on that were for many days and weeks the focus of dramatic and potentially damaging stories in the press. The Boy Scouts of America has had a troop leader charged with child molestation, and the United Way of California has had to defend itself from accusations that it monopolizes workplace solicitation drives. A strategically oriented public relations program must manage such crises and not let the crises manage them.

There are two approaches to crisis management: long term and short term. In the long term, the public relations manager must actively prepare for the inevitable unexpected disaster. This means, first of all, cultivating strong media relations. If the public relations staff truly has a customer-centered approach to its relationships with the media (described further below), it will have established itself as having the media's interests at the center of its public relations program. This should mean that key media people will give the organization the benefit of any doubts and will give the organization a clear opportunity to get its story across.

The other long-term approach is to prepare key managers to deal with the media in crisis situations. This means, first, creating an attitude that regards members of the media not as the enemy, but rather as individuals like the managers themselves attempting to do their job as thoroughly and professionally as possible. Second, it means giving managers advanced training in holding press conferences and being part of stress interviews with the media.

In the short run, public relations experts must have clear guidelines as to how to handle each individual crisis event. The Foundation for American Communications, which has as its mission improving the quality of information reaching the American public through the media, offers a number of suggestions outlined in Exhibit 20–2.

Choosing Specific Public Relations Tools

Here, we want to examine in more detail the major public relations media and tools that can be used in implementation. They are (1) written material, (2) audiovisual material, (3) organization identity media, (4) news, (5) interviews, (6) public service announcements, (7) events, and (8) telephone information services.

Written Material.   Organizations rely extensively on written material to communicate with their target publics. A public library, for example, uses such written material as an annual report, catalogues, employee newsletters, informational flyers, and posters. Many universities now have very extensive publication programs, including alumni magazines (see Figure 20–4).

In preparing each publication, the public relations department must consider *function, aesthetics,* and *cost*. The function of an annual report is to inform interested publics about the organization's accomplishments during the year and about its financial status, with the ultimate purpose of generating confidence in the organization and its leaders. Aesthetics enter in because the annual report should be readable, interesting, and professional. If the annual report is

EXHIBIT 20-2

How to Handle Bad News

Accidents happen. Acts of nature cut wide swaths of destruction. Fire damages property and injures people. You may discover that your agency or an individual associated with it is the victim of a crime. Or an individual who is part of your organization may be identified as the suspect in a crime. Accusations are made, complaints are raised, and you are not immune.

There is also the possibility of a hard news story developing elsewhere that concerns an agency like yours, or involves people like your clients. Just as many nonprofit organizations "piggyback" on news from other places, thoughtful editors will see a problem reported in another community and wonder if that problem could happen in yours.

Reporters and editors tend to think of hard news stories as "real news," and are keen on obtaining all available information when such stories come along.

How can you prepare to survive a crisis, should it take place?

There are three points to keep in mind:

1   Do nothing to make things worse.
2   Get the story over with and behind you.
3   Remember that you will be dealing with many of the same news organizations long after this story is over.

What makes things worse? Wasting time searching for someone to blame. Pretending things are O.K. when they are not. Stalling, stonewalling, or getting in the way of reporters. Telling lies. Speculating. Showing what looks like indifference to suffering. Attempting to cover up a problem. And panicking.

How do you end coverage of a story? Disclosure is the fastest way. Gather information and release it as soon as you can. If information is not available or must be held up for some reason, assure reporters that it will be provided as soon as possible. Reporters get nervous when they think they may miss out on information available to others. Be evenhanded.

Fact-finding is one of the regular public relations jobs. When there is a potentially damaging or difficult story in the works, fact-finding is more difficult, but also more necessary.

And finally, carry out your media responsibilities in professional and self-respecting ways. Every editor has stories to tell about the swarm of public relations people who come around looking for coverage of positive news and disappear at the first hint of controversy or trouble.

SOURCE: *Media Resource Guide*, 5th ed. (Los Angeles: Foundation for American Communications, 1987), p. 21. Reproduced with permission.

FIGURE 20-4

University of California Riverside Magazine

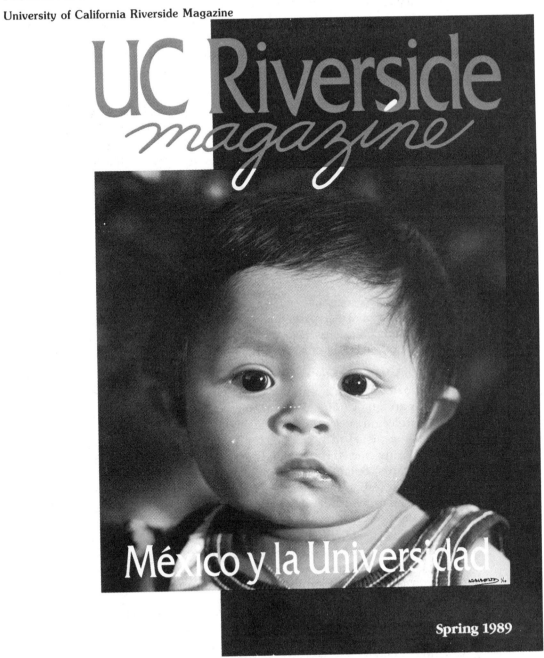

SOURCE: Courtesy of *UC Riverside Magazine*.

published in mimeograph form, it suggests a poor, amateur-type organization. If the annual report is extremely fancy, the public may raise questions as to why a nonprofit organization is spending so much money on graphics instead of needed services. Cost acts as a constraint in that the organization will allocate a limited amount of money to each publication. The public relations department has to reconcile considerations of function, aesthetics, and cost in developing each publication.

Audiovisual Material.   Audiovisual materials such as films, slides, and audio and video cassettes are coming into increasing use as communication tools. In the old days, college recruiters would visit different campuses and present a talk, answer questions, and pass out some written materials to the high school seniors gathered to hear about the college. The students had to concentrate hard on the recruiter's words. Today's recruiter, in contrast, delivers a high-impact audiovisual presentation about the college. A recruiter from the University of Richmond, for example, shows a 16mm, full-color, 12-minute film dramatizing life on the University of Richmond's campus. The film cost $13,000 to produce and has apparently paid for itself many times over in improved recruitment effectiveness. Other colleges use a combination of slides and recorded campus sounds that can be very effective. In all cases, the visual materials should be put together with some care. One of the authors witnessed a college recruiter make a presentation involving 100 slides showing mostly campus buildings, in no particular order, with several slides upside down. The whole presentation bored the high school seniors, and few applications came in.

Organization Identity Media.   Normally, an organization's various visual and print materials lack a uniform look, which not only creates confusion but also misses an opportunity to create and reinforce an *organization identity*. In an overcommunicated society, organizations compete for attention. They should try to create a visual identity that the public immediately recognizes. Visual identity is conveyed through logos, stationery, brochures, signs, business forms, call cards, buildings, uniforms, and rolling stock.

The organization identity media become a marketing tool when they are attractive, memorable, and distinctive. The task of creating a coordinated visual identity is not easy. The organization should select a good graphic design consultant. The consultant will try to get management to identify the essence of the organization, and will then try to turn it into a big idea backed by strong visual symbols. The symbols are adapted to the various organizational media to create immediate recognition in the minds of various publics.

News.   One of the major tasks of a public relations department is to find or create favorable news about the organization and market it to the appropriate media. The appeal of publicity to many organizations is that it is "free advertising"—that is, it represents exposures at no cost. As someone once said, "Publicity is sent to a medium and prayed for while advertising is sent to a medium and paid for." Publicity is far from free, however, because special skills are required to write good publicity and to "reach" the press. Good publicists cost money.

Publicity has three qualities that make it a worthwhile investment. First, it may have *higher veracity* than advertising because it appears as normal news and not as sponsored information. Second, it tends to catch people *off guard* who might otherwise avoid sponsored messages. Third, it has high potential for *dramatization* in that it arouses attention, coming as it does in the guise of a noteworthy event.

Getting news items in the local press or on television or radio is itself a marketing task. As such, the publicist must start with the immediate audience. One must understand what the media are looking for in a news story. Among the prime characteristics they will have in mind are:

1 The interest of the subject to their audience.
2 The possibility for dramatization through pictures, live interviews, and so forth.
3 The clarity and exhaustiveness of any press release (for example, including supporting materials, statistics, etc.).
4 Limited need for further "digging."
5 The possibility of "exclusive" coverage—for either the entire story or for a specific "angle."

Long-term cultivation of media gatekeepers helps get news items reported and assures full and accurate coverage. Favorable attitudes on the part of these gatekeepers can be particularly valuable when a crisis arises or a "scandal" is uncovered. As we shall discuss in the concluding section of this chapter, it is our position that the basic principles of customer-centered marketing apply to public relations as much as they do many other areas of organization management.

Finally, the publicist must learn to think strategically. A clear, continuing program of releases and stories should be developed for each planning period. These should be tailored to end the period with specific communications objectives achieved for specific audiences. Not all stories that are interesting to the publicist or the organization's administrators should be brought out if they do not help promote the organization's long-term interests.

Interviews and Speeches.   An often effective vehicle for publicity is the media interview. It was recently reported that there are 4,250 local news and talk shows on 988 TV stations in the United States. On these shows, 10,200 guests appear annually.[4] Often these guests are not celebrities or especially newsworthy individuals. They are simply experts on some subject or people with a simple story to tell. Nonprofits can usually provide to the media a number of subjects and guests over a year's time to meet the voracious need for program material. An attractive, articulate veterinarian from a zoo can tell of the special problems of dealing with large animals. A college recruitment director can talk about the new competition for students or offer advice on how to get one's son or daughter into their college of choice. Visiting artists at theaters or music performances are always in demand. Anything offbeat generally has a much better chance of getting time or space to tell the organization's story than a subject that has already been worn out in the media. The new public access channels on TV are particularly eager to find and use such guests.

Public Service Announcements.   In addition to their need for guests, TV and radio stations (and networks) are usually quite willing—even eager—to give air time to public service announcements (PSAs). There was a time when they were required to do so by the Federal Communications Commission. They no longer have this requirement, but most still wish to include PSAs as part of their programming. This is in part because they need to fill otherwise empty air time with interesting material, but more so because the stations simply wish to be seen as good community citizens (especially when license renewal time comes about). At the same time, many local and national advertising agencies and production houses are willing to donate some or all of their services to developing such PSAs. The program of the Advertising Council is perhaps the most prominent in this regard.

A 1985 survey indicated that TV stations were most apt to use PSAs under the following conditions:[5]

1   PSAs of differing length are offered.
2   One of the following subjects is dealt with: health, safety, alcohol and drug abuse, child abuse and molestation, family and social relations, education, crime prevention, and drunk driving.
3   There is a possibility for a local tie-in (respondents said they broadcast 56 percent of PSAs for local organizations and 44 percent for national issues).
4   The target audience is children, the elderly, the handicapped, or minorities.

A study by the Health Message Testing Service showed that effective PSAs on health issues had the following characteristics:

• They emphasized both the health problem and the solution in the PSA.
• They used a person typical of the target audience when presenting a testimonial.
• They visualized a reward from practicing the recommended healthful behavior.
• They communicated the psychological benefits of practicing the healthful behavior.
• They used an approach other than humor.
• They demonstrated the healthful behavior (if possible).
• They used a high or moderate emotional appeal.[6]

Events.   A nonprofit organization can increase its newsworthiness by creating events that attract the attention of target publics. Thus, a hospital seeking more public attention can host major research symposia, feature well-known speakers and celebrities, celebrate anniversaries of important events in the history of the institution, create birthday parties for special patients, and hold news conferences. Each well-run event not only impresses the immediate participants, but also serves as an opportunity to develop a multitude of stories directed to relevant media vehicles and audiences.

Event creation and management is a particularly important skill in running fund-raising drives for nonprofit organizations. Fund-raisers have developed a large repertoire of special events, including anniversary celebrations, art exhibits, auctions, benefit evenings, bingo games, book sales, cake sales, contests, dances, dinners, fairs, fashion shows, parties in unusual places, phonothons, rummage sales, tours, and walkathons. The American Cancer Society, for example, distributes a brochure to local units in which they outline the following ideas for special events:

> Dramatic special events attract attention to the American Cancer Society. They bring color, excitement, and glamor to the program. Well planned, they will get excellent coverage in newspapers, on radio and TV, and in newsreels. . . . A Lights-On-Drive, a one-afternoon or one-night House-to-House program have such dramatic appeal that they stir excitement and enthusiasm . . . keep in mind the value of bursts of sound such as fire sirens sounding, loudspeaker trucks, fife and drum corps. . . . A most useful special event is the ringing of church bells to add a solemn, dedicated note to the launching of a drive or education project. This should be organized on a division or community basis, and the church bell ringing may be the signal to begin a House-to-House canvass. Rehearsals of bell ringing, community leaders tugging at ropes, offer good picture possibilities.[7]

Telephone Information Service.   A relatively new public relations tool is a telephone number through which members of the public can get information about the organization. Triton Community College, for example, set up a telephone number which gives prerecorded information about the college, registration times, and costs. Various health organizations have set up telephone numbers that provide health messages about specific symptoms and diseases. The American Cancer Society has set up a national network of offices, called Cancer Information Services Offices, to take calls. Going further, drug abuse centers have set up "hot-lines" to take emergency calls. These telephone services suggest that the organization cares about the public and is ready to serve them.

There are a great many alternatives available for free or low-cost publicity for nonprofits. Sometimes creativity can be stimulated by the use of outside consultants. Rhoda Weiss, a Santa Monica, Calif., based marketing and public relations consultant, has developed a number of tips which she passes along to her nonprofit clients. Several of these are listed in Exhibit 20–3.

EXHIBIT 20-3

Rhoda Weiss's Public Relations Tips for Nonprofit Organizations

Talk Shows

Hundreds of hours of free time on television and radio public affairs programs and cable systems can be used to educate the public, raise money, alter attitudes and make a name for an organization. The key to successfully pitching a story to a talk show producer or guest coordinator is to mix timelines with consumer interest.

- Keep pitch letters to one page.
- Use national, regional, or local statistics and background information to show how and why your suggestion is important to the audience.
- Suggest a few thought-provoking questions to be asked during the interview.
- Provide brochures and related news clippings that help sell the idea as timely and provocative.
- Follow up your letter with a phone call to the producer or coordinator and be prepared to sell your idea.
- Bring along visual aids or props to help enliven a television segment.
- Make sure your representative has seen or heard the show prior to the day of his or her appearance.
- Send stations a list of possible discussion topics and experts to deal with each one. Routinely remind the talk show contact that you exist and that your people are available.

Identify Yourself

If you work in a large city it's easy to get lost in the shuffle with other community nonprofit groups. Even in smaller communities you have to remind the news contacts that you exist. Some people are in the news every day but most of us need to work on setting up and maintaining contact with newspeople.

- Send a yearly letter to reporters and editors in your service area listing your name and address with a short description of your services, including daytime and evening contacts and phone numbers.
- Print your agency's interest on Rolodex cards, and send them to reporters and editors in your area. This makes it easier for them to find you and identify your interests.
- Consider letters to the editor or opinion articles. Ask for editorials on your area of concern.
- Identify all procedures and deadlines for calendar listings, club listings and other regular sections of newspapers or broadcasts where you can list activities and meetings.
- Ask to participate in editorial board meetings with news executives to provide them with your first-hand impressions of current issues.
- Schedule events to take advantage of slow news days such as holidays.
- Encourage supporters to write complimentary letters to the editor about all community activities, not just your own organization's.
- Attend programs where reporters are present to get to know them.

The Other Media

Before modern newspapers and broadcasting, we communicated with fliers, broadsides and by word-of-mouth. It's useful today to look beyond the standard news media.

- Consider asking for mention in telephone books, souvenir programs for cultural or sporting events, bus benches, bus shelters, taxi panels, marquees at schools and private or public buildings, community bulletin boards, grocery bags, milk cartons, restaurant placemats, bowling alley score sheets, balloons, buttons, caps, even T-shirts.
- Send your news releases to church bulletins, chamber of commerce publications, service club newsletters and employee newsletters published by major employers in your service area.
- Leaflets can be inserted in billing envelopes by major employers.
- You might find places for leaflets in doctor's offices, building lobbies, health clubs, libraries, YMCAs and YWCAs, museums, or even grocery check-out stands.

Speakers' Bureau

You can generate many first-hand contacts with the public in your area by providing your volunteers, staff, or members as public speakers through your own speakers' bureau.

- Identify the potential audiences in your area such as service clubs, social clubs, churches, business associations, schools, or cultural associations. Chambers of commerce may have listings of such organizations in your area.
- Develop a list of speakers in your organization.
- Determine how many speakers you might be able to provide.
- Send a notice of your speakers' bureau to program coordinators at your potential audiences.
- Develop a comprehensive checklist or worksheet for each speaking assignment covering the date, exact location, specific start time, whether to expect questions and answers, audience size, program length and the name of the contact person.
- Provide backup information, materials and support for your speakers including audiovisuals, handouts and transportation if needed.
- Don't forget to use your speakers' bureau mailing list for publicizing your programs, fundraisers and for other direct-mail purposes.

Celebrities

Well-known people can spread the word about your cause in public service announcements, publications and personal appearances. They are instantly recognizable, newsworthy and will frequently donate time if they believe in the cause being promoted.

- Many celebrities maintain contact with their hometown or college alma mater—you don't have to live in Hollywood or New York to think about celebrity endorsements. Jack Benny's hometown of Waukegan, IL, and many other communities have benefited from celebrity endorsements.
- The Screen Actors Guild in Los Angeles provides information about members' agents or publicists. SAG can be contacted by mail or phone, 7750 Sunset Blvd., Los Angeles, CA 90046, 213/876-3030.
- Directories of actors, such as the Academy Players Directory, are available from the Academy of Motion Picture Arts and Sciences, 8949 Wilshire Blvd., Los Angeles, CA 90211, 213/278-8990.
- The television networks will forward letters, but will handle them as fan mail, which underscores the value of direct contact.
- Consider local sports, news, television, or radio personalities or professional athletes in your community as celebrity spokespeople.
- When a celebrity performs in your community, request a personal appearance on your agency's behalf or participation in a public service announcement.

SOURCE: *Media Resource Guide*, 5th ed. (Los Angeles: Foundation for American Communication, 1987), pp. 39–41. Reproduced with permission.

Implementing Actions and Evaluating Effects

Public relations actions to be taken have to be assigned to responsible individuals within the organization along with concrete objectives, time frames, and budgets. The public relations department should oversee the results. Evaluating the results of public relations activities, however, is not easy, since it occurs in conjunction with other marketing activities and its contribution is hard to separate.

Consider the problem of measuring the value of the organization's publicity efforts. Publicity is designed with certain audience-response objectives in mind, and these objectives form the basis of what is measured. The major response measures are exposures, awareness, comprehension, attitude change, and sales.

The easiest and most common measure of publicity effectiveness is the number of *exposures* created in the media. Most professional publicists supply the client with a "clippings book" showing all the media that carried news about the organization and a summary statement such as the following:

Media coverage included 3,500 column inches of news and photographs in 350 publications with a combined circulation of 79.4 million; 2,500 minutes of air time on 290 radio stations and an estimated audience of 65 million; and 660 minutes of air time on 160 television stations with an estimated audience of 91 million. If this time and space had been purchased at advertising rates, it would have amounted to $1,047,000.[8]

The purpose of citing the equivalent advertising cost is to make a case for publicity's cost effectiveness, since the total publicity effort must have cost less than $1,047,000. Furthermore, publicity usually creates more reading and believing than ads.

Still, this exposure measure is not very satisfying. There is no indication of how many people actually read, saw, or heard the message, and what they thought afterward. Furthermore, there is no information on the net audience reached, since publications have overlapping readership. Indeed, there is the very real danger that the organization will attempt to maximize *what it can measure.* Success is measured by brochures passed out, articles written, and so on. Distributing more brochures in 1990 than in 1989 is considered great progress.

A better measure calls for finding out what change in public *awareness, comprehension, or attitudes* occurred as a result of the publicity campaign (after allowing for the impact of other promotional tools). This requires the use of survey methodology to measure the *before* and *after* levels of these variables.

Certain PR activities will be found to be too costly in relation to their impact and might be dropped. Or the PR goals might be recognized as too ambitious and require modification. Furthermore, new problems will arise with certain publics and require redirection of the public relations resources. As the public relations department implements these actions and measures the results, it will be in a position to return to the earlier steps and take a new reading of where the organization stands in the mind of specific publics and what improvements in public attitudes it needs to pursue. Thus the public relations process is continually recycling, as shown in Figure 20–2.

CUSTOMER-CENTERED PUBLIC RELATIONS[9]

Marketing is simply an approach to changing behavior. Just as it can be applied to getting donors to give money and clients to consume services so too it can be applied to the task of inducing journalists or news editors to run a story or, in general, to communicate accurately about a given organization, individual, or idea.

To illustrate the use of these principles, let us take the case of a hypothetical public relations specialist for a gun owners' association and consider, first, how a *selling-oriented* specialist would approach the problem of getting favorable press coverage of a story of importance to the organization:

1 The selling-oriented PR specialist would begin by assuming that he or she has a basically interesting story in which the general public would really be interested *if only* the journalist would cover it.
2 If journalists are reluctant to run the story, then it is likely to be either because they do not fully appreciate how truly interesting it is and how much their audience would like to be exposed to it or because they have the usual liberal bias against gun owners and want to run as little as possible that is positive about them.

3   The PR specialist reflects on his or her years of experience with journalists and takes pride in knowing how they think. There will be little need really to explore *in advance* how journalists will react to this particular story opportunity. The specialist will prepare the necessary press releases and rely on his or her well-tested ability to be really persuasive on the telephone or through imaginative direct mailings.

4   Getting coverage will be seen mainly as a matter of convincing journalists of the fact that it is a great story. This means pushing the story hard to make sure that the journalist comes to see the PR specialist's view of its great merit.

5   Different materials will be prepared for print, radio, and television journalists, but one or two treatments for each broad category ought to do it.

What would a customer-oriented approach look like? This PR specialist would proceed in a very different way:

1   He or she would not assume that the likely reactions of target journalists are known nor that they are likely to be the same as the PR specialist's. Further, he or she will assume that there may be major differences both *within* as well as among media.

2   If time permits, when planning the strategy for securing news coverage, the PR specialist would begin with calls to a few key newspeople to get initial reactions to the proposed story and to learn which features seem to resonate with the interests of which kind of journalists.

3   The PR specialist would recognize that getting the story covered means that it must meet the journalists' near-term needs and wants. These needs will differ by journalist and may include one or more of the following concerns:

    a   How long will the story need to be?
    b   How well will the story appeal to the journalists' audience?
    c   How well will the story appeal to the journalists' editor or news director?
    d   What opportunities are there for the journalist to contribute his or her own "spin" to the story?
    e   Will the journalist have to dig further to cover the story well (some may want a lot of opportunities for digging, others none)?

4   Persuasion is not the heart of the strategy. The PR specialist would recognize that the "product" to be offered has to be right in the first place. The journalist should be presented with not only the facts of the story but a range of peripheral material that may respond to specific needs and wants of theirs. This peripheral material could include photos or photo opportunities, profiles of key figures in the story, names of follow-up sources both inside and *outside* the association, lists of reference materials, floppy disks with news release materials in each journalist's own word processing language, and so forth.

5   The PR specialist would recognize that the story is only one of many he or she will want to have covered over the years by target journalists. Thus, each particular story is to be marketed as a part of a longer-term strategy of building *relationships* with the journalists. This often means sacrificing near-term gain for a long-run benefit. For example, selling-oriented PR specialists are usually reluctant to help journalists dig up critical (or even objective) material about the organization for the particular story. This would be seen as just getting in the way of "making the sale." A customer-oriented PR specialist interested in building long-term relationships would see that providing journalists the names of one or more independent outside sources of follow-up information may cause short-run problems but (a) the journalist in all likelihood will find

sources anyway (often more hostile ones), (b) providing outside sources will increase the credibility of the present message, and (c) most importantly, the PR specialist will more likely be seen (except by the most cynical journalists) as someone who is basically concerned about meeting the *journalist's* needs—not just selling a story. The customer-oriented news source is someone who tries to help.

SUMMARY

Public relations is a well-established function in profit and nonprofit organizations. The recent introduction of marketing into nonprofit organizations has raised the question of marketing's relation to public relations. This book assumes that public relations is a tool used to advance the marketing purposes of the organization. As such, it can benefit from careful strategic planning.

The task of public relations is to form, maintain, or change public attitudes toward the organization or its products. The process of public relations consists of seven steps: (1) identifying the organization's relevant publics, (2) measuring the images and attitudes held by these publics, (3) establishing image and attitude goals for the key publics, (4) developing cost-effective public relations strategies, (5) preparing for public relations crises, (6) carefully choosing specific public relations tools, such as written material, audiovisual material, organization identity media, news, events, speeches, and telephone information services, and (7) implementing actions and evaluating results. Just as elsewhere in the organization, a customer orientation is the best philosophy to apply to both long-term and short-term public relations strategy.

QUESTIONS

1. Your telephone rings. A reporter from the local press tells you that she has photostats and affidavits showing that an executive of your charitable organization has been given an interest-free loan from a trust fund managed by your agency. The fund is very large and the loan is very small and for only one month. The reporter says she plans to publish a story on the finding in the next day's edition. She asks for your comments. What do you do?

2. You have built a close relationship with reporters from two of the three network television stations in your area and one of four key reporters at the city's only major newspaper. These reporters are actively interested in your organization and have reported favorably about your activities. You have given each of them exclusive stories from time to time. On a particular Thursday morning, the reporter from the third TV network with whom you have had little contact enters your office and accuses you of favoring his competitors. He demands an exclusive story and hints that failure to cooperate will lead to unfriendly investigative reporting on his part in the near future. What do you do?

3. Traditionally, a journalist is selected as the public relations specialist in many organizations. Make a case for hiring a marketing MBA into that position.

4. Describe ten events that a homeless shelter might develop over a year's period to improve its public image.

5. Your organization's CEO is about to go to a radio interview with a reporter who has a reputation for tough questioning. Although there is no crisis outstanding, you fear that the interview will not help your organization. How would you help the executive prepare for the meeting?

NOTES

1. Some of the material in this chapter is adapted from Philip Kotler and William Mindak, "Marketing and Public Relations," *Journal of Marketing,* October 1978, pp. 13–20.
2. Scott M. Cutlip, "The Beginning of PR Counseling," *Editor and Publisher,* November 26, 1950, p. 16.
3. *Public Relations News,* October 27, 1947.
4. Timothy G. Manners, "TV Talk Show Tour Extends Marketing Reach," *Marketing News,* August 16, 1985, p. 1.
5. "Free TV Time Abounds For Public Service Messages," *Marketing News,* August 16, 1985, p. 7.
6. "Study Identifies Qualities of Effective Health Public Service Announcements," *Marketing News,* April 3, 1981, p. 7.
7. *Public Information Guide* (New York: American Cancer Society, 1965), p. 19.
8. Arthur M. Merims, "Marketing's Stepchild: Product Publicity," *Harvard Business Review,* November–December 1972, pp. 111–112.
9. Material in this section is taken from Alan R. Andreasen, "Communicating by Listening," *Issues & Opportunities,* Vol. 1, no. 5 (August 1989).

21

Managing Personal Selling

The "Welcome Neighbor" program at Good Samaritan Hospital in Downer's Grove, IL, targets new residents moving into rapidly growing DuPage County. Under the program, hospital representatives telephone new residents and offer to make a personal visit to explain hospital services. If the new resident agrees to a visit, the representative brings a packet of literature on services the resident has expressed an interest in. Those who decline a visit are sent welcoming materials. Of the 1,296 phone calls made during the first 10 months of 1987, 260 resulted in visits. The program has generated 500 physician referral requests, 25 inpatient admissions, and 20 outpatient visits. Most physician referrals were to Ob/Gyn, family practice, pediatrics, general practice, and internal medicine. The total cost of the program, including salaries for two full-time representatives, is $47,000—less than one-third the revenues brought in by the program during its first 10 months. A key to the success of the program is follow-up. Residents visited under the program are contacted by phone three and six months after the visit to make sure all their questions are answered. And Welcome Neighbor representatives oversee the admitting process of any of those new residents who require hospitalization. The program also has provided the hospital with data on what services patients would like and what patients thought of the physicians they were referred to.

Source: "The Welcome Mat Is Out at Good Sam," *Healthcare Marketing Report,* Vol. 6, no. 2, February 1988, pp. 1, 6–7, as summarized in *Hospital Marketing Abstracts,* March 1988, p. 2.

It has been our experience that the marketing tool that nonprofit marketers are most often reluctant to employ vigorously is personal selling. This reticent posture seems to follow from two attitudes. First, as noted in Chapter 2, nonprofit managers typically believe that their offering is inherently good and needs simply to be made available to be happily embraced by a grateful public. Second, they often believe that personal selling is synonymous with manipulation and is therefore unethical to a greater or lesser degree. This is less a problem when the selling situation involves an economic transaction such as occurs in museum gift shops or when one is soliciting donations. But, when it is proposed that the nonprofit's workers should personally persuade people to attend a college, or join a political party, library, or church, resistance to using a planned, vigorous approach is quite common.

Not only is personal selling resisted when clear opportunities exist for its use, it is often neglected in more general situations. The best run for-profit service organizations and many retailers long ago recognized that *every time* a member of the organization and a member of a key public interact, there is an opportunity to further or weaken progress toward the organization's marketing goals. How often have our favorable feelings about a hospital been destroyed by the perfunctory attitude of the admissions officer or the cashier? What nonprofit marketers have to recognize is that almost everyone in their organization is at one point or another a *boundary person*. Their personal communication style will affect the organization's success. It is better to manage these communications than just to let them happen.

In this chapter we want to look at strategic management problems involving boundary personnel. These boundary personnel fall within two groups. The first are salespeople, whose job it is to actively influence the behavior of others. Major examples of such personnel are

- *Recruiters* (college recruiters, military recruiters, job recruiters)
- *Fund-raisers* (development officers, door-to-door callers, telephone solicitors)
- *Change agents* (agricultural extension agents, outreach workers, family planners, community organizers)
- *Vote seekers* (politicians, lobbyists)

The second group consists of *service personnel*, those who provide the organization's services to members of the public. The group includes

- *Operators* (bus drivers, librarians, U.S. income tax advisors, ticket takers, museum guards)
- *Protective personnel* (police officers, firefighters)
- *Repair personnel*
- *Receptionists*

We have considered the job of service personnel in Chapter 13. In this chapter we will concentrate on sales personnel and the problems of running an effective sales force.

PERSONAL SELLING

We shall use the term *personal selling* to refer to *all attempts by the organization at using personal influence to affect target audience behavior.* Personal selling is the most effective tool at certain stages of the consumer decision process, particularly in building up preference, conviction, and action on the part of buyers. This is because personal selling has three distinctive qualities in comparison to advertising:[1]

1 *Personal confrontation.* Personal selling involves a living, immediate, and interactive relationship between two or more persons. Each party is able to observe the others' needs and characteristics at close hand and make immediate adjustments.
2 *Cultivation.* Personal selling permits all kinds of relationships to spring up, ranging from a matter-of-fact selling relationship to a deep personal friendship. In most cases, the sales representative artfully woos the target audience. The sales representative is at times tempted to apply pressure to induce an action, but he or she normally keeps the customer's long-run interests at heart.
3 *Response.* Personal selling makes the target audience member feel under some obligation for having listened to the sales talk or for taking up the sales representative's time. He or she has a greater need to attend and respond, even if the response is a polite "thank you."

These distinctive qualities come at a cost. Personal selling is the organization's most expensive customer contact tool, costing organizations in 1988 an average of $172 per sales call in consumer sales, $218 in industrial sales, and $201 in services.[2] Even when the sales force consists of volunteers, there is a cost of recruiting, training, and motivating them, and their time should be used wisely.

We will examine the major decisions in building and managing an effective sales force as part of the total marketing mix. These steps are shown in Figure 21–1 and examined in the following sections.

ESTABLISHING SALES FORCE OBJECTIVES

Personal communication is part of the marketing mix, and as such is capable of achieving certain marketing objectives better than other tools in the marketing mix. Sales representatives can perform as many as six tasks for their organization:

1 *Prospecting.* Sales representatives can find and cultivate new customers.
2 *Communicating.* Sales representatives can communicate useful information about the organization.
3 *Persuading.* Sales representatives can be effective in the art of "salesmanship"— approaching, presenting, answering objections, and inducing action.
4 *Servicing.* Sales representatives can provide various services to customers— counseling on their problems, rendering technical assistance, and reducing service times.

FIGURE 21-1

Major Steps in Sales Force Management

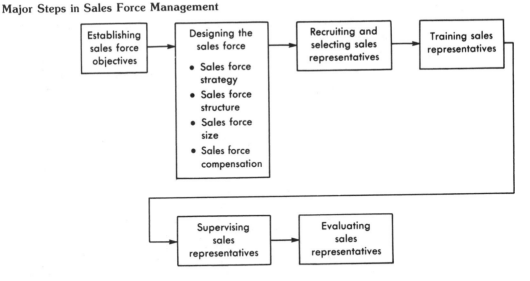

5   *Information gathering.* Sales representatives can supply the organization with useful market research and intelligence.

6   *Allocating.* Sales representatives can advise the organization on how to allocate scarce goods and services to customers in times of shortages.

The organization has to decide the relative importance of these different tasks and coach their sales representatives accordingly. College recruiters, for example, spend most of their time in prospecting, communicating, and persuading. Lobbyists, on the other hand, tend to emphasize communicating, servicing, and information gathering. Each organization normally gets its representatives to set specific goals for each of their activities so that their performance against these goals can be measured.

DESIGNING THE SALES FORCE

Given the objectives, the organization has to make basic decisions on (1) sales force strategy, (2) sales force structure, (3) sales force size, and (4) sales force compensation.

Sales Force Strategy

Sales force strategy deals with determining how best to reach prospects and customers, given the marketing objectives. Suppose a social action program is seeking to increase its grants from the Ford Foundation. It wants to (1) "sell" the

Ford Foundation on funding some immediate proposals, and (2) build up a stronger relationship with the Ford Foundation for the future. The program can use one or more of six sales force strategies to meet its objectives:

1 *Sales representative to buyer.* Here, a program officer talks to a Ford Foundation officer in person or over the telephone.

2 *Sales representative to buyer group.* Here, a program officer makes a sales presentation to a group of Ford Foundation executives.

3 *Sales team to buyer group.* Here, a team of people from the program (president, controller, researcher) makes a sales presentation to a group of Ford Foundation executives.

4 *Conference selling.* Here, a program officer arranges a meeting between people at the program center and Ford Foundation executives to discuss mutual problems and opportunities.

5 *Seminar selling.* Here, a team of experts from the program presents an educational seminar to Ford Foundation executives about recent state-of-the-art developments. The program provides the free seminar to improve relations with the foundation.

6 *Telemarketing.* Individual staff members can regularly call counterparts at the Ford Foundation. Telephone sales solicitation has the advantage of relatively low cost as compared to face-to-face selling, yet it provides the same opportunity to respond immediately to target audience concerns (for example, to the interests they show or the objections they raise). In general use, the development of automatic dialing systems, independently run telephone marketing services, and low-cost wide-area calling systems has rapidly extended the potential and the range of telemarketing.

Two of the nonprofit categories in which telemarketing is used most extensively are the performing arts and fund-raising. In the arts, two examples of successful use were by the St. Paul Symphony Orchestra and the Old Globe Theatre in San Diego.

- The St. Paul Symphony had a subscription renewal rate of 50 percent in the 1980–81 season. By using telemarketing to contact those who hadn't resubscribed, the Symphony raised this rate to 68 percent in just two years. Two calls were used. One was made two weeks before the deadline for renewing subscriptions. On this occasion, nonsubscribers had the option to renew on the spot using a credit card, or if they said they needed more time, they were guaranteed their old seats for an extended two-week period after the deadline. A second last-chance call went to those who were still not responding one week before the season. St. Paul also used a 15,000-name prospect list derived from single-event purchasers and from lists of those attending other arts events in the area. Callers reached 8,000 to 10,000 of those on this list, producing 14 percent of new subscriptions in the 1982–83 season.[3]

- The Old Globe began contacting nonrenewers to its theater season by telephone seven to ten working days after its new season mailer. Between October, 1982, and June, 1984, the Old Globe's telemarketing department was able to generate $750,000 in annual ticket sales and increase season ticket sales by 20,000. Most importantly, the Old Globe's marketing director claimed that the telemarketing program was *more cost effective* than direct mail. He stated that it costs 15 percent of sales for telemarketing versus 30 percent for direct mail. This was due in part to the fact that the Old Globe only called those with a known interest in the theater. They did not make cold calls or buy lists. The Old Globe found that telemarketing worked in part because it allowed nonrenewers to voice some of their concerns. Once they had gotten their gripes out of their systems, they were more predisposed toward renewing. Finally, through experimentation, the Old Globe staff found that volunteers were not as effective at telemarketing as were professional salespeople. They experimented with five professionals and five actors and found that the actors "could talk about the theater but couldn't close the sale." The Old Globe now uses only professional salespeople.[4]

Like the Old Globe, once an organization has clarified the type of selling it needs, it must choose between using (1) full-time paid employees, (2) volunteers, and (3) temporary paid help. All three may be used to advantage. Thus, Stanford University's Office of Development consists of a small employee staff of professional fund-raisers who raise money directly; a very large group of alumni who volunteer their services in fund-raising drives; and temporary help as needed to make phone calls, stuff envelopes, and so on especially at the time of annual campaigns.

Sales Force Structure

Part of sales force strategy is deciding how to structure the organization's sales force to achieve maximum market coverage and effectiveness. This is relatively simple if the organization provides only one service to one type of customer who is found in many locations. The answer would be a territorial-structured sales force. If the organization sells many different services to many types of customers, it might have to develop product-structured or customer-structured sales forces. We shall review here these alternative sales force structures.

Territorial-Structured Sales Force.   In the simplest sales organization, each sales representative is assigned a territory in which to sell the organization's services. Thus, the U.S. Army operates army recruiting stations in different cities, and each station is responsible for planning and attracting enlistments in its area. Likewise, the Easter Seal Society raises money through regional, state, and local organizations, each responsible for fund-raising in its respective territory.

A territorially structured sales force has a number of advantages. First, it results in a very clear definition of the salesperson's responsibilities. As the only salesperson working the territory, he or she bears the credit or blame for area sales to the extent that personal selling effort makes a difference. This tends to encourage a high level of effort, especially when management is able to gauge fairly accurately the area's sales potential. Second, responsibility for a definite territory increases the sales representative's incentive to cultivate local customers and personal ties. These ties tend to improve the quality of the sales representatives selling effectiveness and personal life. Third, travel expenses are likely to be relatively small, since each sales representative's travel takes place within the bounds of a small geographical territory.

Along with this structure goes a hierarchy of sales management positions. Several territories will be supervised by a district sales manager, several districts will be supervised by a regional sales manager, and the several regions will be supervised by a national sales manager or sales vice-president. Each higher-level sales manager takes on increasing marketing and administrative work in relation to the time available for selling. In fact, sales managers are paid for their management rather than selling skills.

Product-Structured Sales Force.   Organizations that produce a large number of products and services often prefer to organize the selling activity by product line. Harvard University, for example, allows each of its major schools—business, law, medicine, and so on—to do its own fund-raising and recruitment. Personnel within each school can do a good job of representing it to prospects and customers. Specialization of the sales force by product is warranted where the organization's offerings are technically complex, highly unrelated, numerous or some combination of these characteristics. It is also warranted if the target market is similarly organized.

Thus, instead of Harvard sending one development officer to the Ford Foundation to represent all of the proposals submitted by Harvard, several development officers from Harvard's different schools would converge on the Foundation to speak with program officers concerned with their specialty. Each will come with more knowledge of the relevant proposals at the cost of high sales force expense.

Customer-Structured Sales Force.   Organizations often specialize their sales forces according to customer type. Cornell University fund-raisers, for example, are specialized by donor category: foundations, corporations, government agencies, alumni, and wealthy donors. By working full time to raise money from, say, corporations, the corporate fund-raiser has a clear incentive to know as much as possible about them collectively and individually and to use his or her time more effectively. Furthermore, the person needed for this job may be recruited directly from the ranks of those to be influenced. The major disadvantage of customer-structured sales forces arises if the various types of customers are scattered evenly throughout the country. This means an overlapping coverage of territories, which is always more expensive.

Complex Sales Force Structures.   When an organization sells a wide variety of products to many types of customers over a broad geographical area, it often combines several principles of sales force structure. Thus, the University of Chicago has a fund-raising staff with personnel specialized by territory, type of school, and type of donor. Each fund-raiser has a line of dotted-line reporting relationship to the development office and various other parts of the university.

Sales Force Size

Once the organization clarifies its sales force strategy and structure, it is ready to consider the question of sales force size. Sales representatives are among the most productive and expensive assets in a company. Increasing their number increases both sales and costs.

Most organizations use the *work load approach* to establish the size of their sales force.[5] The method consists of the following steps:

1   Customers are grouped into segments according to their sales potential.
2   The desirable call levels (number of days on an account per year) are established for each segment. Both existing and *potential* sales levels are considered.
3   The number of accounts in each segment are multiplied by the corresponding call level to arrive at the total workload in sales calls per year.
4   The average number of call days a sales representative has per year is determined, allowing for other tasks, holidays, and so on.
5   The number of sales representatives needed is determined by dividing the total number of call days required by the average annual number of call days a sales representative can make available.

To illustrate, suppose a college recruiting office determines that the recruitment target will require calling on 100 class A high schools, 80 class B high schools, and 40 class C high schools each year. To be effective, a recruiter will have to spend 2 days at a class A high school, 1 day at a class B high school, and 1 half day at a class C high school. Furthermore, each recruiter has only 60 days available per year. Thus, the high schools will require 300 call days ($100 \times 2 + 80 \times 1 + 40 \times 1/2$), and the college will require a staff of five recruiters ($300 \div 60$).

In the case of college fund-raising, a similar analysis can be undertaken. Given the campaign sales target and the potential of different donor groups, the college can figure out how many fund-raisers it needs. Most colleges tend to hire too few fund-raisers rather than too many; an additional competent fund-raiser can usually add more money to the college's coffers than he or she costs.

Sales Force Compensation

The sales force may comprise volunteers, as in many charities or other fund-raising activities. Where paid sales representatives are to be used, the organization has to develop an attractive compensation plan. Sales representatives would like a plan that provides income regularity, reward for above-average performance, and fair payment for experience and longevity. An ideal compensation plan from management's point of view would emphasize control, economy, and simplicity.

Management must determine the level and components of an effective compensation plan. The *level of compensation* must bear some relation to the "going market price" for the type of sales job and type of organization. Nonprofit organizations tend to pay less than business firms, and this may result in attracting less skilled people and achieving lower results. Yet nonprofits feel that they can attract good people who are motivated by nonmonetary considerations and a belief in the value of their work. In the author's judgment, this is usually a mistake. First, nonprofit salespersons who feel they are making a personal sacrifice to work for the organization may be less willing to take direction from management. They may be less efficient and may interfere with management's carefully engineered marketing strategy. Second, underpaid workers who "believe" in their cause may not have a customer-centered attitude. Because they "believe," they may feel that the customer should also believe, and they may be hostile to signs of customer reluctance. Well-paid professionals seldom have either of these problems.

The organization must also determine the *components of compensation*—a fixed amount, a variable amount, expenses, and fringe benefits. The *fixed amount*, which might be a salary or a drawing account, is intended to satisfy the sales representatives' need for some stability of income. The *variable amount*, which might be commissions, bonuses, or sales contests, is intended to stimulate and reward greater effort. *Expense allowances* are intended to enable the sales representatives to undertake necessary selling costs, such as travel, taking prospects to lunch, and so on. And *fringe benefits* such as paid vacations, sickness or accident benefits, pensions, and life insurance, are intended to provide security and job satisfaction.

Fixed and variable compensation, taken alone, give rise to three basic types of sales force compensation plans—straight salary, straight commission, and combination salary and commission. In industry, most plans are combination salary and commission, with 70 percent going to salary. In nonprofit organizations, most salespeople are on straight salary. Army recruiters who are especially effective, for example, tend to be rewarded with badges and recognition rather than extra money.

In general, the more a compensation scheme is oriented toward salary over commission or bonus,

- the more management can ask the sales force to do routine but necessary tasks like market research or prospecting that do not have an immediate payoff.
- the more the salesperson is likely to be farsighted in approaching customers, recognizing that missing a sale (and bonus) now may be desirable so as not to sour a good, building relationship.
- the more difficult it will be to judge performance.
- the less clear it will be to salespersons how they are doing, and the more management will have to develop alternative feedback systems.

RECRUITING AND SELECTING SALES REPRESENTATIVES

Having established the strategy, structure, size, and compensation of the sales force, the organization has to manage the steps of recruiting and selecting, training, supervising, and evaluating sales representatives.

Importance of Careful Selection

At the heart of a successful sales force operation is the selection of effective sales representatives. The performance levels of an average and a top sales representative are quite different. A survey of over 500 companies revealed that 27 percent of the sales force brought in over 52 percent of the sales.[6] Beyond the differences in sales productivity is the great wasted cost in hiring the wrong persons. Of the 16,000 sales representatives who were hired by the surveyed companies, only 68 percent still worked for their company at the end of the year, and only 50 percent were expected to remain through the following year.

What Makes a Good Sales Representative?

Selecting sales representatives would not be such a problem if one knew the characteristics of an ideal salesperson. If ideal salespersons are outgoing, aggressive, and energetic, it would not be too difficult to check for these characteristics in applicants. But a review of the most successful sales representatives in any company is likely to reveal a good number who are introverted, mild-mannered, and far from energetic. The successful group will also include men and women who are tall and short, articulate and inarticulate, well groomed and slovenly.

Nevertheless, the search for the magic combination of traits that spells surefire sales ability continues unabated. The number of lists that have been drawn up is countless. Most of them recite the same qualities. McMurry wrote:

> It is my conviction that the possessor of *effective* sales personality is *a habitual "wooer," an individual who has a compulsive need to win and hold the affection of others.* . . . His wooing, however, is not based on a sincere desire for love because, in my opinion, he is convinced at heart that no one will ever love him. Therefore, his wooing is primarily exploitative . . . his relationships tend to be transient, superficial and evanescent.[7]

McMurry went on to list five additional traits of the super salesperson: a high level of energy; abounding self-confidence; a chronic hunger for rewards; a well-established habit of industry; and a state of mind that regards each objection, resistance, or obstacle as a challenge.[8]

Mayer and Greenberg offered one of the shortest lists of traits exhibited by effective sales representatives.[9] Their seven years of fieldwork led them to conclude that the effective salesperson has at least two basic qualities: (1) *empathy*, the ability to feel as the customer does and (2) *ego drive*, a strong personal need to make the sale. Using these two traits, they were able to make fairly good predictions of the subsequent performance of applicants for sales positions in three different industries.

It may be true that certain basic traits may make a person effective in any line of selling. From the viewpoint of a particular organization, however, these basic traits are rarely enough. Each selling job is characterized by a unique set of duties and challenges. One only has to think about college recruiting, corporate fund-raising, and congressional lobbying to realize the different educational, intellectual, and personality requirements that would be sought in the respective sales representatives.

How can an organization determine the characteristics that its prospective sales representatives should "ideally" possess? The particular duties of the job suggest some of the characteristics to look for in applicants. Is the job mostly order taking, or must a lot of "influencing" be carried out? Is there a lot of paperwork? Does the job call for much travel? Will the salesperson confront a high proportion of refusals? Is creativity necessary? Will the salesperson be closely supervised or be expected to use a lot of initiative? In addition, the traits of the company's most successful sales representatives suggest additional qualities to look for. Some organizations compare the standing of their best versus their poorest sales representatives to see which characteristics differentiate the two groups.

One of the traits that has proved to be particularly valuable in social marketing settings is empathy with the target audience. In social marketing, one is often dealing with extremely delicate subjects. Finding salespeople, or *change agents* as they are sometimes called, from among the population to be influenced is usually very effective. They are more likely to know the audience's concerns, the appropriate language and metaphors for discussing problems and possible solutions, and which motivations can be played upon to bring about needed behavior change. In Ethiopia, for example, as outlined in Exhibit 21-1, the Ministry of Health found that former prostitutes were better at asking difficult intimate questions and communicating information about AIDS to other prostitutes than were traditional social workers.

Recruitment Procedures

After management develops general criteria for its sales personnel, it has to attract a sufficient number of applicants. Recruiting is turned over to the personnel department, which seeks applicants through various means, including soliciting names from current sales representatives, using employment agencies, placing job ads, contacting college students, and discussing needs with similar organizations (e.g., other United Way local organizations).

TRAINING SALES REPRESENTATIVES

Not too long ago many organizations sent their new salespeople into the field almost immediately after hiring them. Nowadays a new sales representative can expect to spend from a few days to a few months in training. Training has the following objectives:

EXHIBIT 21-1

Using Empathetic (if Unorthodox) Salespeople in Ethiopia

In a tin-roofed, shanty-like classroom where primary school students usually struggle to learn math, a smartly dressed prostitute posed her problem to a nurse conducting a seminar on AIDS.

"I don't have a baby and I want one," she said, "But if I use a condom, I Iwon't become pregnant."

The nurse, Etaferahu Kebede, replied that the woman could solve her problem by having only one sex partner. "Then you can have safe sex and you don't need a condom," she said.

The classroom session, during school vacation, was part of an unusual program in the Government's efforts to gather more accurate information on the spread of AIDS in Ethiopia and warn prostitutes about the dangers of not protecting themselves.

The nurse's briefing to the 10 prostitutes seated in the classroom's benches was a prelude to the program's focus:

The Ministry of Health hired the former prostitutes and trained them in the art of asking delicate questions in the hope that they can succeed where social workers have failed: in persuading prostitutes to talk frankly. As confidential interviewers, the former prostitutes are more persuasive in selling the virtues of condoms, epidemiologists said. At the conclusion of the interviews, prostitutes are asked to donate blood for testing and given condoms.

As in other African countries, AIDS is largely a heterosexual disease in Ethiopia; primary carriers are prostitutes, truck drivers and soldiers.

Prostitution has become more endemic in Ethiopian cities because of increasing poverty. Sociologists here say that another result of poverty is promiscuity in general, as young people find it too expensive to marry and so tend to have numerous affairs, increasing their risk of AIDS.

A 20-year-old woman waiting in the dirt schoolyard to be interviewed said she turned to prostitution five months ago. "I'm trying to make a living," said the woman, a kerchief over her head. She knew about AIDS, she said, and was grateful for the seminar. "It is going to help us in prevention."

The Ethiopian medical authorities, confronted with some of the worst public health problems in the world—the rate of child immunization is the second-lowest in the world, according to the United Nations—were prompted to further action on AIDS after a blood survey last year showed an alarming spread of the virus. In one town, Dessie, a major transportation hub, 38 percent of prostitutes and drivers of the Ethiopian Freight Transport Corporation tested positive for the virus.

With money from the World Health Organization, the Ministry of Health started its AIDS program two years ago, focusing mainly on education and tracking the disease.

1   The sales representative should know the organization's history and mission and identify with it.
2   The sales representative should know the organization's offerings.
3   The sales representative should know customers' and competitors' characteristics.
4   The sales representative should know how to make effective sales presentations.
5   The sales representative should know the organization's systems and procedures.

Principles of Effective Selling

One of the major objectives of sales training programs is to train sales personnel in the art of selling. The sales training industry today involves expenditures of hundreds of millions of dollars in training programs, books, cassettes, and other materials. Almost a million copies of books on selling are purchased every year, bearing such provocative titles as *How to Outsell the Born Salesman, How to Sell Anything to Anybody, The Power of Enthusiastic Selling, How Power Selling Brought Me Success in 6 Hours, Where Do You Go From No. 1*, and *1000 Ways a Salesman Can Increase His Sales*. One of the most enduring books is Dale Carnegie's *How to Win Friends and Influence People*.

All of the sales training approaches are designed to convert a salesperson from being a passive *order taker* to a more active *order getter. Order takers* operate on the following assumptions: (1) customers are aware of their own needs, (2) they cannot be influenced or would resent any attempt at influence, and (3) they prefer salespersons who are courteous and self-effacing. An example of an order-taking mentality would be a college fund-raiser who phones alumni and asks if they would like to give any money.

As we have noted, nonprofit salespeople are much more likely to be order takers, but order *getters* are often needed. In training salespersons to be order getters, there are two basic approaches—a sales-oriented approach and a customer-oriented approach. The first one trains the salesperson to be adept in the use of *hard sell techniques* such as those used in selling encyclopedias or military service. The techniques include overstating the offer's merits, criticizing competitive offerings, using a slick canned presentation, selling yourself, and offering some concession to make the sale on the spot. The assumptions behind this form of selling are that (1) the customers are not likely to buy except under pressure, (2) they are influenced by a slick presentation and ingratiating manners, and (3) they won't regret the purchase, or if they do, it doesn't matter.

The other approach attempts to train sales personnel in *customer need satisfaction*. Here the salesperson studies the customers' needs and wants and tailors a proposal to meet these needs. An example would be a museum fund-raiser who senses that a wealthy shoe manufacturer has a strong ego and need for recognition as a supporter of the arts. The fund-raiser could propose building and naming a new room at the art gallery after this person. The assumptions behind this approach are that (1) the customers have latent needs that constitute opportunities for the sales representative, (2) they appreciate good suggestions, and (3) they will be responsive to sales representatives who have their long-term interests at heart. Within a customer-oriented marketing framework, the need satisfier is certainly a more appropriate image for the salesperson than the image of the hard seller or order taker. It is also one with which nonprofit salespersons will feel comfortable.

Most sales training programs view the selling process as consisting of a set of steps, each involving certain skills. These steps are shown in Figure 21-2 and discussed in the following sections.[10]

Prospecting and Qualifying.   The first step in the sales process is to identify prospects. A hospital fund-raiser, for example, could obtain the names of wealthy people in the following way: (1) asking current wealthy donors for the names of other potential donors, (2) asking friendly referral sources, such as lawyers, accountants, and bankers, (3) joining organizations such as country clubs where there is a high probability of meeting wealthy people, (4) giving speeches or writing articles of interest to wealthy people that are likely to increase the salesperson's visibility, (5) examining various data sources (newspapers, directories) in search of names, and (6) using the telephone and mail to track down leads.

Sales representatives also need to know how to screen the leads to avoid wasting valuable time on poor leads. Prospects can be qualified by examining their financial ability, giving history, personality, and location. The salesperson may use the phone or mail to qualify the prospects further.

Preapproach.   This step involves the salesperson in learning as much as possible about each good prospect. The salesperson can consult reference sources, acquaintances, and others. The salesperson should determine *call objectives,* which may be to make an introduction, gather information, or make an immediate sale. Another task is to decide on the best *approach,* which might be a personal visit (possibly with a respected intermediary), phone call, or letter. The best *timing* should be thought out because many prospects will be more responsive at certain times of the year. For example, corporations and foundations are

FIGURE 21-2

Major Steps in Effective Selling

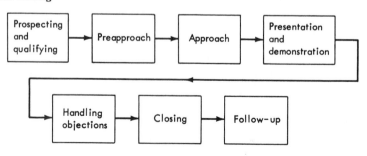

most receptive to grant proposals that are delivered before their own budgeting cycle begins. Finally, the salesperson should give thought to an *overall strategy* to be used at the approach stage.

Approach.   This stage involves the salesperson knowing how to meet and greet the prospect to get the relationship off to a good start. It consists of how the salesperson looks, opening lines, and follow-up remarks. The salesperson's looks include his or her appearance, manner, and mannerisms. The salesperson is encouraged to wear clothes similar to what the prospect usually wears, such as an open shirt and no tie in Texas, to show courtesy and attention to the prospect, and to avoid distracting mannerisms such as pacing the floor or staring. In general, it has been found that the more like the prospect the change agent is perceived to be, the more effective he or she will be. The opening line should be positive, pleasant, and start with the *customer's* interests.

Presentation and Demonstration.   After this introduction, the salesperson can make a brief statement about the organization and the purpose of the call. The salesperson will follow the AIDA formula: get *attention*, hold *interest*, arouse *desire*, and obtain *action.*

There are three contrasting styles of sales presentation. The oldest is the *canned approach*, which is a memorized sales talk covering the main points deemed important by the organization. It is based on stimulus-response thinking, which assumes that the buyer is passive and can be moved to purchase by the use of the right stimulus words, pictures, terms, and actions. Thus, a museum fund-raiser might describe the museum's capital campaign as a "once-in-a-lifetime giving opportunity" and show some beautiful four-color pictures on the present collection, hoping that these will trigger an irresistible desire for giving on the part of the prospect. Canned presentations are used primarily in door-to-door and telephone canvassing and have been pretty much abandoned by most organizations in favor of more flexible approaches.

The *formulated approach* is also based on stimulus-response thinking, but it attempts to draw the prospect into the discussion in a way that will elicit the prospect's needs and attitudes. As these are discovered, the salesperson moves into a formulated presentation that is appropriate to that prospect and shows how the transaction will satisfy that particular prospect's needs. It is not canned but follows a previously thought-out plan.

The *need satisfaction approach* does not start with a prepared presentation designed to sell the prospect, but with a search for the prospect's real needs. The prospect is encouraged to do most of the talking so that the salesperson can really grasp the prospect's real needs and respond accordingly. This is the most customer-centered approach but it puts a premium on good listening and problem-solving skills.

Sales presentations can be improved considerably with various demonstration aids, such as booklets, flip-charts, slides, movies, and samples. To the extent that the prospect can participate by seeing or handling the offer, he or she will better remember its features and benefits.

Handling Objections.   Prospects almost always pose objections during the presentation or when asked to sign up. Their sales resistance could take a psychological or logical form. *Psychological resistance* can include[11] (1) resistance to interference, (2) preference for established habits, (3) apathy, (4) reluctance to giving up something, (5) unpleasant associations with the other person, (6) tendency to resist domination, (7) predetermined ideas, (8) dislike of making decisions, and (9) neurotic attitude toward money. *Logical resistance* might consist of objections to the terms of organization of the proposal. To handle these objections, the salesperson uses such techniques as maintaining a positive approach, trying to have the prospect clarify and define the objections, questioning the prospect in such a way that the prospect has to answer his or her own objections, denying the validity of the objections, and turning the objection into a reason for buying. The salesperson needs training in the broader skills of negotiation, of which handling objections is a part.[12]

Closing.   In this stage, the salesperson attempts to induce action. Some salespeople never get to this stage or do not do it well. They lack confidence in themselves, their organization, or their offering; they feel guilty about asking for the action; or they do not recognize the right psychological moment to ask for action. Salespersons have to be trained in recognizing specific closing signals from the prospect, including physical actions, statements or comments, and questions signaling a possible readiness to close. Salespersons can then use one of several closing techniques. They can ask the prospect to act, recapitulate the points of agreement, offer to help write up an agreement, ask whether the prospect wants A or B, get the prospect to make minor choices among possible variations, or indicate what the prospect will lose if the transaction is not completed now. The salesperson may offer the prospect specific inducements to close, such as a concession or gift item.

Follow-up.   This last stage is necessary if the salesperson wants to assure customer satisfaction and repeat business. Immediately after closing, the salesperson should attempt to complete any necessary details. The salesperson should consider scheduling a follow-up call to make sure everything has gone smoothly. This call is designed to detect any problems, to assure the buyer of the salesperson's interest and service, and to reduce any cognitive dissonance that might have arisen.

Indeed, dissonance theory suggests that the postdecision phase is the time during which customers most actively seek information to justify their choices. This is especially true under two conditions: (1) the choice was personally involving for the decision maker, and (2) the alternatives under consideration were quite similar.

SUPERVISING SALES REPRESENTATIVES

The new sales representative must be given more than an assignment, a compensation package, and training—he or she must be given supervision. Supervision is the fate of everyone who works for someone else. It is the expression of the employers' natural and continuous interest in the activities of their agents. Through supervision, employers hope to direct and motivate the sales force to do a better job.

Directing Sales Representatives

Organizations undertake a number of activities to improve their sales representatives' performances:

Developing Customer and Prospect Call Levels.   Many organizations classify their customers into account types, such as A, B, and C, reflecting present sales and the growth potential of the different accounts. Army recruiters, for example, may classify different high schools into these groups. They establish a certain desired call level per period that their recruiters should make to each account type. The call levels that are set depend upon competitive call norms and expected account responses.

Organizations also like to specify how much time to spend prospecting for new accounts. Organizations like to set a minimum requirement for the canvassing of new accounts because salespeople, if left alone, spend most of their time with current customers, especially if they are rewarded mainly by the number of sales achieved in the current period. Current customers are better known quantities. The sales representatives can depend upon them for some business, whereas a prospect may never deliver any business or deliver it only after many months of effort.

Using Sales Time Efficiently.   The sales representatives should know how to schedule planned sales calls and use their time efficiently. One tool is the preparation of an *annual call schedule,* showing which customers and prospects to call on in which months and which ancillary activities to carry out. The other tool is *time-and-duty analysis* to determine how to use sales call time more efficiently.

Actual selling time in some organizations may amount to as little as 15 percent of total working time! If it could be raised from 15 percent to 20 percent, this would be a 33 percent improvement. Organizations are constantly seeking ways to help their sales representatives use their time more efficiently. This takes the form of training them in the effective use of the telephone ("phone power"), simplifying the record-keeping forms, using the computer to develop call and routing plans, and supplying them with marketing research information on the prospect or customer.

Motivating Sales Representatives

A small percentage of sales representatives in any sales force can be expected to do their best without any special prompting from management. To them, selling is the most fascinating job in the world. They are ambitious and self-starters. But the majority of sales representatives on nearly every sales force require personal encouragement and special incentives to work at their best level. This is especially true for creative field selling. Management can affect the morale and performance of the sales force through its organizational climate, sales quotas, and positive incentives.

Organizational Climate.   Organizational climate describes the feeling that the sales force gets from their organization regarding their opportunities, value, and rewards for good performance. Some organizations treat their recruiters, fund-raisers, and others as being of minor importance. Others treat them as highly critical to the organization's success. The company's attitude toward its sales representatives acts as a self-fulfilling prophecy. If they are held in low esteem, there is much turnover and poor performance; if they are held in high esteem, there is less turnover and high performance.

The quality of personal treatment from the sales representative's immediate superior is an important aspect of the organizational climate. An effective sales manager keeps in touch with the members of the sales force through regular correspondence and phone calls, personal visits in the field, and evaluation sessions at headquarters. At different times the sales manager is the sales representative's boss, companion, coach, and confessor.

Sales Quotas.   Many organizations set sales quotas for their sales representatives specifying sales objectives for the period. Thus, a U.S. Navy recruiter may be expected to produce five enlistees each month. Sales quotas are developed in the process of developing the annual marketing plan. The organization first decides on a sales forecast that is reasonably achievable. This becomes the basis of planning production, work force size, and financial requirements. Then management establishes sales quotas for all of its regions and territories, which typically add up to more than the sales forecast. Sales quotas are set higher than the sales forecast in order to stretch the sales managers and salespeople to their best effort. If they fail to make their quotas, the organization nevertheless may make its sales forecast.

Each sales manager takes the assigned quota and divides it among the sales representatives. Actually, there are three schools of thought on quota setting. The *high-quota school* sets quotas that are above what most sales representatives will achieve but that are possible for all. They are of the opinion that high quotas spur extra effort. The *modest-quota school* sets quotas that a majority of the sales force can achieve. They feel that the sales force will accept the quotas as fair, attain them, and gain confidence from attaining them. Finally, the *variable-quota school* thinks that individual differences among sales representatives warrant high quotas for some, modest quotas for others.

In all cases, care must be taken that quotas are never set at unrealistic levels. This can lead to counterproductive, sometimes unethical behavior just to meet the quota. Several years ago, military recruiters faced with poorly qualified candidates but high quotas bent the test requirements, or in some cases helped recruits fill in answers.

Positive Incentives.   Organizations use a number of positive motivators to stimulate sales force effort. Periodic *sales meetings* provide a social occasion, a break from routine, a chance to meet and talk with the organization's leaders, a chance to air feelings and to identify with a larger group. Organizations also sponsor *sales contests*, with the best performers winning a product or a trip somewhere. Indeed, an entire industry has grown up in recent years whose goal it is to provide organizations with creative and attractive special employee incentive schemes.

EVALUATING SALES REPRESENTATIVES

We have been describing the *feedforward* aspects of sales supervision—the efforts of management to communicate to the sales representative what they should be doing and to motivate them to do it. But good feedforward requires good feedback. And good feedback means getting regular information from and about sales representatives to evaluate their performance.

Sources of Information

Management gains information about its sales representatives in a number of ways. Probably the most important source of information is the sales representative's periodic reports. Additional information comes through personal observation, through customers' letters and complaints, and through conversations with other sales representatives.

Much of this information can now be computerized by issuing portable personal computers to salespeople, and sales and expense data can be recorded on desk top PCs in central offices. Those data bases can then be analyzed by imaginative salespeople with only limited training. It has been the experience of many organizations that once salespeople discover that they can use all of the day-to-day data that management insists they record, the reporting task changes from a resented imposition to a task eagerly carried out for the benefits it can give the *salesperson* as well as management.

Formal Evaluation of Performance

The sales force's reports, along with other reports from the field and the manager's personal observations, supply the raw materials for formally evaluating members of the sales force. Formal evaluation procedures lead to at least three benefits. First, they lead management to develop specific and uniform standards for judging sales performance. Second, they lead management to draw together all its information and impressions about individual sales representatives and make more systematic, point-by-point evaluations. Third, they tend to have a constructive effect on the performance of sales representatives. The constructive effect comes about because the sales representatives know that they will have to sit down one morning with the sales manager and explain certain facets of their routing or sales call decisions or their failure to secure or maintain certain accounts.

Salesperson-to-Salesperson Comparisons.   One type of evaluation frequently made is to compare and rank the sales performance of the various sales representatives. Such comparisons, however, must be done with care. Relative sales performances are meaningful only if there are no variations among sales assignments in market potential, workload, degree of competition, promotional effort, environmental conditions, and so forth. Furthermore, sales are not the only measure of achievement. Management should be interested in how much each sales representative contributed to net surplus. And this cannot be known until the sales representative's sales mix and sales expenses are examined. A possible ranking criterion would be the sales representative's *actual contribution to surplus as a ratio to his or her estimated potential surplus*. A ratio of 1.00 would mean that the sales representative delivered the potential sales in his or her market segment. The lower a sales representative's ratio, the more supervision and counseling he or she needs.

Current-to-Past-Sales Comparisons.   A second common type of evaluation is to compare a sales representative's current performance with past performance. Each salesperson is expected to improve along certain lines, such as producing more sales, bringing down costs, opening new accounts, and so on. His or her progress can be measured and a judgment made about whether there is enough improvement, and if not, what the problem is.

Qualitative Evaluation of Sales Representatives.   The evaluation usually extends to the salesperson's knowledge of the organization, products, customers, competitors, territory, and responsibilities. Personality characteristics can be rated, such as general manner, appearance, speech, and temperament. The sales manager can also consider any problems in motivation or compliance. Since an almost endless number of qualitative factors might be included, each company must decide which will contribute most to organizational performance. Then, these factors should be objectified as much as possible and routinely fed back to the salesperson. Only when they know the criteria against which they are to be judged can salespeople make efforts to improve in the ways that management wishes.

SUMMARY

Many organizations utilize sales representatives and assign them a pivotal role in the creation of sales. The high cost of the sales resource calls for effective sales management, consisting of six steps: (1) establishing sales force objectives; (2) designing sales force strategy, structure, size, and compensation; (3) recruiting and selecting; (4) training; (5) supervision; and (6) evaluating.

As an element of the marketing mix, the sales force is capable of achieving certain marketing objectives effectively. The organization has to decide on the proper mix of the following sales activities: prospecting, communicating, selling and servicing, information gathering, and allocating.

Given the sales force objectives, the sales force is then designed to answer the question of what sales force strategy would be most effective (individual selling, team selling, etc.), what type of sales force structure would work best (territorial-, product-, or customer-structured), how large a sales force is needed, and how the sales force should be compensated.

Sales representatives must be recruited and selected carefully to avoid the high costs of hiring the wrong persons. Their training should familiarize them with the organization's history, products and policies, customer and competitor characteristics, and the art of selling. The art of selling itself calls for training in a seven-step sales process: prospecting and qualifying, preapproach, approach, presentation and demonstration, handling objections, closing, and follow-up. The salesperson needs supervision and continuous encouragement. Periodically, the person's performance must be formally evaluated to help him or her do a better job.

QUESTIONS

1. How can the principles of effective selling outlined in this chapter be adapted to a service context such as where a nurse in a clinic in a rural village in India tries to "sell" a new mother getting a postnatal medical checkup on attending a future class on family planning?

2. What are the disadvantages of treating volunteer fund-raisers as if they were salespeople? How can these disadvantages be minimized or eliminated?

3. You have arranged an appointment to meet the CEO and vice-president for public affairs of ARCO to discuss the possibility of their serving as prime sponsor for a series of rock concerts to raise funds for your AIDS treatment and research program. Two earlier concerts have been only moderately successful. Which of the following selling approaches would you use and why: (a) sales team to buyer group, (b) conference selling, or (c) seminar selling?

4. You have two lists of potential donors to your animal shelter. One list will be used for a direct-mail sales presentation, the other for a telemarketing presentation. Draft a presentation outline for both approaches. How would the sales approaches differ because of the medium used?

5. Outline the major objections a salesperson is likely to face in the telemarketing situation described in Question 4. Offer two responses to minimize the effects of each of these objections.

NOTES

1. See Sidney J. Levy, *Promotional Behavior* (Glenview, Ill.: Scott, Foresman, 1971), pp. 65–69.

2. *Sales & Marketing Management*, February 20, 1989, p. 15.

3. "The Trend Toward Telemarketing," *The Cultural Post*, Vol. 8, no. 7, March–April 1983, p. 13.

4. Kevin Higgins, "Theatre Groups Discovering the Power of Telemarketing," *Marketing News*, June 22, 1984, p. 1.

5. Walter J. Talley, "How to Design Sales Territories," *Journal of Marketing*, January 1961, pp. 7–13.

6. The survey was conducted by the Sales Executives Club of New York and was reported in *Business Week*, February 1, 1964, p. 52.

7. Robert N. McMurry, "The Mystique of Super-Salesmanship," *Harvard Business Review*, March–April 1961, p. 117.

8. Ibid., p. 118.

9. David Mayer and Herbert M. Greenberg, "What Makes a Good Salesman?" *Harvard Business Review*, July–August 1964, pp. 119–125.

10. The following discussion is drawn in part from W.J.E. Crissy, William H. Cunningham, and Isabella C.M. Cunningham, *Selling: The Personal Force in Marketing* (New York: John Wiley, 1977), pp. 119–129.

11. Ibid., pp. 289–294.

12. See Gerald I. Nierenberg, *The Art of Negotiation* (New York: Hawthorn Books, 1968); and Chester L. Karrass, *The Negotiating Game* (Cleveland: World, 1970).

22

Marketing Evaluation and Control

This summer, at its 25th anniversary summit, the Organization of African Unity resolved to achieve "universal child immunization" by 1990 It is well on its way. Today, seven African countries, with a combined population of more than 100 million, have already reached that goal, says James P. Grant, executive director of the United Nations Children's Fund. (Universal immunization is defined as 75 to 85 percent of those under age 1.)

In the developing world in general, immunization rates rose from 5 percent in 1974 to more than 50 percent by May 1987, according to the World Health Organization. The rates grew despite the recession of the early 1980s that sapped health budgets of developing countries.

Development agencies attribute this success to putting their money where it would do the most good. This meant funding mostly primary health care, which emphasizes preventive services that often do not require a doctor, rather than hospitals and curative strategies, and determining which primary care strategies were most cost-effective.

Because of this approach, says Grant, in 1985 the absolute number of children dying annually in Africa began falling for the first time, and it has continued to do so, although demographers had projected that it would rise through the end of the century.

Not everyone thinks that the various development agencies have done such a good job of promoting health care in the Third World. In a background paper published by the Heritage Foundation in Washington (and which does not necessarily reflect the views of the foundation), Carol

Adelman, Jeremiah Norris and Susan Raymond voiced a variety of criticisms of the Agency for International Development, many of which apply equally to the overall thrust of development agencies' Third World health policy. The three have consulted for AID and are officers of the nonprofit Consultative Group on Development in Washington.

One criticism is that there is no hard evidence that the primary care approach has had any impact on Third World health, "given that infant mortality was already declining," as a result of control of communicable diseases, education and better sanitation, says Raymond.

Both sides agree that it is no easy matter to ascertain exactly what works, since conditions vary considerably: from impoverished countries with very high infant mortality, such as Ethiopia, to countries that are on the verge of industrialization, where infant mortality has declined greatly, such as Thailand.

In countries with high infant mortality, children saved from one disease are likely to succumb to another, so the strategies may appear less effective.

Raymond says categorically that only about 50 percent of infant mortality is addressable by so-called childhood survival strategies, and Warren concurs. For example, Raymond says that oral rehydration therapy can have only a tiny impact, because such a small percentage of deaths among the 50 percent are caused by diarrhea, and there are different types of the illness, some of which cannot be treated by the therapy.

But Warren says that most forms of diarrhea can be so treated. And a study of oral rehydration therapy in Egypt, just published in The Lancet, suggests that in some Third World countries the technique can have an enormous impact on childhood mortality (defined as death before the age of 5, excluding babies less than 1 month old). Over six years, the rate fell by two-thirds in one Egyptian village where oral rehydration was introduced; other factors influencing health held relatively constant during this period, the authors said.

Source: Adapted from "Strategies for Third World Care," *Insight*, August 19, 1988, p. 58. Reproduced with permission.

Strategic planning in marketing is crucial in setting the nonprofit organization off in the proper direction, whether for a year's activities or for an entirely new venture. But pushing an enterprise into the stream of competition by no means assures that it will either get to its desired goal or get there as quickly and efficiently as possible. To assure that strategic marketing achieves its goals in a timely and efficient manner, the nonprofit manager must develop and put in place effective control systems for strategic plans and, where necessary, take corrective action. There are two types of control that management needs: strategic control and tactical control. *Strategic control* focuses on larger issues and requires tracking changes in the broad environment, competitors' actions and plans, perceptions of the organization held by the general public, organization strengths and weaknesses, and broad trends in organization performance. This information then becomes input into subsequent rounds of the strategic marketing planning process (SMPP) described in Chapter 3. Regular marketing audits, as described in that chapter, represent one approach to strategic control.

Tactical control requires the development of systems for more or less continual monitoring of program performance for purposes of day-to-day fine-tuning of the strategic plan to correct for undesirable performance. In this chapter, we shall focus on such systems for regular monitoring and corrective action. We investigate several considerations in designing such systems and look at several measures that could be used by specific institutions. We shall look at various approaches to measuring revenue performance and to tracking customer satisfaction. The latter is particularly important since (1) customer satisfaction is—or ought to be—the goal of most nonprofit organizations, and (2) revenue measures may be either inappropriate or unavailable.

TACTICAL MARKETING CONTROL

The purpose of marketing control is to maximize the probability that the organization will achieve its short-run and long-run objectives in the marketplace. Many surprises are likely to occur during the plan's execution that will call for new responses or adjustments. Marketing control systems are an intrinsic part of the marketing planning process since they permit such crucial and timely adjustments.

As indicated in Figure 22-1, the control process is in reality a cybernetic system that will ideally function not unlike a thermostat regulating a building's temperature. Management sets a goal (the desired temperature) and puts in place a device or system for detecting deviations from the goal (a thermometer) and ascertaining causes of the deviations (above or below ideal temperature because the space has warmed or cooled). The loop in the system is then closed

FIGURE 22-1

The Control Process

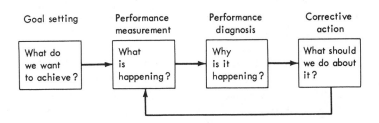

by a device or subsystem that makes the necessary corrections (a trip-switch that restarts the furnace or turns on the air conditioning). Control systems in non-profit organizations, of course, can differ greatly in complexity, timeliness, and precision. A library can simply monitor its total circulation and periodically smooth out irregularities or stimulate increased book usage through radio ads, newspaper articles, or direct mail. Or it can look periodically at the circulation of each of its departments during different parts of the day or week and seek corrective actions that would boost lagging departments or increase patronage in particular departments during off-peak hours or days. At a more complex level, it could attempt to look, not just at circulation, but at *who* was taking out books and develop control procedures that would, say, bring the number of elderly or teenagers coming to the library up to goal levels.

Control systems can also vary as to timeliness. The library can measure its performance daily, weekly, monthly, quarterly, or even annually. Obviously, the faster an organization's environment changes and the more competitive activity that takes place, the more frequently the system should be "read." Thus, libraries can get by with relatively infrequent measures compared to hospitals in major urban centers. In very volatile situations, daily monitoring may be necessary.

Types of Control Tools

Setting in place a control system like that described in Figure 22–1 is driven by an approach called *management by objectives*. Top management starts the process by developing aggregate goals for the planning period, for example, number of customers served, messages delivered, grants made or received, and so on. These goals are broken down into subgoals for lower levels of management. During the relevant period, managers receive reports that allow them to follow whether their subordinates are reaching their goals, and if they are not, to take the necessary corrective actions.

What are the control tools used by management to check on the progress of their subordinates in reaching their goals? In nonprofit organizations that have some sort of revenue objective, the three main control tools are revenue analysis, market share analysis, and marketing expense-to-sales analysis. The first two measures assess effectiveness, the latter efficiency. For nonprofits without sales or revenue outcomes, other measures are necessary.

Revenue Analysis.   *Revenue analysis* is the effort to measure and evaluate the actual revenue being achieved in relation to the revenue goals set for different managers. Thus, the management of a concert hall would compare actual to expected sales of tickets by season, audience type, specific performance, and so on, to understand audience behavior and preferences. If too few students are attending the concert series, if certain areas of the city are underrepresented, or if a certain type of music is not well attended, the reasons should be sought out. Management should avoid jumping to conclusions without some research. Too few students attending the Performing Arts Series could be due to any number of causes: (1) high ticket prices, (2) low interest in this season's performers, (3) many competing social events on the same nights, (4) increased academic pressure for grades, and so on. The proper corrective actions would vary with each cause.

Many nonprofits use revenue or attendance figures as a key measure of effectiveness. There are good reasons for this. First, strategic decisions about allocating resources are often made in terms of revenues. Assuming that revenues are a good measure of consumer interest in particular offerings, then more effort should be expended on programs that are in high demand or are growing. Thus, revenue or patronage data would help in assessing activities involving specific goods and services, such as museum gift shops, Sierra Club book and calendar marketing, and so on. Second, revenue and patronage figures are politically appealing. Nonprofits must typically market their programs to customers and to other diverse publics. Among the latter, regulators, oversight committees, and even donors will find these figures easy to understand. If they are high or growing, the activity they reflect will be thought deserving of continued or increased support and perhaps reduced outside interference. Mass transit systems that serve more citizens (for example, more voters) are likely to be well rewarded and actively praised. Obviously, systems with declining revenues usually find themselves with reduced budgets and more outside meddling in their day-to-day management.

The "objectivity" of revenue data also minimizes charges of bias by groups or factions who might otherwise argue that their constituencies are being slighted. Social service agency directors need only point to usage data to show who is or is not using the organization's offerings and therefore deserving of attention and funding. Finally, there is the "default argument." It is suggested that most alternative methods of assessing nonprofit performance (like those suggested below) are fraught with measurement problems and possible biases. Isn't it safer, then, to measure revenues or patronage than something as amorphous and subjective as customer satisfaction?

There are, however, a number of problems with "sales" or usage data. Where no cash changes hands, for example, "sales" measures may be subject to bias. That is, if measurement of park attendance is left to staff members, they may make subjective judgments that favor their own performance. Even where mechanical devices are used, like hand-held counters, turnstiles, or traffic electronic eyes, unethical staff members can manipulate results by turning equipment off and on at will or tripping the system to count themselves as often as is necessary to achieve desired figures.

A more difficult problem is whether patronage or sales is a true measure of organization performance. Assume for the moment that more attendance is sought by an organization. Those who attend may be those who have already been marketed to, or, more likely, who don't need marketing to at all. For many programs to be really successful, nonprofit marketers need to reach those who are *not* attending or *not* buying the offering. And if past resource allocations have been based on sales, the cycle will be self-reinforcing: those who attend will be allocated more marketing effort, which gets more of them to attend. At the same time, budgets and possibly interest are shifted away from other groups who may be no less interested but who come to be ignored as a result of a fixation on past revenues as a control measure. Revenues will look good, but this scenario suggests that management is really misallocating its effort and wasting scarce resources.

A related problem is that past sales to individuals may not be a good predictor of future sales to the same individuals. An institution can survive for a long time and even grow if it keeps attracting new "triers." But if it gets few repeat customers, its long-term prospects are bleak indeed. This is why many of the more sophisticated profit-centered organizations monitor *repeat* patronage or, more frequently, attempt to directly assess customer attitudes or satisfaction with the offering.

Even more compelling is the criticism that revenues may not be—ought not to be—the organization's ultimate goal. For example, museum or art gallery attendance is, indeed, important. But many museum directors might reasonably argue that simply processing "bodies" through the institution is not enough. It is the *quality* of the experience that is important. Busing hundreds of disadvantaged kids to a violin concert may increase an organization's "body count," but may well have little or no lasting effect on the "bodies" themselves, and indeed might create in them a negative image of concerts. Such a criticism would seem to be equally valid for the performing arts, recreation sites, and even libraries and educational institutions. In such cases, there is a very real danger that sales or attendance figures, because of their "objectivity" and ready accessibility, may simply substitute for what the nonprofit should *really* be striving for.

Finally, many nonprofit marketing programs simply do not have easily measured sales or attendance figures. We said earlier that the goal of nonprofit programs is ultimately to affect behavior. Thus, in theory, one ought to be able to develop a measure of that behavior. Unfortunately, in practice this may be very difficult to do, for three reasons. First, the behavior may be personal and private and very difficult to "observe" objectively. An obvious example of private behavior would be families' birth control practices. One can measure *contraceptive* sales, but major assumptions must be made to translate these into estimates of family planning behavior. Second, the behavior may involve a lifelong change that is economically impossible to track. Such would be the case for high-blood-pressure medication, which in most cases must be taken for the rest of the sufferer's life. Finally, there are cases in which the impact of a marketing program may stretch over a long period and even then may be difficult to trace to the marketer's strategies. Thus, an antismoking campaign designed to acquaint smokers with quitting techniques may help break down a smoker's lack of confidence in his or her ability to quit. Then, later—perhaps months or years later—he or she may be encouraged by a friend to enter a quitting program that is only partly effective. Still later, a physician may offer a warning about a worsening heart, a child may nag, and a favorite TV star may mention that he or she has quit. This combination finally leads to permanent quitting. Deducing the causes of such behavior will defy all but the most sophisticated tracking systems. Clearly, for a nonprofit manager to effectively manage strategies aimed at this ultimate behavior, other interim measures must be attempted.

Market Share Analysis.   Organizations should periodically review whether they are gaining or losing ground relative to their competition. Zoo attendance continues to rise for many zoos, for example, yet zoos are declining in their share of the recreational dollar. They are losing ground relative to theme parks such as Disneyworld and Great America. Market share is a much better indicator of marketing effectiveness than total revenues or sales. It must, however, be used cautiously. The organization must correctly identify its real competitors. Beloit College, for example, should not measure its enrollment performance against that of the large state universities or the elite private universities. Instead, it should measure its enrollment performance against the other colleges to which Beloit applicants also apply. A "perfect competitor" would be another college that students applying to Beloit see as equally desirable.

Marketing Expense-to-Sales Analysis.   Annual plan control also requires checking on various marketing expenses as a ratio to sales to make sure that the organization is not overspending to achieve its sales goals. The ratios to watch are total marketing expense-to-sales, sales force expense-to-sales, advertising-to-sales, sales promotion-to-sales, marketing research-to-sales, and sales administration-to-sales. The organization should continuously check whether these ratios are satisfactory and whether shifting from one marketing tool to another could bring down its total cost of sales. Management has to keep an eye on other performance ratios that say something about the efficiency of marketing effort. An experienced fund-raising director, for example, periodically checks the following figures: revenue per fund-raiser, number of prospects contacted per fund-raiser per day, number of minutes per contact, revenue per contact hour, percentage of closure per contact, percentage of potential contributors covered, and number of lost contributors.

Customer Satisfaction

Customer-centered organizations recognize that customer satisfaction should be a major indicator of organizational success. To keep this goal at the forefront of management thinking, it is important to establish a system for tracking customers' satisfaction as part of the day-to-day control system. First, it is necessary to define the term "satisfaction." Our definition is

> **Satisfaction** is the state felt by a person who has experienced a *performance* (or outcome) that has fulfilled his or her *expectations*.

Thus, satisfaction is a function of the relative levels of expectations and perceived performance.[1] A person will experience one of three states of satisfaction. If the results exceed the person's expectations, the person is highly satisfied. If the results match the expectations, the person is satisfied. If the results fall short of the expectations, the person is dissatisfied.

In this case, the amount of dissatisfaction depends upon the consumer's method of handling the gap between expectations and performance. Some consumers try to *minimize* the felt dissonance by imagining that performance was really better than they first thought or by thinking that they set their expectations too high. Other consumers exaggerate the perceived performance gap because of their disappointment. They are more prone to reduce or end their contact with the organization and/or complain to friends and coworkers.

Thus, to understand satisfaction, we must also understand how people form their expectations. Expectations are formed to some extent on the basis of people's past experience with the same or similar situations and statements made by friends and associates. They are also affected by statements made by the marketer. The latter, therefore, needs to monitor both the performance of its offerings but also the expectations it raises. If it raises expectations too high, it is likely to create subsequent dissatisfaction; if it sets them low enough, it might create high satisfaction—although it risks lowering "sales" by suggesting that its offerings promise only limited benefits.

Consumer satisfaction, in spite of its central importance, is difficult to measure. Organizations use various methods to infer how much consumer satisfaction they are creating.

Complaint and Suggestion Systems. One possible approach is to establish complaint and suggestion systems. A responsive organization makes it easy for its clients to complain if they are disappointed in some ways with the service they have received. Management will want complaints to surface on the theory that clients who are not given an opportunity to complain might reduce their business with the organization, bad-mouth it, or abandon it completely. Indeed, it has been found that dissatisfied customers are likely to tell 9 to 12 other consumers whereas satisfied consumers speak to only 2 or 3.[2] However, the likelihood of negative effects will be reduced substantially if dissatisfied consumers are encouraged to voice their complaints to the marketer, they are more likely to continue to patronize the organization, *even if* the marketer does not respond to the complaint to the customer's satisfaction. Further, it has been found that the faster the marketer responds to a voiced complaint, the more likely it will lead to a favorable attitude on the part of the consumer.

How can complaints be facilitated? The first step is for management to accept the seemingly contrary notion that more complaining is *better* and to communicate this position up and down the organization. Complaints should be seen as customer-volunteered marketing research data to be actively sought, not as information to be squelched for fear that complaints will lead only to reprimands. Once this crucial atmosphere is established the organization can set up systems that make it easy for dissatisfied customers (or satisfied customers) to express their feelings to the organization. Several devices can be used in this connection. A hospital, for example, could place suggestion boxes in the corridors. It could supply exiting patients with a comment card that can be easily checked off (see Figure 22–2). It could establish a patient advocate or ombudsman system to hear patient grievances and seek remedies. It could establish a nurse grievance committee to review nurse complaints.

An organization can then identify the major categories of complaints. It should then focus its corrective actions on those categories showing high frequency, high seriousness, and high remediability.

Consumer Satisfaction Surveys. A major problem with volunteered complaints as noted in a 1977 Andreasen and Best study is that they are unrepresentative of both the types of complaints and the types of complainers. Thus, consumers are more likely to volunteer complaints about problems in which high costs (economic, social, and psychological) are involved or in which they are seriously inconvenienced. Further, they are more likely to complain if they

FIGURE 22-2

A Hospital Comment Card

You are a VERY IMPORTANT PERSON!

Will you let us know how we did?

We strive to provide the best possible hospital care to the patients who come to us. Please take a couple of minutes to complete this questionnaire, there is space on the back for additional comments, which will help us improve our service and continue Memorial's tradition of excellent patient care.

When completed drop it in the mail. It is addressed and the postage is paid.

Thank you for your valuable assistance.

Robert M. Magnuson
Robert M. Magnuson
President

Your room number ________

From ________ To ________

Male ________ Female ________

Your name, if you wish ________

A. Your admission: Yes No

Were you courteously received and processed by the admitting office? ___ ___

Were you admitted to the hospital from the Emergency Department? ___ ___

B. Your room:

Was it ready for you? ___ ___

Was it attractive? ___ ___

Was it kept clean during your stay? ___ ___

Cat No 193540

Yes No

Was the proper temperature maintained? ___ ___

Were lighting and ventilation facilities adequate? ___ ___

Was your room quiet enough for you to sleep and rest? ___ ___

C. Your meals:

Was the food well-prepared and appetizing, considering your diet? ___ ___

Were you satisfied with the portions? ___ ___

Did hot food arrive hot at your bedside? ___ ___

Was your food served attractively? ___ ___

Overall, were you pleased with the food service during your stay? ___ ___

D. Nursing service:

In your opinion were the nurses skilled in the performance of their duties? ___ ___

Were they attentive to your needs and did they explain reasons for medications, treatments, and diagnostic procedures? ___ ___

Was your call for assistance answered with reasonable promptness? ___ ___

E. Were you satisfied with the services given by:

X-ray technicians? ___ ___

Laboratory technicians? ___ ___

Yes No

Housekeeping personnel? ___ ___

Nursing assistants, orderlies and other nursing personnel? ___ ___

Volunteers? ___ ___

Telephone operators? ___ ___

Admitting clerks? ___ ___

Other personnel? ___ ___

F. Were you informed about tests and treatments ordered by your physician? ___ ___

G. Was your schedule arranged so that you could get enough rest? ___ ___

H. Personal:

Were your visitors courteously received? ___ ___

Were visiting hours satisfactory? ___ ___

Were services such as delivery of mail, flowers and packages satisfactory? ___ ___

I. Business office:

Was the cashier courteous and helpful? ___ ___

J. Overall, are you satisfied with your care at Memorial Hospital? ___ ___

K. Overall, are you satisfied with the information given you about your health, your treatments, and follow-up care? ___ ___

L. Would you recommend our Hospital to family members, friends and neighbors? ___ ___

think the nonprofit organization is to blame and they did not contribute to the problem themselves. Finally, they are more likely to complain if the nature of the problem and its source are manifest—that is, if the existence of a problem is not really a matter of individual judgment. For these reasons, a nonprofit is more likely to receive complaints about issues involving large monetary and time costs on the part of clients. Problems involving broken items, delayed services, and discourteous employees are more likely to surface than problems in which, say, medical care is just a bit impersonal or in which the staff of an educational seminar seems underprepared and the seminar is not taught very well.[3] Yet it is just these more minor kinds of unreported feelings of dissatisfaction that management would like to know about. The obvious bad features of any program usually quickly become apparent without much management research. The subtle things that can truly sink a basically good program or institution through poor word of mouth, lack of repeat behavior, and perhaps worse still, just plain apathy, are the very things that don't get volunteered by dissatisfied consumers. People must be asked.

People must also be asked because not all of them will speak up. To voice a complaint, one must not only have a problem or a dissatisfaction, but one has to understand where and how to complain and have the skills to do so and the gumption to speak up. Not everyone has these qualities. Indeed, research has consistently shown that vocal complainers are much more likely to be socially upscale and have higher incomes and better educations. They are also likely to be relatively young. Yet many nonprofit programs, such as those in social work or those requiring long-term behavioral change like stopping smoking or practicing family planning, have *downscale* audiences as their primary targets. Hearing from these people is essential to program success, yet they are the least likely to volunteer information about their dissatisfaction.

Finally, the voicing of complaints is sometimes inhibited by the institution itself. Unless the circumstances are right and the nonprofit marketer sets the right tone, people are relatively unlikely to complain about their church, their doctor, or even their lawyer or accountant. The Andreasen and Best study reported the following dissatisfaction experience rates for medical and dental services compared with rates for all services and all products.[4] While patients

	Medical/Dental	*All Services*	*All Products*
Percentage reporting problems	14.9%	20.9%	20.0%
Percentage with problem voicing a complaint to marketer	32.7%	42.3%	40.2%
Percentage who complained who were not satisfied with marketer response	46.4%	28.7%	23.6%

perceived fewer problems with their medical and dental care than with other services or products, they were significantly less likely to speak up about them. And when they did, they found the medical and dental community much less responsive than other product and service marketers in resolving their complaints. Only one in six of those who had a serious dissatisfaction felt bold enough to speak up about it and were lucky enough to have it handled satisfactorily.

There are many reasons why doctors might not encourage complaints, several of which do not reflect well on the customer orientation of the medical community. Some of these inhibiting perspectives could be described in medical jargon as "syndromes."[5]

1   *The Holier-than-Thou Syndrome.* Many physicians believe that patients do not really know what is in fact in their own best interests. Patients find illness threatening and so have a distorted perception of their true needs. Further, they simply lack the physician's technical knowledge and thus cannot judge what is needed and what is not. Physicians can therefore ignore their complaints.

2   *The They're-Not-Paying-for-It-Anyway Syndrome.* Since third-party insurers frequently bear much of the cost of medical care, patients can (and should) be scheduled for tests, medication, or return office visits that may have only marginal value. The costs to patients in terms of time and inconvenience are ignored, as are their complaints about excessive tests and medicines and about medical costs in general.

3   *The Higher-Opportunity-Cost Syndrome.* Since physicians perceive themselves to be in the business of saving lives, they frequently assume that their time is much more valuable than that of their patients. Patients therefore should not complain about accommodating to the physician's convenience or paying high fees for his or her services.

4   *The I-Want-to-Be-Alone Syndrome.* Four out of five physicians practice alone. Many do so because they cherish the independence that makes them immune to the peer pressures upon which medical community control largely relies.

5   *The They're-Out-to-Get-Me Syndrome.* Many physicians seem to behave as if all patients have a lawyer friend or relative ready to bring a malpractice suit at the drop of a suture. Such physicians schedule excessive self-protective tests and procedures and tend by demeanor to discourage any consumer inquiries about their medical care that might escalate into a malpractice claim.

6   *The Mystique-of-Omnipotence Syndrome.* Since a positive patient attitude toward the illness and its cure is often an important contributor to the cure itself, many physicians believe that unswerving faith in the physician is essential to a positive outcome. Creating a mystique of omnipotence requires that the physician brook no questioning of his or her methods and outcomes.

As a result of these types of factors, the better, more responsive nonprofits supplement the devices described earlier with direct periodic surveys of consumer satisfaction. They send questionnaires or make telephone calls to a random sample of past users to find out how much they like the service. Some organizations also survey clients of competitors or of marketers of unrelated products and services to identify potential market opportunities on which they might capitalize. Through direct surveys, they avoid the several biases of complaint monitoring systems.

Customer satisfaction can be measured in a number of ways. We consider four approaches here:

1 Directly reported satisfaction
2 Derived dissatisfaction
3 Problem rates
4 Importance/performance ratings

DIRECTLY REPORTED SATISFACTION.   A university can distribute a questionnaire to a representative sample of students, asking them to state their satisfaction with the university as a whole and with specific components. The questionnaire would be distributed on a periodic basis either in person, in the mail, or through a telephone inquiry.

The questionnaire would contain questions of the following form:

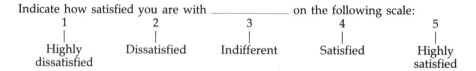

Indicate how satisfied you are with _____ on the following scale:

1	2	3	4	5
Highly dissatisfied	Dissatisfied	Indifferent	Satisfied	Highly satisfied

Here 5 values are used, although some scales use only three values and others as many as 11.

When the results are in, a histogram can be prepared showing the percentage of students who fall into each group. Of course, students within any group—such as the highly dissatisfied group—may have really quite different intensities of dissatisfaction ranging from mild feelings of disappointment with the university to intense feelings of anger. Unfortunately, there is no way to make interpersonal comparisons of intensity and we can only rely on the self-reported feelings of the respondents.

If the histogram is highly skewed to the left, then the university is in deep trouble. If the histogram is bell shaped, then it has the usual number of dissatisfied, indifferent, and satisfied students. If the histogram is highly skewed to the right, the university can be very satisfied that it is a responsive organization meeting its goal of delivering high satisfaction to the majority of its consumers.[6] Finally, if the distribution is bimodal (i.e., two peaks), the organization may need to develop a second offering to meet the needs of the dissatisfied market while retaining the present offering to serve the satisfied group.

DERIVED DISSATISFACTION.   The second method of satisfaction measurement is based on the premise stated earlier that a particular student's satisfaction is influenced by the perceived performance and his expectations. He is asked two questions about each component of the university; for example:

The quality of the academic program:
  a. How much is there now?

| | (min) | 1 | 2 | 3 | 4 | 5 | 6 | 7 | (max) |

  b. How much should there be?

| | (min) | 1 | 2 | 3 | 4 | 5 | 6 | 7 | (max) |

Suppose he circles 2 for part (a) and 5 for part (b). We can then derive a "performance deficiency" score by subtracting the answer for part (a) from part (b), here 3. The greater the performance deficiency score, the greater his degree of dissatisfaction (or the smaller his degree of satisfaction).

This method provides more useful information than the previous method. By averaging the scores of all the respondents to part (a), the researchers learns the average perceived performance. The dispersion around the average shows how much agreement there is. If all students see the academic program of the university at approximately 2 on a 7-point scale, this means the program is pretty bad. If students hold widely differing perceptions of the program's actual quality, further analysis is needed of why the perceptions differ so much and what individual or group factors it might be related to.

It is also useful to average the scores of all the respondents to part (b). This reveals the average student's view of how much quality is expected in the academic program. The measure of dispersion shows how much spread there is in student opinion about the desirable level of quality.

By finding the deficiency score for each component of the university's offering, the administration will have a good diagnostic tool to understand current student moods and to make necessary changes. By repeating this survey at regular intervals, the university can detect new performance deficiencies as they arise and take timely steps to remedy them.

PROBLEM RATES. A third approach is simply to ask respondents three major questions: (1) Have you purchased this product, used this service, attended this program, and so on in the last 12 months?, (2) If yes, did you experience any problems with it? and (3) If no problems mentioned, was there any way in which it could have been better for you? There are several advantages to this approach. First, specific problems or deficiencies can be identified, including many that management may not have anticipated. These can then be the subject of immediate corrective action, especially if respondents indicate how serious a problem it was for them.

Second, respondents reporting problems can be asked about their subsequent actions including whether they complained to the marketer, spoke with friends, or took other actions. This would yield data on how well the organization's complaint-generation system was working. Those who complained to the organization could also be asked how this process turned out so that management could monitor the effectiveness of its complaint-handling operation.

IMPORTANCE/PERFORMANCE RATINGS. Direct and derived dissatisfaction measures do not yield measures of the importance to customers of poor performance on specific dimensions of the organization's offering. Thus, a fourth approach is to ask consumers to rate various components of the offer provided by the organization in terms of (1) the importance of each component and (2) how well the organization performs each component. Figure 22-3 shows how 14 components of a university's offering were rated by students. The importance of a service was rated on a four-point scale of "extremely important," "important," "slightly important," and "not important." The college's performance was rated on a four-point scale of "excellent," "good," "fair," and "poor." The first service, for example, "academic program," received a mean importance rating of 3.83 and a mean performance rating of 2.63, indicating that students felt it was highly important, although not being performed that well. The ratings of all 14 services are displayed in Figure 22-3B. The figure is divided into four sections. Quadrant A shows important services that are not being offered at the desired performance levels. The college should concentrate on improving these services. Quadrant B shows important services that the college is performing well; its job is to maintain the high performance. Quadrant C shows minor services that are being delivered in a mediocre way, but that do not need any attention since they are not very important. Quadrant D shows a minor service that is being performed in an excellent manner, a case of possible "overkill." This rating of services according to their perceived importance and performance provides the college with guidelines as to where it should concentrate its efforts.

Relation Between Consumer Satisfaction and Other Goals of the Organization

Many people believe that the marketing concept calls upon an organization to *maximize* the satisfaction of its consumers. This, however, is not realistic and it would be better to interpret the marketing concept as saying that the organization should strive to create a high level of satisfaction in its consumers, though not necessarily the maximum level. The reasons for this are explained below.

First, consumer satisfaction can always be increased by accepting additional cost. Thus, a university might hire better faculty and build better facilities and charge lower tuition to increase the satisfaction of its students. But obviously a university faces a cost constraint in trying to maximize the satisfaction of a particular public.

Second, the organization has to satisfy many publics. Increasing the satisfaction of one public might reduce the satisfaction available to another public. The organization owes each of its publics some specific level of satisfaction. Ultimately, the organization must operate on the philosophy that it is trying to satisfy the needs of different groups at levels that are acceptable to these groups within the constraints of its total resources. This is why the organization must systematically measure the levels of satisfaction expected by its different constituent publics and the current amounts they are, in fact, receiving.

The organization hopes to derive a number of benefits as a result of

FIGURE 22-3

Importance and Performance Ratings for Several College Services

Service	Service description	Mean importance rating[a]	Mean performance rating[b]
1	Academic program	3.83	2.63
2	Housing quality	3.63	2.73
3	Food quality	3.60	3.15
4	Athletic facilities	3.56	3.00
5	Social activities	3.41	3.05
6	Faculty availability	3.41	3.29
7	" "	3.38	3.03
8	" "	3.37	3.11
9	" "	3.29	2.00
10	" "	3.27	3.02
11	" "	2.52	2.25
12	" "	2.43	2.49
13	" "	2.37	2.35
14	" "	2.05	3.33

[a] Ratings obtained from a four-point scale of "extremely important." "important," "slightly important," and "not important."

[b] Ratings obtained from a four-point scale of "excellent," "good," "fair," and "poor." A "no basis for judgment" category was also provided.

A.

B.

creating high satisfaction in its publics. First, the members of the organization will work with a better sense of purpose and pride. Second, the organization creates loyal publics and this reduces the costs of market turnover. Third, the loyal publics say good things to others about the organization and this attracts new consumers without requiring as much direct effort on the part of the organization.

Efficiency

The measures just described of sales, attitudes, and satisfaction are all designed to monitor the *effectiveness* of nonprofit programs. Equally important is the need to measure the *efficiency* of those programs. As we pointed out in Chapter 1, nonprofits are notorious for having very limited budgets—both in dollars and personnel. An effective control system therefore also ought to track costs and relate them to the returns from the program elements on which they are spent. Where the returns are dollar revenues, this evaluation is usually referred to as *profitability analysis.* Where the returns involve other measures of satisfaction or attitude change, the evaluation is usually referred to by the more general term, *cost/benefit analysis.*

SUMMARY

Nonprofit managers must have in place carefully designed measurement systems in order to track organizational performance and make appropriate adjustments. There are two broad categories of control systems. Strategic control systems monitor the organization's environment, competitors, publics, strengths and weaknesses, and performance. Tactical control systems monitor day-to-day performance for the purposes of fine-tuning current marketing efforts.

Two types of tactical control systems are those that measure organization revenues and those that measure customer satisfaction. Tracking of revenues requires analyses of revenues, market share, and marketing expense-to-sales ratios.

Customer satisfaction should be a major objective of all nonprofits. Complaint tracking systems provide one way of assessing this satisfaction over time. However, complaint measures are typically biased both as to types of complaints and persons affected. Periodic direct surveys of customers do not suffer from these biases. They can measure satisfaction directly as problems, indirectly as derived dissatisfaction, or as a combined measure of performance and importance. Studies of problems can be particularly helpful if they also track performance of the organization's complaint-handling activities.

QUESTIONS

1. The Los Angeles County Library wishes to embark on an aggressive marketing program to develop new markets and to expand service offerings to existing markets. What monitoring system would you recommend they put in place to measure their progress on these two types of initiatives? Make whatever assumptions are necessary but be as specific as possible.

2. Assume that the Board of a major art museum believes that the museum's marketing expenses are getting out of control. It recommends that the organization monitor at least one of the following: total marketing expense-to-sales; advertising-to-sales; sales promotion-to-sales; or sales administration-to-sales. Sales for the museum include annual subscriptions, donations at the door, and gift shop and restaurant receipts. Which of the ratios do you recommend they use and why? Describe any other alternatives which you think would be more appropriate.

3. Critique the hospital comment card presented in Figure 22–2. Propose a revised version that would be more useful for management decision making.

4. There are several ways to measure customer expectations. They could be: (a) minimum acceptable levels; (b) ideals; (c) average of competition; or (d) those anticipated on the basis of advertising, word-of-mouth, and/or experience. Would you suggest that a university use any of these? Which ones and why?

5. A customer's expectations change as he or she experiences the service a nonprofit organization provides. New characteristics are discovered that

should be considered in an evaluation. Characteristics initially believed to be important turn out to be trivial. Should an organization pay attention to this process of change when constructing a satisfaction measurement system? If so, how should it take the expectation-learning phenomenon into account?

NOTES

1. See Ralph E. Anderson, "Consumer Dissatisfaction: The Effect of Disconfirmed Expectancy on Perceived Product Performance," *Journal of Marketing Research*, February 1973, pp. 38–44.
2. Technical Advisory Research Program (TARP), *Consumer Complaint Handling in America: Final Report* (Washington, D.C.: U.S. Department of Health, Education and Welfare, 1979).
3. See Alan R. Andreasen and Arthur Best, "Consumers Complain—Does Business Respond?" *Harvard Business Review*, July–August 1977, pp. 93–101.
4. Ibid.
5. Alan R. Andreasen, "Consumer Behavior in Loose Monopolies: The Case of Medical Care," in Ronald F. Bush and Shelby D. Hunt, eds., *Marketing Theory: Philosophy of Science Perspectives* (Chicago: American Marketing Association, 1982).
6. It is, however, not uncommon for the typical pattern of responses to be more positive than negative or indifferent (the "yeasaying" bias).

Indexes

NAME INDEX

Aaker, David A., 257, 177
Abler, Ronald, 503
Abramowitz, Michael, 380
Abramson, Howard S., 3
Ackoff, Russell, 378
Adams, John S., 503
Adelman, Carol, 615–16
Adler, Lee, 258
Agins, Teri, 33
Ajzen, Icek, 161
Albrecht, Karl, 394, 401
Alexander, J., 33
Alexander, Raymond S., 428
Allen, Chris T., 64
Alpert, Mark I., 257
Anderson, Jack, 34
Anderson, M.J., Jr., 219
Anderson, Ralph E., 161, 631
Andreasen, Alan R., 35, 36, 64, 65, 119, 120, 180,
    184, 200, 241, 245–46, 257, 356, 401, 428, 479,
    504, 592, 623, 624, 631
Ansary, Adel I., 503
Ansoff, H. Igor, 113, 120
Anspaugh, Michael B., 503
Aramony, William, 545, 546
Argyris, Chris, 61, 65
Assam, K., 544

Bagozzi, Richard P., 125, 126, 149, 150, 153, 161, 162,
    194
Baker, George L., Jr., 542–43
Ball, Donald W., 503
Bandura, Albert, 429
Bansley, Marcia, 339
Bartels, Robert, 122, 161
Bass, Frank M., 257
Bauer, Raymond A., 161
Beal, G., 458
Beckham, Daniel, 95, 99
Beckwith, Neil, 200
Beik, Leland L., 180, 200
Belk, Russell W., 32, 65, 161, 184, 186, 245–46, 257,
    271, 479, 567
Bell, Alexander Graham, 1, 2

Bell, Herb, 559
Berkowitz, Eric N., 119
Bertrand, J.T., 543
Best, Arthur, 623, 624, 631
Betak, John F., 257
Black, T.R.L., 478
Blackwell, Roger D., 129–30, 161, 543
Bloom, Paul N., 4, 23, 31, 34
Blueck, Grace, 33
Bohlen, J., 458
Bonaguro, John A., 193
Bonfield, Edwin H., 149, 150, 161, 162
Booth, Elizabeth Mills, 32, 428, 481
Bramel, Dana, 161
Brancoli, David, 331
Brehm, J.W., 543
Brehony, Kathleen A., 32
Breitrose, H., 33
Brien, Richard L., 257
Brockner, Joel, 299, 305
Brown, B., 33
Brown, T., 429
Browne, Joe, 545, 546
Burnett, John J., 543
Burnkrant, Robert, 161
Bush, George Walker, 7
Bush, Ronald F., 631
Butterfield, Fox, 304
Buzzell, Robert D., 219
Bybee, H. Malcolm, 543

Calonius, Erik, 33, 34
Campbell, Donald T., 258
Carlzon, Jan, 394, 401
Cartano, David G., 458
Cash, Harold C., 378
Cassidy, Claire Monod, 428
Champlin, Charles, 33
Chandler, Russell, 222
Chinn, Donna E., 258
Churchill, Gilbert A., Jr., 258
Cialdini, Robert B., 305, 544
Citron, Alan, 202
Clarke, Roberta N., 31, 360
Clotfelter, Charles T., 34, 428
Coates, Susan, 306, 307
Coffman, Larry L., 31
Cohen, A.R., 543

633

ORGANIZATIONS INDEX